JIDDU KRISHNAMURTI

WORLD PHILOSOPHER

What is called Brahman, that is what this space outside a man is; and what that space outside a man is, that is what this space within a man is; and what that space within a man is, that is what this space within the heart is. That is the 'full'—inactive, undeveloping. Whoso knows this wins good fortune, full, inactive, undeveloping.

Chandogya Upanishad III, xii, 7-9

JIDDU KRISHNAMURTI
World Philosopher
(1895-1986)

His Life and Thoughts

DR. C.V. WILLIAMS

MOTILAL BANARSIDASS PUBLISHERS
PRIVATE LIMITED • DELHI

First Edition: Delhi, 2004

ISBN: 81-208-2032-0 (Cloth)
ISBN: 81-208-2033-9 (Paper)

MOTILAL BANARSIDASS
41 U.A. Bungalow Road, Jawahar Nagar, Delhi 110 007
8 Mahalaxmi Chamber, 22 Bhulabhai Desai Road, Mumbai 400 026
120 Royapettah High Road, Mylapore, Chennai 600 004
236, 9th Main III Block, Jayanagar, Bangalore 560 011
Sanas Plaza, 1302 Baji Rao Road, Pune 411 002
8 Camac Street, Kolkata 700 017
Ashok Rajpath, Patna 800 004
Chowk, Varanasi 221 001

Printed in India

BY JAINENDRA PRAKASH JAIN AT SHRI JAINENDRA PRESS,
A-45 NARAINA, PHASE-I, NEW DELHI 110 028
AND PUBLISHED BY NARENDRA PRAKASH JAIN FOR
MOTILAL BANARSIDASS PUBLISHERS PRIVATE LIMITED,
BUNGALOW ROAD, DELHI 110 007

Dedication

For

WARWICK

Who was Jiddu Krishnamurti?
With the greatest respect I offer this story.

Contents

List of Illustrations

Acknowledgements

My thanks to the many librarians who anonymously or selflessly assisted with this work, particularly in the State Library of NSW, including the Mitchell and Dixson Libraries, the State Archives of NSW, the National Library of Australia, The Huntington Library in San Marino, California, the libraries of the University of Technology, Sydney, the University of Sydney, the University of NSW and Macquarie University. I would like to give particular thanks to Naomi and Cai Blumensaadt from the Phyllis Campbell Library of the Theosophical Society in Sydney.

My grateful thanks go to my supervisors, Professor Stephen Muecke and Dr Paul Gillen, to Associate Dean, Research, Dr Hilary Yerbury, and Director of Research, Dr Paula Hamilton, in the Faculty of Humanities and Social Sciences, who encouraged my research during their tenures. My thanks also to my patient partner, Warwick, and my two daughters, Tasha and Jasmine, who nurtured me each in their own way.

No less grateful thanks in kind to other generous people who have offered assistance at crucial times: my agent Lyn Tranter, and Elizabeth McMahon, of Australian Literary Management, John Tranter, Donald Ingram Smith, Merlyn Swan, Tom Molomby, at least forty-five people I interviewed who gave of their time (not all of whom are identified by quotes), Radha Rajagopal Sloss, Peter Blodgett, Andrew Hilton, Dipesh Chakrabarti, Charles T Tart, Graeme Blundell, Paul Evans, Jennie Lees, Celeste Howden and Jeremy Gilling, Paolo Black, Bev Champion, Nick Fisher, Mark Lee, staff of the KFA, KFI and KFT, Sally Cohen, Neville Petersen, Tony Peacock, Bob Walshe, Imre and Felicia Molnar, Phil Wilson, Sucih Das and Robert Lotty. Particular thanks go to Mary Zimbalist who participated in our recorded interview.

Acknowledgements

[illegible]

The Characters

Principal:

Jiddu Krishnamurti - (also known as **G. Krishnamurthi**, as his father's name was 'Geddu', **Alcyone, Krishna** and **K**). He is 'discovered' and promoted as the next World Teacher by the Theosophical Society (TS) in 1909. He breaks away from the constraints of the Society in 1929 at the age of 34, declaring 'Truth is a Pathless Land".

Other characters in alphabetical order:

Dr EW Adhikaram - a well-known educator from Sri Lanka, he works with Krishnamurti from 1947 and later becomes Chancellor of the Sri Jayawardhanapura University in Colombo.

Ramaswami Aiyar - legal counsel to Krishna's father, G. Narianiah, in the custody case.

George Arundale (also known as **Fides** in *The Lives*) - a student of Leadbeater in England who studies Moral Science at Cambridge and becomes Principal of the Central Hindu College in 1909. He marries Rukmini, the daughter of a prominent Hindu pundit in 1920. At first very close to Krishna as his tutor, there is a falling out between the two about 1916 in England. He is General Secretary of the TS in Australia from 1926-1928. Known as a leading ceremonialist, ritualist and bishop in the breakaway Liberal Catholic Church, he holds the Presidency of the TS from 1934 (after the death of Annie Besant) until 1945.

Richard (or Dick) Balfour Clarke - an English engineer who is a tutor to Krishna.

Dr Balusandrum - a young chemist teaching in Bangalore when he is first associated with Krishnamurti in 1947.

Reg Bennett - an office-bearer in the Krishnamurti organisation in Australia, active in the 1960s and 1970s.

Annie Besant - (known as **Penelope** to Madame Blavatsky and **Mother**, **Mum** or **Amma** to Krishna and Nitya, and **Herakles** in *The Lives of Alcyone*). Wife of an English Anglican minister, separating from him in 1873 and becoming the following year an office-holder in the National Secular Society. A close associate of the social reformer and free-thinker, Charles Bradlaugh, Dr EB Aveling and the playwright George Bernard

Shaw, she publicly supports birth control and socialism, joins the Fabian Society and is famous as a prolific writer and extraordinary orator. She meets Madame Blavatsky of the TS in 1889, becoming devoted to her. She moves Blavatsky and the TS to her home at 19 Avenue Rd, Regent's Park and becomes President of the TS after Blavatsky's death. Besant first visits India in 1893. She establishes the Central Hindu College for the education of boys in Benares in 1898, becomes involved in Indian politics on a platform of self-government, but not independence, by 1913 and is elected president of the Indian National Congress 1917-1923. A prolific writer, she translates the Bhagavad Gita on a sea voyage to Australia and it is published in 1895.

Evelyne Blau - a wealthy American woman who becomes a trustee of the Krishnamurti Foundation of America in the 1970s, producing videos of Krishnamurti's life and talks.

Madame HB Blavatsky - a Russian-born charismatic who founds the TS, with Colonel Henry Steel Olcott and William Judge, in the United States in 1875. Author of *The Secret Doctrine* and *Isis Unveiled.* Acclaimed as a psychic, she is also accused of being a charlatan in an investigation by the Society for Psychical Research. Living at 17 Lansdowne Rd Holland Park during the first years of contact with Annie Besant, Blavatsky moves house to live with Annie before her own death in 1891.

Dr David Bohm - Professor of Theoretical Physics at Birkbeck College, London University, a friend whose dialogues with Krishnamurti have been published.

Radha Burnier - current President of the Theosophical Society, she is the daughter of N. Sri Ram, who succeeded C Jinarajadasa as President in 1952. Sri Ram was a brother of Rukmini, George Arundale's wife. (This makes Radha Burnier a niece to George and Rukmini). Leadbeater's biographer, Gregory Tillett, makes the point that the influence of Leadbeater continues to dominate TS thought.

Mary Cadogan - office holder of the Krishnamurti Foundation Trust in England from its inception.

Prof Gyanendra N Chakravarti (or Chakrabarti) - a Brahmin from Allahabad who attends the Parliament of Religions in Chicago in 1893. A mystic and adviser to Annie Besant, he later falls out with her over charges made that he had an hypnotic power over her.

Sudhukar S Dikshit - founder of Indian publishing house *Chetana.*

Jamnadas Dwarkadas - a Bombay politician and businessman from an affluent family from Kutch. A friend of Annie Besant, he wears a white Gandhi cap and is a Vaishnavite. He has a strong involvement in Indian independence politics.

Sidney Field - a friend of Krishna from Hollywood in the 1920s who writes a memoir published in 1989.

G Nityananda (or Nitya) - younger brother of Krishna by three years.

Geddu Narianiah - Krishna and Nitya's father.

Geddu Sanjivamma - Krishna and Nitya's mother.

G Narayaniah - Krishna's nephew, son of G. Shivaram.

Rajagopal Iyengar - a government engineer who is active in Krishnamurti affairs in India from 1947.

Pupul Jayakar - Krishna's friend and biographer and a sister to Nandini Mehta. Pupul meets Krishna in 1948, is President of the Krishnamurti Foundation in India for many years and a good friend of Prime Minister Indira Gandhi. Jayakar is also influential in cultural and arts and craft circles. She publishes several books including a biography of Krishnamurti in 1986 and a biography of Indira Gandhi in 1992.

C. Jinarajadasa - (known as **Raja**) - born into a Buddhist family in Ceylon in 1875, he is 'discovered' by Leadbeater who claims he is his deceased brother. Leadbeater attempts to kidnap him to take him to England and, after the boy is hidden on board a ship for three weeks, the parents agree. Graduating from St John's College, Cambridge in 1900, he is active and prominent in the TS, becoming President after George Arundale's death in 1945. He marries an Englishwoman, Dorothy Graham, in 1916. Jinarajadasa is expelled from the TS by Olcott for moral turpitude and insubordination after stoutly defending Leadbeater in

1906. He is reinstated before Leadbeater's reinstatement, on the basis that the dying Olcott has discovered a letter of explanation and an apology from Jinarajadasa.

Charles W Leadbeater (or CWL) - formerly an English curate in the Anglican Church, he joins the TS in the 1880s and 'discovers' Krishnamurti in 1909, soon afterward compiling an imaginative network of characters (published as *The Lives of Alcyone*). The characters are all said to be related to Krishnamurti in their past lives. Leadbeater is investigated as a paedophile twice in his life (once by a committee of the TS in 1906 after which he is asked to resign, before being reinstated about two years later, and once in 1922 by the NSW police). Criminal charges are never brought against him, although his prominence in the TS is adversely affected for periods of time. By 1915 he has migrated to Australia and becomes the leading figure in the movement, providing fuel for continuing controversy. He is a leading ceremonialist in the TS, aligning it closely with a fringe form of Christianity in his role as a bishop in the break-away Liberal Catholic Church.

Lady Emily Lutyens - joins the TS at the age of 36. The granddaughter of spiritualist writer, Bulwer-Lytton, sister of Lord Lytton, a Governor of Bengal, and wife of the architect of New Delhi, Edwin Lutyens. She becomes devoted to Krishnamurti, twenty years her junior, and something of a surrogate mother to him over a period of twenty years. Her disillusionment with Theosophy is explored in her autobiography, *Candles in the Sun*, published when she is 83.

Mary Lutyens - a daughter of Lady Emily, she is in love with Krishnamurti's brother, Nitya, until his death in 1925, this love being the subject of her autobiographical work, *To Be Young*. She remains devoted to Krishnamurti as 'World Teacher' throughout her life and is his official biographer from 1975.

R Madhavachari - an engineer with the railways in Madras who becomes the representative of KWINC in India. A Brahmin and follower of the Madhava sect. Called affectionately 'Mama', Tamil for uncle and a name used for close male friends.

Nandini Mehta - close friend of Krishna from the late 1940s.

Sister to his biographer, Pupul Jayakar.

Patwardhans (brothers) - their father is a wealthy man from Ahmadnagar in Maharashastra.

***Sahib Rao (eldest son)** - is closely associated with the work of Sarva Seva Singh, a Gandhian service organisation. A gaoled freedom fighter, member of the Congress working committee before Indian independence and friend of Nehru and Patel, he is overlooked for a position in the first Constituent Assembly.

***Achyut** – an intellectual and freedom fighter, during the Independence struggle, who, with Jai Prakash Narain and Acharya Narendra Dev, is involved in the founding of the Socialist Party of India. According to Jayakar, when Achyut tells Gandhi in late 1947 that he is going to spend time with Krishna, Gandhi is very happy about this. In early 1949 Achyut returns to Delhi to edit a Socialist weekly, later breaking with the Party and politics.

***Pama (MH)** - youngest son. He goes into business in Poona, owns a printery and becomes a director of Orient Longman publishers. His wife **Sunanda** acts as Krishna's private secretary in India and takes notes of Krishna's talks, transcribing them up until tape recordings largely take over. She first meets Krishnamurti at the age of twenty in 1947. In later years she is instrumental in establishing a school and study centre at Sahyadri near Poona, and writes a memoir published by Penguin in 1999.

Doris Pratt - a loyal Krishnamurti worker who becomes a trustee of the Krishnamurti Foundation in London.

D Rajagopalacharya - (son of VK Desakacharya) an Ayyangar Brahmin said by Leadbeater to have been St Bernard of Clairvaux and a future Buddha. An intelligent, efficient, dedicated worker, he becomes Krishnamurti's editor and main organiser of lectures. In 1968 Krishnamurti takes legal action against him. Rajagopal later counter-sues. Rajagopal retains his ties with the TS throughout his working life with Krishnamurti. Rajagopal's wife is **Rosalind**. They divorce about 1961.

Rosalind Rajagopal (nee Williams) - married to Rajagopal, she has a 25-year (at least) affair with Krishnamurti. Sexual relations are said to have been cut between Rajagopal and Rosalind after the birth of their daughter, Radha. Rosalind forms a close relationship with Aldous and Maria Huxley and administers the Happy Valley School, of which Krishnamurti and Huxley are founding trustees. Relations between Krishna and Rosalind cool in the late-1950s and are cut by the time he dies in 1986. In 1991 Rosalind's daughter, **Radha Rajagopal Sloss**, publishes a memoir of Krishnamurti and her childhood with him.

Dr MC Nanjunda Rao (or Row) - the trusted physician of Col Olcott and present at his death. He disputes the account by a Theosophist, Mrs Russak, of a Mahatma being present at the death. In 1911 Dr Rao contributes articles to The Hindu, criticising the TS.

Rama Rao BA BL - According to M Lutyens he takes a degree in science at Cambridge. As a boy he runs away from his home in Mysore to go to school at the Central Hindu College in Benares. George Arundale grants him a scholarship. Rama Rao is with Krishna at Varengeville in 1913 and Pergine in 1924. His wife's name is Mano. He dies in 1945.

Rao brothers

***Sir BN Rao** - a lawyer and bureaucrat, advises Nehru in framing the constitution of India.

***B Sanjeeva Rao** - a friend of Annie Besant, educated at Kings College Cambridge. His wife is Padmabai, a teacher influential in women's education in Uttar Pradesh. He is instrumental in buying the Rajghat estate at Varanasi for Krishnamurti.

***Shiva Rao** - a teacher who first meets Krishna in Benares in 1910 and assists Leadbeater at Adyar in compiling 'the Lives'. In 1913, at the age of 23, he is sent to England from India by Mrs Besant to teach Krishnamurti and his brother Sanskrit. In 1916 he is recalled to India by Mrs Besant to help her edit her Madras daily, *New India*. During the 1920s, he becomes the Delhi representative of the Madras paper *The Hindu*. His wife, Kitty, is Austrian.

GV Subba Rao - first principal of Rishi Valley School, a post he holds for thirty years. In 1942/43 he leaves and sets up his own school, accused of having increased retrospectively his allowance for some years previous. His school venture falls through. After Rama Rao's death in 1945, differences are set aside and he is appointed principal of the Rishi Valley Trust school (in Rajghat).

Dr Mary Rocke - a medical practitioner from Australia who is appointed English Secretary of the Order of the Star. She is the main force behind the construction of an amphitheatre at Balmoral, overlooking Sydney Harbour, in honour of Krishnamurti.

Don Fabrizio Ruspoli - a former lieutenant in the Italian navy who gives up his career when he becomes a Theosophist. He is a tutor to Krishna at Adyar.

Mrs Russak, later Mrs Harry Hotchener - a confidante of Annie Besant, she is accused of having hallucinations in claiming to see a Master at Olcott's death.

Dr David Shainberg - an American psychiatrist who holds dialogues with Krishnamurti in the 1970s.

AP Sinnett - a critic of Leadbeater and Annie Besant, who resigns from the TS in 1908 or 1909, founding the Eleusinian Society and a publishing firm. In the summer of 1911 Sinnett and Annie Besant make up their differences and he returns to the TS as Vice President.

Donald Ingram Smith - an Australian involved in early tape recording of Krishnamurti who remains an adherent, publishing memoirs.

PT Srinivasa Iyengar, MA - an ex-Theosophist, principal of a small college in Vizagapatam and Fellow of Madras University who writes a savage exposÈ of the history of the TS in *The Hindu* in Madras in 1911.

SV Subrahmanyam Aiyar - a tutor in English and Sanskrit to the boy Krishnamurti, a close friend of his father, Narianiah, who writes to *The Hindu* in 1911 and is later a supporter of Narianiah in the High Court of India custody case. Wood writes that Subrahmanyam said he heard Krishnamurti tell his father in Telugu, 'The book [*At the Feet of the Master*] is not mine; they fathered it on me'. Mrs Besant gives Subrahmanyam the alternative of recanting or banishment from Adyar and he regrets he cannot deny he heard it. He returns to his village and 'died there shortly afterwards, while still himself little more than a boy', according to Ernest Wood.

(Sir) S Subramania Iyer - Recording Secretary of the TS, a judge of the High Court of Madras and past Vice Chancellor of Madras University who supports Annie Besant for President of the TS after Olcott's death. Honorary President of the Home Rule League in 1916.

Divarkanath (Dwarkanath) Telang - tutor/guard for K in Europe in 1913. He establishes the Vasanta Vihar property for Krishnamurti in Adyar in the 1930s after his separation from the TS.

PK Telang - principal of Central Hindu College and Indian representative of the Order of the Star in 1911. General Secretary of the Home Rule League in 1916.

CS Trilokekar - MA, Principal of Theosophical College, Madanapalle, Krishna's birthplace.

Vigevenos – James & Annie - the couple leaves Germany for Holland in the face of Nazism and runs the Krishnamurti Centre at Ommen in the 1930s. They emigrate to the US about 1939 or 1940 and retain strong links with Krishnamurti's work all their lives.

BP Wadia - a staunch Theosophist and publisher of TS books. Politically active, he is interned with Annie Besant in 1917 and is an activist in the first trade union action in India. Treasurer of the Home Rule League in 1916. He rejects the TS, publishing an exposÈ in Los Angeles in 1922. Despite differences with the Adyar Theosophists, he continues to write in support of a Theosophy based on his interpretation of Blavatsky's writing.

Susunaga Weeraperuma - a librarian, writer and friend from Sri Lanka who compiles a bibliography on Krishnamurti. He later resiles from his adulation, saying a hidden force behind Krishnamurti is that of 'the Devil'.

AE Wodehouse - tutor to Krishnamurti. Brother of PG Wodehouse, he wins the Newdigate Prize for poetry and the Chancellor's Essay Prize at Oxford and is Professor of English at Elphinstone College, Bombay, before moving to the TS at Adyar at Mrs Besant's request.

Ernest Wood, Professor - secretary to Leadbeater and tutor to Krishna. Stands for Presidency of the TS on Annie Besant's death in 1933. In 1936 he discredits Leadbeater.

Evelyn Wood - (according to Jayakar) an Englishman who is a Professor of English at Bombay University and is involved in Krishnamurti activities in India in the 1970s.

Mary Zimbalist - widow of Hollywood producer, Sam Zimbalist, she is Krishnamurti's close companion in his late life.

Chapter 1

Boyhood Dreams

"Thyself art thy master
Inasmuch as thou art acquainted with the Master of all...
Follow thy own way and lose not thy head."
... All we see is One.
Whoever says 'tis two is suffering from double vision.

Masnavi I Ma'navi Teachings of Rumi (trns) EH Whinfield 1979 Octagon Press London.

Memory is a knave ... notoriously unreliable. Most of us carry around static images of ourselves as children, re-thought and re-worked, embellished as thoughts recollected hundreds of times throughout adulthood. How far back can we go? No-one can remember the beginning, the first cries or whimpers we uttered after the trauma of the birth canal and the feeling of discomfort in being outside the womb. We rely on others' stories and hold fast to those projections that we accept as images of our youthful selves.

As an adult Jiddu Krishnamurti could remember very little of his childhood. Some people believed this was a sign that he was a self-realised Master. Others said his fractured personal life was an indication of self-delusion. Krishnamurti lived an extraordinary life – wealthy, travelling the world, delivering lectures on philosophy to thousands of devotees and sceptics alike, a fixed star in a vortex of love. Yet, revered and adored, Krishnamurti continued to refute publicly the international image of himself as guru. His origins were as obscure as for any of us.

Jiddu Krishnamurti was a dreamy child, according to accounts from people who knew him as a small child in the late nineteenth century. He was born in May 1895 at Madanapalle in the

Telegu-speaking Indian state of Andhra Pradesh in the middle of the night when the moon was high in the sky and full.[1]

An eighth child, a son born to a Brahmin family, he was given the name of Krishna, in honour of Sri Krishna[2], who is said to have been an eighth child and a sage considered a reincarnation of Vishnu, the preserving aspect of the Hindu trinity.[3]

Great expectations were laid at the feet of this newborn of the Jiddu family.[4] The Sanskrit horoscope, probably written on a palm leaf, declared him a "gem" of a son, born to the "great" man, Brahmasri Jiddu Narayaniah of the Gotra of Harita. The horoscope waxed lyrical about the birth that occurred under a slightly waning moon: "the full moon to the ocean of Jiddu family, endowed with everlasting day by day growing prosperity, blessed and adorned with the grace of the Lord of Lakshmi; in the womb-ocean of his wedded wife - Srimati Sanjivamma adorned with good luck and pure character".[5] The wording indicates the custom in India that the family is paramount and the individuals within it are bound by responsibilities and duties. This baby Krishna was born into a high-caste religious tradition, not an individual so much as a link in a chain, one budding leaf of a great overarching family tree: Krishnamurti's father held a BA and had become a civil servant in the Revenue Service; an uncle held a senior position in the District Registrar's Office; his grandfather, a civil servant described as "well-to-do", owned a farm; his great grandfather, said to be an eminent Sanskrit scholar, had worked in the judicial department of the East India Company.[6]

Also according to custom, Krishnamurti's astrological chart began with the blessing that there might be good fortune, and the most positive aspects of the position of the planets was set out to show it as an "harmonious" time, endowed with the six *vargas*.[7]

The day of his birth was Saturday 11 May, 1895, according to the Hindu calendar, which is determined by sunrise and sunset. But as the birth was just thirty minutes past midnight, Western calculation puts Krishnamurti's birthday as Sunday 12 May. Western astrologers looking at the chart say it has Aquarius in the ascendent, with the Sun in Aries and the Moon in Sagittarius. With Aries in the fourth house governing communication. Krishnamurti would be a warrior with words and with Sagittarius and the Moon both in the eleventh house governing ideals and wishes, the humanitarian and altruistic aspects of Aquarius are heightened. There are four planets in the fifth house, Venus and Mars indicating sexual attractiveness, along with versatile Gemini and gainful Jupiter. Overall the chart shows a gregarious and affectionate nature. Astrological predictions aside, all that is known for sure is that this little boy was born into and nurtured within a family and community which held to practices and beliefs that had endured for centuries. Krishnamurti's biographer, Mary Lutyens, writes that his horoscope was cast by a renowned astrologer in the region, Kumara Shrowtulu, who told Narianiah the baby would be a very "great" man. Whenever he saw the father he would ask after the boy, saying he had told him the truth, that he would be someone very wonderful and great.[8]

According to custom, mother and child would remain secluded in semi-darkness for eleven days, the baby suckled at the mother's breast and rocked to sleep in a hanging cloth cradle[9], the mother cared for by the midwife who attended the birth: A room with a separate door at the front of the house allowed the midwife to come and go without disturbing the rest of the household which would go on about its daily affairs, with family activities centred on the kitchen, an adjoining puja or prayer room and dining and sitting rooms. Upstairs the baby's father could attend to his business in a study and brothers and sisters could sleep at night without undue disturbance from the intermittent cries of a nursing mother and child. On the sixth day the newborn would be named in a religious ceremony, the naming giving particular pleasure to the baby's mother, Sanjivamma, who was a devotee of the incarnated deity, Krishna.

Over time legends outshine reality and one story repeated often is that Sanjivamma was devout in her Hindu practice. Krishnamurti himself wrote, in a sketch of his life made at the age of eighteen, that his mother had a *puja* room. She worshipped regularly and he said he often went into the *puja* room where she performed her daily ceremonies. Krishna's memory of his childhood at this time, 1913, is reasonably expansive, with the sketch running to about two thousand words.[10]

In the first major authorised biography of Krishnamurti published in 1975 it was claimed that his mother had a premonition that this son was to be in some way remarkable and she insisted that he be born in the *puja* room.[11] This was later corrected and it is now accepted that Sanjivamma spent time in devotional prayer in the *puja* room of the house immediately before going into labour.[12] The biographer, Mary Lutyens, continued to maintain both Sanjivamma's religious devoutness and her psychic abilities. Lutyens writes that the family belonged to the highest caste Brahmins for whom Westerners were on a "par" with the lowest caste 'Untouchables'. Sanjivamma would throw food away if so much as the shadow of an Englishman fell on it, and if an Englishman entered the house the rooms were afterwards scoured and the children put into clean clothes".[13]

Yet the family seems to have had a strong involvement in Theosophy, a 'spiritual' organisation established in India by Europeans, while remaining orthodox Hindus. The evidence that Krishnamurti's father had a strong commitment to Theosophy is irrefutable and his mother's reputation for religious piety remains unchallenged. It would seem that there was no conflict between the values of the Theosophical Society and those of Hinduism in their minds at the time.

The small boy Krishna, a physically weak child, spent a great deal of time with his mother. When he was aged eighteen months the family moved to a larger town in Andhra Pradesh, Cuddapah, which reportedly had a malaria plague, and the following year the boy contracted the illness and was not expected to live. Thereafter he was subject to periodic attacks and is also said to have suffered nosebleeds.[14] A few weeks after Krishna turned three in 1898, his mother gave birth to another boy, named Nitya, to whom the young Krishnamurti is said to have been "devoted".[15] Nitya also suffered several attacks of malaria in his early years. The family moved again because of the father's work in 1900 to Kadiri, closer to Madanapalle, and two years later another boy, Sadanand, was born. This was Sanjivamma's tenth child and is reported to have been somewhat "mentally deficient".[16]

It was at the Narasimhaswami[17] temple in Kadiri when Krishna was six that he underwent the sacred thread ceremony, or *upanayana*, required of Brahmin boys. His father was later to describe the importance of the ceremony as a significant starting point in an "educational career according to the ancient Brahmin custom".[18] The ceremony began at home where the young Krishna was placed upon his father Narianiah's knee while Narianiah held a silver tray strewn with rice grains. Krishna's mother then took Krishna's index finger and traced in the rice the sacred letter 'Aum' in Sanskrit. The father's ring was then placed between Krishna's thumb and finger and again the letter was traced in the rice in Telugu script. Finally the letter was traced three times, mantras were recited by the officiating priest who blessed Krishna, and he was taken off to the temple for prayers for his future success.[19]

The young Krishna would go with his younger brother and mother to the temple every evening if he was well enough, sickness taking its toll in his attendance at school where he missed classes for one whole year.[20]

Further employment transfers followed for the father. From September to December 1902 the family must have been living at Madanapalle since a letter from the headmaster of Krishna's primary school is said to be held in the Theosophical Society's Adyar Archives in Madras.[21] However in 1903 the family was back in Cudappah where Krishna's eldest sister died.

This sad event would provide the occasion for Krishnamurti's sensitivity in matters of clairvoyance to be first publicly acknowledged. Some years later Krishna wrote about his sister's death and his mother's clairvoyant ability to see and converse with her dead daughter in a special place in their garden. At first he laughed and then he saw her too, and was afraid because he had previously seen her corpse burnt. His mother told him there was no reason to be afraid. Krishnamurti was the only other member of the family who saw these "visions" although they all believed in them. he said. His mother was able to see people's auras, and he also saw them sometimes.[22]

In the same memoir Krishnamurti wrote that he had learnt about the Theosophical Society from his mother and father. His father attended conferences at the Society headquarters at Adyar in Madras and also used to hold meetings in their house. In his mother's *puja* room were pictures of the Indian deities and also a photograph of the President of the Theosophical Society. Mrs Annie Besant[23], a grandmotherly figure in Indian dress sitting cross-legged on a *chowki* or small platform covered with a tiger skin. Krishnamurti says that as he suffered so much from fever he was often at home while his brothers were at school - "almost" every day - and he often went into the *puja* room with his mother. She talked to him about Mrs Besant and *karma* and reincarnation and read to him from the *Mahabharata* and the *Ramayana* and other Indian scriptures. He was aged only seven or eight but he believed that he "felt" much which he could not actually understand.[24]

No one can say what drew this conservative Brahmin family to the Theosophical Society at this time but perhaps it was not such an unusual course for an ambitious Indian family in a country suffering a national political schizophrenia – working daily in a British legal system and aspiring to succeed within it while also seeking to throw off this domination by an imperial foreign government. Among the tenets of the Theosophical Society are a belief in the wisdom of ancient religions, the hidden powers of nature, and the brotherhood of Man. This recipe is in no way at odds with the principles which would govern the life of a devout Brahmin who has already come into contact with Westerners in the course of his public life. Annie Besant, who headed up the Theosophical Society. would also become President of the Hindu League, a political body with the aim of Indian self-government through mutual agreement with the British. The fact that she was sympathetic to Hinduism and active in the cause of Indian self-government would at first endear her to many conservative Indian middle-class intellectuals, setting a foundation for their acceptance of Theosophy (in Greek, 'theos' meaning god and 'sophia' wisdom), an elaborate belief system which promoted the slogan, 'There is No Religion Higher than Truth".

The Theosophical Society had been founded in New York in 1875 by a small group of spiritual seekers disenchanted with orthodox Western religion, and drawing their inspiration from the ancient 'wisdom' of the East. Among these spiritual free-thinkers were most notably three charismatic people: Madame Blavatsky, a Russian with an illustrious past; Colonel Olcott, a former colonel in the northern army during the American Civil War; and William Judge, an Irish attorney. The movement became established when Blavatsky and Olcott went to London in 1879 to build support among intellectuals and artists and then set up a headquarters near Madras in India in 1882. By then the objects of the Society had been firmly established, largely those of the present code: a nucleus of universal brotherhood; a study of Aryan literature, religion and science; the importance of enquiry; and, exploration of the hidden mysteries of Nature and the latent powers of Man. Blavatsky's first published books, *Isis Unveiled* and *The Secret Doctrine*[25], outlined the Society's belief system, based largely on archaic occult knowledge drawn from Hinduism, Buddhism and the Ancient Egyptians, as well as her creative imagination.[26] The Society became an influential populariser of Eastern spiritual beliefs in the West, with membership still to reach its peak in the 1920s.[27]

Theosophy's past is fraught with controversy and factionalism: the most notorious founding figures being Madame Blavatsky, with mild-mannered Olcott as her practical deputy. A decade later Annie Besant, a well-known English Fabian and civil rights campaigner, faced a major turning point in her life on meeting Blavatsky and by 1890 she had become the Society's leading light, setting up its London headquarters in her home in Avenue Rd, St John's Wood. This 'commune' became a haven for her and her spiritual mentor, with Besant taking over all Blavatsky's correspondence and most public activities in the face of Blavatsky's failing health. The year Blavatsky died, 1891, she had already appointed Annie Besant Chief Secretary of the Inner Group of the Esoteric Section & Recorder of the Teachings, "in the name of the Master".[28]

Charles Leadbeater, an English curate who was similarly overwhelmed by the extraordinary 'spiritual' manifestations associated with Blavatsky's presence, also became a member of the Society and a Buddhist, in a ceremony conducted in Ceylon, resigning membership of the Confraternity of the Blessed Sacrament of the Church of England in 1884.[29]

Blavatsky, denounced as a charlatan during her lifetime, had at first aligned the Theosophical Society with Spiritualism and 'Himalayan Masters', and then with Buddhism as practised in Ceylon and with a reforming Hindu group in Bombay.[30] The concept of these Himalayan Masters, aged yet looking in the prime of life, and living in Tibet because their bodies were too sensitive for the everyday world, retained its ultimate authority long after Blavatsky's death. The question of the influence on Krishnamurti's thinking of these pivotal images of "Masters" remains open to debate. As Lutyens explains it, the two Masters looked quite unalike. Master Kuthumi had the body of a Kashmiri Brahmin, yet with fair-complexion and blue eyes, whereas Master Morya was a Rajput king with a "dark" and good-looking "Indian" body, with black hair and "flashing" black eyes. Blavatsky reckoned she'd met them in Tibet but it wasn't necessary to travel there in order to encounter them. Her associate, AP Sinnett, was said to be in correspondence with them, and what a lot of striking, and formally English, letters they reportedly wrote to him. These were detailed with direction about Theosophist personalities' factional struggles, evident in the publication of the correspondence, *The Mahatma Letters*. Higher in authority still than the Masters was the Lord Maitreya, who unlike the personage referred to in Buddhist terminology, was not the coming Buddha, but a being who had taken hold of an earthly body to become Lord Krishna in the fourth century BC and later Jesus Christ. The Buddha, it might be reassuring to know, was considered by Theosophists, to be "a still higher entity". Lord Maitreya was thought to be ready to take the body of someone on earth once again, and Theosophists were on the look-out.[31]

T. Subba Row, a Madras lawyer schooled in esoteric knowledge, extended an invitation to Blavatsky to visit Madras in 1882. He joined the Theosophical Society and is said to be one of the main reasons for establishing the world headquarters in Adyar, Madras, the same year.[32] He was soon to have an irreparable falling out with Blavatsky, claiming she "desecrated the Sacred Science" by giving out "Secrets of Occultists"[33] and he worked to have her deported from India in 1885, never to return.[34] In 1883 Subba Row had written that the body of Blavatsky was occupied by a Hindu *chela* or spiritual aspirant and it was working through her, but two years later he described her as "a shell deserted and abandoned by the Masters".[35] He refused to assist Blavatsky in writing *The Secret Doctrine* or to endorse it. She wrote in 1886 to Olcott that she wanted him to secure the help of Subba Row for the book. "Lots there of Adwaitism[36] or old Aryan Religion occult ... We can take the public of India by storm if he helps me with the old quotations and the occult meanings added to mine," she wrote.[37] Subba Row resigned from the Society in 1887, *The Secret Doctrine* was published in 1888 and he died in 1890, the year before Blavatsky. Despite an enquiry carried out in 1885 by Richard Hodgson, which claimed she was neither the mouthpiece of hidden seers, nor a mere vulgar adventuress but "one of the most accomplished, ingenious and interesting imposters in history"[38], Blavatsky's reputation continues to be upheld by Theosophists to this day. A refutation of Hodgson's report, defending Blavatsky, was published by the Theosophical University Press as recently as 1997.[39]

The non-controversial Colonel Olcott, who remained a stalwart of the Theosophical Society, turned his attention to "the sad state of Buddhism in nearby Ceylon and attended to reform in education, including girls' education, and in agriculture, for which efforts he is honoured there still".[40]

The Indian connection had been firmly established by the meeting between Subba Row and Blavatsky and the existence of the Adyar headquarters in India is still a testament to the fervour and financial commitment to the original cause by Theosophists. The headquarters remains a romantic central force in the lives of Theosophists world-wide, a beautiful estate of about two hundred and fifty acres. It is the setting for an annual get-together of members every Christmas and offers to European visitors all year round a pacific haven from the excessive heat, noise, smell, sights and activity of Madras.[41]

During the 1880s, the link between British theosophists and contemporary middle-class Indian society - based on what many consider is the source of theosophy in the wisdom of ancient Indian scriptures - was reaching its acme just as Blavatsky stirred the spirit of "the greatest public speaker in London"[42], Mrs Annie Besant, when she read Blavatsky's *The Secret Doctrine*. Besant's biographer, Gertrude Marvin Williams, says that whether through "hypnotism or some other influence", within two months of joining the Theosophical Society Annie Besant believed she had seen the "Master". Thereafter she gave all her energy to this eccentric, albeit humanitarian, cause which advocated three main principles, already cited: universal brotherhood; the study of comparative religion, philosophy and science; and, the investigation of unexplained laws of nature and the power latent in humans.[43] Gazing at that photo of Besant in his family's *puja* room, could the little boy Krishna have 'felt' how significant Mrs Besant would become in his life? As a result of her determination, intellect and beneficence in the face of a chequered public life[44], Besant had an extraordinary network of contacts among the liberal-minded intelligentsia of Britain and Europe. Within a few years this world would open up and overthrow Krishnamurti's simple, traditional home-life.

This dreamy child, generous to a fault, hated schoolwork and appeared to his teachers to be mentally retarded. According to his biographer, Mary Lutyens, he would stand about looking at trees or clouds, or squat, gazing at flowers and insects. He would give away his pencils, slate and books and give too much of his mother's boiled rice to the first beggar who came along, leaving none for those coming after, so that he would have to plead with his mother to give them some more food. Yet the young Krishnamurti had a practical streak to his nature in his love of machinery. It's said that he once took apart his father's clock to find out how it worked, refusing to go to school until he had put it back together. This is said to foreshadow his interest in cars later in his life. But it has to be acknowledged that the boy may have found any excuse to wag school.[45]

The first major break in the continuity of Krishnamurti's life came with the death of his mother in 1905 when he was ten and a half and the family was living in Cudappah.[46] In his memoir Krishnamurti wrote that his happiest memories centred on his "dear" mother. He said that with her death he was deprived of love and care, since his father was too "occupied" to give his sons much attention and there was no one to look after them. He remembered following his mother's ghost form as it went up the stairs, trying to catch hold of her dress (this is the word used – not sari) and that "she" vanished as soon as she reached the top of the stairs. He also heard the tinkling of her bangles as she followed him to school, he at first half-frightened as he looked behind him, seeing the vague form of her dress and a part of her face.[47] Another account of Krishna's ability to see the dead mother figure, even more clearly than he had seen his sister, comes from Krishnamurti's father, Narianiah, in a statement dictated in 1911 to an English Theosophist at Adyar and signed by him in the presence of two witnesses. Narianiah relates that on the third day after the cremation of his wife, Krishna came running out of the bathroom one morning, and when questioned, said he was following his mother. She was taking off her wet clothes and putting on dry, he said, and then eating. After a time he went towards the stairs and stopped half-way up, saying he couldn't see her any more. He reported that she looked just as she usually did and had not spoken to him.[48]

In another published account, Narianiah said Krishna ran out of the bathroom without his clothes and dripping wet. He went to the room where his mother's "saris" used to dry overnight and stared. He told his father that his mother was "removing" her wet clothes and putting on dry, and then, in another room, she was eating. Narianiah maintained that he too once saw his wife eleven days after her death, following her funeral, when she came to him as he was lying on his bed, talking with his brother. She bent over him, her face caressing his, and passed her hand over his hair. She told him she was going away. Narianah's brother could not see her.[49]

Perhaps there were some other deaths of children in the family as there were said to be ten children – two born after Krishnamurti, who was the eighth child. An older sister was married and the sister whom Krishnamurti had seen after her death, along with Narianiah's four sons referred to in 1909 - Shivaram, Krishna, Nitya and Sadanand - would make a total of six children accounted for, yet there's no mention by Lutyens of who or where the others were. At this time Sivaram was aged fifteen, Krishna ten, Nitya three years younger, and the youngest, Sadanand, almost five years younger again. There's no explanation of the fate of any other children, nor whether Krishnamurti ever saw them, whether they had already died or not.[50]

After the mother's death the family moved back to Madanapalle, considered safer for the children since it was away from malaria country, and Narianiah resumed work, now as a District magistrate, remaining there until he retired in 1907. Krishna is said to have liked walking up a steep hill to a Shiva temple overlooking the town, and would insist Nitya go with him. The hill is named Basinikonda after a legendary thief and is associated with gold, sounding as it does like the Telugu word for gold, 'pasidi'. It stands due east, every morning dominating the sight of the sunrise, viewed from the open rooftop of Krishna's father's two-storey home which is set in the midst of the crowded town. At night, light from a lamp in the Shiva temple shines out across the countryside, a clear beacon giving direction for travellers. Shiva temples are invariably built on the highest natural landforms of any district in southern India, dotting the night landscape like an inverse pattern of the stars above. From Lutyens' account, the boy Krishna was drawn to the temple by day, so that over the two-year period spent in Madanapalle, Krishna, who was in his early teens, and Nitya, three years younger, would often walk the two kilometres to the hill temple after school. Lutyens records that Krishna and his younger brother Nitya were both admitted to the Madanapalle High School on 17 January 1907 where they studied until 1909 when the family moved to Adyar, home of the international Theosophical Society.

With the family's involvement in the Society would come, inevitably, involvement with Charles W Leadbeater, another leading figure of the Society who was dogged by controversy. He was instrumental in 'discovering' Krishnamurti as the next "World Teacher" and would later establish a dominant presence in Australian Theosophy. The 'discovery' occurred on the beach at Adyar, where, in the evenings, Krishna used to play with other boys in the waves rolling in on the sands from the Bay of Bengal.

Leadbeater's past is a patchwork of myth and fact, his biographer, Gregory Tillett, kindly concluding that Leadbeater's imagination got the better of him on both spiritual and physical planes. "Leadbeater's vision world was so much derived from his personality, his culture, his rigid and unvarying view of the cosmos that ... one cannot argue for his objectivity".[51] This seems a generous summary of a man many believed to be a paedophile and liar. In interview, Tillett's view was tougher, in describing Leadbeater as "a good old-fashioned fraud who used his ability to persuade others of his own fantasies essentially for his own personal gratification". Tillett also said that from his thorough research he was "absolutely certain" Leadbeater had sexual relations with boys in the Society but he didn't believe that he had sex with Krishnamurti or his brother Nitya while they were in his care.[52]

In the early 1900s Leadbeater was a "massive, muscular man, five feet eleven inches in height and some sixty inches around the chest" with muscular biceps to match. With grey-white hair. a long straggly beard and prominent forehead. he was altogether a most striking man.[53] He had been involved in a paedophile scandal that was the subject of an internal Theosophical Society enquiry in England in 1906 – three years before meeting the adolescent Krishnamurti in India in 1909. The Committee of Investigation accepted his resignation after debate over whether he should be expelled, but two years later he was re-admitted.[54] His authority was gradually restored by Annie Besant and he returned to Adyar. There, one evening at the beach, while Mrs Besant was away, he spotted young Krishna, a boy who had what he described as "the most wonderful aura he had ever seen, without a particle of selfishness in it".[55] One might be prompted to ask what is the colour of selfishness. Clearly Leadbeater had no doubts about what he claimed as his special clairvoyant faculty and predicted that the boy would become an orator and spiritual teacher even greater than Annie Besant. The boys were said to sport themselves on the beachfront, playing in the scented evening breeze.[56] Perhaps it might be reasonable to think that Leadbeater simply fell in love with the figure, the exceptional eyes or the aura of Krishna, and imagined this extraordinary future for the boy. Certainly he would not have been the last person held by some magnetic power Krishna consciously or unconsciously wielded.[57]

For a worldly woman, Annie Besant was curiously trusting of Leadbeater, just as she had been trusting of Blavatsky before him. Perhaps this loyalty and open-heartedness were the qualities that would in future endear her to the two boys. Krishna and Nitya always showed her great love and kindness, much more than mere duty proceeding from any obligation they might have felt in being adopted by this fond, white-haired grandmother figure they learned to address as "Mother" or "Amma".[58]

It's interesting to view correspondence from Blavatsky to Annie Besant around 1890 in which Blavatsky points out Besant's naivete bordering on gullibility.

"I have acquired almost a conviction," Blavatsky writes, "that my friendship and sincere love for a person (very rare with me) leads that person astray from his right and correct ideas and fills him with *maya* of all sorts". She continues:

> Even YOU, honest like day, sincere and true, you could not escape the thing. It is the more dangerous because you do not seem even to realize the danger. ... May the Masters protect you and open your eyes *before it is too late*.

The letter goes on to describe the possible problems that could arise for members who had assisted by donating funds to Mrs Besant for her mortgage at 19 Avenue Road, Regent's Park, when she established her home there as the headquarters of the Society in London, problems if, for example, Mrs Besant died suddenly. Blavatsky admitted she had forced upon members the decision about the site of the headquarters, but now there were complaints and she wanted Annie Besant to address them.[59]

Blavatsky held extraordinary ideas, about races and subraces descended from a point "in the beginning" when "every class and family of the living species was hermaphrodite and objectively one-eyed", and of people becoming more psychic and spiritual down through the ages.[60] She was also transparently anti-papist and expounded her views in a journal called *Lucifer*.[61] When she died in 1891 these ideas did not die with her.[62] Leadbeater, an eccentric ex-curate whom Blavatsky referred to as "WC", rather than "CW Leadbeater", assumed the mantle of the Society's supreme clairvoyant and adapted Blavatsky's ideas. And Annie Besant seems to have accepted this role for him, as if there was a pact between them.

It was believed by those around Blavatsky that although the cause of her death was a heart attack, "the real facts" were that she was "called away without a moment's warning or preparation" because an accident provided a sudden opportunity for her to immediately reincarnate into another body. Her astral body was present at her cremation, and Leadbeater saw it, "naturally enough". It seems to have been so provocative it frightened a horse, overturning a wagonette with six people aboard.[63]

Annie Besant is said to have deliberately switched off her clairvoyance because the Master told her it would be too dangerous to be clairvoyant while working in politics in India. Wood maintains that Mrs Besant believed she could have been superlative if she practised her psychic powers frequently but she had a policy of cooperation with others and division of labour. so she concentrated on policy and organisation, scarcely using her own psychic powers after the mid-1920s and relying on her co-workers in that respect. Perhaps Annie Besant's early occult experiences had been so strong they allowed her to believe in any and all visions that Blavatsky, Leadbeater and others described.[64]

It's interesting to note that, according to Tillett. Leadbeater had a multiple-occupancy view of Blavatsky. allowing him to overlook her indiscretions, such as smoking cigarettes and hashish, according to whether her views aligned with his. Sometimes she was inhabited by a highly-evolved soul. sometimes by a dark figure. Tillett says one of the great portraits of Blavatsky is cut off at the chest or airbrushed to hide a view of her holding a cigarette. Annie Besant's tolerance of Leadbeater. overlooking his faults, was founded on her trusting nature, and might be likened to the trust she had in Blavatsky, despite the warning she'd had from Blavatsky about "maya". In any case. the theory of a coming and going of higher souls to and from the bodies of spiritual leaders on earth is a significant one when it comes to a consideration of Krishnamurti's later standing as a world spiritual teacher.[65]

For most of his life Leadbeater treated women with contempt, yet his relationship with Mrs Besant was closer than any other in his life. He dominated her life virtually from the time he met her.[66] Their correspondence was always fond as well as businesslike; his letters would use terms such as "with very much love, I am ever yours most affectionately". One of Besant's biographers described Leadbeater as her "astral Svengali"[67] and many of Leadbeater's critics, including Aleister Crowley, suggested that the Theosophist cleric hypnotised her or used Black Magic.[68]

Whatever the source of the bond, it was inordinately close and in many respects provided a protective umbrella for nurturing the youthful Krishna and Nitya. The two Theosophical leaders, Bishop Leadbeater and Dr Besant, taken as a pair, have been described as he being always sure of himself and she modest and yielding, in spite of her skills in public oratory.[69] Unalike as they were, perhaps the balance was beneficial for these poor Indian boys who were being thrust into an international spotlight. Whether the thrust itself was beneficial is another matter.

Krishna was in the right place at the right time to be taken up by this occult three-ringed circus which anticipated the arrival on earth of a Saviour. Krishna's father, we know, was an enthusiastic Theosophist and had taken the family from Madanapalle to the heart of Theosophy at Adyar after his compulsory retirement at the age of fifty-two.[70] Two earlier hopeful choices for the role of World Teacher had been abandoned, so finding another candidate from within the ranks of the Society must have been considered opportune.[71] Lutyens records that having been a member of the Theosophical Society since 1882, Narianiah wrote to Annie Besant offering to work in "whole-hearted" and full-time employment at Adyar, considering his capability - he had been in charge of an area of 800 square miles comprising 160 villages when he had been in government service. But Mrs Besant turned him down, saying that his boys (the four aged between fifteen and five) would be a disturbing influence in the compound and that the nearest school was three miles away. But Narianiah persisted, met Mrs Besant at the annual convention at Adyar in December 1908 and began working as assistant secretary of the Esoteric Section in January 1909.[72] In correspondence to Mrs Besant in September 1909, Leadbeater explains the poor living conditions at the home of Narianiah and his sons, with "the overcrowding in that place ... far from sanitary".[73] Narianiah had had his sister staying with him for a time, but she had left; Narianiah had also asked for a toilet to be built again and again, but "nothing is ever done here!". Leadbeater asked Annie Besant to direct that a house and a printing-press room standing vacant on the

Adyar estate be made available for the family and by the end of October he had word that she had agreed.

Considering the bizarre antics and ideas lived and breathed in the Theosophical Society, when Krishnamurti's father went to work on the Adyar estate in January 1909 the boy's life must have changed irrevocably. Leadbeater believed that a higher purpose for the family being at Adyar was to train the boys. On the day of Nitya's Brahmin thread ceremony or *upanyanam*, which was held in 1909 when Nitya was eleven, later than customary, Leadbeater kept a close watch on Krishna and afterwards asked Narayaniah to bring him to his room one day. Narianiah did so and Leadbeater sat Krishna on the sofa next to him, placing his hand on the boy's head as he related stories from his past lives.[74]

Krishna and Nitya attended the Pennathur Subramanian High School at Mylapore after their father was employed by the Society on 23 January, 1909. They walked the three miles to and from school, but little Sadanand was considered not bright enough to go to school. Even before these two special boys moved onto the estate, though, Leadbeater seems to have taken over supervision of their education. He writes to Annie Besant in October, just before the move, that their father had a "providential" difference of opinion with Krishna's schoolmaster who was said to be inefficient - one of Krishna's teachers at the school is also said to have beaten him. Lutyens writes that Krishna was caned almost every day for not learning his lessons and would frequently be sent out of the classroom onto the verandah, sometimes until the end of the school day when Nitya would come out and find him in tears, take his hand and lead him home.[75]

Leadbeater had Dick Balfour Clarke, Ernest Wood and a local young man, SV Subramania Iyer, teach Krishna and Nitya English and Sanskrit, taking them himself for English when he could spare the time. Their older brother, Sivaram, was also taught English and studied at the Presidency College in Madras in preparation for a career in medicine.[76] Krishna and Nitya must have been confused about their studies in Madras considering their first language was Telugu and their Tamil and English were so poor. But Leadbeater was not so much concerned with how they felt about their education as what "He" ("the Master") wanted of them: the two boys were said to have been taken on probation by the Master on 1 August. This probationary event was described by Lutyens as Leadbeater taking the boys' astral bodies on a visit to the Master while they were asleep. This pattern continued for the next five months and each morning Krishna would laboriously write out "the Master's" wisdom from the night before.

Leadbeater writes to Annie Besant that he is trying to steer a rather cautious course in their education but must carry out the instructions given to him, and then quips, "after all that has happened within the last three years, I must not take too prominent an interest in boys of 13!" He reassures Mrs Besant that when she is in Adyar he will be bolder, and do more of what "He" wishes. If it might be called reassurance.[77]

Ernest Wood, who worked as Leadbeater's private secretary for five years from 1909, describes Krishna when he arrived at Adyar as "a very frail little boy, extremely weak, all his bones sticking out", adding that Krishna's father said more than once that he thought he would probably die. Krishna was having a bad time at school because he did not pay attention to what his teachers said. He was bullied and beaten to such an extent that it seemed he might fade away from life, and the father went to Leadbeater and asked what he could do. As Mrs Besant had already set up the Central Hindu College for boys, providing food, shelter and education, it was not unusual for her to be asked for help. Wood says Leadbeater did not train Krishna in any particular way, except that to be near Leadbeater was training in itself. Leadbeater told Balfour Clarke that they had a difficult job to do, to take the two boys out of an "orthodox" environment, change their diet, and teach them physical exercise and Western methods of bathing. He was particularly concerned to dispel their fears, he said, and to this purpose would tell them "the most bloodcurdling stories of ghosts and vampires", embellished by his own experiences. Once when Krishna avoided a deep hole when swimming, Leadbeater noticed and marched the boys back to the beach to find it and overcome the fear.[78]

Leadbeater made Krishna eat fruit and drink milk, even though he didn't like milk. As well as swimming, cycling exercise was arranged for the two boys. Soon Krishna became healthy and strong and took more interest in the world, according to Wood.[79]

By now Leadbeater had begun to investigate what he claimed were the past lives of this boy, Krishnamurti, whom he named 'Alcyone'[80], and it is no surprise to find that he conjured up "a past of very great importance, indicating far greater advancement than his father ... a better set of lives than Hubert's". (Hubert van Hook was a boy previously set apart as a contender for 'the Coming World Teacher' role, a concept advanced by Blavatsky and in which Theosophists fervently believed.) "I am sure he is not in this compound by accident, but for the sake of its influences," Leadbeater concluded. His ostensibly pragmatic view was that, "if we are to have the karma of assisting even indirectly at the bringing-on of one whom the Master has used in the past and is waiting to use again, we may as well at least give him the chance to live decently!"[81]

Annie Besant was not at Adyar when Krishnamurti was 'discovered' yet Leadbeater maintained that she was spiritually present. "You are often here, but I do not know how far you remember these details, so I am repeating them on the physical plane. I showed you, for example, the lives of Naraniah's [sic] boy, and you were keenly interested; I wonder if you have brought any of it through..."[82]

Mrs Besant first met Krishna, on the physical plane, at Madras central railway station in November 1909, more than six months after Leadbeater's "discovery". Krishna's account of the meeting comes from his essay composed four years later in Varengeville. He writes that the train, due in at about midday on 27 November, was delayed by accident so the group had to wait until about four o'clock. Krishna was barefoot and his feet burned on the sun-drenched stone of the uncovered platform, so after dancing about, he was able to find respite by standing on the feet of a man in the party. But not for too long, as the group went for an extensive drive around the city. Back at the railway station. Krishna was handed a "garland of roses" to give to Mrs Besant, but as there was such a rushing, pressing crowd when she stepped off the train, it was all he could do to throw the garland over her, showing his respect by quickly saluting, hands pressed together, "in our Indian way".

What the over-tired, over-weight, elderly Annie Besant would have spied in the crowd when she stepped onto the platform was a South Indian boy aged 14, who had large expressive *sanpaku* eyes and long lashes, who stood straight and tall, and who, under Leadbeater's tutelage, was spotlessly clean and neatly dressed in traditional Indian silk. It must have been a relief for her to set eyes at long last on this beautiful embodiment of her hopes and dreams for a 'Saviour'. Krishna was of a retiring personality yet spoke politely when required, she would find, once they'd returned to the compound. The boys waited in Leadbeater's bungalow while he talked with Mrs Besant in the main building. Then came the sound of the "peculiar" coo-ee Leadbeater used to call them and they went off nervously to meet her, knowing how great a figure she was. In reverence, the boys prostrated themselves before her but she leaned down and lifted them into an embrace. Krishna recalls meeting his father on coming out of the room with Mrs Besant. She said they were going to the first of the private Theosophical meetings the boys had ever attended and hoped he approved. He said he was very glad. Krishna sat at Mrs Besant's feet facing the audience during the meeting and his nervousness persisted.[83]

Leadbeater usually had the assistance of shorthand note-takers to whom he would launch into dictation for his descriptions of the past lives of Krishna and others, constructing a network of family histories for members of the Society which were remarkably interlocked and also remarkable for their famous predecessors. "None of the real names of the parties concerned appear in the lives, with the exception of the Lord Buddha, Zarathustra, King Harsha, and one or two public characters of that sort," he wrote to Mrs Besant in October 1909. In a letter the previous month he had intimated that he believed Annie Besant and Krishnamurti both came from "the Moon Chain", producing a superior type of person who was self-sacrificing and spent a shorter and more intense period than most in the heaven-world before being reincarnated, irresistibly incarnating back in India "on every possible occasion".[84] Other characters conveniently sharing the same heritage were Nitya, known as "Mizar", Krishna's mother known as "Omega", his father as "Antares", his older brother Siva as "Regulus", Hubert van Hook as "Orion", Mrs Besant as "Herakles" and Leadbeater himself as "Sirius".

The charts based on Krishnamurti's past lives were published in *The Theosophist* from April 1910 and belatedly as *The Lives of Alcyone* in 1924. Wood explained that Leadbeater began on 'the Lives' or 'Rents in the Veil of Time' when he asked him about the intervals between lives and Leadbeater had asked the boys' father for permission to look into their past lives. Leadbeater worked on twenty eight lives in his octagon-shaped bungalow on the estate, one per night. He walked around and around the room dictating to Wood and refreshing himself by lying down for a five-minute catnap. Mrs Besant reportedly wrote two of the total of thirty lives. Krishnamurti was also in the habit of coming around in the morning and writing what he could remember of his previous night's experience. Wood said that Krishnamurti used to collect people's thoughts and he had seen him do some notable feats of conversation with the dead while still a boy and that this capacity developed "quite naturally".[85]

Following instruction by telegram from Annie Besant. Leadbeater had held back publication of 'the Lives' until she had arrived in Adyar in November 1909 and no doubt the general acceptance of the work by those around Leadbeater dispelled any concerns she might have had at first. The close connection between the boy Krishna and "the Master DK" was said to be one of the many remarkable features of the life. and a lot of jealousy and spiritual rivalry erupted among Theosophists close to the centre of power over whether they had been part of this golden circle in past lives.[86] Shiva Rao, who when young had gone to Adyar to help Leadbeater write out the charts comprising about two hundred characters, all related through the thirty incarnations, believed in Leadbeater's clairvoyant powers. He said that the fellow's ability to trace with comparatively few errors the family ties of such a large group of souls through life after life amidst a maze of details struck him as so far beyond anyone's mental resources, however prodigious the memory, as to rule out invention. When he came across discrepancies every few days he would point them out to Leadbeater who would close his eyes and correct them and the changes would be found later to fit the scheme exactly.[87]

However, Ernest Wood who was probably in the best position to know how 'the Lives' were compiled since he was the shorthand note-taker at the very start of the exercise[88], in later years expressed his doubts. By 1936 Wood was saying that he had noticed that Krishnamurti's importance increased the further back in history the past life: "in more recent lives he was a humble individual ... but in the earlier lives he appeared as a personage of great eminence". He also noticed that imagination was seriously affecting the visions. Even so, Wood said that having had other cases of convincing evidence of clairvoyance, he was prepared to give Leadbeater the benefit of the doubt.[89]

Tillett quotes Wood as saying that Leadbeater's filling in the genealogical charts to accommodate newly-arrived Theosophists undermined his confidence in their veracity. He had also noticed other discrepancies. For example, members were originally listed as being intermarried in past lives and the later arrivals to the Society had also intermarried in past lives, but earlier and later rarely intermarried. And of six thousand marriages only a few did not produce children. "When Leadbeater was attracted to ... new people, especially young boys, their names would suddenly be added to the list and places found for them in 'the Lives'," he said. But when Leadbeater went to live in Australia in 1915 and a new set of people came into his circle there was no room for them in the chart of 'the Lives', although they were given special names.[90]

Hugh Gillespie, a Theosophist at Adyar at the time, also claims that 'the Lives' were faked. He said Hubert van Hook assisted in the faking and then talked about it in the United States in 1917 so he was suddenly removed from Adyar. One could reportedly 'buy' exalted past lives. Gillespie said that Ernest Wood found 'absolute proof' of the deception in Leadbeater's room once when he was absent. BP Wadia, who was manager of the Theosophical Publishing House, was shown the evidence, laughed and said he was sure 'the Lives' were fictional. Mrs Besant, at first indignant and abusive in her defence of Leadbeater, finally admitted the wrong in the face of the evidence. 'The Lives' were published progressively in a Theosophical journal, but the anticipated book of 'the Lives', which had been widely publicised, was held up. Advance copies had been sent out, but the rest of the first volume, already printed and ready for distribution was withdrawn and stacked in storage. Theosophical Society lecturer (later Vice-President) Jinarajadasa announced that the distribution was delayed because Krishnamurti feared he would be ragged at Oxford, where he was preparing to sit an entrance examination. *The Lives of Alcyone* was published about fifteen years after the charade began, allegedly at a time when Annie Besant was in need of money. The books were offered at a reduced price and sold poorly despite Jinarajadasa's encouragement of members to buy them. Wadia had had an article published in *The Theosophist* in January 1911 praising Leadbeater's reliable clairvoyance, particularly in relation to ancient Persian names. Again in September 1911 in a review of Leadbeater's *The Inner Life* (for which publication was delayed due to the urgency of getting *At the Feet of the Master* into print), Wadia praised Leadbeater's knowledge as "phenomenal" and his instruction "priceless", although he acknowledged the work was "here and there scrappy" since it comprised a series of talks. Yet in 1923 and again in 1938, Wadia published brief statements rejecting the accuracy of the clairvoyance, feeling "compelled ... wholly to reject" his earlier conclusions. He said his revised opinion was the result of "physical plane knowledge and experience gathered later on".[91] It's hard to argue with physical plane knowledge, after all.

As to Ernest Wood's final position, after spending ten thousand hours before 1913 and some years in the 1920s turning Leadbeater's dictation into book form, his last view is less kindly tolerant of the charismatic's "imaginative" construction of past lives. Wood saw Leadbeater as a politician within the Society who detested argument and criticism, contrary to his own raison d'etre which was "to sift the gold from the ore".[92]

When it came to the book which was produced at Adyar about the same time as the compilation of 'The Lives', Alcyone's or Krishnamurti's *At the Feet of the Master*, the plot thickens. The book was ostensibly compiled by Leadbeater from Krishna's writing sessions in Adyar in 1909 – in other words it was said to have been essentially written by Krishna. Leadbeater maintained that after making a few corrections he sent Krishna's writing to him when he was in Benares on tour with Mrs Besant in early 1910. Balfour Clarke vouchsafed that apart from spelling and punctuation errors, Krishnamurti's notes of his astral experiences comprised this book. *At the Feet of the Master*, published in 1910 under the pseudonym "Alcyone", for which the Foreword contains the statement, "These are not my words; they are the words of the Master who taught me". This testimony is questionable considering later revelations.[93]

Wood first asked Leadbeater about some passages being nearly identical with Leadbeater's own writing and the old fellow told him that he had been present with Krishnamurti when he was being taught in his astral body by the Master and he had made use of these points in his own talks and his book.[94] This seemed to all to be an acceptable type of plagiarism at the time, and Wood said that it was natural that Leadbeater should adopt something of his own Master's style. But after *At the Feet of the Master* created a sensation and practically a new cult - when 'The Order of the Star in the East' was set up by devotees of young Krishna - Wood at first held himself aloof with some other members, recognising that "Krishnamurti did not know enough English to write the sentences in the book". Krishnamurti could not have linked the sentences together and punctuated them so well, nor have written the Preface. But Wood explained away the difficulty with the words of the Foreword, that "Krishnamurti had not written it himself – they were the words of the Master", his rationalisation being that there was no explanation of who that 'Master' was. He also pointed out that this had been noted in a court case and that a friend had heard Krishna tell his father that the book was not his, that "they fathered it on me". The murky nature of the attribution of the book persists to this day, after publication in twenty seven languages and millions of copies sold. The author is still referred to as "Alcyone (Krishnamurti)" in some re-publications despite Leadbeater's admission that he retyped the notes and changed some according to instruction from "the Master" on the astral plane, and his even more preposterous statement that the Lord Maitreya looked them over, approved them and suggested he produce them as a book to introduce Alcyone to the world. [95]

One interesting observation made by Wood is that the book is divided into four parts in the style of Shankaracharya's "four qualifications", expounded as Advaita philosophy in about 800 CE. The four categories are given the names, "Discrimination, Desirelessness, Good Conduct and Love". Wood observes that the book was far simpler than other works on the same subject commonly used by Theosophists, such as *The Path of Discipleship* by Annie Besant, *The Voice of the Silence* by Madame Blavatsky and *Light on the Path* by Miss Collins.[96]

The most unsettling aspect of the whole incident is the curious resilience of the myth that Krishnamurti wrote the book, with Theosophists and Krishnamurti adherents ignoring strong evidence that it was nothing other than Leadbeater's work either directly or by proxy through the young Krishnamurti's hand. Lady Emily Lutyens, who had known the boys since 1911, stated categorically that she was told by an unnamed person closely associated with the boys' early training that the teachings in *At the Feet Of the Master* were dictated to Krishna by Leadbeater. Yet she lamely concluded that the truth would never be known."[97]

In an officially-sanctioned biography of Krishnamurti published in 1995 to celebrate the anniversary of his birth, the author, Evelyne Blau, says that in his later years Krishnamurti denied any memory of writing the little book which has become a spiritual classic. Not that he denied writing it, but denied memory of writing it, a significant point considering other references to Krishnamurti's poor memory in relation to his adept 'spirituality'. However three extracts of comment are included in the Blau biographical work: from Balfour Clarke, Leadbeater and Annie Besant.[98]

The overly-sensitive tutor, Balfour Clarke, explained that he never liked to be rude or inquisitive by peering over Krishna's book but he did know that morning after morning Krishna wrote "something". The question is never raised that Balfour Clarke may not have been competently doing his job of correcting English grammar and spelling if he did not look at the work. This revelation clearly scotches Balfour Clarke's earlier statement that apart from spelling and punctuation errors, Krishna's early morning writing comprises the writing in the book. How could Balfour Clarke know that as fact if he didn't even know what Krishna was writing, apart from an idea that he was writing "something"? Balfour Clarke is also quoted as saying that years later Krishnamurti told Count Keyserling that he didn't remember whether he wrote the book but he did remember writing something very laboriously in English. "Laborious" was, coincidentally, the word used by Balfour Clarke himself to describe Krishna's effort. "Somewhat laboriously" are also the words used by Leadbeater in his description of Krishna's supposed boyhood effort. Krishnamurti was aged fourteen, it must be acknowledged, an age at which most people would be able recall later in life if they had written a book or not.[99]

In the Blau biography, Leadbeater is quoted from a passage in *The Masters and the Path*. In this quotation there are dots [...]

between two parts of a sentence: "I arranged his notes as well as I could, and typed them all out", and "and in due course the book was published" – which usually denotes an excision. The first edition of the book was published in 1925. Later issues, including a 1979 edition, repeat the excision. What the excision hides are significant details - of Leadbeater's references to having checked the notes with 'the Master' and 'Lord Maitreya' - thereby granting Leadbeater's words greater credibility than the preposterous unexpurgated passage warrants.[100]

Finally, in Blau's biography, the extract from Annie Besant's declaration may also be thought misleading in its reassurance about the amount of editing done. She is quoted as saying, "Two omitted sentences were supplied by the master". The use of lower case for "the Master" in this version blurs the fact that Annie Besant used capitalisation because she was referring to an astral "Master". Added to Besant's other quoted explanation - "In two other cases an omitted word has been added", and, "Beyond this, it is entirely Alcyone's own..." - the rebuttal fails to offer a comparison with Leadbeater's explanation from the expunged testimony, an explanation which was much more vague about the details of the editing. In his words they were "connecting and explanatory notes" that he admitted had been added to the text, an explanation inadequate in detail.

The lack of clarity about Krishna's role versus that of Leadbeater in the book's authorship is just one example of the interconnectedness of interest which persists between the work of Krishnamurti and that of the Theosophical Society which he supposedly broke away from in 1929. *At the Feet of the Master* continues to be published; the three versions available in the Theosophical Society's Adyar Bookshop and other esoteric book outlets in Sydney, exemplify its availablity. One published by the Theosophical Society in Adyar has the author as "Alcyone", with no reference to the name Krishnamurti, yet showing a photo of Krishnamurti as a boy. Another Adyar version cites Annie Besant and CW Leadbeater as the authors. A third published by Quest, the Theosophical Society publisher in the United States, gives the author two identities: "Alcyone (Krishnamurti)".[101]

The authorship could have been established categorically at any time over the seventy five years of Krishnamurt's life after the book's publication in 1910 in the form of a brief unequivocal statement from him. This was no doubt hardest to effect in the early years when he was so young and dependent. he and his family in the care of Leadbeater and Annie Besant. It's a consideration which might evoke compassion. for the boy was undoubtedly at the mercy of their ethical and moral code at a time when he was still too young to demur.

Clearly the intense nurturing needed at Adyar to bring the boys' lives into line with middle-class European standards was taking an unusual course and Krishna and Nitya must have soaked up the irregularities of this authorship question as freely as other more academic proprieties required of them. The boys were innocents abroad and had developed few discriminatory faculties to deal with cultural displacement on this scale.

They trusted Mrs Besant, an English woman greatly admired in India. and she in turn trusted Leadbeater. Not restricted to supervision of Krishna and Nitya's academic learning. Leadbeater also took charge of the state of the boys' bodily health. Initially Clarke was given the job of delousing Krishna's eyebrows and hair. part-shaved in the front and part-knee-length pigtail. which was later cut to shoulder-length, reportedly to imitate the Buddha's. Clarke was also given the task of giving the boys clean clothes every morning.[102] When in 1912 Krishna was fitted with an orthodontic plate which Clarke tightened every day. Mrs Besant wrote to him in sympathy, saying it must have been very uncomfortable at first but he must have become used to it over time. She recounted her own difficulty in talking when she had a plate fitted and practised speaking aloud in the train from Waterloo to Esher until she could enunciate clearly.[103]

Leadbeater supervised their personal hygiene. making sure they washed between their legs as he deplored the practice of bathing while wearing a loincloth. Their underclothes were to be made of silk. linen or fine cloth; no wool or flannel was to touch their skin; and, tight-fitting clothing was not allowed. Their feet and heads were also to be left uncovered as far as possible. Leadbeater also taught Krishna good European manners, including keeping his mouth from hanging open as was his habit. But dreamy Krishna would forget, and one day Leadbeater was so exasperated he hit him on the chin. Krishna never felt the same about Leadbeater again. This must have compounded Krishna's initial fear – "When I first went over to his room I was much afraid" – which was born of the gulf between Indians and Europeans and the "political agitation and gossip" he had heard and which he said he had overcome as a result of his fine treatment by them. Clearly the boy's personal relationships with individual Europeans was not divorced from his sense of Indianness, founded in equal but conflicting measure as it was on a belief by Brahmins of their cultural superiority and the political oppression of Indians by the English. Krishna made his own youthful political statement, with an observation that he wished the English in India could understand that Indian boys loved India as deeply as the English loved their own country, and they felt any insult, even if it was unintentional, just as deeply.[104] This recollection made only a few years after the hitting incident is interesting in the light of a statement Krishnamurti made as an old man, an implication that he had never been hurt though many things had happened to him, whether flattery, insult, threat or even security. It was not, Krishnamurti wrote in 1973, that he was insensitive or unaware: but he had no image of himself, which presupposed he also had neither conclusion nor "ideology". He reckoned that when you found the beauty of never being hurt, then all past hurts disappeared.[105]

In those early years at Adyar one of Krishna's tutors, Professor EA Wodehouse, the elder brother of the writer PG Wodehouse, described the boy as very natural without a trace of affectation. He was modest, deferential to elders, courteous to all and serenely unselfish. His charm seemed to lie in his lack of self-consciousness of himself as the "holy" child and when he liked someone he showed a kind of eager affection which was "singularly" appealing. He also kept his body in good condition, enjoying a two-mile run or four hard sets of tennis.[106]

Wood too describes Krishna as extraordinarily unselfish and affectionate for a boy of his age, who would invariably answer, when asked what he would like, 'What *you* like". He was often vague and inattentive to book learning, especially to arithmetic which he didn't think he would ever need, but when he put his mind to it he could concentrate and learn a lesson very effectively.[107]

The boys' education proceeded at a regular pace for a couple of years, Krishna still dreamy while his younger brother was bright and alert. Quite detailed instructions were given by the Master about the daily life of Leadbeater's two young pupils, according to another of the boys' assistants, Dick Balfour Clarke, whose accounts must be taken more circumspectly than those of Wood.[108]

Balfour Clarke offers an English culturally-chauvinist view of the boys' education which must have been prevalent in Adyar at the time. Before their move to a room adjacent to Dr Besant's, the boys' way of living, according to Balfour Clarke, was, from the modern scientific and hygienic point of view rather "deficient", although its ideals were "splendid". Their food was mostly over-spiced with red and green chillies, their diet unbalanced, and their washing more "ceremonially" correct than "chemically" cleansing, was Balfour Clarke's assessment. And their sleeping conditions were hardly conducive either to peace of mind or of body, considering so many slept together in a confined space.

Krishna was gaunt and thin, he said, so there were many changes to be made. Balfour Clarke was given the role of go-between to persuade Krishna's father that the boys' accommodation move was for the best.

Determined as ever, Leadbeater was keen to make progress not only in housing and English studies but also in Krishna's elevation to World Teacher, and in January 1910, while Annie Besant was in Benares, Leadbeater informed her that Krishna was now ready for his Initiation. She instructed Leadbeater to use her room for the period of the private ceremony which would span a day and two nights. Leadbeater locked himself away with the boy on 9 January and they emerged on the morning of 11 January. According to Leadbeater, he had lain on the floor and Krishna on the bed in a semi-conscious state, perhaps what might be called a trance, while Clarke and Nitya waited outside the room in the headquarters building, the outer doors to which were closed until the Initiation had been completed.[109] Krishna was only allowed warm milk (not his favourite food) as sustenance. When he emerged he looked radiant, beautiful in the "fullness" of an "exalted" boyhood, according to Balfour Clarke, and once again dressed in a white silk robe and wearing sandals. The small group waiting eagerly for him, including Krishna's father, Nariananiah, and Dr Mary Rocke from Australia, as well as Nitya and Balfour Clarke, presented him with a garland and some, at least, prostrated themselves at his feet. Leadbeater declared the Initiation a great success, presenting handwritten notes of what Krishna had purportedly said after his out-of-body experience. He described seeing many Masters standing in a semi-circle around Lord Maitreya who was seated. Various questions were asked of the Masters who were his sponsors, and he pledged to keep certain things secret and even help his worst enemy if it was needed. Then a great "Silver Star' flashed and Lord Gautama Buddha appeared. The next day the disembodied being of young Krishna was taken off to see "the Lord" who turned out to be a boy not much older than himself, handsome, shining and glorious, strong and yet nothing but love. There was no mention of the colour of the boy's skin nor his cultural background, even what language he spoke - in other words, no visual or aural details which might jar with the images of personified perfection any and all Theosophists might play with in their own minds, images based on an innocent boy, perhaps even young Krishnamurti himself, created in the image of the Lord.[110]

Having made his debut in public life so successfully, Krishna was now set to be launched onto the world stage. But the familial bond needed to be broken if Leadbeater was to have a free rein.

And so it was arranged for Annie Besant to become the legal guardian of Krishna and Nitya two months later. A new life had opened up for the boys and been formalised within the law – a life of privilege, discipline, regulation, public occasions, courtesy, 'civilised' European manners and, above all, wealth. From now on the streets of heaven on earth would be paved with gold and the ties to family cut asunder.

Chapter 2

A Sentimental Education

In order to achieve this [finding the root-causes of *duhkha* - suffering or unsatisfactory experience], it is essential that we practice in our lives those causes producing happiness, while ceasing to operate those causes giving rise to *duhkha*.

His Holiness Tenzin Gyatsho the XIVth Dalai Lama of Tibet 1971 The Opening of the Wisdom Eye, Theosophical Publishing House Madras p 15.

Born a Brahmin, Krishnamurti must now seek his destiny in a world dominated by Europeans. His touchstones of the past would one by one vanish from his life.

But Krishna was not completely alone – he had Nitya. The boys were never apart for very long and this bond offered them a bulwark against the onslaught of so much that was culturally confronting. They had lessons together, bathed together, ate their meals together.

Their tutor Ernest Wood says that for the Hindus living on the Adyar Theosophical estate, food was cooked in the back quarters of a little old cottage, two rooms of which were set aside as Brahmin and non-Brahmin caste dining rooms. It was not until 1913, he says, when Mrs Besant took up political work in India, that she turned against the caste system. The food served was simple and traditional – rice, vegetable curries, korma, kofta, idli, and bananas in abundance - and for Brahmins all meals had to be cooked and served by members of their own class. Wood recalls stewed guavas constantly dominating the meals as they were plentiful and cheap in Madras.[1]

At first the boys' daily routine began with "orthodox Brahmanical [sic] ablutions with cold water at the side of the well, meditation and then arrival at Leadbeater's bungalow where they received hot milk served to them by a Brahmin caste servant in order to "comply with orthodox feeling". Krishna and Nitya also complied with the caste rules about not eating cooked food in the presence of non-Brahmins and would go to their home for the two main meals of the day. But sometime after Mrs Besant's arrival in Adyar at the end of 1909 the "rigid caste rules as regards the eating of food were finally broken through, and both Hindu and English friends ate their food together in the Presidents' dining room, the food ... being cooked and served by a Brahman [sic]".[2]

The adoption of Krishnamurti and his brother Nitya by Mrs Annie Besant took place on 10 March 1910. Balfour Clarke who had played a role in the initial negotiation with their father, Narianiah, to have them educated at the Adyar estate, writes of Narianiah's initial hesitancy, after which he gladly and willingly assented.[3] Narianiah's reluctance was based on the fact that a child needed to have passed through the school examination system to gain government or professional employment. Yet Narianiah could see that Krishna faced daily problems at school. With the reassurance of Mrs Besant's interest in his sons he accepted the tuition Leadbeater provided on the estate.[4]

Mrs Besant took her role as guardian of the boys very seriously in view of her belief in Krishna's great future as a religious teacher. It was her sacred duty, she believed, to nurture their spiritual and educational lives, and she would take them herself into the shrine-room for meditation. Years later Besant described how she had joyfully answered 'Yes" to the question of whether she would guard Krishna with her power when asked to do so at his 1911 astral Initiation, a ceremony at which she claimed she was present, even though she was in Benares at the time and was not able to be there in the physical body.[5]

Perhaps it was the idolisation of Krishna that had occurred which set Narianiah against the Theosophical remodelling of his sons. Or, as rumours had been rife since the 1906 sex scandal involving Leadbeater, Narianiah no doubt distrusted Leadbeater's conduct. Or perhaps Narianiah was under pressure from orthodox Hindus linked with nationalist political forces. But whatever the cause. sometime after March 1910 Narianiah was having second thoughts about the adoption. and when he turned. he turned with a vengeance. The leaders of the Theosophical Society never seemed to doubt that they were doing the right thing in taking Krishna from his father and schooling him in not only their own strange ideological mix. but also in Western culture. The Western education may not have been so much the contentious issue as the abrupt termination of their Hindu education which accompanied the boys' adoption by Mrs Besant and tutelage by Leadbeater in a Society which always kept its affairs hidden from public scrutiny. Wood makes the point that when Narianiah "had grown dissatisfied and instituted a case for the recovery of the custody of his sons". Mrs Besant could not give them up because they flatly refused to go back to their father. It was thought by some in the Hindu community that Krishna and Nitya had turned against their father and the evidence seems to indicate this.[6]

Annie Besant had her subtle little ways of setting up a division between Krishna and his family. In October 1912 she told him that he needed to write more neatly not only because the Master had asked him to but. incidentally. the *Hindu* newspaper had published a letter he'd written to his brother and it didn't do any of them any credit. It wasn't nice of his brother to give the letter to the press. she said. and she'd only told Krishna so that he'd realise he ought to be more obedient. Two months later she told him she was very sorry about his father's legal action but he should not feel anxious. Wicked men had made a tool of his father and she felt sorry for Narianiah since he had created bad karma. But they could try to help him some day. was her patronising conclusion.[7]

Balfour Clarke supplies the mind fix of most Theosophists at the time. claiming Krishna became the target for attacks from the "worldly-minded".

> Some of his [Krishnaji's father's] friends tried to stir up in him the deeply-rooted pride and prejudice of the Brahman [sic] by whispering in his ear that these two foreigners. Mrs Besant and Mr Leabeater. were

> gradually maturing a plan to cause his two sons to break their caste and to forsake Hinduism that they might become converts to some form of Christian Theosophy. They worked so insidiously and persistently upon his mind that finally he quite changed his point of view and grew more and more antagonistic to Theosophical and occult teaching: though before this he had felt it a great privilege to reside at Adyar and to place his two sons under the guardianship of one whom he had then regarded as his *guru* in all things high and spiritual.[8]

The question of whether Narianiah was supported or manipulated by orthodox Hindus depends on your point of view. Annie Besant was a truly charismatic figure and it's no surprise that Narianiah had taken her as his guru, although a statement from Balfour Clarke is not sufficient evidence in itself to prove that this was true. It's clear that at the very least Narianiah at first showed her very great respect.[9]

Many theosophists must have been devoted to her in a way that might be likened to the link between guru and spiritual devotee present among practitioners of *bhakti* yoga. Besant's powerful presence is attested to by a writer in 1922 who said that he had fallen in love with her on sight when he first met her in Calcutta in 1894. He was twenty five and she forty seven.[10] Yet the issue of Europeans, particularly the English, dominating the religious sphere as well as social and political life must have been anathema to many Indian philosophical students and religious practitioners. Even more than that, the way these bower-bird foreigners picked up bits and pieces of dogma and practice to build their own nests must have seemed ridiculous. It was an issue that had caused trouble for the Theosophists a generation earlier, with Subba Row's rejection of Blavatsky's rough-shod exposure of sacred occultism, and again when Chakravarti was challenged by Leadbeater as the chief confidante of Annie Besant. The best Indian minds were not about to back off now and allow an adulatory cult of Krishnamurti to make a mockery of their beliefs.

The charge that Narianiah was afraid of the influence of Christian Theosophy on his sons also seems quite valid considering Leadbeater's propensity for church ritual and dogma, as a former minister in the Church of England and later developing an interest in the breakaway Liberal Catholic Church, an interest which would become even stronger after his move to Australia in 1915. (George Arundale, Krishna's tutor, who had in turn been tutored by Leadbeater in England in the 1890s and was Principal of Annie Besant's Central Hindu College when he met Krishnamurti late in 1909, would also go on to become a Bishop in the Liberal Catholic Church and President of the Theosophical Society.) It's an interesting perspective to charge that Hindus had worked so "insidiously and persistently" upon Nariániah's mind when it was the Theosophists who were the imposters in a predominantly Hindu country and might be viewed as proselytisers for the Theosophist mind-set.

In any case it's not surprising that a father would be alarmed to hear that "his sons no longer belonged to him and he must not interfere in their lives". Apart from the deep emotions a father feels for his sons, in India, where no effective government social security system protects the aged from penury and where the family is the dominant socialising force, children represent some security for parents in their old age. But Leadbeater overrode these cultural sensibilities in declaring that "the Masters" had ordered that the two boys were to be isolated, associating only with those people who were under 'Theosophical influence', to such an extent no other boys were to touch Krishna's bicycle or tennis racquet for fear of "bad vibrations". Krishna and his father were at times shocked by Leadbeater's rudeness and insensitivity, especially to women. Leadbeater was also seen as having a "liability to irritability, which would sometimes become quite explosive and verging on the cruel". The more diplomatic Annie Besant at first had more success with Narianiah, for example in persuading him in 1909 to return the boys to the estate after spending only an hour at the traditional ceremony which commemorated their mother's death, and in agreeing that they should not participate in the rite in future.[11]

But Leadbeater would not be stymied in his intention to develop a puppet World Teacher and the coddling of Krishna continued. He was kept away from women and peremptory orders were made by 'the Masters' that the boys not enter their father's house. White European Theosophists watched Krishna's every move and listened to him with reverence.[12]

In this state of anticipation of the Second Coming, on January 11, 1911 – one year after Krishna's Initiation - George Arundale, Principal of the Central Hindu College, set up the cult, the Order of the Rising Sun of India. But his fervour was so great that there was a backlash against worship of the Hindu boy among the College Committee members. There was also controversy over members of an inner group, the Order of the Rosy Cross, being instructed to meditate on Arundale to increase his spiritual power. Parents were agitated that this conflicted with their educational ambitions for their 'sons of India', so Annie Besant disbanded the Order and, in a master stroke, immediately set up another, called the Order of the Star in the East. Members wore purple and blue ribbons 'magnetised' by Krishnamurti, and a silver five-pointed star and medallions indicating their rank of 'spirituality' within the Order. A magazine, the *Herald of the Star*, with Krishna as its nominal editor, would spread the message of the Coming World Teacher. But Arundale's excessive zeal led to threats of resignation by some staff at the Central Hindu College, so in order to avoid such disruption Arundale was granted leave of absence to return to England where it was anticipated he might act as tutor to Krishna and Nitya.[13]

Orthodox Hindus in the North of India had been the first to publicly attack Theosophists in the *Hindu* newspaper, claiming a high Initiate was preaching and practising the sin of Onan, or masturbation.[14] The editor, Srinivar Iyengar, opened up the debate and south Indians also took up their acid pens, so that soon Mrs Besant "had all four of the great Oriental religions against her" in a coalition she described as "the ultra-orthodox good people".[15]

Most letters to the editor were unsigned, but SV Subrahmanyam stood by his word. Subrahmanyam, who had taught Krishna and Nitya Sanskrit at Adyar, brought the principal Theosophists into disrepute when he said he heard Krishnamurti tell his father in Telugu, "The book [*At the Feet of the Master*] is not mine: they fathered it on me". Besant gave Subrahmanyam the alternative of recanting or banishment from Adyar and he regretted he could not deny he heard the words. He returned to his village and "died there shortly afterwards, while still himself little more than a boy".[16] Another critic was the physician who attended Colonel Olcott at his death, Dr MC Nanjunda Rao (or Row), who warned readers against the Society's outlandish notions. He advised Hindus to follow the ancient wisdom of their forefathers rather than deify an Englishwoman, regardless of how clever she was, particularly when she allied herself with a man with the character of Leadbeater and offered a little Hindu boy as an object of worship. Rao was accused of being a follower of Vivekananda but would neither confirm nor deny it. The former Theosophist, a college principal, PT Srinivasa Iyengar, claimed many followers were victims of "psychopathia sexualis", a term which had been used by a Madras physician, Dr TM Nair, in a medical journal *Antiseptic*. Krafft-Ebing, Bloch and Forel were cited as proving these abnormalities to be pathological while Theosophists, it was claimed, saw them as an indication of future morality. The *Hindu* even ran excerpts from two articles in the London weekly, *John Bull*, by Annie Besant's former friend, Horatio Bottomley, MP, who had split with her over the "filthy" Leadbeater.[17]

Annie Besant left for England in April 1911 to spend the summer introducing her wards to English society. She persuaded their father of the benefits of such a trip and any fears he had about Leadbeater at this stage would have been allayed by the fact that their chief tutor would remain in India. Before leaving, the boys were fitted out with expensive wardrobes from the most fashionable tailor in Bombay, as was thought fit for 'the Vehicle of the Messiah' and his attendants. Part of the makeover also involved having the holes in the lobes of their ears, the result of a traditional Hindu practice of piercing, sewn up by a doctor, since Leadbeater insisted that Krishna's body was unacceptable as a vehicle for the Lord with holes pierced in it. The local anaesthetic did not allay the pain, it seems, and Mrs Besant sat through the mini operation holding the boys' hands to try to transfer the pain to herself.[18]

Their acceptance of and by the English came as a cultural shock to the boys, a mostly favourable shock but with jarring mismatches at times. They met a woman who would become another foster-mother to them. Lady Emily Lutyens, who, already having a family, had at the age of thirty-six become an avid Theosophist, devoted to the idea of the 'Coming World Teacher'. Lady Emily's husband, leading architect, Edwin Lutyens, was always wary of Theosophy, having a dread of its "definitions and articles". "Why need we suffer the tyranny of creeds and the narrowing beliefs of men in men?" he wrote to his wife in 1911. "The fencing in of God with palings to his ways" was his conclusion about Theosophy's strict institutionalisation.[19]

But Lady Emily was a spiritual romantic, and on the arrival of the Adyar party at Charing Cross station she "had eyes for none but Krishna, an odd figure, with long, dark hair falling almost to his shoulders and enormous dark eyes which had a strange, vacant look in them". She noted that the boy was dressed in a Norfolk jacket. At the first meeting held, she sat on the floor in the front row at Krishna's feet and felt herself fortunate. Lady Emily saw a great deal of the boys that summer, reporting some of the difficulties they faced: shivering cold at an Oxford garden party; Krishna suffering acute stomach pains from the English diet of milk, porridge and eggs, and loading the tasteless food with pepper and salt to try to spice it up in the absence of curries; both boys suffering the pain of walking in shoes after their years barefoot; and jeers from the crowd thrown at the shy Krishna about his shoulder-length hair during King George V's Coronation parade, despite one bystander's exclamation at the boy's beautiful face.[20] This beautiful face was captured in a London studio photograph and has served as a passport to world-wide recognition for Krishnamurti ever since, used in situations as different as gracing the covers of books to its use in press coverage of court cases. Krishna was impressed by the photographic session. He wrote about it to his father, in a letter which was cited in the custody case to come as an example of his naïve writing style, at variance with the style of *At the Feet of the Master*, written eighteen months earlier:

> MY DEAR FATHER We have been photographed to-day and I hope they will be ready to bring them back. He took about 15 of us. I hope they will be alright. Yesterday we went to Maidenhead, there she gave a lecture, also AF Sinnett spoke. We are not going to Genoa as there is a bad cholera. Love to Sada and Siva Ram. Love to all. Yours affectionately, KRISHNA.[21]

Mrs Besant also wrote several letters to Narianiah about the great learning experiences the boys were having, mentioning an invitation from the First Lord of the Admiralty and a meeting with the "late" Prime Minister Balfour, "who is interested in Theosophy".

One letter in particular in which Mrs Besant raised problems about educating the boys as Hindus must have startled Narianiah. The boys certainly wear their threads but they cannot be trained as Brahmins in England, she stated bluntly. That they "keep their Indian hearts" seemed to be all that mattered to her. Families must adjust to the change, otherwise what would be the use of incurring all the expense of the trip? Mrs Besant advised Narianiah to accustom himself to the idea.[22]

Mrs Besant also took the boys to Paris where she gave a lecture at the Sorbonne to an audience of four thousand on the subject of Giordano Bruno, in whose body she believed she had lived a previous life. Krishna wrote to Leadbeater that he saw 'the Count' at the lecture, this vision being one of the Society's adept Masters, the Comte de St. Germain, who had lived in the eighteenth century.[23]

While in England Krishna made his first public speech at the newly-formed Order of the Star in the East, of which he was the head and Annie Besant 'the Protector'. Krishna, feeling fearful and embarrassed before the lecture, was saved by younger brother, Nitya, who saw his dilemma and drafted a few remarks which Krishna memorised. He said little more than that he looked forward to seeing the group again in two years when he would return to study at Oxford University, and he made a reference to the Second Coming of the Messiah. However a smooth entry into the hallowed halls of Oxford was far from assured, whether Krishna knew it or not, as the authorities had "diplomatically put her [Mrs Besant] off" after interviewing the boys.[24]

Back in India in October 1911 Mrs Besant had to face the inevitability of an amalgamation of her prized educational project, the Central Hindu College, with the Muir College at the University of Allahabad to form a National Hindu University. Although she was treated with respect publicly, having a permanent place provided for her on the University's governing body, privately Mrs Besant was bitter in believing her university plans had been stolen and overridden.[25]

The Society's annual conference in Benares at the end of the year was a major turning point for Krishna, his 'occult authority' providing the stimulus for continuing controversy and his father's complete re-thinking of his sons' future. Although Annie Besant and Leadbeater talked up their extraordinary visions of Krishna's 'coming out' (Mrs Besant saw a great coronet of brilliant, shimmering blue like a halo above Krishna; Leadbeater said the hall filled with tremendous power evidently flowing through Krishna), others present saw nothing more than an embarrassed Indian boy before an adoring crowd of over three hundred theosophists. Krishna was simply required to hand certificates to members but, after the first few had filed past him, one eager devotee suddenly prostrated himself at the boy's feet which led to a mass prostration by members, one after the other in the queue, some streaming tears. The day after the December 28 meeting Mrs Besant declared that Krishna's body had been selected by the Bodhisattva for his personal use. As an indication of the disapproval of some of Mrs Besant's strongest supporters at this flamboyant turn of events, the Secretary of the Indian Section of the Society, Babu Bagavan Das, wrote an article pointing out the danger for young students in such a show of emotionalism.[26]

Nor did Narianiah like this deification at all and on the last day of the year he complained to the mother of the boy previously chosen as potential Saviour. Mrs van Hook, that he and his sons would become the laughing stock of India. Narianiah claimed that he also spoke to Mrs Besant, threatening action if she did not separate her sons from Leadbeater.[27] Krishnamurti's official biographer, Mary Lutyens, claimed that anti-British extremists, enemies of Mrs Besant among orthodox Hindus, worked Narianiah up to act. Her claim, the same voiced by Balfour-Clarke, was that they insinuated that Mrs Besant intended that the boys break caste and forsake Hinduism for Theosophical Christianity. Narayaniah went to Benares to demand his sons return to him, which was refused. On returning to Adyar, he threatened legal action and insisted the boys be separated from Leadbeater. When Mrs Besant hurried down to Adyar in January 1912 she assured Narianiah of the separation from Leadbeater and he signed a document allowing them to return to England to study.[28]

But Mrs Besant was hatching a far-flung escapade. She sent Leadbeater ahead to make plans for a safe haven in Europe where she could hide the boys from their father and continue with Leadbeater's occult training. Narianiah was again talking legal action so while he was away from Adyar for a week, Mrs Besant let it be known she was sailing with the boys on February 10 but actually sailed on February 3. She wrote to Narianiah four days out to sea advising him to immediately vacate Adyar – his home for the past three years - and telling him that the boys would stay in Europe until their education was complete.[29]

Annie Besant was facing more than her fair share of troubles at this time, mostly over the idolisation of young Krishna, yet it doesn't seem to have occurred to her to give him up. Certainly there were many respected people who were voicing their scepticism about his deification, both conservatives and visionaries, within and outside the Society.

Mahatma Gandhi, who was developing his Hind Swaraj (or Indian Home Rule) campaign which would ultimately banish the

English from the government of India and transform the country in the process, wrote privately in 1911:

> I do not think that Mrs Besant is a hypocrite; she is credulous and she is duped by Leadbeater. When an Englishman suggested to me to read Leadbeater's *The Life after Death*, I flatly refused to do so as I had grown suspicious of him after reading his other writings. As to his humbug, I came to know of it later.[10]

Claiming there was fraud at Adyar, Gandhi went on to say that it was worth ascertaining what humbug prevailed there "safe under the cover of Mrs Besant's goodness". Her desire to pass off as 'the Master' was understandable, he wrote, but anyone who chased after occult powers couldn't help but become intoxicated.

Gandhi seemed to have a very reasonable and tolerant view of Theosophy, giving credit to Blavatsky's *Key to Theosophy*, which made a good impression on him, and more importantly, had sent many Hindus back to their own religion, he said. Nevertheless, while claiming that he took from Theosophy the lessons which he believed worthwhile, Gandhi was working on a friend who was a staunch Theosophist "to get him out of the hold of Theosophy", hoping he wouldn't be "taken in".[11]

A more significant and public blow to Mrs Besant was the defection of a leading Theosophist in Germany, Rudolph Steiner, who objected to the Krishnamurti cult. In 1912 she lost most of the German membership of 2,400 to Steiner's new movement, Anthroposophy.[12] Writing in May 1912, Annie Besant described criticism from Steiner and his followers as a "hail of attack", as they wanted to blame her. Steiner saw the Society becoming 'Orientalised' and rejected claims of Krishnamurti's special importance. He could not accept such an adoration-based cult, coming as he did from a background of respect for Goethe's scientific writings and study of geometry and having a strong interest in the esoteric experiences and subtle sense perceptions of individuals. Writing of that secession period, Steiner explains that from the time of the 1907 congress an anthroposophic movement developed through artistic expression, creating innovations which upset many old members of the Theosophical Society from England, France and Holland. This anthroposophic movement provided a different "inner bearing" than before. which was the reason the Anthroposophical Society could no longer exist within the Theosophical Society, he said. In a subtle explanation. Steiner emphasised that this was the cause of the split. not. as many people believed. the "absurdities" which had grown in the Theosophical Society over time and caused endless quarrelling.[33]

Although Annie Besant was reported to have taken the loss in her stride. she remained bitter over what she considered disloyalty. Writing in an Australian journal a decade later, Mrs Besant described the storm that broke out against her in 1911 as "part of the Pan-German movement to destroy the Empire of Great Britain in India". An attempt was made to oust her from the Presidency of the Society, in favour of Steiner, she said. (The next Society Presidential election was due in 1914 after a seven-year term.) Somehow, to Mrs Besant's mind, the German-based plot was hatched in the United States under the guise of peaceful reconciliation between Mrs Besant and the American breakaway Theosophists. She believed a dishonest 'emissary' of her American rival, Mrs Katherine Tingley, named Myron Phelps, had revived the 1906 charges against Leadbeater in an attempt to discredit her by persuading Narianiah to take legal action. Certainly Mrs Tingley was a vocal critic of Leadbeater, hounding him over paedophilia even into the 1920s, but if Narianiah was being urged into legal action he didn't by any means rush into a lawsuit. Mrs Besant left India with his sons in February 1912 and it wasn't until after her return in October without them that he took legal recourse to withdraw the guardianship.[34]

Ahead of the breaking storm back in January, Leadbeater had sailed off to the calm waters of the Mediterranean, finding Taormina in Sicily a suitable hideaway since it enhanced his claim that he'd once been a pupil of the ancient, world-renowned mathematician and philosopher, Pythagoras – Leadbeater's past lives being of exalted status.

Meanwhile Annie first took the boys back to London, staying with wealthy friends in South Kensington. It was a turbulent time in the suffragette campaign for women's rights, with female protesters hauled away to prison from street demonstrations. Annie Besant overstepped her usual law-abiding tone in an article in *The Times* by advocating violence to gain political reform. She also spoke at a mass meeting in Albert Hall to raise money for the release of women political prisoners. including Emily Pankhurst. Mrs Besant's old friend. Bernard Shaw. was no use to her in this time of need. his farce *Press Cuttings* being substantially a tract against the feminist movement. The Albert Hall meeting raised 10.000 pounds and forced the release of Mrs Pankhurst. while Mrs Besant's passion was stirred to advocate further militancy by the conservative attitudes that abounded.[35]

The militancy sounds a hollow ring however. considering Mrs Besant's predominantly pro-British Government. anti-violence stance in Indian politics. Gandhi. who was just entering what would become a brilliant and revolutionary public life, seems in the early years of the century's second decade to have been dancing a jig out of step with Mrs Besant in debates over anarchy and political freedom. He'd step in. she'd step out. and vice versa.

In 1913. for example. Gandhi said Mrs Pankhurst had broken all bounds in fighting. advising women to plunder and destroy. He admired her courage. calling her a brave lady after her collapse in gaol from eight days of fasting. but he explained that this kind of fighting to get released was not *satyagraha*. which had instead the object of getting into prison and staying there. Nevertheless, Indians should emulate Mrs Pankhurst's courage, he maintained.[36]

Yet in 1916 at the opening of the Benares University, Mrs Besant interrupted Gandhi as he spoke. fearing he was advocating anarchy and violence. His view was that "if some people had not thrown bombs we should never have gained what we have got" over the partition in Bengal and its annulment in 1911. "Please stop it," cried Mrs Besant. "If Mrs Besant ...suggests that I should stop, she does so because she loves India so well," Gandhi continued. With a reference to mutual love and mutual trust, he then went on to say that the British never gave self-government to a people who would not take it. "If we are to receive self-government, we shall have to take it," he declared, referring to the Boer War, and with Mrs Besant ready to walk out, the meeting came to an abrupt halt. If not for Mrs Besant's hasty and ill-conceived interruption, nothing would have happened and his speech would have left no room for doubt, Gandhi was reported as saying the next day.[37]

Regardless of what alliances and disputes these two titans would have in the future, Mrs Besant was under siege in 1912, with newspapers having a field day in India. So she sent the boys off with like-minded theosophist spirits in Taormina where she joined them after a brief lecturing spin in Holland, France and Italy in April and May. The party of seven consisted of Arundale, Jinarajadasa (a Singalese who had been taken under the wing of Leadbeater years before, had graduated from Cambridge and was now a lecturer for the Theosophical Society), Balfour Clarke, the two boys, Annie and Leadbeater.[38] But far from a typically English beer and skittles vacation, apart from swimming and sunbathing it was a hard 'spiritual' slog during the four months they spent in this holiday resort.[39] According to Balfour Clarke, all present "attained those further expansions of consciousness which are called higher Initiations", Krishna and Nitya moving the fastest through the grades, and Krishna and Jinarajadasa taking 'Second Initiations' (to cast off self-delusion, doubt and superstition) while Annie and Leadbeater worked on a book. The visit was kept secret ostensibly because of the important occult developments taking place but Mrs Besant and Leadbeater were keen to keep the location secret from the boys' father. Once Krishna and Nitya returned to England they stayed at the homes of friends: the Brights at 82 Drayton Gardens, South Kensington; 'Warwick House', St James's, owned by Miss Mary Dodge, a wealthy American spinster crippled with arthritis; and the country house of her companion, Countess de la Warr, 'Old Lodge' in Ashdown Forest, Sussex. A bodyguard of four young men protected Krishna and Nitya from hypothetical kidnapping by agents of their father, maintaining their security vigilance for eight months.[40]

Lady Emily Lutyens was charmed by the Theosophists' plans for their World Teacher but her husband Edwin was more circumspect, writing to her in September with some good advice. He had a dread of Leadbeater and said he believed in a force as dangerous as electricity and as little understood, so that he felt that this force, or occultism, was better left alone. As to Krishna, it too was dangerous to say of a boy so young that he would be a Messiah "and not expect to put the backs up of nearly every white man and the majority of blacks". Krishna must win allegiance through years of patient silent work, he said. No one could help him and prophecies could only hurt.[41]

Whatever the hyperbole and paranoia over the custody of the two boys and the campaign against Annie Besant and Leadbeater in the Indian press, there seems to be no evidence that Narianiah had the means or took steps to kidnap his own sons in Europe. He did, however, make a valiant effort to recover his adolescent boys by lawful means through the courts once Mrs Besant and Leadbeater boldly returned to India without them.

On October 24, 1912, he filed a suit in a local court at Chingleput for the return of his sons from Annie Besant's guardianship. The case was transferred to the High Court in Madras before Mr Justice Bakewell.[42]

Before and during her trip, Mrs Besant may or may not have received correspondence from Narianiah alleging improper sexuality between Leadbeater and Krishnamurti. Narianiah certainly claimed that he had written to her in February challenging a statement drawn up before her by her servant Lakshman in which Lakshman denied he saw anything improper – only that in Leadbeater's room one day he saw Leadbeater half-dressed, with one knee on a chair, Krishna in front of him and Leadbeater dressing his hair. During the court case Mrs Besant said she had no recollection of having received the letter. Narianiah also claimed that the Society's publisher, Mr Wadia, had told him that Lakshman saw Leadbeater commit an act the name of which was censored, "something very nasty", and that the librarian, Mr van Manen, had also been told this by Mr Wadia. In the February letter Narianiah said that he had not heard from the boys and he and his other two sons were anxious to know that they were well. A second letter from Narianiah in February corrected the place of the alleged incident to Mrs Besant's room, a less public place. Again Narianiah asked that his boys write to him. When Mrs Besant had written in February telling Narianiah to leave Adyar she hadn't spared his feelings, saying any decent father would rather have died than publicly accuse his son. She claimed his record of only five surviving children out of thirteen was an eloquent testimony to their home surroundings, the children before adoption being half-starved, dirty, beaten and in terror of his approaching step. If he tried to set aside the adoption she was prepared to prove their lives were made a veritable hell by him, she said. The boys would not return to India until they were men, "able to protect themselves" against him.[43]

Narianiah said that he received no letters from his boys but in May Mrs Besant sent a note to the eldest son, Sivaram, saying his brothers had a very serious piece of work to do for four months so they couldn't write to him but Krishna's love for him and little Sada was always the same. In July Narianiah wrote to her withdrawing his permission for guardianship as the boys' moral character was being undermined by continued association with Leadbeater and he demanded they be handed over to him in Madras by 31 August. Mrs Besant merely acknowledged receipt of his letter.[44]

Once back in India with the legal challenge under way and the *Hindu* in full attack, Mrs Besant drew up a reply to Narianiah's charges that filled five columns of the newspaper. She pointed out that Narianiah had allowed his sons to associate closely with Leadbeater for two years, thus sanctioning the relationship, and that he was an excitable and unreliable character. In declaring that Krishna was not being deified, she drew a distinction between 'the Vehicle' and 'the Person'. Another of her strong arguments was that the Foreword for *At the Feet of the Master* stated that the words were not Krishna's but those of the master. This was a convenient escape clause for her to be able to maintain that Nariamiah's claim - that the book was attributed to his son yet the boy could not yet write "a decent English letter" - was groundless as Krishna wrote as if by dictation from memory.[45] Her overwhelming argument was that the court case was a political plot, in which an enemy within the theosophist movement in America, Katherine Tingley, had joined forces with disaffected Hindus who had been targetting her ever since she took a stand against boys at the Central Hindu College getting involved in "the plots of the Extremists" during the Viceroyalty of Lord Curzon.[46] Certainly Narianiah's lawyer, CP Ramaswami Aiyar, was also the legal adviser to the *Hindu*, even though the paper denied direct acquaintance between its staff and Narianiah until after the court action was lodged.[47]

Once the case went to the High Court in Madras Narianiah was allowed by the judge to make an amendment and drop the charge against his son. Narianiah argued that at the time he signed the guardianship document he was completely under Mrs Besant's influence and control and his delay in taking legal action was due to his belief, shared by many, that she was semi-divine. But he claimed the document did not allow delegation to another person against whom he had an aversion. Mrs Besant argued her own case, emphasising that Krishna's character would be ruined if he were ordered back to his father in Madras. In any case he was just weeks away from turning eighteen, an age when he could decide for himself where he wanted to live. In England, she said, the boys were surrounded by love, mixing with "refined and cultured people, eminent in intellectual, moral and social life". Her conviction was reinforced by a letter from Krishna in which he reiterated his loyalty and devotion to her, surmising that her present difficulties were perhaps trials for the 'Fifth Initiation'.[48]

The trial date was delayed until 20 March 1913 and in the meantime Mrs Besant lost a series of libel suits she brought against the *Hindu* and other journals. She had claimed that the *Hindu*, with a regular "disregard" of fairness had published details of the legal suit to "deprive" her of custody of the boys. But when it came to her performance in the main case dealing with custody, before two to three thousand spectators every day, Mrs Besant was able to trap Narianiah into contradictions and hysterical tears, as well as expose inconsistencies in the testimony of her servant, Lakshman.[49]

The judgement on 15 April was remarkably divided. Although Mr Justice Bakewell said that Narianiah's stories were not to be trusted, he allowed him the right to change his mind over guardianship and ordered his sons be turned over to him by 26 May. But he also ordered Narianiah bear the costs for both sides in view of the protracted court investigation of unproved charges. Mrs Besant was gracious in defeat towards her opponent's legal counsel, Ramaswami Aiyar, but took out her invective against the news coverage in *The Times* in London for 8 May. The judge, she said, had described Leadbeater as a person holding immoral ideas, not as an immoral person, a moot point, one might have thought, and not significant enough to convince anyone of Leadbeater's trustworthiness with young people in his care.[50]

But Mrs Besant was not one to give up her defence of Leadbeater and Krishna so easily. She appealed the decision, lost, and then took the case to the Privy Council in London, where, it cannot be denied, she had friends in very high places. One in particular was Lord Haldane, an old Fabian, who was now Lord Chancellor and Chairman of the Judicial Committee. Krishna and Nitya were ordered to be present for the hearing in the Council Chamber as their interests were vitally affected. Annie Besant sat with Viscountess Churchill on her right and her son, Mrs Bright and Countess de la Warr on her left. The atmosphere was so friendly the boys were not at all shy about giving their reasons for not wanting to return to their father. On 25 May 1914 the Judicial Committee suggested that the Indian court order to return the boys could not stand because it could not lawfully be carried out without their consent – and only the High Court in England could deal with the question of jurisidiction of the Crown over infants in England. By August Leadbeater wrote from Madras to Krishna in Varengeville that they were all waiting day by day for a court decision on jurisdiction. checking the notice board every afternoon. and again in October he said the case was still dragging on and that Mrs Besant had been patiently exposing all the lies and malicious misrepresentations of her opposing counsel.[51] Finally the suit was dismissed. with costs to Nariamiah. Checkmate. Narianiah knew his sons would both have come of age before he won any further court action. as Krishna had already turned nineteen, and Nitya sixteen. Mrs Besant never claimed her costs. perhaps not wanting to add insult to national injury. Not long after, Lady Emily Lutyens held an 'at home' attended by. among others, the Lord Chancellor and Annie Besant.[52]

And what were the states of mind of Krishna and Nitya in this war being waged between their protectress and their father? Certainly, regardless of how they are treated at home. even considering allegations of hunger and mistreatment, Hindu boys do not readily defy the authority of their fathers. But Krishna and Nitya's father was being ridiculed by all around them. by high-class English men and women who were regarded as worldly. intelligent and the cream of civilised society. The boys would have had little resistance to the intense pressure they must have felt to conform to the thinking of the Theosophists whose foremost aims were to love and support them. The boys. always affectionate, returned this love, grateful for their extraordinary elevation in material terms, wanting to please and appease. Correspondence from 1913 shows their innocent outlooks.

Nitya wrote to Leadbeater in March 1913. impressed that the old man he believed a seer had reportedly discovered ten more 'Lives' to add to the network. asking for the names and commenting that he didn't envy the person who had to add these names to the charts. Over the next couple of months Nitya wrote several letters from different homes – Old Lodge in Sussex. a villa near Genoa. from Wimereux near Boulogne, and by July from *Les Communes*. a country house at Varengeville near the Normandy coast owned by friends. the Mallets, which had been designed by Lady Emily's husband. Edwin Lutyens. Lady Emily.

who had thrown herself into the Theosophical cause of preparing for the Coming World Teacher and was besotted by the young Krishna, took her children to Varengeville in the summer holidays to be near him.[53] She acted as surrogate mother to Krishna and Nitya and, having taken lessons in public speaking, was almost as mobile as Mrs Besant and the boys, lecturing in draughty halls across the countryside to spread the word of the Coming Teacher. Before her trip to Varengeville, her husband Edwin, who, as a man of business, kept his ear to the ground, told Lady Emily in a letter home from India that the Minister for Education, Sir Harcourt Butler, had told him there were ugly rumours about the boys at Adyar but he did not think it could be true. "He did not refer by this to Alcyone [Krishnamurti] but he evidently thought the position might prove dangerous ... he made no committal or definite statement and I didn't really want to hear anything unpleasant," Lutyens admitted.[54]

Writing from Varengeville in early July, Nitya says they've settled there and Krishna is playing tennis in the grounds regularly. At the end of the month Nitya says he hopes the court case is "going on alright" and then in August tells Leadbeater he's glad the case is progressing "in our favour", aware that the appeal may have been decided by the time Leadbeater gets the letter. His attitude is entirely open and favourable towards the old man.

Aged just fifteen, this intellectual youth has a lot of questions to ask before he'll be satisfied as a seeker of Truth. He wants to know what makes a Mahachohan, or Master, and what is his work. Can Leadbeater send him a list of all the changes in names, and finally, can he find out about himself, what he is to aim for, what he has to do in the future? "If it is permissable to know, will you please tell me?" asks the polite and frustrated youth.

In another letter from Varengeville in August, Nitya describes a new Order of the Servants of the Star, suggesting that as Krishna himself has authorised its foundation it will be helpful and successful in its aim to draw young people together. Support is being sought from Mrs Besant, Lady Emily, Countess de la Warr and Lady Churchill and as Krishna has definitely expressed his approval, it is taken for granted that the "Higher Authorities" will also approve. He encloses a draft prospectus. What the young ingenue doesn't anticipate is the incessant rivalry and politicking within the Theosophical Society. There will be many spiritual interpreters and administrators to pass opinion on these youthful aspirations to prevent any unexpected changes to the Order being effected.

In September Nitya writes to Mrs Besant that Krishna was photographed by the best photographer in Paris. Nitya seems to have solved his problem about what he is to do in the future, telling her that he thinks he will work for India as a barrister. The following month he writes to Leadbeater that he's glad he approves of him going to the Bar.

Despite "settling" in Varengeville, soon the boys are off on their travels again. In November they visit Genoa and stay at the Hotel Milano in Florence. Then they return to London, where Nitya writes that he does not think that they can go on as they are and they will be leaving London again soon. In January 1914 the brothers are staying in Taormina for a little over a month. Nitya explains that when he last wrote he put his address as Drayton Gardens in London as they were not supposed to tell anyone where they were "because of some legal business". But as they would be in London for the Privy Council Appeal, "The lawyer tells us that we need keep our place of abode for the next week no longer secret". It's a disturbing business, this secrecy and constant shifting ground but the zestful, enquiring Nitya keeps his mind trained on bigger puzzles.

> I want to ask you some questions which I hope you won't think too private to answer. We were talking the other day about all of you being adepts next life. I mean all the people who will be Arhats this life. Krishna, Raja and you will, I presume, be on the same level. But if you are to be the Teachers of different root races with millions of years interval, how is it that the three are at the same stage at a period? In reality I suppose you are the higest [sic], but how is it that the other two are at the same level or rather will be at the same level?

The sweet boy's clear-thinking, honest and probing mind would press against the confines of Theosophy's theories.

Questions concerning the Apostles were also troubling Nitya. Somebody said that Leadbeater had stated that they were all a myth, all except Paul. If Paul did exist, did Leadbeater think it was probable that he would take birth now in order to help in the preparation? Was it permissible for himself, Nitya, to know these things, he asked. And he excused himself for troubling Leadbeater so much. The next day he and Krishna were on a train bound for London, headed for an appointment with a lawyer who would tell them whether they were to attend the Privy Council appeal. But today Nitya wanted to know whether a person on the Second Ray could be a Mahachohan and what the Lord Maitreya said on 17 January about the Servants of the Star. And, as a final note, he explained that Dr Rocke, an Australian appointed English Secretary of the Order of the Star, wanted to know whether the Zoroastrian religion was under the charge of the Master KH. Such a volatile mixture of innocence and ambition, simplicity and complexity was haunting the thoughts of this adolescent as he and his "chosen" brother travelled as fugitives across the map of Europe.

By the end of the month, ensconced again in Drayton Gardens, Nitya has assumed a worldy air, describing his and Krishna's attendance before the Privy Council Committee, sharing with Leadbeater his intimate knowledge of the workings of the British legal system – "Paramour was lately made a peer" and "Sir Robert Finlay who I believe will be Lord Chancellor when the Conservative government comes in". But his exuberance shines through – he writes of the counsels' funny wigs and envious faces (seen through the eyes of someone who hopes to practise law). Nitya is impressed by the immense power of the Lord Chancellor in the way he speaks yet finds it ridiculous that it matters that evidentiary papers are two inches longer than the appointed size. "So far everything is in our favour." Nitya concludes as he anticipates going down to the country for a couple of months before the Appeal is due to commence.[55]

In contrast to Nitya's questioning correspondence to Leadbeater, in 1913 the older Krishna, now about eighteen, is concerned with the practicalities of place and organisation. From Italy in March he writes to George Arundale, whom he addresses as 'My beloved son' despite Arundale being the elder by seventeen years, that he wants to know who will take Arundale's place in the Order once he leaves. He suggests PK Telang for a year as a try-out, followed by Wodehouse. And he wants to write to members of what he knows about magnetism and how to cure the sick.[56] In April from Septeuil, north-west of Paris, Krishna says he's so glad the court case went well and hopes it will be over soon. He encloses a copy of "a little speech" he gave in Paris. Writing from Wimereux in June, Krishna describes the sea view as beautiful, the food as very good and mentions the tennis court they hire. He says their friend Charle [sic] Blech thinks letters should be addressed in someone else's name to avoid attacks by the French press following the Privy Council hearing.

Then in early July from Varengeville he comments that the new T.R.C. [Temple of the Rosy Cross] will be useful when the Lord Maitreya comes. At the end of the month, writing on Order of the Star in the East letterhead, which includes the words, 'Office of the Head, J Krishnamurti', in the top left hand corner, Krishna discloses various manoeuvres. He'd had a "strong" thought that "Bhagat" should not be in the Order, and he'd put it out of his mind but it recurred. So he'd spoken to Arundale, and then they had both spoken to Jinarajadasa and it was agreed that Arundale and Krishna should speak to "Bhagat". They did so and Arundale had been tactful and it was all "settled". No further explanation. That a thought came into Krishna's mind might be reason enough for action. Or perhaps Leadbeater already had some insight into what the trouble was. Thankfully, George Arundale was on hand to do the dirty work.

Then to some money matters – Bibby has given 100 pounds a year for five years and Miss Dodge has given 200 pounds a year for five years towards publishing the journal *The Herald of the Star*. So they are getting on well in regard to money, he says. A few days later Krishna is sending Leadbeater a photo of a young man who is in with a bad lot, and is hoping Leadbeater might help him, presumably by good thoughts from afar.

In August Krishna writes a stiff letter to Mrs Russak, a stalwart of the Society, divesting her of her appointment as an international lecturer of the Order, referring to Mrs Besant's endorsement of his decision, but assuring her that her usefulness will not be diminished.[57]

Signing herself as 'Herakles', Ms Besant sends a telegram to Krishna in Genoa at the end of October to say he should not feel forsaken and that they'd done "admirably". Yet another cable forwarded from Mrs Besant via London announces that the court appeal had failed. The brothers are to return to London immediately to take legal advice. Writing to Leadbeater that same day, Krishna makes it clear he wants to take control of his life, after having been "dragged" about like an infant. Perhaps it's a combination of Krishna's newfound love of golf combined with the disappointing legal news that stiffens up Krishna's attitude. He wants a house by the sea in Devonshire, he doesn't want Jinarajadasa as his tutor, and nothing will induce him to return to his father.[58]

Despite the favours being bestowed on him, Krishna, like Nitya, is feeling rattled by the emphasis on secrecy and constant travel as a security measure. By the end of December 1913, Krishna writes of the difficulty of not letting people know where they are, but gives a reassurance that they are very comfortable and have beautiful views. His loyalties are very strongly with Mrs Besant, who seems to have taken on a martyr's role, seen from Krishna's standpoint. He fears she will be prosecuted for contempt of court and declares that these people seemed to have no "honour". "These" people presumably include his father. He is on the side of righteousness, with the good Mrs Besant, believing that the Government might interfere if the case against them goes too far and public opinion stays with them.[59]

A few months earlier, at the end of September while still at Varengeville and after having spent an agreeable summer, adored by, among others, Lady Emily and family, Krishna does show some small sign of uncertainty – this time over a spiritual matter he wants to clarify with Leadbeater. He "strongly" feels that

George Arundale will be Buddha after him, and after George, Lady Emily will follow. It's been on Krishna's mind for a long time – can Leadbeater tell him if it is right? He also checks whether Leadbeater thinks a certain "Basil" [probably the body-guard cum tutor, Hodgson-Smith] is an accepted pupil of the Master. All these letters show there's not the depth of enquiry as is found in Nitya's correspondence. Krishna is more concerned with organisational matters. But his affectionate respect for Leadbeater is strong. As usual, Krishna signs off giving his "very much "love" and affection and underlines his name.[60]

The affection the boys felt for both Leadbeater and Mrs Besant was evident in their correspondence. They always wrote to Mrs Besant on her birthday and the tenor of their writing was very often yearning for the comfort of her presence and reassuring love. Viewed in the cool ambience of contemporary Western society, these emotional letters from young Indian boys can seem overly sentimental, but almost a century ago such sensibilities were more openly expressed. Signing himself as her "devoted" son, Nitya writes a birthday note to Mrs Besant from Varengeville in September 1913. He says that Arundale has been talking about the problems associated with getting people to "co-operate" in India and he hopes that when he is back there he shall be able to "work" for India and so follow her "example". He hopes too that the court case will be in "our favour". Aligning himself with India, that is, Mrs Besant's India. The concepts in his mind are "us" and "them". And again the same month, he thinks he shall choose the Bar as his profession, if she agrees, for he wants "to serve India". But Nitya's financial security seems to materialise from England now, not a future India. By October wealthy Miss Dodge has settled 300 pounds a year on him, and Nitya is very glad it will relieve his "dearest Mother" of some of her burden, and possibly even assist in the court case. He believes he can live on half the sum he'll receive.[61]

When Mrs Besant is off to India, her loving adopted son Nitya, who expects to go there himself fairly soon, is so sorry he can't travel with her. "It would be wonderful if we could always be with you and work together ... you know how much I love you ... If only I could do something for you ... with all my love".

By March 1914 Nitya is studying hard to go to Oxford and checks with his "dearest Mother" about waiting for another year to improve his chances in the entrance examination. "Responsions" are dominating the thoughts of Mrs Besant's "loving" and "devoted" son.[62]

On the other hand, Krishna is very despondent about his life after the successful yet ultimately disappointing climax of the court case. He is to receive 500 pounds a year from Miss Dodge and 125 pounds a year from Mrs Besant, but what is expected of him in return? To become a Saviour. And he must discover on his own the qualifications for such a role.

Mrs Besant returns to India in June 1913, under instruction from her "Master" to devote her energies to Indian Home Rule. Meanwhile the boys are left with the onerous task of studying for entrance to Oxford, in Krishna's case a seemingly insurmountable goal, as he's never been academically-minded and his name is associated with scandal and eccentricity. There are enough tutors around him to make a success of the most recalcitrant student – at different times these include Jinarajadasa, Arundale and Wodehouse, and Shiva Rao is even sent over from Adyar to teach Sanskrit – but Krishna lacks motivation. In the summer of 1914 the small group of tutors and boys are living at Bude on the seaside in Cornwall and Lady Emily goes down to join them, by this time Arundale becoming impatient with her infatuation.

Lady Emily had been supremely happy during her stay at Varengeville in the summer of 1913, living so close to Krishna. The small community comprises: the Mallets, who had first introduced Lady Emily to the Theosophical Society; Lady Emily's children, including Barbara whom both Nitya and Arundale loved, and the younger Mary who, in turn, was in love with Nitya; plus various others in the group of tutors and helpers. This disparate group forms a hothouse of emotions.

Lady Emily had explained that she loved Krishna as her son and *guru* – he seventeen, she in her late thirties and neither sexually mature. Theosophists believed in higher and lower natures – the lower definitely being primitive sexual urges – and Lady Emily had never enjoyed, but always *endured*, the sexual act for the sake of having children. In her autobiography she wrote that during this time her husband, her home, her children faded into the background. "Krishna became my entire life, and for the next ten years I suffered all the difficulties of trying to sublimate a human love." From Bude Lady Emily wrote to her devoted husband that she had "suffered intensely physically" during her marriage. "I have done my duty to you and my country as regards children," she wrote, believing that every woman had a right over her own body, and to give her body to Edwin unwillingly would be prostitution. She announced the severance of their physical relationship, asking forgiveness for the pain she caused him, her darling 'Nedi'. She must have hoped that the move to a platonic relationship would help her ascent on the Theosophical astral plane's ladder of promotion. Edwin Lutyens had written to his wife just the day before, saying that he did not like ribbons – blue or any other colour – magnetised by Krishna's touch and used for badges of various grades in the Order. "I don't believe they are 'magnetised' – do you?" he wrote, a little too cockily, it would seem from the outcome. Three days after her shocking letter of rejection, Edwin Lutyens replied that he felt ill and depressed and would do anything to retain her love, but he felt less sympathy with Theosophy than ever. The thought of returning to India where he was working on plans for a new seat of government in New Delhi, so far away from her and so alone, made him feel sick at heart, he said.[63]

Lady Emily's love for Krishna was odd and disruptive to her marriage, but Edwin would not give her up so easily. He admitted to his body being "self rampant, aggressive, horrid" but said he hated the Theosophist paraphernalia introduced into his home – "the large photographs".

> How could I all this time do all those things you hate and loathe? How could you darling be intimate and petting with the Krishnaji party? You know how I hate it. I have tried to be just kind and patient. ... I think the plane – if true – on which you and others occupy each other's minds

> and bodies is just as immoral – to me nauseous and horrid – as anything else. Do you hate 'me' because you think it prevents Vedas or whatever you call them occupying you? Heaven knows where (what I believe to be) your absorbing 'follies' will lead you.[64]

It's hard to know what Krishna felt physically for Lady Emily. She was a surrogate mother, it is true – he called her "My dearest Mother" in correspondence. But as a sexually frustrated young man with time on his hands perhaps the "petting", as Edwin describes it, did involve physical union to some degree. It is generally believed that it was during the 1913 summer holiday in Varengeville that Lady Emily and Krishna's love for each other, which had begun as a mother-son relationship, became obsessive, to the point where Lady Emily later destroyed many of Krishna's early letters to her as she considered them "too intimate". Not having the prospect of marriage in his own life, he always scorned others' announcements of intending marriage. And this would not be the last occasion Krishna would witness at very close range the rejection of the marriage vows to a husband by a wife besotted by his beauty.[65]

Krishna wrote to Leadbeater an emotional letter in February 1915 in which he stressed that he loved Lady Emily very *purely*, assuring him that he was not like usual people "in that respect" and never would be. In any case Mrs Besant had warned them not to show their affections openly as it might cause trouble. Krishna also claimed that Edwin Lutyens said Lady Emily should not be so friendly with him as he was an Indian, Krishna describing Lutyens himself as an 'anglo-Indian'. (Lutyens' father was English and his mother Irish). Krishna's letter was entirely concerned with people's emotional states, their loves, their jealousies and his belief that he and others were trying to do their best. He put in many good words about Lady Emily so that she would be "accepted by the Master". Judging by the letter it's a wonder that everyone hadn't collapsed from emotional exhaustion. But not a word about the war, politics, the weather, wildlife or even what he ate for breakfast. He told Leadbeater he loved him "*very*" much. When he was with him he had hurt him in many ways and now that he saw it all more clearly he was "*very*" sorry, was the way he emoted. As if everything depended on this epistle. There were, in the "*whole*" world, four people he loved and they were: Leadbeater, Mrs Besant, George Arundale and Lady Emily and that would never change whatever happened, he said. How wrong he was. Leadbeater was already distancing himself from Krishna, writing less often, and by the time they left Bude, Arundale and Krishna would suffer an irreparable breach in their relationship.[66]

It's true that those within the Theosophical circle, living so closely together and sharing a set of beliefs, also shared their minds, waking and sleeping. Lady Emily describes one incident at Varengeville in 1913 when she dreamt and also had prophetic thoughts which Krishna confirmed had occurred during their sleep, so that she felt the greatest joy in the world.

However there were others who held fears that the love which existed between Lady Emily and Krishna was on a too personal plane. Along with Edwin Lutyens, George Arundale was not keen on their close relationship. He reported this to Mrs Besant and deterred Lady Emily from seeing too much of Krishna. She had "hindered" the Master's work by emphasising Krishna's lower nature at the expense of the higher, he said. The result was, even though she could not see it, that Krishna's higher nature had "kept away" when she had visited. Arundale suggested she raise her own love to that strength which would make it "indifferent" to any return from Krishna.[67]

By 1916 Nitya reported that Krishna's love for Lady Emily was no longer an infatuation but a very steady love. Krishna at this time was professing his love for George as just the same as it had always been, and saying that despite George's jealousy, Lady Emily had not drawn him away from George.[68]

Apart from the bond with Lady Emily, all was not well with Krishna during this period. He had a motor cycle and took golf lessons with a professional but felt at a loose end. But, more disturbing, he seemed to be developing what Lady Emily describes as a "divided personality". There was a different side to the dreamy, spiritual young man – he loved cinema, theatre and motor cars and his sudden changes of mood "from the sublime to the ridiculous" would puzzle her. On looking back on this period from the age of 38. Krishna recognised that he was at first critical behind people's backs and then openly, even of Mrs Besant, describing his life in dissolute terms – being exceedingly fond of fine clothes, attending opening nights and fashionable resorts and careless about diet.[69]

Early in the war Krishna wrote to Mrs Besant that the Germans were not as bad as the papers made them out to be and he had a great sympathy for them. They were brave, he said. And he wanted to know whether Mrs Besant thought he should join the war. She thought it a bad idea, not so much because he might kill someone as he would have to pollute his body by eating meat.[70] That eating meat was anathema to Mrs Besant must have been fairly common knowledge since Gandhi referred to it in 1913. He likened Lord Buddha's body falling dead, when he ate flesh received in alms, to Mrs Besant vomiting if ever eggs were used in her food as a result of ignorance or oversight.[71]

In late 1914 Nitya went off to study with a tutor at Oxford, leaving Krishna, dispirited, at Bude. Krishna longed for a normal life, asking why did 'they' choose him for this extraordinary 'World Teacher' role. Mrs Besant wrote to him that his happiness must lie in 'the work' and that he would be restless and unhappy if he turned away from it. Now grown, he couldn't turn to Mrs Besant for comfort, as she was so caught up in politics in India, including editing a paper she had taken over, *New India*. Nor could he seek reassurance from Leadbeater who had moved to Kodaikanal when the Madras scene heated up. As an imperialist, Leadbeater was out of tune with Mrs Besant's Indian Home Rule aspirations so by the end of 1914 he was making plans to travel to Australia, where, along with California, theosophists believed a new sub-race was evolving.

Nitya too wanted a mother to love him, like Lady Emily, according to Krishna. Nitya studied hard and wasn't well. He at least was able to escape the oppressive atmosphere of Bude, by joining a Theosophist doctor in Paris, and working as a dispatch rider for the Red Cross. There were plans for Krishna to join him, then he was told he could help in renovating a hospital in London, but after a few months Krishna was advised to give up war work and to go back to his studies, since it seemed that as an Indian no-one wanted him. Edwin Lutyens wondered of Krishna in 1915 whether he would continue to submit to the unnatural surroundings - "spoon and apron fed" – when he turned twenty-one the following year, since he was becoming unfitted for all work except the esoteric while "his poor India cries aloud for reliable men of action".[72]

Krishna tried his best to study, and when Arundale went up to London as General Secretary of the Society for England and Wales, other tutors, including Wodehouse, were assigned Krishna as their charge. But by 1917 he failed to get into any college at Oxford – his name was tarnished and his grades were poor.[73]

In India, meanwhile, Mrs Besant had maintained her political activity apace. In June 1917, as a result of her political activism over Indian Home Rule, she was interned at Ootacumund with BP Wadia and Arundale, who had returned to India. Mrs Besant had been an extraordinary tactician and activist for Hind Swaraj or Home Rule, particularly since 1915 when she had had an astral experience with Leadbeater (who was actually living in Australia) in which she saw pictures of an Allied victory and future events in the world for centuries to come. She was so energised by the experience, she took to her political work in India with even greater gusto during the war when many English were very sensitive about any criticism of British rule. Many theosophists back in England tried to suppress her propaganda, including Harold Baillie-Weaver, who was having such an influence in educating Krishna and Nitya about elegance and good taste in clothing. But Mrs Besant was irrepressible, sending lecturers back to England, and holding talks with the leading players in Indian politics.[74]

Recognising MK Gandhi as a rising star, she invited him to a garden party in his honour under the spreading banyan tree at

Adyar, saying he'd told her that he had met her in 1889 at Mrs Blavatsy's. A rift developed between them, however, when she wrote disparagingly of Gandhi's *ahimsa* (non-violence) and *satyagraha* (truthfulness) concepts, as she was concentrating instead on questions of methods of election and representation in a National Congress. Nevertheless Mrs Besant contributed an article to the first issue of Gandhi's *Young India* in November 1915 and the following month organised a conference on Home Rule attended by two hundred and fifty delegates.[75] Her zeal was never dampened by critics. In 1917 the newly-appointed Secretary of State for India, Austen Chamberlain, called her political methods dangerous, she had an altercation with Gandhi at the foundation ceremony for the Hindu University, the police were increasingly harassing her by "protecting" disorderly crowds at her public lectures, delaying and damaging her mail, demanding money from her over her seditious articles, and finally she was interned. She had always made it clear that she believed in Home Rule rather than Self-Government as she wanted India to remain within the British Empire. But her enthusiasm to weld together the disparate political forces of India (by for example joining the more extremist BG Tilak's League simultaneous with membership of her own Home Rule League, and working through the Congress for unanimity) deeply unsettled the Government. Mrs Besant worked hard to have the Madras Parliament's bill, the "The Commonwealth of India Act", considered by the House of Commons and though time was running out she would not keep quiet, describing India as the wage slave of the Empire, and in late 1916, arguing her appeal under the Press Act against charges of disloyalty. She even challenged Baden-Powell's Boy Scout movement, which excluded Indian boys, by setting up an Indian Boy Scout organisation, at first rejected by Baden-Powell but later assimilated into the international movement.[76]

In 1917 as word got about that Mrs Besant was to be interned, supporters in Australia cabled for her to join Leadbeater in Sydney where research facilities would be provided for her. But

Annie was never one to back off from a fight. Besides, by May she was elected first President of the Women's Indian Association following the adoption by the Congress of a resolution for women's suffrage. In mid-June BP Wadia and Arundale were expelled from Madras and forbidden to engage in any public activities and Mrs Besant was offered safe conduct to England for the duration of the war. But she refused this, saying that the Government was striking its deadliest blow against the British Empire in India. The three were interned in the hill town, Ootacumund, Mrs Besant travelling there alone, after a send-off at Madras Central Station which lasted half an hour as her supporters passed before her, bowing in respect, with their hands in *namaskar* or prayer gesture, as she declared "*Vande Mataram*!" (Sanskrit for 'Worship the Mother').

The influence Mrs Besant had on Indian nationalism can hardly be over-emphasised, the diversity of her interests and the range and effect of her personal notoriety difficult to comprehend, set within the confining social practices of the period. She was a model to at least one generation of Indians, future leaders who, even if they finally went beyond the limitations of her British Empire parliamentary model, owed their passion for the enfranchisement of Indians to the courage and commitment Mrs Besant showed in paving a way forward. As Gandhi said, she had "made Home Rule a *mantram* in every cottage".[77]

Once interned, Mrs Besant presented a figure of martyrdom which opposition political leaders of all persuasions could use. Mohammed Ali Jinnah cabled Chamberlain protesting the internment; Motilal Nehru, leading journalist, lawyer, and father of Jawaharlal, who would become independent India's first prime minister, was inspired to join the League; well-known barristers, Joseph Baptista of Bombay and EL Iyer of Madras announced they would take court action in England. Gandhi wrote to the Viceroy's private secretary to say the internments were a big blunder as Madras had been calm before the government acted against Mrs Besant.

> ...now she is on a fair way towards commanding India's identity with her methods. ... no one could deny Mrs Besant's great sacrifice and love for India or her desire to be strictly constitutional ... Many of us have respectfully differed from Mrs Besant but all have recognised her powers and devotion. ...I plead with all the earnestness I can command for the boldest policy, ie to acknowledge the blunder in the frankest manner and to withdraw the orders of internment.[78]

In August Gandhi chaired a Home Rule League meeting of businessmen at Ahmedabad and the following month, in a long statement about *satyagraha,* he wrote that Mrs Besant couldn't be freed through armed action but if she wasn't released within a certain time limit, people would be compelled to follow her path.[79]

Mrs Besant, although not imprisoned, was confined to a small house owned years before by Olcott. She was stifled, yet even under these conditions she turned the confinement to some good. She worked on a design of a flag of green and red, symbolising Muslims and Hindus, which later became the first Congress flag, with a white section and Gandhi's spinning wheel added to represent minorities and cottage industries. The flag was modified to become the first flag of independent India. But apart from this hope for the future, Mrs Besant, hidden away in Ootacumund, found her spirit was weakening. She suffered badly from depression and fatigue so the three were moved to the warmer climate of Coimbatore. The reaction throughout India to the internments was outrage, with public meetings organised all over the country. Back in England, where *The Times* described Mrs Besant as "fanatical", Baillie-Weaver, the Society's General Secretary, set to work to pull the aristocratic strings that had always worked in the past. From India, Mrs Beant's staunch supporter, former Madras High Court judge, Dr Subramania Iyer, even wrote a letter to President Woodrow Wilson which was smuggled through British censorship and caused the Americans to ask some embarrassing questions. Further fuel to the anti-government fire came with the election of Mrs Besant as President of the Congress, a proposal first mooted by PK Telang, General Secretary of the Home Rule League, which gained support from one provincial committee after another across the country. On 18 September, after more than ninety days of internment, Mrs Besant, Arundale and Wadia were released, and the masses rejoiced. In Calcutta it was estimated that three hundred thousand people turned out to see a street procession with the three freedom fighters in a carriage drawn by sixteen horses.[80]

At last Krishna had developed an interest in something outside of the emotions of his nearest and dearest. In the light of Mrs Besant's Herculean effort he is said to have been in favour of Indian Home Rule and sympathetic to the Labour Party in Britain, making friends with George Lansbury, Labour MP. Krishna told Mrs Besant in April 1917 that he was a great pacifist and wanted to be a complete cosmopolitan – a stance he adopted for life. His refusal to believe in stories of German atrocities during WWI, if it is reported correctly, is perhaps not so admirable, indicating a naivete, gullibility or at least immaturity.[81] But the attitude is consistent with his later abhorrence of all forms of party political activity and its extension, nationalism, which he saw as the result of egoistic emotional commitment forcing a person to take sides or hold strong partisan opinions.

Krishnamurti was in a privileged position to see the vagaries of politics simply by observing his "dear mother's" fate over the next decade. Her interpretation of the position of President of the Congress as an opportunity to be politically active throughout the year rather than as a figurehead, was one of the reasons the tide turned against her, led by conservative elements in the Congress. The other reasons were that she was now elderly, and a woman, and after the long internment she was in no mind to antagonise the British administration unnecessarily. Essentially she was a representative of the British in a country struggling to articulate its own nationhood. She wrote in 1918 there was no doubt about the suffering inflicted on her the previous year, describing her whole life as "shattered beyond mending".[82]

Nehru believed that Annie Besant's failure to get down among the people was her major drawback to ultimate political success – she spoke only limited Hindi, and no other Indian language. In effect the people's enthusiasm for Home Rule had overtaken hers, which had been their stimulus, and Gandhi was the perfect vehicle to direct this energy. Nevertheless, Mrs Besant's influence was long-lasting even while her popularity was on the wane. Nehru credits her internment as being the stimulus for his own father, Motilal, and other Moderate leaders to join the Home Rule League. Many later left but Motilal remained as president of the Allahabad branch, in turn influencing his son's movement towards a political life. As Mrs Besant's protégé, BP Wadia, is also credited with having formed the first trade unions in India in 1918, Mrs Besant supporting the cigar-makers strike the year before, just as she had supported the London matchgirls back 1888.[83]

But it was Gandhi who would carry the massive popular wave of independence to its bitter end thirty years later, as Mrs Besant, aged seventy the year of her internment, would fade from the political scene gradually after being seen as an apologist for the British Government, the outcome of her reported reaction to the Amritsar massacre and her acceptance of the Rowlatt Act on sedition aimed at tightening political controls.[84]

Meanwhile in Australia, Leadbeater was creating a few more scandalous headlines. His earlier indiscretions with boys were catching up with him while his roles within the Theosophical Society and the Liberal Catholic Church, of which he was now a bishop, were being flagrantly questioned.

1920 saw Krishna packed off to Paris after failing all his examinations for London University. Nitya had passed his matriculation with honours and begun to read for the Bar, hoping to go to India and earn a living there, whereas Krishna was even more despairing. He was staying with Theosophist friends who would help him polish his French, expected to be useful in his future role as Messiah.[85] It was reported that he suffered periods of great depression and rebelliousness interspersed with inspiration and hope. At this time another young Indian had come on the scene, Desikachar Rajagopal, who had also been "discovered" by Leadbeater, in 1914. There was some talk that this young man was a rival to Krishna. Leadbeater was also promoting the idea in Australia that the Lord might choose different spokespersons in different countries and it might be twenty years before these were chosen, which was a sign that Krishna was perhaps moving out of favour. To add to the pressure, Krishna was at this time struggling with a move by C Jinarajadasa (familiarly known as Raja and not to be confused with Rajagopal) to introduce greater ceremony into the Society. Krishna's exasperation to the point of rudeness shows in his frank letters to Lady Emily about Rajagopal. He called him by his full "blinker", Rajagopalacharya, and referred to rumours that he, Krishna, was fearful or jealous of him. But the "poor chap" could accept his own "notorious" place in his stead for "two sous", Krishna said. "Personellement je m'en fiche de Raja. Rajago!!!" was his reaction.[86]

Krishna was also very impatient about the idea that he was indebted to the Society. IF, and he underlined the word four times, if he was to occupy a leading role in the Society it would be because of who he *was*, not what other people thought of him, he said, and if Raja thought he, Krishna, must return his debt in service, he would tell him he had never asked to be taken out of India, he said. Anyway it was all "d ... d rot" and he was fed up with it.[87] Now in his mid-twenties and with Mrs Besant and Leadbeater in far-flung reaches of the world, Krishna had to shoulder more of the burden of responsibility for running the Order of the Star in the East. He told Leadbeater in 1921 that he had written to many rich people seeking funds and not received replies. He sounded self-righteous and pompous in reminding Leadbeater that it was the duty of every member to subscribe to the *Herald of the Star* journal, as it was the source of their inspiration. And then he was immediately remorseful – it had been greatly his fault for not taking enough interest in the journal, but now his heart and soul were in it and in the Theosophical Society, he reassured Leadbeater.[88]

What Krishna really wanted was to gain what he could from the West and then turn his face to India where he was sure he should work. he told Mrs Besant. He expected to go home the minute he was called. Nitya too was looking forward to returning to India at the end of 1921 to help Mrs Besant in her political campaigning. working on her journal. *New India*. to ward off the "troubles" Gandhi was causing her. Mrs Besant had given a lecture at the Sorbonne in August 1921 to a crowd estimated at 2.500 in 100 degree heat, followed by two lectures in the Theatre des Champs Elysees to about 1,500 each time. Despite the acclaim in the West, her fortunes were reversing in India and Nitya was sorry he could not accompany her back to the subcontinent so she would not have to face the prospect of increasing unpopularity in Indian politics alone. But he had to be careful not to overtax his health as he'd been diagnosed with tuberculosis. By October he believed the disease had abated, he'd been reading Patanjali's *Yoga Sutra*, and was very keen to leave with Krishna for their long-lost, long-missed home the following month.[89]

Meanwhile Krishna had had several flirtatious relationships on the boil – letter-writing to Lady Emily, now forty six, at the same time as being cared for by the attractive Frenchwoman, Madame de Manziarly, also middle-aged, whose husband died of pneumonia in February 1921. Then in September he went to Castle Eerde at Ommen in Holland to meet Baron Philip van Pallandt who offered to give his castle to the Order of the Star. In this fairytale setting Krishna fell in love – according to Lady Emily, for the first time – to a seventeen year old American from New Jersey called Helen Knothe. They spent only a week together. walking in the woods. bicycling or driving in the Baron's expensive car, but Krishna "avowed real love". He covered his face with his handkerchief out of shyness, admitting her into the trinity of his closest friends: his brother, Mrs Besant and Lady Emily, Arundale having been dropped as an intimate by this stage. Krishna and Helen didn't speak of marriage and she doesn't remember kisses or caresses. but rather an attraction that seemed a "meeting of souls". She kept his letters, "so pure and so noble and so beautiful and so eloquent".[90] And then he was off to India. On his way to visit Nitya, under a specialist's care in Montesano, and then to spend a short time in London to say goodbye to friends, Krishna wrote to Helen that he was thinking of her "*all*" the time. In Monetesano he said he'd found two letters from her, the person he most wished to "have", and he nearly "yelled" with pleasure.[91]

Krishna had another taste of love in a brief meeting with Helen in Amsterdam in November before he sailed for India. He gave her a copy of *Alice in Wonderland* with "curiouser and curiouser" written on the flyleaf, a reference to his curious feeling that he had known her for ages, and a copy of *The Oxford Book of English Verse* with an inscription suggesting she was the source of his "bubbling spring-well".[92]

According to Helen Knothe Nearing, theirs was not a physical relationship yet it was warm, deep and passionate, a great outpouring of his love. Krishna wrote out directives for her life: she must be great; keep her body as clean and pure as her conscience; be well-dressed; take exercise for twenty minutes in the morning; not show any depression she might be feeling; show a cheerful face; and play the violin wonderfully well. Yet it was Krishna's influence which she implied would stymie her burgeoning musical career. Krishna's letter to Helen from Amsterdam in which he vowed that he loved her with all his heart and soul and always would, was the first of a "spate" of letters extending over the next six years.[93]

Krishna wrote to Lady Emily from Paris about his love sacrifices over Helen that he thought – no, he knew - she had felt the same way but what else was to be done? And he said she did not know how he was feeling. Apart from an offhand remark about hoping that she wasn't jealous, he seemed to be oblivious of Lady Emily's feelings over his newfound love. Just two months earlier he'd written to Lady Emily that his love for her was as pure and as lasting as the snow on Mont Blanc. Now she was expected to make room for Helen as the shared source of his misery over parting. But there was no time to dwell on these coincidental events; after about ten years away from India, during which time he'd gained an extensive sentimental education. Krishna was being catapulted back home. The business of the Theosophical Society was at hand.[94]

While Mrs Besant's fortunes in India were increasingly unfavourable. so that she was now becoming so unpopular a figure she was a target for protests, her standing within the Theosophical Society continued to fly at full mast. In 1921 she was re-elected for a third seven-year term during which period the membership of the Society would grow from 36,000 to 45.000. its absolute peak, in 1928. But this discrepancy was not the greatest that Krishnamurti would need to deal with in confronting the demons which were closing in on Mrs Besant as the 1920s unravelled her life's work.

Leadbeater had dominated Mrs Besant from afar as well as commanding his associates close at hand in the community living in a large house near Mosman in Sydney. so that criticism from within the Society had to reach a crescendo before it would be heeded. This occurred at the Australian convention in April 1921. wnen TH Martyn was so indiscreet as to leak stories to the press alleging Leadbeater's poor character regarding sexual liaisons. Not only that, but Bishop James Wedgwood, who had consecrated Leadbeater a bishop in the Liberal Catholic Church, and did his bidding thereafter, was publicly repudiated by the Church in Britain since it was said that he had, in turn, been consecrated by a priest unfrocked for sex perversion. Finally, the Church denied the credentials of its entire English branch, which should have left Leadbeater even further from hallowed ground. But this slight setback plus the continuing allegations of his pederasty by Katherine Tingley, from the breakaway Society at Point Loma in the United States, was blithely ignored by Leadbeater, who was setting up youth organisations, describing the fairies and sprites he used to observe on the Sydney Harbour ferry crossing, and dressing to impress, either spruced up for dinner in formal evening dress or in the flowing purple robes of a distinguished priest of the questionable Old Catholic Church.[95]

With the incessant turbulence of political and sexual controversy having become a regular background noise. Krishna and Nitya sailed from Marseille on November 18, 1921 to return to India for the first time since their rushed departure to escape from their father in 1912. Major changes had occurred in the lives of these boys – they had become men, aged just short of 27 and 24 respectively. They had thrown off the cultural clothes of their birthright, for a time at least, and adopted European clothes, manners and education. Their dress was a wealthy Western style yet their skin colour betrayed their oriental origins, and their soulful eyes contemplated a more exotic future than that of their European companions. Brothers together, they would work interdependently. Now they sailed in comfort to the edge of the horizon, right back to the Madras riverbank they'd come from. The façade of their lives was an agreeable stream of pleasantries but there were hidden depths to navigate following this decade-long severance of ties to the "ocean" of their family and culture.[96]

Chapter 3

Antipodean Rudeness

And why beholdest thou the mote that is in thy brother's eye, but considerest not the beam that is in thine own eye?

Matthew 7, 3.

On board ship, bound for India, Krishna wrote in late-1921 of his country "long forsaken" but still his own. As he made editorial notes for the Order of the Star's journal, the *Herald of the Star*, the sea was rough and he a bad sailor. But the young leader, known publicly as Krishnamurti, looked forward to the new year, "ripe" for new effort. And whatever personal misgivings and uncertainties he might have felt, he exhorted members of the Order to look to their duties and make progress with pure vision, remaining true to their "glorious" faith in the "Coming" of 'World Teacher'.[1]

Krishna and Nitya arrived back in India in early December 1921, during the dry season, to a crowd of admirers standing on the dock at the imperial 'Gateway' of Bombay. Mrs Besant was the first on board, hurrying up the gangway with two garlands of flowers. These two handsome young men were dressed in European clothes but changed into Indian dress for the garden party that same afternoon. Later in the month, when they went from Adyar back to Bombay to meet Lady Emily, they looked very strange to her eyes, dressed Indian-style – Krishna in a mauve turban, a long tussore coat and dhoti, or waistcloth, and Nitya having the added touch of a small round velvet cap.[2]

Krishna's first letter from Adyar to Helen Knothe described his homecoming as a scene of people shaking hands and giving prostrations and smiles, with photographs and receptions all in his honour. He changed into Indian clothes as soon as possible and the turban was tied by someone else as he had forgotten how to tie it, he said. In Madras, crowds threw flowers into his car as he sat there, "blushing" and feeling stupid and emotional since he didn't feel equal to their expectations of him.[3]

As well as in dress, Krishna and Nitya adopted other Indian habits: rising early; sitting cross-legged on the floor for meals; and eating using the fingers of only the right hand. Krishna might have tried to revert to his simple former life but he retained his revered status. Many people sought interviews with him in the mornings, "Lord" only knew why, he told Lady Emily.[4]

These daily rituals were only the outer signs of Krishnamurti's adaptation to the cultural restraints he encountered back in India. Actually he felt disturbed and found the atmosphere in the Adyar compound gossipy, with jealous factions at war with one another. So he held tea parties in his room, and progressed to Sunday luncheons on the ground floor of the Russak part of the building complex, co-hosted by Dwarkanath Telang, an Oxford graduate and manager of Mrs Besant's *New India*. Krishna had written to Lady Emily soon after he arrived, saying that life was not "over pleasant" and the future looked "damned" difficult.[5]

Krishna was missing the romantic figure he'd created in Helen Knothe, but the separation suited Mrs Besant's plans for Krishnamurti's future. She wrote to Helen that she knew something of the tie between them and that that affection might have a good deal of pain in it because the world needed Krishna and he could not belong to any one of them. It was a warning that Helen would come to understand within a few years.[6]

Another shock for Krishna and Nitya was for them to confront the state of their family during a visit to their father in January 1922. Nitya had wanted to make an effort to be friends with the old man again – he had asked Mrs Besant months earlier whether they might visit him if she didn't mind. But after the visit, the report Nitya gave to Mrs Manziarly shows little of his usual compassion. "We have seen our father who is doddering, our elder brother who is really not bad and our younger brother who is mad," Nitya wrote in French. Years later all that Krishna was said to remember of the meeting was that he and Nitya prostrated themselves, touching their father's feet with their foreheads which caused him to immediately go and wash his feet as if he had been touched by "pariahs". Krishna himself wrote of the meeting that it followed a break of fifteen years and that his father went out to wash his feet as his sons were "polluted", having eaten food cooked by non-Brahmins. They were shy and their father sent them away when mealtime came as he could not eat with them. Krishna cited the incident as an example of tradition being stronger than love. Yet, claiming that Krishna's memory could be faulty, having fused with what others had told him, his biographer, Pupul Jayakar tells a very different story sixty years later. She maintains that the young men visited their father on three consecutive days and their father embraced them and wept. Krishna consoled him even though he and his brother were both shy and too embarrassed to eat. Sweets and savouries had been prepared but only Nitya took an orange to eat.[7]

Back in Adyar, Krishna and Nitya threw themselves into a role of support for Mrs Besant in the Theosophical Society and in politics. Their plans were to gather about five organisers in each province of India – each man speaking on a specialised subject such as religion, politics, sanitation, child welfare or rural industry – and preach a new doctrine for India. Nitya and Krishna would take responsibility for this consciousness-raising in two provinces and they expected to raise enough money to carry it through, campaigning for six months every three or four years with the intention of outstripping Gandhi in developing "roots among the people".[8] But before they could tackle these longer-term plans, more pressing matters demanded their attention.

The 1919 sex scandal over Wedgwood and the Liberal Catholic Church had not died down with Mrs Besant's crisis of confidence and her deferral to Leadbeater in all matters occult. The repercussions were still being felt when Krishna and Nitya were back on their home ground, with news of discontent brewing across the Indian Ocean in the Sydney lodge where Leadbeater had sought haven. An Australian Theosophist, TH Martyn, who had been the person entrusted to convey the news of Wedgwood's bad behaviour to Jinarajadasa and Leadbeater back in Australia. was outraged by Leadbeater's ability to persuade Mrs Besant to act against her better judgement and endorse Wedgwood after all. Martyn would not keep quiet about it, maintaining the rage sporadically in the Sydney press over the next few years.[9]

In April 1921 the trouble boiled over at the annual conference. Martyn, a well-respected businessman who had opened his home to Leadbeater and a couple of boys when Leadbeater first arrived in Sydney, wrote in May 1921 to Mrs Besant, whom he had revered, asking for an explanation of Leadbeater's scandalous behaviour. Martyn's wife alleged that Leadbeater was continuing his pederast activities since she had seen him in the early hours of the morning with a naked boy in his bed in her own home. She was so upset by the incident, she said, she later had a nervous breakdown which she attributed to her worry. The major cause of her concern was her own son, whom she had named after Leadbeater - Tom Leadbeater Martyn – who claimed to have been the subject of unwanted touching from Leadbeater.[10] Mrs Martyn gave Leadbeater credit for an abnormal memory and the most marvellous brain of any man she had met, but she believed Mrs Besant was under his spell. Mr Martyn, who had been a member of the Theosophical Society since 1891 and had known Leadbeater since 1905, also claimed evidence of having seen a naked boy in Leadbeater's bed, which he had at first dismissed as unimportant. But Martyn, who now also believed Leadbeater was not the occultist he pretended to be, was opposed to the influence of the Liberal Catholic Church in the Society so the charges of immorality against Wedgwood in 1919 and Mrs Besant's inexplicable loyalty to Leadbeater only added fuel to his fire of righteousness.[11]

Instead of offering an adequate explanation to Martyn, Annie Besant was outraged that his 1921 letter to her had been made public and she staunchly defended Leadbeater's honour. They were infamous accusations and she would not discuss them, as no decent person would, she said.[12]

Early in 1922. anticipating more trouble at the Easter annual convention. the Australian Section invited Mrs Besant to preside over the meeting. also extending an invitation to "Mr Krishnamurti". kind friends guaranteeing all the expenses.[13] With a Sydney-Colombo first-class return fare costing 84 pounds and the male living wage set at three pounds 18 shillings a week, it was a generous offer.[14] Whether Martyn. a prosperous businessman, would have contributed to the cost is not known. Mrs Besant accepted. sending a delegation ahead, as Gandhi had been arrested and she wanted to remain in the thick of Indian politics for a little longer. It was reported that she feared riots and bloodshed and did not want to leave at such a critical time.[15]

It had been decided soon after Krishna and Nitya arrived in India in late 1921 that they would go on to Australia. Krishna wrote that it would have been pleasant if Mrs Besant could be there when he first met Leadbeater again after ten years, perhaps anticipating a little difficulty, but acknowledging that he and his brother owed everything to Mrs Besant and Leadbeater.[16]

They sailed in March 1922 from Colombo on the *RMS Omar*, an 11,000 ton liner. accompanied by Jinarajadasa and his wife Dorothy. Fritz Kunz, one of Leadbeater's proteges now in his mid-thirties, and two other women, one an organising secretary for the Order of the Star in India, who was said to be in need of a complete rest after five years of strenuous work. Nitya's view of the company was "a hell of a lot of old women" travelling with them, making him feel ashamed.[17]

It took twelve long and very "boring" days to cross the Indian Ocean.[18] During the voyage Krishna wrote to Lady Emily almost every day, dreaming that things might be different, that he might be alone with her and Helen and fearing the adulation he would receive in Australia. He felt awfully sentimental, he said, and he'd been in the same state since he'd left Adyar. He didn't fancy his fellow passengers, describing them as dirty sort of gentlemen, as cockney as one could make them, and full of curiosity that was offensive. One day one of these "gentlemen" literally buttonholed him – Krishna spelt it "button hold" – even though he hated to be touched, he said. He took exception to the man questioning him in detail about where he'd come from and where he was going, and, in particular, to the fellow dropping his "h's" during the inquisition.

But Krishna's most scathing descriptions were reserved for the sensualists on board. The officers were "appalling" in their manners. They were slack and undignified. There were two "so-called" 'belles' and the officers "flocked" about them like flies around a "stinking" carcass, which he spelt "carcuss". He was shocked that the men "almost" sat on the ladies' knees on deck. He presumed one 'Lady' was married as she had a child. As the officers conducted themselves so poorly you could "imagine" the rest, he said.

'Oh for a P & O!' cried Krishna from the confines of his cabin, leaving his fan on the whole night as he crossed the equator, with Nitya's cough worsening in the tropical heat and humidity, and 800 immigrants on board sharing the bad food and attended by stewards who were "dirty" and had "no manners". He sounded a little fearful for his manhood when one of the 'belles' sat opposite him, writing. She was "vulgar" and "coarse" and only wanted one thing and that was "Man", was his conclusion.

He was a little more cheerful describing the beautiful, deep sapphire sea – it would beat the Mediterranean and every other sea he had seen, he said – but he soon gave way to melancholy. As the blue waters stretched for miles with nothing in sight, spelt "site", it made him "long" for his dear Mum.[19]

A letter to Annie Besant during the voyage shows his boredom and apprehension. He was glad his "dearest mother" was not sailing in that ship, he said, as it was very slow and the passengers were not very exciting. The sea was fairly calm but it was expected to be rough across the Great Australian Bight, to the south of Australia. He wished he was travelling with her, he said, and he would be "very" glad when he saw her again. The letter was in the usual style he sent to his mother/Protector: simple and loving to the point of banality. But it maintained their strong bond.[20]

On board ship Krishnamurti played poker, avoided the attentions of the two 'belles' and indulged in what might be described as 'ennui'. Also on board, although there's no record of Krishna having any knowledge of it, was the artist, Daryl Lindsay and his wife, who were returning to Melbourne.[21] There was also, on the ship, the familiar racism an Indian abroad inevitably experiences. One evening Krishna was disgusted by the racist behaviour of an Englishman towards Jinarajadasa when he tried to sit beside him on a sofa. The seat was engaged, the man told Jinarajadasa, who promptly apologised and moved away. The man declared it was "bloody cheek", and Krishnamurti felt like "thumping" his "ugly" head, he said. His own Brahmin sense of superiority is apparent in his remark to Lady Emily about not knowing what to do with these barbarians. He wished he were a "Lord of Karma".[22]

Krishna's cultural prejudices were strong at this stage of his life. He described a concert given by the stewards as appalling and the usual British taste, with hilarity over nothing being a means to hide their "terrific insignificance". He was feeling severely alienated, and his mood was not helped when he was described as a "dark" gentleman. He wanted his stay in Australia to be 'short and sweet', as Australians didn't attract him, at least not those he'd met on board. He felt more in tune with the sea than his fellow passengers, likening the two to the sacred and profane.[23]

More than anything, Krishna did not want to play the role of demi-god. The day before arriving in Fremantle, the port city for the state capital, Perth, he received a radiogram of welcome from Perth. "I am wishing I was anywhere but here," was his reaction, aware that it would be like this all the rest of his life. He believed he was not fit for the role, it was a torture to him to give public speeches, and the devotional manner of people towards him was abhorrent, he said. The ship landed at Fremantle before six o'clock on the morning of Sunday, 2nd April, and the party was driven to Perth, the state's capital, half an hour away, for several meetings before returning to Fremantle for the ship's departure at

11 pm.[24] Senator Reid, an active Theosophist, travelled three thousand kilometres from Sydney to Perth to greet the group.[25] Publicly Krishna was on his best behaviour, writing later that he was driven about nineteen kilometres to Perth, by a very hospitable member of the Theosophical Society. He was delighted with the change of atmosphere, to see trees and grass and fresh faces. The drive was one of the most beautiful he had ever had, running beside the Swan River and through a park he described as full of luxuriant vegetation, a welcome relief from the everlasting view of the ocean he'd had from on board ship. Krishna was very impressed by the natural bushland around the city – virgin forest where no one was allowed to shoot or pick flowers. Once the official welcome was over the young men went out for a walk in the city, finding muscatel grapes for sale at four pence a pound and a dozen figs for a shilling, the low prices and high quality reviving the brothers' spirits. Later at the official meeting Krishna gave his best talk ever, according to Nitya.[26]

DH Lawrence who came out to Australia a month later on the same sea voyage and, in fact, on the same ship as Annie Besant, also had a strong first impression of Australia's stunning natural landscape. He had not liked Ceylon – "the sensuous spiritual voluptuousness, the curious sensitiveness of the naked people, their black, bottomless, hopeless eyes" and his sense that the "natives" were "in the living sense lower than" the English and would one day swarm over and suffocate them. Lawrence commented that the world of ideas might be all alike but the world of physical feeling was very different, and on his first day in Australia, at the Savoy Hotel in Perth, he described the country as "a queer godforsaken place: not so much new as non-existent" ... though they called themselves very 'alive', he added. The air was beautiful and pure and the sky fresh and high – that part he acknowledged as really good. But he doubted he'd be long in Australia.[27]

Krishnamurti's private views of being stuck in a strange land with even stranger Theosophical bedfellows were much more sour than his public stance. Krishna, Nitya and Jinarajadasa, had what Krishna described as a 'huge argument' in a room set aside for them to rest. Airing his problems to Jinarajadasa, who had recently been appointed Vice President of the Society, Krishna found the older man's solution was to cut back the number of lectures that Krishna would be expected to give. Jinarajadasa mildly overlooked Krishna's complaint that Theosophists did not appeal to him, Krishna explaining that, to outsiders he, Krishnamurti, seemed a "crank of the superlative order". Krishna complained that Jinarajadasa was like a gentle stream that flows down to the sea without going over mountainous regions. But when two people such as himself and Nitya fought against the current, Jinarajadasa was stupefied and amazed. Jinarajadasa, an ambitious Theosophical politician, took seriously his duty to keep his rebellious charge in hand. 'Oh! Cuss,' Krishna declared, facing up to the "torture" of public talks ahead in Adelaide, Melbourne and Sydney.[28]

Back on the high seas the *Omar* sailed across the Great Australian Bight in fine weather but Krishna's comment that the waters were as dark as ink reflected his morose outlook. The ship docked on a Friday in Adelaide's Outer Harbour, five days after leaving Fremantle. The *Adelaide Advertiser* announced that three hundred tons of general cargo, a quantity of mail and a number of passengers were landed before the vessel continued its voyage to Melbourne that same evening. Among the passengers who stayed on board were a group of Italians who planned to find work on sugar plantations in Queensland.[29]

The day Krishnamurti's ship sailed into Melbourne's Port Phillip Bay the Melbourne *Herald* carried an article on Theosophy without mentioning the fact that Krishna was in town, although it did state that he and Jinarajadasa would be attending the annual Theosophical Society conference in Sydney during Easter week. The article's approach was sympathetic to Theosophy, which was obvious from its serious tone and the lack of any allusion to the rifts and scandals which had been publicised elsewhere. There were references to the Society's steady growth and facts and figures - membership of the Sydney Lodge, with 900 members, was the largest in the world and there were 300 members in Melbourne and 2,500 Australia-wide; the Melbourne meeting-place, Queens Hall at 181 Collins St, was a warehouse bought 18 months before and remodelled, for a total cost of 25,000 pounds. The article said the objects of the Society were universal brotherhood, with an aim of stemming the tide of materialism and agnosticism. It had been hoped that Mrs Besant would preside at the meeting but she had cabled to say that she would not arrive until May. The brief article on page 8 must have been a relief to Krishnamurti.[30]

There was some small interest in matters Indian in Australia in 1922 as a film called *Royal India* was being shown in cinemas. The Saturday night of Krishnamurti's arrival in Melbourne hundreds were reported to have been turned away from the Hoyts Theatre de Luxe where the film was showing. "Don't miss the Imperial Government's Photoplay – THE FIRST AND ONLY FILM OF ITS KIND THE SCREEN HAS EVER REFLECTED," an advertisement announced. Patrons were promised "an unfamiliar screen creation which sways the senses with its glittering splendour and its unexpected sweep of thrilling incidents", but only if they made sure of seats by booking. A thousand boy scouts had been to see the film the day before, "gay patrol colours on their shoulders, merit badges on their arms, [with] bunting displayed - and enthusiasm too". This was an image of India that was palatable to Western audiences, especially the young and impressionable, as it was not a reflection of the poverty and hardship faced by the mass of the Indian population.[31]

The day Krishnamurti left Melbourne *The Age* ran an article on the treatment of Gandhi in gaol, an article which ridiculed him and was obviously supportive of the British regime in India. The paper claimed that Gandhi's imprisonment was creating excitement among extremist and moderate papers as a result of reports that he was being ill-treated or not being treated with deference. Yet it said that an official communique "shows that Gandhi is treated with the utmost consideration that he has any right to expect". The paper maintained that he was quite well and he didn't want his prison life discussed in the papers.

> Judging by an account of the various privileges he enjoys one would think Gandhi was an honoured guest instead of a convicted criminal seditionist. Since political prisoners have been granted special privileges in gaol discipline has considerably deteriorated. yet apparently a large section of Indian opinion will remain unsatisfied until the prisoners enjoy every home comfort.

Ignoring the fact that Gandhi's home comforts were no doubt considerably fewer than those indulged in by the journalist who wrote the article, and presuming to be wiser than 'a large section of Indian opinion", the article excerpted the *Civil and Military Gazette* in its mocking tone over demands raised about Gandhi's bedding, and in suggesting Gandhi had a halo that needed brushing every morning. Another brief article in the same column reported the Indian Viceroy, Lord Reading, as dispelling all rumors that his telegram had caused the resignation of the Secretary of State for India. Thousands of miles away from these scenes of political disturbance, *The Age* still felt obliged to toe the British Government line, its racist bias on show.[32]

But the times were changing. The day after Krishnamurti arrived in Sydney *The Age* in Melbourne published an editorial on the remarkable change that World War I had wrought on the position of women in society. It was a rearguard acknowledgement of the strength of women's movement into the public sphere, beginning with the well-worn platitude: "The war has not in any way upset the truth that women's sphere is the home". "It is in the service of homekeeping, in the care and upbringing of children, that the essential qualities of womanliness find their most natural and most useful sphere of service to the State," it said. But the article did raise the question of acknowledging change by looking at plain facts: the war exposed the absurdity of regarding women as fashioned in one pattern; there may be women whose sphere is not the home; there certainly were millions of women who were not given the opportunity of having their own home; there were women with outstanding aptitude in the very spheres most rigorously monopolised by men; women found a great deal of 'man's work' was just as much 'women's work' and, very naturally, that discovery had rapidly moved women towards the goal of economic equality with men.[33]

It's possible that Krishnamurti saw this article, or at least took in the tenor of the times - later events in his life indicate that he was clearly abreast of these modernist ideas about women's rights. But his immediate attention was taken up in confronting the domestic wrangling within the Theosophical Society in Sydney after two days at sea.

The ship arrived in Sydney at 7.30 in the morning on Wednesday 12th April. Krishna was impressed by the natural harbour, with houses built up from the water's edge on what must have been magnificent cliffs, he said. The city he described as ugly, dirty and noisy, like any other town. But he obviously enjoyed the steam ferry into the city across the harbour from where he was staying at Kirribilli.[34]

Sydney was celebrating Easter in warm weather with a pagan festival honouring livestock and produce, fairy floss and sideshow alleys - the Royal Agricultural Society Show - and the populace initially took little interest in the affairs of Theosophists. The Show's grand parade featured a Shorthorn Bull called 'Lindenow' and a Champion Clydesdale stallion named 'Craigie Masterstroke' - echoes of the old country - and never before had there been such a display of penned poultry. But Krishna was oblivious of this agricultural celebration; rather, he was feeling hemmed in by Theosophical teachings. For their part the Theosophists seemed oblivious of the focus of the mass of Sydney's citizens, intent as they were on their own little sideshow of factional in-fighting.[35]

The antics of the Theosophical convention began two days after Krishnamurti's arrival. It would prove a turning point for him, the true test of his mettle in a conflict he felt over loyalty to the Theosophists who had elevated him from his poor Indian life and the overriding opposing view he held about the emptiness and hypocrisy of ritual and ceremony which was divorced from real experience of the esoteric in life.

Krishnamurti had first publicly stated his views on ritual the previous year at the Order of the Star Congress following the World Theosophical Convention in Paris in July. It was resolved then that there should be no ceremonials in the Order since, he said, a ritual, however beautiful, would crystallise the movement and narrow its action.

Krishnamurti had written in his editorial for the *Herald of the Star* in August that an open mind was essential to understand Truth, and Jinarajadasa echoed the view that intellectual detachment from all traditions, ideas and customs was necessary.[36] These views were directly opposed to the trend in the Theosophical Society towards ritualism, led by Leadbeater and Wedgwood.

Krishnamurti's account of his meeting with Leadbeater in Sydney after such a long break was kindly. He described him as "just the same", jovial and beaming with happiness but with whiter hair. Krishna said Leadbeater was very glad to see them. He held onto Krishna's arm and introduced him to everyone with a "Voila" in his tone. Krishna was very glad to see him too.[37]

Krishna, Nitya, Jinarajadasa and Dorothy at first stayed with prominent theosophists, John Mackay and his wife, at Malahide in Elamang Avenue, Kirribilli, a street with a magnificent view of Sydney Harbour. Leadbeater at this time was living with the Kollerstroms at Neutral Bay, whose son, Oscar, was a particular favourite of his.

Krishnamurti's introduction to the way Theosophy had evolved under Leadbeater's reign in Sydney didn't please him. His first letter to Lady Emily from Sydney shows his distaste for ritual and dislike of the strong link between the Liberal Catholic Church and Theosophists. He said Leadbeater did very well as the acting priest. But as Krishna was not a "ceremonialist" and did not appreciate all the "paraphanalia" (as he spelt it), including prayers and robes and "bobbing" up and down, he felt some alienation. Leadbeater wore a red cassock, a heavy cross on his chest and a bishop's ring. But Krishna wouldn't criticise the ritual, he said. What right did he have to attack or disapprove, he asked? He claimed he was so bored during the two and a half-hour service that he nearly fainted, but he would be careful in case he was misunderstood. Describing the factions as fighting like cats and dogs. Krishnamurti's conclusion carried a superior tone, describing the over-zealousness and lack of tact as foolish.[38]

According to Krishnamurti, the division came to a head on the fourth day into the convention when there was a call for a vote of confidence in Leadbeater. During a debate lasting over two hours, Krishnamurti defended Leadbeater; he "thundered" at them, is how he described it. He knew Leadbeater better than most of them there, he declared, calling him the "purest" and one of the "greatest" men he had ever met. His clairvoyance might be "doubted" but not his purity, was Krishnamurti's curious defence. He was also concerned that the debaters were losing all "gentlemanliness" in their behaviour in the dispute. Leadbeater and Krishnamurti's camp won the day, with 86 votes in favour to 15 against. A couple of days later Krishnamurti and Nitya dined with the Martyns, hoping to patch things up, and Martyn is reported to have said that he believed in Leadbeater's purity but had undeniable proof of Wedgwood's immorality. Krishna wrote to Lady Emily asking her to find out what the charges were against Wedgwood in England as he had been tracked by a private detective in Sydney entering public toilets sixteen times within two hours.[39]

The tension over this unsavoury dispute could not have helped Nitya's health, which had been poor ever since a severe bout of chicken-pox in February the previous year. A few months later he had coughed up blood – a sign of tuberculosis. He went to Paris for treatment, was diagnosed as having infection on one lung and was prescribed a strict diet and rest. In Sydney he saw a doctor who took X-rays and found infection on both lungs, advising him to go to the mountains immediately, so on 29 April the two brothers went to stay at the Carrington Hotel in Katoomba, about three hours west of Sydney. Before going, Krishna tried to talk with Leadbeater alone, but there were always too many boys around him for a confidential talk.[40]

Three and a half thousand feet above sea level in the Blue Mountains, among eucalyptus trees said to be a tonic for Nitya's lungs, Krishna was still jaded in his view of the general population – the people staying in the hotel were ugly, uncouth, vulgar and crude.

He was fortunate enough to attend a concert by Australia's darling of the opera, Nellie Melba, and it's difficult to know whether he even enjoyed it, so divided was his reaction to the woman with the "marvellous" voice who "oozed" so much vulgarity that he preferred not to watch her. She even threw flowers to the eager audience; yet when she sang 'Ave Maria' he was almost in "Nirvana". He considered the thunderous applause extremely "brutal"; and he disapproved of her encore,'Coming through the Rye'. He was glad to get away from the audience's joyous ecstasy shown as noisy applause. Again he described the "brutality" and lack of "refinement". He attempted to sympathise with the Australian nature as "young", but had to admit that it was "crude" and "raw". He felt as if he had sand in his mouth and was appalled at the "impoliteness" and lack of "gentlemanliness".[41]

Krishna pitied Leadbeater who had been in Australia for eight years, believing he had made a major sacrifice to stay. To Krishna's ear everyone spoke cockney and it gave him a headache. The noise, of the streets and the people, was terrible and nerve-wracking, he found. So in this mountain retreat he looked after Nitya, took walks in the beautiful, "titanic" countryside among the eucalyptus, sometimes doing exercises 'tout à fait nu' - and pined for his loves. He would spend the same amount of time writing to Lady Emily as to Helen, and denied he was in love with anyone in Sydney.[42]

Krishna and Nitya came back down to the city to meet Dr Besant at Central Station when she arrived on a train from Melbourne on 9 May, and as usual she was a rock of reassurance.[43] Krishna said she was really great, taking everything quietly, and she was far nicer than any of them.

This was not Mrs Besant's first trip to the Antipodes. She had visited Australia and New Zealand in 1894 for a lecture series that was delivered to packed halls. The added personal reason for Annie's trip was to see her daughter, Mabel, married to a Melbourne journalist who edited the *Australian Theosophist*. Sir

William Windeyer, Chief Justice of the Supreme Court of NSW, chaired one of her lectures in Sydney during the 1894 trip. He had delivered a court judgement exonerating her from a charge of having issued an obscene publication, a birth control book by Dr Charles Knowlton, and permitting her own *Law of Population* to be sold in Australia. Again in 1908 Annie Besant visited Australia and New Zealand to lecture, receiving rave announcements in the press about her great intellectual powers. Some controversy was raised over Blavatsky's reputation as one of the great imposters in history but generally Annie Besant was greeted by applause at public meetings and plaudits from the press. In Adelaide she spoke in the Trades Hall on what theosophy had to say to workers and in Melbourne, Prime Minister Deakin, who had previously been a Theosophist, attended a meeting.[44]

The 1922 Theosophical Society reception for her went smoothly and was cloaked in some splendour – Mrs Besant wore a sari and Krishna and Nitya their turbans, and she gave a very reassuring address. In fact her presence would bring the festering abscess in the Society to a head within a week. Nitya summarised the developments after her arrival: Mrs Besant received a friendly welcome from the press on arrival but Martyn gave documents to the Sydney *Daily Telegraph* which caused a bombshell; everything was dragged in – Blavatsky, Leadbeater, Alcyone, the Church, the Masters; Mrs Besant answered some letters to editors and Leadbeater paid little attention; as a result of the publicity Mrs Besant's lectures were packed, attracting up to 1500 people.[45]

But Krishna was more sensitive, describing the articles in a letter to Lady Emily as vulgar and saying that he hated the notoriety resulting from stories with headlines such as "The Mahatmas", "Dandy Coloured Coons" and "Where Leadbeater Bishes" or supposedly written by "Krishnamoorfy". In the street people would nudge one another, pointing him out. One fellow called him the "Messiah" he'd read about in the paper and laughed. Krishna observed that he would have laughed too except that he was the one involved. Another man called him the fellow with thirty lives and Krishna nearly "collapsed" on the floor. In other words, Sydney was having a great time at the expense of himself and Theosophy, "thanks" to Martyn. He hated all the publicity and he could only look forward to having it all his life. What had he done to deserve it, he wondered?[46]

It's true that the press had a running story with the Theosophists. When Annie Besant arrived in Sydney the *Daily Telegraph* greeted her in glowing terms. "Her brilliant brain", "the face of a strong man and the femininity of a woman" and "Power and penetration and the force of concentration have impressed themselves upon her strong, fine forehead. She has a mass of magnificent white hair" – these were just some of the plaudits heaped on her. The article even took her side in describing Indians. "[E]ducated up to a certain standard regarding British law and British rule [but with] ... [their] own desire for independence ... proving too strong for ...[them] to keep still longer," was the writer's attempt to explain her leaving the Indian Home Rule League. The article commented that it was remarkable how a woman of seventy-five could still have the force and power to control large audiences, and gave a tip that she would be giving a lecture at the Grand Opera House. And throughout the world there were thousands who revered and blessed her name, readers were told.[47]

On 11 May a favourable article about the Theosophical school, Morven Garden, was published, and four days later Mrs Besant's lecture on India's claim to Dominion status was given a local slant. "In Australia you will be safer for [admitting India to her place in the Empire] because India's millions can guard you against any other Asiatic attack," she was reported as saying, along with a crack against Gandhi who had "promised them immediate home rule, no taxation, and comfort, and they were an ignorant and easily led people". The crowd was so large many were turned away from her lecture at Fuller's New Theatre.[48]

But the tide turned, and on 17 May the Sydney *Sun* wrote about the Theosophist "crisis", referring to Leadbeater, who was "quite an identity about Sydney streets", and "malpractices of a revolting character". On the same day the *Daily Telegraph* carried a story headed "GRAVE ALLEGATIONS", referring to *Dawn*, the official organ of the Theosophical Society Loyalty League and its allegations that Leadbeater was using the Buddhist holy day, Wesak, or full moon in May, for his own ends. The *Daily Telegraph* quoted Mrs Besant as saying, "...if the circulators of this filth have any justification for making such accusations, they should at once place their information in the hands of the police". The *Daily Mail* carried an article headed 'Storm', including information that Mrs Besant was speaking that night at King's Hall in Hunter Street. The next day the *Daily Telegraph* carried a long article on details of the dispute and the previous night's meeting, with Mrs Besant quoted as saying the Theosophical Society had no connection with the Liberal Catholic Church any more than it had with Buddhist temples. She also said that, except for three "extreme cases", the parents of every boy who had been in Leadbeater's care were unanimous in enthusiastic gratitude to him. The *Daily Mail*'s report of the stormy meeting of the previous night said Mrs Besant had carried the vote and left looking exceedingly tired but smiling quietly. The following day, Friday 19 May, the *Daily Telegraph* published stories associated with Theosophy, Mrs Besant and Krishnamurti or 'Alcyone' (including a photo of him dressed in robes as head of the Order of the Star of the East) across five columns on the main news page. "TAKE IT TO THE POLICE" was the headline for the story about the Theosophists' meeting two nights before. In the midst of the Theosophical news, the paper's readers were also treated to a story about the chief engineer for the Sydney Harbour Bridge project, JC Bradfield, speaking from New York about tenders, Australian labour conditions and the favourable price of steel. Another story about Mrs Besant entertaining an Institute of Journalists' luncheon at Farmers' store dealt with her call for Indian liberty, closing with the word 'Applause' to indicate the approval of the audience. Leadbeater then had a letter published in the *Daily Telegraph* to say that there had never been any connection between the Liberal Catholic Church and the

Theosophical Society. He also wrote that "the great historical churches of Rome and England have recognised our Orders by allowing our priests to minister on their behalf without reordination" so that they were in a better position than the Church of England itself, he claimed. On 20 May the *Daily Telegraph* published testimonies from two of Leadbeater's 'boys' praising his probity. But the press clamour could not be ignored and on 21 May the State Minister for Justice announced he had "instituted inquiries".[49]

Next day the *Daily Telegraph* rushed to describe the Liberal Catholic Church's Sunday service of the previous day, a service based on Oriental luxury and elaborate ceremonial. "The robes are magnificent. Some of them are cloth of gold embroidered with flowers, and encrusted with jewels," the article claimed, without offering any evidence that the 'jewels' were actually precious stones. The description of Leadbeater's attire could only alienate the average unpretentious Sydney Sunday newspaper reader: "Bishop Leadbeater, clad in a stiff gold robe, wearing a high scarlet and gold mitre, and carrying a gold crozier, passes among his flock waving a white-gloved hand, upon which is his bishop's ring, in Apostolic blessing". The debate also fired up when the President of the Public Questions Society of the University of Sydney, AB Piddington, resigned in protest over an invitation to Mrs Besant to address students, saying the invitation should be withdrawn until the matters involved in her defence of Leadbeater were settled. Then a member of the State Upper House and an ex-Solicitor-General, Mr Sproule, was wheeled in by the *Sun* newspaper to give his opinion about evidence in the Madras High Court custody case, the opinion being that Leadbeater's teachings for youth were pernicious and should not be permitted in Sydney. Strangely enough, perhaps out of a false sense of the need for privacy, Krishnamurti, who was the subject of the custody case, was not mentioned in the article. The controversy continued - with a public correspondence carried on between Mrs Besant and Piddington; with the Society being described as a cult; with Martyn addressing a public meeting;

with republication of an article from *The Times* of London in 1913 at the time of Krishna's custody case: and. the Bishop of Goulburn. Lewis Goulburn. weighing in with a plea to reject "crude sexualism" and the "new retrograde humanism which is painting up the vices of a decadent type of society" and. instead, to find "the ideal of Christian purity". Mrs Besant had kept up a heavy schedule in Sydney, addressing thirty four meetings in less than a month, including a Lord Mayoral reception and the lecture at the University of Sydney which had begun problematically and ended in 'thunderous acclamation'. The hectic pace of public activity and reportage continued unabated even while the police announced that the Minister had ordered "the fullest inquiries" into the Leadbeater allegations.[50]

The police file on Leadbeater had begun in 1917 after contact from Katherine Tingley's friend, Joseph Fussell, from the Point Loma Theosophists in the United States. Mrs Tingley felt that the presence of such a man as Leadbeater was a menace to the youth of Sydney, police were told.[51] The police investigation was thorough enough to include: Martyn's letter to Mrs Besant in May 1921 asking her to explain her support for Leadbeater; a 1917 report from Regent St police station citing Leadbeater's reputation as a hypnotist; persuasive documents dating back at least fifteen years, including the letter written in code by Leadbeater to a boy in 1906; Mrs Besant's letter of 1906 in which she supported the decision of the Committee condemning Leadbeater and said it was right that he resign as his teaching was worthy of the sternest reprobation; and, reports of the Krishnamurti Madras High Court custody case, including one published in the London *Law Journal*.[52]

Now, at the end of May 1922, Leadbeater's 'boys' were called in to police headquarters and interviewed in turn, along with other parties to the allegations.

Most of the twelve boys denied any sexual indiscretion or perversion. However the Martyn boy, Tom, gave evidence that he had seen another boy, Oscar Kollerstrom, sleeping in Leadbeater's bed and that once Leadbeater had caught his,

Tom's. "person". deliberately, and attempted to use some friction by a motion of his hand. The boy did not like it and moved away.[53] Another boy, Roy Bassingthwaight, said that he was asked to join the Liberal Catholic Church when he was in the Scouts and although he never actually saw anything happen, he was suspicious that there was something wrong between Leadbeater and three boys, so he left the Church suddenly and wouldn't go back.[54]

Perhaps the most vehement defender of Leadbeater was Jinarajadasa who said that he knew how to masturbate before he met Leadbeater and he thought Leadbeater gave good advice to boys so they could have complete control over themselves. Leadbeater, he maintained, had never spoken to him about it nor ever made any improper suggestion to him in all the period he had known him, between the ages of twelve and twenty-five, part of which time he had shared a small room with him, sleeping in a separate bed. The following year Jinarajadasa wrote to the Minister for Justice that he believed that the interview he gave police was confidential and he was upset that it had been made public and was being distributed by Martyn, among others. The Minister replied that due to the public importance of the matter, interested parties were given the opportunity to peruse the statements but no authority was given for copies to be made.[55]

Krishnamurti and Nityananda also fronted up to the Metropolitan Superintendent's Office of the NSW Police in May 1922 for an interview.[56] A note was included that as they were brothers they chose to make a joint statement, agreeing with each other on every point since what concerned the one, the other had knowledge of. However it was Krishna who was the spokesperson and the statement was taken to be his. Krishna said that he was "shaking like a leaf" and so nervous he was "dotty", as he had become more sensitive. After the interview he was still shaking and his teeth were chattering. But he had the impression that the detectives did not want to corner them, only wanting to find out the truth. Nitya said that they asked the most appalling questions which the youngest boy didn't even understand.[57]

The brothers called back to the Criminal Investigation Branch on 1st June, requesting to be shown the transcript of the statement and they made changes to five of their answers. To the question, "Have you known Mr Leadbeater some time?" Krishnamurti changed his answer from "I have known him for two and a half years" to "I knew him for two and a half years intimately; from the beginning of the year 1909 and have corresponded with him since". The change is curious – certainly establishing that he knew Leadbeater well, but also raising the question of whether Krishnamurti understood the euphemistic use of the word 'intimate' to convey a sexual relationship. It's hard to imagine a man aged twenty-seven would be such an ingenue as to not know this meaning.

To a question about whether he lived at the same school as Leadbeater, Krishna changed his answer to read "Mr Leadbeater did not live in a school. We lived with our father and when the trouble arose we left and lived in another building". He did not elaborate on what "the trouble" was.

To a question about whether his association with Leadbeater had been good or bad, Krishna challenged the transcript, saying he did not remember the question and the answer must have referred to the previous question. His answer would be 'certainly good'.

The previous questions had been about Leadbeater's reputation, that their father knew about it, and that Nitya had read some of the details of the case [in which it was exposed] but Krishna had not. Krishna didn't want to know anything of the details, he said. In regarding Leadbeater as pure, did he not want this opinion tarnished, he was asked?

> A Yes. I don't want to know anything of this sexual question it doesn't interest me.
> Q Why doesn't it affect you?
> A I do not look on women in any way improper I am a Hindu [sic].

Next Krishna quibbled over a question about associating with other boys at school and he said he wasn't aware there was a school, but they associated with other students of theosophy. Finally Krishna tried to clarify a question about educating boys at the Morven school.[58]

There was no uncertainty. however. over his answer that Leadbeater was a very pure man and the finest man he had ever met. Krishna also said that Leadbeater never spoke to them about sexual matters.

Was Krishna ever a student of Buddhism? No I am a Hindu, he replied. What supports you in your keep? The reply was that they were assisted by Mrs Besant and friends of hers.

When asked whether a wealthy lady in London had left Krishna an annuity of 2,000 pounds. he replied, "As far as I know, I don't know. It is not true that I receive an annuity of 2,000 pounds, but I do receive an annuity." He did not revisit that question, wanting changes.[59]

In August 1922, when Krishna and Nitya were long gone from the Sydney fracas, it was announced that on the evidence submitted there was no justification for criminal proceedings against Leadbeater, the Crown Solicitor having the opinion that there was not enough evidence available to obtain a conviction on any charge. There had been some debate within the Police Department over whether there were grounds for believing Leadbeater was a "sexual pervert". It's a significant point that Krishna had written to Lady Emily in June that "people of influence from our side" had seen the Minister of Justice and that Krishna thought he would "play fair".[60]

One curious aspect of the episode is that the State Minister of Justice at the time was TJ Ley, later convicted of the Chalkpit murder in London in 1947, but there's no other written evidence that he intervened in the investigation to protect Leadbeater. Another strange Theosophist bedfellow of the period was Raymond Perdiau, a member of the NSW Parliament, who condoned child molestation and murder in what was known as 'the Puddifoot affair' of 1923.[61]

Writing in July of the events in Sydney over previous months, Nitya admitted that Wedgwood without any doubt had been extraordinarily indiscreet, and had been seen in distinctly compromising company and circumstances, but that he denied all guilt. He could see the amusing side to some of the press coverage but described the reception they got in the streets when they went out as "beastly", being called brown-skinned dandies, and asked who their tailor was, as a result of being well-known figures and so much better dressed than the average Australian. He admitted that they lent themselves to ridicule. He believed Martyn honestly and sincerely wanted to save the Society, but he had told lies and had associated himself with low types.[62]

There was a final attempt to re-ignite interest in the issue in 1923 when the General Secretary of the Australian Section of the Theosophical Society, Jack Bean, (who had the previous year demanded the Sydney *Sun* print a report of Leadbeater's police investigation exoneration) claimed that the report disclosed "a highly undesirable state of affairs".[63]

And there the matter rested: Leadbeater was never charged and his reputation never cleared. Since that time though, Theosophists have continued to publicly assume his innocence. Mrs Besant seemed never to have trouble justifying her defence of Leadbeater, as if all opinion opposed to hers could be simplistically classified as coming from the 'Forces of Darkness' without need for her to apply any self-reflection about her sense of righteousness. In April 1922 she published a stinging attack on Jesuits as the cause of Leadbeater's troubles. Calling on Blavatsky's memory to justify her prejudice, she claimed the Church to be a depository of occult knowledge and the Jesuits its warriors trying to crush those who wanted to attain occult knowledge outside of its discipline. Blavatsky, who had been accused of the vilest sexual life, had actually suffered the outrage of a medical examination which proved her "a virgin intacta", she said.

> Hence HP Blavatsky's furious denunciations: she saw in it the very embodiment and the deadliest weapon of the Dark Forces that ever war against the Light. It is strongest in North America and Australia in its worst form, for in those countries the Roman Catholic Church is striving to win Democracy to its side, and the Jesuist [sic] are its unscrupulous soldiers. ... my Brother Leadbeater ... has passed through a very hell of accusations of the foulest kind. Other lesser men have shared his crucifixion, and just now the Jesuit conspiracy is making its most venomous attack ....[64]

And in what must be one of the most ungainly, strangled sentences in the English language, Annie Besant, used *The Theosophist* in October 1922 to spit out her self-righteous opinion on the favourable police decision:

> I just hear from Sydney by cable that the cruel attempt to involve Bishop Leadbeater in the web of suspicion based on Mr. Farrer's ignoble attempt to cover his own wickedness by accusations against others, repeated by Mr. Martyn in a letter to myself, and published widely in America and elsewhere – he says not with his consent, but a letter shown by him to his friends, though pretended to me to be private, and said to have been betrayed by one of them – has failed.[65]

She spoke of the "shrieks" of the Sydney *Daily Telegraph's* malicious innuendoes driving the Minister of Justice into an "investigation" (which she marked with inverted commas, perhaps in the hope that its status might be diminished over coming years). Malicious gossip, calumny and taking a confession of crime by one man as "evidence" against others could cause any character to be besmirched, she said. That's why she had told anyone with evidence to give it to the police. "Judge not, that ye be not judged," she warned from her 'Watchtower'. And then turned her attention to Indian politics and a jibe at Gandhi over the setback to healthy political life made by the Non-Co-operation movement and the "Swaraj in a year" slogan.

The following month she quoted in full a sycophantic editorial note from *The Star* in Australia on the impression Krishnamurti made during his trip:

> Gracious, beautiful, and of an exquisite courtesy, he has won all hearts, and by his own intensity of life and purpose has fired our enthusiasm anew. ... "Be a God and laugh at yourself," he writes in an autograph book, and those who were fortunate enough to live in the same house during his short visit know how selfless, strong, humble and consecrated was the example he set. ... when he spoke it was the unexpectedness which genius brings, and with the directness of truth which pierces like a rapier ... they could open their hearts to him more freely than to any other.[66]

In December 1922 Annie announced in *The Theosophist* that the Australian Executive had issued a statement that the scandalous chapter was closed. There was not enough evidence to support a criminal charge as a result of the private police "enquiry" so perhaps the scandalmongers would keep quiet in future.[67]

Three years later the Sydney dispute was described in euphemistic terms as "the trouble that had long been brewing came to a head" and "the Convention of that year proved stormy and another parting of the ways". *The Theosophist* explained that the Sydney Lodge split in two, many members forming the Blavatsky Lodge which "valiantly set to work to build up a fresh nucleus of interest, realising with remarkable speed and courage its ideal of having a new platform from which to expound Theosophy".[68] The charter of the Sydney Lodge was cancelled in June 1923, with 600 of its original 900 members leaving to set up the Independent Theosophical Society, and a legal suit was brought to force them to surrender their property, the case later settled for a nominal sum.[69]

Aside from their duties as part of Mrs Besant's entourage and the police interview, Krishna and Nitya filled in the rest of their 1922 visit to Sydney quietly, with Nitya's ill health determining that they should go to Switzerland as soon as possible after a brief stay in sunny California. Apart from the ugly intrusion of the press, the Sydney they experienced was in many ways more protected than that experienced by DH Lawrence on his first trip, coinciding with theirs. Yet in their excursions into the public domain, Krishna and Nitya inevitably suffered the brunt of humour made by these "crude Australians".[70] Arriving in Sydney at the end of May, DH Lawrence and Frieda stayed in Thirroul on the Illawarra coast, about eighty kilometres south of Sydney. Yet there was something of the same experience affecting the 'Englishness' of both Krishnamurti and Lawrence, and its quality of understatement and subtlety, confronted by the brashness or even harshness of this new culture in an ancient country.

> Australia goes from bad to worse in my eyes. Sydney and the Harbour are quite one of the sights of the world, but the quality of the life is absolutely too much, or too little for me. Talk about crude raw and self-satisfied. If every American is a King or Queen Im [sic] sure every Australian is a little Pope all on his own. God's Vicar. 'There is noth-

> ing better than me on earth' he seems silently to proclaim, not with tongues of angels or tones of silver either and not always silently.'[71]

It's interesting that the word 'vulgar' is used by both Krishnamurti and Lawrence in emotionally disparaging the behaviour of Australians, Krishnamurti in his description of the press articles, and Lawrence of society in general:

> This is the most democratic place I have ever been in. And the more I see of democracy the more I dislike it. It just brings everything down to the mere vulgar level of wages and prices, electric light and water closets....

Another English interpretation of Krishnamurti's reaction to Australia uses the word 'vulgar'. In his 1963 biography of Annie Besant, the English writer, Arthur H Nethercot, says Krishnamurti was "acutely uncomfortable at Sydney when outside Theosophical circles" (though letters show he was also uncomfortable within Theosophical circles).

> The Australians, he found, were crude and insensitive, and treated him like a circus sideshow or public curiosity. He wrote Lady Emily long letters telling her how he had shrunk from the inquisitiveness of fellow passengers on ship-board, how he abhorred the Star publicity and the 'devotional stuff'. In England the demonstrations had been more private, in India they seemed more natural, but in Australia they were merely vulgar.[72]

Yet this quality of vulgarity and harshness is relative and, viewed from a socially egalitarian Australian position, the subtlety of overlooking certain indiscretions for the sake of appearances or the health of the body politic, or even out of self-righteousness, may have seemed dishonest. A letter to the editor of the *Daily Telegraph* on the day after Mrs Besant's victorious meeting addressing the Leadbeater allegations, raised the spectre of her riding rough-shod over dissenters in announcing that they should take whatever evidence they had to the police. She had suppressed discussion in order for a vote to be taken.

> Imagine the feelings of many of those listening to the emotional condemnations of slander, who knew that it was Mrs Besant herself who, in London in October, 1919, first voiced the charges of immorality against one of the promoters of the Liberal Catholic Church; who, in fact, sent instructions to her representative in Sydney to secure this gen-

> tleman's resignation ... Perhaps Mrs Besant has acquired this harshness from a long residence abroad. The more gently disposed Australian member would certainly rather make his charges to the officials of his own organisation first, and leave it to them to perform the (perhaps) higher duty of informing the police.[73]

The question of etiquette within and outside the Society must have been confusing. That the Theosophists were a well-mannered lot is indicated by a peculiar development at the 1922 convention. There was a good deal of clapping during debates, so much so that the Vice President, Jinarajadasa, who was chairing the meeting, asked people not to clap so much because it was noisy. So the helpful Dr van der Leeuw came to the rescue with a suggestion that they follow the custom at conferences in Holland, of holding up the right hand to show approval. The convention delegates fell into line and in future "hearty" applause' was indicated by a show of hands, described as very "picturesque". Leadbeater had already, some years earlier, complained of the "noisy shapes" created by hands clapping and the convention had opted for a "grateful" and "cultured" silence, but many still felt there was something lacking. The show of hands seemed to fit the bill.[74] But even within the bounds of decorous, civilised behaviour, individual Theosophists sometimes got out of hand. At one point, when Krishnamurti was in full lecture mode about the virtues of vegetarianism – "we" in the Hindu religion, he said, had been opposed to the idea of killing animals and were not going to kill animals just to please their bodies. He'd been a vegetarian all his life and his ancestors had been vegetarians, he went on. Suddenly up popped a question from the floor, "How about the boots we wear?".

They had not come to the stage where they could take off their boots, was Krishna's confident response, proud as he was now to be wearing fine European leather on his soles, after the dire warnings from Leadbeater when he was an adolescent that his feet must not be deformed by tight shoes. As to taking off his boots, he said he wished we could, but we could at least be idealists to the extent of not killing animals for food. "We" could be brothers; "we" preached harmlessness and brotherhood, and yet these animals which needed "our" protection and brotherly feelings "we" treated lower than any other thing we could imagine. No wonder Krishnamurti disliked public speaking. It was so unpredictable when even those within the fold called on him to justify his morality in action.[75]

Annie Besant's trip to Australia was fraught with tension and she must have felt that the struggle against the 'Forces of Darkness' would never end. But the year was not even half over.

Yet a tremendous event was about to happen to Krishnamurti which would determine his life's course to its end and the stimulus for this was said to have occurred in Australia. Krishnamurti must have met Leadbeater (either physically or on the astral plane) some time before leaving in mid-June because he said that Leadbeater brought through a special message from the Masters. The message was for Krishna to steady and widen himself and strive to bring his brain into subservience to the true 'Self' within. He was to be tolerant of divergences of view and seek that "tiniest" gleam of light amid the "Stygian" darkness of every "ignorant" mind because by recognising and fostering it he might help a "baby brother". Krishnamurti acknowledged that he was inclined to be intolerant and "not look" for the brother. He and Nitya also had a meeting with Mrs Besant, Leadbeater and Jinarajadasa about the "whole thing", including Wedgwood and 'Initiations', which Krishna thought best not to commit to paper in a letter to Lady Emily. He also had a talk with Mrs Besant about himself, explaining that his "mental" body was not developed enough and that he wanted to study quietly and not do any Order of the Star or Theosophical work. Perhaps he would study philosophy, economics, religion and education.[76]

Mrs Besant left Sydney for India on 1 June and Krishnamurti and Nitya left two weeks later for the United States. The General Secretary of the Theosophical Society in the United States, AP Warrington, who was in Sydney attending the convention, believed the Ojai Valley, about eighty miles north of Los Angeles, a predominantly orange-growing district, had an excellent climate for consumptives so would be ideal for Nitya.[77]

The brothers sailed from Sydney Harbour on 14 June on the *SS Ventura*, leaving the "marvellous sky and air and blue clarity and a hoary sort of land beneath it" to its plain-speaking inhabitants and other culturally-confused visitors.[78]

After a confronting stay in Australia Krishnamurti would himself remain 'all at sea' until he reached the peaceful, temperate Californian Ojai Valley, where he was to undergo the strangest, most overwhelming, and some say 'occult', experience of his life.

Chapter 4

Enlightenment

With self by Yoga integrated, [now] he sees
The self in all beings standing,
All beings in the self:
The same in everything he sees.

The Bhagavad-Gita VI, 29.

On board ship on the high seas between Australia and California, Krishna was full of hope for the future but still dogged by low spirits, largely caused by his separation from loved ones, worries over Nitya's health and the low opinions of others, and his lack of purpose in life. He must have been a sorry sight.

He wrote to Mrs Besant that they'd had just four days of rough weather that drove them all to bed and he was worried for Nitya. Although his brother had escaped a relapse, they would check his condition again as soon as they arrived in San Francisco in early July 1922.[1]

Krishna's interest in his fellow passengers was again distant – they were dull and patronising and he was bored. He continued to face blatant racism: one woman told him he and his brother were quite nice for natives and he thanked her for her 'courtesy' doubting that she understood his sarcasm.

Nitya put it more mildly when he wrote that, apart from the Theosophists Kunz and Warrington, there was the usual mixed lot on board who knew all about Krishna and himself. Some were interested in Theosophy, others were merely interested in his and Krishna's features and skin. He observed that overall he and his brother were the subject of a good deal of amusement.

Nitya remarked that he and Krishna were always inclined to enthusiams, and he wished this time their plans for India and the

Star work would last. He hoped they could make their way back to India via Europe after three or four months in California for his health.[2]

On reaching San Francisco, Krishna's mood changed considerably. He was able to give most newspaper reporters the slip, even though they'd been alerted to his arrival by Theosophist agitators in Sydney and boarded the ship as it entered the bay. He saw one *Los Angeles Times* reporter, pleading with her not to disclose where he was, and was pleased to find nothing published. The medical specialist who saw Nitya approved of their stay at Ojai, where the climate was hot and dry, up to 95 degrees at that time of year, and surrounded by a bare, rocky range of hills.[3]

But within a month Krishna was writing of a distinct collapse in Nitya's health, still blaming Sydney for the relapse. He had had a high temperature and he was coughing and spitting. He mostly rested and Krishna read to him for hours. Krishna himself felt stronger and even thought he would like to return to Australia because he was in now better condition, morally and mentally, to appreciate the Society's activities, he believed.[4] Nitya too was soon feeling repentant, writing to Leadbeater that he was not in a proper frame of mind to receive the full benefit of Leadbeater's 'presence' while in Sydney but now he would become a willing servant of the Master.[5]

What brought about this change of heart was an extraordinary occurrence in August 1922 which lies at the core of the rest of Krishnamurti's life, and is pivotal in any assessment of his role as a world religious teacher. For what happened was the beginning of a 'process' which would recur irregularly throughout his life, a physical disturbance to his mind and body which was, arguably, either self-induced or came upon him unexpectedly and which has been the subject of controversy since the time it first occurred. Depending on one's point of view, the 'process' was anything from a trick employed by Krishna for attention, to the appearance of (what might be called) God in a form which could be detected on the physical plane through the senses of people present.

The physical details of what occurred that first time, in August 1922, were detailed by both Krishna and Nitya in separate statements. In a six-page document, Krishna attempted to explain the source of the experience. He wrote that ever since he'd left Australia he'd been thinking about the message that the Master KH had given him when he was there. In the message he had been told to bring his mind and brain into subservience to the true Self within and to seek for a tiny gleam of light in each ignorant mind. Krishna said that he began meditating regularly and found that he concentrated with considerable ease. He realised that he had to destroy the wrong accumulations in his thinking over past years and began to harmonise all his bodies with the Buddhic plane. He kept them vibrating, maintaining the image of the Lord Maitreya in his mind the whole day, while becoming calmer and more serene. A fortnight later he felt acute pain at the nape of his neck and cut back his meditation to fifteen minutes. Nitya noticed a lump about the size of a large marble there at the nape of his neck which seemed to be a painful tight muscle. The pain worsened and two days later it was so bad Krishna had to go to bed because he couldn't think or do anything. Over the next two days he suffered intense pain and was in a semi-conscious state. But the extraordinary sensitivity that he felt allowed him to experience the life of beings and objects about him. He felt that he was not only a man mending the road but the pickaxe being used, as well as the very stone that the man was breaking up, and a blade of grass and a tree. Krishna felt himself to be the birds, dust and even noise. The next day, 20 August, Krishna felt as if needles were being stuck into his head. He was exhausted, weeping and lacked physical control. In the evening he refused to lie on his freshly-made bed, believing it to be filthy, in the evening he went out onto their verandah with them and then went out and sat cross-legged under a pepper tree near the house. He began to meditate and felt himself going out of his body. Then he felt the vibrations of Lord Buddha and saw Lord Maitreya and the Master KH. He said he was calm and felt that he had drunk at the source of the fountain of life and that love had intoxicated his heart. Krishna ended the description with a poem, concluding with the line. "I kiss the hem of thy garment".[6]

Nitya's account of the events that began that evening in the "long and narrow valley of apricot orchards and orange groves" is found in a five-page document in Krishnamurti Foundation archives.[7] He also wrote about a dream of a conversation he'd had with Leadbeater in which he said that something had happened to Krishna's 'pituitary' body and an effect would be the awakening of Krishna's creative instinct. In an account written out in full and finally dated nearly six months later, Nitya described Krishna's evenings following the first experience. evenings filled with tortuous pain. screaming, fainting, a 'Great Being' flooding the room, Krishna calling out in a child's voice for his mother and being electrified by fierce energy. The experiences continued until 8 December except whenever he went down to Los Angeles or Rosalind Williams (the young woman who was housekeeping for them) was not present to assist. Nitya's description in the statements and correspondence included many references to Rosalind – that she would hold Krishna: that he would push her away and then want her close again; that she played the part of a great mother and Krishna called her 'Mother'; that on 20 August she saw the splendour of the presence of Lord Maitreya, her face transfixed, and asked, "Do you see Him, do you see Him?"; that she said, "I will, I will", as if answering the Lord; that over a period of half an hour she trembled and almost sobbed with joy, asking, "Do you see?" and "Do you hear the music?"; that afterwards she fell back in her chair almost in a swoon or trance and when she'd recovered she remembered nothing of the event. The following day, according to Nitya, Krishna lay under the pepper tree in 'samadhi' all day. That evening Rosalind saw three figures near Krishna who took him away, leaving his body sitting under the pepper tree. Nitya did not say how he knew these things if not by seeing and hearing Rosalind and from what she told him. In December Nitya acknowledged that he hadn't seen anything, except once, but he was convinced that 'He' exists and would be 'coming'.[8]

Rosalind's daughter claims that Rosalind did not accept what Nitya 'assumed' she had seen. Not having the preconceptions of the others, Rosalind is said by her daughter to have allowed them their interpetations without accepting them herself. Krishnamurti's biographer Mary Lutyens makes the point that a copy of Nitya's account of the experience was typed by Rosalind's sister and sent to Lady Emily who was asked to find a reliable person who would presumably not spread the story about, and retype it. It seems odd that Rosalind would not refute the account entirely as fanciful at the outset, but it is not impossible that her attitude was as tolerant and passive as her daughter claims.[9]

AB Warrington, the President of the Theosophical Society in the United States, also wrote a two-page statement, saying that he had read Krishna and Nitya's statements and could confirm most of the facts they related. Both he and another man, the American Vicar-General of the Liberal Catholic Church, Mr Walton, saw lights around Krishna's head on the evenings of 20 and 21 August and heard music, as in a single chord. He wasn't disturbed by Krishna's strange behaviour as he had seen such symptoms before in five other people over the previous ten years. He felt a powerful presence, a strong downpouring of force which also seemed to be pouring through Rosalind. When the other man put his hand near Warrington he felt a warmth radiating from him.[10]

Krishna wrote to Mrs Besant that since that most extraordinary experience his whole attitude had changed. For the past five or six years he had not been happy and his mental condition had been deplorable because he did not know what he wanted. It had been seven years since he'd had clairvoyant experiences and he'd felt as if he was in a dungeon without light and fresh air. Now he knew what he wanted, he assured her, and it was nothing but to serve the Masters and her. Since the experience on 20 August he had been slightly clairvoyant and felt he was again in touch with Lord Maitreya. He had seen the glory of spirituality so earthly splendour no longer attracted him. His whole life would be devoted to 'the work', particularly in India.[11] In a similar vein, Krishna wrote to Leadbeater that he wanted to serve the Masters and the Lord.[12] He acknowledged with shame that his feelings towards Leadbeater had not been what they should have been. Now the love he had had for him when they first met at Adyar had returned so that he loved and respected him as few people did. And Leadbeater was not to think that he was writing mere platitudes.

Both Krishna and Nitya were keen to have Rosalind Williams, a nineteen-year old, blue-eyed, fair-haired vivacious woman, accepted by and involved in the Theosophical movement. Rosalind's elder sister, Erma, was the only person in her family who was a Theosophist, the girls' parents having been agnostic and free-thinkers.[13] The family had lived in Buffalo, New York, until Mrs Williams took her daughters to live in Hollywood in 1916. A Theosophist, Mrs Gray, who owned the house in which Krishna and Nitya were living, had invited Rosalind to Ojai. Capable, cheerful and keeping Nitya in good humour, Rosalind was asked to stay on as his nurse. Her teasing nature, her prowess at tennis, and her exceptional blue eyes may also have had a lot do with the decision.[14] Both young men saw the value of having this attractive young woman intimately bound up in their lives, which would mean her being accepted by the principals of the Society and adopting its creed. Nitya sent a photo of Rosalind to Leadbeater, saying she was exceedingly nice and they believed they'd met her often in the past. By November Nitya told Mrs Besant that he loved Rosalind intensely and both he and Krishna believed she was their mother come back. Krishna thought she'd been put on probation and would become a 'first ray' person and they were seeking Leadbeater's confirmation of this. Krishna sent Leadbeater a photo of both Rosalind and of Helen Knothe, whom he admitted he'd 'almost' been in love with when they'd met in Holland and in whom he was very 'interested'.[15]

It's difficult to know Rosalind's state of mind at this early stage. She had strong feelings developing for Nitya and possibly also Krishna, who as a handsome, charming man and with the status he held as the head of the Star organisation. was hard to ignore, quite apart from the 'process' he underwent.

Rosalind's daughter maintains that Rosalind never believed in Krishna's 'process' as anything other than a deliberate act to engage some woman. Rosalind was the first: he wanted her attention and would fondle her breasts and while she was rather appalled by this and was never 'taken in', she went along with it.[16]

Certainly the brothers were close and may not have felt any jealousy over their love. Nitya's descriptions of the events over a couple of months from 20 August show no trace of small-mindedness about Rosalind's role in helping Krishna through his agonising experiences. In October Nitya told Leadbeater that Rosalind had been a godsend to Krishna and had a great love for him. She also liked himself, Nitya added. He described how once Krishna asked Rosalind to leave the room when he felt the pain in his spine coming on, how she returned when she thought it was over but he kept on screaming with pain, claiming that a door had opened in his head, and she had shouted for him to close the door. For nearly forty minutes she could hardly hold him still from writhing. Nitya surmised that *kundalini* was being awakened in Krishna's spine, as the pain was mostly centred there. Every time he fainted Nitya and Rosalind did their best to wake him, touching his spine as a last resort. By November Nitya had told Mrs Besant that he loved Rosalind intensely.[17]

Krishna's nightly performance, as he called it, must have been a strain for Nitya, at once puzzling and unsettling. His correspondence shows a mixture of awe, consternation and faith in the religious significance of the process. Both he and Krishna wrote to Mrs Besant and Leadbeater seeking reassurance but in the case of Leadbeater it was not immediately forthcoming. Nitya recalled Mrs Besant's description of being with Krishna as a 'benediction' and both young men wanted desperately to know where Rosalind fitted into the occult picture puzzle of the 'Lives'. In pointing out that Leadbeater did not reply until mid-November, Lutyens raises the question of whether he had waited to hear from Annie Besant first. Krishna told Lady Emily after the letter arrived that Leadbeater had congratulated him with all his heart and explained that he and Mrs Besant had been through a similar occult trial by fire. Although he admitted in his case there'd been no physical suffering, he said he believed Mrs Besant had suffered a great deal but said very little about it. Leadbeater warned Krishna that there were still dangers and temptations right up to the very threshold of 'Divinity'. Krishna's reply to Leadbeater's news that he had passed another Initiation stage was grateful – it had been like a 'magnificent' dream and now he was realising the reality of it. In a letter to Mrs Besant Krishna wrote about his 'semi-conscious' state and how he was beginning to 'feel' astral forms around him. Nitya also explained that afterwards Krishna remembered nothing of the pain.[18]

At first Krishna didn't mind who knew about the occult process he believed he was going through, telling Mrs Besant that she could do anything she liked with the detailed narrative Nitya wrote of the events. Later, although Krishna wanted close friends to know about the experiences, he was very sensitive about the possibility that the message would spread further afield. Lady Emily wrote to a friend with the news, jubilant that Krishna had at last found happiness and direction. At Krishna's insistence the information was marked 'absolutely private'. Krishna also complained to Mrs Besant that he had asked Warrington not to say a word about the experiences yet Warrington had told two people who were not associated in any way, claiming he'd forgotten Krishna's request. Nitya too warned Mrs Besant that it was a good thing that she hadn't published details of the experiences in *The Theosophist* as it surely would have embarrassed Krishna, but he'd have to get used to the publicity and Nitya thought it wouldn't be too long before Krishna came 'out'. Nitya also explained to Lady Emily that he had left out some amusing and personal details in the account because Krishna didn't want them sent to everyone and he also referred to Krishna's 'end of the corridor' jokes.[19]

Ojai was a sleepy country valley and the brothers were not stressed by a busy workload. They continued to attend to *Herald of the Star* business even though their strange evenings were exhausting.

Elsewhere, the major disquiet in Theosophical circles was the agitation BP Wadia was causing over Leadbeater. Wadia had been a close associate of Mrs Besant and a co-activist in early trade union activities in India, assisting her in editing *New India*. He had been her colleague, during internment in 1917, but his stand over Leadbeater had torn open their relationship. He resigned from the Theosophical Society in 1922 and his accompanying statement was published as a supplement to the October issue of *The Theosophist*. Wadia's words were inflammatory as he clearly stated his own 'Back to Blavatsky' line. He wrote of "saviour-initiates" and "the devil of jesuitical black magicians" found in "Pseudo-Theosophy". Mrs Besant explained in her editorial, 'On the Watchtower', that for some time Wadia had been drifting away from his old moorings and that now the tie had been broken she wished him well. As an addendum she turned his resignation into the even greater sin of fraternising with the enemy when she pointed out that the 'non-co-operation' press was jubilant that he'd resigned as it sought to overturn the government, separate India from Britain and strike at her since she stood for respect for law against mob-tyranny and 'anarchy'. In the same editorial she crowed self-righteously about the failure of the Sydney police investigation into Leadbeater to find enough evidence to prosecute. It was enough of a vindication, she believed, to allow her to go on the attack against those who indulged in 'malicious' gossip. Then in November Annie Besant published a letter from her old friend NP Subramania Iyer, who had known Blavatsky, to try to disparage Wadia's renegades and restore the faith of younger members of the Society in their leaders.[20]

Krishna told Mrs Besant he felt angry about the way Wadia had behaved towards her in making scandalous and ungrateful statements and he had written to him in order to meet him in Los

Angeles. Krishna had earlier tried to meet him in San Francisco when he arrived in America but Wadia had gone to Monterey by that time. Krishna wrote a retort to dispel the idea that Wadia and his friends had that he was on their side, as he put it, and he hoped Mrs Besant would publish the response in *The Theosophist.* The following month he said that he had shown the article to two people who wanted to publish it, and he thought it should be published outside of *The Theosophist,* to reach a greater readership. But he would be guided by her. Aware that these were difficult times for Mrs Besant, with his unusual experiences and Wadia's accusations coinciding, Krishna buoyed her with some words of encouragement, telling her to let the difficulties come.[21]

By early 1923, when Krishna's nightly episodes had died down, Nitya was feeling much stronger due, he believed, to a course of treatment prescribed by a Dr Albert Abrams of San Francisco whose credentials at first sight seemed impeccable. He had been a Vice President of the California State Medical Society and a Professor in Cooper Medical College, Stanford University. He claimed to have invented an instrument based on 'electron theory', which used the vibrations of "an energy produced by the radioactivity of vibrating electrons" to diagnose disease from a single drop of blood and a patient's handwriting. He claimed that as almost everybody had either syphilis or gonorrhea, these were common foundations for disease. He believed syphilis was often contracted from vaccinations. It's estimated that 3500 practitioners were using Abrams machines at the height of his popularity in 1923 and he had the support of many respected medical practitioners and osteopaths. In 1922 articles began to appear in the Journal of the American Medical Association questioning his credentials. So the popular writer Upton Sinclair weighed in in support of Abrams and his Oscilloclast or ERA (Electronic Reactions of Abrams) machines. Sinclair claimed Abrams had diagnosed 15,000 people by 1922 and had cured 95 percent of his patients. However the Nobel prizewinner, Professor RA Millikan, examined Abrams' boxes in October 1923 and concluded that they were contraptions which might have been thrown together by a ten-year old to mystify an eight-year old. *Scientific American* published reports on Abrams from October 1923, even after his death from pneumonia in January 1924. Abrams died a millionaire after his success in what has been described as perhaps the greatest medical hoax of all time, one that still persists today in some quarters of 'New Age' culture.[22]

It's difficult to know whether Krishna and Nitya knew how controversial the treatment was and that Abrams' credentials were under question. Mary Lutyens wrote in 1975 that far from being a 'quack', Abrams had the highest medical qualifications and was believed by a distinguished Scottish physician, Sir James Barr, to be a genius born before his time. Lutyens says that Nitya was diagnosed with tubercolosis in his left lung and both kidneys and syphilis in his spleen and underwent treatment for many hours a day on an Abrams machine which sent electrical waves through the affected parts of his body. After two and a half weeks of treatment he was pronounced free of TB and syphilis but was to continue with the treatment for 45 minutes a day.

Lutyens says Krishna believed "absolutely" in the machine - he was also diagnosed with syphilis in his spleen and nose, as well as 'slight' cancer in his intestines and left lung. Certainly Krishna wrote to Lady Emily that it was curious about the nose diagnosis, as doctors had been puzzled about what the trouble was in the past. He said he hadn't written to anybody about it as it would cause a "row". He too underwent treatment on the machine but didn't mention the syphilis to Mrs Besant or Leadbeater. It's been suggested that Abrams used syphilis almost universally in his diagnosis as there was some shame attached to the disease, and patients who suspected fraud during treatment would be more likely to keep quiet to avoid public embarrassment.[23]

Believing Nitya cured, the brothers made plans to travel home to India in November 1923, via Chicago for the American Congress in May, England for the July Congress, then Switzerland for Nitya's health. They hoped to meet Mrs Besant in Europe. Nitya's feeling for his country is evident in his letters – all the mere words had become realities, he said, and back in India he'd work for Mrs Besant and arrange to export goods for sale in London. He'd never been so homesick for India. California had made an Indian of him, and he understood a little of what Mrs Besant felt for the country. Nitya's whole outlook was now changed. He'd dropped his tendency to depression and life was very simple, to follow Krishna and the Masters. Krishna had already declared there was no place like India in the whole wide world and he longed to return "home".[24] Krishna had checked with the 'Masters' that it was an acceptable time to travel before firming up his plans and they supposedly gave their consent reluctantly as the 'process' wasn't complete. As 1923 progressed both young men felt that they wanted to return to Ojai sometime, ostensibly because it had been so significant in Krishna's occult development, so that the whole place must now be very "magnetised". Rosalind's presence there was no doubt a major contributing factor. Nitya wrote to Mrs Besant and Leadbeater about wanting to buy about six acres of land with two houses on it. As it could not be bought in the name of an Indian, a board of trustees was formed which included the brothers and other members of the Theosophical Society. These two astute young Indians who had whiled away many hours playing 'Monopoly' had at last the opportunity to invest their gifts of patronage. They hoped Leadbeater would not think they were wasting money and assured him Ojai would become a valuable magnetic centre. Perhaps the brothers were emboldened by the knowledge that Lady De la Warr had just given five thousand pounds to the Society. The brothers' sense of Indianness must also have been heightened at this time by a scheme they were trying to launch to educate Indian boys in America. Krishna had been encouraged by his visit to the Berkeley campus in San Francisco and this enthusiasm was giving rise to ideas of a theosophical 'world university'.[25]

Krishna had also hit his straps as a lecturer. He and other speakers, including Nitya, raised money for maintenance at

Adyar at an 'Adyar Day' in Hollywood in February 1923; he spoke on India at the Women's Colleges Club of Pasadena in March; in Kansas in May his eloquence almost brought tears to Warrington and Nitya's eyes; and at the Chicago Theosophical convention in late May where $5,000 was raised, Krishna was, not surprisingly, the drawcard.[26]

Krishna and Nitya both wrote to Rosalind on the same day in May 1923 from Kansas City on route to Chicago. The letters are interesting to compare in terms of the different outlooks and writing styles of the brothers. Nitya's style was light-hearted: he amused Rosalind while conveying some serious subjects, such as cables they'd sent to Henry Ford to try to raise funds, and an approaching row in the Society over money. They'd stopped at all the really good hotels, full of smoke and "awful" women, he said, and it was terribly dull without her because they had no one to 'rag'. Krishna's writing was more ponderous, in line with his earlier letters to Lady Emily, indicating his serious burden of responsibility along with his repeatedly-expressed love for her. This was his first letter to her, he said, his "own dearest".[27] He'd been thinking of her such a lot as he loved her so very much and so intensely. He'd like to write pages to tell her how much he loved her but he didn't have the time. He asked her to tear up the letter in case – in case of what he didn't say but expected she'd understand. Nitya said he felt as if Rosalind was his mother and he her father and he used the word 'love' just once, whereas Krishna used it five times.[28]

What could have been Rosalind's reaction on receiving the two letters? One can only speculate. Rosalind was young and may have felt the situation was nothing more than flirtation. It's clear the two brothers felt some responsibility towards Rosalind, as well as being enchanted by her. Krishna had written to Mrs Besant in February saying Rosalind ought to do great things but the trouble was she was penniless. She was used to earning her own money, he said, and hadn't decided what she would do once they left.[29] In their letters from Kansas, the brothers enquired about whether she'd found a tutor or a house in which to live.

Writing of their visits to Washington, Boston and New York, Nitya said he'd like her to study at Radcliffe, if only for a year, and described Krishna's crying for 'Amma' every morning and weeping in the afternoons because he was missing her. To cheer her, Nitya wrote about the money raised at an auction of Indian paraphernalia at the convention, with people even giving their jewellery to the cause, and about all the "big bugs" like him who had sat at a high table and eaten a "darned" good dinner. Krishna described Chicago as awful and dirty beyond words but he liked New York. He told Rosalind he loved her so very much, underlining the point, and again asked her to destroy the letter. Both brothers had long-term plans to take Rosalind into the care of the Theosophical Society, and there's no sign they were jealous or possessive with each other about her love, as they sailed back to their 'old world' from New York harbour. They embarked on the *Paris* on 6 June, due to dock in faraway Plymouth on 12 June, where they would disembark and travel on to London, arriving about 11.30 at night. For her part, Rosalind was young, at a loose end and possibly emotionally ambushed by these two wealthy, well-educated, well-travelled, exotic, attractive young men. Her daughter maintains that Rosalind was not a Theosophist, not very interested in philosophical matters and that it was Rosalind's sister, Erma, who gave her life membership of the Society. But in any case, in these early days Rosalind was not putting up much resistance to the brothers' charm. Clearly though, she must have put up some resistance to the idolisation of Krishna syndrome, as he refers to them quarrelling and also makes several references to a need for her not to laugh at what he says, but take him seriously. Regardless of how independent-minded Rosalind may have seemed, her life would very soon be consumed by the Society and the dominance and protection that association with Krishnamurti offered. Within a couple of weeks of their arrival in England, both young men had written assuring Rosalind that education expenses had been arranged for her, with an offer coming from Miss Dodge, their benefactress, before they'd even asked.[30]

The murky politics of the Society continued as a background to Krishna and Nitya's newfound enthusiasm. Krishna wrote to George Arundale from Lady De La Warr's West Side House mansion in Wimbledon suggesting they both turn over a new leaf and drop their differences as they were bound together in spite of themselves. The tone was jocular and nonchalant, with references to shaking hands over it and giving thanks to Allah or to any old "bird"! Krishna explained that the base of his spine was active and he didn't know whether to return to Ojai or go on to India.[31]

Nitya was keen for Leadbeater to meet them in Europe, hoping he would give some guidance on the care of Krishna's body. He did see the drawbacks though of Leadbeater becoming the subject of press interest again, in particular the harmful effect it might have on the chances of Oscar Kollerstrom, one of Leadbeater's acolytes, being accepted at university.[32]

Meanwhile, a great gift was being arranged for the Star organisation – Baron von Pallandt wanted to deed his castle at Ommen in northern Holland and some 5,000 acres around it to be used as a European headquarters. Krishna did not want to hold property in his own name so it was planned to set up a corporation.[33]

Krishna at first missed Rosalind but by August, staying in a villa at Ehrwald in the Austrian Alps, he was able to take up where he left off with his old love, Helen Knothe, who filled the emotional gap left by Rosalind. He wrote to Rosalind in early September apologising for not having written in over a month. Now he explained that his evening "affair" had begun again three weeks before and he felt like a chewed rag. He longed to see her again, he said, but there was not the same degree of protestation of love in this letter. Nitya wrote to Rosalind that Krishna's process went on every night after dinner between 7 and 9 pm, and Helen stayed with him while most of the other people in the villa who knew nothing about the 'process' were sent outside. But because there were servants still in the house Krishna couldn't shout, so he would moan and gasp instead. The pain was mostly in Krishna's spine and the back of his neck. Nitya observed to Mrs Besant that Helen was a little nervous at first but became accustomed to it.[34]

Recalling that time about seventy years later, Helen Knothe Nearing said it was something that was hard for her to witness and go through but she did what she could to help. The evenings would begin with herself, Krishna and Nitya sitting on the balcony overlooking the mountains when the brothers would chant mantras and sing. Krishna would then become disturbed physically, feverish and restless, and go indoors with Nitya. Soon Nitya would call her in and she would sit and hold Krishna's hand. At other times during the day Krishna would be wild, gay and silly, she said, and then in these nightly sessions he would not be with them at all, as if he were a different person. Asked if it was an out-of-body experience, Knothe Nearing said that it was very much in the body, with Krishna's body undergoing an experience as if two strange personalities were conversing, Krishna and a child or 'body elemental'. Knothe Nearing said neither she nor Nitya were clairvoyant yet they could feel the benediction of a presence coming into the room from the mountains and delivering messages to them through the voice of Krishna. They scribbled down the messages in the dark. Servants two floors below were told Krishna had epileptic fits, to account for the noise he made. Knothe Nearing said she knew nothing about epileptic fits at the time, and thought what Krishna was going through was an 'esoteric' endurance test. All these years later she didn't know what it was.[35]

In her own memoir, Knothe Nearing is more critical of Krishna. She recalls that her musical education under a violin teacher in Vienna was interrupted after the August 1923 Vienna Congress by Krishnamurti and theosophists who urged her to cut back her violin practice and spend the summer with them in the Tyrol. Krishna was insistent, she says, that there were many good violinists in the world but "he hoped she would go beyond that and work with him". Knothe Nearing says she was persuaded while in Ehrwald that Krishna really needed her and she him. She spent all the evening hours that summer witnessing and assisting at strange happenings she believed were spiritual ordeals involving his physical body and psyche. In this memoir she says Krishna would hold not only her hand but her body close. The whole experience was puzzling to her and came at a time in her life when she felt she had to make a major decision about her future direction. She wrote to Mrs Besant about whether to go to Australia to stay with Leadbeater in a communal house or continue with her musical aspirations. Mrs Besant wrote back asking whether she cared enough for a spiritual life to give up everything else for that aim. This settled Helen Knothe's doubts in favour of devoting herself to learning the meaning of life. But even so, she remained puzzled – about Krishna bouncing from intense holiness to tomfoolery, from serious aloofness to wildness and practical jokes. He would also act as a counsellor to Theosophist girls in one-on-one sessions during which they would voice their problems and he would criticise their attitudes. Often they would cry; none left a session feeling "shining, radiant and fulfilled". With hindsight, Knothe Nearing thought that he was "almost sadistic" in stirring up their emotions. He would talk about fear and she, having few fears, wondered why he spoke of it so often. Knothe Nearing did decide to go to Australia but her parents were upset and would not allow her to abandon her career. She says she encountered the socialist movement in Australia and was able to review Krishna's wealthy life, "far removed ideologically and physically from the masses". She returned home and Krishna "wrote many sad letters", in the hope that she would follow him to Ojai.[36]

Writing to Mrs Besant in September 1923 from the Austrian villa, Nitya says Krishna's pain is the worst he's seen and there'll be three more nights of it before they leave. Strangely enough a note dated three days later, 20 September, purportedly a message from the Master KH, says that "this" is finished for the time being but will continue in Ojai. Addressed to Nitya, the message says that both he and Krishna will have more energy, and success will depend on what they do over the next month; they have to be more "careful", put on more "fat" and have nothing get in the way. As for Helen, she has "come on" well and will be used later. "They" want Nitya in particular. And the house is "sacred" and should be "used" for Austria. It may seem to some an unusual method of increasing real estate holdings. In fact the house, which was owned by a friend of John Cordes an Austrian Theosophist, unlike the Ojai estate, has not become a Krishnamurti Centre.[37]

In August Nitya had asked Mrs Besant whether Leadbeater might come to Ojai, where Ruth Roberts (a girl Krishna had "flirted" with in Sydney), Helen and Rosalind might meet him, chaperoned. Nitya's view of Helen's vital role in the 'process' no doubt reflects Krishna's at the time. Writing to Mrs Besant in mid-September, Nitya says that Leadbeater still had not replied and Helen was, after all, not going to Ojai with them as her parents, believing she had a real genius for violin, wanted her to stay on in Vienna. It seemed a waste of time, he said, but he believed her parents would not stand in her way long.[38]

Mrs Besant had given her opinion that after their European stint the brothers should go back to Ojai, rather than India, and their new plans for the young women were based on that, along with the hope that Mrs Besant herself might visit them there. If Leadbeater met her in California, according to Nitya it would be a great success, even allowing for some scandal similar to that in Australia.[39]

So Krishna and Nitya returned to England and then set sail for America on the *SS Voledam*. With them was a young Indian who was studying at Cambridge, Desikacharya Rajagopalacharya, whom they believed would prove a helpful acolyte.[40] Also in the party were Dr J (Koos) van der Leeuw, a young man from Sydney who held classes in psychology for the Society, another boy who was on his way to see Leadbeater in Sydney, and Helen, returning to her parents in America. Dr van der Leeuw was expected to go on to Sydney after a few weeks stay in Ojai.[41] As to the reason for Rajagopal's presence there, Nitya explained to Mrs Besant that after Krishna had repeated a message from the

Master one night, he, Nitya, had asked whether Rajagopal would be helpful in Ojai and the answer coming through Krishna had been yes, 'very'. Rajagopal had some years earlier shared a flat with Nitya. He studied European and English History and Law at Cambridge, and would go on to graduate with honours. Nitya reassured Mrs Besant in October 1923 that six months in Ojai would not retard Rajagopal's progress with his degree. Nitya surmised that Rosalind would probably give assistance but if she was not needed in Ojai with Krishna she might go to Sydney with Helen. Nitya looked forward to a very difficult time, with Krishna's 'process' expected to be more and more painful in Ojai as he became more conscious through the experience. Nitya nevertheless was filled with 'adoration' and the Master was becoming more real to him, he said.[42]

It might come as no surprise that Nitya's unusual speculation that Rosalind might not be needed by Krishna in Ojai came true. And Nitya also reported in November that he and Krishna had put on weight, according to the instructions given. The 'process' began again for Krishna in Ojai on 20 November and this time Krishna did not seem to want Rosalind with him. She was living next door and studying for entrance to Radcliffe. He still called for his mother but now it was Helen he wanted. Krishna wrote to Lady Emily in November that Rosalind, curiously enough, did not help him. Rather, he said, he did not want her but missed Helen. He didn't seem to understand why he couldn't get on with Rosalind; he found her irritating and didn't see much of her, but would hear her and Rajagopal squabbling as they had an algebra lesson together. Nitya was also said to read poetry to Rosalind which she enjoyed. Rosalind's daughter claims that Krishna was angry when Nitya one day suggested that he, Nitya, might marry Rosalind, Krishna believing that Nitya should devote his life to 'the Work'. She says that marriage was still far from Rosalind's mind and Rajagopal was presumably silent at this stage about his love for Rosalind which had developed from hearing Nitya talk about her. There are corroborated reports of Krishna being against marriage in general, and particularly in the cases of

Jinarajadasa. Arundale. and when Mar de Manziarly intended to marry. It's also reasonable to assume that Rosalind was clearly the object of a great deal of jealousy among Krishna's '*gopis*'. indicated by Mary Lutyen's conclusion that. not content with Nitya's love, Rosalind wanted Krishna's and Rajagopal's love as well.[43]

A message from the 'Master' came through Krishna in late November that the work being done was of the greatest importance and exceedingly delicate – the first time such an experiment had been carried out in the history of the world. Everything in the household must give way to it. Krishna said. Nitya once again sought Leadbeater's advice: did he think Krishna should be with him in Sydney during this period and did he know if something similar had occurred in Jesus' life when the Lord last came to earth, he asked? Was Helen put on probation: and the perennial question, was Rosalind their mother?[44]

Leadbeater had been avoiding giving an opinion on the extraordinary turn of events this 'process' was effecting on Krishna's life. Leadbeater's biographer, Gregory Tillett, takes it as a point in Leadbeater's favour that he was genuinely bewildered by it and admitted he did not know what it was. Certainly Leadbeater did not seek to make capital out of Krishna's experience, but he may also have viewed Krishna as now exerting his independence from previous doctrine espoused by Leadbeater himself and recognised the danger in this for him. But with Nitya and Krishna exhausted and seeking his advice, Leadbeater finally grasped this decidedly painful occult nettle. Nitya had written to Dr Rocke in Sydney to pass on details of the 'process' to Leadbeater and to a Society official in New Zealand. He also wrote to Mrs Besant that when Krishna was "away" he was three separate beings: Krishna in his astral body. the consciousness functioning in speech, and the physical body. The Lord came to visit one night, Nitya said, and ever since there'd been peace and harmony.[45]

Leadbeater's response written on New Year's Day 1924 was direct and unequivocal. I do not understand Krishna's terrible drama and I am very anxious about it, he wrote to Nitya. In Adyar the body needed preparation but not this kind, he said, underlining the word 'this' for emphasis. Perhaps they'd been sent to that secluded spot in the Ojai Valley especially. He dared not take the responsibility of advising them to go to Sydney while the 'process' was under way, and besides, he didn't think the sea voyage could be good for Nitya's lungs. But he'd be more than delighted to see them once all these strange "agonies" were completed. Maybe they could be near Mrs Besant, who he believed had gone through similar experiences, but then Adyar was also near the sea. Leadbeater did, however, equivocate over Rosalind. He didn't know how Rosalind could be their mother as she was born before their mother's death, was his delayed declaration. Yet he tempered this with the view that there was a possibility that their mother used both Rosalind and Helen as mediums to help her son in his suffering. Leadbeater added primly that this was not improbable as it would account for Krishna turning to comparative strangers in this curiously "intimate" manner. He wrote off promptly to Annie Besant that he was very troubled by the affair as it was so opposed to what he had been taught. Krishna and Nitya seemed to have no doubts, he said, yet the messages they received were not in the least in the style of the Masters. Leadbeater made it clear he didn't want these antics in Sydney where he had other ventures in train, including the construction of an amphitheatre overlooking the harbour at Balmoral and a new healing service he had introduced in the Liberal Catholic Church.[46]

Nitya and Krishna clearly were very disturbed by Leadbeater's terse response.

"Disquieting" is how Nitya described it, saying he had had a sick feeling in his stomach. He was convinced of the presence of the Master, yet he felt haunted by the thought of fine people who had been led astray, such as Martyn, and he would hate to join such a crew. Leadbeater's letter gave both Krishna and him the shivers, he said. Then came his description of their arduous endeavours – Krishna was a wreck physically and both their brains had almost ceased to "function". On some nights Krishna had been too tired to bear any pain at all so he would leave his body which bore the pain in his absence, Nitya explained. It was mostly felt in three places, the base of the spine, the nape of the neck and sometimes in the head – not ordinary pain as experienced in a cut, for instance, but a sense of intolerable congestion. Krishna hoped a climax would come and felt he could bear the pain more easily if his mother was with him. Could Leadbeater tell them what was this pain, which came in spasms and caused fainting, as they now thought it could hardly be "kundalini" since they'd had about one hundred and forty nights of it? Perhaps the explanation lay in "spirelli" awakening in atoms which was a part of Leadbeater's theories? Nitya also enclosed some messages from the Master, including one about a neighbour who believed he was almost a Master, whereas Nitya saw him only as a fat man making efforts to appear good, because, in contrast, they'd felt distinctly unpleasant "influences" coming from him.[47]

The tone of this letter indicates severe mental disturbances exhibited by the brothers who must have been feeling alone in all the world in having to cope with these extraordinary experiences their minds wrestled with. They immediately sent off a cable to Leadbeater, who replied, "President say all right".[48]

And so the matter was settled for the time being. Krishna and Nitya tried to get on with business, supporting attempts to raise funds for Adyar, a college at Madanapalle near Krishna's birthplace and other ventures, including fundraising to buy the Ojai land.[49] Krishna wrote to a friend in Europe, Ruspoli, over delays in the handover of the Castle Eerde, saying Baillie-Weaver in England was working like a slave over it and it was better that it was all fixed up legally now as afterwards they didn't want Van Pallandt's mother on their heads – as he knew what the old lady was like! Krishna also asked Jamnadas in India for some money. He didn't say it was a loan, but asked for 500 pounds for some people who were in need. Jamnadas seems to have come into some money about that time, as Krishna advised him not to waste it selfishly. Krishna said he was sorry to preach but that was his job. Then he melodramatically requested secrecy over his request for money – if Jamnadas couldn't manage that he was not to read any further as Indians had a "poisonous" habit of talking, he said. The money was to be sent to Nitya's account in California and the letter of request destroyed.[50]

Although Krishna and Nitya had been somewhat reassured by Leadbeater's cable, Leadbeater and Mrs Besant must have been concerned enough about the state of affairs in Ojai to investigate further. A medical practitioner who was an official of the Theosophical Society in Australia, Dr Mary Rocke, was despatched from Sydney and Nitya sent an ingenuous letter to Leadbeater in March to say everyone at Ojai had been wondering why she was coming. This followed a letter in which Nitya had described how Krishna had seen the Lord and the Master after a "force" travelled up both sides of his spine, curling around his head to create a flame streaming out of his forehead. Nitya believed it marked a definite stage, perhaps "*jnana dhrishti*" described in Leadbeater's *Inner Life*. The process had been going on since November and it would continue until the end of April, Dr Rocke arriving in early April and observing it every evening for a week. Nitya wrote to Lady Emily that he and Krishna were awfully glad to see Dr Rocke as confirmation that they were not entirely mad and she was "tremendously" impressed by the whole episode. Nitya wrote to Leadbeater on 21 April that Dr Rocke's visit was providential as she took the place of Rajagopal who had had a hernia operation. Krishna's last night of the 'process' had been glorious for everyone there. Dr Rocke would give Leadbeater the details but Nitya had never felt the presence of the Lord so clearly or so near before. Dr Rocke must have been convinced of the 'process' being genuine as she continued to be a devout follower of Krishna.[51]

Having established the case for Krishna's 'process', Nitya wrote four days later, again pleading for Rosalind to go to Leadbeater in Sydney: if she went even for a little while she would be financially independent so no extra burden, he suggested.[52]

With uncertainty over Krishna's 'process' now cleared up. Krishna and Nitya waited until after the May date for 'Wesak', a moon festival observed by Buddhists, before setting out for Europe. India and whatever destination might arise after that. They left from New York in early June after a visit to the Grand Canyon from where Nitya sent a postcard to Rosalind in his signature jolly style. but with a philosophical undertone and writing in a little ditty that: it was terribly hot but also cold: they were all so happy but also sad; he hoped to see her soon but didn't think he could: and, Nitya was eating a lot but was getting thin. Then, as the ship sailed from America, with Rosalind headed for the opposite side of the world, having been accepted by Leadbeater in Sydney, Nitya's love and concern for her was evident in his note. Love everyone, but not too much, except Leadbeater and the work, he advised her. He said he felt like her father - he was certain that he'd left $200 to be given to her and he'd send money regularly to a bank in Sydney.[53]

Krishna was able to meet up with Helen Knothe again on the voyage across the Atlantic, her father having relented to allow her to travel again but still disapproving. But once settled in London Krishna wrote to Rosalind to tell her absolutely honestly that he thought of her almost every day - he wasn't joking. He was very glad she was in Sydney but begged her not to pick up the Australian accent which sounded worse than the American to his refined English upper-class sensibility.[54]

A few weeks later in Pergine near Trento in northern Italy, Nitya wrote to Rosalind that he had telegraphed her money – had she received it? There was a chance he and Krishna might come to Australia after London, Venice and India but she was not to breathe a word to anyone.[55]

Krishna and Nitya spent a happy period in Europe, the highlights being that they accompanied Mrs Besant for their first aeroplane rides to Paris, Hamburg and to Holland. Mrs Besant also celebrated fifty years of public work at a special function in Queens Hall, following the Theosophical Society and Star conventions in London in July. The Theosophical convention and the third international Star convention were held at Arnhem and the first Star camp was held at Ommen in tents on Castle Eerde land. Bonfires were ceremoniously lit at night for Krishna to give lectures and then he, Nitya and Rajagopal would chant in Sanskrit. Krishna's talks emphasised the need for people to be passionate, as if falling in love, on the path of discipleship.[56]

The main party, including Lady Emily and two of her daughters, moved on to an eleventh-century castle-hotel at Pergine, near Trento in northern Italy. Krishna brought another message through from the Master there which depressed Nitya because supposedly they'd been failing in their work. As soon as Krishna's 'process' resumed at Pergine, Helen was required by Krishna when he would ask for 'Amma'.[57] Helen's own recollection of the time spent in Pergine is that she, Krishna, Nitya and Lady Emily lived in a separate tower of the castle, the rest of the party in the main building. She and Krishna were together as much as time and other company permitted and he didn't seem to have lost interest in her. She even recalls he said to her, "I could drink the water from your body", and when she was required to lie with him she would think of closeness and solace, holding him "not as a lover but as a mother would".[58]

A message from the Lord Maitreya said to have been received by Krishna in Pergine gave serious advice along the lines of: forget yourself and then you'll find the Lord; the happiness you seek is not far off – it's in every common stone; do not amuse yourself at other people's expense; do not try to reconcile the irreconcilable. There was also mention of that place becoming a centre, but once again, this did not eventuate.[59]

Krishna also had private interviews with the young women about him, referred to as 'gopis'. In a diary entry made by Mary Lutyens she says the talks were wonderful - in one she and Krishna were both weeping as he urged her on to fulfil her vision and know real love, as no one would ever love her as much as he did.[60]

The role of World Teacher which Krishna was now beginning to assume suited certain aspects of his nature such as his extraordinary interest in human emotions. but not other aspects. such as his aloofness. shyness and distaste for public speaking, for although his skill as an orator had increased. his fear had not diminished commensurately. He was playing with fire with these girls' emotions, which comprised such a mixture of artfulness and innocence. Holding the special status of 'Coming Lord' as he did, he was expected by Theosophists to hold these intimate sessions. His protection was the exalted position he held and his own sexual innocence and high-mindedness but even these must have been breached in some part at times. The fact that he was persuaded that he would never marry must also have acted as a straitener to him in crossing the barrier to physical sex. Lutyens says Krishna sublimated his sex drive. At times he expressed concern about rumours of a special attachment to one girl or another and would quickly act to scotch them. In Sydney in 1922 in relation to Ruth Roberts, he acted surprised about the idea that he was in love and said how 'darn' careful he would have to be or he would get a reputation. Later Lutyens said he'd flirted with Ruth. Helen Knothe Nearing also believed that Krishna was influenced by a news story in Indian and American newspapers in 1925 that he was engaged to an American girl whom she believed to be herself. She thought he was given advice to break the relationship as it might interfere with his 'mission'. It is, however, speculative that this was the only reason for their breach.[61]

All these young Indian men were affectionate and many of the European women they came into contact with were not necessarily emotionally prepared for their flirtatiousness. As mentioned earlier, the Theosophist gatherings were hothouses of sentiment – Krishna was very good at reading and fuelling love emotions but others about him were not far behind him in prowess.

To take an example, Mary Lutyens ten years younger than Nitya, was nevertheless devoted to him from sometime before the age of six. She wrote a tribute to this love in her book, *To Be Young*, a gentle, sentimental account of her infatuation during her childhood and adolescence over a period of more than a decade. Yet she said Rajagopal was the first young man she ever kissed, when she was fourteen, and she maintained an adoration for Krishna all her life. In the evenings at Ehrwald in 1923, Nitya would sit side by side on the floor with Mary, holding her hand, while her mother read aloud. The following year at Pergine in September, Mary said she and Nitya had become quite close. In November on board ship bound for India she thought Helen, who was Krishna's favourite, was trying to captivate Nitya as well, so she participated in witty, sarcastic repartee with Nitya which seemed also to engage his heart. He told her he'd first loved her sister, Barbie, then Madame de Manziarly, then Rosalind and now her. They didn't kiss but would meet on deck in the evening and look at the stars, Nitya pressing his cheek against hers. On reaching Adyar, once again they would lie on the floor side by side, holding hands and covered by a large shawl while Lady Emily read aloud in the evenings. Yet during this time Nitya was said to be in love with Rosalind. He sent her money in August and he wrote in October that he loved her, missed her and wanted to feel and touch her. During the voyage Nitya became ill again and by January he was passionately kissing Mary goodbye, as she left to meet her father in Delhi while he was sent up to the hill station, Ootacamund, with Madame de Manziarly, for his health. Perhaps he didn't feel the same way about Mme de Manziarly now; perhaps he did. In any case he was very ill, so much of what might be thought fickleness was no doubt overlooked. Just four years earlier, Krishna too had consulted Lady Emily, for whom he professed a deep and abiding love, about whether it would be the right thing for him to fall in love with Mar de Manziarly who attracted him very much. On board ship again on the way to Sydney in 1925, Nitya was very ill and Mary was prevented from meeting with him but would gaze adoringly from afar. She wanted to kill herself, she felt so jealous thinking that Nitya would see Rosalind again, but Krishna told her not to be "a damned fool".[62]

It must be remembered that this is the emotional atmosphere - among the women rivalry, jealousy and attempts at overcoming these qualities in themselves - that forms the context for Mary Lutyens' statements concerning love relations, and an attempt to corral emotional attachments, within the group. She writes comments such as "Helen was not pretty but had great charm and vivacity", "It was understood from the beginning that Rosalind was Nitya's special friend", "Nitya's love for Rosalind has never been doubted" and "I loved [Krishna] more at that time [in Sydney] than I had ever done before". Yet the patterns of affection are messy, the borders of possessiveness are blurred and there's little evidence that Nitya and Krishna followed any form of conventional English morality or rivalry in the realm of their affections and strong evidence that they both felt strong attachment to Rosalind.[63]

Krishna must have at least subconsciously been thinking of Rosalind a lot in late 1923 as his editorial in *The Herald of the Star* for January 1924 was devoted to the theme of the call of the 'Eternal Rose', a flower he always associated with Rosalind. Although he never mentioned Rosicrucianism, many readers would no doubt have drawn a parallel with that occult order concerned with moral renewal through alchemy. He called on readers to forget their own families, to worship at the divine altar of unselfish love and become lovers and disciples of the 'Rose'. In January 1925, too, Krishna told a group in Adyar that you couldn't understand the rose if you didn't have the capacity to see it. At this time he was suggesting taking the 'Masters' a little "on faith" before making them a reality, a fairly typical Leadbeater baseline for development of what might be called imaginative or fantasy-driven clairvoyance.[64]

In India in early 1923 Nitya was staying in a house steeped in Theosophical memories – the house built by Colonel Olcott in 1890 in which Mrs Besant had lived during her internment in 1917. Nitya recovered a little but wrote to Mary that it was the worst four weeks he had ever experienced, feeling feeble and a failure. She said he told her he would always love her.[65]

Krishna meanwhile was carrying out real estate business, inspecting land near Madanapalle as a suitable site for a university. He would not be able to buy any land until the following year, and ultimately the 300 acres purchased at Tettu Valley, about ten miles from Madanapalle, was renamed Rishi Valley and became a school which is still operating.[66]

By March Krishna and Nitya were reunited when it was decided that the best place for Nitya was the dry heat of Ojai, so they must travel as soon as possible. Mr Mackay in Sydney had offered to pay their passage and a stopover in Sydney would give them the opportunity to see Leadbeater again, which they both wanted, so Krishna decided to take the risk of Nitya's illness getting worse in Sydney. Nitya came down from Ooty on 11 March and the brothers went on to Colombo to board the *SS Ormuz* for another ocean voyage. With a party of Theosophists, they left their old home on the ancient Indian subcontinent, headed for Sydney, where they would pick up Rosalind and sail on to their new home in the 'New World' continent, the United States, to live the *dharma* of their chosen lives.[67]

Chapter 5

Pathless

When you get out of the way of your own love it becomes true. And when it's not fixed, when it's not solidified and when it's not focussed rigidly on another object, it broadcasts in front of you and in back of you, to the right of you, to the left of you, above you and beneath you, and you're in the centre of a forcefield that includes everything that has no inside and no outside, that doesn't look at anything, nor does it need to be looked at. It's like the taste of honey when you're very young.

Leonard Cohen Spring 96 documentary Dir: Armelle Brusq, Lieurac Productions France 1997.

Back on the high seas in March 1925, heading for Australia, Krishna and Nitya experienced a reasonably uneventful voyage, troubled only by Nitya's illness. The ship *SS Ormuz* had battled exceptionally heavy seas earlier in the Bay of Biscay and "received some knocking about" as huge waves swept her from stem to stern, according to the Melbourne *Herald*. From Colombo south, when the Krishnamurti party was on board, the voyage was not as bad but still difficult, with eighty passengers in first class and six hundred and fifty in third. More than a hundred and sixty were migrants, and of these the majority were Italian, bound for Brisbane.[1]

Krishna had written to Mrs Besant before boarding the ship in Colombo that following a bad crossing from India to Ceylon, Nitya's temperature had now come down and Krishna had organised the best cabin for Nitya for the long voyage across the Indian Ocean. Krishna asked Mrs Besant to think of Nitya and cure him, as if her thinking would be sufficient to do so.[2]

From on board ship Krishna wrote to Mrs Besant that Nitya's health had been bad for about five days after the excitement of leaving India and the train journey. Now his temperature was normal but he still stayed in his cabin all day, resting and sleeping, with the Society's Vice President, Jinarajadasa, taking care of him as if he were his "grandmother". Krishna was grateful that Jinarajadasa was with them. Lady Emily was also with Krishna this trip so there was no need for longing letters to her but, even so, Krishna missed Mrs Besant – he felt like crying aloud and his heart ached for her.[3]

Two days out from Fremantle Krishna wrote to Rosalind a serious letter in a friendly tone, asking her to take charge of Nitya's nursing requirements as she used to. He had written to her in January and February, first to ask her to help Helen as she was a new chum in Sydney and then to announce that he and Nitya would be in Sydney in April. Rosalind, far from being indifferent to Theosophy, had taken certain steps in occult initiation which pleased Nitya and Krishna.[4] Now, so close to reaching port, Krishna gave Rosalind explicit instructions about what Nitya's diet must be – a copybook light English diet of the period, consisting of salad, macaroni, rice, vegetables, pudding, cheese, stewed fruits and soups. Dr Rocke would arrange Dr Abrams' treatment, he said, and Rosalind was to organise accommodation as far from the sea as possible. He'd be so glad to see Rosalind again, Krishna said, and now that she was such a "big bug" he hoped she'd recognise him, he joked. Nitya also sent his love, he said. Still with the power of prayer in mind, Krishna said he'd learnt to pray, something he hadn't been good at.[5]

Krishna's 'process' had resumed in India and subsided at sea but started up again a few days before reaching Australia.[6] First port of call was once again Perth's port, Fremantle, where a Star meeting was held. Then on to Adelaide.

The *RMS Ormuz* sailed into Port Philip Bay, Melbourne in a strong wind on the night of 31 March, delivering Krishna into the hands of a more temperate press compared with his last trip to Australia. Among the distinguished passengers reported on board the *Ormuz* were a military general, a British judge from the Indian High Court and Professor Warren, Dean of Engineering at the University of Sydney. On a tour of Europe for eleven months. Englishman Professor Warren's conclusion on arriving back in his adopted home was that the engineering schools in Sydney and Melbourne were superior to that in Oxford since students at that very distinguished university used instruments that had gone out of date forty years before, he claimed. Krishnamurti was listed in *The Age* as among the *Ormuz* passengers. This leading paper described Lady Lutyens as the wife of a famous architect, Sir Edward Lutyens, getting his Christian name, which was Edwin, wrong. It reported that the group of Theosophists was to speak at a public meeting in the Temperance Hall, but as the group was headed for the annual convention of the Society in Sydney and their ship was sailing that day, other speakers would take their place. The party of Theosophists was only in Melbourne one day but it was time enough for Lady Emily and her two daughters to add a touch of class to the pages of *The Herald* in a plain head and shoulders shot. Two newspapers gave the Vice President of the Theosophical Society, C Jinarajadasa, the opportunity to make some political capital on the subject of Indian Home Rule. His line of argument reported in *The Herald* was that Gandhi (and the name was miss-spelt) had had three years to organise direct action and had failed, so Mrs Besant would save the day, with the aid of the British Government, with her version of Dominion status for India. Jinarajadasa claimed Dominion status would have been achieved under the British Labour Party but the Conservative Government was too rigid. Mrs Besant, who worked constitutionally, would organise a convention that very month to draft a constitution, he said. *The Herald* mentioned that Krishnamurti, who held "a remarkable position in the cult headed by Mrs Besant", was part of the Theosophical party. The *Sun News Pictorial* noted the visit of Krishnamurti, a "well-known theosophist and editor of *The Herald of the Star*", along with Lady Emily Lutyens, "daughter of Earl Lytton and wife of the eminent sculptor [sic], Edwin", and Mr Rama Row [Rao], professor of science at Madras University. This article too began with a quote from Jinarajadasa attacking Gandhi – describing him as a fine, simple character who had never shown anger but nevertheless failed. "The end of the non-cooperative movement has cleared the air in India," Jinarajadasa was quoted as saying. The Vice President had visited Australia with Mrs Besant's party three years before, taking a lecture tour north to Queensland, so he must have been familiar with the way the press worked in Australia and wanted to drum up interest in Mrs Besant's current political interests in India. The future of India was a subject of some interest in Australia, but rather than take a stance of colonial comradeship between the people of the two countries, the press generally toed the British line. A report in *The Age* of a debate in the House of Lords the day after Krishnamurti left Melbourne describes the Secretary of State for India, Lord Birkenhead, as "responsive". Swaraijist CR Das had expressed abhorrence of violence and political assassination and Lord Birkenhead replied that he watched with hope Das' appeal to supporters. If revolutionary groups atrophied then the need for what Das called 'repression' would be gone, he said. All the British Government wanted was cooperation for responsible government, with "India as an integral part of the Empire". A more tongue-in-cheek article was published in the *Sun News-Pictorial* the day before of a fantastic interpretation of an Aboriginal "invasion" of a town north of Adelaide. Taking a supposed "English view", the writer claimed there'd been an unsubstantiated rumour that Das had telegrammed congratulations to the blacks who'd caused "an uproar", reportedly demanding beer. Considering this use of humour out of context it's hard to know clearly what the political intention of the writer was but at least the article pointed to a parallel which might have been drawn between the extent of white imperialism that existed in both countries.[7]

While Mrs Besant was in the thick of self-rule developments in India, Krishna retained a non-partisan public stance. She was still hoping for Indian Home Rule under the auspices of British domination while Gandhi had a much greater vision of independence from Britain. Despite their divergent views they maintained great mutual respect. For example Gandhi had written to Mrs Besant before her 78th birthday at the beginning of October 1924 to say he was sorry that he would miss the celebration as he would be fasting. Concerning the Congress passing a constitution, he saw many difficulties, but he was keeping an open mind and they would discuss it when they next met as he did not expect anything "untoward" to result from his fast. And he sent a message which was read out at the celebration in Bombay to say that he was present in spirit and that it was no small gain to India that Mrs Besant had dedicated her "matchless" gifts to the country. He hoped she would live to see the establishment of *swaraj*, for which they were both striving. On the Adyar Theosophical estate too, several people had learnt to spin, influenced by Gandhi's campaign to encourage the growth of home industries such as spinning and weaving. Krishna had observed mildly in the midst of a general election in Britain at that same time, October 1924, that the Tories were expected to win, and he was afraid this would mean a "thin" time ahead for India. Privately, Krishna was very liberal. On his way to Australia in 1925, Krishna was corresponding with Jamnadas Dwarkadas, a wealthy Bombay merchant, whom Krishna had known since 1919 and who was active in the Indian independence movement, and, incidentally, had a weakness for gambling on the horses. Krishna's letters were exhortations to Jamnadas to both pay off his debts and to raise money from schemes involving his "sick" and "innumerable" friends. One scheme to raise 1,000 rupees a month was to be organised through a committee Jamnadas would form with another Theosophist Bombay merchant, Ratansi D Moraji. Krishna told Jamnadas not to let himself go but to stick at it as the Masters were watching him. Krishna still held the hope of working through *Bharata Samaj* for social change to be effected across the countryside.[8]

At each port of call in Australia Krishna was presented with land on which it was planned to construct Order of the Star buildings to be held in the name of a Trust. In Sydney the grandest structure of all had already been built. Dr Rocke, who had been appointed Australia's national representative for the Star back in June 1922, had been largely responsible for fundraising and having an amphitheatre built overlooking Balmoral Beach which was the object of much exaggerated humour. Stories circulated of Theosophists gathering there to watch the coming of Krishnamurti walking on water through the heads of Sydney Harbour. The amphitheatre of 26 tiers held 2,500 people and provided a magnificent view of the harbour as a backdrop to speakers at the Theosophist conference in 1925. It cost more than 13 thousand pounds, provided by fundraising, the sale of seats up to 100 pounds each and the remainder provided from Dr Rocke's own personal finances. Nitya had congratulated Dr Rocke on the scale of the project, claiming no one else would have had the capacity to carry it through to completion. It was a grand landmark.[9]

The other major Theosophical landmark in Sydney was an enormous home in Clifton Gardens, near Mosman, called *The Manor* where about fifty Theosophists lived communally. It was constructed by a wealthy builder who had plans for his children to marry and raise their own families there with him; hence the building was referred to as 'Bakewell's Folly'. Leadbeater first took out a lease on the strange, over-sized building in 1922 and theosophist families began to move in with him, feeling secure in the idea that they were close to heaven, with their own tiny chapel in the midst of rabbit-warren corridors. Krishna described it as a glorified boarding house with a beautiful view.[10]

When they reached Sydney the Theosophical party was greeted by a mere murmur of interest. The *Sydney Morning Herald* reported that Lady Lutyens had arrived in town and referred to Krishna and Nitya among others in the group. Lady Lutyens was quoted as saying that Australia was one of the strongest centres of Theosophy among the 41 national societies in the world carrying a message of universal brotherhood. The marginal, non-inflammatory interest of the press continued with the opening of the Theosophical annual conference at the Balmoral amphitheatre, a visual spectacular perfectly designed to appeal to press photographers.[11]

Krishna told the convention of young Theosophists held that Easter that when lunching with George Bernard Shaw one day Shaw had told him that he thought every citizen should go before a tribunal once every seven years to prove they had done something for the general good. Krishna agreed. He also spoke about being at school in England where he said he had been called a "black devil" but he did not mind, he said, for he had had to adapt himself to the outside world. Krishna put forward his views about the caste system in India and aristocracy which should aim for "spiritual" aristocracy instead of a "worldly" aristocracy.[12]

This trip Krishna had no intention of staying in Sydney – his mission was to move Nitya to the mountains as soon as possible to get him well. Krishna had given Nitya a hard time back in India while he was recuperating in Ootacamund, writing to him that he had told the Master he would sacrifice anything for Nitya's wellbeing. The Master in all his magnificent dignity told Krishna that Nitya would be well. According to Krishna, Nitya had been given what Krishna believed was his final chance so he must give way to Krishna and do the 'minutest' thing that he told him. Nitya was in the world to help him, he said, and he shouldn't waste the Masters' forces. Not that he wanted personal authority over him, of course. Even though Nitya had been told not to have personal 'entanglements' he still got away from the path that was meant for him. Didn't he know by now that he had to work with the Teacher? Why did Nitya think he'd been given all these opportunities? For God's sake, he implored Nitya to think simply and 'intelligently'. He'd been told often enough – why did he want his own particular vision? Krishna knew Nitya would get well.[13]

So when he reached Sydney on April 3, Krishna's fixation was to heal Nitya once and for all. The *SS Ormuz* was met by Leadbeater and his 'entourage', including their old tutor, Balfour Clarke, who looked after Leadbeater, now aged about seventy, and Leadbeater's favourite boy, Theodore St John, aged about fifteen who slept in his room. Krishna and Nitya stayed the first

first few nights with Rosalind at 'Myola' in David Street. Mosman. the home of the Mackays who had paid their passage out. A few days later Nitya saw a specialist who diagnosed both Nitya's lungs as infected and advised that he should leave Sydney immediately. Dr Rocke had found a five-roomed house to rent at Leura and within a few days Nitya and Krishna moved up there with Rama Rao, Rosalind and Mrs Roberts as a chaperone.[14] Krishna wrote to Mrs Besant that the specialist was pessimistic about Nitya's health and their departure for California would have to be postponed. But within a fortnight at high altitude and in a dry climate, Nitya was much better and putting on weight.[15]

Even before Dr Ingelman arrived in early May with his Abrams' treatment equipment. Krishna had taken charge enough to be setting the regime and environment for Nitya's recovery. rather than leaving it to Dr Rocke. Helen only visited Leura once during his stay and he told Lady Emily who was staying down at *The Manor* not to telephone nor come to visit them as Nitya might get over-excited. Krishna spent his time travelling down to Sydney and back – two to three hours each way - to keep in touch with affairs. He wrote to Lady Emily explaining his lack of interest in Leadbeater's and others' activities as the result of his primary interest being in Nitya's health. He wasn't sneering. he said, and was happy that she felt the glory and happiness of her first 'Initiation' but Nitya was everything to him – there was no other like him and Krishna had to make him well.[16]

Rosalind's daughter maintains that the brothers' relationship was at a critical point by the time they reached Sydney, and Nitya had unburdened himself about it to Rosalind. He sobbed and told her he was miserable over what Krishna said about Theosophists and Mrs Besant behind her back. He swore Rosalind to secrecy but she told Krishna because she feared Nitya might die still at odds with his brother. Krishna then went to Nitya and reassured him.[17]

Rosalind was clearly regarded at this stage as a person of some standing among the Theosophists. According to her daughter, she had been in charge of meals at *The Manor* and was well-liked by Leadbeater. Yet Rosalind held that she remained untouched by the Society's philosophies and if she was undergoing any sort of training on a higher plane she was oblivious to it. She was however, aware of Nitya's emotional entanglement with Mary and went down to *The Manor* to explain his illness to her. Mary was still in love with Nitya. A brief meeting was arranged in which Nitya asked Mary if she forgave him, and when he sailed for California he was able to throw her a streamer which broke as the ship moved away from the wharf, symbolically breaking their bond.[18]

May was considered a particularly vibrant month spiritually, climaxing at full moon or Wesak on 8 May.[19] Krishna told Lady Emily that he 'felt' Wesak more strongly in the mountains than in Sydney. To Mrs Besant he wrote that it had been an eventful time and he and Jinarajadasa had proposed five people for Initiation: Lady Emily; Fabrizio Ruspoli, Mrs Kirby Ruth Roberts and B. Shiva Rao. He also wrote to Ruspoli that he was very pleased that they would be working together more and their destinies were bound together – just the previous month he had suggested to Fabrizio Ruspoli that he was badly needed to work at Eerde, the site of the Dutch property.[20]

But whatever the machinations about who would be elevated to higher occult status, Krishna was very much out of tune with Leadbeater's Theosophical regime which emphasised the rituals of the Liberal Catholic Church and Co-Masonry. Lutyens describes Co-Masonry as an offshoot of Theosophy, with its origins in the revolt of several Masonic Chapters in France in 1879. Arundale's aunt, Miss Francesca Arundale, had introduced the order to Mrs Besant who was initiated in 1902 in Paris and later founded lodges in Benares and London, building a Masonic temple at Adyar in 1910. Mary Lutyens describes Krishna in 1925 as out of place at *The Manor*, like a gazelle in the midst of a flock of sheep, and not welcomed there by Leadbeater who found him disturbing. Krishna would make fun of the 'gopis', grinning and winking about the rituals they observed. Tillett says Leadbeater offered Krishna little advice about the 'process' and Krishna preferred to be away from *The Manor*. Clearly Krishna was beginning to express his distaste of dependence on ritual, describing it as having a cheque book but no money in the bank.[21]

These sorts of comments were just the beginning of a period of rejection of ritual by Krishna which stretched through the 1920s – exhibited by comments made in personal communication as well as in public statements. These critical statements sat oddly with the increasing fervour of the campaign to elevate him to the position of 'Coming Messiah' and 'World Teacher' which he seemed to sanction and believe in. By 1925, aged thirty, Krishna was setting the agenda for himself and his brother, with Rosalind in tow, although he continued to defer to Mrs Besant's occult status and to hold her emotionally dear. He believed in her extraordinary powers and goodness as representing the extraordinary powers of the Masters, which were also channelled through him and which he experienced as messages.

For instance on the voyage in July 1925 from Sydney to San Francisco, Nitya's health deteriorated markedly, culminating in one night of complete exhaustion. He felt himself 'slipping away' and 'feebly' asked Rosalind to hold his feet. Krishna describes how she clung onto them as he concentrated on thoughts of the Master. Krishna wrote to Mrs Besant that when he was with the Lord, He had told him that suffering teaches, and that Nitya especially had to suffer before he became wise enough to learn, but all things would come out all right. Now Nitya was much better. Krishna also wrote about the event to Lady Emily who was returning to England from Australia. It had been suggested that she go on with Krishna to Ojai but Leadbeater advised against it as her daughter Ursula was pregnant and needed her, he claimed. Perhaps Lady Emily had also been disappointed about Krishna's restrictions on his time in Sydney but if so, Krishna was oblivious of this, as he wrote to her in July that he missed her terribly as they'd been together for so long.[22]

By the end of July the brothers arrived happily home to their 13-acre *Arya Vihara* in Ojai, after a tiring train journey from San

Francisco. They immediately hired an Abrams machine and within a couple of weeks Nitya's health improved. Even so. Krishna did not want to rush off to England in order to be in India by late October with Mrs Besant for the Jubilee Theosophical Society celebrations at the end of the year. He said that he would prefer to leave Ojai by the middle of October.[23]

In the event, Krishna travelled from Ojai to India via Europe with Rosalind, Rajagopal and others in early October. leaving Nitya behind to recuperate in the care of Madame de Manziarly and Rama Rao. Rosalind is reported not to have wanted to leave Nitya but was reassured about his health by a doctor. She was suffering from a skin rash and had been caring for Nitya for months without a break.[24]

Once on their way, Krishna wrote to Nitya from the train en route to Chicago that he had the desire to jump out and go back to him. He and Nitya were one, and, after all the suffering, now that they'd tasted love, they must keep it fresh. "Nitya darling", he wrote. Nitya was "within" him all the time. Krishna wrote to Nitya at least every few days, sometimes daily, seeming to give him encouragement and bolster his spirits – don't get depressed, get well quickly. nothing matters except that Nitya should get well and then nothing would separate them, they mustn't be prejudiced. they had much to do and thank God Nitya was better. And there was plenty of practical information – Nitya would be sent $60 a month regularly; Nitya's tennis shoes could not be repaired so Krishna would bring him the deck shoes he wanted; books Krishna had bought would be sent in small packages to avoid paying duty. He sent Rajagopal's love and news of a dream Rajagopal had had that Nitya was well and fat again. He hardly mentioned Rosalind, except to say that she liked the "boat" and that George Arundale. Shiva Rao, Rosalind and he played bridge. In his last letter posted in Port Said Krishna called on the Masters to bless Nitya and told him he loved him.[25]

A plaintive cable sent from Nitya to Krishna on board the *SS Ormuz* in Port Said said simply: "Flu little more serious. Pray for me, Nitya".[26]

this. He was confident that Nitya would not die, otherwise he would not have been allowed to leave Ojai, he told Shiva Rao. Besides, Krishna had had to build up an armour of confidence since he was in a struggle with the ritualists in the Society, led by George Arundale, who used any form of emotional blackmail to try to limit Krishna, even subtly hinting that Nitya's life would be spared if Krishna acknowledged them as his Disciples. Krishna had unbounded faith in the Masters' powers to prolong Nitya's life. But that night as the ship entered the Suez Canal another telegram was received, this time announcing Nitya's death. The message was delivered to Mrs Besant the next morning and she went alone to Krishna's cabin to break the news.[27]

According to Shiva Rao, who with Rajagopal shared Krishna's cabin, Krishna went into a state of grief in which he at times lost consciousness, sobbing, moaning and crying for Nitya in his first language, Telugu, which he could not normally speak in waking consciousness. The grief and disillusionment he experienced took ten days to wrack his mind and body, causing an inner revolution which finally carried him to a point where he found a renewed strength. When the ship reached Colombo Krishna made a formal announcement that the pleasant dreams of the physical that he and his brother had shared were over. The old dream was dead and a new dream was being born, as a flower pushes through solid earth, he said. He now had a greater desire to see others suffer less or at least bear suffering nobly. He and Nitya could be separated on the physical plane but now they were inseparable, he declared. He now knew a great love that was permanent, imperishable and unconquerable.[28]

In a poem titled "Nitya" published two years later, Krishna wrote that in his search for his brother, when he cried in "loneliness" and no one could give him comfort, he found the face of his brother – and all the living and the dead – in the "Lord" of his heart. As early as 1922 Krishna and Nitya had signed their names as "Krishnitya" – for a time they had been inseparable. There can be no question that his brother's death must have threatened to tear Krishna's psyche and sense of identity in two, even while he tear Krishna's psyche and sense of identity in two, even while he maintained a public composure, until he was able to develop the idea of their inseparability beyond death. In an editorial written at most about a month after Nitya's death, Krishna said that he believed in life after death, that he had seen his brother and they were inseparable.[29]

But thinking was one dimension – on the physical plane, now that Nitya was gone, Krishna had to face the turmoil and turbulence of life within the Theosophical Society quite alone. He'd been going through major changes in his outlook for some years, at variance with the orthodoxy of the Theosophists, and now the turmoil would increase.

Earlier in the year the ritualists under Arundale's guidance had had a field day in Europe so that Krishna and even Leadbeater had distanced themselves from the madcap capers. After a world lecture tour, Arundale and his wife, Rukmini, had settled in Huizen, the centre of the Liberal Catholic Church in Europe, a few miles from Castle Eerde at Ommen, in Holland. Also there were Wedgwood and Oscar Kollerstrom, who'd been a protégé of Leadbeater. When Mrs Besant arrived back in Europe from India in July 1924 she received news from Arundale that occult initiations and awakenings were happening apace at Huizen. She hurried to Holland with a party of Theosophists, including Lady Emily, Rajagopal, Shiva Rao and Miss Bright, and reportedly tried unsuccessfully to reawaken her own *kundalini*. Arundale organised for himself to be consecrated a Bishop in the Liberal Catholic Church, seeking consent from Leadbeater, but Leadbeater cabled his disapproval after the event. Messages said to have been brought through from the Masters to Arundale included instructions that silk underwear was to be worn by Initiates, and there were other dictates concerning diet. The party moved to the Star camp at Ommen where on 9 August Arundale 'brought through' the names of ten of twelve apostles supposed to assist 'Sir Krishnamurtin Christ'. They were Mrs Besant, Leadbeater, Jinarajadasa, George and Rukmini Arundale, Wedgwood, Nitya, Lady Emily, Rajagopal and Oscar

Kollerstrom. Mrs Besant also spoke of a 'world' religion and 'world' university. Back at Huizen, fervour built up over the question of visiting one of the Masters - said to be a Count living at a secret location in Transylvania, Hungary - so much so that on 16 August 1925 a group set off for Innsbruck to await further orders. This adventure was of course a high jinx and all Mrs Besant would say about it afterwards was that 'black forces' had been too strong for them. It was as if she had been hypnotised by Arundale, according to Lady Emily. Krishna was preoccupied with Nitya's illness at the time but wrote a loving letter to Mrs Besant, though not confirming the validity of the happenings himself, while Leadbeater was reported to be distressed and hoping that Mrs Besant's indiscretion would not wreck the Society. It was an extraordinary time for Mrs Besant to become so caught up in such an escapade considering her active role in the drafting the Commonwealth of India Bill for which she had campaigned to gain the support for the bill from prominent Indian politicans. Gandhi refused to support the bill on the grounds that it was insulting and degrading, since he did not subscribe to a "recognition of the King-Emperor as Sovereign and Protector of the Commonwealth" and he expected that the British would throw the proposal on the "scrap-heap". Gandhi was right, as it "slid gently into a Parliamentary Nirvana" after being introduced into the House of Commons in 1925 by Mrs Besant's Parliamentary supporters.[30]

When Krishna arrived in England from Ojai in October 1925 with Rosalind and Rajagopal, he told Lady Emily he did not believe in the search for a Master in Huizen but did not say anything publicly about it as he would be accused of falling under the influence of "Black Powers". Rajagopal too seemed to have done a *volte face*, sarcasm now taking the place of the excitement he had felt at Huizen.[31]

Krishna is reported to have been unwilling to tell Mrs Besant about his rejection of the "revelations" while believing she should be told. It's reported that he stayed in a car outside her home as Professor Marcault, from the World University, went upstairs and broke the news. Tillett maintains that she became physically ill and thereafter showed signs of rapid aging, such as memory loss, torn as she was by opposing loyalties within the Society.[32]

Back in November, Krishna had written to Nitya that he had had a long talk with Mrs Besant who said his attitude was wrong. Krishna had agreed that he would have to regain his interest in the Masters. Didn't he believe that his body would be used, she asked? She also persuaded Krishna he should try to understand Arundale as he was just as proud as he.[33]

Soon the press had got hold of the news of the disciples and it didn't take much fine-tuning to turn it into an hilarious story. In Australia *Truth* newspaper crowed about a Second Coming at hand, claiming Sydney had been chosen as the city of "The Messiah", who was a Tamil named Krishnamurti.

> And so the infamous Leadbeater has at last decided to bring his strange game, that peculiar admixture of farce and sacrilege that he calls religion to a show-down. If he dares to do so, and if he dares to bring his crew of tricksters back to Sydney, he may be promised here and now that it will be a decidedly unsavory show-up.[34]

The paper made a pretence of taking up the cause of "unfortunate lesser ones in the movement" who'd been led to believe that miracles would occur and the "Vehicle" of the Lord, Krishnamurti, would walk across the harbour to greet them in the Balmoral amphitheatre. In fact the report made great use of sexual innuendo in the article and concluded Leadbeater and Wedgwood were undesirable immigrants.

For once these latest Masters' revelations had not originated with Leadbeater yet he had to bear the brunt of the outrageous claims. Within a few months Arundale would be sent back with him to Sydney to toe the line, bringing Krishna reassurance that he would be spared further "complications and unnecessary and absurd romantic excitement". Wedgwood too, the high "panjandrum", would leave Adyar under a cloud, accused by the *OE Library Critic* in December 1925 of being a "sodomistic sex pervert whose unholy doings were a public scandal in London."[35]

What brought Arundale and Wedgwood's antics undone was an apparent transformation in Krishnamurti himself at the Star Congress following the Jubilee convention at Adyar in December 1925. Mrs Besant had tried to allay a widening rift between Leadbeater and Krishnamurti once they'd all arrived in India by asking if he would take Leadbeater and herself as his disciples and he replied that he would not accept any disciples except perhaps her.[36] In November Krishnamurti had "allowed" himself to be made a Co-Mason to please Mrs Besant, and then, by contrast, three days before the December convention he officiated with enthusiasm in a ceremony to consecrate a small Hindu temple in the grounds of Adyar. He was dressed only in a *dhoti* and a sacred thread and had Rajagopal as his assistant. But the convention got under way with more than three thousand delegates present, and nothing extraordinary occurred, despite expectations having been raised with an article even published in New York.[37] Then on the morning of 28 December 1925 (considered a sacred day ever since Krishna's performance in 1911 handing out certificates which provoked a mass prostration), when the Society's convention had ended and the Star meeting had commenced, the excitement was finally justified. Krishna began his opening speech to a crowd underneath the celebrated banyan tree quite normally but then, dramatically, at the end of his speech when he was talking about the "World Teacher", he changed from third person to first person and his voice "rang" out. "I" come for those who want sympathy and happiness, he said. To reform and build, not to tear down or destroy, were his words. Mary Lutyens writes that it was "spine-tingling" for those who noticed, and although Arundale and Wedgwood overlooked the change, for Mrs Besant, Leadbeater and Jinarajadasa it marked the definite consecration of the "chosen" vehicle. The Lord had returned to earth in Krishnamurti's body, they believed. Krishnamurti himself had no doubts, telling people they had drunk at the fountain of wisdom and they should protect their memory of the 28th December as a precious jewel. Rosalind's daughter, Radha, claims that her mother heard Krishna say, before going in front of the crowd, that he was going to show them something, and he did seem to have an extraordinary magnetic power over the audience.[38]

Writer Lily Heber says that Krishna gave daily talks in the Hindu temple in the Adyar grounds following his transformation, in accord with the ideals of the *Bharata Samaj* for social and religious reforms. These talks, published as *Temple Talks*, encouraged people to live their ideals here on earth, rather than in a distant heaven, and abolish abuses and inequities in India such as those springing from the caste system.[39]

Rosalind and Rajagopal stayed on at Adyar after the convention while Krishna went to Benares and Calcutta where he suffered food poisoning causing high temperature and boils on his face. Rosalind also toured with Lady Emily, and with Raja she met Raja's mother and saw Madanapalle, Krishna's birthplace, where Raja had been a teacher.[40] On Krishna's return to Adyar, Madame de Manziarly bundled him off to recuperate in Ooty, where Nitya had stayed the year before. Krishna wrote to Mrs Besant from there to say that he saw, felt and talked with Nitya and missed him grievously.[41]

Nitya's ashes had been taken to Adyar and a foundation stone for the Star dedicated to him there in acknowledgement of the love many people bore him. Among the obituaries were genuinely grieving appreciations of Nitya's character by C Jinarajadasa ("a brilliantly gifted young man"), George Arundale ("blunt, straight, emphatic Nitya"), Emily Lutyens ("He possessed a rare combination of tenderness and strength, of deep wisdom and boyish fun, of keen intellect with complete self-effacement"). But the business of the Star had to go on and Rajagopal took over Nitya's role as Organising Secretary as well as being appointed to a new position, International Treasurer. While in Ooty, Krishna wrote to Rosalind to say he was sorry she didn't go up to the mountains with him. Hadn't her friends invited her, he asked? He hadn't written because he presumed they had. His tone was flippant but conveyed his anxiety that she might be happier away from him, mentioning the "temptations" and "excitement" of Adyar. He asked about her rash. Ten days later he wrote again, to say that he was pleased her rash had cleared up and also mentioned that Madame de Manziarly was leaving the next day for China. Three days later he wrote again to Rosalind let her know he'd be back in Adyar within the week.[42]

Rosalind's daughter says that her mother turned to Rajagopal after Nitya's death, which hurt Krishna very much. She recounts one incident as an example of Krishna's impatience over their bond, when the couple was sitting on an upstairs verandah at Adyar and he was downstairs with Helen Knothe, listening to their laughter and chatter. He was shocked that they could be so light-hearted so soon after Nitya's death and went upstairs to reprimand them.[43] Nitya had in fact encouraged Rosalind and Rajagopal's friendship, asking her to write to Rajagopal back in 1924 when she was in Australia and Rajagopal had returned to Cambridge where he'd be hard at work and feeling lonely, Nitya surmised. He suggested she write a nice long letter.[44] Nitya also reportedly asked Rosalind and Rajagopal in Ojai to promise that they would always stay with Krishna, which they regarded as a deathbed promise.[45]

By May when temperatures in India were becoming unbearable, the Europeans moved out en masse, sailing back home to prepare for their summer season. Rosalind travelled in Mrs Besant's stateroom on board ship and once she arrived in England, she stayed with Miss Dodge, her benefactress. Rosalind's daughter claims that a school headmistress suggested to her at this time that she might do as well to marry Rajagopal as study at university. Although Mrs Besant wanted Rosalind to study, she also wanted her to marry, and wouldn't let her go to Holland the following year.[46]

Krishna wrote to Rosalind in June 1926, wanting her to join him in Eerde. But she should follow her doctor's instructions, he said. Perhaps he was still giving her financial support since he told her not to bother about the money; he had some money but perhaps she should do the wise thing, he said. Rajagopal had sent out a circular to friends saying that if they could not afford living expenses, arrangements might be made for them – so perhaps Krishna's reference should be read in this context.[47]

There continued to be quite a bit of press interest in Krishnamurti's movements. In May Fritz Kunz had written to a writer with the *New York Evening Journal* complaining about a sensational "Messiah" story. The writer replied that nothing hurts if it isn't true. From Paris Krishna said the reporters were a nuisance.[48]

Krishna kept up his correspondence with Rosalind, writing from Ommen in July that he was in bed with some bronchial trouble and would she please come.[49] The camp started on 24 July and Rosalind did go to Holland earlier, staying with a party of people in the Eerde castle, where Krishna was the only person who had a room to himself. His back and head trouble recurred and once again Rosalind was called on to "mother" him. Krishna would give talks in the mornings, and it was believed that the "Lord Maitreya" frequently spoke through him. Once the Ommen camp got under way most of the party went to live in tents at the camp grounds but Krishna insisted Rosalind and Mary stay on at the Castle with him and Rajagopal. Mary was by this time absolutely devoted to Krishna, believing he and Nitya were now one, following Nitya's death. Mrs Besant and Wedgwood arrived a couple of days later and also stayed at the Castle. Every evening at the camp, Krishna, dressed in Indian dress, would light a bonfire to the Hindu God Agni and chant in Sanskrit before a crowd of about two thousand people. Throughout the camp meeting political manoeuvering continued in the background, with Wedgwood once whispering to Mrs Besant that a "black" magician was speaking through Krishna. She confronted Krishna about it and his reply was that if she didn't want him to speak any more he wouldn't, which distressed her. She never again suggested it. Leadbeater also made his loyalty to Mrs Besant clear at this time, writing to Krishnamurti that he refused absolutely to be set up in opposition to the President.[50]

In August 1926 Mrs Besant decided to go to Ojai as part of a lecture tour of the United States, something Krishna had wanted her to do for years. She was issued with a temporary visitor's visa and the US Government kept a security file on her from information compiled by the American Consulate in Madras. The Vice Consul reported that she was the editor and publisher of *New India* and advocated Home Rule for the country but in the opinion of "certain local authorities" she had recently modified her views and her political influence was "considerably less in evidence". The Consulate had conducted a "careful and discreet inquiry" on the question of whether Mrs Besant wanted to deliver lectures on Home Rule but found no "convincing" evidence. The memorandum included a report from *The Hindu* newspaper that Jamnadas Dwarkadas believed that in America Mrs Besant would, among other things, "popularize the Indian demand for self-government and counteract the malicious propaganda carried on by men like Lord Sydenham against the Indian demand".[51]

On arriving in New York from Southampton, Annie Besant, Rosalind, Rajagopal and Krishna were greeted by news headlines about the new Messiah who wore plus fours and tennis flannels. One story described Krishna as a shy young Hindu boy, despite the fact that he was now aged 31. The group stayed at the Waldorf-Astoria and Krishna held a press conference, after which he was offered $5,000 per week to play the part of Buddha in a film. The *New York Times* also linked him romantically with Rosalind and when questioned about love and marriage Krishna was quoted as saying that people marry because they're lonely but he was never lonely because he had something that couldn't be taken away. Another paper reported that he had been engaged to Helen Knothe, a rumour Krishna "hotly" denied.[52]

After New York, the travellers went on to Chicago for a Theosophical convention and then separated while Mrs Besant went on tour. In September Krishna wrote to Rosalind in Ojai from Virginia, where he and Rajagopal had gone to rest, to say that even though he had been irritable and nasty to her, he loved her very much. Now that she had other people she liked more, he said without naming them, he wasn't jealous. He wanted to be real friends, he said, as they used to be, and wanted to apologise for being nasty and quick-tempered. She had no idea how much he liked her, and was longing to see her, and she was not to smile "sarcastically", he said. He ended the letter with the idea that both he and Nitya loved her.[53]

In October Mrs Besant arrived in Ojai, was shown over the valley, was enchanted and wanted to buy more real estate, to set up a centre for the 'World Teacher'. A Trust called the Happy Valley Foundation was formed and an appeal to raise $200,000 launched. Twenty years later, indeed a school was established and it is still operating, although it does not teach the gospel of the "World Teacher". This was the role Mrs Besant unequivocally defined for Krishnamurti in a press statement sent to Associated Press of America in April 1927 before she left Ojai after a long and restful stay.[54]

The sojourn at Ojai was a solidifying period in Krishna and Mrs Besant's long and loving mother-son relationship at a time when it was beginning to be rocked to its foundations publicly. When Krishna invited Lady Emily and Mary to join them it must have been a very satisfying arrangement for Mrs Besant, now in her twilight years, with these old friends as familiar as family about her. Rosalind may have been less happy, considering the work she had to do, as Mary reported there was a certain amount of friction between the Lutyens's and Rosalind and she complained they did not clean the bath properly.[55] Lady Emily wrote to her husband from Ojai that she had learnt a great deal from being in America as labour conditions had driven people to invent easy ways of running a house.

> The fact of doing things for oneself and not always depending on servants gives one a sense of self respect. ... It is really awful to me to think of Mansfield St and ten servants and I am trying to think how we could manage.[56]

It was so easy there to cook and clean, she said – with electric stoves and bathrooms all white-tiled, with china handles, so everything could be spotlessly clean with the minimum of labour. It's clear from the letter how steeped in the English class system Lady Emily was and how protected her life had been, so it's no surprise that her enthusiasm for labour-saving devices may have overreached her actual achievements in their use.

No doubt friction also arose over emotional attachments among the group of friends. Perhaps Krishna had called for Lady Emily and Mary to visit because Rosalind had cut off from him. In any case, Mary was now the woman called on to help Krishna "relax" when he "went off" in the afternoons, reverting to the age of four and suffering pain in his back and neck. These sessions took place in the *Pine Cottage*, or "Shrine", a small house where Krishna slept, apart from the rest of the visitors living in *Arya Vihara*. Meanwhile Rajagopal and Rosalind's relationship must have been deepening since within a few months Rajagopal was said to be very much in love with Rosalind. There's no record of Rosalind's feelings towards Krishna during this period.[57]

Over that temperate winter and springtime in Ojai, day after day Krishna would spend his time in gardening or writing poetry. The world of nature, often that found in tended gardens, feature in most of Krishna's poetry written during the 1920s. In *The Search*, for example, he writes of annihilating the "self" just as a gardener kills "destructive" weeds, and refers to a beautiful rose which "dieth" tomorrow. Generally Krishna's poetry reeks of sentimentality and enticement to find the happiness he has discovered, couched in a mixture of Vedantic and Biblical language, through words such as "Enlightenment", "Beloved", "Thee" and "Thou". The highly-esteemed Australian poet and scholar, John Tranter, says Krishna's poetry does not impress him; rather, he finds "the archaisms borrowed from the St James Bible ... grating". As theology, it lacks the drama and theatre and the complexity of issues to be found in many Buddhist and Hindu texts. As literature, Tranter's assessment is, "I'm afraid not".[58]

By May 1927 the whole group was back in England, headed for Theosophical and Star activities in Holland in the summer. There was now a community living permanently at Eerde along the lines proposed in 1922. The aims of the participants were to: have a conscious spirit to establish a "New Age"; be vegetarian, teetotaller and self-supporting; devote some time to benefit the community; help to break down restrictions on race, nationality, caste, creed and colour.[59] Five years after this outline of these initial plans, a great barn near the Castle had been converted into accommodation to house about sixty people. Krishna was this year speaking about others becoming liberated, as he had, from within. To get in touch with reality was the only way to expand consciousness – from within and not from outside of a person, he suggested. All experience must be one's own, he said. Mary Lutyens says that Krishna was longing for renunciation, to become a *sannyasi* in India. Perhaps Rosalind's absence not only from the camp, but also from his heart as she was slowly forming a resolution to marry Rajagopal, was a factor in Krishna's desire to renounce worldly attachments.[60]

Rajagopal and Rosalind were married on 3 October 1927 at a registry office in London and again eight days later at St Mary's Catholic Church in the Caledonian Road (London's only Liberal Catholic Church and not licensed to perform legal marriages). Mrs Besant gave Rosalind away and an old friend, a lawyer, David Graham Pole, acted as best man. Krishna was in Eerde at the time and Lutyens says that in later years he had no memory of what he thought of the marriage though by 1927 he was not so adamantly opposed to marriage. A question might be posed here too, considering Mrs Besant's influence over Rosalind, about whether the prevailing attitude towards Krishna as special and needing protection, which had been accepted by his associates for many years, was a factor in the marriage of Rosalind and Rajagopal. Nitya had even written to Leadbeater about Krishna's process in 1925 that they tried to ensure that Krishna was always accompanied by at least one initiate, if not two.[61]

Krishna and Mrs Besant's close personal relationship was a bulwark in this period of Krishnamurti's transformation from a devout but irascible idol of Theosophists to a proponent of complete freedom for individuals - freedom from religious institutions and creeds as well as from social and psychological limitations. Krishna made his way in stages, slowly but inexorably, towards the complete public declaration of his credo as Mrs

Besant dealt with one surprising statement after another in the lead-up. Throughout the political turmoil that resulted from the divergence of their visions, with acolytes taking sides and playing up the tensions, Krishna's and Mrs Besant's fondness for each other was evident. Only a cynic could argue that it was Krishna's political astuteness that caused him to remain on good personal terms with Mrs Besant while undermining her spiritual standing within Theosophy. Such cynics would see hypocrisy in Krishna's fond correspondence and loving actions towards Mrs Besant during the late-1920s. A more forgiving and comprehending conclusion is that Krishna had a very loving personality despite, and in some ways because of, the petting and spoiling he'd been indulged in ever since his "discovery" in 1909. Krishna has been described as "full of affection" and the way in which people were drawn to him is a testament to the loving atmosphere in which he thought his thoughts and lived his life most of the time.[62] He generally felt a great gratitude to Mrs Besant for the extraordinary life he enjoyed; he shared with her a belief in a God or supreme life force which he believed he had experienced in his physical body in exceptional ways; and his affection for this idealistic old lady never waned. The fondness between them is evident in correspondence, particularly over the last few years of the 1920s when political tensions within the Society were coming to a climax.

For instance in May 1927 Krishna wrote to Mrs Besant that he didn't really mind what others thought as long as they understood each other. She had distributed to Associated Press of America a statement saying that the "Divine Spirit" had descended once more on a man, this time on Krishnamurti, who in his life was "literally perfect". In July she wrote to Krishna that she understood that he might feel her and Leadbeater as a kind of restraint when he was at the Eerde camp. She had surrendered to the Lord Maitreya the charge of him she had taken so seriously and now he must be totally independent. She just tried to serve him unobtrusively. A fortnight later she wrote that she felt that only he should teach, as he and the 'Teacher" were one but she would do as he wished. He assured her that he would be able to explain his shyness about her being present when he spoke at Eerde when she arrived there. Mrs Besant did give a talk at the camp in August entitled "The World Teacher is Here" but Krishna went one step further. In one speech he explained that since boyhood he had pictured the Lord first as Sri Krishna, since his mother was Hindu, then as a Master, under Leadbeater's influence, and more lately as Buddha – but the 'Beloved' was beyond all these forms and names. He also criticised Theosophical jargon and then wrote to Mrs Besant saying he did not remember what he'd said but he would write to Lady De La Warr who was upset. He was more and more certain of his vision of Truth and Mrs Besant and he should stick together as nothing else mattered.[63] Jinarajadasa who had a great love for Krishna and also believed in him as a great spiritual leader was at this time arguing about the objects of the new organisation being set up to supersede the Order of the Star in the East. The new body was to be called more briefly, the Order of the Star, and would publish an *International Star Bulletin* and a magazine called *Star Review* (instead of *The Herald of the Star*). Jinarajadasa was of the old school of Theosophists and did not want the new organisation so closely associating Krishna, as the disciple, with the Lord. The following year he was earnestly trying to find some compatibility between Krishna's adamant rejection of ceremonial ritual in favour of direct understanding and the organisation of the Society's esoteric wing, the Esoteric Section. Couldn't ES disciplines be modified, including the teaching of the Upanishads, and Liberal Catholic Church sacramental work be minimised so that each could seek an "inner way for himself", he asked. He would tread a difficult road over the next few years, physically caring for Mrs Besant as she aged and loving Krishna from a distance but maintaining the precepts of the Theosophical Society in the face of Krishna's increasing challenges.[64]

At the end of 1927 Rosalind and Rajagopal toured Europe with Philip van Pallandt, who'd made the Castle Eerde donation to Krishna, before returning to Ojai, while Krishna travelled to

India with Mrs Besant and a party of Theosophists. Dr Rocke was killed on the voyage when she fell down a companion-way and suffered cerebral haemorrhage, casting a black pall over the rest of the trip. Mrs Besant wrote a tribute to her in *The Theosophist*, saying she would be missed in both Australia and Holland where she had shown initiative, and perseverance. Gifts totalling 500 pounds were made by two donors to be spent in her memory on the Sydney amphitheatre.[65]

Krishna's respect for Mrs Besant continues to be evident throughout the difficulties arising in 1928. He writes consistently loving letters: from Bombay in February that he is looking forward to Ojai; from on board ship in March that he has given a talk to passengers and it's difficult to make them see his point of view; from Naples that Lady De la Warr has written to him seeming much better; nearing New York feeling "grieved" that Mrs Besant will not be visiting him in Ojai; finally, from Ojai that the place is more lovely than ever but it will cost about 1,000 pounds to fix water pipes. Back at Castle Eerde in July 1928 Krishna is shocked that people are antagonistic to what he says and wishes they had more affection in their hearts. Four days later he writes to Mrs Besant that it would be fatal to have division between the Esoteric Section and the Order of the Star as he does not want the Star to be a "narrow" organisation. He begs her not to cancel the ES meeting as she's been advised. He loves her with all his heart, he says. The next day he writes that he is going to visit her in London before she leaves for India.[66]

Mrs Besant was reported to be quite unwell at this time and there was speculation that it was in reaction to Krishna's rejection of disciples. Bit by bit he was undermining so much of Theosophist philosophy. When he returned to Eerde by air he wrote to her to say how much it meant to him that he was able to see her. But as if to put paid to the doomsayers, Mrs Besant's health picked up as soon as she heard from India that she was invited to a political conference there.[67] If she had doubted Krishna she may have confided in Lady Emily and others but she never made these confidences public. On the contrary, she wrote to Krishna giving him her loyal support by saying that all their students should devote themselves to the study of his ideals. She had decided to leave aside the older teachings for the present. to suspend the Esoteric Section indefinitely. and leave all the teaching to him. The edict seemed to follow the advice she'd been given by Jinarajadasa in August about modifying ES teaching of the Upanishads.[68] Jinarajadasa. who was touring South America, wrote to Krishna from Chile in February 1929 to say he was glad the ES was closed for the time being but emphasised the need to have workers to organise in each country. He worried that most people, particularly in South America where they were fixated on an anthropomorphic God, had not the faintest sense of what was truly spiritual and were astonished by Krishna's teaching concerning liberation.69

Krishna's public profile was at a high point despite the behind-the-scenes faction-fighting in the Society. He spoke to an audience of about 15.000 people at the Hollywood Bowl in May 1928 which he said he found "thrilling" and the *Los Angeles Times* reported as a "rapt" audience. The talk had been advertised in the church notices a few days before as Krishnamurti speaking on "Happiness Through Liberation". The trenchant reaction from a Congregational minister in his sermon the following Sunday was that in declaring there was no sin, Krishnamurti was "casting to the winds those moral distinctions between right and wrong without which civilisation would be turned to chaos". The next day the paper carried a front page story about the Ojai camp headed "Drama Enacted as Krishnamurti Meets World Disciples" and accompanied by three photos, including Rosalind Rajagopal in a group shot and women pitching a tent. More than seven hundred people were reported to have registered for the camp, with the Order of the Star established in forty seven countries and its magazine published in fourteen languages. The writer said Krishnamurti had been heralded as a second Christ, which he deplored. He described Krishna as a "pleasant-mannered Hindu ... so slight and young-looking as to appear a mere youth". Yet he had just turned thirty-four.[70]

Another example of Krishnamurti's world reputation was the proposal at the end of 1927 by the sculptor Antoine Bourdelle to create a bust of Krishnamurti, whom he had met through Madame de Manziarly. Bourdelle, who was aged sixty six, claimed that if he were younger he would follow him. "Ce visage est un fruit si pur de la grande et antique souche Hindoue, si mystérieuse et profonde que le compas occidental y voit hésiter ses deux pointes," was just a part of his glowing praise of Krishna's features. Krishna sat for him in September 1927 and again a year later.[71]

But behind the golden glow of Krishnamurti's public image, the Theosophical internecine strife continued through 1928. Writing to a Star official in India in May, Krishna advised him not to worry about Arundale's manipulations and the World Mother developments which had promoted Arundale's wife, Rukmini, as a major spiritual figure to head up an organisation in the future. Krishna held his nerve in dealing with Arundale, keeping Mrs Besant and Leadbeater on side as far as possible. He had offered Leadbeater the position of Australian National Organiser of the Star, which had become vacant on Dr Rocke's death, and Leadbeater accepted it in a back-handed way in July 1928. His acceptance letter was amusing in his pointing out that he had no idea of the duties and responsibilites of the office, implying a lack of direction. He raised the matter of the "World Mother" work in raising the status of women, saying he didn't think that Mrs Besant had any intention of involving Krishna in it. Krishna replied the following month that he didn't know anything about the "World Mother", what he wanted to do was quite distinct and he didn't want to be dragged into unnecessary problems over unessential matters. By now Krishna agreed that the Society and the Star should be separated and told Leadbeater that he had asked Rajagopal to write to him about what direction the Star was taking in other parts of the world.[72]

Krishna was back in India by November 1928, anticipating similar factional difficulties to those encountered in Europe and finding them. He'd suffered quite a few bouts of bronchitis over the past year and again he took to his bed.[73] He wrote to Mrs Besant about people on both "sides" – sides being an unfortunate word. he suggested - making mischief. On his way back from India via the Suez he called in to Cairo and Giza, the magnificence of the Pyramids and the Sphinx, a sobering reminder of the pettiness of quarrelling egos in the face of all-conquering time.[74] It was tough going for Krishna. Seemingly he no longer had a love interest in any woman, not anyone he could trust absolutely, nor even Nitya to love, hector and bicker with. Although he was back on good terms with Rosalind, judging by his correspondence since her marriage he could no longer speak of his love for her. He would write notes to her about practical matters such as car parts or Rajagopal's health and never mention his heart's desire. Typical is an undated letter from Krishna at Montroc in the French Alps to the couple probably written in July 1928, sending them both his love and asking Rosalind to make sure Rajagopal took enough rest.[75]

Jinarajadasa, who probably understood Krishna better than most people in the Theosophical Society, had written kindly to him a letter marked "June 28", in sympathy with his lack of love's expression. "And your thumping and overflowing heart wanting to overflow," were his words. "It's grim loneliness for you, I suppose, most of the time." He said that being fifty, he was mostly over the problem but Karma still sometimes sent along someone who was covered in "paradisical" rainbows.[76]

Krishna tried to keep Leadbeater as a friend and advisor, irregularly writing frank and affectionate letters, but Leadbeater was now very old and a politically-conservative church ritualist to the core. And he was very disturbed about the anarchic directions in which Krishnamurti was headed. Writing to Krishna in January 1929, Leadbeater again pointed out that he had no idea what he was expected to do as Australian organiser for the Star. He cried poor, as a result of Arundale when he was General Secretary for Australia, "draining" the coffers. He played his usual civilised little games – hoping Krishna would come to Australia yet knowing his arrangements for the year were already settled and pointing out how inappropriate the amphitheatre would be if used for the spectacular bonfires Krishna lit at camps.[77]

Back in Ojai, Krishna was still not well in early 1929 and abandoned the idea of giving weekly talks in April, in the lead-up to a camp at Ojai in May. A doctor advised him that the bronchitis he'd suffered had weakened his lungs and if he continued to work so hard he'd have TB within a couple of years. Krishna kept the news under wraps but went on a brief holiday in the San Bernadino mountains with Rosalind and another couple, putting on some weight but still weighing in at less than eight stone - or just under fifty kilos - on his return. He seemed to have dropped the idea of becoming a *sannyasi*, seeing the need to work in the world. He wrote to Mrs Besant about the beauty and peace at Ojai. He told her that people were annoyed with what he said and that they wanted him and Mrs Besant to quarrel and when they did not, would make up stories that they had anyway.[78]

Much is made of Mrs Besant's disillusionment with Krishnamurti yet at the most crucial time of his definitive statement dissolving the Order of the Star she was with him.

Krishna made his ground-breaking speech on 3 August 1929, the second day of the Ommen camp, with Mrs Besant sitting beside him, three thousand members in the audience and thousands more tuned into Dutch radio for the broadcast. His statement was unequivocal – after two years of patient, careful thought he, as the head of the Order, was disbanding it. It was no magnificent deed, he said, because he did not want followers. The moment you follow someone you cease to follow "Truth", he said. According to him, everyone was depending for their spirituality on someone else, for their happiness on someone else, for their enlightenment on someone else. Why have an organisation, when the key to the "Kingdom of Happiness" lay in your own self and in the development and the purification of that self? Krishnamurti said that he wasn't concerned whether other people formed organisations or created new cages or new decorations for those cages. His only concern was to set men absolutely and unconditionally free. **"Truth is a pathless land,"** he declared, **"and you cannot approach it by any path whatsoever, by any religion, by any sect".**[79]

When Mrs Besant had returned to London Krishna wrote to her on 12 August to say that he hoped she had come to a decision about an important matter they'd discussed. The very next day just a few hours before leaving for America she wrote to him a secretive letter concerning Wedgwood, about her needing to meet with someone, and sending Krishna her reverence. Once she'd arrived in Chicago she wrote again an extraordinary letter of support, saying that the world's press was recognising him as a teacher of outstanding wisdom and unique power. According to her, many realised that his destruction of outworn forms was necessary if the "Life" he was pouring out in rich abundance was allowed to express itself in the lives of people he came in contact with. She spoke of reason and love and that as individuals solve their problems, so the problems of the world were solved.[80]

Krishna wrote to his old and dear adoptive mother in September to say that he'd heard that many pupils had replied to her letter to Wedgwood, which he thought was ridiculous. The following month he had a long talk with her before embarking for India. In spite of the many splits that others had imagined would sink their friendship, it held firm.

The significant other woman in his life also steered a steady course. Krishna's letter to Rosalind from on board ship bound for India - in which he told her he thought of her constantly - is evidence enough that she had been a fundamental strength for him during his difficult and radical transformation into a great spiritual leader - and that he was still very much in love with her.[81]

Chapter 6

Ménage

Knock, knock, knockin' on heaven's door.

Bob Dylan 1973 Ram's Horn Music

Krishnamurti had made a major, radical statement about politics and spirituality, particularly in relation to the Theosophical Society, yet there was remarkably little change in his life immediately afterwards.

He retained the income Miss Dodge had settled on him for life and he would soon be returning to Ojai to live with Rosalind and Rajagopal. He resigned from several Trusts and gave back the Castle at Ommen in Holland to Philip van Pallandt who now had an heir. However a parcel of 400 acres of the estate was kept by the Star Trust and van Pallandt refunded all costs associated with renovations to the Castle. The Star Publishing House and the Star Bulletin moved from Eerde into a house near the local town of Ommen.[1]

About two months after the dissolution of the Order of the Star, Mrs Besant reopened the Theosophical Society's Esoteric Section, prompting Krishnamurti to resign from the Society.[2] Their diverging views did not, however, cause a split in Krishna and Mrs Besant's personal relationship. He returned to India with her in October 1929 and faced the opposition to his views and his presence now evident not only from Arundale and Wedgwood and their followers, but also from Leadbeater. The old man had travelled from Sydney to Adyar for the December convention and there he made it clear that he thought the "Coming" had gone wrong. The basis of this opinion seems to have been that Krishnamurti's ego had got in the way of God's will – in other words it was based on the idea that Krishna had failed, rather than an acknowledgement that the theory of the "World Teacher" inhabiting Krishna's body was faulty. Could not God have foreseen that Krishna would not be able to cut the mustard? Leadbeater's stance of opposition to Krishnamurti is entirely understandable. Since Krishna's philosophy was about looking within for enlightenment it did not include a role for someone such as Leadbeater who played the powerful game of interpreting for others messages from the Masters. This pious, rigid, stuffy old Englishman had too much at stake to see how ridiculous his world-view had become to all but the most self-deluded Theosophists. It was comforting to Wedgwood and Arundale to have Leadbeater at last closing ranks with them. Wedgwood had already told Lady Emily in London that Mrs Besant was often "non compos" so her opinion of Krishna could not be relied upon, whereas he could always tell when the Lord was speaking through Krishna and when he wasn't.[3] Krishna wrote to Lady Emily that Mrs Besant's reaction to this piece of information was that she wished people were more kind and said that strong beliefs hardened people. Mrs Besant was so reverential to Krishna she sat at his feet rather than on the dais with him when he spoke but she would not give up her belief in her Master Morya.[4]

Krishna wrote to Mrs Besant in February 1930 from on board the *SS Ganges*, sailing back to Europe, that she was not to worry about Leadbeater being against him since it was inevitable. It didn't matter what a million people might say or not say, he was certain and was going on his own way. He knew she hadn't been well in India and he didn't like to disturb her but hoped they could have a long talk in England when she returned.[5]

Lady Emily was trying to bring Theosophists in England round to Krishnamurti's viewpoint without success and he reassured her. He had resigned but was not urging her to do the same, he said – which had a catalysing effect in prompting her to resign. Lady Emily's statement of resignation was a clear, chronological outline of events concerning Krishnamurti as the "World Teacher" and a clear example of both her dilemma and her honesty. She accused Theosophical leaders of clinging to a theory of "dual consciousness" of Krishnamurti sometimes being a 'World Teacher" and sometimes not, so that they could take from his teaching only what appealed to them. But it must have been evident even to the most stupid that there was a "cleavage" between the majority of Theosophists who were "credulous sheep" and "Krishnaji", she said.[6] Lady Emily was to go through a period of several years of doubt and unhappiness, not able to be Krishna's disciple, as he said he did not want followers, yet finding it difficult to adjust to the new era of self-help. She took much greater interest in her children's problems than she ever had in the past, before finding contentment again with her husband, Edwin, who had never wavered in his love for her. She retained a steadfast friendship with Krishnamurti, attending the Ommen camp in 1930 and again in 1931, writing to Edwin that Krishna had left the Castle for the last time, walking out as the moon eclipsed. Lady Emily said that Krishna wrote to her in December 1931, urging her to detach from her family and free herself from all human ties, but she did not want to lose personal love in favour of love for all, which she felt was cold, arid and dull. All at once she realised her husband's extraordinary understanding and patience. She felt remorse that Krishna might be disappointed in her but believed he had moved into another sphere where she could not follow.[7]

Mrs Besant missed the 1930 Ommen camp, sending her cordial regards, as she had to remain in London for a series of treatments on her eardrum. She probably believed it was for the best that she stayed away, as it allowed Krishnamurti to develop independently of her influence. Lutyens makes the point that Krishnamurti was now beginning to attract younger people who were interested in what he said rather than who he was.[8]

Krishna returned to Ojai in March 1930 and stayed for a camp opened up to the public in May, followed by a brief American tour, but was back in England preparing for his first ever public camp at Eerde from 26 July to 7 August. He travelled with Rajagopal, his editor, advisor and all-round aid-de-camp. The two men had developed a strong bond during this period of transformation. Radha Rajagopal Sloss says Rajagopal loved Krishna dearly but he never resigned from the Theosophical Society. He always believed Mrs Besant's predictions that Krishna would be a "World Teacher" and kept his promises to her and to Nitya that he would take care of Krishna. Rosalind, too, remained a Theosophist, although her daughter says she did not accept its philosophy.[9]

Krishna's travel movements in 1930 listed by Mary Lutyens are a little vague about his whereabouts following the Ommen camp on 7 August. According to the Krishnamurti Archives of America he gives three talks in Eerde on 24 and 25 September and then on 16 October there is some question about whether he has given a talk in Strasbourg. Yet from 15 October Lutyens reports him in France and Switzerland until 5 November.[10]

It's interesting to consider where Rajagopal and Krishna were in early October because that is the date that Rosalind would have conceived her daughter, forty weeks before Radha's birth date on 12 July 1931, if the birth occurred at full term.

Rosalind's daughter, Radha, explains in her book that Rosalind had gone to Paris to attend the "summer" fashion shows, after an invitation from Madame Barrero whom she had met in Cuba. Krishna was in France at this time and Rosalind wrote to her mother on 23 October from Paris to say that he had given a marvellous lecture in Strasbourg to good reviews. He read it in French and with his ability to attract "thousands" he was compared with the actor Maurice Chevalier in popularity. Radha describes how Rosalind, rather than feeling delighted when she found she was pregnant, as she and Rajagopal had hoped for a child for some years, was in despair. Radha says that it was curious that her mother could not discuss her situation with "the person who should be most concerned – her husband" and puts the explanation down to Krishna's antipathy to those close to him having children instead of devoting themselves to 'the Work'. Radha believes that a physical incompatibility between Rosalind and Rajagopal accounts for Krishnamurti taking the greater interest in her from the moment she became pregnant despite an initial "displeasure".[11]

Krishna had written to Rosalind in Eerde on 7 October from Rebais in France asking her to bring him two cashmere shawls when she came to Paris, and also his hat for the country. Rajagopal had returned to Eerde so that he could have a really good rest, Krishna told Rosalind in the letter, and he hoped that she was making sure that Rajagopal did so – early to bed at night, an afternoon spell and plenty of exercise, he told her. Rajagopal should be completely rested before he returned to Paris because the next tour would be very strenuous, he said.[12]

During the period he spent in France and Switzerland, Krishna suffered badly from bronchitis and cancelled a tour in Italy, spending the period 6 to 30 November in the Sicilian resort town, Taormina, according to Lutyens.[13]

However, contrary to that information, Krishna writes to Rosalind from the Hotel Bristol in Genoa on 11 November to say that he has been in bed for five days with bronchitis that developed from a cold he caught through sudden changes in room temperatures in Montreux. She is in Geneva. Krishna had given talks in Geneva on 29 and 31 October and travelled to Montreux for three days of talks from 3-5 November. Krishna tells Rosalind that he's postponed a visit to Milan until 14 November. Rajagopal, who's with him, looks well and cheerful and is enjoying the Italian cheeses. So Krishna and Rajagopal must not have reached Taormina until sometime after mid-November.[14]

Krishna's letter to Rosalind from Genoa marks a distinct return in the tone of his correspondence to the fond terms used before her marriage. He is a little philosophical and nostalgic, saying that he'd been thinking that afternoon that he'd known her for eight years and she is in his heart. Please believe me, he adds. One sentence is pregnant with import, saying that he is "sorry that _ _ _!" using three dashes and an exclamation mark, followed by the words "well, well". He sends his love to their friend Arthur who is with her and tells Rosalind that this is the first letter he has written for days and there are many waiting.

They would see each other soon enough as Krishna. Rosalind and Rajagopal did take a holiday with John Ingelman in Taormina that November. Taormina was a special place for Krishna since he'd first visited that seaside resort as a boy when he was being hidden from his father during the adoption trial. Leadbeater had believed it was a sacred place. It was in this setting that Krishna especially helped Rosalind through the first uncomfortable weeks of her pregnancy.[15]

By early December Krishna and Rajagopal had travelled without Rosalind to Greece where Krishna was to give a public talk in Athens on 9 December. Rosalind returned to Eerde. The trip to Greece was significant to Krishna for his ecstatic response to the sight of the Parthenon, where he fell to his knees and kissed the ground. It was also the scene for a major confrontation he had with Rajagopal over breaking arrangements they had with their hosts in Athens. Radha Rajagopal Sloss quotes Rajagopal as saying to Krishna, "You ought to be exposed," to which Krishna is alleged to have taunted him. "Go ahead ... who would ever believe *you* against *me*?" Radha does not give details of the dispute except to say, "Krishna had gone back upon confirmed arrangements which put Raja in a very bad position with their hosts". She explains Rajagopal's loyalty to Krishnamurti as result of a sense of responsibility and commitment to what he believed was his *dharma* or duty, his role as a Brahmin which he should never shirk. According to Radha the tension between them would grow with the years despite Rajagopal's love for Krishna and Krishna's pleading and apologies.[16]

Rosalind received a letter from Krishna from the 'Hotel Grande Bretagne' in Athens written the day before his lecture. He had intended to write to her on the boat, he said, but then thought that her husband should be the first to write and he "long after" with his protestations of affection. He wished she were there – being the "whole" of his love. He didn't know what had happened to him but he felt that he wanted to hug everyone, he said. What a letter for him to write, he declared. In any case he was in love and wished she were there. He wasn't in the habit of writing such stuff, he believed, and thought that he'd said enough. He added that he would like to bear the baby for her. He described Rajagopal as a little seasick from the boat pitching and in missing Rosalind. Krishna wanted to say so many things, but to what "avail", he asked? He said he would write again, indicating it was at her discretion. He wouldn't be seeing her for a long time but she would always be in his heart, he said, ending the letter with all his love.[17]

Krishna's next letter from 'Constantinople' was in the same longing vein. He seemed to have forgotten that he'd written to her from Athens as he apologised for having been too busy. Krishna referred to himself as a "stranger" and a friend, a comment he would make in future correspondence. And how strange and dream-like it was, he said, with Rosalind going to the other end of the world just as he was getting "in —!" "Enough said", was his comment, otherwise he thought he might become too sentimental and that would be too terrible. He had half a mind to go to Eerde to see her before she left for America. Wasn't he allowed the pleasure of seeing her, he asked? A husband had the right but for them, "a cat may look at a king". She was in his heart and they must wait until they met again. He said he couldn't imagine her going away and not seeing her. "Steady old boy," was his advice to himself. Beggars couldn't be choosers and he was the beggar, he concluded.[18]

Radha says that Rajagopal had a hard decision to make that December. He had returned to Rosalind in Ommen while Krishna went to Romania on an invitation from the Queen. A plot by what Lutyens describes as "nationalistic Catholic students" resulted in him having a police escort. Radha says Rajagopal received a cable saying Krishna had been poisoned and after pacing the floor, Rajagopal took the decision to go to Krishna instead of accompanying Rosalind back to Ojai.[19]

Krishna wrote to Rosalind at the end of December from a sanatorium in Budapest saying he would like to use many expressions of affection but he would refrain because it might bore her and an ocean of distance lay between them. It was a last epistle before she sailed, to let her know how pleased he was to have been able to speak to her the day before by phone. He admitted he was getting sentimental but he wouldn't write to her in this way very often. She had no idea how he felt and he wished he could see her. So you are going, he lamented, making his familiar comment that life was strange. She was in his heart always, he said, and sweet was the rose.[20]

He had telephoned the Star office in London from Budapest the day before to say he was well, but there were more threats of disturbances in Budapest following the protests in Bucharest. There, according to reports, students who believed he was pro-Jewish and/or anti-Christian had thrown a stink bomb into the audience before his lecture and a cordon of police gave him protection in the street afterwards. When he arrived in Budapest from Bucharest he had "ptomaine" poisoning. Krishna had not mentioned any of these disturbances in his letter to Rosalind, no doubt having given that information by phone, except to say that he would be well in a few days and would have been well long before if Rosalind were with him. Rajagopal was still in London on 2 January 1931 to see Rosalind off.[21]

Krishna wrote to Rosalind again in mid-January a letter beginning with a dramatic line: "So" she was "gone," he said. He thanked her for a letter she sent by Rajagopal and one sent to him following their Taormina sojourn which had only just caught up with him. He was sorry that it was terrible for her to leave Rajagopal, he said, but it was not his fault, and he pleaded not guilty. His talks in Prague were cancelled but he hoped to organise them later, and he was on a strict diet of liquids, potatoes and spinach, with only half an hour of walking allowed every day and an enema every second day, for the next month. He wrote to her of the sunset he'd seen and two ducks pursuing each other to make love, the "eternal" game. He wanted to write about so many things and wouldn't but she was in his heart, he said. Again the dramatic expression, "So" she was gone. Lovely was the rose, he said, but he wouldn't be sentimental. He reminded her that he had offered her a bud at Taormina and it was still a bud and she'd left. He wished her well over her sickness and the difficult voyage and hoped she didn't feel smashed into a "thousand" pieces. He repeated the "stranger" label for himself, linked with the idea that she would "produce" and "multiply".[22]

Krishna wrote again ten days later again repressing his declamations of love for her. He wouldn't bore her with affectionate expressions, he said, so she was not to get anxious – but he thought of her. Again he referred to the eight years he'd known her and how it was all changed from those first days when they'd met. How it was all transformed, he declared. He said Rajagopal had gone to Berlin for a couple of days and he was sorry he'd gone, as she'd also gone.[23]

In early February 1931 he wrote again apologising for not having written the previous week, not that he must write weekly but he would if she didn't mind, he said. Referring to Rajagopal as "the father" he described him as full of zest and amusement. As for "the mother", he dreamt that she said she could feel the baby. He would prefer she were with him, he said, and ended with the same reference that a cat may look at a king. Krishna was still on a diet of light food, mashed vegetables and soups, and had grown a beard which he said was the envy of Rajagopal and had nothing to do with the Masters. Perhaps it was his badge of rebellion.[24]

Krishna was still very much in contact with Theosophists even though he had officially broken away from the organisation. Jinarajadasa wrote to him in early January 1931 or 1932 partly out of affection and partly for business as with most of his correspondence. He said that when Mrs Besant read his letter referring to Rajagopal's "nice" baby she asked what did he mean. Jinarajadasa, trying to retain ties as always, wrote that although Krishna had published a general statement about freeing himself from attachments, he hadn't officially resigned as President of the Rishi Valley Trust so he would have to stay on for a year. He wanted to put out a statement that Krishna's interest in the welfare of the schools was as great as ever but understood that Krishna would not like his name used for fundraising.

Jinarajadasa wrote again a month later to sympathise over the Bucharest incident, regretful that it was a group of college students who were "Jew-baiting" – even while Theosophists had been preaching that it was young people who would save the world from this type of racism. He sent Krishna his love, saying he wished he was with him to fuss over him, to pat his pillows and act as a valet, as he was happiest then. He tried to approach him on the astral plane through the Lord Maitreya, he said. It was his way of sending him his love. The tone of Jinarajadasa's letter is in accord with that of the fond correspondence between Mrs Besant and Krishna. It was as if business had to be dealt with and principles held to, but nothing would stand in the way of the genuine expression of their mutual love and respect. In another letter from Jinarajadasa dated 14 January, he writes of Mrs Besant saying that she didn't know there was any dispute between her and Krishna when Krishna wrote to her about such rumours. She had a deep love for Krishna, he said, and when she reopened the Esoteric Section she insisted on a clause that members must accept that Krishna was the "vehicle" of the World Teacher and she would not budge over this. She saw it as a fact and believed he would need a group of people to stand by his work. Jinarajadasa also held that Leadbeater privately believed Krishna was doing "magnificent" work which might have been a little harder for Krishna to accept.[25]

Krishna kept up his correspondence to the expectant mother, writing in March that he and Rajagopal were in a sanitorium in Amsterdam. He seems preoccupied with their health at the very time when Rosalind would have been most conscious of her body's needs - no doubt his health and vigour had not bounced back after the poisoning. This time the diagnosis for them both was colitis, with Krishna having it more severely. Krishna said he'd dreamt of Rosalind a few nights before – he was rubbing her tummy. He reminisced about Ojai, especially when just the three of them – Rosalind, Krishna and Nitya - were there. Yet the memory was all a blank to him, he said, except for the feeling for her in his heart. Lilac had reminded him of her at Ojai, and his nurse had also given him some tulips which he sent to her in the wording of his letter, he said. Twelve days later he wrote again, seeming not to have a recollection of his earlier letter. By now he was back in Ommen and had been dictating replies to over a hundred letters accumulated over the past seven months. He wished he was with her, but there was not so much overt longing in his letter. He'd been staying with Lady Emily, he said, and she too had colitis. In other news of Theosophists, he reported that Wedgwood was practically "cured" - to begin the "game" all over again, he commented, without giving any particulars.[26]

In April he wrote again, apologising for the letter's brevity, saying he knew Rajagopal had written to her fully. Again the letter was rather restrained although he did say she was constantly in his thoughts. In June from Eerde he again apologised for not writing but said he'd dictated over 150 letters and had had a lot to do. He tried a jocular tone to explain away criticisms that he kept himself in cotton wool, having had a cold. Some friends might think they could be better world teachers - it was an old song and she could sing it too, he said. The Arundales were polite and nothing more and he understood that Mrs Besant was in a bad way, reading novels. He was looking forward to seeing Rosalind the following year and it seemed a long way off, he said. He hoped she was happy and expected she would go to Hollywood [to her mother's] for the "great" event.[27]

And then the great day arrived. Rosalind, across the sea and another continent away, gave birth with neither Rajagopal nor Krishna present. They would not see the baby Radha for weeks, Rajagopal going home first in early September, with Krishna following in October.

Krishna had sent a telegram from Ommen the day after the birth to say that "Daddy" was well and he hoped Rosalind and the baby were too. "Daddy" and he would be back in Ojai in November. No doubt Rajagopal also sent a telegram.[28]

Rosalind had intended to give Radha to her mother to care for but once she was born her maternal instincts took over. The birth was said to be difficult and in addition, a sore on Rosalind's back became infected and was diagnosed as skin cancer which she was told would cause her death within ten years.[29]

Radha's description of the scene when Rajagopal returned home in September 1931 is curious. Rajagopal seemed more excited about the world economic situation, with the United States going off the gold standard, than seeing his new baby. But when little Radha opened her eyes he was "overwhelmed" and then remarked that now that they had a baby there was no longer any reason for them to live as man and wife. Whether he meant it as a joke or was espousing an orthodox Theosophist view of only having sex to produce children, Rosalind did not enquire, but according to her daughter, she took his ban on sexual relations seriously and believed she was now free to have sex outside the marriage. The question that springs to mind is what Rajagopal saw when he looked at this six-week old baby. Radha claims her mother did not understand the reaction in him that produced the comment. Whatever the motive, clearly the couple communicated poorly about their feelings.[30]

Krishna, on the other hand, was as explicit about his emotions as he dared to be. In August, after the birth and after the Ommen camp had finished, he wrote to Rosalind from Italy to apologise for not having written for so long, and blaming the fact that he had to dictate letters and he couldn't do that with letters to her. He explained that "Daddy" was awfully excited, wanting to talk about the birth all the time, but also rather shy about it. Rajagopal read to Krishna the descriptions of the baby with great restraint and a trembling voice. Krishna told Rosalind that Rajagopal had said he, Krishna, was as responsible as himself, and Krishna had replied that if there was no pleasure, then there was no responsibility! It would amuse him, he said, to see father, mother and child together. A child is born to "us", was his quote from the Bible. Oh, it would be nice to see Rosalind again, he told her, and he would be one of the admirers. It was all very extraordinary, he thought. Krishna sympathised with her suffering during the birth, which no man could understand, he said. He thanked her for knitting a jersey for him and said he would have to be careful not to be sentimental now that she was a dignified mother.[31]

When Krishna arrived back home in Ojai he asked Rosalind whether Radha might be Nitya returned to them. He assumed the role of protector of the baby, acting as an "Amma" or nurse, playing games, giving her oil rubs in the sunshine and even changing her diapers. Radha makes the point that it was Krishna who took on this role rather than Rajagopal, who spent most of his waking hours attending to business. Krishna on the other hand led a quiet life, spending the time he wasn't with Rosalind and Radha in *samadhi*, or retreat. Mary Lutyens says that in this period of what she called Krishna's *samadhi* he seemed to reach a culmination of his years of physical pain, to reach an ecstasy that never left him again. She maintains that he reached a new state of consciousness which coincided with his loss of "memory of the past almost entirely". She points out that this was consistent with his own teaching that memory, "except for practical purposes", was a dead weight. It is difficult to understand what she means by this as all memory is of the past and it would seem to be impossible to determine which parts might be used for practical purposes and which not.[32]

Rajagopal had a sinus operation in December 1931 and Rosalind spent her time between their two homes: in Hollywood where Rajagopal was recovering and Ojai where Krishna remained in retreat. Krishna wrote solicitous letters to Mrs Besant during this period, about her immense efforts in the past towards Home Rule which were now coming to fruition and her need to remain peaceful, as he was, but he cut back most other activities except on Sundays. By January 1932 he was giving talks on Sunday to crowds of up to 700 people.[33]

Krishna was not so much at peace in his relationship with Rosalind, however. He wrote to her in Hollywood in December asking when she expected to return and sending his love to Rosalind's family (which included her mother and sister Erma) and Radha, commenting that it was a good thing the baby didn't understand yet the giving and taking of love. At the end of the month he wrote again impatiently asking what she meant by saying she would see about coming back to Ojai. Why had she got it into her head that he couldn't be alone if she were there? She must come on Saturday or he would have to go and fetch her which would be a waste of time and money, he said. She would break their friend's heart if she did not come for dinner as expected – his heart was broken long ago. He sent his love to all and sundry, to anyone she cared to give it to, and hoped Rajagopal was better.[34]

Yet Lady Emily Lutyens believed at this time that Krishnamurti had transcended personal love to reach a state of "universal" love. She uses a quote from a statement she believed he made in 1931 in which he said that pure love is like the perfume of the rose, given to all, and that the sun does not care on whom it shines, in support of her view.[35]

Krishna wrote to Lady Emily in December 1931 to say that he had wanted to conquer sorrow and the pain of attachment and detachment and that he had conquered them. And in February 1932 he wrote to her that he saw that family life with all its charms and entanglements was not necessary for him so he kept out of it. Why should he plunge into a blind rush and jealousies, he asked? Then in March he wrote that in the last month he had realised something that gave greater fullness to life – the way out of chaos and misery was in life itself. He was bothered about his inability to express his 'realisation' and wanted to express it clearly as a bridge for others. And in April he said that what he was talking about was an emptiness that was light, intense energy and vitality, when one was wholly empty of personal ideas and feelings. About this time he also wrote to Jinarajadasa that a reporter had asked him whether he was the Christ and he said he was in the "true" sense but not in the traditional sense.[36]

It is sometime in the spring of 1932 that Radha maintains that her mother and Krishna began their sexual relationship, some nine months after she was born. By 1932 Rosalind and Rajagopal slept in different rooms. Radha writes that Rosalind remembered the night of that first talk for the spring Ojai camp as the time when Krishna moved into her bed, allowing Rosalind "to slip into a love affair that would last for more than twenty-five years". Radha says Krishna's actions were inexcusable, even taking into account his unconventional attitude to marriage and the condition of Rosalind and Rajagopal's marriage. She is also critical of the "chaste" image he maintained thereafter. She writes that it was a miracle that so few people suspected the relationship and offers evidence that at least one person was aware of it, Madame de Manziarly, who had called Krishna "a cuckoo in the other bird's nest". Radha also maintains that Rajagopal suspected nothing until he was told twenty years later. This is very difficult to believe but perhaps not impossible in view of her description of Rajagopal's attention to work and the gulf of sexual intimacy between him and her mother.[37]

Mary Lutyens wrote in 1996, after Krishna's relationship with Rosalind was disclosed by Radha in her book, that Krishna was not looking for a relationship since he wrote about enjoying his solitude. She even says that Krishna told her before his death in 1986 that "Rajagopal had not only condoned it but had manoeuvred it into taking place" to get a "hold" over him. She quotes from a letter Krishna is said to have written to Rajagopal, reportedly dictated to Mary Zimbalist but not sent, which states, "You connived, manoeuvred and encouraged that lady and myself". Mary Zimbalist also says that Krishna said late in life that he had only one regret and that was having anything to do with Rosalind and Rajagopal, and she believes they were "in cahoots".[38]

Yet despite Krishna's memory of that period and of his relationships with Rosalind and Rajagopal, the evidence from correspondence of the time shows that he cared deeply for them both. He had a deep and long-lasting love for Rosalind, regardless of when the sexual intimacy began, and it seems, according to what he wrote to her, to have been linked with his ecstatic experiences. It might even be likened to the relationship an artist has to his or her Muse. Radha too testifies to her mother's love for Krishna in her early childhood, and "as the years passed", when Rajagopal "would become more and more the far point of the triangle".[39]

Lutyens' rebuttal of the Rajagopal Sloss book includes a comment that for "fifteen" years in their happy home, Rosalind had no complaints about Krishna, the man she had wanted so much she had chosen to imagine he was in love with her. Yet it did not take much imagination to read that love in his correspondence by the end of 1930. Lutyens also writes that Rosalind's daily presence does not seem to have been a necessity to Krishna even when they were in California together, citing a letter he wrote in 1937 when the Rajagopals were in Hollywood about having a good time by himself, writing, reading and going for walks in the evenings. Whether Krishna wanted Rosalind's "daily" presence is not worth debating. What is indisputable, judging from his letters, is that during the 1930s he was clearly in love and his letters to Rosalind indicate that she was the recipient and focus of much of that love. The quality of his affection and daily relationships with the three people in his life with whom he held the most intimate relationships over the longest period are of greater interest than either moral defenders or detractors of Krishnamurti choose to recognise. Even the question of whether Krishnamurti was a parent cannot be settled by Lutyens' quote from a letter he sent to Lady Emily in 1937 in which he said that Radha might almost be his child (using exclamation marks) but that he was afraid she wasn't. Krishhna may very well have been afraid that Radha was not his child. Radha herself says that Rosalind's letters to her friends at this time give evidence of the closeness of the three of them and the structure of their lives, "strange" in conventional terms but evidently not to any of them.[40]

In 1932, the year when the affair between Krishna and Rosalind is said to have begun, he left Ojai for a trip that would take him across the United States, to Canada then England and India. Krishna departed nearly four months before Rajagopal for the lecture tour, meeting Rajagopal in New York for the voyage to England. During the trip Krishna's letters to Rosalind maintained the same loving tone that had been present over the past couple of years.

From Seattle in July he wrote that he had dreamt of her twice and couldn't imagine that he wouldn't see her for another two years, limply suggesting she might meet them in India. He didn't think that, over the last ten years, two years had passed when they didn't see each other, he said. From Canada he wished that he was back in Ojai to see Radha walk for the first time. In August from Alberta he wrote to say that again he'd dreamt of her and it would be two years until they met. He hoped Radha was well and enclosed a letter from Lady Emily which he asked Rosalind to show to Rajagopal and then to destroy.[41]

Lady Emily wrote a few days later to Krishna about his attitude to a lack of support for what he said. He seemed surprised that people didn't understand him, but she would be surprised if they did, she said. He was knocking down foundations and replacing them with nebulous abstractions. How did he expect people to understand what he himself said was indescribable, she asked? He was "ego-less", she said, and he advocated the destruction of the ego, but people preferred their egos to something they knew nothing about. His fourth dimensional world and an abstraction of "bliss" meant nothing to people who wanted to live in the three-dimensional world as they knew it. She regretted the gulf between them and felt it would be a joy to see him in England.[42]

Letters from Jinarajadasa indicate that he and Krishna's personal and business relations continued. In February 1932 he wrote to Krishna that not many people understood what he was saying, including reporters, so Krishna would continually have to issue corrections. People would tear their hair out over the documents dealing with Krishna's "experiences" during the period before he liberated himself from the Theosophists, as they tried to understand his "volte face". But anything to get away from an orthodox world, he mused. Jinarajadasa said that he worked like the Devil and gave advice to others but hadn't anything for himself, not even from Krishna. In another letter in May, Jinarajadasa wrote that if Rajagopal's arthritis became too bad he would come over and be Krishna's valet and bottle-washer. Apart from the loving tone, and a reference to his own love who had committed suicide in 1928 and he missed sorely, the letter was a little lecture to Krishna that he should not doubt the "real" thing beyond the glimpse that the physical world offered.

He referred to Plato's archetypes and "Maya", which when you hit upon it, he claimed, knocked the bottom out of everything, leaving only a body-less, form-less centre, "You". He wasn't raving but giving Krishna tips, he said. He also quoted Mrs Besant as saying that they should try to cooperate with Krishna and clear difficulties, but it was a strange business. One ought not to be disappointed, but she had thought he would do bigger things, she said. Jinarajadasa said he too had hoped the millions of poor in India would expand to the "Light" and be swept up by Krishna, and although Krishna's present teaching was pretty "stiff", he hadn't lost hope, but Krishna should, after all, know who the Master was. In July he wrote to Krishna to say the Rishi Valley Trust was completely committed to Krishna's policies and he believed Krishna had big ideas in education. It was a pity Gandhi took away general interest in education, he believed.[43]

Jianrajadasa is not the only Theosophist who wants to hold onto Krishna despite his categoric statement that "Truth is a pathless land" in 1929. Rama Rao, BA, BL, who had been connected with Krishna since his childhood, wrote an article for *The Theosophist* in 1932 trying to explain the philosophy behind Krishna's words, so "simple" and yet so "difficult" to understand. What Krishna called "the Beloved" was for him "the God", he said, and what he called "the Goal" was "the Beloved". Rama Rao was keen to interpret what Krishna said in talks and had written as poetry within Theosophist philosophy, and to set that philosophy within traditional Hinduism. It's interesting, although possibly only a coincidence of names, that a Rama Rao wrote to Mahatma Gandhi in 1929 to ask whether he agreed with Krishnamurti's belief that the "individual problem is [the] world problem". Gandhi replied that he enitrely agreed. What Krishnamurti said was a paraphrase of the aphorism, 'as with microcosm, so with macrocosm'. The problem persisted that the theosophists had found Krishna as the 'world teacher' and then they lost him, but, despite the rejection, they would never give him up as lost to them and their philosophies. Gandhi was certainly not fixed in his attitudes about theosophy. He had written to Krishna in 1928 after Krishna cancelled not only a meeting with him but also his tour due to illness. Gandhi replying that it would give him much pleasure to meet him whenever Krishna could find the time. However there's no evidence that they ever met.[44]

Late in 1932, as Krishna tours the United States and Canada, he suggests to Rosalind that it would be nice if she could come to see him off from New York. Don't worry about the cost, he says, as Rajagopal could take it out of Krishna's money from Miss Dodge, which is also Rosalind's money, he reminds her. He is playful about Radha, writing that if he can't marry her mother at least Radha can be his fiancée. He wonders whether Rosalind can bring Radha to New York or leave her with Rosalind's mother, suggesting they all rent an apartment instead of staying in a hotel. And then his disappointment shows clearly when he finds she has not come with Rajagopal to meet him in New York and all he has is a letter in her stead. He acknowledges it must be hard for her to let Rajagopal leave as the three of them must have been having fun together.[45]

On board ship he writes that he saw the conductor, Leopold Stokowski, and Lillian Gish, who was very nice. He had met and talked with Stokowski in the 1920s at Castle Eerde and they had had a formal, discussion, later transcribed, which ranged over the esoteric subjects of art, intelligence, intuition, truth and beauty. Krishnamurti concluded that beauty exists in itself, beyond all forms and appreciations, just like the perfume of the rose, and that freedom and happiness were humans' ultimate aims.[46]

Krishna and Rajagopal's lives were busy as usual on reaching England, then they stayed with friends in Paris before travelling to Naples to board a ship "full" with maharajas and their "flunkeys" who considered them "communists". On arrival in Bombay they were greeted by a crowd bearing garlands and, on their way to Madras, at many stations people met them with flowers and fruit. Once at Adyar Krishna's description of Mrs Besant's fragility in mind and body at age 85 – her shrunken chin, her arms thin and frail, her comment that she had been responsible for raising Krishna and then moving on to talk about soap – show how touched he was by her "tragic" condition. He was so sorry Rosalind and Radha were not with him but there was no point in repeating that. he said. "I say." he told Rosalind. "I love you." he declared.[47]

Rajagopal's account to Rosalind carried the same sad tone. There were formal greetings but a big change from the 1925 visit and it was a shock to see "Amma". She recognised Krishnamurti and himself momentarily but her mind wandered. Jinarjadasa worked day and night and was kind to them but their minds were not in tune and he reflected Leadbeater's views. Krishna had decided to resign from the Rishi Valley Trust, he said. His letters to Rosalind were always full of the business of the day.[48]

Then came the politics. Rajagopal was the intermediary, trying to explain to the dogged Theosophical leaders. Arundale, Leadbeater and Jinarajadasa, that Krishna must go his own way. They were all so rigid and set in their ways and Adyar was beautiful but now a sad place, the people "withered". Krishna thanked Rosalind for sending her love to him in a cable to Rajagopal and hoped she was not too lonely as she had Radha with her.[49]

Then the meetings began – he gave six public talks in Benares, and then faced audiences of 3,000 at Bombay, 5,000 at Ahmedabad and 7,000 at Karachi. No sooner were they over than he fell ill with chicken pox. The great sweep of landscape and humanity encountered on a motoring trip across the sub-continent once again deeply affected Krishna, the riches and extreme poverty, the explanations of *karma* and reincarnation. Krishna said the audiences would listen in great silence - he hoped that signified understanding. He told Rosalind that Leadbeater had told Rajagopal that to follow the Master he must love "Krishna" as Mrs Besant had done. Krishna himself thought Rajagopal should have a rest from the Theosophists. He told Rosalind she was his first love and last love and must not forget it, though it might be best not to tell his fiancée, Radha, as she might be jealous, he joked. He was looking forward to seeing them both back in Holland in a couple of months.[50]

Krishna was worried in June that Rosalind and Radha may not come to Ommen since Radha was so young. Still he sent his loving thoughts to Rosalind and his "fiancée".[51]

Rosalind did take Radha to Ommen in July which meant Krishna did not have to last two years without seeing her, after all. Rajagopal was suffering badly from rheumatism at this time – he'd been to Salsamaggiore for mud baths. After Rosalind left for Ojai, he and Krishna went to Oslo where Krishna gave some talks, then Paris and Rome, where they stayed in the luxurious home of a wealthy American friend. In July 1933 Krishna also stayed in Lady Emily's home as her husband wrote to her to say he had wondered who was in the house when he got home late and met "Krishnajee" in the bathroom the next morning.[52]

At Ommen Krishna would sometimes ask Rosalind to join him in his cottage, and, according to Radha, Rosalind complied, even though it made her nervous, believing secrecy was more in his interests than in hers. Yet, Radha says, Krishna was undaunted and Rosalind did not feel guilty about Rajagopal. Radha also maintains that Krishna wrote a letter about their relationship to Rajagopal, showing it first to Rosalind, and saying Rajagopal had laughed in his face. Radha says Rajagopal never suspected the relationship was anything more than a "special" feeling between them and implies that Krishna never actually showed Rajagopal the letter but Rosalind believed he had.[53]

Krishna wrote to Rosalind in September to ask if he could say he missed her, or would she consider it too personal? He told her he'd planned to see Miss Dodge in Brighton but his elderly friend telephoned to say she was too tired – he believed she was now too nervous to see people. Back in India Rajagopal would have some traditional treatment for his rheumatism.[54]

They arrived back in India in November 1933, a little over a month after Mrs Besant's death on 20 September. Jinarajadasa had written to Krishna on 11 September to say that Mrs Besant was taking nothing except a little water so matters were approaching a crisis.[55] At her bedside at the end, on 20 September 1933, were Jinarajadasa, Leadbeater, her secretary Sri Ram, her physician and her servant Lakshman. who had testified in the Krishnamurti custody case many years earlier but whom Mrs Besant had retained. The following morning her corpse was placed on the stage in the hall of the main building, a selection of prayers from several religions were recited and hundreds of people passed through the hall to pay their last respects. A Masonic service was held for her funeral and the flags of fifty four countries where the Society was represented lined the road of the Adyar estate down to the edge of the river where her corpse, wrapped in white silk, was cremated on a funeral pyre. Verses from the *Bhagavad Gita* were chanted as Leadbeater ignited the pyre of sandalwood. Her ashes were subsequently dispersed in a garden of remembrance at Adyar, in the sacred Ganges at Benares, and at Huizen in Holland. When news of her death was announced, the business houses of Bombay shut down with even the Bombay Stock Exchange closed for the day. At Benares, the Hindu University suspended classes and office work and in Simla where the Assembly was meeting, politicians paid tribute to her. Jawaharlal Nehru attended a convocation in Lucknow and telegrams and letters of condolence poured in to the Theosophical Society. The newspapers of India were filled with tributes for three days.[56]

In fact Mrs Besant's death was world news and even though Krishna had been told by Jinarajadasa that she was very frail he actually read of her death in the *New York Times*.[57]

Among the outstanding obituaries was one from Gandhi in *The Bombay Chronicle*. He declared that as long as India lived the memory of Mrs Besant's magnificent services would also live, and she had endeared herself to India by making it the country of her adoption and dedicating her all to it.[58]

A major biography of Annie Besant had been published by Gertrude Marvin Williams just two years earlier, acknowledging the brilliant accomplishments of her career, including her contribution to the Indian National Congress, while damning the influence of her "evil genius", Charles Leadbeater. Finally Annie Besant was beyond the plaudits and congratulations of Prime

Ministers, Viceroys and Lord High Chancellors, beyond the influence of occultists, beyond even the fiction she read during those final years to escape the turmoil she had never shirked in over fifty years of public life. At the end of her days she stood by her esoteric experiences and visions and was cared for by that rarity, an affectionate man "as tender as a woman".[59]

Jinarajadasa, who had cared for Annie Besant through the pathos of her final weeks and days, soon after her death assured Krishna that he considered him Mrs Besant's "son". Krishna's rooms would be kept open for him to stay in, just as she had wished, and Jinarajadasa also assured Krishna that Leadbeater had no objection to him staying at the Adyar estate. Jinarajadasa was struck by the Ommen talks, he said, and pointed out that although Krishnamurti "disowned" followers, he actually had them, and they put into capitals what he said in fine diamond point. That Krishnamurti was a guru with followers who disavowed other gurus who had followers was a charge that would be levelled against him for the rest of his life. Jinarajadasa realised the inescapability of the situation.[60]

Krishna and Rajagopal at first did not stay at the Theosophical estate, instead living at 64 Greenways Rd, Adyar, just across the river, in a house built recently on six acres and named *Vasanta Vihar*.[61]

Krishna wrote to Lady Emily from India that Leadbeater had met him at the Madras station but it was an "empty" show, as was his reception by Arundale at Adyar. It was a false atmosphere without friendliness, he said. Some old friends kept a safe distance from him in case their proximity affected their occult progress in the Society. He had huge crowds all over India, he said, but this was quantity without quality. There'd also been an article in the paper saying he was spoilt.[62]

In September Jawaharlal Nehru had written to the loyal transcriber of Krishna's talks in India, Mrs Patwardhan, that the talks had found a responsive chord in him. In that they criticised organised religion and as he was not religiously "inclined", what Krishna said had suited his own mentality – and yet he had a feeling of something lacking. Nehru quibbled over the idea that each individual needed to free him [or her] self, wondering whether the concept went far enough, as the education system, the press and radio were moulding individuals into one pattern, he said, and it may not be possible to break those bonds. He said Lenin's ultimate aim had been a kind of anarchism and yet the way to it that he advocated was the intensification of the state principle. He agreed with the behaviourists who believed that we were the outcome of impressions and it was impossible to shake off these influences. His conclusion was that Krishnamurti's words were pleasurable, like music, but did not appear to solve the problem of life.[63]

Rajagopal wrote to Rosalind in December about Patel's funeral taking up space in the press in lieu of news about Krishna's talks, and also described Nehru's visit to Krishna (or Krishnaji as he called him). As Nehru was very much in favour of mass action he found it hard to understand Krishna's point of view, he said. Rajagopal's summary was that although Nehru was likeable he could not draw the masses as did Gandhi's religious nature, so that as long as he lived Nehru would have comparatively little influence. Rajagopal was very critical of the cost of a certain Maharaja maintaining his palace, but not of the Raja of Sanghi, the brother of a friend, Patwardhan, whose guest they were for several days. Their schedule was heavy with talks and discussions, moving on every few days. Rajagopal was critical of the discussions which he found very boring and futile with new points of view arising rarely. He thought that perhaps they might be discontinued, as Krishna himself had suggested giving up touring after the American trip as there were a lot of "crazy" people attending.[64]

Krishna attended the Adyar convention in honour of Mrs Besant after insisting that he would speak only if Leadbeater really wanted him to do so, but after all, he did not give a speech about her as he did not want to deal with personalities, he said. Warrington spoke with sincerity about Adyar being Krishna's home but Rajagopal said it sounded odd as it should have been unnecessary. Instead of genuine friendship, everyone was carefully guarding against any impact Krishna's talks might have. After the convention Krishna gave six public talks from 30 December, at eight in the morning under the famous banyan tree, not as well attended as the previous year, perhaps because the Theosophists were "sheepish". Calling on Leadbeater in his room for ten minutes, Krishna and Rajagopal were only able to talk about "airy" things with him and the Arundales avoided them entirely. Warrington supported Krishna to an extent, referring to the life that was pouring from him and the importance of giving him a good hearing. Former good friends saluted Krishna at a distance and Wood, being close to Krishna, was an outcaste. One advantage, though, was that Krishna's friend, Dwarkanath Telang, who was thrown out as General Secretary of the Society in India, would be freed to work on a new headquarters building for the Star Publishing Trust. After the Adyar talks Krishna went to the Rishi Valley school, where GV Subba Rao was the first principal, talking to the teachers for five hours a day for a week. Raja's assessment of Krishna was that he was full of vitality and spoke with great power.[65]

Krishna and Rajagopal, who could only have become closer from the isolated position they found themselves in, travelled on to Colombo where on 27 January 1933 they sailed once again the long sea route to Australia.

First port of call was Fremantle in the early morning of Tuesday 6 February. The *SS Otranto* would leave for Adelaide that afternoon, arriving four days later, and again departing for Melbourne the same day. The ship would stay overnight in Melbourne on Tuesday 13 February, arriving in Sydney two days later.[66]

From Fremantle, Krishna went up to Perth to give an address in the Perth Town Hall which was broadcast on radio 6WF at lunchtime for fifteen minutes, a brief announcement of the talk having been published by the *West Australian* the previous week. As a precursor to the talk, the *West Australian* had also published three days earlier, a long biographical article remarkable for its accuracy except for the figure of 100,000 membership of the Order of the Star before it was disbanded. The writer called 'Proctor' said that Krishnamurti had perfect manners and a complete absence of the desire to impress. His books were listed as including *The Kingdom of Happiness*, *At the Feet of the Master* and works of poetry. Proctor said Krishnamurti's teaching appeared to be of the "synthetic" order, "perhaps described as a link between Eastern and Western ways of thought". He also said Krishnamurti's teaching seemed to be that man had within himself all that was necessary for his final salvation. Krishna and Rajagopal must have been happy about the article as this part was republished by the *Star* newsletter a couple of months later.[67]

In his Perth talk Krishnamurti spoke about belief and fear and being "critical". As to God or truth: we might say we look for masters or teachers to help us, he said, but they became exploiters because that comfort could not be described. Like a description of the wind, you could not give one, he said.[68]

The day after Krishnamurti's visit to Perth, the *West Australian* carried another long article – a personal profile of him which was full of praise. It emphasised his smile which indicated he had found great happiness in living, his striking and forceful personality, his voice which was never raised beyond ordinary talking pitch and his expressive hands held palm to palm and his "flashing dark eyes". In answer to a question about whether he was the Messiah, he was quoted as saying, "I am no vehicle of any outside divine power ... I am merely a teacher, owning no organisation". Asked about the "hereafter" he is reported to have replied, " ... the hereafter does not matter ... It is this life that matters". Krishnamurti told the reporter that he could not remember when he was last in Australia and confessed to a poor memory, but said it didn't matter as the past was nothing - only the present and future mattered. At the end of the interview Krishnamurti was said to have left the room, smiling, "in search of something very material – an apple".[69]

The day Krishnamurti spent in Perth, the paper carried a culturally elitist article about a woman who had had spent a year in

India and reportedly talked with Gandhi. Miss G Dowson, who had returned to take up an appointment at a girls' high school, said she had met Gandhi at a place which was a "hotbed of sedition and rioting" and anyone seen conversing with Gandhi was immediately suspected of being a convert and was under police watch. Miss Dowson was reported as saying she hadn't quite settled in her mind what was her real impression of Gandhi but "he was certainly not as ugly as many of his photographs show him to be". "There is no doubt about his being a very sincere and good man, but a mistaken one. ... His influence, although still great, is fast waning and it is generally felt that the days of his greatest ascendancy are past," she is quoted as saying. It's curious that this article reflected Krishnamurti's and most Theosophists' view of Gandhi's influence, which was the result of Mrs Besant's political stance. But then the Western press was generally predictable in supporting imperialism.[70]

Arriving in Adelaide, the 38-year old Ḳrishna was greeted by an article in the morning daily paper describing him as "a normal young man who has broken par on a golf course, who swims and plays tennis and abhors being thought eccentric". The article highlighted that he sought no disciples and gave the venue and time of his public address at lunchtime. At the public talk he began by telling people that when he'd finished speaking they might think he'd given them nothing constructive, systematic or conclusive, and that wasn't his intention. He believed that the acceptance of systems tended towards stultifying thinking. His message was neither Eastern nor Western – it was about criticism or discovering the essential value of something. The talk at the Freemason's Hall in North Terrace was one of two recorded addresses. In the other, on radio 5DN, he spoke of the walls of the prison of our minds and that only by becoming conscious of actions, which were the result of your thoughts and feelings, could you destroy the prison. Krishnamurti reiterated his message about living "fully", without division between thoughts, feelings and actions.[71]

A brilliant meteorite with all the colours of the rainbow had been seen in the South Australian sky that week. Listeners to Krishnamurti may have been forgiven if they thought they had been struck by a comparable intellectual burst of colour.[72]

In Melbourne he spoke to a capacity meeting in Queen's Hall in Collins St, answering written questions rather than giving a discourse, since he would return to Melbourne in March, although his answers were, as usual, very long. Asked what was the difference between his philosophy and Vedanta, he said he did not know. Nor did he know whether it was like Schopenhauer or Kant or others. It was a waste of time comparing philosophies, he believed, whereas criticism was really a perception ... and wisdom came in meeting life with a mind that was absolutely unhindered by an idea. He was asked if he wrote *At the Feet of the Master*, and if so, how his ideas differed from it now, and his reply was that he did not really remember writing it. He was always asked the same question – it was used like a whip on him, he said. But that did not mean he didn't write it – he remembered so little about it. In any case, he now almost entirely differed from the teachings found in it – the whole idea of Masters, guides, teachers was utterly wrong, he said, because man was his own saviour. But people engaged in Freemasonry were helping somehow, weren't they; the "force" helped, didn't it, he was asked? Why do you want to help people, Krishnamurti responded? There was exploitation in the very idea of thinking you were doing good to someone. To a question about choice, his response was that we choose between opposites such as fear and courage but only when the mind was not looking to gain was there immediate perception. To sum up, he said that as long as mind was pursuing gain there was conflict, then memory, then choice but if there was real understanding, not created by opposites, the mind was free to "wander" unhindered, and in that infinite wandering there was "Ecstasy".[73]

The policy Krishnamurti's publishing arm was taking to the matter of copyright of *At the Feet of the Master* at this time was proprietary. The Star Publishing Trust wrote to the Theosophical

Publishing House pointing out that Krishnamurti had given it copyright to all works published both before and after its formation. He wished this book and *Towards Discipleship* to go out of print as fast as possible but would allow old stock to be sold. This matter of trying to wrest publication from the Theosophists while denying complete memory of its authorship would be raised from time to time but was never completely resolved.[74]

An article in the Melbourne *Herald* the day Krishnamurti visited the city described him as a "vital, rather naïve-mannered and entirely earnest Indian". It said he did not propose to found any sect or order for the carrying out of his teachings as it would be directly opposed to his beliefs. No mention was made of his publishing house. nor the role of Rajagopal who handled his business affairs. Krishnamurti's purpose, according to the article, was to expound what he had learned in order to inspire others to understand what life was. He was both arresting and elusive and had a dazzling smile, was the reporter's description of him. He was said to have criticised Gandhi's passive resistance as an inverted form of violence, which held the qualities of the thing it hoped to vanquish, and that Russian Communism, in trying to abolish possessiveness, was headed towards his objective, yet he was not a Communist.

> "Possessions mean nothing to me. They are of no use in life," he said. "I would give you this coat," he offered an interviewer, and he obviously meant it."

Having given up golf, even though he was said to have "gone round at North Berwick in 77", Krishnamurti said his only exercise now was walking. He also took pleasure in cooking, and the reporter observed that perhaps this Indian visitor was the one man in Australia who could claim the secret of complete happiness.[75]

The simplicity of this article was in stark contrast to an article devoted to historian and novelist, HG Wells's address on the BBC which was published in full. In it he spoke of the need for world planning and closer co-operation between the major nations of the West and the reasons for the failure of the League of Nations. The ideas were plausible and the language was erudite. By contrast, Krishnamurti's subject matter was always dense - the words he used were clear and simple yet the sum of his language was at times incomprehensible – but he never moderated the meaning. The confusion that arose would lead him to try to redefine words, in an attempt to dispense altogether with connotation or the memory of what the words had meant in previous contexts. The way that most journalists approached their task was to simplify Krishnamurti's message even further and trivialise his image.[76]

Another article had appeared in the Melbourne *Herald* at the end of January presaging his arrival. Written by a "Special Sydney Representative", the story turned Krishnamurti into an undemanding, unobtrusive boy next door. Krishnamurti's hosts in Sydney, the Mackays, were interviewed and happily obliged by showing the writer over their Mosman home where Krishna and his "business manager D Rajagopal" would be staying. Krishna's room would be "an ordinary bedroom, with wide windows looking out across the Harbor to South Head and the Pacific." The room was plain and pleasant, with no texts on the wall or anything to indicate it would be the headquarters of a "prophet", the paper said. And would he be a difficult guest?

> "None easier," said Mr Mackay. "He has no fads about food, except that he is a vegetarian. In the home he is delightful. He will take a vivid interest in all our little possessions. I know he will even want to help with the housework. When he stayed with us in 1924 [sic] he insisted on going into the kitchen to help the girls shell peas and do odd jobs like that."

The main concerns shown in other published material are included here: he was not the vehicle of any divine power; he belonged to no organisation; he had no followers; he would evade an answer about whether he believed in an after-life. Nevertheless he was a "vivid, young man".[77] Yet Krishnamurti was almost 39.

When Krishnamurti reached Sydney on 15 February after two days sailing up the eastern Australian coast, he continued his cracking pace of daily lectures and discussions from 17 February through to 2 March - on two of the days giving two sessions per day. The venues ranged from the Conservatorium, a 'business girls' luncheon' at the Blaxland Gallery at Farmer's department store, the Savoy Theatre, the Mackay's home in Mosman, the Warringah Hall and outdoors at the Morven Garden School or alternative venues when it rained.[78]

Krishnamurti's message, delivered extemporaneously using different words from one talk to the next, changed little in substance over a number of sessions or even years. He would talk of fear, of conformity of ideas in religious organisations, of the need to intelligently 'criticise', of appreciating the now of life rather than a hereafter, of a bliss reached when the mind was empty; of not being able to define God or Truth, as it was ineffable; of not working to a system of meditation.

With his break from the Theosophists complete since his last visit, this time in Sydney Krishnamurti covered new ground, and there were some provocative statements: that the whole structure of civilisation was based on the 'I'; that there was only one thing people were really afraid of and that was death; that there were lasting values and you could only find these out when you came into conflict with established conditions and habits of thought. On the 19 February Krishna said that most people at the end of his talk would conclude that he'd given them nothing constructive, no remedies for their troubles, but to him, offering systems was so much "dust". Yet to understand causes there must be criticism. In the 20 February Q & A session in which Rajagopal joined in a two-person method of stimulating thought, with Krishna and Rajagopal working off each other, the subject matter was worth noting: jealousy. Krishna put forward the proposition that he was jealous of Raja but he liked him so there was a disturbance: he was unhappy and all he wanted was to come back to when they were both happy. Rajagopal said that if he was jealous he wanted to be rid not of jealousy but of that particular unhappiness and so Krishna came to him and said to go to the fundamental. To go to the fundamental, Krishna went on, you had to be rid of the idea of possessiveness and consider that you might lose the person you loved, he said. To all intents and purposes the discussion did not have any deeper personal dimension than a hypothetical discussion technique.[79]

At the business girls' luncheon Krishnamurti again referred to jealousy. He also mentioned the preparations for war going on in Europe and how people were waiting for a miracle. Again he took the subject back to the individual, saying that fundamentally most of "us" were not willing to be responsible. How was mass opinion created, he asked? By individual thought, integrity and responsibility, he said. Starvation would be solved when nationalism, class distinction and possessive rights had vanished, was his conclusion.[80]

At the next talk at Savoy Theatre, Krishnamurti said individuality was necessary for the full expression of life. He also used a classic technique he used in discussion mode (his non-system, as he was supposedly not using a system) which was to put a proposition in the negative. It was part of his larger lecturing scope of beginning with a negative - with the sorrows of this world, the anger, the heartache, the misery – which many in the audience would identify as from their own thoughts. He was asked what was 'thought' and his reply was that to find out what was 'thought' you had to find out what was 'not thought'. Why would this audience, eager to embrace new ideas, disagree with what might have been for them a novel approach? The focus for Krishnamurti was to stir their questioning minds, to whet their appetites for testing shibboleths, as he did not really want the crowd to go away satisfied with answers. He wanted them to go on questioning: he wanted to disturb their familiar thoughts and behaviour. Was the ego a fact, he asked in one discussion session? Did it have any reality?[81] The individualist Krishnamurti, iconoclast and anti-traditionalist, was part of a great tradition. The Socratic method was based on a teacher questioning matters pertaining to ontology, teleology and epistemology, as students sat about him, their minds wrestling with the issues raised, and ending in perplexity. The Indian tradition of oral discourse had laid down the pattern of students' arduous thinking and listening to a teacher long before Plato chronicled Socrates' philosophical sessions. Today we think of 'Q&A' as an abbreviated mode of conveying information but all the great philosophers have been able to create oceans of dissertation from the barest of questions. Krishnamurti was no exception. His answers went on artfully, tortuously, endlessly, leading listeners on until ... Was there, after all, a conclusion that could be reached? A summation? A definitive answer?[82]

People present at his talks said you could hear a pin drop, as Krishnamurti led the discussion, yet he always cajoled the audience into believing they were working together. Perhaps he was as dependent on the audience for the unravelling of wisdom as individual members were dependent on him. When he felt he was losing rapport he would say so, and grab attention and accord once again. If the attention could not be maintained he would close the session or comment afterwards that the audience did not seem to understand. But he never seemed to move out of fear – having been through these processes so many times, once on the platform, he knew he could always take command and lead the audience to an inconclusive place, having them believe that they were moving of their own volition. Could the process be called hypnotic? Hypnotism implies an evil motive. But if Krishna's purpose was only to have people question the status quo and perhaps move to a state of wisdom, what was the harm? I don't want you to accept anything that I am saying, but let us approach it with a freshness, he would suggest. Yet it might be after nine o'clock at night.[83]

It's interesting to note a quotation from Krishnamurti speaking in the summer of 1926 in which he warns his audience not to become over-emotional and hypnotised by words.

> I would ask you to look at ... what I am saying ... not emotionally, not sentimentally, not mesmerised by words, but with your minds, not to be carried away by mass hypnotism, not to act as one of a crowd, but to use your minds individually and think the problem out for yourselves.[84]

In Sydney in 1934 Krishnamurti would say that 'becoming' exists when the mind is not conditioned – he pleaded that he couldn't explain it any further than that. So as long as all our minds were conditioned it was useless to do anything except uncondition the mind, he said.[85]

In the Sydney Town Hall, in front of 3,000 people, Krishnamurti told his expectant audience that only in thinking could a person find an answer, but if the mind was concerned with the "servitude" of the answer, the answer would only satisfy for the moment. Rather, if a person thought of the problem itself, they would find an answer. In answering questions put to him, Krishnamurti said he was not going to give solutions but, instead, show the way a person should think.[86]

The following day at Warringah Hall, never letting off the pressure, he said the process of self-introspection and self-analysis did not give comprehension. What gave understanding was to give one's whole being, one's whole mind and heart, to the present.[87]

Two days later at the Morven Garden School he was asked whether the messages from the Masters did not assist in living. He was afraid that was true, he said. A person could not act unless there was intelligence, which was freeing the mind and heart from all false standards and instincts which had been cultivated, and from false ideas of progress. Did talking do any good, he wondered? Yes, yes, he was assured from the floor. Krishnamurti's only conclusion was that it had to be felt with understanding.[88]

At the Morven Garden School he was asked why he went to a wedding if he was not in favour of ceremonies. After ten years, he wanted to see if human beings were the same or there'd been any radical change, but there'd been none, he deduced.

Krishnamurti returned to Melbourne on 3 March and started all over again. At the Garrick Theatre, Princes Bridge, he continued the theme of radical change. To create opinion, to bring about change, one must start with the individual, he said. The same venue the following night and a strong idea which came out of the written questions was that to bring about a different civilisation one had to begin with oneself. Two nights later in the same theatre he disputed the idea of "gaining" or "attaining" Truth or liberation: instead he proposed discovering the conditions governing the mind to free the mind and the heart for the ecstasy of living. On and on Krishnamurti talked and people listened and began to question their faith in organisations they'd previously identified with. Six pages, ten pages, twenty three pages of transcript, twenty eight pages, thirty three pages – the sessions moved forward relentlessly and the transcriptions file expanded, filled with documentation which could be added to earlier files of talks, all to be published at some time in the future. Rajagopal worked industriously, as Krishna also cast an editor's eye over the papers, and so the oral teaching became a paper mountain.[89]

The day before reaching Sydney Krishna had written to Rosalind to say that he hadn't written to her earlier as life had been so hectic in India. At Colombo he'd talked for ten hours and when he went to bed at 1.30 am his throat was so sore he'd spat blood. Rajagopal was also not well – his rheumatism had been so bad he almost stayed for treatment in India rather than sail for Sydney. At Adyar Krishna had seen Leadbeater twice and talked polite nonsense. The old fellow had left for Australia a week after them but they'd just heard he was dangerously ill in Perth. Krishna was very sorry and hoped he would pull through. He sent his love to Rosalind and Radha but his letter-writing seems to have tapered off.[90]

Rajagopal wrote to Rosalind from Sydney describing the reception of Krishnamurti in Colombo, with three public talks in a "packed" Town Hall. They went to visit the sacred tooth in Kandy, said to be that of Buddha, and Rajagopal scoffed that it was two inches long so it could not possibly be human yet people's devotion before it was extraordinary. Rajagopal described the Mackay's great care of "Krishnaji" in their home in Sydney. He said Krishna had given a talk on the Theosophists' radio station, 2GB, and would speak again the following Sunday. The press had been friendly and gave him a lot of publicity. Writing again on 1st March, Rajagopal said the news from Perth was that Leadbeater was very near the end, and the Manor people were distressed – they would be like lost sheep when he died. The letter went on to say that a telegram had arrived that night announcing Leadbeater's death. Rajagopal's comment was that it ended a long and interesting chapter and he wondered about the future of the Society. There was no nostalgia in his tone. and certainly no sentimentality. He said Leadbeater had developed dropsy. he did not suffer much and was unconscious for several hours before his death."[91]

Returning to Sydney on 9 March. Krishnamurti attended Leadbeater's funeral although he is reported to have remained outside the chapel. Leadbeater's corpse had been sent back to Sydney for cremation. Krishna wrote to Lady Emily that the Manor residents were "bewildered" and wondered who would tell them when they had taken "steps" on their spiritual path.[92]

Beyond his death Leadbeater is still today the subject of controversy over his integrity or lack of it. Mary Lutyens wrote in the Foreword to her biography of Krishnamurti in 1975 that he remained an enigma to her. She believed implicitly in his clairvoyance during the nine months in 1925 she spent in Sydney at 'The Manor' and did not disbelieve fifty years later. Leadbeater's biographer. Gregory Tillett, quotes Balfour Clarke as saying that Krishnamurti believed only Mrs Besant to be sincere in working with him in preparation for the "Coming". Tillett also says that Mary Lutyens told him in an interview that Krishnamurti had told her. "Leadbeater was evil". Tillett also maintains that Leadbeater taught people that there were two sets of moral standards - those required by the occult system and those required by other people - and that lying to protect occult matters was acceptable.[93]

Krishnamurti's final public talk in Australia on 21 March in Sydney's Adyar Hall, explained in part his relationship with the Theosophical Society. He said he and Dr Besant had had many talks but he wouldn't say what they'd discussed because if he said she agreed with him, they would agree. but if he said she disagreed. they would disagree. He had never denied being the world teacher. he said. and she had warned them to keep an open mind. and that he might say things quite contrary to what they expected. Members had prepared for him for twenty years yet none had found out for themselves. Krishnamurti was asked why he passed for a human if he was really Divine. What is human and what is Divine, he posed?"[4]

Krishna and Rajagopal sailed to Auckland, New Zealand, from Sydney on 23 March on the *SS Wanganella* to stay and give talks over a period of ten days. This was to be an eventful trip.

In his first talk in the Auckland Town Hall, Krishnamurti again explained, as he had in Australia, that at the end of the session people might say he had given them no system to follow, and, it was true, he had no system as he thought systems were "pernicious". To be able to criticise and question was the first requirement for any "thinking" man, he said. And to be critical demanded a great deal of "intelligence". By questioning "rightly" one would find out what "truth" was and would live richly, completely and "ecstatically", he said. Patriotism divided people, and to find the glory of living you had first of all to be an individual."[4]

At the Theosophist *Vasanta School Gardens* on 30 March he spoke about the absurdity of religions and the need for individuals, by their own "understanding", to bring about a humanity in which there was real understanding. To a question raised that only a few people in the world were able to grasp his message and Theosophy was necessary as a secondary teaching, he replied that the questioner had to find out what he would say before branding it impossible. The whole system of thought and living was based on individual self-aggrandisement. That wasn't difficult to understand; the difficulty was in putting what he was saying into action. Most people waited for the world to change instead of beginning to change themselves. But if people carried his ideas into action they would see that they were practical, not just theoretical, he said. To a question about whether there was a future life, Krishnamurti was not so much evasive, as he'd been described in Australia, as forthright that this question had little importance to him. What if you discovered there was life after death? Would you be any happier, more intelligent, more human, thoughtful or affectionate, he wondered? Immortality was not in the future, it was 'now' and you could only understand it when the mind was free of time, not burdened by memories of yesterday and fear of death, he explained."[96]

The following day, at the same school, Krishnamurti gave a talk in which he again referred to the "prison walls" that enclosed the mind and heart, and of freeing the hindrances on a mind caught up by authority. But some way into the talk he said that by looking at the faces around him he could see there was little understanding of what he was saying. Wait a minute, "sirs", he said. What brought about understanding was not listening but action, he maintained. By continually questioning, by constant awareness people, could free the mind from the environment and master it. And if you tried to find out what was the fundamental cause of fear, the mind would not get caught up in opposites. Asked about communism, Krishnamurti said not to look from the point of view of an "ism", but from the point of view of an "ordinary" human condition. If the questioner considered himself a "New Zealander" and Krishnamurti considered himself a "Hindu", how could there be a "vital" relationship between them?[97] Later the same day he spoke to Theosophists, challenging their beliefs in ceremony, higher planes, service to the world and angelic superstitions - skirting the question of whether he wrote *At the Feet of the Master* and claiming he did not know Blavatsky's writings. As for Masters or guides, if you wanted to find out what truth was, and asked a guide, then you and he must know what truth was, so why ask, he enquired? Returning to the question of the "World Teacher", he reiterated what he'd said in Australia: Dr Besant had said the world teacher might contradict what they thought. It didn't matter whether he was the teacher or not, and he had never refuted it, but the important thing was to look at their attachments to their beliefs and dogmas, and then there would be no need for a teacher. He would be happy when there were neither teachers nor pupils.[98]

The next day back in the Auckland Town Hall, Krishnamurti began with the supposition that people were there out of suffering in their minds and hearts – again adopting a negative approach. Rather than seek an immediate remedy, his advice was to seek the cause of the suffering through acuteness of mind and intense questioning within that suffering. As to whether he was a theist or an atheist, both were absurd, he said. With a different approach, they as individuals could find out something real for themselves, beyond the limitations of beliefs or the illusion of words. To a question about reincarnation he asked what remained when the "I" disappeared – in love or when really happy. That tremendous feeling of love or ecstasy was real, he said, and everything else false. Was he a Messiah – again, what did it matter? True security in the world would occur when individuals destroyed nationalities and governments that caused continual wars."[9]

The New Zealand talks may be considered a fair summary of Krishnamurti's core views on a range of subjects articulated over decades. In his third talk at the *Vasanta School* he outlined his views on meditation. He believed that in trying to concentrate on one idea others would try to creep in, and so conflict arose. His advice was to complete each thought, not try to "banish" it. This "meditation" was not limited to a few hours but was a continual alertness of the mind and heart throughout the day, which was peace and joy. Again, Krishnamurti was advocating a pseudo-system – a system that dare not be named as such. He did not base his advice on traditional practice, nor did it seem to conform to his own meditative practice which is said to have prompted, or at least preceded, his 'process' in 1922. Krishnamurti's advice about not undertaking a system of traditional, formal or tutored meditation was given recurrently throughout his life. It was open to misinterpretation and obsessive practice by many people, some of whom reached states of high agitation, trying to track their every thought and reaction to every sensation they detected. Krishnamurti's advice may also have left many people feeling helpless since his criticism of traditional forms of meditative practice left them with little more than a memory of his hectoring advice, whereas meditation as practised and advised by some Vedantic Masters can cause changes in consciousness which in turn can lead to ecstatic states (which Krishnamurti does refer to in his talks). He never read philosophy, he said, and the essential thing for action was to liberate the mind and heart from hindrances. Late in life Krishnamurti would explain that meditation was not an "absurd" repetition of words, but it was to "discover" the relationship of thought and silence, of thought and that which is timeless. He indicated a purpose but not a means to discover it.[100]

Krishnamurti's last talk to businessmen in Auckland on 6 April 1934 covered the same old ground – the link between individual thinking and collective action. As long as individuals continued seeking their own self-security there would be exploitation, he maintained. There could not be real happiness in the world if individuals treated the world's human affairs as separate from business, he said. He fielded the same questions about the hereafter and brotherhood. His conclusion was that when a human being lives fully without trying to achieve or succeed, then his action, which is reflected in society, will not reach a pinnacle but be constantly moving and increasing.[101]

Krishnamurti was to have given some talks on Radio IYA but the New Zealand Broadcasting Board banned them on the grounds they would be controversial. The *Auckland Star* reported that he was not "allowed to use the microphone from that station". *The Dominion* in Wellington reported that it was a unique experience for Krishnamurti and he said he could do nothing about it.

> If the Government does not wish me to speak through its microphone, that is the Government's business. It is like somebody asking you not to go into his private house. You do not go, and that is an end of it. It certainly seems absurd.

George Bernard Shaw was also in New Zealand at the time and suffered a ban on the broadcast of the epilogue to his play *Androcles and the Lion*. The Auckland *Evening Post* reported that he was not as disturbed by that as by the ban on Krishnamurti, calling it "far less excusable".

> He is a religious teacher of the greatest distinction, who is listened to with profit and assent by members of all churches and sects, and the prohibition is an ignorant mistake.

Shaw claimed the excuse the Board used that what Krishnamurti said was controversial was "nonsense" as "everything that comes over the wireless is controversial except the time signal and the weather report". He believed the authorities were racist, classing Krishnamurti as "an Indian heathen" and they would be sorry once he became well-known in New Zealand.[92]

Shaw had met Krishnamurti the year before in Bombay and had declared him "the most beautiful human being" he'd ever seen. He had an indirect connection with him, of course, through his former very close relationship with Mrs Besant. Shaw thoroughly approved of him rejecting the "new Messiah" role, pointing to his"high character and common sense". Shaw's biographer, Hesketh Pearson, claims they had a conversation in which Krishnamurti said Mrs Besant had become so old she couldn't think "consecutively" and Shaw whispered that she never could.[93]

Krishna and Rajagopal left Auckland on 7 April on the *SS Mariposa*, arriving in California in late April. At first Krishna stayed in Los Angeles with Dr Ingelman who gave him massages and looked after his health. Rajagopal stayed with Rosalind and Radha at their home in North Beechwood Drive, Hollywood, a flat above the headquarters of the Star Publishing Trust in America. Rajagopal also received recuperative medical treatment for his rheumatism-arthritis. By May the family of four, three parents and little Radha, were happy to return home to their quiet life – and for Krishna "bliss" - on their orchard farm in Ojai.[94]

Chapter 7

In Love and War

The rather indecent display of personalities which has become so unpleasantly common now is something which, if I have any say, shall be avoided. ... What may happen many years hence is the affair of posterity.

Aldous Huxley referring to his selection of letters written by his friend DH Lawrence published posthumously in 1932, Sybille Bedford 1987 Aldous Huxley A Biography Vol I Collins London p 235.

Wrapped in the cocoon of family, Krishnamurti could let the world go by for a time – and an increasingly dark world it was becoming, throughout the Depression leading to WWII.

Rajagopal was drumming up business – seeking donations, producing newsletters, publishing talks and organising a tour of South America for Krishna and himself planned for the end of 1934. Rajagopal explained in a newsletter to *Star* members some of the difficulties of running an international organisation: the bills for printing and postage, the constant fluctuation of currencies, the clearance charges on cheques. He thanked those people who sent more than the actual subscription in guilders or florins. He also said that Krishnamurti did not need money for himself but the capital outlay for his publications must come from donations. He found it curious that while generous donations had been given during the preparation period of the "World Teacher", now that Krishnamurti had arrived and was giving his message, funds had dried up.[1]

However the threesome was not entirely strapped for cash as Miss Mary Dodge – the wealthy American who had lived with Lady De La Warr and settled annuities on a number of her friends, including Krishna and the Rajagopals - made provisions for them all before she died in 1934.[2]

Lady Emily wrote Krishna a rather stiff letter following Rajagopal's plea for funds. She said that Krishna might not deny being a world teacher but he constantly denied being *the* 'World Teacher' for whom Theosophists had given money. Thousands of pounds had been collected in his name and schemes begun by Rajagopal and others with Krishna's approval – schools, the amphitheatre, Star gardens – but they'd all come to nothing. So he could no longer expect Theosophists to give money. She also challenged him about the possibility that he was escaping from life. You cannot face life as it is, with its ugliness, having been protected as if in "cotton wool", she suggested. And he was always "retreating". She wasn't criticising him to be unkind, she assured him. How could she know whether he was more "right" than other people who said they'd found ecstasy, she asked? Since he maintained that no one could be taught - even though he spent his life teaching – she would go her own way, she said. Even so, her conclusion in her second letter was that he had passed "far, far" beyond her into regions she could never enter, but she still loved him with all her heart.[3]

He replied that he had never denied being the world teacher or "W.T.". He had simply said that people should examine what he was saying. As to schemes, there were very few they had deliberately started, he said, but these had grown out of the Theosophical Society's past. And he was not "fighting" with Theosophists but had simply bought land opposite their grounds because it was the best to be found in Madras. He would go on saying what he said about people's illusions because he was in love with "it". "It" was more immense, profound and unforeseeable than ever and he was "bursting" with it.[4]

Krishna may have been in another realm of love but it certainly included Rosalind. Judging by his correspondence to her, they had to deal with the small daily incompatibilities that any couple faces, quite apart from the added complication of their love for Rajagopal. In a letter which was meant to be destroyed, written by Krishna in Ojai to Rosalind in Hollywood in August 1934, he showed how much their petty disputes upset him and damaged their love. He'd telephoned her the night before, he said, just to hear her voice. He didn't know why but he almost jumped in the car to go to Hollywood - a drive of about two hours - to see her that morning. He supposed Rajagopal and she were the two people he loved most but he, Krishna, and Rosalind were always "wrangling", misunderstanding and being sensitive about each other. His heart was "bursting", he said, and when he'd got back home the day before, he'd cried. Not that he was miserable, but something she'd said had "stirred" him so. But with no quiet time available in Hollywood, they couldn't really talk. Let's be friends, he implored her. She knew how much he loved her, he said. It seemed absurd to say it, and she would probably laugh, and then he'd feel better. When he'd thought about her recently something occurred in him that transformed him – it was so "tremendous" that there was now nothing to regret or get over with. It was all very hard to put into words.[5]

He'd slept out under the stars the night before and wished she could have shared it with him. Life was a throbbing, pulsating ecstasy, he said. When there was love, missing someone didn't occur. The only way he could explain this inward happening was through the image of stars seen through dark leaves, the hooting of an owl or the dark stillness of the night. And he wished she were there to talk to even though he knew she would be bored by it. He wasn't ashamed of what he wrote, he said, but wanted her to tear up the letter because anyone who read it wouldn't understand, and it would sound absurd.

Krishna appeared very excited in a letter to Rosalind written five days later in which he said he'd see her within twelve hours. The letter seems to be a call to the real world from the depths of an ecstatic reverie, and as usual, labours to find the words to express the extent of his feeling. Here, as happened sometimes, Krishna had left off the word "you" after the words "I love". At times he would put a dash to replace a word. He was scrappy in his attention to spelling and grammar but it's difficult to believe that dropping the object in the sentence was not deliberate. Most likely, it indicated he did not want to identify Rosalind by name.

and/or that his love was objectless. He was intoxicated, transfigured, overwhelmed and astonished, his heart was utterly open and defenceless, he said. He was lost in an ecstasy of love in which he worshipped (again a sentence without an object). Yet he was very aware to whom he was talking – he told Rosalind not to laugh since what he wrote was absurd or sentimental, or rather, let them both laugh. Krishna told her that just as there was pure sound, the source of all music, so he had touched the love from which all else was derived. He had seen the world in that love, he said. He wished he could talk with her that very night and he would show her the "open" heavens. The pity is that we do not have Rosalind's responses to any of these passionately moving epistles of love; the fact that his love poured forth so abundantly, expressed so fully to her, is evidence enough that she must have accepted it and, at least in small part, returned it. Clearly, she could not have been a 'tabula rasa', merely soaking up the attention, as her complaints and demands become known from his responsive correspondence through the 1930s and 1940s. He refers often to her sceptical attitude to his high emotion, indicating that she scoffed at his sentimentality, but she must have expressed at least sufficient love in action, if not in words, to fuel his desire.[6]

In November Krishna writes to Rosalind that he has never known how much he loved [another dash without an object] until alone among the hills of Ojai. On his walk he could think of nothing except [two dashes], and he had it "rather" badly, he was afraid. He couldn't write any more just then, he said, because he was almost bursting. His love was being sustained by thoughts of Rosalind with some help from the Bible, judging by the quotes from the *Song of Songs* he was to include in correspondence to her over the next few years. "Stay me with flagons, comfort me with apples: for I am sick ... [with] love." The next night Krishna wrote to say he was sorry that she had had to stay in Hollywood while Rajagopal wasn't well and Krishna hoped the doctor would let Rajagopal come back to the healthy environment of Ojai.[7] Krishna said that if either of them felt that he irritated them by his "irregularities" or upset their plans, he could go off and they could stay there alone. The *Song of Songs* was just a collection of words compared to what he was feeling, he said, and he adapted the quote, "Come with me from Lebanon", by changing the words "from Lebanon" in the original text to "to Lebanon". What Krishna wrote carried strong erotic connotations and it's impossible that he was not aware of this. He wrote of a fern shyly showing itself in the "dark places", the noise of running waters filling a canyon, and that he loved [again without the "you"]. How could he go on, he wondered? And then the waters "overflowed" and were wasted. He felt ashamed to write about it and advised Rosalind to destroy the letter. Love came darkly, like a thief in the night, he said. The following night he wrote again and warned himself of the dangers of forming such a habit. His heart was overflowing, and she might laugh, but with him 'to' Lebanon, with him 'to' Lebanon", he repeated.[8]

Krishna had also referred to the *Song of Songs* in correspondence with Lady Emily but not in the same intimately ecstatic way. He said he was "intoxicated", in a state of intelligence and wisdom, and that she might imagine the state of the person who wrote *Song of Songs*, or Buddha or Jesus. No, he wasn't being bombastic, he assured her.[9]

Krishna, Rosalind and Rajagopal, who was still in pain from rheumatism, took a holiday in September and October 1934 in the seaside town of Carmel, about 260 miles north of Ojai. There Krishna met the major American poet, Robinson Jeffers, whose poem "Credo" is thought to refer to Krishna, as Jeffers' 'friend from Asia':

> The God in his mind, creates an ocean more real than the
> ocean, the salt, the actual
> Appalling presence, the power of the waters.[10]

In an interview with Rom Landau, Jeffers said he didn't think Krishnamurti's message had matured enough to be intelligible to most people. "In writing, his arguments are irritating and his logic unconvincing. And yet they sound so true when he uses them in conversation," he said. "Others will have to find a clear and convincing language to express his message." Jeffers remarked that light seemed to enter a room when Krishnamurti walked in. Landau had long talks with Krishnamurti about his teaching, quoting him saying that his inner awareness was always there although it had taken him time to feel it more and more clearly, this inner "unity" remaining, as if behind a screen, even when he was sitting and talking with people. Landau concluded that "truth" could only be found through permanent inner awareness of thoughts, feelings and actions but few could endure this mountain top of "continuous ecstasy". He said Krishnamurti hoped that more and more people would be able to endure the clear air of the mountain top, just as he had said that "a man infinitely greater than any of us had to go his own way that led to Golgotha ... no matter whether his message could be accepted immediately or had to wait for centuries".[11]

Landau also quotes Krishnamurti as saying that personal love did not exist for him as love was his constant inner state. He had the same feeling of affection for everyone and disliked no one. Love was simply "there" like the colour of his skin and the sound of his voice. He also believed it was wrong to assume there was one truth for the masses and another for the elect, as all people were spiritually equal.[12]

Although Krishna spoke to strangers about his generalised love, he felt privately that this love was intricately bound up with his bond with Rosalind. In January 1935 he wrote a note one morning just after giving her a camellia, referring to the night before. He was still concerned about their fights during the day, their "tearing" at each other. He did not want to stop them, he said, but explore them further to understand why they occurred. He even wondered whether they weren't a way of expressing affection. There was no doubt of his "intense" love for – [again he used a dash] and that it was a true and steady flame, he said. The ecstasy of his love for Rosalind, and he identified her this time, was there all the time, he said. She maintained that their differences arose over race and birthplace but he disagreed. He identified her concerns with "aluminium" – worries over the house and dresses and hats. He was actually marking out her materialism as a problem. while acknowledging that her attitude was that these were superficial matters that needed to be attended to. But he felt "choked" by all the "curtain" talk. he said. When the "infantile" talk stopped, he could feel again a simple flow of effortlessness between them. He was disturbed that their precious days were rushing by and the deep "flow" of their lives was being lost. He wouldn't go away because there was nowhere to go. he said. expressing a fear that Rosalind must have held, judging by the correspondence. His mistake was in wanting her to share in his immense experience, for everyone must have their own experience. he realised. Come with him to Lebanon. and set him as a seal about her. he quoted. And, again, advised her to tear up the letter.[13]

Correspondence the following month indicates Krishna's growing intensity and his attempts to convey what he was feeling in words to Rosalind, continuing to be peppered with quotes from the *Song of Songs*. There was an ever-increasing depth to his love for – [dash]. it seemed to be a continual "crescendo". he explained. Out of the fullness of his heart he wanted her as he had never wanted anything so much, he said. He hadn't been able to work and all that he had written, and much more. was completely "consuming" him, he believed. The effect of these letters on Rosalind is not known. What is known is that "early 1935" is given as the date that Rosalind found she was again pregnant. She had been warned that another childbirth would "threaten" her life and decided to have an abortion, visiting an osteopath friend east of Los Angeles, to Krishna's "obvious" relief. He was said to have been compassionate, putting her on and off the bus, but not offering to accompany her. As Rajagopal was recovering in February 1935 from a second operation on his sinuses, Rosalind then accompanied Krishna to New York and Philadelphia where he gave several lectures. She returned to Ojai when Rajagopal and an assistant, Bryan Casselberry, joined Krishna in New York for an eight-month tour of South and Central America. The trip would take in Brazil, Uruguay, Argentina, Chile and Mexico.[14]

While Krishna had been in the throes of sentimental expression, protected in his beautiful orange grove from harsh material living conditions, intermittent news of the rampant nationalism that was building up in Europe broke through into his insulated life. In July 1934 Rajagopal had received up-to-date information about conditions in Germany from *Star* staff in Holland: that many Germans were lying "at the feet of the master", thinking Hitler was in God's grace. Then at the end of June they suddenly awoke as if from a dream to the fact that people could no longer defend themselves before the law when Goering had imprisoned and killed political foes and the press was stifled by Goebbels' propaganda. As a result of this climate the writer did not think it wise to publicise their international cause in case all *Stern-Verlag* publications were "forbidden". At the very least they would have to edit out "Krishnaji's" comments on religion, nationality authority and exploitation which would void its message. The advice given to Rajagopal was for Mrs Vigeveno to translate works into German and wait until the situation in Germany was more "settled". But Rajagopal was not satisfied with this delay. He wrote in 1935 to Mrs Vigeveno to say that he thought Krishnamurti's reports should be issued in German – they should test the consequences of issuing the reports and not remain "apprehensive". Finally he agreed to deletions, but only after a protest that they cut up Krishnamurti's thoughts so much the result might be weak and "twisted".[15]

Rajagopal was a fluent letter-writer, reporting on conditions of living wherever he visited, as well as being an astute observer of character, in particular Krishnamurti's idiosyncrasies. On their trip to South America, which had been put back to March 1935, Rajagopal's letters home make the two travellers to Rio de Janeiro sound like 'the odd couple'. Bryan Casselberry, who travelled with them, stayed in nearby hotel accommodation while Krishna and Rajagopal shared a three-roomed apartment. The pattern soon evolved that as Rajagopal played the dionysian role for the duo, Krishna was in equal measure spartan. Rajagopal loved Brazilian coffee and knew "how to eat food and like it" without analysing its chemical composition, while Krishna was "suspicious" of most meals. Rajagopal said Krishna would declare as he saw the food appear on a platter in the distance, "Oh, that's starch again". Rajagopal said he had never seen anyone suspect food and its chemical reaction on the body as Krishna did. Rajagopal perpetually put off doing daily exercises, although he did go for walks with Krishna. People would recognise Krishna and point at him, which caused him to walk stiffly, head erect, chin up, as if wearing blinkers, moving so fast on the narrow footpaths that Rajagopal and Casselberry would have to fall behind, so they looked like security police. Rajagopal said he found it painful to go for walks with Krishna, not because his legs got tired but because of Krishna's sensitivity; Rajagopal wished Krishna would become a little "hardened" so that his public life became bearable to him and to them. Rajagopal couldn't deter Krishna from his regular walks. In fact Krishna was in everything "painfully" regular, Rajagopal moaned. He told Rosalind he was perhaps beginning to envy Krishna his regularity, which was the start of a hope for a regulated life for himself. At night, the odd couple's differing inclinations became even more pronounced, causing problems. Rajagopal was a night owl and Krishna liked to retire early. A curtain between their bedrooms was transparent and had a tear in it so that when Krishna was ready for sleep Rajagopal had to crawl into bed too. But the Brazilians were a whole race of night owls so noise from the street would keep them awake. Then soldiers would turn up in the vacant lot next door for a game of football at 5 am, so Krishna would wake and Rajagopal would struggle to stay asleep until 8 am. Rajagopal reported that Krishna would spend hours, morning and night, watching "like a hawk" people enjoying themselves in the YMCA restaurant next door and he would say what a mad world it was. "Come and look at this," he'd call, and Rajagopal would tell him not to encourage them.

> And when he is not looking at them he is fixing his hair and creaming his face, and at rare intervals he sits down at a table in front of the window, and looks alternately at the manuscript and at the sky, and nearly

> bores us by saying repeatedly, 'What rot all this is, how can I correct this? It is not worth correcting.'

Rajagopal would say that if it was worth telling five thousand people, it was worth publishing and the only solution was to be more careful in how he spoke to audiences. Meanwhile Krishna wrote to Rosalind every night in what he referred to as his 'daily diary', the handwriting so small it was difficult to read. Rajagopal told him that from a distance it resembled a wall-paper pattern – he only wished Krishna was as regular about correcting his talks as he was about writing to Rosalind. Undoubtedly, Krishna's right-brain creativity was highly over-developed while the brake and self-critic of his left-brain thinking remained sadly neglected.[16]

Rajagopal's travelogue observations are pithy and sympathetic. He liked the Brazilians, especially their friendliness and lack of racism in social and sexual relations and he was pleased to get away from people who knew him as Krishna's business manager so that he could get to understand the locals better. His letters indicate his compassion for Krishna, as well as his sense of humour. One day on the main avenue he saw a procession of students dressed as ancient Romans. There in the crowd, he spotted a placard with the words, "I am the naked Truth, Krishnamurti". Rajagopal also reported that there were two kinds of nuts in Brazil – those you ate and enjoyed and the others, tough Theosophists, who were so keen on the concept of reincarnation that they were hurt when anybody criticised it.[17]

Rajagopal seems to have been puzzled and a little miffed about Krishna writing so much to Rosalind. He commented on it several times, saying that he wouldn't repeat what Krishna wrote as it would bore Rosalind, what was the idea anyway, was she to be Krishna's biographer, and that instead of he being Krishna's chronicler, Krishna seemed to have become his, even asking him where he went in the afternoons when Krishna was giving interviews.[18]

The odd couple stayed in Rio until mid-June before sailing for Montevideo and then flying on to Buenos Aires. They filled in their time in planning new book projects, one being Krishna's proposal for a concise summary of his ideas, with no repetition. But Rajagopal was wary of taking Krishna's ideas for new projects too seriously as he had made so many plans in the past. Rajagopal believed that Krishna's talks in Rio were not his best – one time he had felt very little rapport with the large crowd and another time he had had a stomach upset. They were also not well-publicised, according to Rajagopal, so the agent decided to charge a small fee. Rajagopal's initial optimism waned over their stay, so that by 17 May he was saying that the Theosophists had thought Krishna a "God" until he'd visited and then they realised he did not want to be worshipped. Now they were in their own "narrow" shells and Krishna felt it was futile being there. Rajagopal also commented that possibly what Krishna said was beyond their comprehension as Brazilians were not like Indians, who were both devotional and intellectual. He said that Krishna got restless unless he was holding discussions with people, but when he had them, he'd become bored.[19]

Krishnamurti was invited by the Minister for Education to Montevideo and his talks were broadcast on radio there. He was also invited to the home of the "Dictator" Terra, whom Rajagopal described as a nice, elderly, alert, clever and humorous person who didn't like Catholics. Krishna also said he seemed a very "nice" man. Rajagopal was very amused that Krishna's ideas should suit such a "Dictator", suggesting that that was the advantage of being so general, and probably a characteristic of a "Christ", he said, so that "nothingness" suited everyone and the world could go on with its fights and "knaveries".[20]

Rajagopal's critique of Krishna's talks are very useful as there could hardly have been a more informed and astute listener than he, with his academic background and complete knowledge of all Krishna's teaching. In Montevideo Rajagopal wrote to Rosalind that Krishna was wrestling with the mentality of the audiences. In his opinion, Krishna should not use a discussion form, he said, because he did not know how to do it. But he liked it because it gave direct contact with people. What surprised

Rajagopal was the "extraordinary" fascination people had for Krishna, even when they got thoroughly confused. If anyone else stood there for two hours and said "nothing" they would be thrown out or the audience would leave, Rajagopal joked. But people were charmed by him to the extent that they mobbed him, he said.[21]

By the time the party reached Buenos Aires they despaired of their task. Krishna wrote to organisers in Costa Rica, Nicaragua and Guatemala that he was cancelling planned visits to their centres. He asked that before any future visit, preparation be undertaken in distributing his talks beforehand so that the material would not be new and "puzzling" to the audiences. Rajagopal professed to be "amazed" at the cancellation and wondered whether Krishna had told Rosalind the reason for his change of plans. He believed Krishna wanted to be back in California to rest and think out his ideas "anew." Rosalind wrote to a friend that Krishna believed there was little point in staying in each place just one week since it took weeks discussing the old ideas of Theosophy before Krishna could explain his ideas.[22]

In Buenos Aires Krishnamurti also got a lot of publicity in newspapers, but several Catholic priests worked actively against his visit, publishing their views in the press and issuing a pamphlet titled *Contra Krishnamurti.* Krishna said that Catholic priests dominated the country and there was some talk in the papers that he was a Communist and anti-religious. But the attendance at his talks was excellent, with over three thousand people attending one talk, and one newspaper even translated a talk into Spanish. Krishna elaborated in one letter, saying the newspaper *Critica*, which had a circulation of 500,000, published part of his talks, one Catholic bishop held a special meeting to protest against him and there was lively debate in the city, with pamphlets distributed on both sides. At one meeting there were plain-clothes police because they'd heard that a priest intended to "break up" the gathering, but everything finally went off in an "orderly" way, Krishna said. As in New Zealand, one of his radio talks was abandoned, this time by the decision of a co-owner of the station to ban it. But friends of Krishnamurti arranged for a radio station back in Montevideo to broadcast the talk instead.[23]

Still not fully recovered from his operation, and after allegedly having a big argument with Krishna in which Krishna "slapped" him, Rajagopal returned to the warm weather of California from Buenos Aires.[24] Krishna continued on with Casselberry, flying over the Andes in a twin-engined plane, considered a very dangerous flight at the time. In Santiago Krishna's talks were translated into Spanish phrase by phrase as he spoke. Krishna alleged that at one meeting some men from a Catholic organisation came in with "tear-gas bombs" but did not throw them.[25]

Lutyens says that transcripts of Krishna's talks in Latin America show that his views had not changed since his dissolution of the Order of the Star more than five years before, except in one aspect and that was his attitude to sex. She says sex no longer filled him with horror as it had done in the early twenties. When asked about the problem of sex, so dominant in daily life, Krishnamurti said that it was only a problem when people had lost the sense of true affection and profound love in which there was no sense of possessiveness. It was only when they "yielded" to mere sensation that there were problems concerning sex. Most people had lost the joy of creative thinking, he said, so that in turning to sex it became a problem, eating away their minds and hearts. In his book on mystics and teachers, Rom Landau had said that Krishnamurti told him the previous year that there was nothing wrong with a strong sexual urge. Follow it, he said, if it was burning within you. He maintained a problem arose only when something that was real was opposed by intellectual considerations. According to Krishnamurti, suppression could never solve the problem. But he was concerned that in modern society it wasn't sex as a vital inner urge that dominated people so much as images and thoughts of sex. The degradation of sex had made it the servant of unimaginative salesmanship, he said, where in every shop, cinema and café, girls were made to look like harlots in order to stimulate the sex instincts. It might be argued that although Krishnamurti had made a valid point in condemning the commercialisation of sex, in his censorious tone there was still more than a glimpse of prudishness and sexism left over from his previous "horror" of sex. It's worth noting that he expressed a view of young women as whores but not young men, despite their equal responsibility in sexual role-playing, and their interest in fashion and the cut of their clothing to accentuate certain physical features. After all, he had a strong sense of fashion himself.[26]

While Krishna was touring, the Theosophical Society president, Jinarajadasa had also been on the road, in Australia, New Zealand and the United States and the two parties managed to keep in contact. Jinarajadasa had caused a stir in Australia acting in what many Theosophists considered a high-handed way to make changes to their radio station, 2GB. Krishna received complaints about this, replying mildly to one correspondent that he could not comment as he knew nothing about it. He took the opportunity to describe the church opposition to his South American visit and sent his and Raja's love to the letter-writer whom they'd met on their last trip to Sydney.[27]

When Rajagopal found out that Theosophists in Los Angeles were not making his old friend Jinarajadasa (also known as Raja) welcome he cabled to him offering accommodation in Hollywood, and Raja cabled back to accept. Rajagopal wrote to Rosalind to explain that he had made the offer of "her" apartment and would she tell Jinarajadasa that he loved him still even though he wished Jinarajadasa would be less suspicious of his motives.[28]

Krishna was also keeping up contact with the President of the Theosophical Society despite his public rebuttals of its credo. Jinarajadasa wrote to Krishna in June 1935 to say that his attack on him over the Rishi Valley school came as a shock and Krishna was quite wrong in his view that Jinarajadasa was in conflict with him. Jinarajadasa followed up this letter the following month with an explanation that legal advice had already been sought in the matter of objections to the transfer of the school to Krishna so all he could do was seek further opinion which might find a legal flaw in the case. Jinarajadasa was a wily fellow, now aged 60, and although he might feel the heavy responsibility of the Society office, he loved and believed in Krishna as Annie Besant had. He said that he was startled to hear that Krishna had cancelled the Central American part of his trip – all because theosophists had insisted on "misunderstanding" his teaching, he said. Humanity in its present stage needed ideas to be "crystallised" in personality, he believed. He'd been working forty seven years towards greater beneficence for the world through the Society and although Krishna denounced his work, he saw Krishna's way as just one way and not the only way. He hadn't budged from his conviction about "WHO" was "behind" Krishna. He believed that all that Krishna said was but a "brilliant" repetition of what Buddha and the Shankaracharya had said. When Krishna allowed himself to "pour" out his love, India and the world would at last have the power they needed to put things right. On a personal level, Jinarajadasa said he would love to see Krishna before he sailed from New York in October if it were possible.[29]

Jinarajadasa once again explained his view of Krishnamurti's importance as a spiritual leader in a letter in January 1936 in which he said that there was no conflict for him between his Theosophical work and his belief in Krishnamurti. He said he read the facts differently from Rajagopal and Krishnaji. Annie Besant had seen no divergence between the Esoteric Society and Krishnaji's teachings but closed the ES to ease pressure on people who felt a divergence. Then she re-opened it because the Society was "de-vitalized". Krishnaji was a representative of the "Great Lord", he said, but not every statement of his was direct from the Lord. Many people who had "enrolled" under Krishnaji's "banner" had attacked the Society and he found it necessary to defend it. And there were many movements being given to the world simultaneously.[30]

Jinarajadasa had been a powerful figure in the Theosophical Society over three decades, a political animal given to doing deals as well as a devout believer in the values of the Society. Yet he had a deep affection for Krishna and would defer to the younger man's spiritual power as he did to no-one else living. In 1938 he wrote something of a desperate letter to Krishna from the trials of a lecture tour in Colombia, for his eyes only, asking if he might work for Krishna as an organiser, or possibly even as his valet and "bottle-washer". This brilliant man, who had graduated from St John's College, Cambridge, who spoke five languages fluently, who was past his prime but would actually hold onto his Presidency of the Society for another fourteen years, was humbling himself before the love that he saw in Krishna. He would throw everything overboard if Krishna wanted him, if he was ever in need of his services, he said. It's significant that Jinarajadasa wrote the letter directly to Krishna, asking him not to show it to others, including Rajagopal, yet the letter today forms part of the Rajagopal archival collection. Presumably Krishna would have had no reason to keep it from Rajagopal at the time. Although Krishna was publicly critical of the Theosophical leadership, he must have held onto his personal bond with Jinarajadasa, judging by Jinarajadasa's continuing candour with and unswerving loyalty to Krishna as expressed in his correspondence.[31]

By October 1935 Krishna and Casselberry were in Mexico and Rajagopal had rejoined them on tour. He found a lack of interest in their work, particularly by the press. He described the attachment of theosophists to their opinions, and how Krishna would staunchly defend his argument. This is perhaps surprising in view of Krishna's advice about the futility of debates where each side took an unflinching position. The devotional "mentality", lacking intellectuality, which Rajagopal saw in Latin American theosophists did not suit his or Krishna's own mentalities, it seems. By 23 November when Krishnamurti gave his last public talk in Mexico he'd been on the road for nine months so his patience with audiences that misunderstood him had no doubt run dry. He was drained from the exertion of the tour, having lost weight from his poor diet, and it would take several months back in California before he felt strong again. He went for a month with Rosalind and Radha to Carmel by the sea in the early months of 1936, leaving Rajagopal at work in his office in Hollywood, and it was not long before Rosalind was again pregnant. Rajagopal Sloss describes an argument the two men had in Hollywood in front of Rosalind's mother after the Carmel trip which upset Rosalind so much she believed it caused her to miscarry Krishna's baby in a field, on driving home to Ojai with Krishna one night. He was said to have been "tender, kind and loving and helped her as best he could". Sloss maintains that Krishna and her mother's relationship remained undetected.[32]

By April Krishna was fussing over little Radha in hospital in Los Angeles when she had her tonsils and adenoids removed. Then in May he gave talks at the Oak Grove at Ojai. Afterwards came talks and visits to New York and Sarobia on the East Coast, where the Krishna entourage stayed with friends, the Logans, with whom Rosalind had formed a close bond. Rosalind wrote to a friend from Sarobia about the success of "Krishnaji's" talks there and in New York. She and others thought they'd never heard him speak so well, she said.[33]

Krishna's old flame, Helen Knothe Nearing to whom he had written so passionately over a period of years, tried to see him when he passed through New York but she received what she felt was a "laconic brush-off". Helen had changed radically from the naïve girl Krishna had known in the early-20s at Castle Eerde, a change which seems to have begun during her stay in Australia for two years in the mid-20s. She says that this was where she encountered the socialist movement and spent a "felicitous" time, from playing violin at recitals and on radio, to visiting slum areas and going to meetings with socialist friends. Clearly, she had begun to question the material lifestyle Krishna led, along with his rejection of social and political reform in favour of change occurring from within the individual. She'd begun to recognise his distance from the masses and would reflect on the impression she had that while Nitya had been "tremendously human". Krishna was "a flashing star. hardly human". and although gracious, polite and loving at times. he could be "extremely forbidding". They had met in California after her Sydney sojourn and she realised the spark in their relationship was no longer there - but by 1936 she wanted contact with him again. She wrote from Vermont to say that she would like to see him very much, not the "little peeks and pecks" she'd received on and off over the past six years but to really be with him "for more than an hour!" For quite a while there'd been a vacuum between them, she wrote, but she felt "something else growing up again" and someday she was "going to be something". She was as eager as a baby bird to fly – "I want you to witness my flappings and do some swoops above me". She planned to travel to the USSR to stay on a collective farm and from there go on to Berlin and their old haunt, Ehrwald, to see a "peasant woman friend". Where would he be, she asked? She wanted to see him alone, not always with Scott, her husband. The letter was misplaced, its political exuberance and vivacious invitation for intimacy hardly appealing to Krishna in his current circumstances. His reply was polite and warm but not enticing. Many things had changed since the point where they had all been together, he said. At least he had radically changed, he believed. He couldn't visit her and her husband, Scott Nearing, (who was incidentally a leading American socialist thinker) in Vermont but perhaps they could meet in New York. He sent Rosalind and Rajagopal's love to her and also sent his love to Scott. This was probably a significant dampener on Helen's understanding of his use of the term "love". He hoped she wouldn't fly too far, Krishna added. The letter nipped in the bud Helen's passion to see him, she told him in her reply. Her letter addressed to "Dear Friend" immediately placed them on the same level, pulling him from the exalted position of a great, spiritual bird flying above her. She explained that she could not make herself call him "Krishnaji", yet "Krishna" would shock his secretaries. She and Scott were sorry he wouldn't come to visit them in Vermont; when did he ever visit the sub-soilers, she asked? She loved the Logans, she said, but they were Pennsylvanians, unlike the wild, hard folk of her home. But his refusal to visit her wouldn't put her off – she and Scott could come to New York in June to see him, she said. Krishna replied from Sarobia, which was something of a stronghold for Rosalind, whose friends, the Logans, were their hosts. This time his correspondence was polite but hardly gracious. He thanked Helen for her letter, told her the dates he'd be in New York so they could arrange to meet, expecting these would be convenient to her. He hoped she didn't mind if he didn't write much as he had a lot to do, he said. Helen's reply thanked him in turn for his letter, and observed that it was strange how he had changed with the passing years. A subtle reference indeed to his epistles of a decade earlier, in which he'd declared that as his "beloved" she would always be with him, whatever he was doing or thinking". Perhaps it was at this point that Helen began to form the opinion that "he was half in love with love itself instead of with her". There's no evidence that in 1936 she suspected Rosalind as the focus of Krishna's earthly passion, although years later she wrote that she never knew "quite when or why he lost interest in her [self] and severed connections, whether it was a gradual letting go, or a considered decision to dispense with her when there was no longer the need – or when someone else took her place".[34]

On 1 July 1936 Krishna and the Rajagopals, with Radha in tow, left New York for Holland, first to Rotterdam and travelling on to Ommen. Krishna flew over to see Lady Emily in London in August, travelling with Rosalind while Radha was left with Rajagopal and some other carers in Ommen. The couple returned in time for what was said to have been an "invitation-only" Ommen gathering of just sixty five people.[35] Whether Helen Knothe Nearing's motive for trying to renew her link with Krishnamurti was romantic or political, whether it was her own impulse or her husband's, Scott Nearing himself took up cudgels for her in attempting to meet Krishnamurti in Ommen. His version of events is explained in a letter written once he'd returned to New Jersey in October. He told Krishnamurti that when he tried to stop in Ommen to meet some old friends [he and Helen stayed with Philip van Pallandt] and acquaintances, including Krishnamurti, he had been summoned by the police and treated like a dangerous character.

> I do not complain about such treatment. Rather I take it as a matter of course that the representatives of a decaying social order should object when anyone tells the truth about the system under which they hold their property and from which they secure their privileges.[16]

Nearing said he had it on "good authority" that Krishnamurti took responsibility for calling in the police. It would have been a simple matter for him to request Helen to ask him not to stop in Ommen and he would have respected the request, he said. Krishnamurti had invited him to supper, pointedly not inviting Helen or van Pallandt, and he had only gone in ignorance about Krishnamurti contacting the police, he said. Could double-dealing or perfidy go further than this, he asked?

Krishna wrote to van Pallandt two months later to say that Nearing had written to him about the "troubles" that Helen's activities caused at the Ommen camp – without specifying what they were – and that he would reply to Nearing.[17] Krishna's reply in December explained that he had invited him to dinner not as an act of "perfidy" but because he wanted to tell him about how Helen had "unfortunately" created the disturbance, perhaps unintentionally. He could not have asked for Nearing not to go to the camp, he said, since he'd only heard a few hours earlier of the meeting that had been organised and at which Nearing was to speak. Many people believed he was to speak, rather than simply meet people, as Helen maintained afterwards, so his staff were obliged to tell the police of this activity. Helen had never asked the Ommen camp manager, Folkersma, whether a meeting was permissible. He thought Nearing was being unjust to Folkersma about his informing the police. Krishna said that Helen knew he, Krishna, had made an announcement that there was to be no propaganda, and as Nearing was well-known, his meeting would not have been considered a "social" matter. Krishna said he deeply regretted that Helen had created trouble not only for him but for them all, as all their passports had been examined by government authorities. There had been wild talk based on hearsay and he was sorry there had been a misunderstanding between them.[38]

In terms of Americans' deep beliefs in the importance of freedom of speech, and the Nearings' radical socialist outlook, the repression of their activity must have seemed insufferable conservatism on Krishnamurti's part, as Scott Nearing expressed so potently in his letter. But other more subtle considerations must have been uppermost in Folkersma's mind at the time, namely survival in a place so geographically close to a regime which was vicious in its attacks on certain minority groups. The people of Ommen were actually living with both the fear and actuality of the rise of Nazism in Germany daily, rather than merely grandstanding before making a hasty retreat to the comfort of a liberal democracy in the United States. A letter from a staff member in Ommen to Rajagopal in January 1936 describes the caution that was necessary to go about the business of publishing in German. The writer, most probably James Vigeveno, explained that the situation of the Jews in Germany had become much worse over the past six months. Still considering the publication of Krishnamurti's teaching in Germany, he was glad that they had not taken the decision to go ahead as it was now more dangerous than ever. Nationalism [which Krishnamurti often attacked in his talks] had surged, the authority of those in power had become more "forceful" and most people fell in with the new order, although they were "anxious", he said. There was tight control of book publishing and the press by the Ministry of Propaganda and anyone not thinking "nationally" was attacked. In line with this, he had noticed a drop in interest in Krishnamurti's ideas, either through fear or lack of knowledge. They didn't dare to publicise or publish in Germany as there was direct interference and a need to pass censorship rules set by the Ministry. So they had decided to publish German translations of Krishnamurti's "Verbatim Reports" only within Holland and without publishing the name of the translator. This way they hoped the book, which would not need deletions, would also reach Germany. Switzerland and Austria. The translators of the work were Mrs Vigeveno and a Mr von Fielitz-Coniar who had arrived in Ommen only two days earlier as he had had a nervous breakdown in Germany. He had left with no assets and would stay about two months. Vigeveno said that he would like to find someone who would take over the responsibility for distributing Krishnamurti's teaching in Germany but it was difficult to find anyone because besides the "non-arian-question" [sic]. the general situation was so difficult.[39]

The importance of staying on the right side of authorities was also evident to Rajagopal and Krishnamurti as they needed passport renewals, travel and residence visas updated frequently, spending so much of their time circling the globe and also setting up their homes in the United States. Evidence of this is to be found in a deposition by Rajagopal in 1936 in which he explained that over the past 13 years he had been absent from the United States for 13 months, in order to visit his family in India and to study and lecture on historical and religious movements. He assured the authorities that as President of the Star Publishing Foundation he received no monetary compensation. he had independent means and he maintained no residence other than a property he shared with his wife in Gower Street, Hollywood. For Rajagopal and Krishnamurti. compliance with authorities was one thing. the purity of the teaching another. They had learned many years before that as representatives of subaltern cultures in respect of European values. they needed to put effort into the administrative requirements of the powers-that-be in order for Krishnamurti to be free to express his message attacking authority. organisation, government and nationalism, so that the message was sanctioned by those very authorities.[40]

There's no doubt that Krishnamurti and his associates were under surveillance by the FBI during the war. Krishnamurti had first been mentioned in a US Government security file in 1926 in a note from the American Consulate in Madras to the Secretary of State in Washington regarding a visa for Annie Besant to travel to America. At that time he was said to be "a subject of Great

Britain" holding a British passport issued five years earlier. Krishnamurti continued to update his British passport throughout the period of WW II, when he came under increased surveillance as a result of the pacifism expressed in his lectures.[41]

After the Ommen camp in August 1936, Krishna and the Rajagopals stayed on in Europe, keeping a low profile while on holiday. By late September Krishna was staying with friends, Carlos Suares and his wife Nadine, in Paris. There he also met Marcelle de Manziarly, a talented pianist, who with sister, Mima Porter, was devoted to him.[42]

In October, the Rajagopals went with Krishna to Villars near Montreux to rest before their trip to India and then Rosalind and Radha headed home to Ojai. There they met a devotee who had been to the Bircher-Benner clinic and showed Rosalind the benefits of eating muesli, unfamiliar to Americans at that time. Perhaps feeling the pressure of public talks, Krishnamurti had written to Dwarkanath Telang in India in July suggesting that they needed to concentrate on finding a few people to carry on his work rather than undertake a lecture tour of India. Krishna must have felt somewhat plagued by disagreements in the Indian organisation which sometimes even boiled over into misunderstandings between himself and Dwarkanath who had been a loyal follower of Krishna for many years, his dedication dating from his role as a guard/tutor in 1913. They were real friends, he told Dwarkanath in 1934, and regardless of what others might say, Dwarkanath must also understand Krishna's close relationship with Rajagopal, having known the two of them for so long. Rajagopal didn't manage him, but consulted about everything they did – and that was to be the end of it, he said. It's clear that Krishna wanted to build up a loyal base in India and also wanted to review and make his teaching more concise, along the lines of his aim expressed in Latin America. He needed time to do this and he needed loyalty among his friends and helpers. Perhaps Krishna was considering a biography. He had asked Madame Blech for material which she had passed to Professor Marcault to hand on to him and Jinarajadasa was also having other material copied. In addition, Ernest Wood had asked for a copy of Krishna's pivotal speech in 1925 to use in an article. Jinarajadasa assured Krishna at the end of 1936 that he was delighted to have Krishna's correspondence copied but it would take at least three months. There were matters of spelling and names to attend to and the work would not be charged to Krishna, he said, but it would be impossible to employ someone from outside his office to do it, as there was confidential material involved. The negotiation over the issue of ownership and copyright would go on between these two loving titans for some years to come.[43]

In India in early 1936 Krishna gave public talks in Madras and Jinarajadasa came to visit him several times at *Vasanta Vihar*, across the river from the Theosophical Society's Adyar estate. Krishna felt it peculiar that most of the people he used to be 'intimate' with had dropped away, feeling antagonistic. There were few new friends as yet. He used the term "choiceless awareness" to refer to smashing of the "old" in a letter to Lady Emily; it was a term that would move into his vocabulary as a hallmark of his advice. Lutyens explains it as awareness from moment to moment of what was taking place inside oneself without any effort to direct or change it, as pure observation.[44]

Krishnamurti's love letters to Rosalind had continued industriously through 1936 since June when he wrote from the Sulgrave Hotel in Park Ave, New York, that he thought it was absurd writing to her but she would understand, he believed. There was a tremendous thing in his heart, he said, and it was hers.[45] The next month he implored her not to build walls between them. It would be a thousand pities for that to continue, he said. Since their stay in Sarobia [from where he had written to Helen] many things had happened for the better. Their flame could be kept alive or smothered by "futile" resistances, he said. Krishna also wrote an impassioned letter to Rosalind saying she didn't know how deeply and truly he loved her. He didn't think his love for her had ever wavered, and he likened it to a water lily, alternating between summer flowering and winter dormancy. Through misunderstandings and wrangles, through months of absence, still the flame was "ever" there, he said. Rosalind was disillusioned and had no trust, he said, but he didn't think their love would die so easily. He knew he was to blame for a lack of "timely" action, he said, but he really loved her and "deep" things, strange and "powerful" things, had happened in this love. If their relationship wasn't settled, he said, everything else would go "awry". He had no sense of wanting to escape from their love, an absurd idea. He might have been nervous at times, but he had never wanted to run away, be casual about their love or enjoy it only for the moment, he said. He had wanted to talk with her the previous night and if they agreed, he would "tell" Rajagopal. He wasn't frightened, he said. He was even willing to "give up", and he asked her not to misunderstand him. But his next point was that the three of them had to live together, he had always felt that, he said. Even the palmist, Cheiro [he misspelt the name as 'Cairo'], had told Rosalind this, he said – it would be a "calamity" if they separated. Any fool could break up, he believed, but they needn't and he was willing to move their relationship onto a different plane. He hadn't wanted them to "break" each other while they watched the sunset the previous night. People did "break" each other and he didn't want that. Krishna's abject position, his willingness to hold out an olive branch, is evident in the letter. According to him Rosalind didn't want any advice and he was only offering this letter "in case" she wanted to talk. He would consider it a great show of "affection" if she responded, he said. The intensity of love was evident to him and she was in his heart as the scent in a flower. Life was strange and cruel and they didn't need to add to it, he pleaded. The letter ended in poetry. Krishnamurti's letters written in small, increasingly near-illegible handwriting, would continue through 1936, including a letter from on board ship, all based on the theme of love and the senses, drawing on the poetry of nature as he experienced it. These declarations may not have been read in full, but even the sight of them, like tiny wallpaper print, as Rajagopal had described them, could not have failed to wrench the heart of even the most resistant lover. A clinical assessment of the form and style might even have produced a diagnosis of obsession.[46]

Rosalind was leading an enjoyable life between Hollywood and Ojai in late 1936. Back from Europe she had what her daughter called a full life in Hollywood, playing tennis and going to parties, often leaving Radha in her mother, Sophia's care. As an attractive woman wearing "elegant" clothes, many of which she made, married to an Indian, having a beautiful part-Indian child and closely associated with Krishnamurti, she had an exotic image that appealed to the Hollywood set.[47] Many of her friends were from the film and art world, Los Angeles at that time a magnet for creative, bohemian and artistic personalities. The Austrian architect Richard Neutra, who by the 1930s was living in America, designed Rosalind's apartment above her mother's house in Gower Street.[48] Rosalind was also friendly with the German film director William Dieterle, the actress Luise Reiner, who won three Oscars, composer Arnold Schoenberg, screenwriter Dorothy Arznar and artist, Galka Scheyer, who gave her art lessons. The ceramicist, Beatrice Wood, was a particularly close friend, moving to Ojai and maintaining a bond for life.[49]

After Krishna and Rajagopal's stay in India in 1936 they returned to Europe in the spring of 1937 before the heat set in in Madras. On the way they spent three weeks in Rome at the home of Lord and Lady Berkeley. As public talks had been banned by Mussolini, Krishna spoke to a small private group at the home of Contessa Rafoni in the via Morgani. There he met Vanda Passigli, the daughter of a prominent Florentine aristocrat, who would a few years later marry a marchese, Luigi Scaravelli. Krishna and Vanda, who was a pianist, got on well together and would remain very close friends for many years. That first year Vanda's father invited Krishna and Rajagopal to Florence, where they were accommodated in a luxùrious hotel and went to the Passigli's home in Fiesole for meals. After this pleasant interlude, the annual camp at Ommen was the major engagement for Rajagopal and Krishna that summer, but Krishna also spent some time in London visiting Lady Emily. Krishna had already decided not to return to India late in the year as he didn't see the point of it. He was clearly despairing at the disparity between theosophists' ideas and his and felt the less he had to do with their "mentality" the better. He felt there was a lack of interest in his work in India and saw major difficulties in fanning interest while the country was concentrated on the immediate "problems" of politics. He warned Dwarkanath Telang not to take an almost life-size painting of himself that George Arundale had offered for their new building, *Vasanta Vihar*, saying they could throw it in the river, as far as he was concerned. Krishna had already given notice that the building was not to be turned into a shrine in his honour. but was to be an office, focussed on work. This making holy the places he had stayed was a pernicious attitude, he believed. Clearly, the egalitarian attitudes of the democratic West sat more easily on Krishnamurti's slight shoulders. On the return of the two men to the United States, Rosalind and Radha met them in Sarobia where there was a gathering which lasted about a fortnight. At summer's end the Krishnamurti party – he, Rosalind, Rajagopal and Radha - took an overland trip home to Ojai in their new Lincoln Zephyr. Radha says they were cooped up for weeks, staying in new-concept accommodation called 'auto courts' or 'auto camps', later known as 'motels', which were often roadside cottages in country areas. But Krishnamurti loved this style of travelling, as he loved cars. He was able to take an acute interest in technical details such as fuel consumption, acceleration speed and distance covered each day. Krishna said that they travelled about 300 miles per day and took a fortnight, but they could have made it in ten days if they hadn't stopped off along the way. They spent two days in Washington and called in for a couple of days on Frieda Lawrence, the widow of DH Lawrence, who was living in Taos, New Mexico. Whether Frieda and Krishna shared stories of their impressions of Australia back in 1922 is not known. Rosalind too had visited Australia just three years later, so the subject may have come up. But the whole party had travelled so much as individuals they had virtually the globe as their subject matter. It's unclear whether Krishna and Lawrence ever actually met, even though a story of his was published in *The Star Review* in late 1929, following Krishna's break with the Theosophical Society. In the article, titled "Men and Women", Lawrence suggests that what passes as love between people is often the thought of the other person rather than the person in their real actual body. Characteristically, he deplores mechanisation, giving Soviet Russia as an example of "anti-physical insanity", and advocates men and women get back to their bodies to preserve a "flow of warmth, affection, and physical union". Krishna had suggested in the editorial in the issue that if people were to be free in thought, leading to freedom in life, they would need to remake their world of ideas and a first step was to realise that good and evil were not absolute but relative. Ignorance was at the root of all so-called sin, he said. The tone was attuned to Lawrence's passion for life but it's doubtful that the two men collaborated in any way. Frieda would later write to Rosalind that she read a biography of Krishna and it reminded her of Lawrence – that all "big" men had the same ultimate source of "the vision", each in his own way. In 1937 Frieda's home, built by her loving partner, Angelino, was hung with Lawrence's art and his ashes were treasured in an urn.[50]

Late in 1937 back in California, Krishna was determined to keep a low profile, apart from seeing good friends, among whom would be the leading British writer, Aldous Huxley and his wife, Maria, who had gone to live in America. The initiative for contact had come from Huxley who wrote to the Secretary of the Star Publishing Trust [Rajagopal] in September 1937 saying that it had been suggested that he, Huxley, should meet "Mr" Krishnamurti when in Holland, but as he was now in California, he would greatly appreciate an opportunity to meet him there. Huxley expected to be in Ojai the following week and asked if Mr Krishnamurti would receive him with his friend, the writer, Gerald Heard.[51]

Krishna had replied from Sarobia to say he would not be back home until the end of October. But it would give him great pleasure to meet Huxley and Heard, he said. Heard wrote in January

1938 to say that Huxley then was on the east coast but he, Heard, had returned to Hollywood and would like to see Krishnamurti. The reply was prompt, inviting Heard to Ojai. Krishnamurti asked that Heard phone Rajagopal in Hollywood who might be able to drive him to Ojai as he came "quite often". They met in early February and Krishnamurti's reaction was that Heard was nice and well-informed about science. Huxley was suffering bronchial pneumonia about this time but within a couple of months would be back in Hollywood and have the opportunity to meet Krishnamurti. Heard wrote to Krishna in April to say that Huxley would be delighted if Krishnamurti called to visit him at his apartment in North Laurel Avenue. Heard said he was also relieved to hear that the turkey on their farm had recovered and the baby chicks were well. No doubt this was a reference to Radha's gobbler and hen, given to her in lieu of cooked turkey at thanksgiving, which in turn produced forty chicks. Krishna's response to Huxley after visiting him with Rajagopal was very positive, describing Huxley to Lady Emily as an intellectual but not "merely" that. They talked about a wealth of subjects, from propaganda to yoga and Krishna said it would be nice to continue their friendship. Huxley and Heard returned the visit in May and June, cementing a strong bond of friendship, especially between Aldous and Krishna and Maria Huxley and Rosalind. Radha makes the point that Maria loved Rosalind for herself, apart from the connection with Krishnamurti. She says that living with a 'great' man such as Huxley, Maria understood the complications that that involved, and she admired Rosalind's practicality.[52]

Maria was said to have been a lesbian, so there must have been a certain amount of freedom and acknowledgement of openness in the Huxley marriage. This may have added to the freedom of Maria's expression of admiration for Rosalind, in that she would not have felt the repressive sexual morality of most marriages.[53] Huxley had good friendships with Heard and Christopher Isherwood, both homosexuals and also devotees of the Swami Prabhavananda, head of the Ramakrishna Order or *Vedanta*

Center in Los Angeles. Huxley was himself a disciple of Swami Prabhavanada for a time. but his healthy intellectual scepticism prevented a full flowering of his capacity for *bhakti*, or a devotional spiritual path.[54] His intellectual approach was more in tune with Krishnamurti's teaching and the two men would share hours of tramping across the countryside together, following the tracks of each others' minds through their dialogues. Writing in the third person about his walks with Huxley, Krishnamurti said that Huxley was extraordinary. He could talk about modern and classical music, science and civilisation, was well-versed in Vedanta, Zen and other forms of Buddhism, and would comment on the flowers along the path or a nearby animal, even though his sight was poor. Krishnamurti said they had a strange relationship – affectionate, considerate and non-verbal, as they often sat together without saying a word.[55]

Radha Rajagopal Sloss writes that Huxley based one of his characters in *After Many A Summer Dies the Swan* on Rosalind. Radha says that Huxley would not tell Rosalind which character this was and was surprised that she did not recognise herself. When he asked her about the book, she told him she couldn't honestly say she liked it. It was not meant to be liked, he is reported to have replied.[56] There's no question that Huxley and Rosalind developed a strong friendship – she was one of the two people present at his death more than twenty years later.[57] It's also a tenet of great literature - and Huxley's contribution to the form is difficult to dispute - that although characters might be based on one or several actual living people, there can be no direct transposition of common characteristics between the living and the fictionalised by making an assumption that they are one and the same. The creative capacity distorts the features of the living to produce a fictional character in its own right.

It is, however, interesting to look at the only female character of any note in *After Many A Summer Dies the Swan*.[58] She is introduced into the story teasing an English don in a swimming pool – all sensuality, she dives, plunges, glides and pulls the man, a stranger, under the water. Her behaviour might have been considered impertinent. but is forgiven as playful in the context of her youthful beauty. clothed in a white satin two-piece. and viewed up close through the "translucent water" by the Englishman who is without his spectacles. Her eyes are large and blue and her mouth has a short upper lip that conveys an adolescent quality whether she is "telling smutty stories or making conversation with the Bishop. taking tea in Pasadena or getting tight with the boys". This character. "Virginia", aged twenty two, has a relationship with a Hearst-type character, aged sixty, and lives with him in a mansion among orange groves. She is not interested in wanting "long-range" things – "the best part of Virginia's life was spent in enjoying the successive instants of present contentment of which it was composed. ... Besides, it was obvious that Uncle Jo got a tremendous kick out of her not wanting things; and to be able to give Uncle Jo a kick always made her feel good". She had had "accidents" in having relationships with two women – "she really wasn't that way at all" – and she fancied a male doctor about the house. Before long her "addiction to pleasure" had led her into sex with the doctor and, as a result, into "deliberately and systematically double-crossing" the Hearst-type character. This made her feel unhappy and ashamed, "and one of the reasons why she had to do it again was that it stopped her feeling bad about having done it before". At the end of the novel, Virginia, having got mad at her lover and fought with him again and again, at last, tired and miserable, recognised that he always got what he wanted and it seemed to be what she wanted too, or rather, what her "unhappiness" wanted.[59]

Huxley's biographer Sybille Bedford says that in this novel Huxley came as near to making use of living models as he ever did. "Hearst's young woman friend, Marion Davis, was, at least to contemporary Californians, 'as recognizable as she is in Orson Welles's film [*Citizen Kane*].'"[60] Bedford makes no reference to Rosalind as another living model.

Bedford also says that Huxley mixed categories of writing styles in the novel, sliding from slapstick into philosophic dissertation, eroticism, pastiche and esoteric moralising.[61]

A slab of essay-style occurs on the subject of whether there is such a thing as normal sexual behaviour. The argument Huxley offers is that even when humans think they are being exclusively animal in their sexuality, they are still "on the human level ... still self-conscious, still dominated by words", which means there is no one type of human sexuality that can be called 'normal' as experienced by other "instinctive" animals. Huxley couldn't help parading a little essay-lecture within his fictional tale. The section concludes with an observation that the conceptions of 'normality' for those whose chief preoccupation is with enlightenment and liberation, "of passing from the human level to the level of eternity", would not resemble those of other men and women.[62]

Regardless of whether Rosalind recognised anything especially characteristic of herself being used as a basis for any character in the book, perhaps she took a little comfort from Huxley's appraisal of human variation in sexuality, particularly his views about those people focussed on enlightenment, whose actions may have been incomprehensible to others who were tied to the practicalities of daily living and perhaps even bound by a consciousness of atheism.

The contact between the Huxleys and the family at Ojai was intermittent but not any the less warm as a result. It would continue through the 1940s while the Huxleys remained in the United States and become even more intermittent through until the 1960s.

Rajagopal had left Ojai by the time of the Huxleys' first visit there in April 1938, having decided to begin his summer in Europe early. No talks were held in Ojai in May that year and Krishna followed Rajagopal in July, travelling alone for the first time.[63] The most likely reason for Rosalind staying behind was the cost, as funds were low during the Depression even for those with guaranteed annuities. On arrival in Plymouth, Krishna wrote to Rosalind to say how curious it was that he now had no feeling of intimacy with England; except for India and Ojai there was no place that held him, he said. He described having tea with

Lillian Gish and reporters fluttering about, trying to make something of it. He claimed the people on the ship were "empty" and would chase around theatres, museums and shops. Whereas he was filled with love. Rosalind couldn't imagine how deeply and fully he loved – [dash], he wrote. There was a steady burning flame, needing no artificial stimulation but which was "self-illumined". It was its own "eternity" and "enrapturing".[64] Krishna's bond with Rosalind was as strong as ever and he still seemed unable to separate it from his 'illumination'. In April he had written to her that he understood that she wanted to be alone for a while so he had not gone right away to see her (presumably in Hollywood where she had her apartment). He understood the feeling, he said, and that was the reason he had left the previous day, but he hoped she would return within a few days.[65]

Radha says her mother was restless in 1938. She stayed behind in California while Rajagopal and Krishna were attending the Ommen camp. Krishna then went on to India in November and Rajagopal returned home. Rosalind's close friend, Sara Logan, from Sarobia, died at the end of November and, writing to another friend, Rosalind said she hadn't known she had felt so deeply for her, and afterwards felt a great sense of loss. It was at this time that she went to Galka Scheyer's art classes with Beatrice Wood, Beatrice writing to Krishna that Rosalind was the most extraordinary person she knew. If everyone was as affectionate and wise as Rosalind, the need to change the world from the outside would not be necessary, was Beatrice's assessment. She didn't believe Rosalind carried any hatred as others did. Krishna replied, delighted with Beatrice's appreciation of Rosalind. He went on to describe the insanity and hate being manufactured in Fascist Europe.[66]

Rajagopal and Krishna had been in London in September 1938 the day the Prime Minister, Neville Chamberlain, brought back a peace agreement from Munich, but they were undoubtedly in the majority in recognising that the opportunity for peace was fragile. Rajagopal and Krishna separated after their European trip, Rajagopal to return home while Krishna went on to India. Once he was back in Hollywood. Rajagopal wrote to the Vigevenos, still in Holland, to say that although there seemed to be peace for the time being at least, they must all be suffering, but he hoped not directly, from the terrible "outrages" in Germany.[67]

On his way to India, Krishna fulminated against nationalism, viewing the events in Germany as an exaggeration of the nationalism that existed among all countries. He travelled by P&O on the *SS Strathallan* with an Indian nationalist, a good friend, V Patwardhan, known as 'Pat', but this didn't inhibit Krishna's strident criticism of all forms of nationalism. On board ship the distinction between "natives" and "whites" was marked, he said; Protestants prayed in first class and Catholics in second, and the altar was draped with a Union Jack. What was the good of fighting the Germans when it was the same the world over, he asked? To talk about the brutal Germans, persecution and injustice – yet all on board were prejudiced and separated by nationality or religion. It was a cruel world and Krishna said he saw individuals as the only hope. Once Krishna got to India he felt little better, but described himself as "out of joint" with the Gandhian politics of the country. The British press howled over Japanese horrors in China and devastation in Spain but ignored "imperial" brutality in Palestine and India, he said. Lutyens says Krishna saw no difference between German aggression and British imperialism and believed that the British, having "grabbed half the earth", were as "brutal and greedy" as any other nation. Although Krishna had criticised nationalism many times before, he had not particularly targetted British imperialism, so these observations indicate that although he was feeling out of tune with Indian nationalism, he was being influenced by Indian nationalistic opinion nevertheless. He wrote again on 21 November to Lady Emily from Malabeleshwar, where he was staying with the Raja of Sangli, to say that he agreed that the "poor" Jews were having a horrible and degrading time in Germany. But he wasn't going to leave the question merely in the realm of resigned sympathy for that group alone – he pointed out that dominant races exploited others all over the world: the Kaffirs were treated brutally and inhumanly.

the Brahmins in certain southern parts of India had lost all sense of humanity in regard to Untouchables, and the "negroes" in the south of the USA had a bad time. That humans should behave in such a "bestial" way was revolting. He understood that it was difficult for an individual not to be sucked into the "storm" of hate and confusion. He saw hope only in individuals not belonging to any particular race, country or ideology. Debate over the looming war would go on for months between intimates, friends and enemies, at all levels of society, in all countries. Lady Emily wrote to Krishna in March 1939 saying that there could be no peace while a madman ruled Germany. Krishnamurti's response was that it was easy to curse Hitler and Mussolini but the attitude of domination and craving for power, in the hearts of almost everyone, led to wars and class antagonism. Until the source, the human heart, was cleared, he believed the hate and confusion would remain. The philosophy was as ancient as Shankara but the expression was pure modernism, with the emphasis on "the individual", as that concept became understood in the twentieth century's Western world. Unfortunately, unlike Shankara, Krishnamurti offered no practical aids for the clearing of the human heart.[68]

Krishna stayed on the subcontinent through until the end of March 1939, visiting Bombay, Madras, Karachi, Lahore, New Delhi, the Rajghat school in Varanasi, and finally Colombo. He had told Dwarkanath Telang that he wanted to travel about this time, having all but given up the idea of training a small group in any one place to carry on his work in his absence. He had also given Dwarkanath a little lecture on financial administration before the trip, saying that he did not like to mix up funds to finance his visit there - now Mrs Besant was no longer around to organise funding he thought "the Indian people" should pay his passage and tour expenses if they wanted to hear him speak publicly. He was travelling alone this time but next time the trip could involve the expenses of two people, he said.[69]

This was about the time that Jinarajadasa wrote to Krishna from South America to offer his services if they were ever needed. in a letter marked for Krishna only. Perhaps he had heard that Rajagopal was setting his own travel plans these days. In any case. Krishna set sail with Patwardhan from Colombo on 1 April for a tour of Australia and New Zealand. with a plan for Rajagopal to meet him in Sydney.[70]

Krishna made the usual circuit, visiting Fremantle, Adelaide and Melbourne before reaching his haven with the Mackays in Sydney. His South Australian talks included two at "Holiday House", Mt Lofty and one in the Adelaide Town Hall on the night of 16 April. In Melbourne in mid-May he gave a public address in 'Central Hall' as well as discussions. In Sydney his schedule was heavy, involving discussion every day from 22 to 30 April at a camp at Newport, a northern beach suburb. These were followed by lectures in the Conservatorium of Music and the Theatre Royal in the city.

In one question and answer session in Sydney, Krishnamurti was asked what he had to say that would help a man on the dole. Some in the audience laughed, but Krishnamurti didn't think it was funny, saying people laughed because they thought it was not their problem, just as they thought that wars going on in China, Spain and trouble in India were not their concern. This was the very reason they had the dole, regimenting themselves to a particular ideology which prevented human relationships, he said. But he had not answered the question, came a voice from the audience. The solution was simple – allow people access to the wealth of the land, the voice called out. Krishnamurti immediately assumed the lead again and claimed there were innumerable systems which would not solve poverty. The solution lay in our attitude to change, he said. The next question may also have been considered provocative – what did he have to say about sex? But Krishnamurti was not put off, suggesting they look at the question comprehensively, not "one-sidedly". "Let us go into it sanely and intelligently", he said. Sexual impulses were excited by cinemas and before we knew it we were "entangled" in a particular habit, he explained. There was an emotion that was different from an intellectual sensation, but we had created deep intellectual sensations and lost spontaneity, he said. So habit had become the only means of escape, he argued, and it had become an "immense" problem. He explained that seeking to realise God through celibacy, and believing celibacy assisted purity, was a self-confined and self-limiting process. But when one could live without fear, the problem ceased. In another discussion he reiterated this view – that our minds were bound by the idea of celibacy and we needed to be free of fear. A man who loved a woman in all her being was more than just a man who practised celibacy, he said. Love gave complete fearlessness. These did not sound like the words of a person advocating or even practising celibacy, yet many in the audience would continue to see Krishnamurti in the image of a messiah, as they had formed this image under the influence of Theosophist principles years before. Admittedly, Krishnamurti did not elaborate on the particulars of how he knew about loving a woman "with all her being" but these were publicly sexually-repressed times, and Krishnamurti had always been a private, even shy, individual. One would not have ever expected him to have divulged any details of his own sexual experience.[71]

In contrast to his visit to New Zealand five years before when he had been banned on radio, this time Krishnamurti's trip warranted a mayoral reception in Auckland. The Mayor said many people cherished recollections of that visit and Krishnamurti's message of hope and inspiration. Acknowledging that Krishnamurti's teachings were known throughout the "civilised" world, perhaps a compliment inspired by Wells' comment on the racism shown to Krishnamurti on the last visit, the mayor's enthusiasm went a little too far in view of Krishnamurti's private views of British imperialism so recently expressed. The Mayor said those present were glad to have Krishnamurti in their midst "as an ambassador from one of the component parts of the British Commonwealth" and hoped the visit would "assist the closer linking-up of the bonds of friendship" between Krishnamurti's great country and New Zealand, presumably referring to India, although it was no longer where Krishna was resident.

With few new substantive ideas in Krishnamurti's public talks and discussions, the language he used was always fresh and there were some references to current affairs. He was asked if he was a pacifist and, even though he was to write privately that he was a pacifist, here he wanted to make it more complicated, no doubt so the audience would think on the question afresh. He'd been sailing from Europe to India when the October crisis occurred, he said, and all the passengers prayed twice a day, which was absurd, he maintained, since they had created the war out of their own nationalism. When the crisis was over they forgot all about it. When laughter and applause came from the audience he restored decorum by reminding them this was not a political meeting. He continued by saying that pacifism was a reaction to war and if a person was not inclined to violence they were neither pacifist nor war-monger.[72]

In another talk in Auckland, he was asked about duality and agreed it was a "fact". The mind created pleasure out of discomfort, in this way cultivating duality indefinitely. But when the mind saw the falseness of the lie, it became aware of the process of its own thinking. Communism, he said, took thesis, antithesis and synthesis, as an explanation, but this was still thinking within duality. The explanation must have been confusing to the audience. How many might have experienced this truth of the duality of human thinking, a basic tenet of Advaitism, which was to be found outside of language so that they might understand his words? All that Krishnamurti offered was an invitation to explore beyond the particular system – Communist, Fascist or Social Credit – and the narrow point of view. In his typical dialogue style he asked the audience to go with him – "you and I talk this over reasonably … if ... you merely listen I am afraid it is rather futile … whereas if you think of the problem as an individual listening to a talk in which you are reasonably taking a part, and with that attitude, let us go into this question …".[73]

By mid-June still in Auckland, Krishnamurti seemed to be getting somewhere in these intensive talks and discussions which had been going on for a fortnight, sometimes attended by 250 people. If a person's consciousness was merely the result of self-protective values, then whatever social actions flowed from that had to be anti-social, didn't they, he asked? Nearly five pages later in the typically-long transcript, someone asked whether Krishnamurti would explain what "being ourselves" was. That's what he'd been trying to do for the last four nights, he replied, with a sense of exasperation. That was one of the most difficult things to do, and if you could do it, you were "God". he said, since you had to penetrate through "layers", but in that penetration there emerged the "reality". That's why he had taken, one by one, their ideas of growth, individuality, virtue, pursuit of power and possessiveness. They had not followed in the exploration of these ideas yet they wanted him to tell them what was the real "I", he exclaimed. Finally Krishnamurti came clean in the seemingly endless word game. What he was suggesting over these five days of discussion of values, conclusions, explanations - of growth, individuality and more - was that the mind was really seeking protection. When it was "outwitted" in one place it set up new sets of values and took cover there," he said.

> We have built up a structure and in that structure we are trying to find reality. All that I say is, the mind must cease.

And a few pages later he tried to give the message again, another way. When you loved someone, he asked, were you thinking about your beliefs or abstractions? It was these abstractions and beliefs that perverted your heart, he said. You could not drop the past because you were your past – your every action and thought was of the past, he maintained.[74]

Krishna described his Australasian tour as "much too much". He'd been ill in Melbourne and had to cancel visits to Brisbane. Christchurch and Dunedin. Rajagopal had returned to Europe from Sydney and Krishna said he would have to take a good rest back in California in July as he couldn't go on the way he had been. There'd been more questions and discussion this tour, as he had developed more of a discussion-style for public talks, for more direct and individual contact and to link his ideas with the "actual" in life. Patwardhan had written a review of the changes that were taking place in Krishnamurti's lecture style in the April issue of the *Star* newsletter. Certain words or phrases, such as "spirituality", "love" or "emotion" acted like drugs as they carried fixed and conventional ideas, so Krishnamurti avoided them, he said. Other words, such as "relationship" or "spontaneity" he invested with "fresh" significance, Patwardhan wrote. The focal point of Krishnamurti's discussions was always the same – the individual in his [or her] environment – but as no two discussions were the same, they had a quality of dynamism, he said. It was important not to give the mind the satisfaction to which it was accustomed. He said that according to Krishnamurti, psychological conflict could only be understood when the mind ceased to crave a solution. As a result of this perpetual variety in what Krishnamurti said in public discussions, he needed to be alert; he could not rely on hackneyed speeches, memorised and delivered without a genuine mood of intellectual investigation. As a result he would become exhausted. He had already been warned by a traditional Vaidya doctor in India that he must take a rest from public speaking for three months to recover from the flu he'd had in Bombay. At the end of the New Zealand talks, Krishna had a little respite with his friends, the Tidswells, in the hills behind Auckland, relishing the lush forest with its Kauri pines, tree ferns and palms, where he was free to go tramping without fear of encountering snakes or panthers. Krishna thought New Zealand was a beautiful country but the people showed an amazing ignorance about India.[75]

Having articulated as well as he could the mysteries of the mind, in June Krishnamurti returned to Ojai to explore further the mysteries of the heart. The summer of 1939 was spent with Rosalind and Radha in a palatial home belonging to friends in Santa Barbara, while Rajagopal was in Europe. The Huxleys visited often, and Bertrand Russell visited at least once. Maria Huxley wrote to a friend of Krishna that he was charming, amusing and so simple, and that he must suffer when treated as a prophet".[76]

That summer Rosalind again found she was pregnant. She considered keeping the baby, as the threat of cancer suggested by doctors after the birth of Radha was no longer raised. But as she was then aged 36, not young for undertaking a pregnancy, she was "partly testing" Krishna for his reaction when she told him her feelings about wanting to continue with the pregnancy. She said he didn't think it was a good idea to have the baby, so once again she went off on her lonely bus ride to have an abortion, and he was as loving and solicitous as ever when she returned.[77]

Another sad event occurred when Krishna's friend, the Indian patriot VC Patwardhan, died at the end of August 1939 of a brain tumour which doctors said he'd been suffering for perhaps a couple of years. On a trip to San Francisco, he had a fever and doctors did not know what caused it until, on his return to Hollywood, the symptoms became acute and his spinal fluid was examined. Krishna and Rosalind were with him the last few days of his life, when he was in a coma, while Rajagopal, back from warring Europe, was still in New York. Krishna cabled the news of Patwardhan's death to his brother in India and communications were difficult due to the onset of war. Patwardhan was cremated in early September and Krishna wrote to Dwarkanath that he was really distressed by his death. The knowledge that thousands of people were being killed in warfare in Europe provided a pessimistic background for any personal loss. Krishna commented that it was appalling to think of being told in India the previous year that England's trouble was India's opportunity, and he wondered whether the United States would stay out of the conflict.[78]

For Krishna, the declaration of war by England was a sorry, "nonsensical" path and, being a pacifist, he did not want the madness to become cumulative. He believed that if India became independent and aided the violence being carried out by either England or Germany, this would not produce a happy world. He felt it would be disastrous for India to become a militaristic nation. Was his philosophy simplistic? Certainly from his safe haven in the United States he could afford to be philosophical. Lutyens maintains that Krishna was never violent and, if attacked, would probably not even have defended himself as a physical reflex. Krishna wrote to Dwarkanath that it was only "unmilitarized" individuals who could create a decent world.[79]

Krishna saw his other old friend. Jinarajadasa. in Santa Barbara and Ojai that summer. They had long talks but avoided controversial subjects such as ownership of the schools. Krishna reported that Jinarajadasa had the difficulty of travelling back to India in December, when shipping was on stand-by for war alert, and he had also rented a house for the Esoteric Section of the Society in London. Jinarajadasa would see out most of the war in London, enduring the risk of bombing raids, caught away from his homeland by his loyalty to the cause of Theosophy.[80]

Meanwhile, by the end of the year the English pacifists holing up in California were able to enjoy favourable weather and a picnic or two. There are several accounts of one large picnic, which included the Huxleys, Krishnamurti, the Rajagopals, the Viertels, Bertrand Russell and Greta Garbo, in the setting of Tujunga Canyon, outside Los Angeles. Christopher Isherwood, who was working at Goldwyn's studio, made the observation that Garbo was very silly, gay and sympathetic. If she weren't Garbo he could be great friends with her. he felt. But she was isolated, always needing to cover her face with her hand or a hat for fear of being recognised. Her fame was so great it was for him like going about with someone wanted for murder. Huxley, whom Isherwood had only known a short while, he said he was getting to like better. Huxley made great efforts to be pleasant but was "so very very donnish". Bertrand Russell seemed to Isherwood a typical English aristocratic eccentric but he didn't have a chance to speak to him. On the subject of eccentricity, Isherwood's impression of Krishnamurti was that he was most unassuming and must have "disliked being a Messiah". Isherwood described Krishna as "a slight, sallow little man with a scrubby chin and rather bloodshot eyes, whose face bore only faint traces of the extraordinary beauty he must have had as a boy". He said Krishnamurti never talked in ordinary company about philosophy or religion. Isherwood also claimed that Heard had said that Krishnamurti got violently upset about trifles, such as catching a train, and showed little inward calm. He didn't impress Isherwood as Prabhavananda did but Krishna did have "a kind of simple dignity which was very touching" - Isherwood gave Krishna credit for refusing "to become a god". Isherwood said that Garbo had been anxious to meet Krishnamurti, being "naturally drawn to prophets", and had gone to the picnic in the belief that it would be just a few people. Salka Viertel, according to Isherwood, said Garbo was unhappy, restless and frightened, wanting to be told the secret of life in one lesson. She and Krishnamurti were sat next to each other but they hardly spoke together and Isherwood thought they were both scared. Isherwood went on to describe the antics the party got up to, digging a small pit under the forestry authority's high wire fence, joking that they might have been in a "concentration camp", and then splitting up into pairs and small groups to get under the wire and trespass through the forest. Isherwood took his place with Garbo and on the way back Garbo pulled down her wide hat brim when they ran into a forest ranger who was collecting firewood for his cabin. He didn't seem to care that they were trespassing so it was something of an anti-climax. But Berthold Viertel was pulled up by another ranger who fined him for smoking in a fire hazard area. Much ado about nothing – not even enough for a puffed up screenplay, but Isherwood was enchanted enough by Garbo's fame and acting out her elusiveness, to detail the encounter in his diary.[81]

Screenwriter Anita Loos's account of the picnic included a preliminary discussion about vegetarianism and Krishnamurti and Rajagopal's Brahmin sensibilities which meant they had to go and buy new utensils as the Indians could not eat out of cooking pots.[82]

It was all light-hearted fun, typical of the aimless pursuits of the Hollywood set. As Krishnamurti so often said, "What a strange world" - in which politicians in his old homeland weighed up the question of support for their Imperialist oppressors against Fascism while in Krishna's new home, the cradle of the "free world", life was lived as if in a Hollywood dream.

Chapter 8

Relationships

God is. That is the primordial fact. It is in order that we may discover this fact for ourselves, by direct experience, that we exist.

Aldous Huxley "Seven Meditations", Christopher Isherwood (ed) Vedanta for the Western World, Unwin, London, 1948 p 130.

Home on the farm. Krishna had chosen the place where Rosalind lived as his home back in the 1920s, although he continued to tour the world, making his denunciation of nationalism and nationality easier than it might have been for others who paid particular allegiance to place and government. But with the outbreak of World War II Krishna would be grounded at Ojai for its duration as shipping and international communications were under the control of military authorities – and in 1940 he had no idea how long the conflict would last. Physically Krishna was a South Indian. Geographically he was a resident of the United States. As regards nationality, he held a British passport. Krishna had not sought citizenship in the United States, and the task of having his residency permit renewed fell to Rajagopal, as Krishna's secretary.

In March 1940 Jinarajadasa wrote to Krishna from the house he had rented in Ovington Square, a few streets away from Harrods, to say that Rajagopal had told their old friend, Miss Bright, that Krishna's permit to stay in the United States would expire in September, but he might yet be given an extension. Ever hopeful of personal intimacy, as well as public reconciliation between Krishna and the Theosophical Society, Jinarajadasa proposed that Krishna could go with him to India in the autumn if he faced immigration problems. What a sensation they would create arriving together, he suggested. He delighted in the consternation he imagined it would cause the press.[1]

Krishna's reaction to the war was unusual in the West. Although he called himself a pacifist, his view of non-violence was perhaps philosophically different from the understanding of most Westerners, steeped in an ethic derived from Christianity in which turning the other cheek was based on a moral conviction about the nature of being 'good'. In the face of statistics about numbers killed, ships sunk and bombing carried out, he adhered to his view of a need for radical, fundamental change within individuals to bring about a cessation of conflict, both within and without. He acknowledged that change in the individual consciousness was a long process but it was the only way – superficial change would not suffice, he told Dwarkanath Telang in India.[2] The repetition of this view was little consolation to the millions who lost loved ones fighting Fascism - but few heard Krishna's cry in the comparative wilderness of Ojai. One person who remained a great friend but was upset by his views was Lady Emily. Mary Lutyens writes that her mother went through the Blitz and lost family members in fighting, and Krishna's pacifism "irritated" her. The feeling was undoubtedly stronger than this.[3]

Krishna must have gained an extension of his residency in the United States because the matter of residency came up again in 1941. Krishna's Hollywood friend, Sidney Field, says that Krishna had had extensions to his visas granted without difficulty up until late in 1941 when "certain elements" in the Immigration Department opposed it. He says they were "no doubt influenced by critical reports from FBI men who had stood watchfully under the oak trees the previous year listening to Krishnaji propound his anti-war views". Field says Krishna suggested on the phone that it would be helpful if, as the Costa Rican consul in Los Angeles, Field could support Krishna's application with an affidavit. Krishna wrote formally to Field to request his assistance, saying he was really very sorry to bother him. Field wrote directly to the "Immigration Authorities", referring to his own father, who had been an upstanding businessman of Vermont, as having helped Krishnamurti set up his centre in Ojai.

Field's character reference claimed "Southern California was indeed fortunate in having a place where a man of the moral and spiritual stature of Mr. Krishnamurti could come and express his ideas". The extension was granted and Krishna was able to stay in Ojai for the duration of WWII.[4]

Lutyens maintains that in making a visa application in April 1942, Krishna was unperturbed by the prospect of having to return to India. She suggests that he might have wanted to get away from a "claustrophobic" atmosphere in Ojai, although she gives no evidence of what he found claustrophobic. Krishna's personal relations with Rosalind seem to have been harmonious during this period. He had been with Rosalind to Martha's Vineyard in Massachusetts in October 1940, staying with a friend at Seven Gates Farm, on land held jointly by a number of people who had agreed to keep a large part of it wild. He also travelled with "the Rajagopals" to the Sequoia National Park, about 250 miles north of Ojai in the summer of 1941. Krishna was kept under surveillance by the FBI, who sent an agent to Ojai to ask him why he took so many walks and whether he met anyone, the questions purportedly prompted by fears that there was a plot to assassinate President Roosevelt. Perhaps the claustrophobia Lutyens referred to was caused by this security surveillance. The FBI did hold information on dates of his arrivals in the country through the 1920s and 1930s. In any case, Krishna must have been considered as offering no security threat and in November 1941 he was granted a "long" extension to stay. Even so, in 1943 the FBI kept a file on Krishna concerning a Brazilian writer, C. Lustoza de Lemos, who confirmed the spread of Krishna's teachings in Brazil and neighbouring countries, and "pacifist activities in the Argentine inspired by Krishnamurti". In 1945 the FBI referred to a belief that the Star Publishing Company might be "distributing literature favourable to the subject's pro-Nazi organization in Brazil" but decided to close the case. Clearly the implication had been that if you were a pacifist you were opposing Allied involvement in the war, ergo you were pro-Nazi. Krishna's FBI file remained active until at least the end of March 1945, when an agent reported that Krishnamurti was a citizen of British India and a Hindu religious leader believed to be the reincarnation of Jesus Christ, but that credit and criminal investigations had turned up nothing on him.[5]

Aside from the security surveillance, Rosalind herself had written to a friend in 1938 that she wanted very much to take Radha to India to live where she could attend a famous traditional dance school run by Udai Shankar. Rajagopal was said not to be keen on the idea but perhaps Krishna's lack of concern about the prospect of living in India might be traced to Rosalind's interest in living there.[6]

Radha remembers her childhood at Ojai as a treasured realm. She was an only child in a family of three adults and she saw nothing irregular about this at the time. In fact she says that all three disdained conventional respectability. A strong memory of her earliest years was of Krishna – whom she called 'Krinsh' – laughing with her mother in a world of joy and gentleness on holiday in Carmel. She doesn't remember her father's visits there but recalls the image of Krishna rubbing cream into her mother's face as he sat on the edge of her bed. In Carmel they had adjacent rooms and he would climb from his balcony to hers at night. In Ojai Rajagopal was often absent from family life, rising late morning and working long into the night. Krishna would bring Rosalind flowers in the mornings and a single rose on her birthday. He told Radha she shouldn't smell a rose before giving it to someone as this would detract from the gift. Family dinners were fairly formal, Krishna sitting at one end of the table and her mother the other, giving up her seat to visitors such as Aldous Huxley or another close friend, Robert Logan. Radha doesn't remember her father ever occupying an end seat. After dinner they might play poker dice or *Monopoly* and Radha says Krishna must have liked the game or he would not have played. Rosalind was an excellent player and one game when Beatrice Wood was present stands out as Rosalind's triumph in taking all the players' real estate and bankrupting Krishna. He would never have played chess, Radha said, as he preferred games that needed no thinking. Perhaps she meant that he avoided the kind of rigorous thinking or even determination needed to compete against an opponent to win. At nine o'clock Krishna would check his Patek Philippe watch and go off to his house next door, *Pine Cottage*, for the night. Yet Radha depicts Krishna as a great playmate in other respects, pretending shock or surprise and joining in the game when she hid in a tree to throw a bucket of water on his head. The strong bond between them was weakened, however, over an incident when she went swimming in a reservoir without permission and confided to him about the adventure. Radha says he promised not to tell but broke his word, passing the information on to her mother. Radha felt betrayed and lost her trust in him, in future turning to Rajagopal for advice with any personal problem, particularly in adolescence.[7]

In May 1940 Rosalind's mother died; this old woman named Sophia, who had advised her daughter to leave Krishna and go away with her husband to save her marriage, would no longer be there as a backstop for Rosalind. Over the several weeks during which Sophia's health declined, Aldous and Maria Huxley visited Rosalind, who with her sister Erma, was nursing the dying woman in her home in Hollywood. After Sophia's death Rosalind took a break with Rajagopal and Radha in the mountains of Sequoia National Park – the first of a number of summers spent there during the war years. Radha says that Krishna accompanied her mother and herself most years, with Rajagopal visiting for just a few days towards the end of their holidays.[8]

By 1941 the Huxleys had become firm friends with Krishna, Rosalind and Rajagopal. Before Aldous signed up with MGM to write a screenplay of *Pride and Prejudice* he was agitated about whether to take the job as it seemed unfair for him to earn so much money in California while his family and friends suffered the hardship of war in Britain. Anita Loos advised him to take the money and send most of it to England and Krishna also gave good advice, as Maria wrote to Rosalind afterwards to thank Krishnaji and tell him he was a great help. Maria also refers to a picnic "dans un bosquet d'eucalyptus sur l'herbe succulente" in

1940 with their friends, Chris Isherwood. Gerald Heard, Peggy Kiskadden, the Rajagopals, Krishnamurti, their little girl and two geese, and her goats.[9]

In 1941 Maria Huxley was distraught over her family's dire situation, in need of basic foodstuffs in occupied France. Should she try to bring them to America, or leave them there in distress, and if they came, should she ask Aldous to support them, she wondered? She said she was close to tearing out her heart – Aldous was feverishly lost in finishing a book, Gerald Heard was too busy preaching to help her, and Krishnamurti was "full of sympathy" but couldn't make her decisions for her. She also wrote in July 1941 about going to Rosalind's for the weekend. Rosalind and Krishnamurti and the children (probably a reference to Radha and her cousin) had been away for a month and Maria said she had missed them greatly. "Her blue innocent eyes…" was her comment about Rosalind. In another letter in July, to Isherwood, she described the family as "those poor Hindous" staying in a cabin in Yosemite, all in one cabin. Rosalind cooked and cleaned, Rajagopal was irritated by the close quarters and Krishna spent his time in the woods, except to send his "earthly body to dry the dishes". As Maria described it, the whole situation was "gloomy" as the children were not well but could not be given cod liver oil as they were vegetarian. Krishna was waiting on certain documents from India needed for immigration. Maria must have got some version of these events from Rajagopal who was at her place for lunch that day.[10]

The families' mutual contact remained close. Huxley wrote to "Krishnaji" in March 1941 to say how much he got out of Krishna's recent book, particularly the dialogues between questioners and Krishna at the end of each talk.[11] Huxley said it went to work so "delicately and yet so powerfully". He had often thought, he said, that the most valuable religious and philosophic literature was found not in formal treatises but in "letters of spiritual direction" in which the writer answered specific questions. He suggested that Krishnamurti could provide something "extremely valuable – records of real cases" which could remain anonymous.

> Such records would show the thing, not as a theory abstracted from reality, but alive and in action - not pickled in alcohol, which is the fate of philosophies when they become systematic, but running about in its native habitat.[12]

Huxley believed Krishnamurti could make something "very wonderful" from this style of writing. He said both Maria and he had got a great deal from the book – they had read it aloud.

There's no question that Huxley's opinion would have greatly influenced Krishna and Rajagopal and it's not difficult to draw a parallel between this particular advice and the series publication, *Commentaries on Living*, the first volume of which was published in 1956. Huxley may also have provided an impetus for Krishnamurti's later publication by the mainstream press, as Rajagopal approached Gollancz with an attractive proposal to publish, offering to buy any unsold copies at the end of the financial year.[13]

The Huxleys visited Ojai often by the mid-40s, sharing a love of animals and plants and at one period an interest in vegetarianism, and their mutual pacifism creating a strong bond. Aldous had outlined his attitude to armaments in *An Encyclopaedia of Pacifism* published in 1937 in which he said the desire of arms manufacturers to make profits was a standing menace to world peace. He elaborated his pacifist views in *Science, Liberty and Peace*, written in the spring and summer of 1945 and published in 1946. This book is a treatise of the way science is applied to technological centralisation and war, and it carries a dire warning that any government that enjoys a monopoly of political and economic power is "exposed to almost irresistible temptations to tyranny".[14]

No doubt both families felt blessed to be living in the relative affluence of America while others were experiencing such hardship during the war. Radha describes how Rosalind had an idea to accommodate British orphan children in unused *Star* buildings in Ojai but the British government decided the sea voyage would be hazardous. Rosalind then turned her hand to the heavy manual work required for close to self-sufficiency on the farm, her motive not to be a burden on the world's food supply during the war years, as well as contributing to CARE food donations. She had a farm hand, Willie Weidemann, to manage the place, while Krishna worked with her in the vegetable garden, cleaned the chicken coop, shovelled cow pats and hosed out the barn, even though he was said to be 'in retreat'. Radha's chore was milking a cow. Rajagopal, by contrast, took no part in farming, keeping himself occupied in his office. Rosalind produced butter and cheese from their cows' milk in a butter churn given her by Maria Huxley. Frieda Lawrence, who kept in touch with the Huxleys, wrote to Rosalind to say she'd heard the small-scale dairy production was a success. Frieda also made a comparison between Krishna's refusal to be bound by the ideas of "dumb theosophists" and her deceased husband's view, saying that all "big" men had the same source of vision although they expressed it individually.[15]

Throughout the period that Krishna lived at Ojai, and despite his statement that he did not want followers, devotees would take up residence nearby in order to be close to their idol. Radha writes about single ladies who would discreetly take a cabin in the valley for the summer, happy to catch a glimpse of Krishna on his way to the post office. They would buy produce from the Rajagopal garden in the belief that it was blessed - the eggs that Krishna collected, the cows' milk, apples and oranges off the tree that he had touched. Krishna laughed at them and took pleasure in tending his roses, the pride of his garden.[16]

There might be considered to be a fine line of distinction between loving followers and obsessive devotees, and all his life Krishna had what were referred to as "nuts" congregating about him. Rajagopal commented on it during the Latin American trip. Radha writes about "unbalanced" people, most of whom were harmless but some creating problems, mostly, she maintains, because Krishna did not deal with them decisively initially. One woman, for instance, who accused Rosalind of having a skeleton in her closet, would walk along the road in front of the house at night chanting Krishna's name. Another sent anonymous threatening letters to Rosalind which resulted in legal action banning the woman from the state of California.[17]

Perhaps part of the problem for those who took undue notice of Krishna was the confusion that could arise over what might be viewed as his dogmatism over experiencing self-awareness. He was unequivocal in his advice about what to do for self-awareness – and that was essentially to notice every thought and feeling you experienced - while at the same time claiming that all 'methods' were doomed to failure. Mary Lutyens says that Krishna gave no talks between 1940 and 1944, as he was on 'retreat'. Lutyens believed Krishna went very "deeply" into himself over this 'retreat' period, even though he met many friends and gave personal interviews, since the talks of 1944, 1945 and 1946 were concerned with "self-knowing".[18] In the third talk in 1944, Krishna advised the audience to try to write down <u>every</u> "thought-feeling" and see how difficult it was. The next year someone from the audience claimed he had done so for several months but was none the wiser. Thought must cease to condemn, deny, compare, judge or seek comfort, Krishnamurti responded, because that interrupted the flow of "thought-feelings". Understanding was only in the present, he said. But how to stay in the present? Krishna never gave an answer, apart from an exhortation to be meditative, but not practise any accepted or taught form of meditation. Use "right" meditation he said, which gave the activity an imprimatur of sanctity but explained nothing. It left many 'followers' with dubious advice about checking their every thought or feeling, which might only lead to nervous agitation.[19] Sidney Field writes that Krishna kept aside a voluminous file of "nut" mail which was a great source of amusement. One time when Field stayed overnight alone with Krishna at Ojai, he said he was so keyed up by Krishna's "roaring" kundalini he had to go out for a long walk, because if he did not he thought he'd go out of his mind. It reminded him of one follower called Fenn Germer who had had a nervous breakdown and been admitted to a mental institution. When Field told Krishna the next morning, Krishna laughed and said the trouble with Germer was that he had repressed his sexual urge. No doubt he was not alone among followers in doing this, as many

Theosophists believed they should live celibate lives. At one stage of his life Field himself, while tramping in the hills near where he lived found, as he sat quietly in a favourite spot, that he experienced something he called a joyous "Presence" which came upon him regularly every afternoon. It came in rhythmic waves as long as he maintained what he called "passive" vitality, trying to quieten his restless mind and emotions. At its height it was a superb "trip", he said. Krishna had told him some time before, in answer to a question about whether he was in constant touch with the reality called "Liberation", that there was no separation. He said he had taken a long road to find simple "Union" and was an example to others – since he had "attained", others could too. It was a message which carried echoes of the words of that great spiritual sage, Jesus Christ, who offered salvation through the example of his life and crucifixion. Some years after Field's own daily "spiritual" experiences he told Krishna about them. Krishna's reaction was that Field was probably close to a breakthrough and it was a pity he just didn't let it happen, instead of being anxious.[20]

Field reports another conversation with "Krishnaji" about sex. Asceticism as a goal was destructive, Krishna said, and there was a biological need for sex. If you recognised that sex was simply energy, you could see that a person needed to conserve energy to reach a goal. When they considered the question of DH Lawrence's view that 'liberation' was only possible "momentarily" through sex, Krishna laughed and said that 'liberation' was sex inverted.[21]

In 1942, Rajagopal moved the *Star* office from Hollywood to Ojai, having a 'fire-proof' room and office built next to Krishna's nightly abode, *Pine Cottage*. Radha says Rajagopal had no inclination to move into the "ménage" in the main house with Rosalind. He would go to dinner there but never lunch. Sometimes Krishna would take him a breakfast tray. According to Radha there were signs of Rajagopal's discontent with Krishna – he never liked being referred to as Krishnamurti's secretary or manager (although he acted in that capacity as well as editing talks) nor being asked personal details about Krishnaji by devotees. But he put up with it, even when he had to take the blame for Krishna's speeding while driving or was considered by Krishna as the 'bagman' since Krishna could not sully his own hands by touching the filthy lucre of donations.[22]

In one capacity or another, Rajagopal was in charge of a range of significant financial assets. The war-time FBI file on Krishnamurti refers to a person vouched for by the stockbrokers, EF Hutton, who was "a man of considerable money, holding investments in seventy-five to one hundred different high-grade US stocks such as US Steel, Standard Oil, etc". His average bank balance was reported to be over $1,000 in 1945. When interviewed by the Retail Merchants' Credit Association, the "secretary to Krishnamurti" and his wife, who reportedly each received permanent life trusts of $1,000 per year, declined to disclose the figures.[23]

By 1943 Radha was aged twelve and attending a private school in the Ojai Valley. Krishna had been a devoted helpmate to her during her childhood, walking her to the school bus stop but keeping at a distance so as not to embarrass her. He wrote to Lady Emily in August 1943 that Radha was probably tall for her age and intelligent and considerate, all qualities he found admirable. Radha seems not to have been conscious of the unusual marital arrangement of the Rajagopals. She says Rajagopal enjoyed that part of his life he could keep separate from Krishna and Rosalind. She also recognised that despite some quarrelling, Rajagopal retained his strong affection for Krishna. But she was aware of Rajagopal experiencing feelings of isolation and pessimism, which she partly attributed to the war, a pessimism that was felt generally.[24]

Rosalind, for instance, showed fear and confusion over the prospect of the United States entering the war. She was afraid, she wrote in 1940, that movements starting up in Europe could easily lead Americans into the conflict. She was concerned that people were so taken up with "outside" chaotic problems they had no time to understand what "living" meant, she said. By

February 1941 she felt that, politically, everything was more and more "confused" and the more a person tried to have an "open" mind, the more everything went right through it and the person was left with nothing at all. The language is woolly but the sentiment is strong. Rosalind felt powerless in the face of the great war machine. After America's entry into the conflict with the bombing of Pearl Harbour in December 1941, Rosalind advised a friend that same month that if she was coming to the East Coast she had better stay with them in Ojai as the world was mad. In many ways Rosalind was living a blessed life at that time – working hard manually but psychologically comforted within a pocket of pacifist intellectuals at odds with the harshness of the larger political realm.[25]

The last camp in Europe was at Ommen in 1938 (the last ever held there as it was taken over by Nazis for internment) and Krishna had not been able to travel due to war restrictions, but he resumed his public talks in Ojai in 1944.[26] They were published in India in 1945 by Krishnamurti Writings Inc (KWINC - a "charitable" organisation which had succeeded the Star Publishing Trust). In June 1946 Krishnamurti signed a statement declaring KWINC to be the central Foundation for his work throughout the world. At that stage Krishna and Rajagopal were the two main trustees who had the power to appoint another three.[27]

Krishnamurti's 1945 and 1946 talks were published in an abridged form in 1947 by KWINC, and Krishnamurti wrote a preface, saying he had written the talks down immediately after delivering them, with revision later. These were the last talks that Krishna revised or helped to revise. Krishna wrote to Lady Emily in June 1945 to say he had taken discussion groups in Hollywood and written them down himself. The Ojai Sunday talks were also under way, with a crowd visiting in spite of petrol rationing. As well, discussion groups were held on Wednesdays, transcripts of which Krishna also wrote out himself.[28]

One woman who attended the 1944 talks for the first time would become a major figure in Krishnamurti's later life. Mary

Taylor, who would later marry film producer Sam Zimbalist and be widowed by 1958, was in an unhappy period of her life in 1944 and was deeply moved by what Krishnamurti said in the public talks and in a personal interview she had with him.[29]

The horrors of WWII provided an ever-present background for the smaller efforts at peace and goodwill made by pacifists seeking refuge in California. Krishna's correspondence indicates the fragmentary information that the press reported on world affairs and how events in Europe were of such horrific dimensions they affected the lives of anyone with connections there. The Vigevenos were able to get away from Holland to California to save their own lives but more than forty members of their family were killed in Nazi gas chambers.[30] Krishna wrote to Dwarkanath Telang in India in 1940 that the camp in Ommen was lost to them and they were trying to sell all the land they had at Ojai except that necessary for public talks. As it was so difficult to raise any money in India they would have to close the office and rent out *Vasanta Vihar* in Madras. In this wounded state, Krishnamurti's organisation in India was no match for the Theosophical Society, and Sanjeeva Rao signed an agreement between the Society and the Rishi Valley School Trust. It would not be the end of Krishnamurti's plans for the Rishi Valley School however, as the Trust, by 1945, had still not been legally transferred to the Society, remaining a separate body. Krishna replied to Rama Rao in July 1941 that it was an "ugly" business and everyone was going through sad times. Further details of the malleability of accounts and a lack of funds and direction at the school in the early 1940s would emerge later.[31]

Krishna received another spate of correspondence from his old flame, Helen Nearing in 1944. Writing from a Florida sanitarium, she said she'd had a minor operation and while chanting mantras to ease the pain, she had strongly felt Nitya's presence. She wrote to Krishna for old friendships' sake, she said, and there was nothing calculated in it. She didn't deny that years before she had "suffered agonies of bewilderment and desolation" when she felt him "drawing away". But life goes on, she said, and she drew a pretty picture of her life in the woods of Vermont with her husband, Scott. Krishna was moved to write a letter that happened to arrive on her birthday, sent on from Florida to her, back home in Vermont. She sent him a quote from Shakespeare, "When forty winters shall besiege..." and declared that her husband, who had returned from a trip to the Mid-West, was the most energetic guy she knew, and he was sixty. In April she wrote again to say that since contact with Krishna, things had speeded up and she was convinced she was "in touch with something tremendously real". "Communications from Nitya and Master Morya are piling up," she wrote. She asked for her last letter and the "slips of paper" on which she'd written accounts of what had occurred, to be returned to her. She wondered whether Krishna would like to visit them and judge for himself. Her next letter a week later was written en route to Florida to visit her father who was very ill in hospital, so she suggested that if Krishna did intend to visit her in Vermont, he should put it off until after mid-May. She added, enigmatically, that she'd been told to tell him that, "the child will be born November 1st". Krishna replied just as soon as he got the letter, politely and decisively putting paid to any supernatural connection between them. Since she took her automatic writing very seriously, and to prevent any misunderstanding, he said he wanted to emphasise what he'd been saying for years. Without deep self-knowledge, the messages she'd been receiving were dangerous and misleading; and with deep self-knowledge it had no value for it did not exist, he explained. She had a difficult problem on her hands, he said. Since she'd invited him to visit, he hoped she didn't mind that he wrote so candidly, but he thought it best to tell her what he thought. A week later Helen had the last word. She thanked him for returning her letters and for what was not an easy letter to write, she imagined. But the curious thing from her point of view was that he hadn't had much success in working on her to be "alert" yet now she was "continuously cognisant of high purpose", and it was of her "own making & feeling & determination". She thanked him for his friendly greeting to her father – he'd died the day before.[32]

The Huxleys had moved to Llano in the Mojave Desert in 1942 where Aldous wrote a book about the Bates' method for better eyesight called *The Art of Seeing.* He practised eye exercises and experienced a remarkable improvement in his sight. Krishna also took up the method, continuing to do eye exercises all his life, and never needing glasses, according to Mary Lutyens. The Huxleys enjoyed their desert home and the incessant writer in Aldous, who was working on *Time Must Have A Stop*, published in October 1944, even gave way to a little physical interest – in picking figs from their tree and drying tomatoes outside his terrace. The couple remained in touch with the Ojai group, with correspondence mostly between Maria and Rosalind, and in 1943 the Huxleys took a pied-à-terre back closer to the coast, in Beverley Hills. Their friendship is evident in October 1944, for instance, when Huxley wrote to "Krishnaji" to say how much he looked forward to seeing him at Llano, and that he and Maria hoped he would stay a long time. Krishna had less contact with Gerald Heard but did visit Heard's "monastery" in Trabuca in 1944. Heard thanked him for the visit, and observant of Krishna's wish for privacy, explained that although some people arrived unexpectedly last time, he could always arrange complete silence for him if he wished.[33]

In March 1945 Huxley wrote to Krishna about a troublesome person who had sent him an extraordinary letter denouncing Krishna. The letter had included a "psychiatric report" which tried to prove that Krishna was suffering an advanced form of "dementia praecox". Huxley dispensed with the correspondent efficiently but was concerned enough to let Krishna know. He returned the report to the writer, Miss Helen Boardman, saying it was of no interest to him. "Though written in elaborately medical language," the report was "pretty silly" even to someone who did not know Krishna personally. It was deplorable that the "wretched" woman should bother to send the report to strangers, Huxley said. Then he turned to more important matters – they'd had six inches of snow at Llano, and with the sun shining brightly, the effect was wonderful. He'd also finished his latest book and got it off to the publisher. And finally, he asked Krishna to tell Rosalind to keep Radha's outgrown clothes and other household rags so they could send them to family in France who were suffering great hardship.[34]

On 14 August 1945, the end of the war just declared, Maria Huxley expressed to a friend the sentiments the whole group of pacifists must have shared at the news that, "Le jour de Paix est arrivé".

> Everybody was smiling - or crying. There is much grief made harder to bear by this exuberance of deliverance. All the shops closed spontaneously.[35]

That month, with a new-found vitality, the Huxleys made a rather sudden decision to buy a "hideous little house" at Wrightwood, about twenty miles from Llano in a small mountain resort not far from Mt Baldy, outside Los Angeles. Huxley wrote to 'my dear Krishnaji' that, as he had told Rosalind the other day, he said, if Krishna wanted a retreat in the mountains, either alone or with Rajagopal, he could use the first cabin they'd bought there which was available. For those who, "unlike Americans", could still make use of their legs, he said, there were beautiful walks, and "splendid" panoramas just a five-mile drive away. Huxley loved the place but Maria preferred the desert. "Please like it when you come," Maria wrote to Rosalind, of the house not yet connected to electricity nor insulated, set among pinewoods and sage brush. Maria felt remote – one time she waited on Krishna's arrival to drive her into town to the garage. In another letter Maria said their "dearest friend Krishnamurti" would be staying there during June 1946. Maria's affection for Krishna can be seen in a teasing letter she wrote, thanking him for some roses he'd given her. Their scent was so strong she and Aldous had decided there was a "sur-natural" perfume about them, she joked.[36]

Huxley's *The Perennial Philosphy* was published in September 1946 and sold 23,000 copies which pleased Aldous as a sign of interest in the subject of mysticism. He wrote to a friend that its greatest merit was that about forty percent of it was not written by him but by "a lot of saints, many of whom were also men of genius". Among them were Taoists, Buddhists, Christian mystics – Lao Tsu, Asoka, Plotinus and St John of the Cross, Francois de Sales, Eckhart, St Teresa, Boehme, George Fox, William Law, Jesus Christ. He wanted to show what the best and most intelligent humans had agreed on over the last 3,000 years, and he insisted on including on the 'blurb', which he rewrote, that he had made no attempts to "found a new religion".[37]

Chapter One of *The Perennial Philosophy* is titled "That Thou Art", a translation of the Upanishadic teaching '*tat tvam asi*'. Huxley writes that the doctrine of the 'Perennial Philosophy' belongs to autology rather than psychology – "to the science, not of the personal ego, but of that eternal Self in the depth of particular individualized selves, and identical with, or at least akin to, the divine Ground".[38]

Huxley said someone who wished to know the "That' which is 'thou' could set to work in three ways: to look inwards and die to the self in reasoning, the self in willing and the self in feeling; to look to 'thou's and try to see their essential unity with God; and to do both of the above. He quoted from Shankara's *Viveka-Chudamani* ('The Crest-Jewel of Wisdom') passages such as:

> The Atman is the Witness of the individual mind and its operations. It is absolute knowledge ...
>
> Supreme, beyond the power of speech to express, Brahman may yet be apprehended by the eye of pure illumination ...
>
> 'I am he who experiences.' This notion is the cause of bondage to conditional existence, birth and death. It can be removed only by the earnest effort to live constantly in union with Brahman. By the sages, the eradication of this notion and the craving for personal separateness is called Liberation.
>
> When a man follows the way of the world, or the way of the flesh, or the way of tradition (i.e. when he believes in religious rites and the letter of the scriptures as though they were intrinsically sacred), knowledge of Reality cannot arise in him.[39]

There's no question that these ontological questions were the substance of Huxley's long discussions with Krishnamurti, just as he engaged in debate with Isherwood and Heard on these very same matters, at the heart of the purpose of life. Huxley had written to Isherwood in 1942 that in some recent conversations he'd had with Krishna he had talked about his experiences in an illuminating way and these were better than books. Huxley was very much bound by his intellectual discrimination, yet he could see that it wasn't this faculty that most easily allowed one a view of 'the immortal'. Huxley's own view was that just as a child has direct awareness of God, so the habit of analytical thought was fatal to the intuitions of integral thinking. "A few people work their way out of the prevailing preoccupation with matter and through the prevailing habits of analytical thought into the direct experience of the spiritual Ground of things," he wrote in *The Perennial Philosophy*." Sidney Field describes Huxley and Krishna's philosophical and metaphysical discussions as lively. Krishna would make a general, sweeping statement, minimising the importance of intellect, and Huxley would rebut it quietly with an arsenal of historical and scientific evidence. "This, Krishnaji, isn't quite the way it happened," he would say. Field said these conversations were among the most fascinating debates he'd ever heard – Huxley "brilliant" and Krishna "a man with great feeling" for what he was saying. According to Radha, Krishna described Huxley's mind as like a "wastebasket" and, harsh as it might seem, perhaps Krishna was implying that Huxley's strong intellect was the very characteristic which prevented his attainment of direct experience of 'God'.[40]

Maria Huxley was beginning to be greatly interested in these spiritual questions too. She would write to a friend a few years later that pure "intellectuality" was as much an obstacle to spiritual concerns as anything else.

> *Savoir et pouvoir* – to know and to do – are two different things ...And we must look everywhere to find what we are looking for ... The Perennnial Philosophy is the most helpful ... And yet I've got to tell you what Krishnaji indefatigably repeats – that it is in ourselves that we shall find the answer if we know how to listen. Where Krishnaji doesn't give us any help is in learning to listen and how to prepare the ground. Krishnaji has so well understood the error of Theosophical directions by the ... Masters etc that he himself will indicate no system. And yet we are all so buffeted by the speed of living that it seems to me that a technique is necessary to eliminate the *fragmentation, the unnecessary tensions*, caused by the details of daily life.[41]

Meanwhile, Krishnamurti, who seemed to have all the answers, was tussling with his personal attachment to womanhood, principally in the form of Rosalind. In October 1944 he wrote to her from Ojai to say that when she returned he thought they all should meditate regularly together. He thought it would "quicken" mind and feelings so that, with "detachment", people could look at events, relationships and the whole environment about them. It was important to clear up "darkening clouds" and bring clarity, he said. The next month he wrote to her that as a person became older, without "wisdom", tendencies were exaggerated while finer qualities were submerged. That was the reason he suggested meditating, he said. Later in the month he proposed that Rosalind might need another holiday as she'd been looking after Radha who'd been ill.[42]

In an undated series of letters about this same time written in Sarobia, on the East Coast, Krishna tried once again to explain to Rosalind, and include her in, an understanding of the ecstasy he experienced in his mind, or simply, the joy of his thinking, of which she was an integral part.

He'd had two thoughts all day, he said, or rather, not two but one thought, in which she was included. It was a thought in which, if he penetrated deeply enough, he found an extraordinary sense of wholeness in which she was present too. But to refer to her sounded rather ridiculous, he said. He had felt so "lastingly" close that nothing could break it, though on the surface it might seem to be division. He felt like singing tonight as his heart was full. "Stay me with flagons ... sick of love, " he quoted again from the *Song of Songs*. Although the flame might appear dull, the churning went on without being seen, he said. And he told her he loved her, adding that it sounded absurd to write it. His love had no beginning and could have no end, he assured her.661

Krishna, Rosalind and Radha visited Sarobia in 1946 for his first public lectures there since 1940. Afterwards Krishna attended a discussion with some high-powered thinkers such as Erich Fromm and psychiatrist, Harry Stack Sullivan, organised by Dr Benjamin Weininger in Washington. The Krishnamurti Archives does not provide any record of these discussions but, according to Radha, Krishna tried to challenge these esteemed thinkers about their old conditioning and their attachment to a certain style of language. Radha, who was aged about fifteen at the time, says that Krishna found the sessions arduous. During their stay at the Weiningers, Krishna would go to Rosalind's room at night which his long-time lover considered indiscreet and which made her feel "uncomfortable".[44]

Radha's view is that Krishna was feeling desperate by now as he was no longer Rosalind's sole focus of attention. He, Rajagopal, Robert Logan, Louis Zalk and Aldous Huxley had encouraged her in the idea of establishing a school adjacent to Ojai, in the Happy Valley, a venture which had been first mooted when Annie Besant launched an appeal for $200,000 to buy land there in 1927. By the mid-1940s the mortgage was $90,000. A dedicated group had kept alive the idea for the school and the money was found to get it started. A retired philosophy professor from Vassar, Dr Guido Ferrando, had moved to Ojai and had ideas for a Socratic method of teaching, and so the nucleus to actually establish the school was formed, with the responsibility for its administration falling to Rosalind. The first year there were nine pupils at the co-educational, secondary school, their parents attracted to the gravitas that Krishnamurti and Aldous Huxley lent to the school as trustees. This small, pacifist, libertarian institution opened in September 1946, and the first students were accommodated in Rosalind's home, *Arya Vihara*. Soon afterwards Krishna fell ill with a kidney infection, and Rosalind, who had a broken ankle, with plaster up to her knee and on crutches, looked after him and the students, as well as administering the school. Krishna, who had intended to go to Australia early in 1947, had to postpone the trip. The duress for Rosalind was great, with Krishna refusing hospitalisation and medication. Maria and Aldous Huxley visited often to sit quietly and show their loving support, just as they had when Rosalind's mother was gravely ill. Radha remembers one starry night walking with Rajagopal who expressed great love for Krishna, saying their lives would be so strange and empty if he died. Radha believes Krishna and Rosalind's relationship underwent a significant change during this illness as she found his constant presence and needs taxing and looked forward to space and time apart from him.[45]

That time came the following year. After Indian independence in August 1947 all Indians with British passports were given the choice of retaining them or taking up Indian passports. Lutyens says that Krishna did not think much about it as he considered nationality an evil, yet he clearly took the decision to identify himself as an Indian. She says he subsequently regretted the change since travel for him as an Indian meant a greater need for visas in Europe.[46]

Krishna had kept in contact with his Indian friends although he had not been able to visit throughout the war. The 1940s would prove a decisive decade in the renewal of Krishna's bond with his native culture. Despite the fact that Krishna had ostensibly cut his links with the Theosophical Society, its President, Jinarajadasa, remained a loyal friend. In 1943 Jinarajadasa had been diligent in keeping Krishna informed of disclosures over authorship of *The Lives of Alcyone* in the *Canadian Theosophist* and his stout defence of Mrs Besant and Krishna. Jinarajadasa wrote to the editor of the *Canadian Theosophist* that, all those years before, Mrs Besant had ordered *The Lives* withdrawn from publication because Krishna had been nervous that he would be "ragged" if he got into Oxford. She had not withdrawn it out of fear over fraud by Leadbeater, he said, and maintained it was pure myth that Mrs Besant was the dupe of Leadbeater. He, Jinarajadasa, had seen her original drawings for the book *Occult Chemistry*. Jinarajadasa sent Krishna a copy of his letters to the editor and to the General Secretary of the Canadian Theosophical Society, warning Krishna that he might be asked what he knew of the affair.[46]

Their communication by post continued despite Krishna's distancing. In early 1944 Jinarajadasa referred to a letter Krishna had written the previous November complaining that

Jinarajadasa should be more "with" him. instead of "against" him. He wasn't against Krishna he said. but went only part of the way, not the whole way with him. Jinarajadasa knew a lot about the teachings of great teachers of the past, and he said Krishna's teachings in their intellectual "fundamentals" were not new, even though they had an infinitely attractive "newness" and sprang to life through him. But he did not go along with Krishna's "sneering" and depreciation of the Masters. Every night when Big Ben sounded nine o'clock and people concentrated on something good during one silent minute, Jinarajadasa would concentrate on Krishna. He dreaded that when peace finally came the old vice of greed would rise again, unless Krishna "entered" the scene. He had seen Krishna give out waves of love and knew the world was in need of the message to love neighbours and rivals. He had a vision of Krishna's possibilities. In 1916 he had even taken 'K' as his Masonic mark. "J'y suis, j'y reste," he concluded.[48]

Jinarajadasa wrote Krishna a moving description of his experience during an air raid in London – looking out at a square flooded with light from converging searchlights as a bomb hit eight blocks away and he read the *Encyclopaedia Brittanica*, especially a section on the French revolution, to keep his mind occupied.[49]

Late in 1944 Jinarajadasa wrote to Krishna explaining how he had been accepted for travel, before applications closed down for passage to India, by the High Commission of India in London. There was a waiting list of hundreds but he impressed on Krishna that he might be given priority if he were returning to his homeland. It had taken Jinarajadasa eight months to get a passage even with medical certificates confirming his arthritis and after his pressure on authorities to act. He suggested alternative routes, direct from America or from Australia, if Krishna wanted to return to India. Jinarajadasa painted a bleak picture of England's rigid control over some foodstuffs and he bemoaned the fact that potatoes were a penny a pound. At this time Krishna was making plans to travel to Australia and New Zealand in 1946. He had word that his old friend Rama Rao. who had been principal of the Rajghat School, died in November 1945. Rama Rao had TB, was nearly blind and had to remind Jinarajadasa of a promise he had made to him to look after him in case of need, out of respect for the memory of Mrs Besant and his loyalty to her. For the last six months of Rama Rao's life, Jinarajadasa paid 125 rupees a month so that the old man could be looked after in a sanatorium, as he was bedridden. By 1946 Krishna's Indian friends were all keyed up about their idol's expected visit to the subcontinent, following a trip to Australia, happy to pay his passage even in late-1945. Jinarajadasa warned Krishna what to expect from the press and suggested a basic kind of media release of background information, joking that, if asked, he would declare that the "Avatara" had arrived. Jinarajadasa made no end of fuss in trying to induce Krishna to mend fences between himself and Theosophists. After Jinarajadasa's re-election as President of the Society in February 1946, he sent a telegram welcoming Krishna back to Adyar, and over the following months, several letters explaining the renovations being undertaken and the accommodation waiting for Krishna there. In January 1946 he explained how it had come about that Sanjiva Rao had asked him to be President of the Rishi Valley Trust, to counteract Congress involvement, and that as there seemed to be no conflict between what was taught at the Theosophical school and the Rishi Valley Trust school, he was acceptable to Krishna's people. After all, Krishna had never given the "groundwork" of what true education should be, he said. In an emotional letter to Krishna the next day he described the sacred thread ceremony that had been performed for Sri Ram's son at the *Bharata Samaj* temple Krishna had inaugurated in 1925. He reminisced about the young Krishna's suggestion, in his "unregenerate" days, to have the prayers of all major religions recited at ceremonies every day. Jinarajadasa had immediately organised prayers to be printed, in order of chronological age: Hindu, Zoroastrian, Jain, Judaic, Buddhist, Christian, Islamic and Sikh, followed by four lines composed by Annie Besant about the hidden life vibrant in every atom. The next day

– January 11 – was the anniversary of Krishna's 'Initiation' in 1910 and the establishment of his order in 1911. "Never mind: if there is no one else. there is me who believes not only in the Masters but also in you," Jinarajadasa concluded. In May 1946 he sent Krishna a note about his birthday according to his horoscope, which was different from the date on his passport. In the same letter Jinarajadasa said he was "astonished" to find Krishna had become an incorporated society [KWINC], since Krishna had said he did not want to be labelled. Krishna's friends had certainly put him in a cage, he observed. Jinarajadasa reassured him that if it had been a matter of preserving copyright and earning money from his work, Jinarajadasa could have raised all the money needed and published the books free. He was disgruntled, he said, because he believed in Krishnamurti, not Krishnamurti 'Incorporated'. Later in the year Jinarajadasa said he'd heard that the Auckland Town Hall had been booked for Krishna in October and wanted to know when he might arrive in India. In Australia too, Krishnamurti 'followers' were getting ready for a vigorous round of dialogues, issuing a new pamphlet. *Voyage*, in plenty of time for the visit.[50]

By the time Krishna actually set off for India a year later than originally planned due to his illness, the expectations were high. Krishna hoped to create something "vital" and effective. He suggested to Rao Bahadur Madhavachariar, who was in charge of making all the travel arrangements, that he would fit in with whoever would put him up, in case Ratansi Morarji was not in a position to offer accommodation, as in years past, and not wanting to take up the offer of accommodation at the Theosophist headquarters. In 1947 Krishna held no talks in the springtime at Oak Grove. Ojai, nor any interviews, preferring to quietly restore his strength for his arduous travelling. He did try to get his message out to a sympathetic readership, however, as indicated by a letter from the Vedanta Society of Southern California in mid-1947. Christopher Isherwood's guru, Swami Prabhavananda, wrote to Isherwood with the news that Krishnamurti had sent a copy of one of his talks to be published in their magazine.

Rajagopal said Krishna had himself selected it. The Swami was amused to comment that he could not understand the talk but he thought people would like it "as long as they do not understand". The Swami also mentioned that the Huxleys had come to lunch and he had taken great care to give his whole attention to Maria since he'd heard that she was shy and avoided him, and as a result of his care she was quite at ease and they enjoyed themselves.[51]

In September 1947 Krishna sailed with Rajagopal to Southhampton, staying with Lady Emily en route to India, while Rajagopal remained in Europe about six months, perhaps not wanting to jeopardise his permanent residency in the United States with a return to India. Lady Emily was now aged seventy three, and three years a widow, while Krishna was fifty two. They had not seen each other for nine years but their bond remained extraordinarily close. This is clear from Lady Emily's conclusion to her memoir, *Candles in the Sun*, in which she described his visits in later life as the two of them sitting and holding hands, at peace with one another. She said that for her Krishna was unique – "the purest and most beautiful being she had ever come across, the perfect flower of humanity". However she did acknowledge in the book that back in 1913, when she wrote to her husband from Varengeville about her one purpose in life being to prepare for a World Teacher to manifest through Krishna, she was not conscious of the true nature of her feelings for him. She had spent ten years trying to sublimate a human love.[52]

Before leaving Ojai there must have been an understanding between not only Krishna and Rosalind but also Krishna and Rajagopal that their relationships were moving onto a different footing, or at least that Krishna would be away some time and the Rajagopals' security needed to be addressed. Krishna had been through a very severe illness and no doubt these concerns had been raised in the Rajagopals' minds at the time. So Krishna wrote a long, formal letter to Rajagopal in August 1947 outlining their relationship and administrative and property rights and responsibilities. Several times before starting out on long journeys he had written to Rajagopal, he said, to indicate his intentions regarding the activities with which they'd been associated for 25 years. It might have seemed unnecessary or even unfriendly to make such a testament, he wrote, but recognising that ambition and ill-will could creep into human activities, and to prevent future "misrepresentation", he was stating that in the event of his death, Rajagopal was to be in complete [underlined] control of KWINC and the teachings. KWINC would be the only legal body in charge of properties, including the Ommen Camp if it was returned to them. The sole purpose of KWINC was to maintain and spread the teachings, he said, and not for personal ambition. *Arya Vihara*, their home in Ojai, had been given to them personally by "Amma", Miss Dodge and one other person. It should be considered always as the place for Rajagopal, Rosalind, Radha and himself to live, he said, and was not for public use. If he died he hoped it would be their home for as long as the three of them were alive. He suggested that after all their deaths, it should become part of KWINC. Since Rajagopal had always, voluntarily, taken a vigorous and creative part in their activities, Krishna hoped Rajagopal would continue to act as President until his death or ill-health might prevent it. This was Krishna's last will and testament, he said, and he did not intend to write any future documents of this type. He added that he had made a separate formal will in respect of any personal property he might have at the time of his death, and Rajagopal was the executor and beneficiary of that will.[53]

Krishnamurti's correspondence to Rosalind in the year before his 1947 visit to India seemed as attentive and sentimental ever. But his life would change considerably as a result of his journey which lasted eighteen months. There he met a woman who had a considerable effect on his life, Nandini Mehta, and her sister, Pupul Jayakar, who would go on to become another of his biographers and a close friend. His relationship with Nandini was exceptional and would become the cause of much dissension both in India and back home in Ojai.[54]

Nandini's description, in her sister's Krishnamurti biography, of her own meeting with him is a moving account. She went with her father-in-law, Sir Chunilal Mehta, a distinguished industrialist in Bombay, to a discussion where Krishna sat, dressed in a long white *kurta*, in a room full of people. Krishna turned and looked at her "steadily" for a few seconds. Time stopped for her, she said. He continued talking. Then he turned back to her and looked "deep" into her eyes. Again time stood still. He continued with the discussion but she was by then totally unaware of what he was saying.[55]

Nandini has been described by an Australian who knew Krishna for almost forty years as the most beautiful woman he's ever seen. Aged thirty in 1947, Nandini was a loving mother caught in an unhappy marriage. Krishna was aged fifty-one.[56]

According to Nandini's description of that first meeting with Krishna, when he finished speaking he walked across the room to her. Her father-in-law, who was devoted to Krishna, introduced them and Krishna was laughing - the sound like a "Himalayan" stream falling across rocks to "mingle" with another stream, is how she described it. He asked her why she had come and tears streamed down her cheeks as he held her hand. She told him she had waited thirty years to see him. Krishna placed the palm of his hand on her head for a few seconds. Back in the car, her father-in-law seemed bewildered and told her that it was a great privilege that Krishna noticed her and she should not let it go to her head. She accompanied her father-in-law every day to see Krishna while he was in Bombay and one morning he asked her if she wanted to see him. He left shortly afterwards for Madras but on his return she saw him privately.[57]

Krishna had much to attend to as this was his first visit since 1938. British India was partitioned at independence on 15 August 1947 into two separate countries - Pakistan as a Muslim state and India predominantly inhabited by Hindus - and immediately erupted into racial violence. By the time Krishna arrived in October the mass migration of ten million people in the north of the country was under way in chaotic and heart-rending conditions. The idea of partition had been so anathema to Gandhi that he had even proposed to the Viceroy, Lord Mountbatten, in early 1947 that to avoid it, the Muslim leader, Mohammed Ali Jinnah, might be asked to form a government, placing the 300 million Hindus of India under Muslim rule. But Gandhi's idealistic, or perhaps wily, solution to Jinnah's demands for partition was, predictably, rejected by the Congress Party, led by Jawaharlal Nehru and Valabhbhai Patel, who had not believed that partition would lead to mass violence. Jinnah had been intransigent about the need for Muslims to escape domination by a Hindu majority, through the formation of Pakistan, a new country to be formed from the partition of the Punjab and Bengal. For two bloody months from September 1947, eleven and a half million homeless people – the greatest ever single column of refugees in history - would take to the roads, most on foot, seeking safety from mass religious killing. Their hopes were to build their lives anew, as a coalition of religious hatred and political expediency carved up the states of the Punjab and Bengal. Estimates of deaths range between a quarter of a million and two million – so many who'd escaped butchery in their towns and villages died of starvation, exhaustion or devastating illnesses such as cholera and typhoid, along their route to freedom. The road between Lahore and Amritsar, forty five miles of hell, turned into an open graveyard as people collapsed under the duress of carrying their few possessions and the corpses of their loved ones who had died in the mass migration.[58]

At this revolutionary time, political leaders could do little more than look on as an hysteria of hatred swept across the country and its main force was spent. The turmoil on the ground was matched by the inner turbulence in the minds of everyone from Prime Minister to simple villager. Perhaps only the assassination of Mahatma Gandhi, who had embodied *swaraj* to become the greatest possible personification of non-violence, was sufficient to quell the killing of neighbour by neighbour across the Indian countryside.[59]

Krishna had flown from London to India via Istanbul, Damascus and Karachi in October 1947. His first impressions were of an India chaotic and poorer than ever. He told Aldous Huxley that he believed Communism was spreading but not "violently". He did not think the country's political leaders knew what was ahead. Huxley's reply was critical of people's concentration on fabricated problems while ignoring the real problems of Man's destruction of the natural world, his preoccupation at the time. He commented that Rosalind had told him that Krishna had found India very "sad" this trip.[60]

Krishna was in Bombay on 30 January 1948 when Gandhi's assassination was announced. Pupul Jayakar describes the moment she heard of Gandhi's death during a discussion session with Krishna at his friend, Ratansi Morarji's house in Bombay. Achyut Patwardhan was called to the phone and returned, his face "ashen", as he announced the news. Krishna became still, watching everyone for reactions. All were thinking the same thought, whether the assassin was Hindu or Muslim, she says. In fact the assassin was a Hindu fanatic. Achyut's brother, Sahib Rao Pawardhan, asked if there was any news of the assassin, and Achyut said he did not know. Everyone rose silently and filed out of the room. Two days later when Krishna was asked at a public meeting what were the real causes of Mahatma Gandhi's death, his reply carried not an ounce of sentimentality. What was your response, he wanted to know? Concern over personal loss or over the trend of world events? These were interrelated, he said. The real cause lay in each one present, since they encouraged the spirit of division – through property, caste, ideology – thereby causing conflict in the world. Pupul says that in the days that followed, the groups discussed violence, Krishna making it clear that non-violence was an illusion and violence the reality. He spoke of callous and hypocritical relationships between husband and wife, alienating some traditional Hindus, and refused to discuss abstracts such as "eternity" or "God" while people's minds were caught up in lust, hatred and jealousy. In early April 1948 Krishna gave a talk on All-India Radio on the subject, 'Conditions of Peace'.[61]

Krishna gave twelve public talks in Bombay through until 28 March, held in the grounds of the home of Nandini's father-in-law, Sir Chunilal Mehta. Krishna would be dressed in a long red-bordered *dhoti*, or male skirt, a long white *kurta* shirt, and an *angavastram*, or shawl. With about five hundred people assembled, he would walk to a small platform, take off his sandals and sit cross-legged as silence descended on the group. Jayakar says that his vocabulary had changed and even people who had followed his teachings over many years found it difficult to understand him. He patiently tried to move the audience of mainly prosperous middle-class merchants to think about their own thinking. Jayakar says he established contact with individuals in the audience with his gaze. And he was fearless; he chastised them over their wealth, declaring they could not mix god and mammon. Jayakar claims that it was during the months Krishna spent in Bombay in 1948 that the dialogue form of exploration of his teaching was born. Yet he had been using this more interactive form since his trip to South America, when Rajagopal had declared that he should leave discussions alone as he didn't do them well. Certainly in Australia and New Zealand, Krishna had stretched the minds of those dialogue audiences. Nevertheless, the technique was new to Indians, used to the passively-receptive, *bhakti* mode of mind usually required in attendance before traditional gurus, and their intellectuality thrived on this new challenge. Perhaps Krishna felt more at ease with this mentally highly-charged group, which allowed them greater verbal response. But he never permitted the group dialogue to move off the well-worn tracks of his incessant themes: the source of fear, narrow-mindedness, conflict and duality, and the immensity of the 'Reality' that was beyond words. He always held the reins, while impressing on individuals that he was not their guru, and that they could have direct perception. In one session when Sahib Rao claimed that the ideals and beliefs that had carried him through all his years of political struggle had crumbled, Krishna jumped up to sit beside him, leading him to face a point where he could not find any answer nor any longer did he look for an answer. So what was the state of mind when it was no longer looking for an answer, Krishna asked? Pupul Jayakar's notes showed she still hadn't quite grasped what Krishna was getting at. Pupul also quotes a man who later became a spiritual *sannyasi*, Mukund Pada, who says that in 1947 when he first heard Krishna speak he was stunned and rocked to the point of trembling. Krishna's words opened an immense space in his head and he realised that the seeds of Krishna's message were already there in his brain.[62]

Unused to the humid heat of India, Krishna found it wearing and planned to go to Europe in the summer. But in March his plans changed. Early in the month, Maria Huxley had written that she and Aldous were looking forward to seeing him in England, but by the end of April he wrote to say that Rosalind had probably written to them that he was not going to Europe after all, and would stay the whole year in India. Also in March, Maria had written in glowing terms about Rosalind – how she brought so much joy to people, how the Happy Valley school was running smoothly and not a burden to her, how she seemed so calm and serene. There was no sense in the letter of Rosalind missing her absent lover.[63]

When Krishna moved on to Madras in April he invited Nandini and Pupul to stay with him at *Vasanta Vihar*, writing to them both about travelling on with him to Ootacamund, along the lines of 'if the mountain won't go to Muhammad...'. Nandini's husband agreed that she could accompany Pupul for the visit. They stayed one night and there was a significant occurrence after they went to bed. The sisters heard Krishna calling from the verandah where he slept and when they went to him, he didn't seem to recognise them and spoke in a child's voice. After a while his normal voice returned and he accompanied them back to their room. During his stay in Madras, Krishna held private discussions at *Vasanta Vihar*, preferring not to visit the Theosophical estate but taking long walks on Adyar beach. Jinarajadasa visited him, no doubt again going over old times and his view of Krishna's mission. Jinarajadasa had written to Krishna from

London before he himself left in mid-October saying that he'd wondered why Krishna and Rajagopal had arranged to talk with him there, as it seemed like flogging a dead horse. The gap between Krishna's and Theosophical teachings was as wide as the Atlantic ocean, and he wanted Krishna to concentrate on his own future work. Krishna could help the world in "travail", he was convinced of it, even if he was the only person left in the Society who knew it.[64]

In May Krishna went to stay with friends, including Maurice Friedman, a former Theosophist, in the hill town, Ootacamund, and, at his request, Nandini and her sister, Pupul, along with their children and Nandini's father-in-law, visited him, staying in a nearby hotel at their own expense. They went for long walks with him in the pine-forested hills. Soon further evening episodes of the 'process' occurred, spanning a period of about three weeks. Similar to the occurrence in Ojai in 1922, Krishna suffered head, neck and spinal pain and his stomach was hard; he called in a childlike voice for his mother; he shouted and tossed about in bed; he fainted. On the final night Pupul says that after excruciating pain, Krishna fell back on his bed, intensely still, and his face became suffused with a beauty, stillness, vastness and immensity. His body radiated light, she says, and she felt the stillness "pour" into the room and into her mind and body. She draws an analogy with the two disciples of the founder of Advaita Vedanta, Adi Shankaracharya, who, as legend has it, watched over his body while he was out of it, as a shape-changer. She implies that she and Nandini were Krishna's protectors during his transforming ordeal to open up previously "nonoperative" areas of his brain. Krishna asked them afterwards if they'd seen a face – confirming that the Buddha had been present and they were blessed. He asked them to keep the experience secret, but Pupul says that by the 1970s he had begun to talk about it, thereby excusing her own account published forty years after the occurrence. Krishna spoke about a face being beside him and of energy pouring in to his brain, but when the brain cells were not "large" enough to receive the energy, it "polished" up the brain.[65]

A small nucleus of people dedicated to Krishna formed around him during the year and a half he stayed in India. In Bangalore, Krishna stayed in a house that belonged to the Chairman of the Atomic Energy Commission, Vikram Sarabai, with Maurice Friedman taking care of him. A group of young people, including Sunanda, a young teacher, Balusandrum and his wife Vishalakshi, and a young dancer Shanta Rao, visited daily. Soon an energetic Englishwoman, Miss Payne, came on the scene and offered to get the Rishi Valley school in order. She went on to alienate various people, including Evelyn Wood, an Englishman who had stayed on in India after Independence, and Sanjeeva Rao, who had been educated at Kings College, Cambridge, and resented Miss Payne's ignorance and poor spelling. Miss Payne would return to England within a year but ructions over Rishi Valley, whether it might be sold and how it was to be managed, would continue for some years between different factions of the Krishnamurti following in India. Krishna claimed he didn't hold property and washed his hands of the disputes. Instead, he concentrated on the inner lives of people around him.[66]

Krishna was very fond of Sunanda, who had completed a degree at Madras University and was now "enraptured" by the atmosphere of dialogue and ecstasy she found in Krishna's circle. She was soon to marry Pama Patwardhan, the only brother who went into business in Poona rather than politics, but was she being enticed out into the world by Krishna, who gave her a shawl and 400 rupees as a symbolic gesture of her coming out.[67]

In her biography of Krishna, Pupul Jayakar wrote a detailed account of what had been her first meeting with Krishna in January 1948. She went with her sister, Nandini, and their mother to visit him in the hope that the older woman would become free of her depression over widowhood. Krishna gave her no simple, obvious comfort. When she said she wanted to see her dead husband again, Krishna asked which husband that might be – the young man, the man he was when he died, or the man he would be today if he'd lived. He encouraged her to drop the memory that caused her such sorrow. The meeting disturbed

Pupul and it wasn't long before she sought a private meeting with him, during which she told him of her emotional agony and then felt an extraordinary healing within herself. This was the beginning of their long and warm association.[68]

Krishna also continued to have a deep relationship with Nandini following their first unusual encounter, and there was considerable controversy over the nature of the relationship. Jayakar says many women with troubled marital lives sought interviews with Krishna. In his public talks he spoke about marriage and the hypocrisy of Indian society in which men dominated their wives economically. It was undoubtedly an American sensibility that he brought to an observation of Indian marital relations and it was not received with equanimity by traditional Indian men.

In the case of Nandini, Krishna spent a lot of time with her in 1948. He would go on to correspond with her from mid-1948 until at least March 1960 and possibly longer. Within a few months of meeting Krishna, Nandini told her husband that she no longer wanted a sexual relationship with him. Her father-in-law was confused and asked Krishna to intervene but the situation did not improve. One night Nandini's children were taken from her and she left her home physically bruised. The following morning she went to see Krishna and he told her that if she acted out of "self-knowing" she would be alright but if she had been otherwise influenced, the "guru" was gone. Pupul pointed out to Krishna that her sister was penniless without her husband's support, and although she would not return to her husband's home, if there was legal action over custody of the children, Krishna's name would be brought up in court. He didn't need protection, he said, and Nandini should fight for her children if it was right to do so. Nandini filed for legal separation and custody of the three children, aged between three and nine. The case was heard in late 1949 and passages from Krishna's public talks, which Pupul describes as "religious" sermons – the same material he'd been delivering to audiences for almost twenty years - were quoted by lawyers for Nandini's husband, Bhagwan Mehta. Nandini appealed the decision against her, and when Krishna returned to Bombay in early 1950 she saw Krishna alone several times, and took her children to see him, without her husband's knowledge. Krishna even laid his hands on the eyes of the eldest son to try to aid his sight in one eye which had a faulty optic nerve. Nandini lost her appeal and the case received wide publicity, considered a scandal among the elite of Bombay and stretching across the world to astonish loved ones in Ojai. It was almost as if there'd been no progress in women's rights since Mrs Besant had fought for custody of her children in Britain so many years before but the role Krishna played in "liberating" Nandini from her marriage vows remains a question still.[69]

Krishna was a curiosity in India that first visit after the war as he was revered by many upper-class Indians yet refused to accept a role as guru. When the "Mother" guru, Anandmai Ma, visited Krishna in Delhi and spoke to him through an interpreter, they held hands and she assured him he was a guru. But he refused to allow her followers to touch or kiss his feet. The new Prime Minister of India, Jawaharlal Nehru, also met Krishna in 1947, first in Ootacamund, Krishna visiting his residence with Pupul and Maurice Friedman. Sitting in front of an open fire, with bowls of carnations for the two men to admire, they talked, at first a little shy and hesitant. Nehru was in anguish over the violence that had erupted over partition. He spoke about transformation and asked Krishna to define "right" action and thought. Silence lasting about three minutes followed. Krishna then slowly explained that right action could only come from a silent mind, free of motive. Krishna leaned forward and pressed his point that in the midst of the chaos in India and the world, a few individuals had to free themselves from corruption and "transform" themselves, as world chaos was a projection of individual chaos. Clearly Advaita Vedanta or 'non-dualism', this must have touched a nerve for Nehru. From the ashes, said Krishna. Phoenix-like, commented Nehru. It was the tenet of the age-old belief in Shiva, that from death comes renewal. In December 1948 Nehru wanted to see Krishna again, inviting him to his official residence in Delhi, once again accompanied by Pupul. Nehru asked Krishna how to regenerate the individual, how to begin to "watch" oneself in relationships, as Krishna had told him that relationship was the mirror in which the self was revealed. They also talked about fear as well as the desire for happiness and avoidance of pain. Jayakar says they seemed to really communicate only once or twice as Nehru was tired. Krishna seemed sad on the way home from the meeting, saying Nehru had a fine, sensitive mind that was wasted in politics.[70]

In 1949 Krishna travelled from Delhi to Varanasi, staying at Rajghat, close to the banks of the confluence of the Ganges and Varuna rivers and the site of pilgrimages by so many seers over the centuries. He must have been impressed by this ancient lineage, writing about it over the years in his notebooks. On this trip he was accompanied by Pupul, Nandini, Achyut and Rao Sahib Patwardhan, Maurice Friedman and Sanjeeva Rao. After the stay in Varanasi he returned to Pupul's home in Bombay and then went on to Rishi Valley.[71]

Early in the year a Bengali woman called Chinmoyee, who had been on a spiritual search with several gurus, met Krishna, and following a trip to Tibet, returned to be with him. From that time she changed her name back to Tapas and whenever he was in India she would arrive without notice and take it as her job to look after his wardrobe, buying good quality cottons and wild silk cloth. When he was away she would live in the mountains. Pupul tells the story as an example of the great esteem in which Krishna was held by spiritual seekers in India.[72]

Krishna's older brother, Sivaram, whom he had not seen for over twenty years and who was now a physician and surgeon, even came to see him with his own son, G Narayan, and asked if he was "self-realized". Krishna did not reply directly but said the self was just a bundle of memories. The two brothers sat and held hands for some time – the long-standing breach healed.[73]

Radha Rajagopal Sloss says herself that Krishna transmitted a highly-charged energy that could awaken within an individual a capacity to confront the depths of their being, but some people just used it to adore him. Clearly many Indians recognised something of the greatness of a guru in Krishna, something that they either imagined or which was a true reflection of the guru within themselves.[74]

Krishna flew to London on 9 April 1949, staying three days before going on to America. As he'd been away for nineteen months, perhaps his sense of "home" had changed over that time. But he was pleased to be back in such a beautiful place as Ojai, where in spite of lack of rain the landscape was green. He sent Lady Emily the news that Radha had completed senior schooling and was off to school on the east coast. She was really very nice, he told Lady Emily, and began to philosophise about the extraordinary things that had happened in his personal life, and that were still happening. At least their love for each other hadn't broken, he told his elderly friend. And that was all that mattered, he said. Most people were only concerned with the person they loved, rather than that "strange" thing called love, he said. What passed for love faded so quickly under difficult circumstances, with people's thinking merely the slave of jealousy and envy. In those cases, the person dominated and love disappeared. He did not mention names and one might speculate that Rosalind, and even Rajagopal, were not as attached to Krishna's person as they had been before their extended break.[75]

The sentiment in this letter is strangely reminiscent of the slightly bitter conclusion of his former sweetheart, Helen Nearing. She said that she came to believe that Krishna was in love with love itself rather than with her. By the time Helen visited him in India, some years after their 1944 correspondence, she had to make a formal appointment with his secretary to see him. When she entered Krishna's room he'd virtually forgotten who she was and asked her if it was her first trip to India. She might have reminded him that she'd come on her first visit practically in his arms, she thought, but did not tell him . He was "distant" and not even friendly, in sharp contrast to the young man who had once promised to love her forever. "I kiss your hand, if I am permitted. But otherwise, I merely bow, very low down," he had written in the 1920s. He had told her not to doubt his love, and that all his ardor and what might be called infatuation were perfectly "true".[76]

Certain rivalries and antipathies are evident in the different memoirs and accounts of Krishna's life that have been published. Although Krishna clearly had an intimate relationship with the Rajagopals over a major period of his life, and his correspondence shows his continued fondness during the 1940s, Lutyens writes in 1983 that in 1947 Krishna felt imprisoned by "the Rajagopals" who, she says, bullied him and ordered him around. She claims that his long solitary walks were his only "escape" from them, which puts a decidedly negative slant on what seems from his writing to have always been a very great source of enjoyment and creativity for him. Lutyens' biography of Krishna was authorised and his view of "the Rajagopals" had significantly soured by the 1970s and 1980s. Jayakar, too, writing in 1986, says Krishna's 'outer' life had been taken over by Rajagopal and Rosalind and the nine years he spent in Ojai over the WWII period had separated him from his friends in India, although she tempers the criticism by implying that different people at different times acted as protectors of him since he was a special person.[77]

But in contrast to his later reflections about his return to Ojai in 1949, Krishna made it very clear to his friends back in India at the time that there were no differences between him and Rajagopal. He stated explicitly in several letters to Madhavachari, for example, that, as he had already explained to him in Bombay, he had the "completest" confidence in Rajagopal. Krishna said he sincerely hoped Madhavachari would work cooperatively with Rajagopal – not just superficially but deeply. Rajagopal had voluntarily for many years "given" his life to the work; Krishna had left it in his hands and Rajagopal had not put himself forward but freely undertaken the task, he said. Madhavachari was to understand that the Rishi Valley Trust existed for education and experimentation with "Krishnamurti's" teachings, Krishna said, using the third person reference to himself. And his orders were that he did not want an ashram, so *Vasanta Vihar* was to be sold.[78]

Krishna went with Rosalind and Radha on holiday to Wrightwood in the spring of 1949. Radha says that she had always felt the "true" marriage in her home was that of Krishna and her mother, and on his return from India that year they seemed genuinely happy to be together again. Radha graduated from Happy Valley School in June and would go east to Swarthmore College in Pennsylvania. On her departure she would receive the only "material" gift she believed she'd ever received from Krishna, a one hundred dollar bill for her to buy a warm coat.[79]

There were changes afoot and not only in the intimate relations between members of Krishna's circle. Technological changes were having effects in some unlikely places and unseating people from established positions of authority in a new age where information was power. Before the advent of television and video, new sound technologies such as tape recording, the phonograph and radio were forging the way forward to an information revolution. Already in 1948 there was a whisper that someone from Australia was going out to India – at his own expense - with a "recording machine" to tape Krishna's talks, with the idea of allowing those who could not see and hear him in the flesh to hear his talks in their own surroundings. One of the earliest to recognise the opportunity to disseminate Krishna's talks by tape recording was an intrepid radio producer, Donald Ingram Smith from ABC Radio in Sydney. He would be bowled over by his first meeting with Krishna and spend the next fifty years living the seeds of that experience day by day.[80]

Krishna spoke of the conditioned mind and the need for its revolution in order for a person to die to the past, but his own past kept pace with his present life. Jinarajadasa continued to remind him of his Theosophist roots, asking in July 1948 for permission to publish Krishna's poems *The Pool of Wisdom* as a book and his major 1926 speech in *The Theosophist*. Other Theosophists remained devoted; one fellow asked if Krishna minded him publishing a comparison of his and Theosophist beliefs and he received a curt reply from Krishna that he did not agree with the

Theosophical Society. And a judge from Chittoor who had gone to school with Krishna even wrote to remind Krishna that he used to try to copy the nascent lawyer's examination answers and yet within a few months of being taken out of school Krishna was reputed to have written *At the Feet of the Master*. Krishna's reply was prompt and muted, claiming he remembered none of it. But along with these troublesome figures from the past, Krishna's circle of introspective seekers was ever-widening and his force-field of influence strengthening. His image was being projected by devotees via tape recording and playback, for broadcast over global space and time. But without control over his past – neither over its substance nor its public projection - Krishna and his minders could hardly expect to keep control over his future, which would consistently become the subject of public admiration and even adoration as well as speculation and conflict.[81]

Chapter 9

Self-Transformation

Though lovers be lost love shall not

Dylan Thomas 1936 And death shall have no dominion.

The mid-point of the century would find Krishna back on Indian ground at the start of what would be a turbulent lecture tour. In November and December 1949 he gave three talks at Rajahmundry, north of Madras, and a fourth in Madras. During one talk he was challenged over the question of self-transformation creating world transformation for peace. Krishna tackled it head on, although the questioner may not have been satisfied with his answer. You are the world, Krishna pointed out. In transforming yourself you produced a transformation in society. He wasn't talking propaganda, he said, but fact. One man couldn't change the world but this man and he could change it together. When they found "truth", it would dissolve the miseries of the world.[1]

At New Year Krishna was in Colombo where he was giving a series of talks running from Christmas Day through to 22 January, as well as two radio broadcasts. In University College, Colombo Krishna faced heckling as he began to speak, a rare occurrence at any of his talks, as an expectant hush would normally fall as he ascended any podium. In the face of this reception Krishna smiled and asked what they wanted. To cries of, "Are you the Christ?" Krishna departed from his usual subjects and shared with the crowd the "poignant" story of his life, including his loneliness and longings, his struggles and searching, and finally his realisations. Applause, cheers and even tears were the immediate response, as the audience repented their aggressive mood. An academic who gave an account of the talk said Krishna had a radiant spiritual personality without the need for organisation. ceremony priest. *puja, darshan.* magic or mystery.[2]

The Australian radio producer, Donald Ingram Smith, first met Krishnamurti in Colombo in 1949 and it was a self-revelation for him. Ingram, who had been studying Krishna's verbatim talks for years, approached ABC Radio's Director of Talks in Sydney, BH Molesworth, about going to interview the Prime Minister of the newly-independent Sri Lanka, as well as Krishnamurti. Smith thought he was doing well to have organised some dub editing facilities with Radio Sri Lanka, but no sooner had he arrived than he was offered a job as Controller of Programs, so his entrée was assured thereafter. Smith was aged thirty eight and he'd landed the best job he'd ever had but he walked away from it five months later to follow Krishnamurti around India, then to Rome, France, England and the United States.[3]

Smith says that his first meeting with Krishna was when he visited to make arrangements for a talk to be broadcast. Smith "fumbled" about, didn't know whether to shake hands or not, asked Krishna whether he had a script, which he had, and in picking it up they spilled the unnumbered pages on the floor. They talked for about half an hour about whether it was too long and whether the window should be open or shut and other matters concerning the recording but Smith was very confused. His only memory of the meeting was that they had managed to make an arrangement for Smith to return the next day with recording equipment. As Smith left and took a long walk beside a nearby lake he felt very agitated. He'd believed he was going to meet a "great being" and instead had found a nervous, fumbling man.

> Suddenly it was as though I'd walked smack into a brick wall. I realised for the first time in my life that I'd met myself. And then I realised that Krishnaji is the mirror. I didn't really fully understand this at the time but it was going to become clearer and clearer ... you discover what you are. Most people, if you do the wrong thing, will tell you what you should do ... but ... I had met myself in the clear mirror of Krishnamurti.[4]

Smith says he "knew a bit about recording" and recognised the efficiency of taping Krishna's talks rather than taking them down by shorthand. as Sunanda Patwardhan had been doing. He decided to tag along with the happy band of people who surrounded Krishna for the insight into themselves that contact with him brought them. What Smith brought to the group was new technology.

A sign that Krishna himself recognised the value of this new recording technology can be seen in his letter to another person who taped his talks a few years later. Krishna pointed out to a Mr Solness in 1953 that he had been allowed to tape material in Benares on condition that all the records would be given to himself. Yet afterwards Solness had gone about Europe addressing groups and using Krishnamurti's name. Krishna sent copies of his letter to organisers, Tidswell in New Zealand and Spencer English in Australia, in dissociating himself from Solness. No doubt the astute Rajagopal was also disturbed by this potential for copyright infringement through advances in recording technology.[5]

During his stay in Sri Lanka Krishna wrote to dear old Lady Emily in January, exclaiming over the beautiful countryside, so green and "luscious". He reported that in Colombo the halls were packed for his talks, with many Buddhist monks in the audiences, and that he had met Nehru to talk about war and "disintegration". Nehru had a great burden to carry, Krishna said, and he believed he was a very "nice" person. About ten days later he wrote again to say that Jinarajadasa, looking old and "fragile", had visited him in Madras. He was a little sad that Krishna would not visit the Theosophical estate in Adyar. Jinarajadasa had already asked for permission to reprint certain questions from Krishna's 1947 and 1949 talks in India, and a few days after the visit Krishna would write to him formally asking for copies of his correspondence from years past, to be used for biographical notes sometime in the future. The subtleties of copyright and the power of "teachings" would continue to create a bond of rivalry and mutual respect between these two titans.[6]

Jinarajadasa soon replied to say that Krishna's request was a large order, as he had only one secretary and she was already regularly occupied. These were days before photocopiers so each letter had to be retyped or copied by hand. Jinarajadasa assured Krishna that he did not want to call in any outsiders and he would have the letters copied piece by piece. He reminded Krishna that in about 1938 he had sent to Rajagopal Krishna's early letters to Mrs Besant and Leadbeater and those from Nitya, as well as Krishna's Varengeville autobiographical writing from 1913. Wouldn't it be best to wait until Krishna returned to Ojai to check this, Jinarajadasa wondered? But he sent an extra copy of the Varengeville work in any case, along with copies of letters describing Krishna's "process" in Ojai in 1922. Jinarajadasa reminded Krishna that some material had already been published in *The Theosophist* so it could not be suppressed. Having gone back through his correspondence, Jinarajadasa also noticed that he'd asked for a copy of one of Nitya's letters sent to Rajagopal in 1936 and hadn't received it so he wrote to Rajagopal now, asking for the copy and keeping him up to date on Krishna's latest request. Krishna did in fact follow it up once he was back in Ojai, claiming that Rajagopal had received none of the correspondence and he asked again for Jinarajadasa to send it. Krishna included an invitation for Jinarajadasa to visit Ojai when he was next in California, so the rebuff should not have seemed harsh. The issues of copyright and possession would drag on. Later in the year Krishna upped his claim by thanking Jinarajadasa for having the letters copied and sent to him and then asking for the originals, since he did not want them to fall into the hands of Jinarajadasa's successors. Jinarajadasa replied that he was keeping them in trust as Mrs Besant had asked him to. He knew Krishna was writing an autobiography and he felt he had to safeguard the integrity of Mrs Besant and Leadbeater in case other people said they had exploited Krishna, as had been rumoured back in 1927. Some people even thought it was the Theosophical Society which had put Krishna forward as the "Vehicle" of the Great Teacher, whereas the Society was not involved, according to Jinarajadasa. Always one for legal correctness, he suggested placing a codicil in his will so that no one but himself could see the material for fifty years, when Krishna would be 105, so presumably no longer alive. Jinarajadasa's trustees would be his successors as Outer Head of the Esoteric School of the Society. But this was not a solution that would in any way appeal to Krishna who immediately responded with the moral argument that "Amma" would have given the letters to him if he'd asked. He did not want Jinarajadasa's successors to have anything to do with them, he said, and denied that he was writing an autobiography. He dismissed the "stupid" gossip Jinarajadasa had heard so many years before. However, Jinarajadasa would not be deterred. He didn't think Krishna realised that with this stupid gossip continuing, Jinarajadasa's obligation to "Amma" and Leadbeater remained. And it was a little too late in the day for Krishna to hide his past, he advised, as all the instructions Mrs Besant received from the Masters were tendered as part of the Privy Council appeal over custody in 1913. He had also published these instructions in *The Theosophist,* as well as the happenings at Eerde in 1926. Krishna retorted that he was not trying to suppress or hide from his past. He wished they had talked about publication beforehand and he certainly was glad Jinarajadasa had not published anything about the "past" in Ojai. He lamented Jinarajadasa not coming to Ojai for a holiday. Krishna said he would write more about it all later and asked that Jinarajadasa publish nothing more about him without checking with him first.[7]

By February and March, 1950, questions were being raised among Krishna's friends about whether he should speak in Bombay, since Nandini's court appeal had recently caused a stir. Krishna wanted to speak in the outdoors, rather than a "rich" man's house, so a venue was found on the terrace of Sunderbai Hall, which was open to the sky. Pupul Jayakar says Krishna showed Nandini no special sympathy. He met her alone several times and refused to let her indulge in self-pity, telling her to face the fact that one life was over and she must awake to the new.[8]

Nandini's divorce case was linked to Krishna's influence over her in a report in *TIME* magazine in January, published while he was absent from Ojai. It came as a great shock to Rosalind. The article, headed "Revolt of a Doormat", began with a brief history of Krishnamurti's fame as a new Messiah. "Bunkum and Nonsense", "Resentment and Rupture" were the sub-headings. Krishnamurti, close to fifty and still handsome, the article claimed, had returned to India to lecture, with the help of "a few wealthy followers". After nearly ten years of marriage, the wife of the Bombay textile millionaire, Bhagavandas Chunilal Mehta, asked for a legal separation, testifying that he "beat her, locked up her medicines and used insulting language". His side of the story was that his wife had become a "disciple" of Krishnamurti who had called the sacred Hindu wedding verses "bunkum and nonsense". Krishna was quoted as saying to males in the audience: "Do you know what your relationship with your wife is? We all know this relationship – sex nagging, bullying, dominating, the superficial responses of marriage ... If you are dominant and you make her a doormat, you say: I am happily married". The *TIME* article claimed that as a result of listening to such teaching Mrs Mehta's attitude had changed "sharply".

> "Before she was always strong but good," said Mehta. "Afterwards ... she became aggressive. I trusted my wife completely but, I did not know what Krishnamurti was up to ... I had come to the conclusion that under the guise of teaching, Krishnamurti was running after my wife."[9]

The article said Mrs Mehta had declared her eyes had been opened by Krishnamurti's teachings and she would live a celibate life. Judge Eric Weston, who was said to be one of the few remaining "Britons" among India's judiciary, observed "dryly" that he did not think there was any room for doubt that teachings suggesting the wife revolt from her doormat position must have had "their effect upon her mind". Her refusal of marital relations must have caused considerable resentment and the inevitable final rupture was "largely of her own creation", the judge concluded.

Jayakar says that while Krishna was in Bombay, the small group of people meeting regularly for discussion consisted of herself, Nandini, Rao Sahib, Achyut, Maurice Friedman, and an Englishwoman, Mrs Lucille Frost. Jayakar says that on Krishna's return to Ojai later in the year, Rosalind and Rajagopal questioned him "relentlessly", wanting to know more about his "new" friends.[10]

Before returning to Ojai, Krishna had flown to Paris, where he was joined by Rajagopal. He saw old friends, Marcelle de Manziarly and the Suares. Writing from Fontainebleau, outside of Paris, in March, Krishna said that the "nonsense" in TIME magazine was unfortunate. He put the press interest down to the fact that those involved in the case were wealthy and, on the husband's side, "unscrupulous" – there were other cases coming up in court of women standing up against their husbands but they wouldn't be reported in the papers.[11]

A sign that the reporting of the divorce case caused alarm back in Ojai is a letter written by James Vigeveno to Rajagopal in KWINC suggesting an urgent Board meeting. He wanted to find a way to overcome what he described as a continuing "ironical" attitude of the press towards Krishnamurti. It had a devastating influence on millions of people all over the world, he claimed.[12]

In India the response was muted. Jinarajadasa said that the American Theosophical Society General Secretary had protested to the *TIME* editor but nothing had appeared in print. And Madhavachari, who was the KWINC representative in Madras, said some friends in Bombay had offered to send in a protest but were dissuaded as they did not want any further attention. Meanwhile certain elements were keen to be pro-active in the new field of 'public relations', to gather biographical information about Krishnamurti and his teachings to send to the press as the need arose, mostly to coincide with his talks. A Public Relations Committee was formed in Bombay with Evelyn Wood, an Englishman living in India, taking on the role of an active researcher and writer of background material. He wrote a draft 'hand-out' giving advice to people who would be attending discussions with "Krishnaji" that they needed to be more involved rather than just passively listen. At first people resisted the idea of changing themselves radically, the background sheet said, but Krishnaji would raise a storm of revolutionary thinking and feeling and show how to control it and reduce its chaos to "eternal" order. Wood also wrote a piece about Krishna, the "noted" Indian philosopher, having addressed a meeting attended mostly by "the working classes", where Rao Sahib Patwardhan had acted as interpreter into Marathi. Clearly the object of the press release was to turn attention away from Krishna's links with the ruling and middle classes and towards his message for the common man and woman – just as Krishna had wanted to speak in the open air rather than a rich man's house. In January Krishna wrote to Wood to say that he thought it might be best if he gave a verbal explanation at each discussion, instead of having it printed and distributed. By the time Krishna was in Paris he must have been having second thoughts about the whole exercise, possibly as a result of Rajagopal's reaction. He and Rajagopal hadn't had enough time to meet and discuss this "propaganda" business, Krishna wrote to Wood, pointing out that the press wanted "sensationalism", not facts. Having dispensed with the *Star*, they'd have to be careful and would need to delay a decision on it. Wood replied that no publicity should contain anything but facts, even if released anonymously, and he attached a copy of a Reuters' story that had appeared as a result of their first press release. Wood wrote to Madhavachari the same day an outline of the "facts" he needed to rebuild Krishna's public relations, also enclosing a copy of the Reuters' story. He acknowledged that Krishna had just written from Paris calling for a rethink. And he also wrote to Rajagopal, the letter addressed to Ojai rather than Paris, saying he realised it might take months for Rajagopal to attend to the details of the public relations outline that Krishna had suggested he check. Wood also encouraged Rajagopal to return to India the following year as no one was able to give such a practical base to Krishna's day-to-day living as he could give, Wood believed. By August, Wood had to extricate himself from this visionary public relations exercise in the face of the lack of interest or funds, with both Krishna and Rajagopal urging reconsideration. It was uncertain whether Rajagopal was assembling facts about Krishna's life and this should be ascertained, Wood told Pupul Jayakar. and the public relations committee might be disbanded as he himself was leaving the following month.[13]

The lack of direction over public relations is just one outward sign of the deep rift that was developing between Krishna and the Rajagopals in the early months of 1950. Radha says her mother had felt a change in her relationship with Krishna when he returned from India in 1949. Twice he called her "Nandini" - she did not disclose the circumstances – and Rosalind had been "perturbed". It had not occurred to Rosalind that Krishna would be disloyal, Radha says, even though she believed he told lies sometimes, as he himself had said his lies arose out of fear. Rosalind did not consider herself unfaithful to Rajagopal, according to Radha.[14]

When Rosalind arrived in London in the spring of 1950, she met old friends and heard rumours about Krishna and his new friends and activities in India which disturbed her, as he had not written to her about certain details. She went on to Paris to see Rajagopal, who was arriving from America, before meeting Krishna. In talking with Rajagopal, she was so distressed that the story of her long-standing relationship with Krishna "burst" out, according to Radha. This was a "tremendous" shock to Rajagopal - and then Rosalind herself was shocked to discover Rajagopal had never known of her relationship with Krishna.[15]

These were grave and deep-seated disclosures about the three-way relationship that had formed the foundation of their lives for more than twenty five years. On the face of it, it seems astounding that Rajagopal did not know that the bond between Krishna and Rosalind was more than platonic. If, as Radha maintains, Rosalind and Rajagopal's sex life was over, so that she did not feel betrayed by any "liaison" Rajagopal might have had, it seems incredible that Rajagopal knew nothing about Rosalind's sex life. It had been going on, perhaps in his own home or even right next door, at least since the early 1930s, if not earlier. After all, Radha says she saw the true "marriage" as between Rosalind and Krishna, with Rajagopal as the person outside the magic circle of daily domestic life and love.[16]

Rosalind was so distressed about her situation she insisted on talking with Krishna about it when he arrived in Paris the following day. They walked for hours beside the Seine, away from the home of friends, the Suares, with whom Krishna was staying. According to Radha's account, Krishna was at first "horrified", then angry, and finally relented in saying he would talk with Rajagopal. But he didn't, she says. Rosalind returned to the United States on 19 April 1950 and Rajagopal stayed on to attend to business in London, Rajagopal assuming that Rosalind's "affair" was over, according to Radha.[17]

Krishna may not have talked with Rajagopal but he did try. He wrote to Rajagopal on 19 May from France to say that his attempt to talk had been a "fiasco". Rajagopal knew all about "it" from Rosalind and Krishna saw that he had hurt him deeply, though it had never been his intention. he said. It had happened and there it was. He would do everything he could to heal the wound, consciously and unconsciously, he said, and he would like them to remain friends and brothers. When Rajagopal had asked him at the hotel if he had anything more to say, Krishna had said he didn't, not because he was frightened, indifferent or callous, but because he was anxious that he might say the wrong thing. He really wanted them to be brothers, ne said, and sent his love, emphasising in a postscript that he did not write this "casually". Krishna also wrote about his cold and fever, and the pouring rain, as if taking on the role of a poor fellow in need of sympathy. He did not raise any question about whether Rajagopal had known of his relationship with Rosalind.[18]

Krishna returned to Ojai in May but was back in New York for a series of talks in June. He wrote to Lady Emily that he believed the talks went off well, as he'd been told that for New Yorkers to attend such serious talks was rare.[19]

Radha writes about meeting Rajagopal and Krishna at Sarobia at the end of the spring school term and overhearing a quarrel between the two men. Rajagopal threatened to walk out and finally, after "sharp" exchanges, Krishna "begged" Rajagopal to stay, agreeing to put in writing that he had lied to him over the years and would never do so again. Radha says harmony was restored during the New York talks. Rajagopal explaining to her years later that he did not want to leave suddenly which would have exposed Krishna and Rosalind and upset her work at Happy Valley school.[20]

After the New York sessions, Rajagopal went home to Ojai while Krishna went with Radha to meet Rosalind in Seattle. Before a series of talks there they had a ten-day holiday on Orcas Island, during which time the tensions between Krishna and Rosalind seemed to fade. In Seattle they saw a white Ford convertible they loved and rang Rajagopal to its arrange purchase, which he did.[21]

Donald Ingram Smith, who had travelled from Sri Lanka to Seattle to hear Krishna's talks, says that when he met Radha with Krishna he had the impression that she was his daughter. It was not so much from physical characteristics (although of course she was part-Indian), as from the easy and familiar way they related to one another. About this same time Krishna observed to Lady Emily that Radha was quite a young lady, after her year at Swarthmore, clearly proud of her confidence and achievement.[22]

By now Krishna had decided to go into retreat for a year, which meant he would miss a trip to India in the winter. In September he officially informed Madhavachari about his decision, saying he was worn out, and asking him to tell friends there and send out a circular to that effect, and he wrote to Jinarajadasa that it would be something of a "silent" retreat. His letter to Pupul Jayakar in September 1950 advised her that he would go into retreat without interviews, private or public discussions or talks, 'and Rajagopal told her that Krishna was observing complete silence.[23]

In December Rosalind and Radha went alone to spend Christmas with their old friend Robert Logan in Sarobia and Rajagopal reported to Rosalind that arrangements were working out well at home, with Krishna tending his garden of all sorts of flowers, especially roses, while he was busy minding his own business.[24]

But Krishna still had Indian business to attend to. The troubling Englishwoman. Miss Payne, who had become so involved in Rishi Valley affairs, was now waging war with her pen. Krishna wrote her a soft admonition that her letter to Madhavachari was "utterly" unnecessary and unfriendly. He was sorry things were turning out this way. Then he wrote "strictly" confidentially to Madhavachari to say that Miss Payne should not be given complete charge or there was a danger the school could be dominated by the whim of one person. By early 1951 Krishna, still in retreat, was becoming agitated over the direction of the school and ideas about experimenting with his teachings, which he found "absurd". Miss Payne had no business to be there, and if they weren't careful the whole place would be "wrecked", he said. It was meant for the "right" kind of education, and if people wanted to undertake other activities, such as supplying milk and butter to a sanitarium, they could go elsewhere. Krishna also wanted to know why "Mr Frydman" owed so much money to KWINC, pointing out that such debts were a burden on the organisation.[25]

Krishna had always had an interest in fostering education, ever since the scheme for a university with Professor Marcault back in his Theosophical days, but, as Jinarajadasa had so directly pointed out, Krishna had never given clear direction about education methods to be followed. Now Krishna was working with Rajagopal to discover and extract what he'd said about education from his talks over a period of many years. It might be considered curious that he never simply sat down and wrote a treatise on education, and, instead, always felt compelled to fall back on what he had said in public talks. Granted it's generally easier to talk than to write formally. But it is a significant point that the people close to Krishna always considered his "teachings" to be those words uttered in a public forum, either in a talk or discussion. These attitudes set by Leadbeater and followed by Arundale and even Jinarajadasa, that he was a great teacher but not everything that he said was sacred, persisted right through his life and Krishna seems to have accepted them as much as anyone else did. So it may not have been out of laziness that Krishna did not write his teachings. From the mass of correspondence and private writing extant, it's obvious that he spent a great deal of time writing, but it was more of a creative outlet for his thoughts and feelings than a disciplined exercise in essay-writing.[26]

Aldous Huxley had a major influence on how Krishna's thoughts on education were edited and prepared for public consumption at this time. They shared a strong interest in education through the Happy Valley School, as Huxley was an original trustee along with Rosalind and Krishna. The school's motto was *Aun Aprendo*, 'I Am Still Learning', and in June 1951 Huxley gave the Commencement Address on the subject of learning which he said should go on from the cradle to the grave, and beyond. One of Huxley's nieces attended the school and Maria Huxley hoped their own son, Matthew, would send his children along to "such a happy atmosphere" where they had a Russian cook who was a virtuoso pianist, and which seemed "mad" but worked well.[27]

Radha says that Huxley had introduced Rajagopal to his publisher, Harper & Row, and Rajagopal buried himself in the work of preparing manuscripts for publication. She maintains that Krishna took not the slightest interest in the work and would not even look at the manuscripts.[28]

However a letter from Huxley to Krishna in mid-1951 concerning "chapters on Education", which both Krishna and Rajagopal had been compiling from talks, makes it clear that Huxley needed to address his advice to the source, Krishna himself. Huxley advised against publication in the form in which the talks had been compiled as they had "neither the life of a spontaneous talk directly recorded nor the coherence of a composition". He suggested a volume of aphorisms or short statements that would have a logical sequence. Applying the complexity of his mind to the matter, Huxley suggested a central idea of self-knowledge or "the awareness of things as they are in themselves, undistorted by passion or self-interest". From that principal idea could spring different contexts, such as personal relationships, education, class, national relations, war and so on, as branches on a tree. It was a classical form, used by Marcus Aurelius and in the *Dhammapada*, among others, he added.[29]

The copyright for *Education and the Significance of Life* was held by KWINC for publication by Harpers' in New York in 1953, although it would take another two years before it was published by Victor Gollancz in Britain. In the meantime Gollancz published *The First and Last Freedom* in 1954, with a Foreword by Huxley. Donald Ingram Smith says Rajagopal approached Victor Gollancz in 1953 with an offer to buy up any unsold books so that Gollancz did not need to take any financial risk. The first book published went into a second printing.[30]

Education and the Significance of Life is set out in a form which deals with the central theme first, as the title suggests, followed by other aspects such as types of education, schooling and parenting. But Krishnamurti finds it almost impossible to think along traditional pathways of thought, and includes chapters on sex and marriage, art, beauty and creation. His central theme is principally that education of a human being should awaken its capacity for self-awareness, rather than be an accumulation of facts for self-expression.[31] The "right" kind of education is in understanding a child without imposing an ideal of what we think the child should be. The "right" kind of teacher will not depend on a method but study each individual pupil, he says. Current education does not encourage an understanding of inherited tendencies and environmental influences so it cannot break through this conditioning to bring about an "integrated" human being, he explains. In regard to world peace, a world crisis existed because of wrong values in relation to people, property and ideas. Under the heading "Sex and Marriage", Krishnamurti maintained that the "problem" of passion and sexual urge was complex and difficult and if educators had not probed it for themselves they could not help those they were educating. One of the main reasons sex so controlled our lives was that we were not creative and were dominated by the intellect. While sensuality was developed through books, advertisements and cinema, chastity was upheld, which caused a contradiction. The hindrances and escapes of the mind constituted the problem, not sex or any other specific issue, he said.[32]

Krishna spent most of the year 1951 in retreat, no doubt trying to heal the intimacy of his relationship with Rosalind and Rajagopal. It was decided that Rajagopal would travel with him back to India in November 1951 and Krishna wrote to Dwarkanath Telang to let him know. Ever since his aborted attempt to become involved in *Bharata Samaj* back in the early 1920s, Krishna had eschewed politics and his year of retreat no doubt left him even less interested. The less talk about politics the better, he told Dwarkanath. Only small and weak countries were pacific, he said; the others were all intent on "butchering" each other.[33]

Radha says that the year Krishna spent back in Ojai had helped heal his and Rosalind's relationship and he wrote long and lovingly to Rosalind after he'd left America. When Krishna arrived in Bombay, after a brief stay in London, he was still maintaining his public silence, according to Pupul Jayakar, and he did not break it until he went to Madras where he gave twelve talks from 5 January to 12 February 1952. Jayakar says Rajagopal was very wary of her and Nandini, grilling them about the details of Krishna's "process" in Ootacamund in 1948. Rajagopal lived in the Theosophical headquarters compound while Krishna stayed upstairs at *Vasanta Vihar*, with Pupul Jayakar and Nandini sleeping on a closed-in verandah and sharing a bathroom with Madhavachari, as the rest of the building had been let. Jayakar says Krishna tried to impress on them how much Rajagopal had sacrificed for him and was anxious that they all be friends.[34]

Biographer, Mary Lutyens' view is that during his retreat Krishna had been trying to find new words and expressions for solutions to complex living – advising people to break with the past and hear the "whisperings" of their own prejudices. As always, words were inadequate to convey what Krishna wanted to say about the power of forces beyond the capacity of the intellect to comprehend them. A professor from Travancore

University in Mylapore wrote to Krishna saying that his talks seemed negative, except for his references to "love" but, even so, he didn't understand what Krishna meant by it. Meanwhile, Jinarajadasa never let up on his hope for reconciliation between Krishna and the Theosophical Society. He questioned Krishna about what he meant by "Truth", pointing out the Upanishadic quote, "Satyam eva jayate, na anritam" which he translated as, "Verily Truth conquers, not untruth". Jinarajadasa also impressed on Krishna that he should put his correct birthdate, from his horoscope, on his passport application and sent him the "original" Sanskrit version which he said Krishna's father had given him years before. Finally he issued the umpteenth invitation for Krishna to visit the Theosophical estate, challenging him with his own words about discarding old mental concepts. Jinarajadasa asked Krishna if he dared step through the gates to call on an old friend.[35]

But Krishna did not visit, despite Rajagopal being accommodated there. The two left for London in March 1952 and Krishna gave a series of talks at the Friends' Meeting House in April. Writing to Rosalind about the death of the English King, Rajagopal said that the English were queer people, not grieving, but going about their work satisfied with the Queen who had replaced the monarch. He said Krishna's talks had been good even though their six weeks there together had not been wonderful and he would go on to Switzerland for his health before returning to Ojai, while Krishna went directly home. Rajagopal also impressed on Rosalind that he needed to return to India, that it was important to him, and afterwards he hoped that they would "stay put" in one place. Radha says that Rajagopal's mother was still alive and he wanted to see her as well as keep his eye on Krishna's activities in India.[36]

Krishna's hay fever was bad in Ojai in June 1952 so he went with Rosalind to stay at Santa Barbara. Radha, by this time returned from Swarthmore College, was studying at the University of California. After an engagement of about five months, in July Radha was married to James Sloss, a student who had stayed in Radha's home when he first attended the Happy Valley School with her in 1946. Krishna gave ten talks in Ojai on Saturdays and Sundays during August and Rajagopal left for Europe in September after a brief sojourn at home, with Krishna following him in October. During the summer, back in India, Nandini had been diagnosed with cervical cancer and was flown to London for an operation. Pupul Jayakar sent a telegram to Krishna and received no reply. It was if he had vanished, she said. Yet she felt that his silent "presence" was with her sister throughout the operation and recovery period. Nandini became strong again and went on to establish a play school for street children, called *Bal Anand*, which was later incorporated into the Krishnamurti Foundation in India.[37]

According to Radha, before leaving Ojai in the autumn of 1952, Krishna gave Rosalind a pencil copy of a letter he said he would deliver to Nandini. It had been prompted by Rosalind's belief that he was infatuated by the younger woman, and was presumably an explanation of his commitment to Rosalind. Rajagopal was asked by Rosalind to check that the letter was delivered and he agreed to carry it. Krishna allegedly stated in the letter that he had had a relationship with a woman for more than twenty years and did not intend to break it, and apologised for any misleading impression he had given Nandini. But once in Bombay, Krishna is believed to have never delivered the letter, even though his bond with Rosalind remained strong, as he wrote to her almost daily.[38]

When, in early 1953, Krishna and Rajagopal were staying with Ratansi Morarji in Bombay, Jayakar says that, publicly, there was no hint of trouble between Krishna and Rajagopal. Krishna held many private meetings with people who sought interviews with him to ease their sorrow and he gave a series of public talks. But privately there was obvious discord between the two men, Rajagopal often angrily raising his voice and Krishna remaining passive. After one incident Krishna went for a walk with them and declared the trouble was his fault. (Radha also writes of an argument she witnessed in Ojai in 1951 when Krishna pummelled Rajagopal's chest, so it's clear that relations were increasingly difficult, regardless of who was taking the physical action.) Another problem which may have arisen as early as 1953 was Rajagopal's problem drinking, which had reportedly begun after a doctor in India prescribed whisky to ease his pain from oesophagitis. A clear sign that there was great resentment between the two men is to be found in the fact that Rajagopal did not tell Krishna of the birth of Radha's baby in February 1953 until twelve days after he'd heard the news, which, understandably, hurt Krishna.[39]

During this trip to India Krishna was able to develop discussions with a group of intellectuals who gathered at Vithal Wadi, near Poona, at the home of Rao Sahib Patwardhan, an ardent, prominent political activist in the years leading up to Independence who had by now broken with the Socialist Party. Jayakar says those present, some of them Socialists, were tough-minded and focussed on poverty and social action in India, whereas Krishna tried to persuade them that problems could not be solved through ideology.[40]

Krishna also turned his attention more to education issues. Rishi Valley was still in a mess, with the teachers, who were caught between Theosophical views and Krishna's teaching, not thinking clearly about subjects such as authority, freedom and order, according to Krishna. Krishna also asked Achyut Patawardhan to work at the other Rishi Valley Trust site, the Rajghat estate in Varanasi, to try to improve its focus. He told Achyut that his mind was choked with the syndrome of social work and that unless the centre of his being changed, all his social work was useless. Soon, with Achyut's support, an agricultural school, a medical centre and hospital for the poor were established. Krishna and Rajagopal visited Rajghat in the winter months of 1953-54 where Krishna had fifteen sessions with the children. In order to convey his message about complex subjects such as fear, authority, sorrow and death, Krishna spoke gently and with great affection and the children reportedly remained quiet and listened intently.[41]

In Bombay in 1953 Krishna met his nephew G Narayan again. asking him if he'd like to teach at the Rishi Valley School. G Narayan relates how that night he had an experience in which his chest was infused with white and blue light, and a great sense of calm. Although he was trained as a lawyer and economist he decided to become a teacher and six months later took up a position at the school.[42]

On this trip to the Indian sub-continent Krishna also met a young man who would become a "tireless" worker for him, publishing a 2-volume bibliography of works by and about Krishnamurti. As a boy, a few days after his mother's death in Colombo in 1949, Susunaga Weeraperuma had heard Krishna give a public talk. Then in 1953, at the age of eighteen, he travelled to Poona and Bombay and had the opportunity to meet Krishna face to face. Weeraperuma, a librarian, was devoted to Krishnamurti's teaching for the major part of his lifetime, yet in old age he is now completely disillusioned about him. He even accuses Krishna of hypnotising him when he was eighteen by staring into his eyes with an intense gaze. knowing instinctively that he was a very vulnerable and malleable boy. Believing Krishna to be a "pure being" caused Weeraperuma to allow Krishna to penetrate deeply into his psyche, he says, and to use him for his "work, glory and worldwide publicity".[43]

Regardless of who he might have influenced for good or ill during his Indian tour, by June 1953, Krishna was back in California and trying to enjoy his family life, with Radha, James Sloss and their baby visiting at weekends. The young couple had both graduated and Sloss was about to take up a position with the Atomic Energy Commission in northern California. Krishna and Rosalind spent a large part of the summer at Point Lobos near Carmel, enjoying their family which now included a poodle, named Coco, as well as a grandchild. Radha says that Krishna, at fifty eight, still wanted a sexual relationship with Rosalind whereas she looked on their relationship as a habit, with occasional "sparks" of their old love. Krishna happily acted as father to Radha, as usual, and took on the role of grandfather to her baby, nicknamed Tinka. Radha felt the same sense of family she had known as a child, with Rajagopal included whenever he was present. But she describes Rajagopal as irascible and Krishna as only "ostensibly" trying to make peace.[44]

Krishna was giving talks in the Oak Grove at Ojai in June and July 1953 when news came through of Harpers publishing *Education and the Significance of Life*. It was a breakthrough into mainstream publishing under the auspices of a very well-known and respected publishing house, as Krishna recognised. Harpers had also agreed to a run-on for a special, lower-priced Indian edition. In addition to this coup, Chetana Publishing in India would release Carlo Suares' book, *Krishnamurti and the Unity of Man*, translated from the French. Pleased with the developments, Krishna was nevertheless wary of others cashing in on his and Rajagopal's work, warning Madhavachari not to release their mailing list to Chetana.[45]

The odd couple, Krishna and Rajagopal, were soon off to Europe again in the autumn of 1953, travelling on to India, and with tentative plans to visit Australia the following year. Radha says that Krishna wrote to Rosalind more philosophically, but continued to assure her of his love. Rajagopal met with the Harpers' editor and arranged translations and copyrights.[46]

In June 1953 Jinarajadasa died suddenly in Chicago, at the age of seventy eight. He had resigned the Presidency the previous year but was still very involved in the Society, writing to Krishna just ten days before his death that he was still organising copying of Krishna's correspondence. With this death Krishna's link with this formative Theosophical aspect of his life was suddenly cut and he reflected to Lady Emily that a great deal of the past had gone with Jinarajadasa. Krishna marvelled though that he and Lady Emily still loved each other forty years since they'd met.[47]

Their love would be tested by a book Lady Emily was writing about Krishnamurti and Theosophy. A son-in-law of Lady Emily was a partner in the publisher, Hart Davis, and in October 1953 she had published by the company an autobiographical work about her adolescence, which sold about 10,000 copies. She and the publisher were keen to publish another biographical work. Mary Lutyens says that Krishna gave Lady Emily permission to quote from his correspondence and his and Nitya's accounts of the 1922 "process". Krishna wrote Lady Emily that he was not "ashamed" of the past but he hoped that what she wrote did not cause animosity among Theosophists.[48]

Krishna and Rajagopal flew on to India after a brief stay in Holland and then Italy, visiting Vanda Scaravelli and her husband, first in Rome, and then moving on for a fortnight of discussions in Fiesole, outside of Florence. On reaching Madras they received by mail Lady Emily's typescript of the book, since Krishna had asked to see it before publication. Rajagopal's reaction was that many people would be disillusioned by it and as he had many suggestions to make, and Krishna was very tired and had a busy schedule in India, it might be best to wait until Rajagopal was back in London in April when he could help Lady Emily with editing. Lady Emily was not satisfied with this response and set to work with her daughter, Mary, and an editor, to revise it. In February 1954 Krishna went to Bombay and saw the free school for poor children Nandini had established, which was incorporated into the Krishnamurti Foundation activities that year. By March when he and Rajagopal were in Athens, Krishna wrote to Mary suggesting it might be wiser not to publish the book, or at least to talk it over "leisurely" before deciding to go ahead. Rajagopal also wrote a confusing letter, not clearly stating his view about publication. So Lady Emily waited until May 1954 when Krishna and Rajagopal were to spend a fortnight in London, after a visit to Vanda Scaravelli in Rome and Fiesole. When the time came Krishna did not talk about the book so Lady Emily presumed that he had no objection. Its title, *Candles in the Sun*, carried the meaning that Krishna, as World Teacher, or the sun, had dimmed the lights of all those "candle-holders" who had proclaimed him. Mary sent off the final manuscript to the publisher while Krishna was still in London, knowing that it would be the first time the events of Krishna's process in 1922 had been made public.[49]

Krishna's second book, *The First and Last Freedom*, was published in 1954, first in the United States and then in England, to good reviews in *The Observer* and the *Times Literary Supplement*, among others. Aldous Huxley's Foreword set the mood to take the work very seriously. He wrote that even the best cookery book was no substitute for even the worst dinner – yet even the most learned fell into the error of imagining symbols as more real than what they stood for. Every system was a standing temptation to take symbols too seriously. He explained that Krishnamurti offered the only solution to this fundamental problem – that everyone find truth for and by himself, and not in systems or organisations. Huxley pointed out Krishna's belief that transcendent spontaneity or "creative Reality" revealed itself only in a state of "alert passivity" or "choiceless awareness" since judgement and comparison irrevocably committed a person to duality. He ended the Foreword with Krishna's recurring idea that the still mind knew what love was.[50]

Krishna's book, which would prove to be a compelling entrance into general publishing in Britain and pave the way for many books to follow, had taken Huxley's cue from a decade before that the immediacy of specific questions and answers about conduct in particular circumstances was a successful way to convey philosophical truths. The first part of the book comprised extracts from Krishna's talks on particular themes while the second part was a selection of questions and answers. Subjects covered included how truth becomes a lie, the confusion of the mind, superficiality, the meaning of life, and transformation.[51]

Once back in the United States Krishna spoke to large crowds in New York, many attracted by having read his book. He wrote to Lady Emily from there without mentioning either his or her book. But once he'd returned to Ojai and received a proof copy of *Candles in the Sun*, he wrote to Lady Emily to say the book must not be published. She replied that his sudden and unexpected opposition was distressing and it was probably too late to withdraw the book. His reply was immediate and emphatic: he was deeply convinced it would not help what he was doing; it would cause bitterness and sensation; and, as it was about him, what he said must be taken into account. So out of love and respect she must stop publication. The publisher finally released Lady Emily from her contract but the company had to be reimbursed. Krishna offered to pay in instalments out of his annuity from Miss Dodge, but Mary Lutyens found the cost of reimbursement from other sources. Krishna wrote to say how sorry he was to have caused such unhappiness. The following month he went to London and was reconciled with Lady Emily and Mary, who both gained the impression that it was pressure from Rajagopal that caused Krishna to write refusing approval. However, Rajagopal wrote to Dwarkanath Telang in October that it was Krishna who had made the decision at the eleventh hour. Six months later Rajagopal claimed Lady Emily was still in the dark about whether her book's publication would come later or never. And then another three months on, he said Lady Emily had agreed not to publish the book during Krishna's lifetime.[52]

Krishna went on to Rome to see Vanda Scaravelli in October 1954 and Rajagopal joined him there before they both went on to India for the winter. Rosalind wrote to Krishna in February a letter ostensibly from their poodle, Coco, complete with inked paw mark, announcing that she had sold her puppies to raise $1,000 for his school at Rishi Valley. Krishna was deeply touched.[53]

Another significant event in February 1955 was the death of Maria Huxley, who'd remained a close friend of Rosalind. She'd been having radiation treatment since the previous summer and saw Rosalind whenever it could be arranged, considering the distance between their two homes: hers at North Kings Rd, Los Angeles, and Rosalind's in Ojai. Maria had written in September 1954 that she and Aldous had got away for a weekend, and "Krishnaji" was there. She felt so much calmer, she said, and Aldous was stimulated and optimistic. Maria had always had Aldous's emotional life as her main focus – she had been both a conduit and a protective bulwark in Huxley's social relations with the intellectual and social elite of California. During their years there directors, actors and arts luminaries such as Edith Sitwell and Stravinsky, as well as scientists of the calibre of Edwin Hubble and Fred Hoyle were the mainstay of their social circle. At her deathbed Aldous Huxley sat with her for hours on end. He would repeat to her over and over that he would always be with her in that light which was the central "reality" of their beings, that she was enveloped and sustained in love, and that she should let go and forget her poor body and the past. Rosalind had helped bring Maria home from hospital two weeks before she died and after her funeral Aldous went to stay at *Arya Vihara* for a few days, Radha describing his grief as so intense it was difficult to know how to help him recover. Huxley's biographer says Aldous went away with his son, Matthew, the day after the funeral.[54]

Krishna missed direct involvement in this trauma in Huxley's life as he was in India in February 1955. By March he was quite ill, and as the heat intensified it was arranged that he would go for about a month to Ranikhet, a hill station in the Himalayas. There he spent the first few days with Achyut Patwardhan who would read the *Mandukya Upanishad* to him in the evenings. When Achyut returned to the plains, Krishna stayed on alone to walk among the mountain forests by day, with a cook employed to provide his meals.[55]

Soon after Krishna came down from the Himalayas to the heat of India in April, he was off again to a more temperate clime. He spent a couple of weeks in the Scaravelli Fiesole home and then travelled to Holland to meet Rajagopal. He gave five talks in Amsterdam at the Bellevue Hotel and then went on to London where he gave six talks at the Friends' Meeting House. At the end of May Krishna flew back to the United States while it was arranged for Rajagopal, who wasn't well, to stay on in Europe at a sanatorium for a few weeks. By now, Krishna was looking forward to talks in the oak grove at Ojai in August, followed by a trip to Australia and New Zealand and on to India with Rosalind late in the year. Rajagopal wrote to James Vigeveno, who was still quite involved in Krishnamurti activities in Ojai, that there would be no need to advertise Krishna's Ojai talks, as word of mouth would suffice as usual. He then relented and said that if Vigeveno wanted to advertise in the *Citizen News* or *Sunday Times* he could.[56]

About this same time Krishna wrote twice from Ojai to Mary Lutyens in London to say that he wanted an assurance that Lady Emily's book would never be published, not even after his and her deaths. He wanted an answer before he left with Rajagopal to fly to Sydney in the first week of November 1955. Mary Lutyens tried to put him off, but he wrote again from Sydney to say that future biographies may or may not be written but neither his nor Nitya's accounts could be included in Lady Emily's book without his permission. He was not bullying them, he said, but even if Rajagopal had given permission, he, Krishna, was now withdrawing it. Mary now felt there was no alternative but to withhold the material and Lady Emily's book was finally published in 1957 minus Krishna's correspondence and any account of the Ojai experience. Lady Emily wrote to Krishna in November 1956 to say that as a result of his disapproval, she and Mary had thoroughly revised the book, leaving out his goings "off". She hoped the memoir would be published while she was still alive, as it had been impossible to stop the book at the eleventh hour. Radha says there were "endless" discussions about Lady Emily's book in the summer of 1955, with Krishna convincing Rosalind that the publicity about her role in the 1922 "process" would bring undesirable publicity to the Happy Valley School. Rosalind suggested her name be left out. According to Radha, Krishna took on a protective role for Rosalind, yet Rosalind did not feel strongly either way about publication of Lady Emily's book. She did not even believe in the "process", it seems, yet had played an active role in it. This attitude is difficult to comprehend. If she viewed it as a bizarre pretence on Krishna's part in order to have a physical bond with herself as a woman, why did she take no responsibility for dispelling the contrary view that it was an example of Krishna's extraordinary spiritual power? After all, she had been intimately connected with him for the duration of his public role as a spiritual advisor, a role he'd carried out for over thirty years. Out of honesty she might have declared her scepticism there and then, even if it meant putting an end to the material comforts that Krishnamurti's public image brought her. If she believed it was a harmless, youthful game that she and Krishna played in order to be physically close, she could have said so, regardless of the disillusionment of Theosophists. She had no reason to continue to pander to their illusions, if that's what she thought they were. Radha suggests Krishna may have been pretending to protect Rosalind in the hope that his 1922 "process" would not be disclosed to Nandini, who had experienced something similar more recently. Yet, judging by Nandini's sister's account, it was explained to them both that this type of occurrence was explicable in the life of a great sage, such as Shankaracharya, so it might be expected that Nandini would not have been surprised about earlier occurrences. She may even have heard about them from Theosophists who knew they had occurred several times in the 1920s, in Holland and California, even without Rosalind being present. In any case, Rosalind remained publicly silent about her views.[57]

Rajagopal was Krishna's helpmate in Sydney for the talks but, according to Radha, he had no desire to return with Krishna to India and witness the 'devotion to guru' shown Krishna there. Rosalind, on the other hand, wanted to see it for herself, and in particular to meet Nandini.[58]

Krishnamurti was greeted in Sydney by an article headed,

although her conclusion might arguably stand as a basis for debate, in view of Krishna's record for international travel and smart clothes:

> But there has never been a world teacher who did not prefer to sit quietly under a tree with his begging bowl and his disciples, while the chanting processions of purple-robed and jewelled priests swept on their way somewhere else.[59]

In Sydney Krishnamurti gave six talks from November 9 - 26, 1955. He began in the usual way, inviting people to listen with an intention to understand but without seeking an end or answer. All problems were individual, he said, and the individual problem was the world problem. If we did not understand our own urges and compulsions they produced conflict. Relationship was the mirror in which to see ourselves. These ideas were all conundrums, perhaps, to the European audience, but they are tenets of Advaitism. The petty, conditioned mind, according to Krishnamurti, could never find that which was beyond the mind. Anger, jealousy, envy and lust - all these reactions existed only in one's relationship to another, he explained in answer to a question. Relationship was used as a means of security and self-perpetuation, self-expansion and self-aggrandisement, he said. And he reminded people that if they were really listening they were bound to experience the truth of it. In answer to another question, Krishnamurti talked about listening, to follow the actual functioning of your own mind as you sat there: to know that you were sitting there and he was speaking; then to go deeper and become conscious that the mind was registering and naming; then deeper, to recognise hidden motives; then to understand what you were in the mirror of relationship, without condemning. At this point you could go beyond your mind, he maintained. In his second talk he went on to say that a mind that was occupied could not pay attention, and most minds were occupied with an idea, opinion or judgement, so most people never put serious questions to themselves. By the third talk he was very concerned to follow through with the idea that we sought authority from others to relieve us of our confusion – people followed tradition, dogma, gurus, religious beliefs. He made a salient point in answer to a question about whether he had experienced freedom. It was irrelevant, he said, since people could only judge this according to their own psychological inclination. One did not learn wisdom from books or teachers, but by "uncovering" the mind and heart, which was self-knowledge. In the fourth talk Krishnamurti posed the question whether change came about at a deep level of consciousness, and he concluded that radical change could only happen without effort, when the mind was not trying to become something. As a parent and teacher, one needed to comprehend that freedom was at the beginning and not at the end. In Talk Five Krishnamurti led the audience to recognise the "known" - our minds crowded with conclusions, knowledge, experiences – and to be free of it so that another state - the "unknown" - might come into being. Krishnamurti reminded people not to take notes as he and they were trying to experience directly. The mind, being the result of time, had its being in the area of the "known", he said. When the mind was aware that it was conditioned, only then was it free to give its attention to the conditioning. If it was aware, without trying to be free, then that very awareness brought its own freedom. Finally in the sixth talk, Krishnamurti tackled time, and the [false] idea of a gap between what is and what should be, of making an effort to achieve or improve. Was love, goodness or beauty something to be achieved through effort, he asked? If you practised love now would you get it next week? When you saw the process of becoming as illusion, the "other" was, a "love" which could not be measured by the mind, he said.[60]

The impression of one young man, aged just fifteen, was that he came away from the lectures at the Conservatorium of Music with a "marvellous sense of energy". He remembers Krishna being very calm in dealing with one woman who hectored him from the floor, calling out that he was not speaking the truth about God.[61]

There must have been some uncertainty about whether Rajagopal would go on to India after his visit to Sydney in November 1955, as a circular to raise funds and announce the

Australian visit said he would fly out with Krishna direct to India. Krishna also wrote from Sydney to Madhavachari in Madras to apologise for a misunderstanding that had casued Madhavachari to organise Rajagopal's wardrobe for his stay. Just Mrs Rajagopal and he would be coming, Krishna explained. He said that they had paid their airfares already but would like Rs 200 sent to Calcutta to pay any excess weight plus their *Grand Hotel* bill for an overnight stay before flying on to Benares. The Sydney circular, authorised by Spencer English, estimated the expenses for the Australian visit at 1,500 Australian pounds and asked for "voluntary" contributions to meet the costs of airfares, advertising, hall rentals, printing and mailing, as well as recording and transcribing Krishna's talks. Once Krishna was in India his accommodation and meals were free, taken care of by friends and the administration of the Krishnamurti centres.[62]

Rosalind arrived in Sydney as Rajagopal was returning to Ojai. A big crowd saw her and Krishna off from Sydney and another greeted them in Jakarta. In Singapore the couple had a day to themselves for once, staying at the *Raffles Hotel*, and seeing the sights as tourists, a rare activity for Krishna.[63]

Rosalind wrote to Rajagopal from India to say how strange it was that she was there and he in America. She hoped he had the family with him and they were all happy. Many people were disappointed that he had not gone to India, she said. Some people were very nice to her – the Madhavacharis and Sunanda – and the food was delicious – she was probably putting on weight. She also did some sightseeing with Kitty Shiva Rao, whom she had known for many years. But Rosalind was clearly surprised that the organisation was in such a state of disorder. Everything was tense, there were daily meetings, Rao had cried openly, there was a proposal to close down the schools, everyone talked and criticised, but she did not let herself get involved. She told Rajagopal that Krishna had said he wished Rajagopal were there to talk the situation over with him. She listened to others and learnt a lot but would not give an opinion until she had seen the whole thing, she said. Pupul had been to visit and gone away "hurt", but not because of her, she added.[64]

Radha says that Krishna became ill in Madras and Rosalind nursed him. She hoped to meet Nandini but Krishna said she was in a state of "*samadhi*", whereas Rosalind believed Krishna had arranged for Nandini to be inaccessible to her. But Rosalind did meet Nandini at one of Krishna's talks and believed that while Nandini was "innocent", Krishna had been deceptive about his feelings for her. Krishna expressed his physical love for Rosalind and wanted her to enjoy her time in India but her "confrontations" with Krishna over Nandini were met by a "stony" silence from him. Rosalind was also upset that Krishna travelled by first-class rail while Madhavachari did not, and she was deeply disturbed that the devotees and adulation, which he had so often publicly disparaged, was so evident in India.[65]

In Pupul Jayakar's version of the 1955 visit she sees a marked deterioration in Krishna. His astonishing, awesome beauty was absent, she says, his face aged and his hair greying. Krishna told her later that he often became silent and passive when faced with Rosalind's anger, which made her even more furious. Jayakar says that Rosalind had taken Krishna for granted for many years and now she found there was suddenly no Krishna with whom she could establish a relationship. This is a curious statement which implies Jayakar sanctioned his silence and attributed to him some great spiritual authority in what many would view as simply an interpersonal relationship.[66]

Krishna and Rosalind left India in April, spending a week in Alexandria with the Suares. In Rome they were met by his old friend, Vanda Scaravelli who was trying to find an Italian publisher for Krishna. Rajagopal had failed to send money for Rosalind and Krishna so they were at first "virtually" penniless but stayed with the wealthy Countess. Once their money came through Rosalind went to Paris for a week on her own and Krishna wrote imploring her not to be superficially agitated and over-emotional. But, according to Radha, her mother had had a major change of heart, and by the time she met Krishna and Rajagopal in Stockholm she wanted to be completely free of Krishna. She told Rajagopal that Krishna could live elsewhere whereas she needed to stay in Ojai as she was director of the *Happy Valley School*. Rajagopal thought she was being unreasonable but Krishna agreed not go back to Ojai. After her return home Krishna wrote to her as if nothing had happened and assured her that she still had his love, and that only when one lost love did things go wrong. But their split would have major repercussions in Krishna's personal life and in the administration of the organisation set up to disseminate his teaching. Rosalind's independence was reinforced when her close friend, Robert Logan, died in June 1956, leaving her financially secure for life. In August she made a will leaving everything she owned to Rajagopal and Radha, with Rajagopal as her executor.[67]

Krishna was ill with an allergy and bronchitis in Brussels and Amsterdam, and went on to stay in the French countryside near Perigueux, with a French textile merchant and his wife, for about a month. That summer of 1956 Radha and James Sloss flew to Copenhagen to meet Rajagopal. Krishna was waiting in Holland to see them, but communication had broken down between Rajagopal and Krishna, and Krishna waited in vain for them to call him. Harmony was restored in Paris where Radha and James stayed with old friends of Krishna and went out to dinner with their two father figures, Krishna and Rajagopal. This brief period seems to have rallied their love. When Radha got the flu Krishna tried to pull the fever out of her feet as he had done when she was a child – a technique Rosalind had used on Nitya. Their idyllic sojourn in Paris over, Krishna returned to friends in the Dordogne and Radha and James went on to Rome where Countess Vanda Scaravelli took them on to Assisi, Venice and Florence. During talks in Hamburg with Rajagopal in September 1956, Krishna was planning ahead. His public talks that summer had been, as usual, ranging over the subjects of inward revolution and self-knowledge through the overthrow of the accumulation of experience so that a free mind could discover and experience anew. Krishna's own inner revolution was already in train. He sent a detailed schedule for talks in India the following month, and proposed giving group personal interviews rather than individual interviews, obviously with a view to cutting down his workload.[68]

Also that September, *Commentaries on Living* was published, again to fine reviews in respected journals such as *New Republic* and in the *Times Literary Supplement*. As mentioned earlier, Aldous Huxley's suggestions were the foundation of this book, and the next two in the series. Huxley's proposal had been to edit Krishna's talks and discussions in such a way as to elicit the immediate and practical advice Krishna gave, for people to face the problems of daily living. Rajagopal drew on reams of transcribed material to edit the book into one to two-page segments on 88 topics as diverse as "Three Pious Egoists" to "Respectability", "Politics", "Life in a City", "Self-esteem", "The flame and the Smoke", "Stillness and Will" and "Suffering". In "Politics" Krishna set the scene of meeting a leading politician and ended by minimising his power – saying that by manipulating outer effects, people hoped to bring about order but it wasn't as simple as that because life was a total process, inner and outer. In "The Flame and the Smoke" Krishna described the mother of several children who had never felt love. He said that what was open and vulnerable was beautiful, and dullness was a form of self-protection. But it was best to remain as you were, even if insensitive, and become aware of it, to let the "story" unfold. The doing was not important but the listening was, he said. The battle was not between the flame and the smoke but in different responses within the smoke. If you observed the smoke, even insensitivity, the flame, or sensitivity, would arise. In "Beauty" Krishna described a "fairly good" dancer who was proud of her art and wanted to talk about beauty and the spirit. His conclusion was that the search for beauty and incessant talk of art was an escape from life. If any of these seekers after truth who had come to see Krishna recognised themselves – politician, disillusioned mother, young dancer – it might be hoped that they gained as much from Krishna's unsentimental and direct advice as did the thousands of readers who could identify with these unidentified characters.[69]

Krishna would respect Rosalind's wishes and keep away from her and Ojai for a total of four years. During the first year after their break he continued to write and assure her that his feelings for her had not changed. He returned to Delhi in October 1956 alone and Jayakar saw a major difference in his physical appearance. He was filled with beauty, she said, and drew diplomats, *sannyasis*, bureaucrats, professors and more young people than previously to his talks. A small group followed him about the country and Kitty Shiva Rao kept Rajagopal informed of Krishna's schedule, commenting that Krishna quite often questioned what he was doing, since people attended his talks but very few understood them. Kitty was enthusiastic about Krishna's new book, sending along a local review. Two major radical intellectuals in Maharashtra, Javdekar and Bhagwat, had written in 1948 that Krishnaji was a "realized" human being, recognising in his talks Advaita Vedanta philosophy cast into contemporary language. Their approval was a valuable imprimatur for other major Indian thinkers and writers to build on in the 1950s. Krishnamurti now commanded great respect. An indication of this is the fact that in December 1956 His Holiness the Dalai Lama, aged just twenty and travelling in India for the first time, was keen to meet Krishnamurti when he was in Madras. His companion, Apa Sahib Pant, from the Indian Foreign Service, described as "breathtaking" watching the electric affection that instantly flashed between these two great sages. The Dalai Lama was said to have called Krishnamurti a "great soul".[70]

Also that winter a young devotee of Vinoba Bhave, Vimala Thakar, went to hear Krishna speak in Benares. Vinoba Bhave, who had been a trusted aide to Gandhi, began the Bhoodan movement which advocated that all land belonged to God. He was considered a saint and established an ashram in Paunur in Maharashtra. Vimala Thakar had once been a disciple of the guru, Tukroji Maharaj in Maharashtra, and then marched with Vinoba Bhave across northern India, speaking to village people about poverty, non-violence and a revolutionary interpretation of traditional religion. She suffered pain in her ear and would later become deaf following an operation, regaining her hearing after Krishna performed a healing act. This occurrence, along with another startling act of healing on Shankar Rao, another former Gandhian, both extraordinary happenings still ahead in Krishna's remarkable life, would by the mid-1960s cement his standing as a major guru figure in India.[71]

But by 1957 Krishna was still struggling to retain an identity in harmony with his two closest companions over the past thirty years. After a fine start to Krishna's year with five public talks broadcast in Sri Lanka, Krishna and Rajagopal made arrangements to meet in Rome in March, at the outset of what was planned as a heavy program of talks in Europe during the summer. But the two men were at odds as well as exhausted so the talks were cancelled. Krishna told Rosalind he would write to no one but her and Rajagopal. He also said that even with age creeping on he would not return to Ojai until both she and Raja asked him. He continued to profess his love for Rosalind. Rajagopal's increasing testiness by 1957 shows in correspondence. In January he'd written to someone who was complaining about not having a private interview with Krishna to say that the simple fact was that if Krishnaji had wanted to see the man privately he could have done so, so why blame other people? During the summer he wrote straightforward letters that Krishna was recovering well, he had fairly regular contact with him and they expected to go to India later in the year.[72]

Krishna stayed in Europe for the summer of 1957 while Rajagopal returned to Ojai and Rosalind spent a large part of the season at Carmel. Rajagopal had hoped to spend a couple of weeks at the Bircher-Benner health clinic[73], famed as the home of muesli, before going to India late in the year but Krishna was keen to return to the sub-continent, even though he did not give talks and stayed in "semi-retreat" once he arrived. During this trip to India Rajagopal concentrated on tidying up copyright matters with Krishna. Jayakar said Krishna was vague about copyright rights and responsibilities and gave Rajagopal whatever power he wanted. Krishna was more interested in the unkempt condition of *Vasanta Vihar* which was being looked after by Madhavachari, who was now retired and spartan in his material needs. Krishna stayed on in Delhi and by the summer of 1958, returned to Ranikhet in the Himalayas. Jayakar's daughter, Radhika, and her nephew, Asit Chandmal, who would in future years become loyal friends to Krishna, visited him in Ranikhet that summer. He taught them yoga *asanas*, or postures, and how to "see" from the back of the head.[74]

Rajagopal had left India in January 1958, saying he would spend a short time in the "wretched" Bircher-Benner clinic not so much for his sake as for that of everyone else. While in India he had visited his mother, whom Rosalind had sent money from her inheritance and who would die soon after this trip to India by Rajagopal, his last. Krishna continued to write to Rosalind reassuring her about Nandini, until suddenly he decided it was absurd that he should continue to do so. Radha says that Rosalind sometimes didn't even read his letters anyway.[75]

Krishna kept a busy schedule in India during the last few months of 1958 – there were private discussions and then public talks in Poona in September, Madras in October and November, and Bombay in December. In September, Rajagopal's assistant, Bryan Casselberry, sent a bundle of mail for Krishna which had been acknowledged but not answered while Krishna was in retreat. It wasn't necessary for Casselberry to emphasise that some of the letters might have been very important and people could be wondering why they hadn't heard from Krishna, but he did emphasise it anyway. It was a pointed way to demonstrate the work that Rajagopal was no doubt tired of attending to - and the point was not lost on Krishna. In November he signed a document that gave full copyright in all his writings up until that time and into the future to KWINC, and authorising Rajagopal to make all arrangements for all publications. Krishna had earlier ceased to be a trustee of KWINC, and Rajagopal was already its President.[76]

By early 1959 Krishna was still in India, with a stand-off soon to develop over his return to Ojai. By April he left Bombay for Lonavala, a hill resort near Poona, staying alone in the home of Pupul and Nandini's youngest sister, with a servant to cook his meals. In May he moved up to Srinigar with Madhavachari and then on to a rest house built by Nur Jehan at Achebal, a sacred site from ancient times. Pupul Kayakar joined him, living in a hut next door, throughout June. There was no electricity and at night they used kerosene lamps. Krishna would wake at dawn to do his *asanas* and *pranayama* (yoga postures and breathing exercises), he'd share delicious *idlies* and *sambhar* or *dosas* and rice-and-lentil cakes with Pupul for breakfast, and then they'd go for a long walk. Pupul said she became aware of how difficult it was to live with Krishna - like a laser beam, the intensity of his observation and listening might scorch and shrivel his companion. Jayakar remembers him talking about speaking with the whole head - not just from the throat or mouth. Sometimes Krishna would recite poetry, especially Keats' *Ode to a Nightingale*, and sometimes chant in Sanskrit. He loved the vast glory of the sun setting behind the snowy Himalayas but he couldn't stop from being critical of some monks he'd seen who had passed by, oblivious of the splendour, their eyes focussed on the ground.[77]

Meanwhile, back in Ojai in the spring of 1959, Rajagopal fell in love with Rosalind's assistant at the Happy Valley School, Annalisa Beghe, a Swiss-Italian woman twenty five years younger than him. According to Radha, Rosalind seemed happy about the affair and that Rajagopal had someone to love him. Nevertheless she was depressed. Rajagopal too was depressed, and Annalisa would ask Rosalind for advice about how to assist him. Rosalind wrote to Krishna asking him to return to Ojai to help, but he replied that he would not return unless Rajagopal asked him. It might have seemed significant to Rosalind that her poodle, Coco, so well loved by the family, and especially by Krishna, died that summer.[78] Krishna too became ill with a kidney infection and fever in the middle of August and was taken down to Delhi and then Bombay. He returned to Srinigar in

October but was soon back in Bombay again with fever. He resumed public talks in November through until March 1960. Then he flew to Vanda Scaravelli in Rome and went on to the Bircher-Benner clinic in Switzerland in April, at last writing to Rajagopal from there about a return to Ojai. Rajagopal had been anxious, not knowing Krishna's whereabouts, since he'd become tired of acting as Krishna's travel agent, so he handed over this responsibility to Doris Pratt, who lived in London and had known Krishna since the 1920s. Doris too was thinking of retiring and had asked Mary Cadogan to take over the London office (which was transferred to her home as she had an infant to care for) with responsibility for arranging the European talks and distributing books. Doris had to send detailed accounts for all Krishna's bills to Rajagopal, and by 1960, with relations breaking down between Krishna and Rajagopal, wealthy friends of Krishna were paying his bills.[79]

Once Krishna was home in Ojai, the players on three sides of the human triangle made a pact to have a moratorium on recriminations, to keep each other informed of their plans, and for Krishna not to hold talks before meeting again the following summer. Krishna stayed for six months and his health improved markedly. He was concerned during that time for Rosalind to continue to run the school and for Rajagopal to remain living at *Arya Vihara*. He emphasised to Rosalind and Radha that this was their home for life. If he saw major changes ahead he did not rush to embrace them, wanting instead to spend a harmonious summer with his family in the place that for close to forty years he had assumed was his home.[80]

Rishi Valley School, Chittoor District, A.P.

Krishna's Secondary School, Chennai

Krishnamurti Foundation India, Chennai

Leadbeater's Bungalow, Adyar Estate, Chennai

Mrs Besant's Quarters, Adyar Estate, Chennai

Krishnamurti Foundation India, Rajghat, Varanasi

Krishnamurti Foundation India, Rajghat, Varanasi

The Manor, Sydney

Chapter 10

Out with the Old, In with the New.

When all desires which shelter in the heart
Detach themselves, then does a mortal man
Become immortal: to Brahman he wins through.

Brihadaranyaka Upanishad IV, iv, 7.

Krishna's spell in Ojai in 1960 might have been called an Indian summer - he was now aged 65 and although his stay extended long after the summer was over, from May through to November, it must have lacked the true human warmth of his family life at its height. Correspondence leading up to this period reflects the tensions between Rajagopal and Krishna over financial arrangements that inevitably spilled over into many facets of their relationships.

Rajagopal had been ignorant about much of what Krishna was doing since he'd seen him last in India in early 1958, except for what he gleaned from second-hand accounts. For instance, Rajagopal wrote to Madhavachari in Madras in January 1960 trying to find out what expenses Krishna had. He understood a return air ticket to London had been paid for, he presumed from the KWINC travel fund, and he wanted to know what other funds Krishna needed for his European trip. Madhavachari replied that Krishna himself would let Rajagopal know his expenses. Meanwhile Krishna kept very quiet about his plans.[1]

In February 1960 Rajagopal wrote to a long-time friend, Kitty Shiva Rao, with whom Krishna had been staying in India, to say that there were rumours that Krishna was to go to Europe and perhaps to a clinic. Rajagopal was worried about Krishna's health and he himself was in some turmoil, he said. Kitty explained that Krishna had been very ill the previous August in

Kashmir, had been treated in Delhi with acute kidney infection and returned to Kashmir, only to find that by October he had to return to Delhi as his weight was ten kilos below his normal weight of 52 kilos. Several discussions had been cancelled as Krishna's "vitality" was low but he did manage to give a couple of talks with up to 1500 people attending. In fact Krishna gave thirty-one talks in Madras, Bombay, Benares and New Delhi from late November 1959 to early March 1960.[2]

When Krishna slipped away to Italy in March, Rajagopal tried to track him down there, writing to Vanda Scaravelli that he was sad and worried that she had not answered his two recent letters asking about Krishnaji's plans. He advised Vanda to advance whatever amount Krishna needed and let him know. Yet when Krishna went on to the Bircher-Brenner Clinic in Switzerland to rest, Rajagopal said the fee should be paid for out of the London KWINC account. Considering these difficulties, some friends of Krishna from Puerta Rica, Enrique and Isabel Biascoechea, footed the bill.[3]

It was left to Doris Pratt, the KWINC manager in London, to try to articulate the difficulties that she felt existed between Krishna and Rajagopal, and herself, as part of a kind of "triangular" connection while he was in London in May 1960. Krishna would only accept minimum help from her (spending just 21 pounds), and she had seen his attitude to her, which was at times short-tempered, as linked with his attitude to Rajagopal. But this was only her own mind's doing, she believed. She said she did not blame Krishna for showing anger, irritation, scorn or negativity. And this lack of blame was not because she idolised Krishna, she said, but because she did really feel – and she underlined the word "feel" – him as a mirror of herself. Nor did she blame Rajagopal for Krishna's terseness, she reassured him. In another letter she said that Krishna was still so very sick it was easy to believe that he nearly died in India and he was in no fit state to give talks in Ojai in May.[4]

In any case the impasse between Rajagopal and Krishna was relieved when Rajagopal agreed to Krishna's return to Ojai.

Krishna flew from London to New York on 9 May 1960, staying there with Frederick Pinter, who urged him to look into the affairs of KWINC, over which Rajagopal had complete control as President of the Board, as some previously generous donors were beginning to question the financial affairs of KWINC. When Krishna returned to Ojai in mid-May, he asked for information about the financial state of KWINC, and to be reinstated on the Board, but Rajagopal is said to have refused both requests. Krishna gave only four talks in the Oak Grove, cancelling the last four for the season. Enrique Biascoechea, was alarmed to hear this and fussed about Krishna going back to the Bircher-Benner Clinic in Switzerland. He made a reservation and wrote to Krishna that he was happy to pay the fees since he was so grateful to Krishna for changing his life. Rajagopal wasn't pleased with the cancellation of the talks, saying that Krishna was not "acutely" ill but cancelled only because he felt he did not have enough energy to complete the whole series. But Krishna seemed alright to Rajagopal; he was eating well and having a long rest. Krishna himself sent a telegram to Biascoechea to say that he regretted that he was unavoidably delayed in Ojai and the reservation should be cancelled.[5]

Mary Lutyens wonders whether Rajagopal had any understanding of Krishna's inner life and the "special" energy he needed to give public talks to large audiences.[6]

Krishna did not go to Europe in the summer or autumn of 1960, staying on in Ojai until his departure for India in November. He continued to give interviews, and one of those who had a private interview was Mary Zimbalist (nee Taylor), who had first met Krishna five years before, and whose husband, Sam, the producer of *Ben Hur*, among other major Hollywood films, had died just two years earlier. She found what Krishna had to say about death profound and moving. Whether Krishna knew he'd reached an irreconcilable turning point in his relations with Rosalind and Rajagopal is hard to judge. He certainly restricted his public speaking in India as Radha suggests was agreed on, alternating discussion sessions with talks to students and teachers, rather than public talks to large audiences. The venues were schools and centres in Madras, Benares, New Delhi, Rishi Valley and Bombay. But Radha claims that within two months the numbers attending limited discussion groups increased from sixty to two hundred. It must have seemed senseless to turn away people genuinely interested in what he had to say.[7]

By December Krishna wrote from Rajghat to Doris Pratt in London that Rajagopal had told him he could not organise talks in Europe the following year and had suggested Krishna ask Doris if she could do the work. Krishna made it clear that he could not give any public talks until the following July – without explaining why – but could talk with "gatherings". He expected to leave India by mid-March and take a rest in Italy but would be ready for work again from the end of April until early June. He hoped she could arrange gatherings outside London and was writing to her early enough to begin the necessary organisation. Mary Lutyens says that Rajagopal was in London in December 1960, when his refusal to organise the spring talks for Krishna was made clear, and he was also abusive about him, which shocked her and her mother.[8]

After India Krishna again stayed with Vanda Scaravelli in Italy in March and April and went on to London in May. Doris Pratt rented a house for Krishna for two months at Wimbledon so that he could take walks on Wimbledon Common and she arranged for twelve "small" meetings in the town hall. Doris and a Dutch friend, Anneke Korndorffer, cooked his meals and escorted him to the meetings. Lutyens says these were the first that he allowed to be taped for later publication.[9]

When Krishna left for California via New York in June 1961, Doris wrote to Vanda Scaravelli that he was dreading his return to Ojai and might be back very soon. Doris also wrote to Rajagopal of some strange and difficult happenings during the Wimbledon stay. Though Krishna's health was mostly good, at times all his energy seemed to drain from him for a few moments and he felt ill and weak and had to rest. Or during a meal he would drop his knife and fork and sit transfixed and then go limp. Or he would call out in bed at night. Krishna would not explain what was going on but told Doris not to touch him and that it was linked with the happenings described in Lady Emily's "unexpurgated" biography. Doris felt many times that she was watching a profound and tremendous "Mystery". Her description of several Krishnas within the one person was moving: first the man who helped others to look into the human mind and heart, building scaffolding which towered dizzily into the heavens to stretch the capacity of others to reach out to the hand of God; another Krishna who "rapped" out concise instructions and stood no nonsense; another who was as tender as a mother with some-one in distress; another who was frantically trying to combat his physical disabilities; and the incessant traveller grumbling about his clothes. Finally, there was the meditator who would spread a "mantle" of intense quiet over the house.[10]

Krishna wrote to Nandini of his inner events in Wimbledon as the "wheels" of Ootacamund working, powerful and strong again, without anyone being aware of it. These wheels were also furious and painful, he said.[11]

The day before Krishna flew to Los Angeles from New York, en route to Ojai, he began an extraordinary diary of his inner experiences. The journal, published sixteen years later as *Krishnamurti's Notebook*, begins with the statement that "it" was there in the evening and that other people had noticed "it". The journal, written and dated over a period of seven months, fluent and with few erasures, simultaneously describes impressions of the world of nature he was experiencing and his reflections on meditation, the mind and an otherness which he calls "it" or "benediction". There is such an emphasis in the writing between the workings of the mind and the beauty Krishna finds in nature, and on a balance between them, that the chronicle offers some insight into the relationship between the two. The account has a dream-like quality, immersed in descriptions of streams swollen by rain, sunsets exploding with colour, massive rocks, trembling leaves, a smelly pig-sty, a cawing crow. And throughout, Krishna muses on loneliness, humility, belief and other esoteric subjects such as harmony of the brain and body. At times he borders on the florid sentimentality of his early poetry, using "poetic" words such as "innocency" and "communing". At other times his descriptions are exacting. Very often he writes anthropomorphically, for example, saying that a flower is surprised at its redness. Then suddenly a succinct insight will strike the reader as an ancient truth – a saying such as, 'life is the active present, while time belongs to the past or future'.[12]

Krishna kept up his journal for the nineteen days of 1961 he spent in Ojai. He does not record that he again tried to persuade Rajagopal to allow him back on the Board of KWINC nor his interactions with Rosalind. What he does record is a lack of centre in his experience of vastness - with sights startlingly clear and colour painfully intense on the drive to Ojai, and in a dentist's chair, feeling his quivering brain and looking with the whole head, as if from the back of the head. He relives an experience he had at Vanda's home and writes of waking, shouting and groaning, in the middle of the night. His comments about love are moving – it cannot be made respectable, he says, and when it is not present, "travail" begins. The urge to possess another person springs from loneliness, and trying to escape through drink or organised religion won't erase the existence of love. He writes too of isolation, and that, unrelated to the "twists and turns of self-contaminated consciousness", there is an immense solitude in which all creation takes place. Krishna feels his body is disturbed by his travelling, as he leaves Ojai on 8 July for London, but the sensation of benediction is never far away, even during the flight.

It must have been about 1961 that Rosalind divorced Rajagopal, not that she wanted it, according to Radha, but because she thought it was right for Rajagopal. She arranged a Mexican divorce as she wanted to claim incompatibility as the grounds, without any rancour.[13]

In London Krishna finally got his dissatisfaction with Rajagopal on paper, writing to him to ask for reinstatement to the Board of KWINC and that his letter be shown to trustees.

Krishna visited Aldous Huxley, who was glad to see him. Huxley described him as looking well, but curiously different from former times, for he was now "a small bright old man, with a bald head ringed by white hair". Huxley made plans to hear Krishna's talks in Gstaad, Krishna's destination after London. Vanda Scaravelli met Krishna in Geneva and from there they went on to a chalet she rented at Gstaad, near Saanen. He gave talks in the Saanen Town Hall to about 350 people at gatherings which would become an annual event.[14]

Krishna's process was ongoing in Saanen. In his *Notebook* on 14 July 1961 he wrote sagely that the urge for repetition of a pleasant experience was the soil in which sorrow grew, and the brain had to stop making its own ways and become passive. On 16 July he described a sacredness or power that filled the room, which Vanda also felt. This was what everyone craved – monk, priest, *sannyasi* – and because they craved it, it eluded them. Vanda also wrote about her experience of Krishna's 'process'. He fainted and there was a change in his face, his eyes becoming larger. Then she felt a powerful "presence" of another dimension – simultaneously empty and full. Krishna did allow Vanda to touch him during the experience, she said, but no-one else. Again, the next day, Vanda took notes to explain to Krishna what happened when he "went off".[15]

Aldous Huxley and his second wife, Laura, visited Gstaad to hear Krishna speak several times at the end of July 1961, along with Huxley's friend, Yehudi Menuhin. Huxley said the talks were among the most impressive things he'd ever listened to. He likened the experience to that of listening to a discourse by the Buddha: "such power, such intrinsic authority, such an uncompromising refusal to allow the *homme moyen sensual* any escapes or surrogates, any *gurus*, saviours, *fuhrers*, churches." Krishna showed one how to end sorrow but if one didn't choose to fulfil those conditions, sorrow would continue indefinitely.[16]

The Huxleys met Krishna again in India at the end of the year. After Gstaad Krishna had gone on to Paris to give nine talks, staying with his friends, Carlo and Nadine Suares in the Avenue

Labourdonnais, and then on to Vanda's home *Il Leccio*, Fiesole, outside of Florence. By October he was back in India and Huxley wrote to him about the possibility of meeting in Madras after a conference Huxley was to attend in Delhi in November 1961. He was so happy to have caught "fleeting" glimpses of Krishna in Gstaad, he said. Krishna immediately invited the couple to stay at *Vasanta Vihar* and measures were taken to spruce up the austere accommodation there. It might be recalled that Huxley by this time was a revered literary figure, his standing indicated by the fact that about six hundred students went to a reception to pay him homage and collect his autograph during the conference celebrating the great Indian poet, Tagore's centenary of birth. Yet he was happy to listen in awe at Krishna's talks. Laura Huxley too was impressed, particularly about what she heard of Krishna having thrown over his deification by the Theosophical Society in the 1920s. At her request Madhavachari gave her a copy of Krishna's statement announcing the dissolution of the Order of the Star in 1929, but put paid to a story she'd been told and wanted to pass on to others in New Year greetings, that Krishna had spoken to audiences of 30,000 people. It was more like 2,500, he said.[17]

Vimala Thakar, who had first met Krishna in 1956, had gone to see him at the end of 1960 and had healing sessions for her ear, which despite treatment in England, discharged blood, causing deafness in the ear. She had had another three sittings in March 1961 and met Krishna again in London to ask him about his healing power. He told her she would not understand it. She went on to Gstaad in August of that year determined to find out about his healing power and also find an explanation for an experience she had "pulsating" through her mind and body. All Krishnaji would tell her was that he had had a power to heal since childhood but rarely exercised it. Love had played the major part in the healing, he said. Then, attending one of his talks, she found out the "folly" of trying to understand the experience she had been going through, of trying to analyse it in terms of previous experiences. Vimala Thakar says that she was experiencing vibrations and something within her was let loose, freeing her from all personal, national, racial and ideological preoccupations. In December 1961 Vimala met Krishna again in India and he encouraged her to speak publicly. Old people at the helm of every sphere of life had no fire, he said, but if she had fire within her she should not let it die out. He advised her to shout from the "rooftops". In 1962 Vimala found she was writing poetry and was "staggered" by this "phenomenon". Again she went to Gstaad and met with Krishna and again he encouraged her to speak, to put "ginger" into people's minds and bombs under them. Soon she was speaking in England, Norway, Germany and Holland and then met Krishna in Geneva at the end of the year. There she talked with him about people believing that she was his disciple and spreading his message. He said he was afraid that would happen. It was not easy for her to stand alone but the world needed *sannyasis*, he said. After Vimala Thakar first heard Krishnamurti, some of her friends thought she had been hypnotised but she described it as two minds experiencing the same state. At one point in *An Eternal Voyage*, Vimala writes that Krishna told her that the talks were sinking deep into her being, operating all the time, and one day she realised the truth. Now Vimala Thakar maintains that when Krishnamurti gave discourses or conducted discussions he used to get transported into a different dimension of consciousness. She felt the presence of that consciousness within her occasionally before 1962 and since then it has never left her. "That consciousness or Presence does not belong to Buddha, Christ or Krishnamurti. It is a natural consummation of human refinement," she explains.[18]

In the winter of 1961-62 Krishna gave 23 public talks as well as holding private discussions and interviews. His public audiences were estimated at 4,000 capacity each talk, so it might be argued that there'd been no diminution in his fame as a result of his break with Rajagopal, just as he had not really suffered from his break with the Theosophists thirty years before. Krishna had struck out on his own in 1929, and in a sense he was repeating the experience in his current distancing from Rajagopal's management of Krishnamurti Writings Inc.

Madhavachari kept Rajagopal informed of all of Krishna's affairs, and showed particular concern over Krishna's health once he'd returned to Vanda in Europe in mid-March 1962. Krishna was suffering a recurrence of a kidney infection and at one stage Madhavachari even considered going to visit him and later told Rajagopal that he was the best person to be with Krishna to attend to his good health. Rajagopal agreed that Krishna needed someone other than an admirer or devotee to look after him. Rajagopal also kept track of Krishna through contact with other mutual friends, such as Biascoechea. Madhavachari also took up the pen in defence of Krishna after an article in London's *Daily Mail* in February 1962 about an "authoress" and daughter of a brigadier, who had "joined a strange cult". The paper was concerned about Rowena Farr sitting beneath a banyan tree and listening to Krishna, whom the paper dubbed "The New Messiah", and implied that it caused her "abdication from life and its responsibilities". Madhavachari wrote to the Managing Editor to say there was nothing strange or oriental about Krishnamurti and he did not call himself "The New Messiah".[19]

Soon after Krishna arrived in Rome on 15 March 1962 he suffered fever and Vanda recorded an unusual statement he made when his eyes were closed or partly closed. It was not like the transformation she had seen on the earlier occasion. He spoke, using a "natural" voice, of himself as if he was someone else, describing his nice face and eyelashes, how he had wanted to come back to Rome for her and that he loved her and she must look after him. He was ill for some time, with kidney trouble. In May he was recovered and went to London, staying in another furnished house in Ridgeway Place, Wimbledon. He spoke at the Friends' House and Wimbledon Town Hall and Community Centre. He visited Lady Emily and would sit holding her hand and chanting.[20]

Krishna went on to Gstaad with Vanda for the second Saanen gathering of ten meetings from 22 July to 12 August 1962. He was still not well after the talks concluded and rather than go on to India in October he stayed on in Gstaad to see a urologist in Geneva. Rajagopal visited him but their differences were not reconciled, although Rajagopal left enough money with Krishna to pay his medical and dental bills. Rajagopal had by now married Annalisa and his future happiness in the new relationship was the hope of many old friends. Perhaps Krishna was not so happy about the match, however, as it left Rosalind on her own and Annalisa a powerful influence on Rajagopal. Annalisa was said to believe her husband had as much talent as Krishna and should have been 'standing in his shoes'. Krishna said he'd been told she was 'mad'.[21] Rajagopal went on to Amsterdam and tried to explain his feelings about Krishna to their mutual friend, Anneke Korndorffer. She wrote to Doris Pratt that Krishnaji was a phenomenon and, like a whirling fire, would scorch all those close to him. Mary Lutyens' reaction to the comment was that Krishna did not drop people, they dropped him after they had become possessive and then found that psychologically or emotionally he was not dependent on them. When she met Rajagopal in London she was shocked to hear Rajagopal speak harshly about Krishna as hypocritical and caring too much about his appearance. She urged him to leave the Krishnamurti work.[22]

Krishna spent the winter of 1962-63 with Vanda Scaravelli in Rome, where he met, among other prominent people, Federico Fellini, Alberto Moravia, Carlo Levi, Bernard Berenson, as well as Pablo Casals and Andres Segovia, who played for him. At the beginning of the year he had mumps, a serious illness for adult males at any time, and particularly, following Krishna's bouts of illness over the past couple of years. Aldous Huxley was in town in March and they met several times, both old men now, and Huxley well aware that he had cancer. These were their last fond meetings. In February it had been announced that Krishna would concentrate all his European talks at Saanen, so that in May, when he went to London, he held only ten small discussion groups of eighty people each at the Marlborough Hall in Wimbledon. He visited Lady Emily several times. Even though she had lost her memory, her face would light up on seeing him and he would sit with her, holding hands and chanting to her for comfort. Krishna returned to Gstaad near Saanen for ten talks in July. Mary Lutyens, who visited him there said he took her and her husband for a drive in his Mercedes, or rather, the Mercedes owned by the Saanen Committee. Krishna had always loved expensive cars, and he would clean and polish it after every drive.[23]

That summer of 1963 a South African who would have a close relationship with Krishna came to hear him speak at Saanen for the first time. Alain Naudé, aged thirty-five, a pianist and lecturer at the University of Pretoria, was to resign his position early the following year, after a trip to India. Before long he would become Krishna's secretary, a role which would bring him into conflict over the administration of KWINC.[24]

Another Gollancz hardback was published in London in 1963, *Life Ahead*, described as a "comprehensive collection" of Krishnamuti's talks to students, teachers and parents. In "an era of world-wide confusion and general demoralization", Krishnamurti's simplicity and directness was publicised as a "welcome beacon in the prevailing darkness".

In August 1963 Krishna had already tried to revive the idea that his teachings were the foundation for the Happy Valley school in California, which was administered by Rosalind. He wrote to Louis Zalk, a member of the Board of Happy Valley who was Rosalind's sister Erma's husband, reminding him that Dr Besant had set up the Happy Valley Foundation with a "definite" purpose in mind: that his teachings should be its major concern. He said he'd dropped a few hints that it had "wandered" away from its purpose, when he visited the school in 1960. He was worried it might fall into the hands of people not primarily concerned with the teachings, he said. Zalk replied that it was a dead piece of land until Rosalind, with "unstinting" effort had developed the school. It was her very life, he inveighed dramatically, and to destroy it would be to destroy her. Krishna never had any thought of destroying the school or in any way harming Rosalind, he promptly replied, and such an impression was entirely wrong. Rosalind, Rajagopal and he were responsible for starting the school and he and Rajagopal naturally had a great interest in it still. There was no question of starting another school, but he would like the Foundation members to carefully see that the teachings were introduced into the school.[25]

Concerns were being raised over educational and financial aspects of the schools in India and Happy Valley. Madhavachari cast about for funding, writing to the Minister for Education in the state of Uttar Pradesh seeking government assistance. He also wrote to Rajagopal asking him to raise funds in the United States and Rajagopal responded immediately, sending out letters to some wealthy supporters of Krishna, including the Biascoecheas. They replied that they hoped Rajagopal would be able to raise the money Madhavachari needed from his funds. Madhavachari also pointed out that Rajagopal had raised money for Ojai needs and Mr Pinter from New York believed there was enough to spare from those funds. Rajagopal came up with $2,250 or Rs 10,000, from donors, the largest donation coming from James Vigeveno, who was living in Ojai. The problem persisted and the following year Madhavachari had to send to Rajagopal a resolution from the Rishi Valley and Rajghat schools foundation asking for more money. The year before, Madhavachari had got wind that the house in Madanapalle in which Krishna was born was for sale at a good price and began to arrange to buy it, before changing his mind, on thegrounds that it was a sentimental decision. Rajagopal heartily agreed with the about-face. He was keeping a firm hand on the KWINC purse-strings.[26]

Meanwhile pressure on the management of the Happy Valley school was building. James Vigeveno wrote to Krishna in October 1963 that the rumour that KWINC wanted to take over the school Foundation was completely false and he asked to meet him. Vigeveno then received a personal message from Krishna endorsing his re-election to the Board and Vigeveno found himself at odds with Rosalind. Krishna wrote a letter to Rajagopal saying that Rosalind had claimed the situation was very "ugly" and he must do something about it, but he didn't know what the situation was. He said he'd explained to Rosalind that no one had any thought of destroying the school or harming her. He sent a copy of the letter to Rosalind. In November Vigeveno sent an account of what had occurred at the Happy Valley Foundation meeting, quoting Rosalind's words to the best of his memory. She was angry, he said, and claimed Krishnaji changed his views all the time. She reportedly ended with a challenge that she'd known Krishna for forty years and knew more about him than anyone else there, and Vigeveno said she threatened to tell some things she knew about Krishna. Krishna then told Vigeveno that someone had asked him to write to Rosalind about school matters but he would not, except through him. He found it all extraordinary. And the following month Krishna wrote to Vigeveno that he was pleased he'd been re-elected to the Board as he would be a thorn in their side and some good might come of it. As long as hate and antagonism continued, nothing much could be done, he said.[27]

At the end of 1963 a controversy within Theosophical circles was revived on the publication of a pamphlet called *there is no religion higher than truth*, which was the Society's credo. As Doris Pratt explained it to Rajagopal, someone she described as an elderly gentleman, EL Gardner, had been asked by the Society to publish a pamphlet concerning certain discrepancies found in correspondence between Annie Besant and Charles Leadbeater from 1916 to 1920. Doris says that Gardner disclosed that he had interviewed Mrs Besant in 1930 and found she realised "the devastating truth" that Wedgwood and Leadbeater had been deluded, and soon afterwards "became mentally and physically ill", before her death in 1933. No wonder the Theosophists wouldn't let Rajagopal see the early letters, Doris Pratt told Rajagopal.[28]

In the pamphlet Gardner writes that with the advantage of forty years perspective, it's clear that the Lord Maitreya and Masters which Leadbeater quotes for his authority were his own "thought-creations". But Gardner is kind enough to believe Leadbeater was honest and sincere and had no intention to deceive. Gardner refers to *kriyashakti*, or the power of creative thought, as Leadbeater's weakness. It was similar to the power of mind that could create stigmata, and the pity for Annie Besant was that as she had shut herself off from occult investigations after 1912, she loyally accepted statements by Leadbeater and others without checking them.[29]

A refutation of the pamphlet by Geoffrey Hodson and pupils of Leadbeater was soon published under the title, *C W Leadbeater A Great Occultist*, making the claim that the pamphlet had done great harm. The fact that Gardner had used the credo of the Society as its title was especially irksome, and he was accused of having a false memory of his conversation with Mrs Besant thirty years before. One writer, Hugh Shearman, disputed that Mrs Besant had renounced her clairvoyance, quoting her as saying that she could make a special arrangement to return to the "higher" worlds when she needed. The Society's President, Mr Sri Ram, also dissociated himself from the views expressed by Gardner.[30]

This kerfuffle was merely Theosophical Society squabbling which had been going on throughout its history, with arguments first over whether Blavatsky was a fraud and then questioning the authenticity of Leadbeater's pronouncements. But Krishna's name was inevitably dragged in since most factions still saw Krishna, despite his breakaway, as the shining 'star'. Gardner was keen to quote Krishnamurti's statement from 1927 about 'The Beloved' as identical to Blavatsky's 'Ever-Present' God.[31]

About the same time as this Theosophical dust-up, Arthur H Nethercot's weighty biography of Annie Besant, *The Last Four Lives of Annie Besant*, was published, with several references to Krishnamurti. Nethercot had interviewed Krishna at *Vasanta Vihar* in Madras in December 1956 during the period when he, probably unknown to Nethercot, was refusing to agree to publication of Lady Emily's account of his 'process'. Nethercot takes a reasonably mild view of Krishna as an ancillary character in Mrs Besant's life but raises questions about his sincerity. He makes a major point about Krishna not remembering his past, especially before 1929, concluding that Krishna had had to struggle to get his mind under control – or even perhaps hypnotised himself – so that he could "relegate to oblivion most of the things he does not want to remember". Nethercot quotes people who'd known Krishna to support the divergent arguments that he is either a "phony" or a "Teacher" with "integrity". He also raises an allegation that Krishna had been "organised into a concealed commercial enterprise, under the disguise of Krishnamurti Writings Inc., managed by D Rajagopal and his successor, R Madhavachari". Nethercot says he does not know who benefits from royalties from Krishna's books. Nethercot also describes raising the question with Krishna of whether he was "exploited" by Annie Besant and says Krishna "flared up in what I would have called an angry denial in any less philosophic a person". Nethercot's conclusion is that Krishnamurti is a "schizophrenic, or at least a man of a now permanently divided dual personality". He says he had long esteemed Krishnamurti for his courage and independence but his whole public life was now in contradiction to his philosophy, and he would have done better to have become an Indian holy man or recluse. As if in reply to Gardner's interpretation, in his so-recently published pamphlet, of the Theosophists' long-standing claim on Krishnamurti as one of their own, Nethercot ends his conclusion about Krishnaji by saying that he no longer speaks, as he used to, of his "Beloved". Yet Nethercot overlooks the fact that Krishna still talks of benediction and the 'Unknown'.[32]

Doris Pratt's response to the references to Krishna in Nethercot's book is forgiving, in that she says that understanding Krishnaji was beyond Nethercot, and, all things considered, he hadn't done too badly. She writes to Rajagopal that the reference to KWINC as a concealed commercial enterprise might be libellous and the footnote misleading. She explains away the question of Krishna's memory loss as him not strengthening his memory cells through use, as other people do. But she ignores Nethercot's references to schizophrenia and dual personality. As Krishna was at that time in India, there's no indication that Doris was influenced by Krishnamurti in her view of the book, nor that any legal action was undertaken.[33]

In late 1963 Krishna was in India when he heard of the death of his close friend, Aldous Huxley in California. Over the last few weeks of Aldous's life, his wife, Laura, contacted Rosalind who would bring fresh oranges down to him from the orchard at Ojai and also give him massages, between his attempts to work on his last article, *Shakespeare and Religion*. Rosalind was there on 22 November when, aided by oxygen, and becoming weaker, he asked for LSD "in extremis". Laura took it as a sign of his final awareness and acceptance of death, just as he had written about death in *Island*. Laura sat by him for hours, telling him to 'let go' with ease, just as he had helped Maria at her death. Rosalind and a nurse were also in the room and doctors moved in and out. An extraordinary coincidence had occurred with the assassination of President Kennedy that morning, and a television in the hall was kept on to follow the dramatic events. But the news was kept from Aldous, who was slipping from consciousness. Radha says that Rosalind too tried to use the same words with Aldous as he had used to whisper to Maria at the end of her life, words about emptiness and letting go of this world to move into peace and clear light. Rosalind's description of the experience was "uplifting" as she felt a sense of awe and love, and shed no tears.[34]

Aldous's brother, Sir Julian Huxley, asked Krishna to contribute to a memorial volume on Aldous but Krishna declined. He wrote to Sir Julian that he and Aldous had known each other for nearly thirty years, and in Ojai they had shared long walks, talking about all manner of things. Aldous had told him about his cancer of the tongue a couple of years before. Krishna said that they had seen each other every day for a fortnight while Aldous was in Rome the previous spring and he had seemed so well, and said so often that he was feeling well, that it was a shock to Krishna to hear of his death. It was good of Sir Julian to ask him to contribute, he said, but he offered as an explanation for his refusal that he found he couldn't write about Aldous, as their relationship was strangely personal yet impersonal. Krishna said that right to the very end, their affection for each other never varied. The letter was hand-written on 25 February and typed in March with the date left open for Krishna to add it with his signature.[35]

It's worth noting here that Krishna refers, in a talk in Madras four years later, to a "very learned" doctor who took a "minute" dosage of LSD. Krishna does not identify the doctor but says that two other doctors with him at the time recorded what he said on a tape, which suggests it was an experiment. The experimenter said there was no space between him and flowers on a table in front of him. This accords with Huxley's account of his first experiment with mescalin. Krishna told the audience he was not advocating taking LSD as it had deleterious effects. But there was a simpler, more direct and "natural" way to look, so that space became non-existent – and that was when there was "love", he said.[36]

Another dear friend to Krishna, his mother-surrogate, Lady Emily, died of an aneurism in January 1964 after an extended period of dementia. There's no question that for Krishna it was the end of an era, with so many of the loved ones of his early life gone. He couldn't have wished for "Mum" to go on living, he told her daughter Mary, but London would never be the same. Theirs had been more than a friendship, extending over nearly fifty-two years - almost his whole life. Krishna was now aged sixty eight. He had loved her, he said.[37]

That winter of 1963-64 in India, Krishna was a changed person, according to Pupul Jayakar. She says that when he left India in March 1962, the Krishnaji who had laughed with his Indian friends and been overwhelmed by the beauty of the land also disappeared. When he returned, a new Krishnaji had emerged – stern, impatient, questioning – and his great laughter and play had finished. He seemed more distant; he said that he had been speaking for thirty years and yet there was not one person who was living the teaching. Jayakar observed increasing tension between Madhavachari and Achyut and Rao Sahib Patwardhan, and saw, too, Krishna's impatience with old associates and a need for young people around him. He wanted change, not lethargy, in the schools. Alain Naudé and Mary Zimbalist went to Rajghat that year. Krishna was "horrified" at the poor standard of the room Mary, a wealthy American, was to stay in so she was invited to stay in a room in his house instead. Jayakar says Madhavachari was "unruffled" by Krishna's "explosion" over the standard of the room.[38]

Rajagopal continued to work through Madhavachari to find out what public engagements Krishna had in India. In May 1964 he wrote asking for details of talks late in the year, advising that they should be published with the talks early in the year as *Talks in India 1964*. He also wanted to know sales figures for *Talks in India 1963*. An English edition of *This Matter of Culture* had recently been published and he sought Madhavachari's reaction. Then there were All-India Radio talks which he asked Madhavachari to obtain from the broadcaster for the purpose of "long-playing discs" or 33-1/3 records.[39]

By the summer of 1964 Krishna was back in the Chalet Tanneg in Gstaad near Saanen, and Radha and James Sloss arranged to visit him there. Radha wanted to "clarify" outstanding problems between him, her father and Rosalind. Radha describes a formal dinner, with Vanda away and the three of them served by a butler in white gloves. After an initial stiffness, the affectionate bond between Radha and Krishna returned and he took enjoyment in watching and listening to their children, aged ten and eleven. When Radha explained how Krishna's criticism of the school had fomented discord against Rosalind, Krishna seemed genuinely "stricken" and insisted that he had not intended to harm her. He promised to write to Rosalind, but Radha says he never did. However the archives show that Krishna did write to Rosalind acknowledging a letter from her and saying he wanted to clear up any misunderstanding at once. He couldn't understand how she or anyone else got the impression that he wanted to hurt her or the school; he had only wanted to point out the original intention of the Happy Valley Foundation. Krishna regretted that the misunderstanding had continued for a year and if he had been the cause of this, he wanted her to please accept his sincere regrets. He asked that she send the letter to all members of the Foundation to clear up the matter at once. (By September Rosalind would give up the position of Director of the school, exhausted from years of emotional turmoil, according to Radha. But she stayed on the Board and kept up the task of finding funding for the school. In November James Vigeveno resigned from the school Board, citing its disregard for the original purpose, and Rosalind accepted the resignation, expressing regret that he was resigning over educational policy. Krishna wrote that it was unfortunate and unnecessary.) Radha and her family stayed three days in Gstaad with Krishna, and on the last morning Krishna told Radha that Rajagopal and Rosalind should never have divorced. They should all have stayed together, he said. She could not understand why it mattered so much to him. Whenever she tried to clarify what he was saying he would despair and say she did not understand, and then move on to a related subject. He criticised Rajagopal for not paying his medical bills and then gave her $3,000 to use on her holiday in Europe. She found out later that the money probably came from a fund of $50,000 that Rajagopal had given Krishna to buy land in Saanen where summer camps could be held.[40]

Alain Naudé was with Krishna in Gstaad in the summer of 1964, but Radha says she did not meet Krishna's new circle of friends until 1966. Naudé had resigned his position at the University of Pretoria early in the year and was free to stay on with Krishnamurti, along with Mary Zimbalist, after the talks were completed.[41]

Also that summer of 1964, Doris Pratt threatened to resign from KWINC over Rajagopal's tight hold over the accounts. Rajagopal had given her shares, which no longer paid dividends, to cover Krishna's expenses, and when she asked for a "trifling" sum of 160 pounds, Rajagopal had insisted on financial information even to the extent of knowing who had bought a tape recorder. Rajagopal's tight rein is indicated in the correspondence over a period of a couple of years. For example, Doris acknowledged a cheque for $750 for Alain Naudé in March 1965, and Rajagopal wrote the same month to say Mr Naudé's travelling expenses should come from the KWINC London account. By July the following year there were problems over Rajagopal sending Naudé a money draft sent on to Rishi Valley for scholarships which needed endorsement by Krishna and could lead to questions from income tax authorities. So the draft was returned to Rajagopal who claimed it would have been quite simple for Krishna to endorse the cheque. Rajagopal sent another cheque directly to India.[42]

Doris also insisted that Krishna should travel first-class for reasons of health. By early 1965 she wrote, at "Krishnaji's" request, asking for KWINC to provide Alain Naudé with an allowance of up to 700 pounds p.a. plus a travel allowance of 500 pounds in order for him to accompany Krishna, who was 70, wherever he went. Rajagopal engaged in a psychological chess game, sending a cable to say that the allowance seemed like a good idea, but he wanted a letter directly from Krishna about the matter. Luyens claims he sent no reply to the first-class travel proposal. Doris also raised the question of getting a copy of the KWINC's mailing list, kept in Ojai, maintaining that there was no question of competition, and she also acted as a go-between on the matter of funding the purchase of land at Saanen for a centre.[43]

In April 1965 Krishna returned to Wimbledon for talks, staying with Naudé in a rented house where Doris Pratt and Anneke Korndorffer again took care of domestic chores. Mary Zimbalist provided transport for trips to the country and some of the sights of France in a Mercedes. Mary continued on with them to India later in the year.[44]

In the meantime, Madhavachari had offered to resign his position as KWINC representative in India, being now 75 years of age, and had also written, without Krishna's knowledge, a personal note to Rajagopal suggesting he invite Krishna to Ojai the following year, 1966. The request came from the bottom of his heart, as he sincerely wished Rajagopal to make up with Krishna.

It took a while but Krishna at last received, at the end of 1965, Rajagopal's invitation for him to speak in Ojai in October the following year. Madhavachari stayed on in his pivotal Indian KWINC position.[45]

Generally the correspondence between the head office in Ojai and other workers for Krishna in other parts of the world was polite and efficient, perhaps softening Rajagopal's apprehension about new people on the scene. They wrote about tapes, Krishna's attire, Naudé's appointment as secretary and even an increase in his salary. Doris Pratt was certainly effusive about Alain Naudé in his role as secretary to Krishna, informing Rajagopal that he was a real asset – a willing helper with plenty of life and conversation. But that old warrior for Krishna, Madhavachari, wasn't so keen on the new group of Europeans around his idol. He told Rajagopal in March 1965 that Naudé had been collecting all available books to prepare an anthology of talks; and by the end of the year Madhavachari was worried that, with rumours of a new headquarters in Europe and "enormous" funds being held in Ojai, Krishna would not travel to India as often as in the past. Madhavachari was now old and did not want Krishna to place greater trust in the people connected with the Saanen gathering than those in KWINC. Rajagopal kept tabs on affairs as best he could, sending messages to Krishna workers across the world. Naudé was recording Krishna's talks and Casselberry, Rajagopal's assistant, impressed on Doris the importance of the tape transcriptions being exact for archival purposes, however incorrect or incomplete they might seem.[46]

Meanwhile, in Sydney a May camp was being organised for people to listen to tapes of Krishna's talks and Donald Ingram Smith was impressing on anyone who had the authority to send him tapes or records that the listening sessions were a worthwhile experiment, in the absence of Krishna in the flesh. Smith invited Krishna to Australia the following year, 1966, but Krishna replied that he had to fly to India immediately after Ojai as there was a "serious" responsibility to attend to at Rishi Valley.[47]

By October 1965 the disturbance in communication over the Happy Valley school between Krishna and Rosalind still had not settled, despite Krishna's letter of reassurance over a year before. Doris Pratt wrote a confidential letter to Rajagopal to say that Rosalind had rung her asking about a Dr Leybourne-White. Doris understood that Rosalind still wanted to carry out what she believed was Annie Besant's purpose in establishing the Happy Valley Foundation.[48] Of course Krishna as the 'World Teacher' had been integral to Mrs Besant's purpose but that was a major factor that was being deliberately overlooked in charting a future purpose for the land. Annie had declared in 1927 that she was acting on the wish of her Master in buying a large amount of land to create a "model" in miniature of the coming "Civilisation" to train the new human type she expected, the "sixth sub-race" now "multiplying" in California. The Happy Valley School was dedicated to that work, but it would be "incomplete" without the "Bodhisattva", or World Teacher, to shape the religious side of the "Civilisation", she'd explained.[49]

Alain Naudé and Mary Zimbalist were with Krishna in London and on the continent in the spring of 1966, and Naudé corresponded with Rajagopal as usual on matters dealing with recording Krishna's talks. There'd been tensions between Naudé and Madhavachari in India the previous winter and when Krishna proposed that Naudé and Zimbalist be elected to the Rishi Valley schools board, Naudé was refused, until his general "behaviour" and attitude was considered improved. So Krishna wrote a stiff letter to Madhavachari in April 1966 and Madhavachari was shocked enough to send a stern reply, before Krishna cabled him to please forget his letter, suggesting they work together in friendship. Again Madhavachari offered his resignation to Rajagopal and again withdrew it, even though he felt the atmosphere around Krishna at times poisonous. Jayakar points to the problem that Krishna had been told that the Indian Foundation was supporting Rajagopal in his stand against Krishna, but she does not name any one person as generating dissension.[50]

Meanwhile Krishna was generating interest in a curious project that might be called 'the Brahmin boy experiment'. In about 1966-67 Krishna had the idea of replicating his own childhood - finding two boys from religious families, taking particular care with their food and clothing, and educating them as he and Nitya had been educated. They were to be sensitive, dreamy, affectionate, delicate, respectful and religious. Two boys aged about ten and seven were found, living about fifteen miles from where Krishna had been born, with just such qualities, including large, soft eyes. Their parents were very keen for the experiment to go ahead and the boys were sent to the Rishi Valley School and separated from other children there, living in a special house, and given special food, clothing and curriculum. Of course the commanding influences of the living personalities of Leadbeater and Mrs Besant were absent and that factor, along with the egalitarian values of a more liberal era, may have been the major reasons the experiment failed. After about a month the boys discovered that they were missing out on the "real" life being lived by other children in the school – including "rough and tumble sports and hot pickles in the dining hall" – and they asked to be returned to a normal life. Their requests were at first resisted but after about six to eight months they were allowed into the regular hostel and school life of the school and went on to graduate from university and live settled family lives in the United States.[51]

Radha visited Krishna in Gstaad again in the summer of 1966. By this stage she said Krishna was openly critical of Rajagopal with her – he did not refer to him as her father but would call him "Rajagopal" or "he". When asked why he had allowed Rajagopal to devote his life to the work, Krishna said he had carried him along because Rajagopal could not make another life for himself. This shocked Radha who viewed her father as very capable - a Cambridge scholar as well as an efficient manager of the worldwide KWINC organisation. One day she observed two large suitcases of silk "monogrammed" shirts and ties from a Savile Row tailor delivered for Krishna and his current "favourite" person. She said she had an intuition that his association with this person, whom she does not name, would lead to trouble. She also recalls asking Krishna why he continued public speaking after forty years and he replied that he spoke to live and that if there were no more talks he would die. She believed that the older he became the more he felt he must have a life "sustained" by listeners – that he needed more and more of an audience. Perhaps she did not understand what he said, just as she had not understood what he had meant on her visit two years earlier. If he saw it as his purpose to give talks it does not necessarily mean that he needed the audiences. As early as 1927 he said that a message to make humanity happy had been entrusted to him and he took this message to be his task. Perhaps he still believed it, despite his rejection of Theosophy's outward forms.[52]

Krishna's health in Europe was a real concern to Madhavachari – bronchitis, hay fever, an enlarged liver – and he clearly did not approve of Krishna's meals being cooked by Mary Zimbalist. He wrote to Rajagopal in June 1966 asking him to go to Gstaad to arrange proper care for Krishna. It was as if Madhavachari was oblivious of the deep chasm that had developed between Rajagopal and Krishna and the new life Krishna had been leading, away from Rosalind and Rajagopal, for about a decade. Younger audiences, too, were a feature of Krishna's talks now. Jayakar says that in Saanen many young people initially came to the talks but they drifted away without seriously joining in Krishna's work. Naudé was keen to encourage more young people to take an interest and arranged six lectures at the New School for Social Research in New York as well as discussions at Harvard. Mary Cadogan observed in a letter to Naudé that many "exhibitionistic" young people probably came to talks out of curiosity as Krishna had been linked with Zen. In New York Krishna also met the poet Allen Ginsberg and writer, Timothy Leary, as well as two other men who would become closely associated with him, Count Hughes van der Staten, a Belgian industrialist, and Gerard Blitz, founder of the Club Mediterranée.[53]

On 18 October Krishna flew to California to give talks at Ojai. He and Naudé stayed at Mary Zimbalist's home in Malibu before setting out on what was for him a nerve-wracking meeting with Rajagopal. In diary entries Mary Zimbalist refers to her memory of an earlier phone call between the two men – Rajagopal in Ojai and Krishna in New York - when Rajagopal was shouting so loudly that she could hear his voice from across the room. Arriving in Ojai, Mary and Naudé were accommodated at *Arya Vihara* and were witness to the tension between the three former intimates. At one point Krishna recalled quarrels in 1960 over Rajagopal wanting a divorce, which he said had caused him to cut short his talks in the Oak Grove. Krishna said he had no one he could talk to then but now he had Mary and Naudé. Mary records in her diary that she could hear Rajagopal's strident, angry voice through the wall when he and Krishna met to talk. There was also some mention of Krishna saying that Rajagopal had claimed Krishna had put a curse on him, and that he was as much a Brahmin as Krishna. She also commented on Rosalind's "nagging" and "chivvying" of Krishna. Mary says that on 22 October Krishna wrote Rajagopal a letter about the Board and disclosure of assets, and that when they talked about this a few days later, Krishna warned him that if he ignored it there would be "consequences". Krishna walked out of the meeting. The next day Krishna and Naudé said that they would not accept money from KWINC and would keep the tapes of the talks. James Vigeveno, vice-president of KWINC, was called in to assist in restoring harmony. Krishna gave six talks at Ojai and held a final public discussion on 14 November. Mary says that the following day Krishna failed to obtain the manuscript of *Krishnamurti's Notebook* and tapes of the talks and he left Ojai after a "dreadful" day.[54]

The breakdown in talks between Rajagopal and Krishna must have been a major disappointment for Krishna's followers and friends of Rajagopal. Mary Cadogan, who was now doing much of the London KWINC business and Madhavachari in India had both sent encouraging notes about the Ojai trip. Later, Reg Bennett in Sydney said he would cooperate with Madhavachari without letting his personal feelings intrude in the task of disseminating Krishnaji's message.[55]

In the midst of these internal wrangles, the public persona of Krishna was still greatly admired and he still carried a charismatic power on the shoulders of his slight frame. A BBC radio interview with Krishna was broadcast in October and, in New York, National Educational Television had requested filming one of his talks and in Ojai Krishna agreed to filming for the first time. His visits to the New School and Harvard were considered a success in drawing interest from a younger generation. KWINC was also tracking plagiarism and copyright of his work. In August Byron Casselberry, KWINC office manager in Ojai, mildly reminded the editor of the *Theosophical Review* in Varanasi that he had used a Krishnamurti quotation, with only the initials "JK" appended, without giving the date or source. As Krishnamurti's thoughts were now expressed quite differently from formerly, it was important to date any quotations used.[56]

But the situation at the heart of the organisation only got worse in 1967 with spot fires breaking out all over the world while the main conflagration between Rajagopal and Krishna smouldered. Doris was critical of the editing of Indian talks, which offended Madhavachari. Rajagopal told Madhavachari he was not prepared to spend money on temporary facilities in India and he didn't know what inspired Krishnaji to have such "vague" and "ambitious" schemes. Naudé informed Rajagopal that Krishna had instructed him not to send any tapes to Ojai until certain matters were "cleared up". Then Rajagopal sent Madhavachari $20,000 because of "impending" difficult situations, but he hoped it wouldn't be "squandered" on "absurd" schemes. He said he had no confidence in the people immediately around Krishna. Then in August Madhavachari reported to Rajagopal that Pupul Jayakar had seen Krishna and come away with notes about what Krishna wanted from Rajagopal: that it not be the prerogative of any one person to take decisions on archives, tapes and writing; that in Krishna's lifetime it should be himself who decided on what group would make these decisions; and he should decide the members of the Board of KWINC. Madhavachari wrote again the same month reminding Rajagopal of Pupul's notes and saying that as they were all getting old perhaps Rajagopal could be magnanimous for the sake of peace. The following month Madhavachari said he feared two openly opposed camps. By October he told Rajagopal that he was not right in thinking that Krishna's "seemingly" reasonable demand was only a façade. But when Rajagopal required Krishna to account for all monies or there could be trouble from the US Internal Revenue, Madhavachari said it went against the grain for him to ask Krishna, whom he held in such high esteem, to sign receipts for all his personal expenses over the past year, since it had never been required in the past. Finally in November Madhavachari again reassured Rajagopal that rumours about intrigues and legal action were unfounded.[57]

But by December 1967, Rajagopal had Casselberry write to Madhavachari to say that he believed Madhavachari was misinformed. He enclosed a note about a visit from Gerard Blitz, of Club Méditerranée fame, to California demanding Rajagopal agree to Krishna's wishes or resign, otherwise legal action would follow.[58]

In January 1968 Naudé wrote to Rajagopal on behalf of Krishna, now in India for the winter, complaining that *The First and Last Freedom* and *Commentaries on Living* had been published by the Theosophical Society in America. Rajagopal had allowed this without even consulting Krishna, knowing that he had had nothing to do with the Theosophists for forty years, he said. He felt it a betrayal and would now consider what action he might take over copyright. He also wrote to James Vigeveno telling him Krishna had said that as long as Rajagopal was the head of KWINC he would not have anything to do with it nor accept its money.[59]

Rosalind had tried several times during 1967 to restore harmony between Krishna and Rajagopal. She wrote conciliatory letters, pleading that differences between them in their old age would only lead to mischief and calamity. There was too much pride on both sides, she believed. She said the Happy Valley school was bursting with his ideas and that every cent of KWINC could be accounted for if only he saw all the records. Rosalind said she couldn't talk to Rajagopal as he would get angry over she and Krishna "wrecking" his marriage to her. She suggested Krishna go to Ojai alone as he was getting "stupid" advice from others. She then visited him in London in the autumn of 1967 and found him "impervious" to her, "withdrawn" and "haughty". Ten days later in Rome she found him loving and willing to talk. He told her he would return to Ojai and see Rajagopal alone. Krishna's last letter to Rosalind was full of concern for her and a promise to set things right when he returned to Ojai the following summer. His love was with her always, he said.[60]

But by the spring of 1968 in Paris, Krishna asked Mima Porter, now Vice President of KWINC after James Vigeveno's resignation, to help settle the dispute with Rajagopal. According to Radha, Krishna warned Mima that without cooperation from him, he would dissociate himself from KWINC. Rajgopal's reaction was that Krishna must talk directly to him, not send messengers.[61]

By the end of June when Krishna heard back from Mima Porter that everything would be settled in the autumn after he came to Ojai, Krishna decided he'd had enough of procrastination. He sent a final letter to Rajagopal revoking the document he had signed in Madras in 1958 giving authority to Rajagopal. The legality of the document was finally settled after a lawsuit. An announcement was also read out at a public gathering at Saanen on 8 July that Krishnamurti completely "disassociated" himself from KWINC and that he hoped people would support the new Krishnamurti Foundation of London. The new body was legally constituted on 28 August 1968. Its trustees were Krishna, Mary Zimbalist, Alain Naudé, George Digby, Dorothy Simmons, Count van der Straten and Gerard Blitz. Doris Pratt and Mary Cadogan became associate trustees and Cadogan began to seek funding independently of KWINC.[62]

Now the hard decisions had to be made regarding funds and positions held in KWINC offices in England and India. Mary Cadogan froze the assets of the London office, after writing to

Rajagopal and Casselberry that she was shocked that Krishna was refused a position on the KWINC board.[63]

At this late stage in relations between the two men many people were involved in attempting to effect their reconciliation. But no ordinary mortals were able to persuade Rajagopal of the crux of the irreconcilability. Krishna was who he was, and would do what he wanted. He preached freedom for the individual and, finally, he had thrown off whatever personal controls and inhibitions had formerly bound him.[64] It was not a matter of opposing camps, as Madhavachari had described it. Krishna was the goose who laid the golden eggs – golden both in wealth and love. Even if he was banished from Ojai, he would keep on laying eggs, giving talks all over the world attended by thousands of people. It was only natural that people would be drawn to his elixir of life. Rajagopal may have been a proud Brahmin but his life's work had been to preserve Krishna's golden eggs. He could neither produce some himself, prevent further laying nor claim sovereignty over the new eggs laid. The creative force was with Krishna. It was very hard to justify keeping control over the writings of Krishna when Krishna was alive and well and every year producing more writings. Some people pointed this out to Rajagopal, questioning his stand. Madhavachari certainly encouraged Rajagopal to back down, keeping him informed of developments in the first half of 1968. Krishna's attitude had become more hardened, he told Rajagopal in March, and he, Madhavachari, would not work for any organisation if Krishna broke away from KWINC. In April he said people would be justified in saying that those who'd been nearest to Krishna were now leaving him to fend for himself, and that Rajagopal should restore Krishna's control of KWINC. In May he told Rajagopal that if KWINC had no more talks to print it had no right to collect donations or claim that it was helping Krishna. Then he said that regardless of the legal position, his moral position was in favour of Krishna and he would resign from KWINC, relinquishing his power of attorney given by Rajagopal. He did so officially in August, suggesting the American consul look after

KWINC's interests, as he hadn't heard from Rajagopal. Meanwhile Dwarkanath wrote to Casselberry that a Mrs Jayalakshmi had been appointed as Krishna's representative in Madras, and she had support from the United Nations Secretary-General in New York, Mr CV Narasimhan. Whether the link was strong or not, it's an indication that the main pro-Krishnamurti players in India thought the stakes were high, involving property and copyright, and reference to prominent members of society rarely harmed a cause. Jayakar says 1967 was a gloomy year, with Krishna pointing out there had not been a "flowering" of his teachings in India or in Ojai. Madhavachari had clashed with Naudé in January 1967 and when Krishna returned the following winter, Naudé did not accompany him. Krishna appeared agitated and critical; he said he wanted to save his centres as oases for his teachings in a "mad" world and wanted his friends to consider how to save the schools when he was dead. Then in 1968 when the break with Rajagopal came, Balasundaram was appointed Secretary of the new Krishnamurti Foundation in India, and Jayakar President. In October Jayakar said the Foundation received a letter from Krishna in a language and style "alien" to him. It stated that there had been mistakes in the past and he had drawn up a list of requirements for the future. He emphasised that the new Foundation was not a "psychological" organisation but simply a committee responsible for diffusing the teachings. After a new Krishnamurti Centre was set up in Madras, with Mrs Jayalakshmi as Krishna's representative, Jayakar had great difficulty making contact with Krishna. She says she had to confront the fact that her "guru" had disappeared. She heard second-hand that Krishna had severed all connections with Naudé in August 1969. Finally Krishna replied to her in January 1969 to say he would be back in India at the end of the year for a couple of months.[65]

Kitty Shiva Rao, a close friend of both Rajagopal and Krishna for many years, visited Ojai in April 1968, and the following month she wrote a heart-felt letter to Rajagopal to say she recognised that he felt that he had been chosen or entrusted to carry out his work. But, she explained, Krishna had also been chosen in a very definite way and any organisation was meant only to cooperate with him. To put it bluntly, Krishnamurti could deliver his message without Krishnamurti Writings Inc but Krishnamurti Writings Inc without Krishnamurti seemed to be an anomaly – and what really counted were Krishna's teachings.[66]

Another friend posed a question to Rajagopal about whether Krishnamurti's teachings worked – if so, could he dissolve the enmity, and if not, why did he publish the teachings?[67]

In August an intermediary, Frank Noyes, put to Krishna a proposal from Rajagopal but again the stumbling block was Rajagopal's insistence that he meet Krishna alone. In September Rajagopal even wrote to Krishna about personal "denunciation" he said originated with Krishna and asked for a face-to-face meeting, otherwise a public "airing" would inevitably result which would damage the spread of the teachings. Perhaps he was referring to Krishna's sexual relationship with Rosalind. Krishna replied that it was not a personal matter between them but that over the previous eight years he had been asking to be consulted about the affairs of KWINC. He said he would not see Rajagopal alone as he had been violent and abusive. Now all he would accept was the resignation of Rajagopal from the board of KWINC.[68]

Over the period of this dispute, there grew up among Rajagopal's supporters the view that Krishna had a dual personality. Casselberry wrote to Reg Benett in Australia, for instance, that "Krishnaji" had encouraged false rumours about Rajagopal and that Krishna seemed to have two "distinct" personalities. He said Krishna had hurled his "anathema" at KWINC Ojai – but Rajagopal was bearing up and KWINC was placing copies of Krishna's works in college libraries all over the United States. Casselberry also wrote to Chetana Publishers in Bombay that KWINC was planning to publish Krishna's collected works through an American publisher involving world rights, so Chetana could not reprint the 1927-1933 talks without permission.[69]

When Krishna was staying with Mary Zimbalist in Malibu in November 1968 Rosalind made another attempt to help heal the breach between Krishna and Rajagopal. She visited Mary's Malibu home and Mary remained present at the meeting. The next day Rosalind wrote to Krishna that she had told him he was a "dual" personality because he was "often" different people. She accused him of "vicious" inciting, saying that people should not air their problems in public but deal directly with the "principles". Although it must have been clear that Krishna did not need her care, she said she had a grave responsibility resulting from her pledge to Nitya, to see that Krishna had whatever care was necessary.[70]

James Vigeveno, who also tried to bring Rajagopal and Krishna together, was sorely disillusioned, writing an open letter the following year highly critical of Krishna. He accused Krishna of a "double-faced" attitude, in refusing to meet the trustees of KWINC once Rajagopal had dropped his insistence on meeting him alone. However the invitation to Krishna did not include his new friends Alain Naudé and Mary Zimbalist – he was required to come alone. Vigeveno deplored the fact that tapes of Krishna criticising Rajagopal had been sent around the world and he refuted an allegation that Rajagopal had not made KWINC funds available to Krishna. He said there was a gap between Krishna's teachings and his actions and questioned whether Naudé had a "magic" influence over Krishna. Vigeveno even referred to "psychologists" and "graphologists" noticing an unhappy change in Krishna and a "decline" in his strength, "spiritually" and "physically". Vigeveno also wrote a personal covering letter to Krishna in a more ingratiating spirit, begging for an answer and hoping with all his heart Krishna would agree to meet him and Rajagopal the following year. If Vigeveno seriously wanted to mend relations, he must have been oblivious of how deeply offensive the open letter was.[71]

It might also be observed that Vigeveno, despite his use of the respectful term "Krishnaji", felt on an equal enough footing with his teacher to criticise him roundly, perhaps understandable within the context of the egalitarianism of the 1960s. Possibly Vigeveno felt aggrieved that he had not been effectual in bringing about a reconciliation of two sides in a dispute. It's interesting to note that years later the guru Rajneesh, or Osho, said of Krishnamurti that he was a Master who said he was not a Master, and that he followed the 'Royal Path', with no methods, no techniques and no scriptures.

> And the people who listen to him and follow him are disciples who think that they are not disciples. ... For the egoists who cannot drop their egos, he opens a door. He says, "You keep your ego, you don't need to be a disciple ...". The egoists feel very good that they need not bow down to anybody."[72]

Followers and devotees of Krishna, regardless that they did not describe themselves as such, would step in to take the place of others who might become disenchanted or overlooked by Krishna. It was reported among friends in early August 1969 that Naudé would no longer be Krishna's secretary nor accompany him on travels. Naudé's physical proximity to Krishna was certainly broken but he remained loyal to him. Lutyens says that Naudé ceased working for Krishna in the autumn of 1969 and went to live in San Francisco, at the time the gay capital of the world, where he taught music. He currently resides in Texas.[73]

New friends who would be powerful protectors of Krishna were Erna and Theodor Lilliefelt who had first heard Krishna speak in India in the late 1940s and early 1950s. They moved to Ojai after Theodor's retirement from the United Nations in 1963 but finding that Krishna no longer gave talks there they made contact in 1968 to offer their help. Krishna asked Erna to establish the Krishnamurti Foundation of America (KFA) in 1969, with Krishna, Erna Lilliefelt, Alain Naudé and Mary Zimbalist among the original trustees.[74]

In December 1968 Krishna had at last sought legal advice from a retired Attorney-General for California, a friend of Sidney Field. Then in February 1969 Krishna saw the Deputy Attorney-General, Laurence Tapper, in Los Angeles, who in March 1971, became a co-plaintiff in a suit against Rajagopal. Tapper cited "misconduct as trustee over $1 million in charitable assets". A settlement was agreed in the Superior Court of the County of Ventura in 1974 to dissolve KWINC and for all its assets to be transferred to the KFA, except for certain publication rights that went to another trust called K&R, which Rajagopal had formed in 1967. On Rajagopal's death all assets, including the Oak Grove and 150 acres at Ojai, were to pass to the KFA. Legal action was also taken in India to claim *Vasanta Vihar* in Madras from KWINC. The matter was settled in 1976 when the Madras High Court ordered that the property be handed over to the Krishnamurti Foundation of India for Krishna's use.[75]

During the years of dispute between Rajagopal and Krishna both men had kept an eye on their publication turnover and rights. *Life Ahead* was first published by Gollancz in 1963, as a collection of talks to students, teachers and parents pointing to a "central fact", that human problems could only be solved by individuals themselves. Krishna wrote a Foreword for the book and there was no mention of editing by Rajagopal. But when Rajagopal arranged for its republication by the Theosophical Publishing House in 1967 as a Quest book, with funds from The Kern Foundation, he was credited as the editor. Once the Krishnamurti Foundation London was established in 1968 arrangements were made with Servire Publishers in Holland to publish *Talks and Dialogues* which had been conducted in Saanen. It was reprinted by Avon Books in the United States in 1970. The book published in England as *This Matter of Culture* was published in 1964 in the United States by Harper & Row as *Think on These Things,* with an editor's note by Rajagopal. He told readers that what Krishnamurti said was without bias and universal and he provided definitions for the words 'guru', 'sannyasi', 'puja' and 'mantram', words that may not have been familiar to western readers. Meanwhile other people were coming up with their own views of Krishnamurti's work. In 1967 AD Dhopeshwarkar, describing himself as a devoted student of Krishnamurti's teaching, published *J Krishnamurti and Awareness in Action* through Krishna's friend, MH (Pama) Patwardhan, who owned a printery in Bombay. Dhopeshwarkar said that he was not "trying to make out" that Krishnamurti's teaching was a kind of philosophy and he had submitted his manuscript to the scrutiny of two friends, one of whom was an acknowledged authority on Krishnamurti. By these standards the book could be said to have been very much an in-house Krishnamurti publication. Also in 1967 Krishna asked Mary Lutyens if she would write a book for him based on the talks, and she found herself working on talks from 1963 and 1964. She indexed them under themes such as 'Awareness, Conditioning, Consciousness, Death, Fear, Freedom, God, Love, Meditation' and chose those passages she thought showed most clarity and beauty. The book, *Freedom from the Known*, was published by Gollancz and Harper & Row in 1969, with Lutyens credited as editor.[76]

When Krishna returned to India at the end of 1969 he was recognised as a great teacher and welcomed back by his devotees – in particular Pupul Jayakar, Nandini, Sunanda and Achyut Patwardhan. Krishna had written to Balasundaram in March warning him not to let Madhavachari become involved in further work. He said Madhavachari had thought he could keep 'the teacher' and 'the organisation' apart, and even manage Rajagopal, but that was impossible. But he hoped he could still be a friend of Madhavachari. Jayakar says that in 1969 Krishna talked about the Theosophical Society for the first time in twenty-one years, questioning how the boy that he had been remained unaffected by all the special privileges bestowed on him. Suddenly he stopped speaking and asked if people could feel "it" in the room. Jayakar says she could feel the room pulsate as if strong forces were alive and in movement. When he began to speak again it was as if the room had transformed, with an active quality of goodness. Krishna spoke of still being a boy, his character unformed, and still being specially protected from evil.[77]

Although Krishna might still gainsay devotees, it was clear that in India he had *guru* status. This was the decade of major cultural revolution and many young Westerners were travelling in India seeking alternative models for living. It was as if the revolutionary philosophy that Krishna had talked about since the 1920s had come to fruition, yet its form of uncontrolled, undisciplined 'dropping out' was anathema to Krishna's approach to life and the result must have seemed like wasteful turmoil rather than change as a solution to social wrongs. In 1928 he had spoken about the necessity for a change in morality to keep pace with "ever-forceful" life. If women, as the keepers of tradition, decided on change it would happen tomorrow, he said. Women were strong and more self-sacrificing than men and they should strike over things that mattered. He cited child marriage and widow marriage[78] - women were responsible for these sorrows because they allowed them. And in 1929 Krishna spoke against racism – there was no question of white man's land or brown man's land, he said, but just selfishness. One should not be limited by fear of external authority. And in the sphere of religion, that same year Krishna saw a new generation breaking away from creeds and dogma, in revolt against authority and traditional forms that could not be adapted to the "modern" world. Even Lady Emily Lutyens, in 1928, under Annie Besant's and Krishna's influence, had written about the revolt of women and the revolt of youth against all authority and the need to create "liberty" of individual perceptions, or a "freedom" from beliefs imposed from outside of oneself. By the 1960s, there gathered about the *gurus* of India the product of Western children imbibing these humanitarian values at the knees of their parents. An educationist who had worked with Krishnamurti since 1948 and was in charge of the Rajghat Centre in the 1960s, Miss Ahalya Chari, believed that Krishna had a "tremendous" influence on youth movements. He tried to heal people by dealing with their personal problems and explaining that 'you are the world and the world is you', so they would understand their own consciousness rather than create further conflict, at home, at work, in all their relationships. She saw him working with compassion with the oppressed, with the poor and with women, treating every person equally and with the same intensity of interest in his interviews. Jayakar describes the 1960s flower children as "barefoot wanderers" and a "lost generation" seeking consolation in drugs, music, yoga and sex. She claims Krishna saw a general decline in values and responsibility, observing a link between "inward" disintegration and a growing indifference of humans for their natural environment. Krishna continued his demand for a "revolution" in the "ground" of the mind and questioned whether humans were even individual or simply a "movement of the collective".[79]

Many people had heard about Krishna's healing powers. In 1964 Shankara Rao Deo, who was President of the All India Sarva Sangh, the Gandhian service organisation, became ill, losing his power of speech and communication, even through writing. In early 1965 he had four "sittings" with Krishna. At the first he burst out crying when Krishna touched him and he emerged calm and able to speak again.[80]

Krishna's reputation as a healer is supported by testimony further afield than India alone, although most of the people who claim that he helped them physically or psychologically are not prepared to be identified. Reports abound of people who were disturbed by a compelling worry or physical pain, only to be relieved of the disturbance upon meeting Krishnamurti. One man believed he was Jesus Christ until he realised the absurdity of the idea when calm imbued his mind as he stood beside Krishna. The legends persist. An English girl had leukaemia which went into remission under Krishna's influence. An American man regularly found relief from agonising pain when Krishna massaged his back. Two Indian men, one a prominent official of the Theosophical Society, suffered paralysis which disappeared under Krishna's touch. Krishna would place his hands on the eyelids of a woman who was going blind. He would talk quietly with a young man who suffered hallucinations about being in communication with satellites. He could reportedly ease both psychological and physical pain.[81]

Krishna's close friend and private secretary for many years, Sunanda Parwardhan, also benefitted from his healing power. She says that if it hadn't been for Krishna's "passes", she would have been crippled after a severe attack of rheumatoid arthritis. She had also known him to heal other people, but he'd stopped the practice, saying it was much more important to heal psychologically. He referred to physical healing powers as *siddhis*, saying it was easy to acquire them, but they were "a deviation for a person interested in meditation and liberation". S Weeraperuma, the former Krishnamurti adherent now critical of him, also believes Krishna had the power to physically heal the sick. He cites several examples of healing - what Krishna in the early years referred to as "helping" and which he later claimed occurred without him doing anything. A man with a son aged four who was suffering epilepsy and a speech defect wanted to have a private meeting so Krishna could heal the boy, but on being refused, the pair attended Krishna's talks. The boy did not understand English yet his ailments disappeared. A Dutch man with leprosy once grabbed at Krishna in the street to touch him and was cured, even though he was later imprisoned, so Krishna would tell the story as an example of the man's mind needing the healing rather than his body. In Saanen a man in a trilby hat would attend Krishna's talks every year to show his gratitude for Krishna having saved his life when he had had tubercolosis. Another man in Bombay who had cancer of the mouth was cured after Krishna examined his mouth. A woman in Sri Lanka insisted Krishna touch her deaf ear and regained some hearing. Yet Krishna sometimes refused "pleas for help from people who were in great physical pain". Weeraperuma conjectured that perhaps Krishnamurti's rejection of certain cases stemmed from a view that some illnesses should not be arrested as they purified and regenerated the body.[82]

In the mid-1960s Vimala Thakar gave details of how Krishna healed her infected and deaf ear after she went to see him on the advice of friends in December 1960. At the first healing session, once Vimala was seated and ready, Krishna washed his hands, walked gently toward her, stood behind her chair and laid his right palm on her head and his left over her left ear. She said she was alert and saw a very strong and forceful current of vibrations pass through her head and whole body. Her body became wonderfully relaxed. Her eyes closed of their own accord. When he took his hands away, she found it hard to open her eyes and focus and felt she was coming back from a land of peace and light. She drank a glass of water and, feeling sleepy, went home to sleep for two hours. The following year when Vimala told Krishna she felt indebted to him, he said she didn't owe him a thing in the world. The healing was not necessarily related to her new experiences of vibrations in her body. She had been listening to the talks, she had a serious mind, and the talks were sinking deep into her being.

> Look here – you were walking in a forest. You came across another person. He said: 'If you walk this way you might arrive earlier.' You walked. You arrived. You thanked the person. It is as simple as that. Why should you feel you owe something to me?83

The explanation has the same tone of transpersonality as his quip in 1962 to Mary Lutyens: "We do not all have to be Edisons to turn on the electric light". Lutyens also cites his remark to a journalist in Rome who suggested that other people could not attain Krishna's state of consciousness: "Christopher Columbus went to America in a sailing ship; we can go by jet". Krishna's own trek through a pathless land had been arduous but others might benefit from his travail in making their own way.[84]

Chapter 11

Science and Revolution

A background of dark matter – all that is not said – remains, buzzing.

John Updike 1989 Self-Consciousness: Memoirs Penguin London p ix.

The 1970s would prove to be a decade of trial and tribulation when all of Krishna's and Rajagopal's skills in the game of Monopoly would be called in to play, with the help of legal advisers. Yet for all the concentration on property disputes, Krishna, in his mid-seventies, found a new lease of life in building up a fresh organisation to spread his teaching. His interest in education came to the fore, his reputation for iconoclasm finding favour with youthful revolutionaries. And in Krishna's exploration of consciousness he found new partners from among the leading scientists and thinkers of the time.

Jayakar says that even in 1969 Krishna was asking whether there was such a thing as an individual or whether humans were merely a movement of the collective. He said that to be an individual, there had to be a revolution in the collective as it was revealed in knowledge and tradition, so humans had to discover their own incorruptibility. It was necessary for people to ask questions to which there were no answers. That way a person would be thrown back on him or herself and on the way the structure of thought operated. Jayakar says that Krishna's interest in exploring the traditional Indian approach to liberation was evident from the autumn of 1970. He spoke of the tenacity of the Hindu mind, which despite conquest and repression, had kept alive its ancient teachings. Krishna was interested in mythological stories and the Brahmins' understanding of their role as teachers who should give freely so that their poverty was an honour. The pity was that he saw its degeneration.[1]

Krishna's letter-writing had tapered off in recent years, as first Alain Naudé and then Mary Zimbalist attended to much of it. However he would often write to close friends, sometimes in order to outline the current impasse with Rajagopal, sometimes to offer sympathy, sometimes to remind someone of their responsibilities, delivered in a clipped tone.

In March 1970 he wrote several letters in the same vein, giving his version of attempts to have talks with Rajagopal, who, he said, was using the fact that Krishna had begun litigation through the Attorney-General, as an excuse to avoid a meeting. At this time Krishna was staying in Malibu with Mary Zimbalist and had given talks in Santa Monica attended by about 3,000 people, with a few hundred turned away. Krishna commented to Mary Zimbalist afterwards that he felt he'd been singing to the deaf.[2]

Since the mid-60s Krishna had been keen to talk with students and young people. In September 1968 he had gone with Alain Naudé to Puerto Rico, where they stayed as guests of the Biascoecheas in San Juan and Krishna gave talks at the University of Puerto Rico.[3] In October he moved on to the New School for Social Research in New York, then Brandeis University, and Claremont College in California in November. In February 1969 he gave talks at Berkeley, then Stanford, then the University of California, Santa Cruz. Naudé wrote about many of the students at these meetings as being deeply religious, wanting a better world and understanding that that would mean changing their own minds. At the end of 1969 the Brockwood Park school had been established about sixty five miles from London at Bramdean, in Hampshire. It's remarkable that this location is in the same county, not twenty miles as the crow flies from Leadbeater's former parish at Bramshott, where he lived before joining the Theosophists late the previous century. It's hard to know whether this coincidence was contrived or random. Mary Lutyens says that she and Mary Cadogan had been charged with the task of finding a residence and the site was the third proposed as suitable. The property belonged to Lord Chesam and Lutyens simply explains it as "a third property was found which seemed ideal" – reasonably close to London and with enough land for privacy. The Brockwood school, a late-Georgian building painted white, is set in a beautiful estate of 36 acres, planted with magnificent trees, including sequoias, beeches and copper beeches, and an extensive azalea garden. The estate had cost 42,000 pounds, largely a donation from a wealthy friend of Krishna who wanted him to have a permanent home on retirement. But Krishna's purpose, despite his protestations about institutionalisation, was to solidify his teaching in an efficiently-run school. Typical of the pace of Krishna's lecture schedule are the 119 talks he gave in 1969. Peppered among these were talks specifically focussed on young people. In May and July 1969, Krishna held eight discussions with students in Amsterdam and Schoenried; at the new Brockwood Park school in September-October he held ten sessions with students and staff; at Benares Hindu University he gave a public talk in November and another two talks to students at Bombay University in December, before four discussions with young people in Madras in December 1969 and January 1970. Through the 1970s the opportunities for Krishna to mix with students, both outside of, as well as within, the Krishnamurti schools, increased. In April 1970 he gave four talks in San Diego and conducted one dialogue at San Diego College. The same month in England he spoke to students and staff at Brockwood. In Saanen in July he included two talks with students among the nine talks and eight dialogues he gave; back in Brockwood he talked with students and staff through September and went on to Perugia and Rome, then giving a talk to students in Florence; in Madras he spoke at the Indian Institute of Technology and with young people at Mrs Jayalakshmi's home, at Rishi Valley school with students, and in Bombay with young people at Pupul Jayakar's home; back in California, he appeared at the University of Southern California; then he moved on to Brockwood speaking to students and staff separately; in Amsterdam, one discussion with young people followed four general talks. In 1970 when he was aged 75, for instance, Krishna made about 130 public appearances over the year, speaking at forums ranging from recorded discussions with school staff or students to large public lectures. He would continue at this pace over the next decade. The list of venues stretched ahead, with Krishna increasingly feeling his mortality and consciously trying to make contact with serious-minded students, mostly in his schools but also at college venues whenever he was invited. The undeniable stamp of Krishnamurti's teachings was also set on the Rishi Valley school in India early in 1970 when Krishna was staying there. The name, the Foundation for New Education, as the Rishi Valley Trust had become known in 1953, was changed to the Krishnamurti Foundation of India so that there could be no sliding away from its original purpose, as had occurred at Happy Valley in California.[4]

Krishna was very concerned to set up these places where his teaching could be kept safe, and to interest younger generations in what he had to say. He was also very aware of his advancing age and consequent declining strength. He wrote to KFA trustees in March 1970 about the responsibilities of the Foundations during and after his lifetime. He'd referred to the dissemination of his work through publications, records and tapes, and now he wanted to add video to the list, which his advisers realised would be an important medium in the future. Videotape had not become an affordable and therefore common medium for communication until the 1970s. While he felt his mortality, Krishna still looked to the future. He commented to Anneke Korndorffer in Amsterdam that he would like to hold talks there in May, if he were still alive, just as he exhorted Mary Cadogan in England not to invite only people from the old list, but new people who would be vitally interested in his talks.[5]

1970 was also the year of publication of *The Only Revolution*, a title certain to appeal to a younger generation. The publication by Victor Gollancz was based on Krishna's personal interviews in India, California and Europe, interspersed with his reflections on the value of meditation and descriptions of the natural world. The book was edited by Mary Lutyens and the inside dustcover announced that change must come and it must come first within individuals.[6]

Krishna visited Sydney in November 1970, on a flying visit scheduled between a brief rest in Malibu and a heavy program of talks in India. Mary Zimbalist had written to Donald Ingram Smith in July to make some arrangements. Her instructions about their domestic situation were quite explicit: both she and Krishna liked a firm mattress. He liked a very hard pillow but she carried her own. For his diet: whole grains such as rice, wheat, buck-wheat and millet; dried beans, lentils or peas; he liked almonds more than any other nuts but ate all kinds; soy powder or flour he added to his porridge; for breakfast he also ate fresh fruit, dried raisins, honey, wholewheat bread and a hard-boiled egg. Krishna usually had his breakfast and supper in bed so a large tray would be useful. As Donald might have known, for lunch Krishna ate in sequence, fruit, salad and then a hot dish. Sometimes he ate a little cheese or yoghurt.[7]

The Krishnamurti adherents in Sydney must have been very excited by the visit as it was the first Krishna had made in fifteen years. In the meantime certain individuals had managed to walk a fine line, maintaining contact with Rajagopal while others stayed in contact with Krishna. Reg Bennett had written to Madhavachari in 1968 that most of the credit must go to him for making the teachings easily accessible. He also had correspondence that year with Casselberry who had complained that Krishna had engaged in a character assassination of Rajagopal. In 1969 Bennett and Spencer English both kept up correspondence with the Ojai office, Casselberry commenting about the London office being childish, that it was absurd "ballyhoo", about having Rosalind to dinner and that Rajagopal was bearing up and would see matters through to their end.[8]

In preparation for Krishna's visit, his followers in Sydney put out an information sheet in May calling for "liberal" donations from interested friends. The local committee had offered to pay his airfares and suitable accommodation. There would also be the costs of hall hire, amplification, publicity, printing and postage to be taken into account. Spencer English and Reg Bennett collected the funds.[9]

Another statement, possibly intended for the media, was written by Donald Ingram Smith in the week leading up to the visit. He maintained that after watching Krishna for over thirty years he had found him indifferent to success. Krishna had collected no funds, founded no institutes "to back him up", recognised no body of followers and had not even "cast his teaching into a fixed shape for purposes of easy propaganda". (While each of these points was debatable in terms of degree, it might be acknowledged that Krishna's talks were free in Australia and his accommodation had always been in the homes of friends, rather than in expensive hotels. Now that he lived and travelled with Mary Zimbalist, a wealthy woman in her own right, it was not unreasonable to expect the standard of his accommodation to be suitable to them both on this visit.) Smith made the valid point that myths were built up around Krishna as a young man and they persisted in the public mind, yet his actual life had been legendary. Why did the stories overlay Krishna's teaching, Smith asked? He put it down to Krishnamurti adamantly denying organisations and authority and making no effort to bring the teaching to a popular level, so that its meaning eluded the casual listener. He exhorted people to take the first step suggested by Krishnamurti and listen. "Do not believe or disbelieve ... accept or reject. ... [U]nless this step of listening openly, freely is understood, Krishnamurti will remain misunderstood."[10]

In Sydney Krishna gave five 90-minute talks in the Town Hall to capacity audiences, held sessions with small groups at Mona Vale and conducted two dialogues at Manly. A half-hour interview was broadcast on ABC TV and the current affairs program, *This Day Tonight*, ran a segment by Caroline Jones who also interviewed Krishna. The precis described him as a man who, forty-four years earlier, was "supposed to be the returned Messiah" but arrived at Balmoral by quite conventional means. "A massive cult was built around him which has since crumbled but the need for a belief in a Messiah-to-come is still around," it read. Several people who attended a Town Hall talk remember they considered the behaviour of interjectors as rude and counter-productive – Krishna seemed to have an impressive but very gentle personality. Mary Zimbalist recalls a heckler in the audience with whom Krishna dealt swiftly and efficiently. She said Krishna was very good at handling these interruptions. One person who attended a Town Hall talk said that she had a question to ask but was too shy, yet she found that while Krishnamurti was talking, once he looked directly at her, and she found he was answering her question. One adherent who was involved in organising Krishna's visit said that on meeting him she felt he looked right into her, as if by x-ray. Another adherent described coming upon Krishna as he was walking down a hallway of the Town Hall ready to go on stage and feeling a "holy communion" when he'd asked Krishna a question and Krishna had grasped his hand. A question had arisen in the man's mind - "What is love?" - and the immediate response came not as a thought, but as the scene itself, with the realisation that people communicate through love and that love creates the scene, whether we realise it or not.[11]

Krishna and Mary Zimbalist stayed in an apartment in Manly with a spectacular view of Sydney Harbour and the Heads. Mary says that one day an aircraft carrier sailed out of the harbour and Krishna watched it from their balcony, declaring wouldn't it be wonderful to be the captain. Mary spoke of the incident as an example of the child-like quality he had.[12]

One Sydney adherent described waiting with Krishna before his ABC interview when he said that it didn't suit who he was to be kept waiting. Her perception was that he was very humble and modest in his personal life but he considered his public persona as important as it was linked to his teaching.[13]

Perhaps during this visit the seed of an idea to set up a branch of the Krishnamurti Foundation in Australia was discussed, since Donald Ingram Smith worked toward the venture over the next few years. Smith says Krishna was encouraging, that he said 'go ahead'. But, in contrast, he later signed the letter abandoning the idea once lawyers had been engaged to study the proposed articles of association and it was established that under Australian

Government regulation, any international organisation represented would have its funds frozen in the event of war. A school was also set up near Castle Hill based on Montessori, Steiner and Krishnamurti teaching but it only catered for at most twenty students for a brief duration. High hopes have produced very little in the way of lasting monument or organisation in Australia.[14]

Although Krishna's supporters were able to gather enough interest in his talks to fill the Town Hall, this trip to Australia, his last, was not a highlight either for Krishna or Sydney. The problem may have been the timing, as his stay coincided with the eve of the first-ever visit by a Pope to Australia. The media reported that hundreds of thousands of "modern-day pilgrims" were pouring into Sydney, and millions were expected to line the streets for his cavalcade from the airport. In the popular press, Krishna was clearly overshadowed by the greatest living religious figure in the world, as Krishna flew out the day Pope Paul arrived.[15]

Krishna departed Sydney alone, as Mary was not going on to India with him. One of the people present at the airport said Mary was like a mother watching the tiny figure walk alone to the aircraft. Mary Zimbalist was a very capable companion, taking great care of his diet and making sure that his clothes were in immaculate condition, as he liked them.

Back in India he donned traditional clothing and took up the challenge of Indian audiences, with their quicksilver minds and devotional attitudes, some people saying that he was even tougher on them than he was with Western audiences. Vimala Thakar certainly observed that he was different with different audiences. In Wimbledon in 1961 she recognised that the content of his talks was the same but "the overtones and undertones had a noticeable emphasis on science and psychology".

> He was, as it were, fully aware of the full impact of the industrial civilization on the minds of his audience. Indeed he seemed to feel the stress and strain under which their whole nervous system was being crushed.[16]

Jayakar too observed Krishna's positive reaction to the Indian mind in the smaller dialogue groups, sensing in this form of discussion a new approach to the teaching. Much of the material was the same - dealing with subjects such as beauty, God, dying and living and conflict - but much of the material had a decidedly Indian sensibility, in discussion of subjects such as consciousness, *sadhana*, the *guru* and tradition, and even the mind and the heart. Krishna wanted the 1970 Dialogues to form the basis of a new book so they were corrected by her and Sunanda Patwardhan and published in India in 1972 as *Tradition and Revolution*. They wrote in the Preface that Krishnamurti began questioning from a tentative position of "not-knowing" and that a "delicate wordless communication" would take place. "An exposure of the movement of negation as it met the positive movement of thought", they called it. Jayakar maintains that there was a recognition in the book of the importance of dialogue in awakening the questioning mind – that there were no answers to life's fundamental problems but only the awakening of intelligence by asking fundamental questions. Lutyens says that although there was nothing new in the ideas in the book, the approach was new, particularly the inclusion of a glossary of Indian terms. She sees the book as a way for Indians to reclaim Krishna as one of their own, a Brahmin, to see him as an Indian teacher, and to emphasise the affinity of his work with its ancient teachings, even though he considered himself as without race or nationality. Lutyens pointed to Krishna's teaching about not trying to avoid sorrow as the book's significant contribution.[17]

Also in 1970 a respected Indian philosopher published a work on Krishna, *J Krishnamurti and Mind in Revolution*, which placed Krishna in the Indian tradition. AD Dhopeshwarkar, whose early philosophical education had been with EA Wodehouse, had later taught in colleges in Karachi and Dharwar that were affiliated to Bombay University. He had published three books on Krishnamurti, and the first in 1956 had been reprinted three times, as recently as 1968. In this latest work, Dhopeshwarkar opened with a quote from the *Bhagavad-Gita*, "Whoever has not jettisoned concepts will never be Yogi (attain spiritual insight)".[18]

Vigeveno continued to try to act as an intermediary between Krishna and Rajagopal, but he completely mis-read Krishna's mood. In March 1970 Krishna called one of his letters "scandalous". Vigeveno wrote again in April and July, reiterating his views expressed the year before, warning about "unpleasant" consequences coming out of litigation and the many things, if they became known, which would damage Krishna's reputation. It was a personal problem between Krishna and Rajagopal, he maintained, and Krishna was trying to ignore this. It was in 1971 that Rosalind became so worried about disclosure of her relationship with Krishna that she told her daughter, Radha, about it. Radha says her mother did not want her to first hear about it in court. Radha phoned Krishna in Malibu that year in the hope of brokering a peace. She told him about her Aunt Erma's death and says Krishna seemed not to know the identity of Rosalind's sister until she reminded him. She told him the problem between him and Rajagopal was "private" and should be settled in a closet rather than a courtroom. Then she told him it was a conflict of ego and pride. She says Krishna was "outraged" and his voice became angry. He said he had no ego and who did she think she was to talk to him like that. Radha felt like a stranger. In May 1971 Casselberry wrote about Rajagopal being accused of all sorts of "dreadful" deeds and his name "dragged" in the mud. It happened to "saintly" people on the "occult" path, he said, just as Leadbeater had explained. He even drew a parallel with Gethsemane and Christ's crucifixion. Vigeveno wrote to Krishna again in January and July 1972, reminding him of the irony of Krishna's former denunciation of lawyers and his need to recognise that the dispute was "only" a personal matter. Krishna replied that an out of court settlement would be the best solution as long as it were arranged legally to avoid any future problems.[19]

Krishna must have been bored by this fuss over the "personal" references, which no doubt implied knowledge about his sexual relationship with Rosalind. After all, Krishna had himself known about this "affair" for about forty years, had tried to find solutions twenty five years before, including breaking the triangle, and the few people he'd recently told about this problematic relationship hadn't seemed too concerned. He had never been interested in conforming to conventional moral standards and had never advocated celibacy since leaving the Theosophical Society in 1929. Vigeveno's anxiety smacked of prudishness at a time when traditional morality was coming under scrutiny from a younger generation more sexually-liberated and articulate than their elders.

Mary Lutyens was also helpful in bringing Krishna's views about sex out into the open. She was working on a biography of Krishna, inheriting a mass of papers from Shiva Rao, who had carried out research in the Theosophical Archives at Adyar. He had intended to write Krishna's biography but became ill and willingly handed over the project to Mary Lutyens whom Krishna had asked to write the book. She had agreed, after stipulating that there must be no requirement for her manuscript to be cleared by anyone, no doubt remembering her mother's difficulties with Krishna over publication of *Candles in the Sun*. Krishna agreed, she said, and he gave her written permission to quote from his correspondence and the accounts of his 1922 Ojai experience.[20] No doubt Lutyens was aware of his sexual relationship with Rosalind as he had informed people close to him when he decided to take legal action against Rajagopal. Krishna agreed to have an article which he wrote in the form of Q & A published in the third issue of a new quarterly, *Krishnamurti Foundation Bulletin*. It canvassed the question of whether leading a celibate religious life was a kind of puritanical conformity. Clearly Krishna believed it was, and maintained that such austerity and harsh suppression did "brutal" violence to a person's finer instincts. Why make sex a problem, he asked? Get on with it or drop it but don't make a problem of it, he advised. Better to ask whether you would stay in some "sordid" little room of pleasure all your life – go into the slavery of pleasure, stay with it and see what happened, he suggested. Loneliness existed before a person fell in love, which was merely a stimulation, he said, and people's problems stemmed not from their relationships but from their own emptiness. Being in love was without conflict but loss of energy came in the jealousy. possessiveness and fear of losing that love. It was possible to be in a sexual relationship with someone without the nightmare that usually followed, he concluded. Krishna made no comment about his own personal life, but surely must have wondered how his own relationship with Rosalind would have stood up if it were scrutinised as a case study. It's interesting to note here a discussion Pupul Jayakar discloses in her biography of Krishnamurti. In December 1969 in Bombay, Krishna described to Pupul, Nandini and Asit Chandmal his early years with the Theosophical Society. He apparently had no trouble remembering many details of his life lived according to the Society's beliefs and theories, although he questioned how that boy had remained 'unaffected" by the special attention he received. He spoke about the initiations he had gone through, explaining the belief that after two initiations things could go "wrong", but after a third, the "being" could not be affected by anger, sex or money as these were too trivial. Jayakar also describes an occasion in 1979 when Krishna talked with teachers at Rishi Valley school, picking out one male teacher in particular who was living a life of chastity and grappling with the resulting tensions. Come down from your platforms and tell your students you have fears, jealousies and hurts, just like them, so that they can really trust you, Krishna said. Then, after an outburst from the teacher, Krishna patted the teacher's hand gently and with affection, as if he understood his turmoil, saying sex was like a tender flower or an intense flame, so delicate and rare, that had to be nurtured and cherished. He advised neither denying nor succumbing, but watching and nurturing so that it could unfold.[21]

Mary Lutyens became the mainstay of Krishna's literary presence from the time of the publication in 1970 of *The Urgency of Change*, which comprised the edited answers of questions put to Krishna by Alain Naudé. Lutyens says that because of their method of production, with Krishna listening to and correcting his answers, these talks are more valuable than those he never revised. In the chapter headed "Love and Sex", Krishnamurti establishes his often-repeated view that the word is not the thing, and any amount of explanation, however subtle or clever, is incapable of opening the heart to the "immensity" of what 'love' is. So he suggests that by seeing what love is not, through negation, one might come upon the positive - rather than pursuing the positive which led to assumptions. To the question of whether you could have sex without the desire of thought, Krishna replied that there was pain and strife in all relationships except in the act of sex. But it was so different and beautiful that it was addictive, causing bondage. People were so hedged about - by intellectuality, by the family, the community, social morality, religious sanctions – that they wanted the freedom and intensity of sex and attached tremendous importance to it, he said. But it was old society that called new society "permissive", he said, for in new society sex was a part of life.[22]

The Only Revolution and *The Penguin Krishnamurti Reader* were both published in 1970. *The Only Revolution* comprised Krishna's own writing and Mary Lutyens said she found it easy to edit. She explains that it was based on discussions on three continents. Krishna's style of writing was equally candid and imaginative in his descriptions of the natural environment and the people who came to him for interviews. Comments could include observations that: the bearded man who wore a turban looked prosperous and well-fed; the bare-footed Brahmin school-teacher, who wore a clean *dhoti* and a western shirt, was sharp-eyed and showed humility in his salutation. Or Krishna might describe a day beginning cloudy and dull with the "naked" trees silent in the wood, and as you came closer to a patch of yellow forsythia on a green lawn, you were blinded by the brightness of the yellow – which was "God". The Penguin *Reader* was more difficult as the publisher required excerpts from the three previous books, *The First and Last Freedom*, *Life Ahead* and *This Matter of Culture*, to be whittled down into one book. Lutyens said that as they were dissimilar it was not easy to make an homogenous whole. It was presented in three sections, 'The

Problems of Living', 'For the Young' and 'Questions and Answers'. The middle section was something of a misnomer, for although it dealt with questions that young people might wrestle with, the treatment of these questions was as intellectually taxing as anything else that Krishnamurti ever said. However the Penguin *Reader*, in particular, achieved for Krishnamurti a mass circulation and a reputation in mainstream society as a philosopher. In 1972 the *Second Penguin Krishnamurti Reader* was published, comprising excerpts from *The Only Revolution* and *The Urgency of Change*.[23]

This was a coup in terms of his acceptance by opinion-leaders in Western society, bringing him to the notice of intellectuals who were embarking on simultaneously broad-based and locally-intensive challenges to the status quo of prevailing ideologies. Although what he said did not exactly square with the political and social counter-cultural discourse that flowed from the 1960s, his challenging stance made a major contribution to what cultural historian, Arjun Appadurai, has termed "ideoscapes". Krishnamurti's published work was a significant contribution to what Appadurai calls a "discourse of democracy" carried out by "the growing diasporas of intellectuals who continuously inject[ed] new meaning-streams" into that discourse. It might also be argued that Krishnamurti stood on the threshold of a fresh approach to understanding consciousness, at a point where Huxley's 'Doors of Perception' would open up popular and academic enquiry, generating, or at least embellishing, many new streams of investigation into the concept of the mind and personality, in the fields of neurophysiology, psychotherapy, transactional analysis, ontology, epistemology, theism and peace studies.[24]

Historian, Peter Washington, makes the point that having become popular, particularly through Californian university campuses of the 1960s, Krishnamurti might be described as "a star of the New Age synthesis". But it took a little while for people to realise that his views were at odds with the "narcissism, idealism and libertarianism" of the 60s youth movements.

Washington says Krishnamurti was the guru of the wealthy classes and was ascetically disapproving of the self-indulgence accompanying "flower-power". Yet Washington also points out that Krishna distanced himself from "ensnarement" by the rich who all too often think that they own those they patronise. Perhaps unworldly, undoubtedly self-referential, Krishna never considered censoring his lectures to accord with the values of his wealthy benefactors or government security agencies. It might be argued that Krishnamurti's consistently trenchant criticism of nationalism over a major part of the course of the twentieth century, without fear or favour from any government, seeped into the minds and writings of influential intellectuals so that when Appadurai writes of "transnation" or "squaring Enlightenment universalisms and diasporic pluralism", he is pursuing an agenda to delineate a global commonality of interests and culture between individuals as "Other", which Krishnamurti, among other major thinkers, foreshadowed. For Krishnamurti not only spoke about recognising the common issues in the minds of people of all countries which might free them from the values of their respective cultures, nations or religions, but he was a living example of an outsider infiltrating the 'heart of whiteness". Krishna recognised that he was an outsider, whether in Europe, the United States or India, and that people who followed any religion or political creed were interested in what he said "up to a point". He was dark-skinned, had been uprooted from the culture of his birth and had been "stolen" and "assimilated" into European upper-class culture. Yet in accepting certain material comforts, he refused to condone the values which produced them, setting his own ground of debate on questions of international chauvinism, violence within societies, cultural difference, beneficial modes of education, civil liberties - including individual freedom of speech - and the need to question authority. When people listened to him they forgot that he was a "little brown man" (as articulated by one adherent to represent the prejudice of status, race and gender) and related instead to the humanitarian understanding he shared with the audience.[25]

The BBC broadcast a television interview with Krishna at the end of 1970. It began by showing the interviewer. Oliver Hunkin, and Krishna walking outside the main building at Brockwood Park, an obviously wealthy setting, and then moved inside for the interview itself. Krishna was animated and eager to convey his message but the intellectual demands of the interview were no less for all the enthusiasm. At the end of the program Krishna described meditation as occurring when the body was so completely quiet that the brain cells themselves became quiet. In that silence, everything happened. That was real meditation, he said, not just a phony acceptance of authority and the repetition of words. Hunkin asked if he might recapitulate, in his own words, on what Krishna had said, and Krishna agreed, which was out of character, as he would normally plead with people to listen, rather than bring what he was saying back within the language of their own conditioned minds. Hunkin began, "Meditation is the essential deconditioning process ...," and Krishna agreed. "If I discard this deadweight of authority, if I discard everything that I've been told," Hunkin went on, "I shall be totally alone at that moment but in my solitude there's a chance I may understand what I really am". Krishna was beaming in accord. And you would understand what Truth was, or God, or whatever name you liked to give it, Krishna concluded.[26]

Krishna had always carried the taint of his origins in the Theosophical Society, with the sensationalist "Saviour" image revived by the press whenever he provoked interest. In some countries the taint of 'cult figure' still hung about him. Harold S Blume of Humata Verlag publishers complained in 1975, for instance, that Krishnamurti was still regarded as an "obscure" preacher of a sect. He said that journalists did not regard him as a "News-Personality" as they did Sartre and Marcuse, for example, and no notice of the tent-gatherings at Saanen appeared in the press. Similarly, many bookstores did not want to carry his books. Blume, publishing for KWINC, was clearly currying favour in telling Rajagopal that he knew how to spread Krishnamurti's message through the mass media but was prevented from carrying out his ideas. But other people were also trying to assist in spreading Krishna's ideas, and in other major cities in the West, Krishna was slowly becoming broadly enough known as a public speaker and writer to be able to throw off the cultish image. Now he was considered something of a venerable figure, and it was not before considerable effort on his part. In view of his fifty arduous years of criss-crossing the globe to deliver his teaching to audiences ranging from a dialogue group of ten to audiences in the thousands, he was at last being adopted by the media as a reputable philosopher, even while he refuted the "philosopher" label. But as he'd been a celebrity, a figure of fun, a world "Saviour" and a sage, he must have learned by now not to pay attention to the vagaries of the media. He was always finding new followers as others fell away; he cultivated non-attachment in most relationships yet his links with old friends and acquaintances still needed his attention.[27]

Krishna's letters to friends were mostly solicitous. He wrote to his long-time friend, Jamnadas Dwarkardas, in May 1970, commiserating that Jamnadas had broken his thigh when he fell in the bathroom. And in 1973 he wrote to Jamnadas, who was by then aged 84, to say he hoped he was looking after himself and they would see each other in India. To "Kittyji", Shiva Rao's wife, Krishna wrote comforting letters hoping Shiva Rao would recover from a severe illness. Rajagopal, too, had written to Shiva Rao, whom they both respected for his devotion to Mrs Besant and Krishna since their childhood years. But to Motwani, another old friend, who had said his stay at Adyar was becoming uncertain, Krishna couldn't make any promises of help, saying he did not interfere with appointments to the Krishnamurti Foundation, India, and Motwani should write directly to Pupul Jayakar or Rishi Valley to see what they could do. The following year Krishna had Mary Zimbalist reply, sending thanks for Motwani's book, *Towards Indian Sociology*. But by March 1974 Krishna wrote to Motwani, following despairing letters from his wife, that he was sorry that he was feeling so low, but they were all getting old, and he hoped they could accept the inevitable with grace and without self-pity. By November Motwani had picked up enough to ask after Krishna's health but said he was not strong enough to attend Krishna's Madras talks. Krishna hoped everything would be well with him and sent him his best wishes. The following year he wrote to say he was sorry that things were becoming so difficult for Motwani but one had to make the best of it and get on with it. The correspondence gives just a glimpse of the competing and demanding forces of affection that surrounded Krishna all his life. He might give out love but not so much that a devotee should not remain independent, to draw on his or her own resources. Donald Ingram Smith describes it as tying up your own shoelaces if you are able to.[28]

In 1966 Krishna had changed his yoga instruction from the renowned South Indian teacher, BKS Iyengar of Poona, to Iyengar's nephew, TKV Desikachar, whose father, T Krishnamacharya, of Bombay, was also a revered yoga master. Krishna rarely spoke about his *hatha yoga* practice, and even today some of his friends speak of the *asanas*, or exercises he did every day, rather than calling it "*hatha yoga*", in case there is a misinterpretation that Krishna was working towards *samadhi*, or enlightenment. Yet the exercises he did were pure yoga – a regimen of postures and *pranayama*, or breathing exercises, and he did them at least as far back as the 1950s. Jayakar writes of Krishna following the instruction Iyengar had given him in *asanas* and *pranayama* every morning at daybreak in Kashmir in 1959. Some years later, Krishna wanted to study with Desikachar's father, T Krishnamacharya. Instead, T Krishnamacharya, who was very old, sent Desikachar along to see Krishna. Desikachar asked to see what postures Krishna could do and was impressed to see the difficult postures he did over the period of an hour. Krishna was aged seventy and frail yet he was still supple and flexible. Desikachar went home to his father and told him about Krishna's ill-health, which was the reason Krishna sought instruction, and Desikachar went back the next day and told Krishna that his father had asked him to stop all the postures, and to begin a new regime by first practising simple breathing exercises. Desikachar says that Krishna was a very good student and, as his teacher, he learned from him also how to be a good student. Desikachar was young and inexperienced, with only four years of practice behind him, yet Krishna treated him with great respect. Krishna would lay the best mat for him and sit only after Desikachar had sat down. This formality was the norm in India and Krishna carefully observed the etiquette of respect for the teacher. Desikachar said that Krishnamurti was the best model in his life because he was a very distinguished person yet he showed respect for Desikachar as a teacher. He knew Krishna was showing the respect he had for the great tradition of yoga. Krishna also advised him never to become a guru.[29]

Six months after meeting Desikachar, Krishna invited him to go to Europe and his fare and several months' accommodation was paid for. He went to Krishna's room twice a day to help him with his practice. Back in India late in the year, Desikachar, a very serious young man, was at that stage of his life facing decisions about his future work and purpose in life as a dutiful son. He wrote in correspondence that he was concerned about Krishna's liver problem and hoped he had no doubts about his practice. Desikachar was also worried in case he was taxing Krishna in any way. Desikachar writes in the biography of his father, *Sri Krishnamacharya The Purnacarya*, that Krishnamurti told him he would offer him a scholarship - even if it meant selling his shirt – so that Desikachar, as a son, could learn everything possible from his father. Krishnamurti had asked Krishnamacharya the meaning of yoga, and he had replied that for him it meant *santi* or mental peace.[30]

From Krishna's correspondence to Desikachar in 1970, his fondness for his young teacher is evident. He would like Desikachar to come to Brockwood and Saanen, he said, but finances were rather low. But he and Mary Zimbalist would send him a little note about the exercises they were doing so that he could make comments or changes if he thought they should. Krishna said that he had been doing the *asanas* and *pranayamas* very regularly and they had certainly helped him a great deal. By June of 1970 congratulations were in order, for Desikachar's wife was pregnant. Krishna sent his affection and best wishes to her.[31]

The bond between Krishna and Desikachar continued right through Krishna's life. Desikachar travelled to Saanen several times and could call on Krishna without notice in Bombay. He remembers one time in Switzerland, Krishna took him for a drive in his 2-door, 300 SL Mercedes Benz, and he drove very fast. Desikachar emphasised that Krishna was an "ordinary" human being experiencing the same feelings that everyone did. He was good and passionate, he said.[32]

Other correspondence showed the affection Krishna held for old friends. He wrote to Maurice Friedman in 1970 about an interview that had been suggested. He teased Friedman with the comment that he hoped he was looking at the blue sky sometimes and not saving too many souls.[33]

Krishna's attitude to Vimala Thakar, who claimed Krishna had healed her hearing and began giving talks in a similar vein to Krishna, is complex and worth noting. Krishna was told that she had published a book describing the healing and other works that gave spiritual advice, in correspondence from Madhavachari in 1966. Krishna wrote in 1970 about Vimala Thakar to Dr EW Adikaram of Sri Lanka, who had been a devoted friend of Krishna for many years. With a PhD from the University of London and as a Pali scholar and writer, Adikaram had given up teaching and lived as a *sannyasi*, visiting ashrams and studying Krishnamurti's works. Krishna told Adikaram that many people in different parts of the world thought that Vimala Thakar was a representative of his, but she was not a special disciple who would carry on his work. Whatever she said was on her own account, and was not to be confused with any Krishnamurti Foundation publications, he advised Adikaram. He asked him to treat his letter as confidential.[34]

KFA lists in its archives several conversations between Krishna and Vimala Thakar recorded in 1968, unpublished and held in Ojai, but nothing involving her after this date. Lutyens' biographies of Krishna's final years make no reference to her; nor does Jayakar's biography make any reference to her after her meetings with Krishna in Europe in 1962. That year Vimala Thakar had met Krishna in Saanen and Geneva, after sending him poems she had written out of a kind of spontaneous inspiration, with a message not dissimilar to Krishna's. She described an experience of words gushing out of her heart, such as,

> I have drunk deep
> At the fountain of life
> I am no more thirsty,

and

> The mind that creates its own bondage
> The mind that invents its own freedom.

According to Vimala Thakar, Krishna had told her in Benares the year before that the words would not come if she waited. At first she might use the wrong words and make a mess, but she shouldn't wait, as she had the fire within her. In Saanen he told her to put ginger in people's minds and bombs under them, and in Geneva they discussed the fact that someone Vimala Thakar referred to as "X" had been financing her travel and then wrote to her to say she was Krishna's disciple and an interpreter of his teachings. She assured Krishna that she was not. He told her that he had been hoping she would not have to go through the game where people needed authority to believe what was said. "They" had played it on him. If he had money he would give it to her but he had none, he went everywhere as a guest, he said. They also talked about the rise of Indian militaristic nationalism, that Indians loved and hated just as people in the West did, and once they tasted the poison of nationalism, they would be the "worst" jingoists. What the world needed were *sannyasis*, he said.[35]

Vimala Thakar says that she was told in 1970 what Krishna had said about her but it did not hurt her because she had never called herself his disciple or successor, nor the disciple of any spiritual celebrity, though she had met many. She had no personal relation with Krishnamurti so there was no reason for a definite breach in relations with him – when she felt she had understood the

"Truth" behind his communications, she stopped attending his gatherings. At Krishnamurti's discourses he was transported into a different dimension of consciousness, she said. That consciousness, which had never left her since 1962, did not belong to Buddha, Christ or Krishnamurti but was a "natural consummation of human refinement".[36]

In the light of Jayakar's observation that Krishna was interested in the resilience of Hindu teaching and wanted to know more, in February 1971 he held a dialogue with a 93-year old swami who had closely studied the Vedas. The swami told Krishna that his teachings covered a part of the Vedic teaching. The old man was nervous and was happy to listen to Krishna rather than talk, but once Krishna questioned him it was apparent that he was erudite in Vedic scripture, although his English was not good enough to be able to discuss without the services of an interpreter. For all that he publicly rebuked gurus, Krishna seemed genuinely keen to find out from the old fellow the answers to certain questions which perplexed him. Suppose there were no scriptures – how would a man, feeling the misery of the world, come by enlightenment in himself, Krishna asked?[37] If he has sufficient *samskara* he would come upon it, the guru replied. Krishna was dissatisfied with that response. So if a man had to depend on his past, did it mean his freedom was denied, he asked? Not 'has to' depend but 'is' dependent, the guru replied. And in this subtle difference in meaning lay the very crux of the difference in the arguments put forward by each of these two great thinkers. The swami tried to explain that the word "man" itself implied a place in time, that 'Man' was time-bound. So was Man a slave of time? Slave or master, it is left to him, the swami explained. Krishna carried forward the view of the self-willed, independent person and thought the swami did not 'get it' when asked the question, was Man a creature of time or the creator of time?" But in the definition of 'Man" lay the secret to understanding. In their discussion, to make *samskaras* a different entity from "Man" was out of place, the swami said. He drew a parallel between a person who has woken from sleep and an enlightened man. which made Krishna impatient. What was the factor that was instrumental in the breaking of *samskaras*. Krishna asked? The swami could not say, as all *samskaras* differed. One man might break the *samskaras* through the effort of studying the teachings, or another might break them right here and now, according to the capacity of the man. A man might be afraid and then think, 'Why should I be afraid? There is no 'other' to fear'. A man might wake from sleep and not know how he awoke. There was no question of 'how?' in these occurrences. Krishna fell back on his old stance of negativity and asked how the ordinary man could ever get out of his misery? But who says man is a bundle of miseries, asked the swami? Man was not a miserable creature, he said. Man also enjoyed pleasures. He could come out of the misery, he could make a Master of the situation; it depended on himself. But what was the factor that made him depend on himself and not on teachers and books, Krishna asked? Oh the *shastras* were not so inimical as all that, the swami advised. It all depended on the *samskara*, and here the swami returned to the point about looking at the definition of a man placed within time, which was a metaphysical question. Krishna made a last effort, claiming he wasn't metaphysical - and the swami concluded that it was no sin to be metaphysical. Questions could be put from different angles, and to explore them by transcending physical matters and becoming metaphysical in defining the terminology, where was the harm in that?[38]

Surely Krishna could not have overlooked the comic value of the scene. Two old codgers sit down together to discuss the meaning of life. The 75-year old who believes he's enlightened, asks the 93-year old how it came about. The older man tells him that's the wrong question.

One puzzle remains – was Krishna enlightened?

If Krishna was enlightened, why did he not know the answer?

If Krishna wasn't enlightened, why did he ask the question?

If he was/wasn't, why did he need to ask that and so many other questions?

Krishna used to like to tell a joke about three saints meditating in a cave in the Himalayas. Several years went by and one said to his friends, "I see it's going to rain," and then he got up and walked out of the cave. Several more years went by as the two yogis sat meditating, until one said to his friend, "Perhaps it's time I was leaving," and he got up and walked out of the cave. Several more years passed and then, suddenly, the yogi came out of his meditation and said, "It would be very peaceful here if it weren't for all the idle chatter".[39]

At some stage Krishna began to refer to himself in the third person. It may have started during his public talks, in the way one might use the word "one" to move beyond the personal dimension. When he wrote his *Notebook* in 1961 he used the word "I" at the beginning and also "one", but as the work progressed in his informal style of writing, he would mostly drop the subject of his sentences, often beginning a sentence with a verb, e.g. "Woke ...", to describe himself waking in the night. Or he would use an impersonal form of description e.g. "It was a lovely evening..." or "There's that mountain ... to see there must be....". He would often use the words "you", "the body", "the brain" and sometimes "we" and "our", but most personal references were absent from the descriptions – at least in the published edited version accessible to scrutiny. The Krishnamurti Archives believes it was about 1971 that Krishna began to refer to himself in the third person – yet back in 1949 he had referred in correspondence to "Krishnamurti's teachings". As early as 1925 the question of Krishna's role beyond the personal dimension had been raised when he moved from the third person description of a "World Teacher" to first person in saying "I" had come for those who wanted happiness. It's as if Krishna's mind reached full circle, after so many years of rejection of deification, to an acceptance of the legend of his youth. Lutyens reports that in 1977 Krishna used rhetorical questions to liken his life to the lives of Buddha's disciples.[40]

Perhaps Krishna's actual understanding of a phenomenon that is one of the tenets of Advaita Vedantism – the observer is the observed - had a bearing in his movement away from the personal in his observation and expression. Lutyens says it was the concept Krishna spoke about that she found the most difficult to understand, referring to other statements he had made such as: 'The experience is the experiencer' and 'The thinker is the thought' and concluding that the conditioned mind sees a replica of itself, so that what we are is what we see. Krishna had been speaking about this concept of non-duality for forty years and whether he'd read Sankara's texts or their interpretations by other philosophers, again and again he related this to contemporary social situations and the experience of living.[41]

A radio interviewer, Tara McCarthy, taped an interview with him at Brockwood in 1970 in which she asked socially-directed questions and he replied in philosophical terms. They began on the subject of education and the possibility of a different approach to living, and Krishna spoke about the need for a radical change in education in which one had to educate the educator to bring about a total understanding of the whole human being. An educator needed to see the fragmentation in the student and in himself, he said. One fragment, the observer, assumed authority, and liked or disliked - as a censor, analyser or entity who would decide what was right or wrong - so there was always a division between the observer and the thing observed. People had an image about themselves and about the 'other'. These images were constructed out of past experience and, as memories controlled thought, it was rare for any two people to investigate things together as they each took a "position".[42]

Krishnamurti took up a similar point in a discussion in 1976 with Dr David Shainberg, a New York psychiatrist, and Dr David Bohm, Professor of Theoretical Physics at Birkbeck College, the University of London. He asked the two men whether they had an 'unconscious', being mindful that there was a difference between the word and the thing. Krishna said he didn't think it had played any important part in his life at all. He suggested the mind might be one "unitary" total process or movement, and then raised questions about whether a fragmented mind was breaking consciousness into categories called 'hidden' and 'open'. He spoke of image-making and hurt done to the self-image. People hoped for a self-image that brought pleasure, he said, and they were always giving new shape to the image. If they had no self-image, they wouldn't get hurt, Bohm concluded. The three men also discussed image-making in relationships in families. Where a parent and child had images of each other, the relationship was governed by those images, so the question arose about the reality or "fantasy" of that relationship. Could the thought which produced these images, destroying relationships so there was no love, could it stop, Krishnamurti asked? A man who had an image about himself spoke of loving his wife or children but it was just sentiment and fanciful emotionalism, he said. He reiterated the question – could it stop? Then came a statement which might be interpreted as his own experience. Krishnamurti said he had no image about himself, while everyone about him was building images and so destroying the earth. He said that of course it could stop. As long as there were images there was not going to be peace in the world – whether the Christ image, the Buddha image or the Muslim image. In the following talk Krishnamurti tried to tackle with Shainberg the question of who he was, the person sitting there and looking. Shainberg decided that what was an actuality was only an image of himself as a developmental sequence, developed from whom he thought he'd been earlier in his life. They agreed that the image he had of himself was not reality. Whereas nature was reality, Krishna pointed out. So was the perceiver different from the perceived, Krishnamurti asked? Was there an image when there was no observer? Since the observer made the image, the observer was the movement of thought, he said. What Krishnamurti really meant, Bohm suggested, was that thought was moving and creating an image as if it was looking, but nothing was being seen - and Krishnamurti agreed. So if there was no experiencer, was there an experience? The maker of the image was the past, it was the observer who liked and disliked, Krishnamurti said. So were the images hidden? Shainberg said that you didn't have to unearth them once it was clear that the observer was the observed. At this point they agreed there was no 'unconscious', finding an answer to the question which had been their starting point. Krishnamurti said that the moment you saw that the observer was the observed, that the observer was the maker of images, it was finished. Yet as long as people lived their daily lives in image-making, whatever they did would still be in that area of consciousness. But what happened when there was no movement of thought? Complete transformation of consciousness, without fear or pursuit of pleasure. By the end of the following dialogue, the final in the series, Krishnamurti had taken Shainberg and Bohm to a place of understanding of the "sacredness" of life, agreeing that their dialogue had actually been a process of meditation. There is only that, Krishnamurti concluded.[43]

Krishnamurti had explored the question of what meditation was in one of a series of 18 dialogues with the Emeritus Professor of Religious Studies at San Diego State University, Professor Allan W Anderson, in 1974. Krishna was scathing in his description of the proliferation of thousands of schools of meditation. You practised to get something *"over there"*, he said – various forms of breathing, a mantra or practising Zen would dull the mind. What was implied was a path to truth, but truth wasn't static or a dead thing. He advised discarding Hindu, Buddhist, Christian and guru-led meditation in favour of asking what meditation was. In asking the question one began to meditate, he explained. He rejected meditation that was divorced from life and said that it must include the whole field of existence and not be separated from daily living. His advice was to allow desire to flower without control and watch it – neither yielding or resisting since both had repercussions. This was a reiteration of Krishna's "choiceless awareness" which he'd been talking about for decades, and which he explained more fully in the last session with Anderson. It was a matter of deep inward seriousness to see rather than run away from suffering, so that with choiceless awareness of the "flowering" of desires, would come their natural death. The professor had provided a sounding board for Krishna, questioning, agreeing, offering examples as Krishnamurti maintained a "stream of consciousness" over the period of eleven days and all that was left for Anderson to do at their conclusion was to concur with Krishnamurti that in silence time stopped, and to express his gratitude. Krishna complimented him on taking the time to listen.[44]

Krishnamurti had not gone to India at the end of 1971 as usual. He was concerned about war between India and Pakistan and that with increased security provisions, he would not be able to speak freely. He was also aware of his body becoming weaker. He wrote to Pupul Jayakar in November from Rome to say that since his summer spent in Gstaad he'd been getting more and more tired and "hypersensitive", and now he was vomiting every day.[45] So he spent the winter in Malibu with Mary, going to the cinema, walking on the beach, watching television and reading, mostly, crime stories. Lutyens says that at this time "the process" was going on in a mild way: his head was painful, he would stay awake for hours some nights, and would often wake feeling that the room was filled with "holy" beings. Mary Zimbalist says that once in Switzerland in the 1960s she saw Krishna "go off", when he spoke in a child's voice. Lutyens says just such an incident occurred at the end of June 1967 at Vanda's home, Les Caprices, in Italy. But Zimbalist also describes other experiences of being with Krishna, in the company of other people and often when he was talking about his youth, when "something" unusual was felt in the room. He would ask those present, "Did you feel something?" Mark Lee, Director of Krishnamurti Publications of America also describes being in a room with Krishna and four other people when "something" came into the room and "enveloped everyone in what I can only think of as a solid mass". "No sight, no sound, nothing to see or hear ... everything and everyone and the whole room, the whole building seemed to have no time and space," is how Lee describes it. He says it lasted for at least twenty minutes. Lee experienced it twice in the twenty years he knew Krishnamurti. Mary Lutyens says that in

February 1973 when she was working on the first volume of Krishna's biography and dealing with the experiences at Ojai in 1922. she had misgivings about publishing the work, and went to Brockwood to discuss her doubts with him. As they sat quietly alone together in the drawing room, which was his part of the house, he asked her if she could feel "it" in the room, saying that was her answer. She did feel slight "throbbing" she said, but thought it could have been her imagination. But Krishna "evidently" felt "it" was giving its approval. She asked him what it was and he said it was there as if behind a "curtain" and he could lift it but didn't feel it was his business to. Later, on going back to fetch her coat she felt a "great power" rush out at her. She was certain then that this great force was not imaginary or auto-suggestive. Krishna had been questioned the previous year about the "power" behind him by the trustees of the KFA and explained in the third person, that "K" had never enquired into it and the conscious mind could never understand this tremendous "reservoir". It would be "blackguardly" and a stupid "childish" trick to make a mystery of it and he wasn't. Either one created a mystery when there wasn't one or there was a mystery which one had to approach with exceptional "delicacy" and "hesitancy", he said. You couldn't invite it, it wasn't progressive achievement and the brain couldn't understand it, was his conclusion. Lutyens also quotes from notes Mary Zimbalist has of Krishna's experiences of a light "burning" in the mind, and a vast "space" of unimaginable energy as though in the very centre of his brain or head.[46]

Despite the experiences that had been going on in Krishna's mind since the 1920s, he kept an ordered approach to his daily living. He would rise early, setting aside time for his daily breathing and yoga practices, enjoy his health food breakfast, attend to business or give talks or dialogues as arranged, take a healthy lunch followed by a rest. He might write letters or keep a diary and then came a vigorous walk in the late afternoon, usually at sunset, in all seasons and weather, unless illness prevented it.[47]

Krishna was now surrounded by people who not only cared for him personally but took care to build up the Krishnamurti Foundation business. Mary Zimbalist was an intelligent, astute thinker; Mary Cadogan, a former BBC employee, became Secretary of the Foundation in England; in the United States, Erna Lilliefelt had a rare legal sense; Vanda Scaravelli, a yoga enthusiast, provided a comfortable European environment with a sensibility for the nuances of Indian culture; in India, Pupul Jayakar remained President of the Foundation, providing an overseer role, while Sunanda Partwardhan acted as Krishna's secretary and her husband, Pama, became a partner in the publishing firm, Orient Longman, and was instrumental in publishing a number of Krishna's works. By 1978 Dr Balusundarum had resigned as principal of the Rishi Valley school, to be succeeded by Krishna's nephew, G Narayan, the eldest son of Shivaram.[48]

At the end of 1972 Krishna was back in India and held a discussion with a former Jesuit priest, Ivan Illich, an Austrian who'd set up a centre in Mexico where he developed his ideas of social revolution to overthrow the dominance of technology, capitalism and consumerism. His book, *Deschooling*, had been published the previous year and he'd been invited to visit India by the government. Pupul Jayakar had visited Mexico in 1971 and was instrumental in organising the visit through her close friend, the Prime Minister, Mrs Indira Gandhi. Jayakar included a discussion with Krishna in Rajghat, Varanasi, in the itinerary. The two iconoclasts soon found a common symbol for their dialogue about society and the individual – the river Ganges flowing outside their door. All human beings were dragged along in the stream, Krishna said, whereas the individual stepped out of the stream. He pointed out the Latin root of the word 'individual', meaning indivisible, whole and not fragmented. Illich said he'd spent some time down by the river in Varanasi, watching people washing and praying, all in the same river below the burning ghat. People would come out of the river and sit for a while, conscious of their distinction from it, but acceptance of the river would carry them off again. The river had become a metaphor for society for the two men. Krishna was interested in something new happening when a person stepped out for good, since the whole of humanity was caught in a stream of great violence and sorrow, he said. Illich recalled a Mexican poem that repeats a refrain, "Only for a short time have you loaned us to each other".

> Because it is in your drawing us that we take shape
> It is in your painting us that we get form
> It is in your singing us that we take voice
> But only for a short while have you loaned us to each other.

Illich said it was an illusion that you could create a new society. It was the same stream with the same current, Krishna said, in a reference back to the idea of the same water in different pots. Was it possible to tell students and young people all over the world to follow neither one stream nor another, but to be "free" of streams, Krishna asked?[49]

Also in 1972, Krishna's talks from three years before – in London, Amsterdam, Paris and Saanen – were published by Harper & Row under the title, *The Flight of the Eagle*. The book took as its common thread a quote by Krishnamurti that the eagle in flight does not leave a trace, but a scientist does. The world had a marvellous beauty and he exhorted people to live in an ecstatic, blissful way. Not to be narrow and separate and frightened. One compelling image was of meeting not one tiger, but a dozen in human form, all to be killed and all within oneself. There were a thousand "me's" inside, a thousand snakes, he said. So how to get rid of all the snakes at once, he asked? The mind looks. Then he told a story about a master speaking to his disciples every morning. One day a little bird came and sang on the windowsill. When it flew away the master said the sermon was over. The book concludes with the question of whether people really wanted to explore the unknown or hold on to the "apron-strings" of pleasure. Take a journey into what you know, Krishna advised – one's pleasures, delights, despairs and sorrows.[50]

You Are the World was also published by a devotee of Krishna's, Mr Verhulst, a senior partner with the Dutch publisher, Servire. He had published six volumes of Krishna's talks, including *The Flight of the Eagle*.[51]

Two significant books of Krishna's work were published in 1973 but, as Lutyens notes, the press largely ignored them. *Beyond Violence* was reviewed in the *Sunday Telegraph* in March favourably and with the advice that Krishna's message didn't come in a neat sentence and he had to be read, as the act of reading him worked a change in the reader. The subject of the book was perfect for Krishna's style of moving from the negative, from the 'we'll all be ruined' stance to a position of calm and wisdom. Was it possible to end the violence in oneself that showed itself in the pain and brutality of the world, Krishna asked? Unless the mind was absolutely "free" of fear, every form of action would bring more mischief, misery and confusion, he said. Again he mounted a challenge to the idea of 'the conscious' and 'the unconscious', saying water was all the same, whether in a golden jug or an earthenware pot. It was important not to divide, but to see 'the whole', he said. These talks from 1970 canvassed many of the ideas at the core of his teaching - including education being "mechanical", of the need for a revolution in thinking, of not turning to outside agencies to solve problems, of the futility of thinking that we can gradually come to a position of peace - returning again and again to the image of a "clear" mind. Such a mind did not need drugs, drink, sex, worship or escapes, he said. It did not follow psychologists and gurus from the East. The moment you said that you were admitting your confusion, there was an entity admitting it, he said. When there was no division between the observer and the observed there was an absolute stop to the confusion.[52]

The other book published in 1973 was *The Awakening of Intelligence*. It was remarkable for the use of photographs of Krishna, which he had not permitted since the 1930s.[53] They were taken by Mark Edwards, a young freelance photographer who was able to get even big close-ups of Krishna – depicted as a slight, neat figure with an intense expression and white hair immaculately combed in a scoop across his balding head, hands gesturing in the midst of a group of school students or walking in the grounds of Rishi Valley school, dressed in a partly transparent cotton dhoti with an umbrella held aloft. A sense of Krishna's intensity and power matched by frailty and sorrow are conveyed in the series of photographs. And the text of more than 500 pages moves relentlessly on, with Krishna in dialogue with the lowly and great, with unknown questioners and the famously intellectual. Krishna leads Professor Jacob Needleman, Professor of Philosophy at San Francisco State College, to understand the importance of not depending on a teacher or anyone else to find out what is true or false. Swami Venkatesananda, a Vedantist, is delighted by Krishna's point that rather than tell people they must "realise" this or that, sages might tell them to get rid of their fear and antagonism, and once that was effected, nothing more would remain, so they'd find beauty. "Fantastic, fantastic!" Swamiji exclaims. They agree on the definition of Vedanta, being the end of the Vedas, or the end of knowledge. As Krishna says, "freedom" from knowledge. Yes indeed, declares Swamiji. They commiserate too that many people in India can recite the *Bhagavad Gita* without realising its meaning, which was: *I am seated in the hearts of all beings*. Krishna feels it is extraordinary that there has always been an emphasis on teacher and disciple without the knowledge that you are the teacher as well as the pupil. Swamiji says that occasionally this is explained, to which Krishna insists that if you depend on anybody else you are lost. With Professor David Bohm, Professor of Theoretical Physics at Birkbeck College, London University, Krishna is on common ground in seeking to discover the nature of 'intelligence'. Bohm says a question that recurs is whether intelligence and matter are different or merely a distinction within the same thing. Krishna says that thought, matter and intelligence have a common source but thought dominates the world while intelligence has very little place in it. Bohm agrees that thought has made the brain very chaotic and noisy, in seeking security, while intelligence is the "silence" of the brain. Krishnamurti declares that the activity of "wholeness" is intelligence. At the end of the book, Krishna tells Bohm that he's not been listening to Bohm's words but to his meaning, he's been open to him, listening with ears that hear deeply. Bohm agrees that to reach the unconscious one has to have an action that does not appeal to the conscious. Yes, that's affection, Krishna concludes. That's love. Not appealing to the hard, clever, subtle, brittle waking consciousness but penetrating it with feeling.[54]

Lutyens says that in 1973 she suggested to Krishna that he write another journal, as he had done in 1961and he immediately bought a pen and notebooks and began writing the next day. Being in England at the time, his first entry describes the countryside at Brockwood, but the very next day he was describing a scene in Switzerland. Lutyens says that Krishna described the place where he was currently living in only three entries over the six-week period that he kept the journal. It was an example of the clarity of his recall of natural countryside, which she said arose from his "acuteness" of observation. Krishna resumed the journal a year and a half later. First published in 1982 as *Krishnamurti's Journal*, the work eschews the word "I', using second or third person even when it's quite apparent Krishna is talking about something he is actually experiencing, such as looking at the sky through branches or stopping on a track to witness the silence of redwood trees. He also uses the third person to marvel at the vacancy of his own mind while walking, as no thought "entered" his mind, he said. The journal is extraordinary for its balance between his fond description of the natural world and his observations on human thinking and living, as if he was trying to express their interconnection. This had been a characteristic of his first journal. The descriptions of nature – mountains "heavy" with snow, the rich and beautiful "whole" earth, a tiger's long tail with a black tip moving slowly side to side – are a gentler way to move into the epistemological questions he raises than the direct and challenging talks and dialogues. He will segue, for instance, from the detailed description of a tiger, full of "majesty" and "power", to a view, as if from above looking down on Earth, of tyrants and ideologists shaping the minds of men. That day's journal entry will have grown out of a stimulating first sentence about "consciousness" being its own content.

After the description of nature. the journal entry is completed with the observation that all activity of thought is to cultivate fragmentation whereas love is not a fragment of thought.[55]

Relations between Krishna and Rajagopal and Rosalind remained fractious in the 1970s leading up to the property settlement and beyond. Rajagopal had served a cross-complaint on Krishna in 1972 with a summons for a deposition. Krishna gave the deposition in Malibu over two days from 12 April in the presence of lawyers for both sides, a court reporter, Mary Zimbalist, Erna Lilliefelt – and from KWINC, Rajagopal, Mima Porter and one other KWINC trustee. The following day Krishna drew up a statement to prevent Rajagopal from having anything to do with his work after his death.[56] Rajagopal was clearly emotionally injured as a result of his protracted conflict with Krishnamurti. Lutyens says that he even telephoned from Ojai to Krishna in Rome in November 1972 to say that whatever happened he still loved him. Krishna told him he could settle the case immediately if he wanted to but Rajagopal claimed it was out of his hands. As well as the main battle in Ojai. Rajagopal also tried to hold onto *Vasanta Vihar* in India, but Krishna's advisers found a loophole in the legality of KWINC ownership, by reviving the Dutch Stichting KWINC and claiming the Indian estate as its own. Shiva Rao wrote to Rajagopal in 1974 to say he'd heard that efforts were being made to settle the dispute with Krishna through negotiation. and he hoped Rajagopal would drop his involvement in legal proceedings in India over *Vasanta Vihar*. It was such a pity the place was not being used. he said. speaking as a friend who had always had an affection for him. Madhavachari also wrote to Rajagopal that the government wanted the land for housing "homeless people like slum-dwellers", and as Rajagopal had bought and built the property for much "nobler" purposes, Madhavachari would be glad to know an agreement with Krishna had been signed and goodwill restored.[57]

In his correspondence. Shiva Rao also mentioned that he'd met Radha when she'd visited in the winter of 1973-74. He hadn't seen her since 1945, and although he was fond of Rajagopal, and would have been very friendly towards Radha, these matters did not interfere with his straight-talking on the matter of what he believed was Krishnamurti's property. The situation was by that time becoming extreme, leading Krishna to make a statement in August 1974 that he had felt forced "morally" to seek legal advice as thousands of people at great sacrifice had contributed funds yet had no voice in or information about KWINC's funds. A final settlement was agreed in December 1974. KWINC was to be dissolved and all assets -150 acres including Oak Grove, *Arya Vihara* and the *Pine Cottage* - transferred to KFA except for certain publication rights which went to the K&R Foundation and were to pass to KFA on Rajagopal's death. Rajagopal's costs were paid by KWINC and he was allowed to remain in his house until his death. The hand-over of the Ojai property was effected, but not without some negotiation over final conveyances and easements. Rajagopal replied to an "affectionate" letter from Spencer English in Australia in March 1975 that while a settlement "of sorts" had been reached, there was no real friendliness and "bickerings" continued. The representative of the K&R Foundation in India reported that the legal position put by Krishnamurti's lawyer was that Krishna was keen to associate himself with his new Trust and his wishes should be respected in view of his advanced age. He also reported that the judge said he expected that Krishnamurti and the KFA would contribute half a million dollars to the new Trust out of the "several" million they received from KWINC in Ojai.[58]

In California, Rosalind maintained a fortress position about how she believed the Happy Valley school should be run. In 1972 Krishna had been discussing with KFA how it might establish an educational centre in Ojai. In April he gave two talks there – the first he had given in the Ojai valley since 1966, but they were not in his old haunt, the Oak Grove. Then in 1973 Alan Hooker, a proponent of Krishnamurti's teaching who was on the Board of Happy Valley, wrote to Rosalind asking for land in the upper valley to be made available for a school where

Krishnamurti could come and hold talks and discussions. As Chair, she sent a curious reply - that Krishna had not wanted his name used when the Happy Valley school was established, but for people to use the ideas when they became a part of themselves. For those who had lived according to these ideas for over forty years it would be impossible to dissociate from them, she said, yet not defining what the ideas were. The implication seemed to be that she had been living them. Rosalind asked that Hooker send an official letter to the Happy Valley Foundation outlining a prospectus. Krishnamurti never took legal action against her in respect of property rights over the Happy Valley Foundation and it continues to operate a school and cultural centre. Radha says that Krishna did, however, send a verbal message to Rosalind through a friend that she should vacate *Arya Vihara* as he had plans for it. By this time Rosalind had decided to build a house on Happy Valley for her use using funds from the sale of her other house, left her by the Logans.[59]

During Radha's visit to India in 1974 she and her husband and two teenage children visited Krishna in Bombay. She had written to him asking him to phone her hotel and he rang. When she arrived where he was staying he was standing out the front, concerned that they might get lost. He was his usual affectionate self with her, holding her face in his hands and gazing into her face for a "potent" moment, Radha says. A friend of Krishna's who knew Rosalind asked after her, but at lunch Rajagopal and Rosalind were not mentioned by Krishna. Radha left feeling she had not really had any meaningful contact with "Krinsh", as she called him. Perhaps she was looking for a return to the relationship of her childhood and in its absence, could find no satisfying substitute.[60]

Yet others felt they had very meaningful contact with the old man. Krishna's friendship with Dr David Bohm developed in the mid-70s along with his interest in the ending of time and thought, as the two explorers could find common ground in their different approaches to many epistemological questions. Bohm would often offer the linguistic derivation of a word to stimulate a dialogue and this appealed to Krishna's curious mind, but sometimes conflicting definitions of words such as "truth" and "reality" might cause some confusion in the minds of listeners. Their friendship and mutual exploration of consciousness also reflected Krishna's concern to reach a communion between the scientific and the religious minds to achieve truly valuable education. In *Krishnamurti On Education*, published in 1974, the editors said that Krishna believed a "new" mind was needed in which the scientific attitude and the religious spirit were not two parallel processes but were fused as "intelligence" or a "creative" mind. The book's Foreword argued that existing models of education had failed as there was a lack of relevance for humans in contemporary society, indicated by an ecological crisis and increasing poverty, hunger and violence. The book was based on talks he gave in his Indian schools at Rishi Valley and Rajghat. Another important text on education, *Beginnings of Learning*, was published the following year, consisting of conversations with students, teachers and parents at Brockwood Park, and laid an emphasis on differentiating between learning for life and merely finding information.[61]

Also published in 1974, Krishna's talks in Saanen launch straight into the ineffectiveness of politics in solving contemporary global problems. Krishna had, ever since his youthful attempts at political action, been apolitical in the sense that he criticised all political solutions as never going far enough. In this first Saanen talk he begins with the same techniques of inclusiveness he'd been using for forty years to bring about audience involvement. He gives politics as an example of why solutions within the realm of thinking will not suffice. Krishna starts with negativity - the world is in a dreadful state, he says. There's confusion in politics and education. Even in religion there is now denial of the assumed authority of the priest - which is of course what he has been encouraging for years. In India they have poverty and the nuclear bomb – in the West there's also poverty and the decline of social morality. Krishna and the audience are investigating this together, he says. They must be involved, not just listen to the speaker. Thought has created the world, he goes on. Whether in politics, economics, morality. Jewish thought or Arabic – it's all essentially the operation of thought as *matter.* Politicians are trying to find reformation within a field which thought has created, he says. Thought divides the world into American, Communist, Socialist, German, Swiss, Hindu, Buddhist. But thought can only operate within the field of time and can give no answer to the problems, he says. So where to find an answer?[62]

Krishna had tackled this question again and again, in his dialogues with Bohm, and particularly in *The Impossible Question,* published in 1972. There a quote from one of his talks is lifted to the front of the book. It states that people are always putting the question of what is possible. But if you put an impossible question, your mind has to find an answer in terms of the impossible. Shades of Zen and the *koan.* Krishna gives an example of the impossibility of going to the moon, which caused 300,000 people to work cooperatively so that it became possible. Similarly, the impossible question of whether the mind could empty itself of the "Known" might be put with earnestness and passion to discover new horizons.[63]

In 1974 a group of scientists spent a week at Brockwood to hold discussions, among them David Bohm, Karl Pribam, George Sudarshan and Fritjof Capra. Capra had first met Krishna in 1968, and wrote in praise of advice Krishna gave him at the time, when he was confused about being free and also working as a scientist. Krishna had told him that he was first a human being and second a scientist, which solved Capra's dilemma "Zen-like with one stroke". Capra said that by 1974 he became aware of some of Krishna's shortcomings – in particular that he would speak but would not listen. Nearly a decade later Capra saw Krishna again in Madras when he spoke for seventy-five minutes without a break and with almost the same intensity he had witnessed fifteen years earlier. Capra took away a message that the only way to be free of desire was to be free of thought. Capra was disturbed that Krishna, unlike the Buddha, did not show "a clear path toward liberation". yet he was grateful for the "decisive influence and help" Krishna had given him and he had felt "richly rewarded".[64]

Krishna was still way ahead of his audience, his readership, and most serious thinkers in the sciences and humanities. Or was he caught back in ancient thinking, in the void that produced the Vedas? During a flight from Rome to New Delhi in November 1974 Krishna had an opportunity to meet the Maharishi Mahesh, founder of 'Transcendental Meditation' or TM as it's known by adherents in the West. As Krishna boarded the plane he had seen the Maharishi sitting cross-legged on a tiger skin, and later the air hostess brought Krishna a rose sent to him by the yogi. Later, returning from the toilet, he passed by the Maharishi who stood and greeted him with a *namaskar,* which Krishna returned, cupping his hands as a sign of goodwill. They sat and talked for about an hour, the Maharishi explaining that he was going to Nepal to announce a world revolution in consciousness and he wanted Krishna to join him. Krishna politely declined. Jayakar tells the story in her biography of Krishna and follows it with a reference to Krishna being asked, that same year in a group discussion, what was the essence of his teaching. His reply was that his teaching said that where *you* were, the *other* was not. This idea, as a statement about ego transcendence, lies at the core of Advaita Vedanta, as it is understood by teachers and students of Advaita, whether taught by the Shankara, the Maharishi or even Krishnamurti. *Eka,* or 'one' - a basic tenet of Upanishadic or Vedanta teaching – refers to the singular transcendental Self beyond the ego-bound individual. Krishna could not acknowledge the power of an outside guru, since he had found this truth of transcendence within himself. And he believed others could do the same. Exercises and practices were trivial, he said. The mind evolved through time and could not see that which was not of time. So what was it that perceived something that was not of time? Or put another way, as he had explained it in a talk in Madras in the late 1960s: through complete negation, the thing that alone was the positive – love – would come into being.[65]

Krishna's interaction with the Vajrayana or Tibetan Buddhist and founder of the Naropa Institute in Colorado, Chogyam Trungpa Rinpoche, certainly was not memorable for its evident intellectuality as the meeting of minds on the subject of meditation. If they met at all, it was not reflected in a balance between the two men in their verbal expression. Krishnamurti dominated the dialogue, with the Rinpoche's contribution restricted to cryptic rermarks, such as "you can't use intellect to solve intellectual problems" and "if you see disorder then it becomes order" and "when you observe then you are judging" and "I don't see any particular importance in laying emphasis on the stillness of the mind because if one is able to see the non-dualistic way of looking at situations then you have further energy that will flow out". Chogyam Trungpa wanted to emphasise "absolute peace", he said, and when Krishna replied that complete order was complete quietness of the mind, which in turn was the most "active" mind, Chogyam Trungpa responded with, "That's what I want you to say". One person present said that the Rinpoche appeared as if he might have been intoxicated, but in any case, the two great minds reached some compatibility, with Chogyam Trungpa not registering any disagreement, rather, concurring with Krishnamurti's exposition. Krishna's impatience to describe the indescribable shows clearly in this dialogue – his need to convey a communication for the recording, for history, in contrast with the quietness of his Buddhist counterpart.[66]

Mary Lutyens' biography of Krishna was published in July 1975, disclosing for the first time his extraordinary inner experiences that had begun so dramatically in Ojai in 1922. Lutyens took an advance copy to him and he seemed pleased, looking again and again at the illustrations and asking what an ordinary stockbroker might think of the book. Clearly, not enough to have caused a run on bookshops.[67]

The question might be posed how such a man as Krishna, by this stage in his life living as sedately as any of us - someone who had found this treasure of meditation burning in the space at the centre of his mind - how such a man could live within the confines of regular society without confiding these experiences to others? It must have been frustrating at first to find that other people did not share his hyper-sense and looked at him in shock or in awe, treating him as a freak or a god. But after fifty years Krishna must have been well and truly inured to the reaction of others, and would have described the experiences to his close associates only when there was variation or some other exceptional quality about them. But publicly, he felt more than ever a need to chronicle or explain the 'otherness'. His honesty has been questioned, not least by the woman who spent her childhood as his surrogate daughter. Radha does not however give any significant examples of his dishonesty in relation to herself, rather concentrating on her mother's impression of him as having been wanting in fidelity as a lover. The major accusations seem to rest on his failure to admit to, or deliver, certain letters concerning their relationship – first to Rajagopal and later to Nandini Mehta. Radha also writes that both Rajagopal and Rosalind had "occasional" quarrels with him, usually when he "lied". She says Rosalind once asked Krishna why he lied and he said that it was out of fear. There is no further elaboration about what Radha calls Krishna's "astonishing frankness". It might be argued that the statement is convincing as an observation of human nature, but that it is not a water-tight proof of Krishna's deceitfulness, as frankness usually indicates honesty, even if after the event.[68] It might also be pointed out that Krishna and Rosalind did share a sexual relationship over a period of possibly thirty years, which might be considered not an inconsiderable duration of fidelity, considering their attractiveness, their libido, the non-traditional views they held and the milieus in which they mixed. If Krishna's honesty in recording his inner experiences is accepted, whether he suffered self-delusional or narcissistic states all his adult life might be the next question posed. This is a conundrum that might be answered by psychotherapy. However the question might still be only partially resolved, given that psychotherapy is a relatively new medical science, having reached maturity only during Krishna's lifetime, and it is still searching in the unknown of human consciousness for answers to many of the puzzles of human behaviour.[69]

Setting aside for the moment whatever faults Krishna is accused of having, it is clear that he was prepared to explore human consciousness with an energy and daring that few have shown. Krishna was willing to match some of the finest minds of science and the humanities in sessions recorded for posterity, disregarding the possibility that his mental agility might fail or his "teaching" might be exposed as worthless or fraudulent. A number of these great thinkers sought out Krishnamurti and he responded readily to the prospect of holding dialogues with them, particularly over the last decade of his life.

Chapter 12

Yoga and the Nameless

I have always had a great suspicion of charismatic holy men. ... They know how to gather people around them – that's what their gig is. They make you think that something important is going on and you're hooked. I was always suspicious of them because I was able to do it in my own small way ... I know it can be done. It's just a kind of gift – it's like hypnosis.

Leonard Cohen Spring 96 documentary Dir: Armelle Brusq, Lieurac Productions France 1997.

That brilliant light, seen sometimes late in the afternoon, which bathes the world in full flush, - a vibrant golden glow heightening what we've ignored the rest of the daylight hours - this is perhaps an image for Krishna's final years. He worked incessantly to bring his vision to others. Not by sweet words and comforting sympathy but by advocating firm discipline of the mind and body and a need to face fears. And above all, he prompted his listeners by posing questions.

In the mid-1970s Krishna began to hold dialogues with learned Buddhists in India. He had told an American writer who met him in 1958 that although he did not follow any religious leaders, the one who "came closest to teaching and realising the ultimate truth" was the Buddha.[1] Susunaga Weeraperuma who had a Buddhist upbringing in Sri Lanka and became devoted to Krishnamurti before rejecting him in recent years, says that in the 1960s and 1970s Krishna asked him questions about Buddhism and he gave Krishna a lot of information about the great Buddhist philosopher of the third century, Nagarjuna. Weeraperuma claimed, too, that the Buddhist scholar, Walpola Rahula, also said Krishna questioned him a great deal about Nagarjuna. But Weeraperuma, who was a librarian, said Krishna found it difficult to read religious and philosophical books and "avoided" them. But sometimes in Colombo Krishna would ask for a copy of the Bible, saying he only read Ecclesiastes and Psalms. Weeraperuma also says that Krishna had a very good knowledge of the six schools of Indian philosophy, particularly the Advaitic school, but Weeraperuma believes Krishna got this information not from reading, but from "getting snippets of philosophical and religious knowledge from the thousands who visited him". A friend of Weeraperuma, the Sri Lankan Buddhist scholar, Adikaram, was so devoted to Krishna that he once said that for him, Krishnamurti was the Buddha. Adikaram gained a PhD from London University for research on the early history of Buddhism in Ceylon and spent as much time as possible with Krishna whenever he visited India and Sri Lanka. Krishna had thoroughly read and loved Huxley's *The Perennial Philosophy* and, as a young man, had enjoyed reading *The Gospel of Buddha*, compiled from ancient records, by Paul Carus, according to Weeraperuma. No doubt Krishna's youthful belief that he'd been chosen as a Maitreya/Messiah figure coloured his response to the book. In any case, Weeraperuma's conclusion about Krishna's religious integrity later in life is that in claiming that what he said were his original insights, rather than the teaching of ancient Masters, Krishna was a "liar".[2]

However a recorded dialogue between Krishna, David Bohm and Walpola Rahula, who was an international authority on Buddhism, as well as three other people, indicates only Walpola Rahula's great respect for Krishna's teaching. Rahula begins by citing similarities between what Buddha taught and what Krishna said, using the idiom of the day. Walpola Rahula listed the common elements as: not accepting the notion of a creator-God nor an everlasting soul; beginning the teaching from the premise that human life is suffering, conflict and sorrow; comprehending that these spring from a wrong idea of self; that freedom from desire and attachment frees one from suffering; that when you see reality you are free of conflict; that you must not depend on others' authority; and, an emphasis on awareness or mindfulness, impermanence and finding realisation neither through discipline nor without it. The dialogue proceeded respectfully, with Krishna challenging the need for the Buddhist scriptures. Walpola Rahula said that to see the truth one had to be free from all knowledge and Krishna asked why one should accumulate knowledge only to abandon it. His conclusion was to suggest that one might "look" at a feeling, for example, greed, without giving it its name, which inevitably invoked past associations. That way you might find out what the feeling was and be free of it, rather than have books or gurus tell you how. During the discussion, Krishna said that duality was the invention of philosophers. His argument was that violence was actual while non-violence was an ideal, or non-fact. He advised dealing with the fact rather than "running away" to non-fact.[3]

It is arguable that the concept of duality was not "invented" by philosophers as it is believed that the terms *dvaita* and *advaita,* or duality and non-duality, were terms applied to knowledge gained by ancient sages who moved through levels of consciousness to discover the schism in the mind between subject and object, or viewer and viewed. The schism is understood to be made by the thinking mind which is normally in a state of ignorance about formless and supraconscious 'Reality'. An explanation of 'duality' is, as Krishnamurti himself said so many times, that it is a split between the experiencer and the experience. Judging by Krishna's descriptions of feeling at one with a rock on a road, or a tree, he had experienced this state, yet his advice was, as always, practical rather than mystical. Many people, including both saints and imposters, have experienced such a heightened sense of reality at certain times in their lives, feeling an accompanying ecstatic sensation. It might be pertinent here to refer to a criticism of Krishnamurti made by his former long-time devotee, Susunaga Weeraperuma. He argues that many people have mystical experiences of communion with nature or what they believe to be "God" but as these are still within the field of human consciousness – the world of form and of name in which imagination can play a part – these sensations are of little value. They are merely part of the cycle of *samsara*, or flow of cycles of birth and death, much like a protracted delusion or dream. Whereas once an *arhat*, or Master, finds Nirvana, Liberation or Enlightenment, it never goes. Krishnamurti's experiences of 'otherness' came and went like the passing clouds, he claims. The mind plays a thousand tricks and it is easy to delude oneself into thinking that Nirvana has been attained, he says.[4]

Weeraperuma also cites a discussion Krishnamurti had with Professor Dopeshwarkar who told him that the existence of the world was all *maya* or illusion. Krishna is said to have shouted, "It's a bloody fact that the world exists. It's right in front of you". And yet Krishna must have heard the old story of different parts of an elephant – the tail, the trunk, the ears, the leg - being touched by different people who were blind-folded and who gave different descriptions of the animal, or different names according to their own limited experience.[5] And even as far back as June 1926, Krishna had referred to *maya* as the realm of the physical which was transient, fleeting and entangling. Perhaps one explanation for Krishna's apparent questioning of concepts which he had encountered and explained previously is that his questions may have been completely dependent on the audience or partner in discussion at the time. If he said violence was actual while non-violence was an ideal, he may have been reflecting the pre-occupations of a Buddhist scholar's mind. If he questioned the explanation of the phenomenal world as being *maya*, once again he may have been reflecting the doubts or concerns held in the mind of a Vedantist. Krishna's predominant role was as a questioner; this is what he had been doing ever since his break with Theosophy in 1929.[6]

It might also be relevant to examine here another observation by the lapsed-Krishnamurti-ite, Weeraperuma, that Krishnamurti would suffer "stage-fright" immediately before appearing on a public platform. According to Weeraperuma, Krishna would become extremely "jittery" and would sometimes ask, "Will the words come into my mouth?" or "How do I look, sir?". Weeraperuma says he would make small-talk and reassure Krishna, even telling him that he looked young and handsome, although he did not mean it. Mary Lutyens also mentions this apparent lack of preparation by Krishna for his talks. She cites accounts by Shiva Rao that on occasions in Delhi when he was driving Krishna to a talk, Krishna would ask, "What on earth am I going to talk about?", yet when he stepped onto the platform he could talk for an hour or more, "as if inspired". Lutyens also witnessed this in Amsterdam in 1981 before he spoke for an hour and a half to an audience in the thousands, and she wondered where his "inspiration" came from. Leadbeater's biographer, Gregory Tillett, sees Krishna's ability to give public talks without much preparation as a skill he "inherited" from Leadbeater, and possibly Annie Besant as well, and which occurs in people who genuinely believe that they are "God's spokespersons" or that "a message is coming through them". Weeraperuma has also criticised Krishna over his vanity, saying he used cosmetics to hide his wrinkles, he would shave before a lecture, and he feared he would be ignored as an octogenarian. Yet the people close to Krishna were as devoted to him as ever and the organisation that had been set up for him in the latter years of his life worked exceptionally smoothly as a disseminator of his teaching and as an organiser of his public talks. This is evidenced by the fact that thousands of people still attended the talks held on his regular international circuit, right up until the year of his death in 1986, for example his two September 1981 Amsterdam talks in front of a total auditorium plus overflow video audience of 5,000. And although Krishna's physical appearance had changed radically since the 1920s, when he would criticise devotees for coming to meetings "dressed anyhow" and "unshaved", he was still carrying out the mix of Brahmin emphasis on cleanliness of the body and Leadbeater's advice about hygiene, regular exercise and a strict diet. Since beauty is in the eye of the beholder, Krishna's adherents of the 1970s and 1980s loved him no less than the devotees of earlier decades, in spite of their refusal to call themselves devotees and Krishnamurti their guru. He was no more or less than the outgrowth of the mind and body he had been previously. Weeraperuma's testimony has something reminiscent of

Donald Ingram Smith's anecdote about meeting Krishnamurti only to find that he was "a nervous, fumbling man". Smith recognised himself in Krishna whereas Weeraperuma may not have. Perhaps Weeraperuma accepted Krishnamurti as his "guru", despite Krishna's rejection of the role, while ever Krishna reflected the search for goodness in his mind, as is clear from the hagiographic accounts Weeraperuma published about Krishna. But on discovering Krishna as an old man with frailties and vanities, the same qualities that are shared by all of humanity to greater or lesser degree, Weeraperuma rejected the image and turned against his idol. In the same spirit that Krishna told a Buddhist scholar, "violence is a fact", Krishna might equally have said "vanity is a fact – let's start our self enquiry here" to any spiritual seeker who sought to idolise him, just as he had bluntly pointed out to Theosophists their belief in their spiritual superiority back in the 1920s.[7]

Krishna's teaching had always had a strong connection with Buddhist teaching. But it wasn't until 1974 that formal dialogues were organised between him and Buddhist scholars at Rajghat in Varanasi. One man who was present then, Professor Krishna Nath, who is now an editor of a journal of the Krishnamurti Foundation India, played a helpful role in bringing the mind wrestlers together. Krishna Nath, who was about forty at the time the first dialogue was organised, had had an active involvement in the socialist movement in India and had recently practised Vipassana meditation when Achyut Patwardhan told him that Krishna wanted to have a dialogue with Buddhist scholars. So the meeting got under way in an assembly hall at Rajghat, Krishna sitting in the centre of the room and in a semi-circle around him, the scholars – among them Jagannath Upadhyaya, founding Professor and Dean of Buddhist Studies at the Sanskrit University in Varanasi, Professor Samdong Rinpoche, a Tibetan monk who was Director of the Tibetan Institute of Higher Studies in Varanasi, another Professor of Buddhist Philosophy, Pundit Ramashankar Tripatti, and a Professor of Sociology, Ramesh Chandra Tiwari. Not far into the dialogue it looked to

Krishna Nath that the discussion might founder over some incompatibility between the different approaches taken by those present. Krishna would ask a direct question and Pundit Jagannath Upadhyaya would take a traditional circuitous route to answer it. Krishna asked whether an observation came first and naming an object came later. The Nyaya school of Indian philosophy, founded by Gautama in the early years of the common era, follows rules of logic, and posits that the word and the thing are created together simultaneously, which was Pundit Jagannath Upadhyaya's reply to the question. Krishna said he was posing a simple question and the pundit was bringing in theory. Krishna even considered abandoning the dialogue. But then Krishna Nath, who wanted the dialogue to continue, said, "Sir, it occurs to me that we give the name later". The impasse was broken, and Krishna turned his whole attention on Krishna Nath. Professor Nath says that when Krishna concentrated on a person he communicated far more than words, focussing his whole body, mind and intellect as a loving presence. Krishna would have a heightened energy and a "special kind of glow" from the quality of attention he would give to the dialogue. Krishna Nath also observed subtle differences in Krishna's interaction with people in groups of different sizes. In a small group the conversation would begin between Krishna and one other person, and if a third person intervened even then the three would make a unit, as Krishna turned to look at the new entrant into the dialogue. In a larger group there continued to be "a quality of participation" so that those listening would feel that he was going into 'my question'. In a format in which Krishnamurti was speaking to hundreds of people, although the verbal communication could not be two-way, there was a sense of togetherness since the problems of relationship, loneliness, frustration and anger were common to all, according to Krishna Nath. He recognised a "participatory consciousness" emerge in the group in Krishna's presence.[8]

Krishna Nath sees Krishna's dialogues as following a Western tradition rooted in those Socratic dialogues that took the form of short exchanges between master and pupil. Yet he acknowledges that there is also something of the Indian tradition of dialogue to be found in Krishna's talks - in the form of a brief question and a long answer or discourse which raises further questions. "Krishnaji was born in India and some of those traditions would be well within him." is how the Professor explains it. The tradition of a Master giving his oral teachings to a group of disciples who would pose a brief question with the Master responding at length through story or discourse, stretches back to the revelation of the Vedas themselves, said to have been composed in 1500 BCE. Later, the Buddha's discourses would often begin as a dialogue with a few people about him but would blossom into a major discourse, for example, that on awareness or mindfulness, the *Satipatthan Sutra*. But Socrates too, according to Plato's rendering, conducted dialogues which were in effect long monologues containing direct speech, for example: "'How so?' he asked. ... 'Well, then,' said I ...". These were storytelling dialogue devices to create variety within the monologue. And the work *Apology*, Socrates' defence at his trial for impiety and the corruption of young men, is in effect a speech or monologue although it is numbered among his great "dialogues". A quality Krishna and Socrates do share in their lengthy public addresses is a protestation that these are not of their making, although they credit the source with different nomenclature. Krishna speaks of the 'sacred', the 'immensity', the 'otherness', the 'other', the 'vastness', 'benediction', while Socrates more succinctly and consistently calls it "the god".

> For the bystanders always believe that I am wise myself in the matters on which I test another; but the truth really is, gentlemen, that the god in fact is wise, and in this oracle he means that human wisdom is worth little or nothing, and it appears that he does not say this of Socrates, but simply adds my name to take me as an example, as if he were to say that this one of you human beings is wisest, who like Socrates knows that he is in truth worth nothing as regards wisdom. This is what I still, even now, go about searching and investigating in the god's way, if ever I think one of our people, or a foreigner, is wise; and whenever I don't find him so, I help the god by proving that the man is not wise.[9]

Professor Krishna Nath says that it is believable to him that Krishna gained ontological truths through his own "direct perception". He cites a conversation Achyut Patwardhan said he had with Krishnamurti while the two of them were alone together for a week. He asked Krishna how he could have dialogues with philosophers, scientists and psychologists without having studied these subjects through reading. He didn't want to hear the same old answers Krishna always gave about listening and attention, he said. Krishna then told him that all the "rubbish" about "the incarnation of Maitreya, the coming Buddha" had no meaning in a concrete sense but there was a Buddha consciousness that could be invoked to see through another and have a dialogue at his or her own level or depth of understanding. Professor Krishna Nath had great respect for Achyut Patwardhan, a man who had given his life to the ideals of his country, and he saw no reason why this account should not be true. He had himself met several holy men who were enlightened, he said.[10]

Krishna's talks with Indian religious philosophers continued almost annually until the year before his death. Samdong Rinpoche would later tell Jayakar that when he asked a question, Krishna would negate it. At first he did not understand Krishna's approach but over the years he came to realise that fundamental questions had no answers but still needed to be asked. Samdong Rinpoche never saw Krishna provide an answer but his challenge touched a germination point in the listener for an awakening and unfolding of "what is" to occur. On a similar note, Jayakar cites a discussion with Krishna in November 1981 in which he enquires into what he calls the original "Indian" mind which emphasised doubt. He saw Christianity in the West as based on faith, viewing doubt and scepticism as heresy. Whereas in India and other parts of Asia doubt was a principle of religious investigation, he said. It was suggested to him that in the West doubt took the form of scientific research. Krishna said he was concerned that in India the "mind" was being carried away by the same outer or materialistic wave - expressed though materialism, technology and nationalism - that was threatening the Western world. The Indian mind, which had produced the *Upanishads* and the Buddha, had been a storehouse of something "very, very" great. he said. Was that essence gradually being corroded by the West?"

These were concerns that must have troubled the mind too of the Indian Prime Minister, Indira Gandhi, who met with Krishna several times in the last decade of his life. She had known Pupul Jayakar since adolescence and it was through Pupul that she first met Krishna at a dinner in the late 1950s. Jayakar writes of Mrs Gandhi's fine sensory perceptiveness – that she could "drown in colour", for example - being dulled by her worldly responsibilities, particularly high political office. By 1975 political pressures on Indira Gandhi in her role as Prime Minister came to a head when the Allahabad High Court declared her election null and void. Ordinarily an aloof personality, Indira Gandhi's reaction to cut off from criticism became extreme, as she worked out a strategy to cope - since she'd retained Prime Ministerial office, but not her right to vote in Parliament, while an appeal was being heard. Soon, with the support of her son Sanjay, she declared a state of emergency, no doubt fearing her own downfall or death as much as national violence and upheaval. Krishna wrote to Pupul about this "serious" matter, pointing out that the world press was reporting India as a "totalitarian state", with thousands in prison and the freedom of the press almost gagged. Referring to himself in the third person, Krishna said that if "K" went to India at the end of the year, he would talk as usual about freedom of speech, of thought, and of expression. He could not modify what he said to suit a government. Neither could he "allow" himself to go to prison, nor accept any favours or exemptions. Krishna's next letter posed an even more far-reaching question. He'd been considering how his next ten to fifteen years might be spent and wondered why, after forty years, there was not one person in India totally and completely involved in the "Teachings". He didn't blame Pupul but was concerned for his work. He must have been alarmed that in the country that he credited with being the source of so much wisdom, so many of his contemporaries lived under a shadow of nationalist and religious division, against which he'd been railing for so long. As Lutyens observes, by now Krishna's attitude to the importance of his teachings had turned around since the 1960s when he had said "everything" could go after his death. Now he wanted some lasting effect. It wasn't as simple as preserving books and keeping archives. He wanted the "perfume" to go on, yet he didn't want anyone to "interpret" his teaching. A function of the Foundations was to have people working together to bring about a "different" human mind, he said. Some might even call his preoccupation possessive or territorial, and might question whether there wasn't a large portion of egoistic attachment in Krishna's view of his "Teachings".[12]

Krishna did not go to India that year but returned in October 1976, after Mrs Gandhi assured Pupul that as he was a religious teacher he could speak freely. He stayed with Pupul, and Mrs Gandhi came to dinner the same month. Also present were Nandini and her daughter Devi and granddaughter Aditi, Sunanda and Pama Patwardhan, LK Jha and Achyut Patwardhan, who was a strong critic of the state of emergency. Mrs Gandhi stayed alone with Krishna for about an hour, much of it in silence. She wrote to Pupul the next day asking her to arrange another meeting with Krishna, and then arrived soon after, unannounced. She met with Krishna for over an hour and emerged with tears streaming down her face. She told Pupul afterwards that she had talked with Krishna about how she felt she was riding on a tiger's back and he had said that if she was more intelligent than the tiger she would know how to deal with it – to look at the conflicts and wrongs as a problem and then act without motive. She said that that day she had felt a "frail" movement in herself that suggested an end to the emergency. Yet it was almost three months later, in January 1977 as Krishna was ready to leave for England, that Indira Gandhi announced an election and then ordered the release of prisoners held under an internal security act. The announcement came as a shock to her confidantes, including her son, Sanjay, whom she had "directly overruled". A biographer of Indira Gandhi, Katherine Frank, says that despite Indira's irrational belief that only she could lead and control the country, "on some level she remained committed to democracy". Frank does not explore the possibility that Krishnamurti's advice influenced Indira Gandhi's decision to call the election which led to the loss of both her seat and government. After the defeat, Krishna wrote from Ojai to Pupul to say that he felt a little responsible, and sent Mrs Gandhi his love. But Krishna would not have felt her political loss was very unfortunate, as he had already told Pupul that he'd sensed something very fine in Indira which politics was "destroying". This attitude is consistent with his view of her father, Jawaharlal Nehru, after their meeting in 1948 and his view of politics in general.[13]

Later in 1977 Mrs Gandhi was arrested and spent a night in gaol but was released the following day. She wrote to Krishna, but by accident the letter went by surface mail and he did not receive it until months later. She told him she had found a "measure" of quiet within herself but it was not enough to deal with the pressures she was experiencing. Her family was under constant scrutiny and "harassment".[14]

When Krishna returned to Bombay in November 1977 Indira went to visit him in Pupul's home again for over two hours. The following year, after her win in a by-election in Chikmagelur in Karnataka, Indira Gandhi wanted to visit the Rishi Valley school for a meeting with Krishna, but she was gaoled for a week following arraignment by Parliament. Soon after her release she followed Krishna to Madras. He met her on the porch of *Vasanta Vihar* and took her to his first-floor apartment to talk. When she emerged she told Pupul that he'd advised her to leave politics. But she said she did not know how to do it. She had been charged with twenty eight crimes, including the theft of two chickens, and she felt she had two alternatives – to be destroyed or to fight. These were to prove an extraordinarily eventful and challenging few years for Mrs Gandhi. In January 1980 she won elections after a barnstorming tour of the country and became India's Prime Minister for the fourth time. During this period the presence in Mrs Gandhi's life of her spiritual adviser and yoga teacher of twenty years standing, Dhirendra Brahmachari, was said to be ubiquitous. The swami's influence over her reportedly grew with her son Sanjay's rise to power, and the swami's business interests developed beyond his two ashrams - one in Delhi and a luxurious establishment in Kashmir – to include an aircraft trading company.[15]

About this time Krishna told Pupul gravely that Indira would face great sorrow that year and Pupul must also be watchful of herself. In June Mrs Gandhi's son Sanjay was killed in an air accident.[16] A telegram from Krishna was among the thousands of condolences she received on news of his death. Pupul says that the shock and grief noticeably aged her close friend but she continued to carry the heavy load of public office. At the end of 1980 Mrs Gandhi at last visited Rishi Valley school, along with her son, Rajiv, his wife and their children. In introducing her with a formal speech to teachers, children and parents who were present, Krishna said that he thought it was important to have a "global" mind that was not limited by nationality, religious orthodoxy or "worn-out" creeds, and at the same time to live a life of "sacred" religious responsibility. Mrs Gandhi referred to what he had just told the audience about technological confrontation and fighting over religion, language and nationality. The true purpose of education, she felt, was to be able to face these problems with a "balanced" mind and to remain oneself. Each person had within them many attitudes and personalities, she said, and these should all be allowed to "come up" and blossom. Having due regard for Hindu orthodoxy, she cited the *Gita*, and said what she thought was important in a person was how much they could feel, yet also rise above pain and pleasure. "We are all of this earth – we are made of the same stuff as the earth, trees, rocks, [even though] the proportions differ," she said. Krishnaji was a great teacher, but so were the trees, the breezes and all the other people you might meet, she said. Her speech ended with a home-spun joke. Her grandfather had told her there were two kinds of people – those who did things and those who took credit for it. Try to be in the first category, he'd advised, as there was far less competition. Afterwards Indira had a private meeting with Krishna in his room.[17]

In October the following year, 1981, when Krishna returned to India, he spoke to Pupul about Indira Gandhi, asking if she could become global in her thinking and cease to be nationalist. He was concerned about the arms race and the danger it posed for humanity. Pupul told him Indira could not be global in her thinking in her role as Indian Prime Minister. He said he had held Indira in his consciousness for some time and felt that he could silently commune with her. Indira invited Krishna to tea and they were alone together for two hours. In November Krishna was invited to lunch by the President of India, Sanjeeva Reddy, and when Indira arrived Pupul observed that she was like a "nimble girl", her eyes sparkling. She and Krishna delighted in speaking in French during the meal which caused the President some frustration as he did not understand the conversation. Then in early December, the day forty five children were killed in a stampede in the Qutub Minar, Indira went to visit Krishna directly from the scene of the accident. Looking grim when she arrived, her face "softened" after an hour with him.[18]

She wrote to Krishna for New Year in 1982 and he returned the greeting, sending his love. She wrote again in June 1982 and then again the following month as the letter had gone astray. It was a depressing time, she said, when a handful of people had the power to affect the lives of millions who were willing to be pushed along in the illusion that they were free. The world needed Krishna's compassion and direction to look within themselves, she wrote. Back in India again in November 1982, Krishna, Indira and her son, Rajiv, met over dinner. Indira had been sleeping badly. Again, three days later, after his last talk in New Delhi on 7 November, Krishna visited her home, which surprised Pupul. as she said that normally he never went anywhere after the rigours of a public talk. Indira began to sleep more soundly.[19]

Indira wrote to Krishna in Madras from New Delhi in January 1983 to say how sorry she was that, due to some urgent matters, she could not visit him, as arranged. The letter dealt with philosophical questions such as "intelligence" being "outside". Inside and outside what, she asked? When one looked within, who was looking, and didn't this "I" permeate the whole of one's being? The more she thought about it the more confused she became, she said.[20]

His reply, addressed to "Indiraji", was like a private lesson in philosophy. "Intelligence" was not "crafty" thought, he said. It was everywhere and existed where there was compassion and love. The "I" was a series of words, symbols and images. Actually it had no reality, he said. In looking within, the observer was the past – an accumulation of remembrances. The observer was "disassociating" himself from what was observed, but the observer was not different from what he observed. The thinker was the thought.[21]

The demands of high office on Indira Gandhi's time and energy increased during 1983. The religious conflict that had plagued the sub-continent since before her own father's administration was now at flashpoint and by the end of the year it was focussed on Sikh militancy in the Punjab. Indira met Krishna in November for a long talk and from Rishi Valley, where he went at the end of the month, he sent her a box of custard apples and a letter, carried by Pupul. She replied on December 12 that she did not know what to write as she was filled with anguish. So many people came to his lectures but what did they do afterwards, she asked? It was difficult to keep hope or faith in the face of peril, she said. There were few people with whom she could talk – but with him she didn't need to talk. She treasured their brief meetings.[22]

Krishna wrote back in early January 1984 from Madras clearly affected by her distress. He wrote that with the threat of nuclear war, murder and torture, the world was becoming insane and he was concerned that she was involved in it. If it would help her <u>in any way</u>, as he underlined the typed letter, he would go to Delhi before his departure from India in mid-February.[23]

Mrs Gandhi replied that she had many formal functions to attend but would like to meet him in Bombay in February. This was their last meeting, and as Krishna saw her to her car he held both her hands. In April Pupul arranged for him to speak to

Indira by phone from New York. The call was brief but he gave her his love. Within two months, in the beginning of June 1984, Indira Gandhi had taken an irreversible step towards her own destruction. She sent in troops to occupy the Golden Temple in Amritsar, the Sikh's holiest shrine, where the fundamentalist Jarnail Singh Bhindranwale and thirty of his followers were holed up. After more than a hundred government soldiers were killed in a first attempt to storm the temple, tanks were ordered in and destroyed a significant part of the sacred shrine, considered by many to be an unforgiveable act of desecration. Bhindranwale was found dead and none of his soldiers survived the onslaught. It's been estimated that about five hundred government troops and more than one thousand civilians were killed in the raid. Retribution was inevitable and Indira Gandhi, as the person ultimately responsible for the slaughter, would become the most likely target. Katherine Frank observes that despite the foreboding that now surrounded Indira, she was "calm and collected". She even vetoed an order to have Sikh security officers removed from duty at her home. By October Pupul noted that Indira seemed at peace with herself. Perhaps she had at last found the full "measure" of quiet within that she'd spoken to Krishna about. Or perhaps it was simply the result of rest before preparations for another election campaign which would begin in November. She was due to meet Krishna again, this time with the Dalai Lama, at Pupul's home on 3 November. But first a trip to Srinigar, and, before leaving, she told Pupul that she looked forward to it as she was a "daughter" of the Himalayas, and when she died she wanted her ashes scattered on their peaks. Prophetic words. Back in Delhi she was shot by two of her own security guards, both Sikhs, as she walked in golden sunshine in the garden between her residence and her office on the last day of October, a chilly month in northern India. She was gunned down by twenty-nine shots fired at point-blank range as she gave a *namaskar* greeting to a security guard she knew well, an officer who had been protecting her since 1980. "What are you doing?" she asked him directly, alarmed at the sight of his revolver, before he shot her. When the onslaught was over, he said in Punjabi, "I have done what I had to do ...". On hearing the news of Indira's death, Krishna spent the day quietly looking out at the garden in Pupul's home, and said that at four in the afternoon he had felt Indira's presence. However another account has Krishna watching television all day. The following night Pupul was still grief-stricken and Krishna consoled her with advice not to hold Indira in her mind but to let her go free of the earth.[24]

Back in 1977, when Indira Gandhi had been defeated as Prime Minister, Pupul had also felt a loss in vitality and went through an inner review of her work and life, asking Krishna for advice. The following year she asked him to take over as President of KFI, something she'd opposed for many years, believing that he should not be burdened by the responsibilities involved. But Krishna was not daunted by the role, despite his admission that he was not an organisation man and did not conform to a "pattern". After all, it was his organisation. In Jayakar's account of the meeting in which they discussed whether he would take her place, she describes Krishna in part calling himself "K" and in part "I". He asked her to remember that "K" had once dissolved all organisations saying they would not help the world. But, said one staffer present, the Foundation was not an organisation. Jayakar raises no question, in her account of the meeting, concerning this curious statement which denies the fact that the Foundation was, and remains, an organisation. If "K" were to become president what would happen, Krishna asked? He (or as he said, "I") would be in the country for only three months. The discussions went on for two days.[25]

Afterwards Jayakar felt freed and began work on Krishna's biography. She asked him if she could explore the way his mind operated. He explained that when he received a question his mind was empty but he heard it with his ear and also with a "non-ear", a new capacity he might call "insight". That insight actually transformed the brain cells, he said. Listening with the ear involved remembrance from past knowledge; listening with the non-ear was not fragmented but, rather, could be likened to a tranquil pond with a stone dropped into it. The reply was the wave or ripple it caused. The discussion persisted to the point where Krishna volunteered that the mind of "K", the inner nature of "K" was nothing ... like measuring the "immeasurable". Jayakar also refers to a discussion on perception and wholeness, drawing a comparison with the holographic model in which a fragment contains the whole. Krishna said that in total perception of sorrow or pleasure there came a freedom from it. In fully attending to something, all senses were awake – and able to experience a soaring ecstasy and a great volume of energy.[26]

Krishna had maintained a strong yet subtle connection with Pupul's sister, Nandini. In March 1961 he had been with her alone in his room in Bombay when she felt a force described as a "river" of silence and a silent, roaring "wind" enveloping and saturating her. She had felt the strength to hold this wind, but did not know how long it lasted before she again became aware of her surroundings at the sound of Krishna's voice. Jayakar believes Krishna's periods alone in the Himalayas triggered these "immense rivers of energy" which were later instrumental in the production of his *Notebook*, begun on 18 June, 1961. A few days after the incident, Krishna wrote to Nandini on a flight to Rome, apologising if he had made a "nuisance" of himself before leaving Bombay. Writing from Rome he told her not to push her body with exercises, but to give complete attention and keep the "flame" alight. After his visit with Vanda Scaravelli in Rome and Florence[27] and then a stay in the Bircher-Benner clinic in Zurich, he wrote to Nandini in May and June 1961 from London about "wheels", or *chakras,* working. She was not to smother the flame or be smothered by mediocrity, and she should be aware of every movement of thought. She should not let any thought escape without observation, he said. From New York later in the month, he advised her to be explosive inwardly and outer things would take care of themselves. His communications kept pace with his travels. In July from Ojai he referred to that "strange" energy in the room she'd experienced, and from

Gstaad he told her to be aware of every form of fear and wash it away. Jayakar follows her reference to Krishna's letters to her sister with a passage from Krishna's *Notebook* which describes a tremendous sunset at Rishi Valley as if there's a link between these fires – within and without. Krishna writes of the brilliant colours of a sky blazing fire: green, purple and gold, violet and indigo, and the reflected, or "counter", sunset of cardinal red and burnt ochre, magenta and "fading" violet. Its intensity and vastness had penetrated everything - the "heavens" were the earth and the earth the heavens.[28]

Krishna would see Nandini whenever he returned to India in the 1960s and she visited him in Switzerland in 1967. She was a trustee of KFI and would remain a firm friẹnd all his life. When Krishna wrote to Pupul in 1975 about the state of emergency, Nandini was distressed, along with Pupul, that Krishna's involvement in Indian affairs might be over. Yet by 1980 Nandini was still a close associate, visiting Pupul's home to meet Krishna and chat, recalling on one occasion advice he'd given her, while he was ill and she held his hand, about how to help a person die, to help free them of attachments, worries and accumulations.[29] Krishna's relationship with Nandini never interfered with his close relationships with other women such as Vanda Scaravelli, on whom he relied for travel in Europe in the 1960s, especially, or Mary Zimbalist, who became his companion for most of the last twenty years of his life. It was Mary who was able to help Krishna with difficulties which arose from his choice of an Indian passport rather than a British, after Indian independence in 1947 – difficulties over travel in Europe and the length of his stays in the United States. In 1977, after assisting him in Los Angeles in his application for an immigration visa while he was in India, Mary Zimbalist flew to London for an interview alongside him at the American Embassy. On arriving back in the United States with her at the end of January, he was granted permanent residence, or a 'green card', which would allow him to apply for American citizenship five years later. When asked by the author if Krishna's relationship with Rosalind had been the only sexual relationship in his life, Mary Zimbalist said that she was not going to disclose anything from his private life. Her job had been to protect his privacy and that hadn't changed after his death. In any case, regardless of intimacy, the women in the latter part of Krishna's life were supportive of him and each other, so that jealousy of the kind that Rosalind is said to have exhibited over Nandini never recurred as a problem. Krishna had seen Rosalind for the last time in the autumn of 1966 and according to Radha when he left he held her hand tightly for a "brief" moment and said with a "strange finality" that first love was the best love.[30]

In 1977 Mary Zimbalist unequivocally committed to the cause of Krishnamurti's teachings when she sold her luxurious home in Malibu and built an extensive addition to Krishna's home, *Pine Cottage*, at Ojai. She agreed that on her death the property would revert to the KFA. About this time Krishna had a prostate operation. Back in the recovery ward he "went off" for about an hour – talking with Nitya and what he called the "personification" of death. The next day he dictated notes to Mary about the experience. The body realised it was not responsible for itself, he said, as there was another "entity", that was much stronger and more vital, engaged in a dialogue with death. Krishna confided in Mary who responded willingly in the role of confidante, taking notes and physically assisting Krishna in recording his experiences, in a way that the more incredulous Rosalind never could.[31]

By 1982, with legal disputation still going on between Rajagopal and Krishna, Rosalind made what Radha calls a "final" effort in contacting Krishna by letter, as she "dreaded" that her life would be laid "bare" if evidence had to be given in a court case. Yet details of her relationship with Krishna were not made public by any Krishnamurti adherents, even though a handful of people knew of it prior to legal proceedings. Instead, the "affair" became known through her daughter's book a decade later. The historian, Peter Washington suggests it's difficult to believe that Rajagopal really knew nothing of the affair that lasted more than twenty years, and that if that was the case, he must have been indifferent or wilfully blind. Washington says the Rajagopal family puts the worst construction on Krishna's later career.[32]

. Rosalind's 1982 letter was written following an abortive attempt to bring about a meeting between Krishna and Rajagopal at the home of Annie Vigeveno in March 1982 to discuss the dispute over archives. Krishna, who had had a hernia operation the previous month and was still spending his days in bed, went to the meeting, accompanied by Mary Zimbalist. On arrival he was told that Rajagopal would not be coming. Whether Rajagopal was himself ill, or simply changed his mind about attending, it was a rude tactic to stand Krishna up. Krishna was aged 86 and Rajagopal now 81 – they were both too old to be playing at brinkmanship, and Rajagopal could have avoided the drama by phoning to postpone the meeting before Krishna left home. Disappointed and angry, Krishna left Annie Vigeveno's house immediately but phoned Radha two days later as he had promised. She invited him to their old mountain retreat, Wrightwood, to see the snow, clearly oblivious of his poor health, and she tried to defend Rajagopal. But Krishna told her he was too sick to go to the mountains and there was nothing more he could do about the split with Rajagopal. Following this, Rosalind's letter, written in June, was an account of her and Krishna's former relationship and was sent in a sealed envelope to Vanda Scaravelli for Krishna to read in her presence. Krishna handed it to Mary Zimbalist to read and she made a note of the scene in her diary, saying the letter was titled, "A Sad, Sad Story". Mary wrote that it was a self-serving account and a justification of what Rosalind might be "driven in desperation" to say in court. Regarding an accusation in the letter that Krishna was a "congenital liar", Krishna told Mary that he had lied when "they" attacked and brutalised him. He was revolted by the letter, saying it was "unclean". Mary said that she felt sickened by its tone and would never have anything to do with "those two people" after the case had ended. The letter was later reported to have been torn up in front of Vanda.[33]

In Krishna's lawsuit against Rajagopal over archive documents, parties for both sides continued to negotiate over matters such as an apology for Rajagopal and an undertaking that the KFA would never sue him in the future. Then in April 1983 the lawsuit against him was withdrawn which meant that papers that Rajagopal had sent to the Huntington Library would be held there and he would retain papers he considered belonged to him. But six weeks later Rajagopal filed a counter-suit against Krishna and, soon after, also against the trustees of KFA. The suit claimed the 1974 settlement had been breached by the second lawsuit regarding missing archives, that his publishing activities and business had been interfered with, and he had suffered emotional distress. He claimed damages of $9 million. A settlement for an undisclosed sum was only reached four months after Krishna's death in 1986.[34]

In a newspaper report of the settlement – which had followed the three separate lawsuits spanning sixteen years - Rajagopal was said to have been cleared of any charges of wrongdoing. Rajagopal was quoted as saying that it was the least that could have happened in the interest of truth and justice. They'd all been friends and had "sprouted from the same tree", Rajagopal said. He was described as a Cambridge law student when he met Krishnamurti in London, and had "devoted the ensuing 50 years" to editing the writings of Krishnamurti, "a native of India, for whom English was a second language". English was of course a second language for Rajagopal too, but no indication was given about which of the two men had mastered it more fluently.[35]

In the period between the counter-suit and Krishna's death, Krishna had a lot of work to do, lecturing and travelling, despite his frailty. His cracking pace on the international circuit did not slacken. Whether speaking to his "converted" at the schools and centres, or to public gatherings, Krishna continued to deliver hundreds of recorded talks and dialogues – averaging about one hundred and twenty every year up until the month of his death.[36]

Krishna came gradually to make his peace with the Theosophists, to restore the contact he'd broken in the early

1930s. He had met Radha Burnier, a beautiful woman, niece of Rukmini Arundale and the daughter of Rukmini's brother, Sri Ram, who succeeded Jinarajadasa as President of the Theosophical Society in 1953. Krishna had seen Radha as a small girl and met her first as a woman in 1960 when she went to Saanen to hear his talks. She says that he remembered her, and asked her what brought her there, but she does not know whether he recognised her or someone pointed her out. They became close friends and when she stood for the Presidency of the Society, against her aunt, Rukmini, in 1980, Krishna told her that if she won he would visit Adyar, after his long self-imposed exile. In November of that year when he went to Madras, he walked with Radha Burnier on Theosophist ground once more, from the gates of the estate to her home on the beachfront, followed by a group of joyous Theosophists. After an absence of about fifty years, Krishna had given his imprimatur to public reconciliation, although Radha Burnier says she would not use the word 'reconciliation' as it implies there'd been continuing conflict. If it was not conflict, the reader may wonder what Krishna's oft-paraded break with Theosophy in 1929 was – as it underpinned his most famous statement, "Truth is a pathless land", which carried him into the hearts and minds of agnostics and independent thinkers and kept him away from the Society's headquarters for decades. What was this public stand about if not conflict over Theosophical ideology as well as ritual? Perhaps Krishna's return to Leadbeater's and Annie Besant's spiritual home, the place where his own father had brought him for spiritual nourishment, marked the point at which Theosophists could begin to erase from history Krishna's former trenchant criticism of the Society and its followers. Every year after 1980 when he was in Madras he would visit the Theosophical Society estate most evenings to walk with Radha on the beach where he had been "discovered" by Leadbeater in 1909. Radha Burnier describes Krishna as a person of great wisdom, warmth, purity of body and mind and an absence of self. She believes he had a profoundly religious mind which was non-sectarian and in "contact" with the hidden or sacred nature of existence. She felt that as his consciousness was in contact with this different "dimension", he had a great energy flowing through him. She pointed out that the Theosophical Society Presidents had always maintained contact with Krishna. Jinarajadasa and Krishna kept up correspondence during WWII, and her father, Sri Ram, would always call on Krishna when he visited India as a mark of respect. Radha Burnier believes Krishna did not hold any ill feeling towards Leadbeater, although he disagreed with him over ritual and the Liberal Catholic Church. In describing Krishna's first visit, after the fifty-year break, to Annie Besant's room which is now private sanctum - when he stood by her desk and looked at Leadbeater's photograph - Burnier says she did not hear him say, "Pax". She does not know the source of the story that he twice said the word as he faced Leadbeater's image, a description included in Pupul Jayakar's biography of Krishna. The rewrite of history is neither conclusive nor concluded, however. Leadbeater's biographer, Gregory Tillett, says he had an opportunity to meet Krishnamurti through Mary Lutyens but Krishna said he would not discuss Leadbeater or the past. Krishna reportedly told Mary the biography shouldn't be written and that Leadbeater was an evil man.[37]

It is worth questioning here Leadbeater's continued influence on Krishna through the disciplinary attitude he'd instilled into the impressionable boy which carried on throughout his life, and even the possibility that Leadbeater hypnotised his young charge. As both the subjects and practitioners of hypnotism can verify, the effects of such mind possession can last a lifetime or as long as the hypnotist specifies.[38]

It's worth speculating too on what Leadbeater actually saw about Krishna, the boy playing on the beach at Adyar, that might have led him to believe that Krishnamurti would be, if not the next Maitreya, a person with the charisma to lead thousands of followers on a "spiritual" quest. Much has been made of Krishna's aura and his "vacancy" of mind. Much has been written, too, of Krishna's exceptional eyes – that they were large, dark and had a vacant look, that they would gaze into the distance. What is rarely mentioned is that they were *sanpaku* eyes – where from a view level with the eyes, the whites of the eyes are seen not only beside the pupils but also between the pupils and the lower lids. Some significant "spiritual" figures in history have had such eyes – Rasputin, Steiner, Gurdjieff, the palmist Cheiro and Madame Blavatsky among them. These are also the eyes of some famous hypnotists, such as 'The Great Franquin' in Australia. There is a belief which originated in Japan that white showing beneath the iris of the eyes denotes a condition called *sanpaku*, which is "not only an illness of the body but a dangerous condition of the spirit and psyche". It is said that a *sanpaku* person's system is out of balance, making him or her prone to accident or tragic death. An exponent of the *sanpaku* theory who advocated a macrobiotic diet to correct the imbalance, George Ohsawa, cited a dozen or so people who had the condition, including President Kennedy, his brothers Robert and Edward, Abraham Lincoln, Archduke Ferdinand of Austria, Marilyn Monroe, the Iraqi revolutionary Abdul Karim Kassem and the Vietnamese President Ngo Dinh Diem.[39]

Some people who have such eyes and lead perfectly respectable and innocuous lives say that people sometimes approach them in the street and speak to them – some even tell them they have 'the devil's' eyes or 'bedroom' eyes. That Krishna had such eyes is certainly not definitive proof that he had hypnotic power, or that he would die a violent or early death – after all he lived to the age of ninety. But it is remarkable that although many people commented on the effect on them of his stare or gaze, no biographers investigated the fact that his eyes were *sanpaku*. That some hypnotists may have such eyes is also no proof that anyone with this physical characteristic uses them to influence people, either adversely or beneficially. Clearly Krishna was aware of his effect on many people: he said that people fell in love with him, with his face, they were attracted to him personally and wanted to advance spiritually. Mary Zimbalist, Krishna's closest companion in his later life, who loved him devotedly and believes in his goodness, acknowledges that Krishna had a majesty and presence that could be felt and which was so awe-inspiring it was almost like hypnotism to an audience. And it's curious that many people who are clearly "followers" of Krishnamurti's teaching vehemently disclaim the obvious, in accordance with his denial that he had or wanted followers. It might be likened to the way some people under hypnosis claim that they have not been hypnotised yet display behaviour, in their speech or actions, which offers proof that they have been.[40]

In fact hypnotism is little understood by Western science and is still considered a dark art except as it is used in hypnotherapy. As Margaret Goldsmith contends in her biography of Franz Anton Mesmer, in the great healer's *rapport* theory, the emphasis on the correlation between the minds of the patient and the physician "was the first groping step towards therapeutic suggestion". Even Jesus of Nazareth, she maintains, "gave His disciples that perfect confidence, needed by all mental healers, that they would indeed cure the sick, and their conviction, in turn, was transferred to the sick who came to them".[41]

The psychologist Anthony Storr suggests the possibility that the extraordinary views that some 'gurus' have of themselves – the sense that they are special or chosen - may be symptoms of schizophrenia or manic depression. Yet these classic symptoms of delusional behaviour - voices and messianic beliefs - are the foundation stones of most of the world's great belief systems. Idiosyncratic belief systems shared by only a few adherents are likely to be considered delusional, while equally irrational belief systems shared by millions are called world religions.[42]

Martin Gardner seems to hint that Krishnamurti had a malign influence over the physicist, Dr David Bohm, in an article about their "strange" relationship. The only evidence he offers of its strangeness is secondary, based largely on Radha Rajagopal Sloss's biography of Krishna and David Peat's biography of Bohm. From this research, all of it secondary, Gardner casts doubt on Krishnamurti's credibility, calling him a "compulsive" liar, and brands Bohm gullible. Yet there is little evidence, beyond hearsay, that Krishna had a compulsion to tell falsehoods. The relationship between the two men would have had to be strange, by definition, as they were both exceptional men. Bohm gained his doctorate under J. Robert Oppenheimer at the University of California, Berkeley, and went on to play a significant role in quantum physics. His life was not without trauma and sadness, however. He was called before the House Committee on UnAmerican Activities and indicted for contempt of Congress for refusing to name names – a courageous act in the hysterical political climate whipped up by Senator Joe McCarthy. Gardner claims no university in the United States wanted him. Bohm moved to London and held the position of Professor of Theoretical Physics at Birkbeck College, the University of London. He suffered three bouts of severe depression in his life and finally died of a heart attack in 1991 at the age of seventy-five. Bohm's biographer, David Peat, whose work Gardner drew on for his summary, is not so black and white in the way he deals with the relationship between Bohm and Krishna. He says Bohm compared Krishnamurti to Einstein "in his ability to explore deeply in a spirit of impersonal friendship". Bohm even went so far as to tell Peat that he had seen some of the things Krishna talked about, that he had "looked at reality and seen it is an illusion". Peat concluded that Bohm believed he had undergone some kind of inner transformation, that came often but was "fragile" and "not consistent". The biographer quotes a teacher at Ojai who saw Bohm "saturated in the spiritual" which was said to have left him vulnerable to Krishnamurti's influence. Krishna is described as brutal in distancing himself from Bohm following Bohm's heart surgery in 1981 when his physical and psychological health was poor. Following Krishna's death when Radha's book exposing Krishna's sexual relationship with her mother was published, Bohm was devastated. He felt Krishna had been hypocritical as he had spoken to Bohm about the importance of celibacy. Peat says Bohm saw Krishna as an imposter whom he had placed on a pedestal and he was concerned that he himself had been guilty of falseness. But Peat tempers this claim in saying that it is important to note that Bohm expressed such opinions "during the agony of his depression" and they did not reflect his "final and more reflective opinion of Krishnamurti". In fact, just weeks after writing that Krishnamurti was conditioned differently than most people, making certain insights possible for him, yet he was even more "caught up in nonsense (especially when he thinks about 'that boy')", Bohm asked that what he'd written be destroyed as it could lead to "false impressions". Fritjof Capra's view is that Bohm was singularly influenced by the "philosopher and sage, Krishnamurti" who, he says, became Bohm's "spiritual mentor".[43]

Overall, Bohm had had an extremely productive friendship with Krishnamurti following his first significant encounter in 1959 when he read *The First and Last Freedom* and was struck by Krishnamurti's insight into the question of the observer and the observed. On meeting Krishna, Bohm felt Krishna's "intense energy" as a listener and his "freedom from self-protective reservations". At the height of their friendship, they met whenever Krishna was in London. In view of Bohm's susceptibility to depression, or perhaps because of it, he was very interested in Krishna's view that sorrow had its source in the fact that humans were ignorant of their thought processes. Bohm developed the idea of giving close attention to the act of thinking rather than its content. In his book, *Wholeness and the Implicate Order*, he concluded that "original and creative insight within the whole field of measure *is* the action of the immeasurable". Bohm credited Krishna with describing with "force and clarity" the idea that harmony required a man to give full creative energies to inquiry into the whole field of measure.[44]

In 1980 Bohm went to stay at Ojai and eight discussions between the two men were recorded. These, together with another five recorded at Brockwood, were published in 1985 as *The Ending of Time*. What these two thinkers were heading towards was Krishna's preoccupation, particularly strong late in his life, that it was possible to change the brain cells through "insight".

Bohm said that modern research into the brain and nervous system lent support to the idea.[45]

Over the years and through their friendship and discussion Krishna and David Bohm had gone about as far as two great thinkers could go in exploring consciousness. Mary Lutyens says that by the year before his death Krishna's interest in discussions with leading thinkers had palled. She maintains that he needed new inspiration from someone who would challenge him, as often the more learned a person was the more frustrated Krishna became about communicating with them through the maze of knowledge that their minds held. She says Dr Shainberg's conferences with psychologists in New York and even the talks with scientists such as Dr Jonas Salk and the writer, Iris Murdoch, did not hold great challenges for Krishna any longer.[46]

Instead he was setting about getting his house – the Foundations in different parts of the world – in order and trying to find lasting means to disseminate his work.

Krishna had always had a high profile in Sri Lanka, the capital Colombo having been on his lecture circuit in the early Theosophist years and Krishna's close friendship with Dr EW Adikaram since the 1930s offering a conduit for visits. But he had not travelled there since 1957 and in 1980 the government of Sri Lanka invited Krishna as a state guest to give lectures at the Sri Jayawardhanapura University. Old friends Pupul Jayakar, Nandini and Mary Zimbalist stayed with him at the official guesthouse of the Sri Lankan Government, *Auckland House*. Krishna was invited to tea by the President and met the Prime Minister. He also gave television interviews and public talks.[47]

In 1983 Krishna met a millionaire who would be instrumental in having an adult study centre built at Brockwood Park in England. Friedrich Grohe, a German bathroom and kitchen fittings manufacturer, approached Krishna in Tannegg about establishing a school in Switzerland but Krishna was not keen as it was difficult to find teachers. The following year when Grohe visited Brockwood and offered funds to build a study centre there Krishna accepted with alacrity. The architect Keith

Critchlow was asked to submit sketches and after one meeting with him, Krishna decided he was the man for the job. He was a Fellow of the Royal College of Art and had designed religious centres overseas but was not qualified to practise in England so the firm of Triad was brought in to implement his plans. There was a hitch when planning permission was initially refused in February 1985 so a second application was submitted and permission was finally granted in February 1986. about a week after Krishna died. An important feature of the design is a 'quiet room' at its centre, Krishna's idea being that it would act as a meditative "furnace" to heat the whole building.[48]

With the United States and English Foundations now working smoothly, Krishna turned his attention to India. He had only a few months to concentrate on those who would be entrusted to carry on the administration of the schools and other Foundation activities after he was gone, and he knew he needed some new blood. Radhika Herzberger, Pupul's daughter who had a PhD in Sanskrit and Buddhist Studies from an American university, was in charge of Rishi Valley School. She was appointed to the International Publications Committee, along with Dr P Krishna, Radha Burnier's cousin. Asit Chandmal, Pupul and Nandini's nephew, who had expertise in information technology, would also become very close to Krishna, writing a biography in his honour, *One thousand suns, Krishnamurti at Eighty-Five*.[49] Krishna's health was flagging by early 1986 in India, where he was surrounded by the usual group of carers but lacked the daily attention and closeness of Mary Zimbalist, who remained in Ojai.[50]

Radha Sloss was also travelling in India in early 1986 but was oblivious that Krishna had died in mid-February after his hurried return to California. Radha read Krishna's obituary in the *Calcutta Telegraph* five days after his death. The article was written by Pupul Jayakar. Radha says she had not expected the wave of grief she felt; she had never realised how deeply she looked on him as a parent. Radha recalled her recent meeting with Rukmini, George Arundale's widow, who had told her

Krishna paid her a visit at Adyar - for the first time in over forty years. It had been at the urging of her nephew, Professor Krishna. Rukmini impressed on Radha the importance of reconciliation between Rajagopal and Krishna, whom she believed was close to death. Radha rang her father to ask him to be receptive if Krishna phoned him. He told her 'of course'. But he did not believe Krishna would call him and told her she should not have false hopes. Rukmini herself died a week after Krishna. Radha says that she remembers "Krinsh", the father figure, as he was when she was a girl growing up in Ojai, when he'd wear a blue denim shirt and jeans, his face laughing under a big straw hat. He brought her love and happiness, and later, disharmony and sorrow. She believes he let her be free of him and also claims he taught her not to be afraid. So free, in fact, that she did not know what age he was when he died and was not invited to his inner circle of loved ones at his deathbed.[51]

Rosalind outlived Krishna by a decade. She died on 24 January 1996 at the age of 92, five years after her daughter's biography of Krishnamurti and her life in his shadow, was published. Radha was quoted in Rosalind's obituary as saying that her mother drew from theosophy a sense of internationalism and deeper understanding between people, and that she'd believed in individuality and community. This had been a hallmark of the Happy Valley School which she'd founded with Huxley, Krishnamurti and Guido Ferrando. Over the last 26 years of her life Rosalind had lived in a home adjoining the home of her close friend, artist and potter, Beatrice Wood, overlooking the Happy Valley school.[52]

Rajagopal had died on 22 April 1993 at the age of 92. In a brief obituary, the *Ojai Valley News* 30 April, 1993, described Rajagopal as a Brahmin, the son of a theosophist and judge, who "completed his formal education with an LL.D. from Cambridge University in England". The local paper reported that with Dr Besant's encouragement, Rajagopal had "devoted most of his life to organizing and guiding *the* foundations affiliated with Krishnamurti". [author's italics][53]

Krishnamurti's last companion. Mary Zimbalist, is still living. In 1972 Krishna had told her that she must outlive him. She did not belong to herself anymore, he said, cryptically. He told her in 1985 that he knew when he would die but would not say when that would be. As it happened, he died on what was thought to be Leadbeater's birthday the following year. He had also asked Mary Zimbalist to write a book about what it was like being with him. She has many notes and is working on a memoir, at first finding it difficult to put her experience of the "immeasurable" into words. She experienced a "presence" in the room when he would talk about his youth, an unseen "force" or "fragrance" which she experienced perhaps ten times in twenty years. She says compassion characterised the man and his teaching. He was a mystic and he was mysterious; and if there is a level of human consciousness that can perceive and touch the "eternal", he had such a mind, she maintains. As an intelligent and courageous woman, now aged and frail, she is prepared to go on record to say that Krishnamurti stands in the same rank as Buddha, Mohammed and Jesus Christ. But it's not all sweetness and light. Mary Zimbalist also claims that Krishna told her he had only one regret and that was having anything to do with Rosalind and Rajagopal.[54]

There's no question that Krishna was bitter about his continuing rift with Rajagopal. In 1985 he is said to have dictated to Mary Zimbalist a letter to Rajagopal which was never sent. Lutyens quotes the final paragraphs in her version of events surrounding Krishna and the Rajagopals, and the vehemence of the letter might come as a shock to anyone who thought Krishna was a fount of goodness and light. Its unequivocal censure is no doubt equal to any vitriol that might have been found in Rosalind's earlier letter to him. Rajagopal must have schemed for years, "deceiving" everyone and "manoeuvring" to get the properties for himself, Krishna's letter stated. What he had was not given to him and he had exploited those who had made sacrifices, it went on. The letter referred to people calling Rajagopal an "embezzler" and accused him of attempting to "blackmail"

Krishna. "Look." Krishna said, he was not "frightened" of a court case. And he claimed Rajagopal had "exploited" him. On an even more personal level, Krishna referred to Rajagopal's status as a Brahmin, of which he knew Rajagopal was proud, saying he had sunk very low for personal "power" and out of "egotistical" jealousy. The letter was not written in a spirit of "vengeance" nor to hurt Rajagopal's "vanity", he said, but to point out the "deep" abyss between Rajagopal and anything "sacred" or "decent". The reader might consider what level of bitterness and sorrow must Krishna have fallen to, to prompt such unmitigated abuse. Setting aside for a moment the rights and wrongs of the litigation, one can only wonder at the lack of compassion evident in this self-righteous and passionate insult. Was it typical of the tenor of argument Krishna had engaged in with Rajagopal in the past, or an isolated representation of the repressed anger he felt? Did he actually dictate it? Only the cassette recording of Krishna's voice would answer that question and the author has not been privy to that degree of accessibility to the Krishnamurti archives to determine an answer. The release of the quote was authorised by Mary Zimbalist and the KFA so it might be presumed that they do not feel the tone of the letter in any way tarnishes Krishna's character. The fact that it was neither destroyed nor sent is curious, however, possibly placing it in a similar category to problematic letters from the past which Krishna was encouraged to write but which are said to have never been delivered, such as that to Rajagopal regarding Krishna's relationship with Rosalind and another to Nandini to explain this same relationship. But whether Krishna intended to send the letter or not, if genuine – and there's no reason to presume that it is not – it indicates a deep canker in Krishna's spirit of charity, in the original sense of the word, i.e. of 'love', of which he had spoken so often. This was 1985 and with less than a year to go before his death, it might be presumed that this unresolved conflict with Rajagopal was still in Krishna's heart to the bitter end.[55]

But publicly Krishna was held in high regard and his adherents gathered about him, busying themselves with spreading his word. He was particularly keen to see a younger generation take up the work of commitment to his teaching and carry it forward after his death. This could indicate an attachment to his teachings which might be considered an expression of ego and not consistent with the ego-less state of an 'Enlightened Master', even though it must be pointed out that Lutyens says he always spoke of "the" teaching, not claiming it as his own.[56]

Over the last few years of Krishna's life he would describe to close friends the strange qualities of his mind which had been manifesting all his life. He told Pupul Jayakar that Leadbeater and Mrs Besant used to talk about the face of the Maitreya Boddhisatva. It meant nothing to him at the time but many years later he suddenly saw the beautiful face. It began after Krishna's brother's death, quickened after Krishna's move from Ojai and was still with him over recent times. It was like cleaning his body, his face and the air. He'd seen the face in the dark, in the light and while walking. When there was quietness something happened in his brain - at times as if it were exploding. People might say that it was "cuckoo". He claimed that as a child he had had the capacity to read people's thoughts and even the contents of an unopened letter. He could make objects materialise, see visions and foretell the future. Krishna could remember this even though he might have forgotten a lot of other events and people from his past. He said he thought there was a "force" which the Theosophists had touched and which they lost when they tried to translate it into something material through symbols and vocabulary. Krishna described it as the universe pouring in, as though his head was stuck in the universe. The body could only stand so much of it, and he'd never felt it as close as he did then, in 1981. He wondered whether the "Maitreya Boddhisattva" was Leadbeater's fictitious legacy or whether it was something completely different from that theosophist indoctrination. Certainly he felt protected by the sensation as well as feeling a certain hesitancy about this mystery. Did it sound crazy, he asked shyly?

Mary Zimbalist says that many people felt the "presence" and it occurred when Krishna talked very seriously about the phenomenon of that presence.[57]

Krishna remained a mystery to Mary Lutyens, the biographer who must have studied him most closely. It's been suggested that her task was not made easier by the fact that she and her family, particularly her mother, played central roles in the drama of Krishnamurti's life.[58]

But Mary Lutyens, despite her mother's background of belief in the Theosophical Society aim of international brotherhood, was an Englishwoman with a great deal of cultural baggage of rationality, which ran counter to the "Indian" sensibility which was grounded in a great veneration of spiritual philosophy. Mary might have tried to cast Krishna in a role as the bridge between East and West, an acceptable concept to internationalists. But he would not have it. He demanded recognition of the fact that what he spoke about was shared by human beings of all cultures, pointing out that the "concept" of East and West was one of division and therefore faulty. Mary Lutyens saw that Indians liked to claim him as an Indian teacher but she would never give up the concept of him as 'World Teacher' perhaps because Krishna himself never privately gave it up, despite his public rejection of gurus. Professor Krishna Nath points out that what might at first seem to be a contradiction - in Krishnaji's rejection of gurus while understanding the power of invocation through chant or meditation – might be explained as his knowledge that *guru* simply means light, which is not necessarily found in bodily form. It is up to each person to recognise it or not. As the Buddha said in the *Mahaparinirvana Sutra*, "Be a light unto yourself". Krishna Nath says that perhaps Krishna was groomed as a world teacher in the modern scientific age to be in tune with the modern temper of rejection of tradition. Perhaps Krishnaji ridiculed the rites and rituals of tradition in order to suit the tastes and temperaments of modern young men and women for whom outdated rites and rituals would have no meaning. Krishna Nath himself felt that Krishnaji communicated ancient Hindu wisdom through the modern senses and sensibilities of the West at the same time that he brought to India "vitalities" from the West. Speaking with traditionalists he would bring in elements of modernity, while to a group in Washington, for instance, he would speak of an Indian traditional chant – to make a whole of the fragments, according to Professor Nath. There are many testimonies of Krishna 'singing' traditional Sanskrit chants throughout his life. Back in 1931 after Krishna told a reporter that he was the Christ, not in the traditional sense but in the "pure" sense of the word, he wrote to Lady Emily that he had never denied being the "World Teacher". And he never would. Yet while seeing himself as special, he would not acknowledge that this capacity was beyond that of others. Although he didn't use the term 'World Teacher', by the end of his life his mind was entrenched in a recognition of the importance of his teaching to the world. Krishna had told Mary Lutyens in 1974 that he was absolutely certain she and Mary Zimbalist could discover "truth" – likened to a "reservoir" – if they began to "enquire" with an "empty" brain.[59]

Did Krishnamurti reach that state of enlightenment called *samadhi* at the end of his life? *Samadhi*, the final point of the path of yogic enlightenment, bestowed through the grace of the teacher – an ecstatic condition in which consciousness shines through the object, or where there's a merging of subject and object so that only the "Self" remains. How anyone could explain this state without experiencing it is a puzzle. How anyone could recognise such a state in another without experiencing it is another puzzle. Krishna claimed in 1980, with "complete humility", that he had experienced the "source" of all energy during a period from the end of 1979 through January 1980, waking up in the night with a sense of the "absolute". Jayakar says she asked him in 1984 about *samadhi*. He told her that the brain did not accumulate – what arose was full. There was no movement within the brain as time, but an infinite movement, the rhythm of brain, and a sense of timeless, eternal protection.[60] Was he speaking of his own brain or of what he had heard or read? Krishna had certainly for many years been describing his inner experiences and speaking publicly in terms that had been likened to the teachings of great sages. The pundit Jaganath Upadhyaya said that in the 1950s in Varanasi when Buddhist scholars first heard Krishna, they believed he was speaking Buddhism whereas when Vedantists heard him they heard Vedantism. Later the pundit Upadhyaya thought Krishnaji spoke in the stream of Nagarjuna, in negation. But Krishna said there was no understanding of the teaching, only understanding of yourself. In discussion with Samdong Rinpoche about the nature of sorrow, Krishna had said that it was "here", indicating his heart. First of all one had to carefully see the mind and its functioning and listen within and without. Sensitivity would then arise and from that, insight, which would wipe away sorrow, he explained.[61]

Peter Washington who wrote about his view of the emergence of the western guru from its origins in Madame Blavatsky's Theosophical "Masters", said that Krishnamurti resolved what others may have viewed as contradictions in his life by locating the spiritual source within the self. This had been the solution of mystics of all ages, from ancient Buddhists and medieval Christians to Krishnamurti's friend, Aldous Huxley. "More significantly", Washington said, this had appeared "among the Hindu doctrines of Advaita Vedanta, which identifies the soul as an aspect of that absolute reality to which it aspires".

> Krishnamurti had always insisted that individuals must work out their own destiny. But in doing so, he had simply revived an ancient doctrine – just as Theosophy said he should. By listening to the voice of his deepest self, Krishnamurti was perhaps returning to the ascetic ways of his Hindu ancestors.[62]

And to take the concept of the personal or *jiva-atman* linked to the Supreme *parama-atman* one step further, as Krishna said in 1981, the content of our consciousness is the common ground of all humanity. Even though for years he'd been exhorting people to act not as part of a mob through nationalist-political or religious mentality but as individuals, he now explained that we'd been trained to think of ourselves as separate souls, striving for ourselves, but this was an "illusion". We were not separate entities with separate psychological content, but each one of us was the rest of mankind, he said.[63]

Some people close to Krishna may have called his *asanas*, physical "postures" or exercises in order to distance the activity from Hinduism but there's no doubt that he had been taught traditional yoga over many years by two leading Yoga Masters: BKS Iyengar of Poona and his nephew, TKV Desikachar, whose yoga centre is just a few streets from *Vasanta Vihar* in Madras, now known as Chennai. Desikachar saw Krishna a few months before he died and says that he had been continuing his practice right up until that time. Krishnaji believed in his practice so much he asked Desikachar's father, Sri T Krishnamacharya, to teach his son as much as possible so the teaching would not be destroyed. The physical discipline was important to Krishna but so too must have been the philosophy that underpinned it, whether he acknowledged it publicly or not. His physician, Dr Vikram Parchure, takes a public view of the *asanas* as simply physically health-giving, saying he would run through a series of exercises with Krishna in the mornings, including skipping and running backwards. However Scott Forbes, the principal of Brockwood, witnessed Krishna's discipline and capacity in *hatha yoga*, taking lessons from Krishna in 1985 when the sage was aged ninety. Forbes said he would have found Krishna's suppleness extraordinary even in a much younger man. Krishna was a stern teacher, particularly in probing Forbes about his own teaching practices in the school, telling him that the students might have opinions but he should not, and should not react out of his own cultural background. Krishna was still very concerned that the organisation of the schools might be overriding the teaching. He would ask where were the "young lions' to carry on the work. In India, Miss Ahalya Chari, who had known Krishna since 1948 and worked mostly in the Rajghat school, says Krishnaji was a man of great discipline, rising at about four in the morning to do his yoga and breathing exercises for an hour and a half. He took intelligent care of his body, taking the right food and exercise, walking every evening. She admired his ability to be attentive to everyone with equal intensity, even in answering questions from children. She says to watch him was a lesson in how to relate to children. He was hard on the teachers, as he was on himself, asking why they had not changed nor helped others to change. It was "like walking on fire," at times, she said.[64]

Krishna could be irritable, angry, demanding, provocative. The staff at the Krishnamurti Centres acknowledged this yet remained loyal and devoted. Few were interested in his private life, they said. As one staff member at Brockwood put it, seeing Krishna at close quarters completely demolished the ideas he had about how an enlightened person should behave – perhaps having a permanent smile, for instance. Krishna never measured up to his expectations of 'enlightenment'. He found instead a shy man, at times passionate, at other times irritated, and someone who had great charisma and showed a tremendous energy and compassion without seeking a result. Significantly, the more this staffer understood his own limitations, the less important the question of whether Krishna was enlightened or not became to him, so that it faded from his mind. The focus was on yourself, as if Krishna was a mirror to look at yourself, he said.[65]

Other staff members commented on Krishnaji's seriousness, integrity, lack of ego, that he could see through people, and that there was something special going on in his talks. Yet the staff were also aware of his 'lightness', his sensitivity, his love of jokes and his interest in what was going on in the world. Michael Krohnen – a chef at *Ayra Vihara* – would give Krishna the news of the day along with a lovingly-prepared lunch. He relates in his book, *1001 Lunches with J Krishnamurti*, several of the jokes Krishna liked to tell over a meal – often on a religious theme such as St Peter at the pearly gates, or the devil at work, or jokes centred on deflating the pomposity of a political figure. Krohnen likened Krishnamurti's visits to Ojai to powerful storms, stirring people up. Significantly, for all the practicality and light-heartedness of his book, Krohnen took Krishna's standing as a figure of great religious wisdom very seriously. He writes that when Krishna was very ill in February 1986 and he was allowed in to see him, he saw that "a subtle light visibly shone through him" as they held hands. Granted that it was a very emotional moment for Krohnen, his book demonstrates that he had been an acute, though devoted, observer of Krishna and his own emotions for over fifteen years. There's evidence that Krohnen had acuity of sight and thought, but whether his mind was working within what might be called Krishna's command or domain must remain a question, as he, too, wrote that when he first met Krishna in 1971, and their eyes met, he felt a jolt, "as if a current of energy had suddenly been switched on between us". This is the sort of testimony that devotees of guru figures often provide, explaining it as *kundalini* being awakened.[66]

One explanation of Krishnamurti's role as teacher and mystic might be found in the work of those great observers and thinkers in the fields of cultural, social and psychological studies, such as Carl Jung and Joseph Campbell. Perhaps Jung's explanations of the unconscious, including his ideas about the collective unconscious and "numinous" archetypes, can help the reader to understand what seem to have been Krishna's extraordinarily knowledge-gaining quests through different realms of consciousness. In his essay, *On the Nature of the Psyche*, Jung refers to Ignatius Loyola's apparitions of bright light and multiple eyes and the Rig-Veda's "thousand-eyed" *Purusha* to demonstrate how introspective intuitions can capture images from the state of the unconscious.

> Since consciousness has always been described in terms derived from the behaviour of light, it is in my view not too much to assume that these multiple luminosities correspond to tiny conscious phenomena. If the luminosity appears in monadic form as a single star, sun, or eye, it readily assumes the shape of a mandala and must then be interpreted as the self. ... the symbols of the self have a "uniting" character.[67]

Later in the essay Jung confronts the problem of the impossibility of proof for psychological theory since the human organ of consciousness is both a transformer and a transformation of original instinctual images or archetypal knowledge. Or as Krishna would put it, "Water can never find out what water is".[68] Jung's conclusion, meticulously arrived at by tracing archetypes, resonates with the conclusions of physicists:

> Since psyche and matter are contained in one and the same world, and moreover are in continuous contact with one another and ultimately rest on irrepresentable, transcendental factors, it is not only possible but fairly probable, even, that psyche and matter are two different aspects of one and the same thing.[69]

Perhaps too these concepts help to explain Krishna's command over his own mind and the mind or minds of large audiences. His talks demonstrated his own understanding, explanation and practice of ideas such as 'the word is not the thing' and 'consciousness as the common ground of all humanity for thousands of years'.[70]

Joseph Campbell has studied the role of shamans in society and the power that emanates from their ability to access states or dimensions of consciousness not available to most people. As he wrote in 1959,

> ... in contrast to the life-maiming psychology of a neurosis ... the shamanistic crisis, when properly fostered, yields an adult not only of superior intelligence and refinement, but also of greater physical stamina and vitality of spirit than is normal to the members of his group.[71]

Campbell also spoke of Eden, "the Kingdom of the Father ... spread upon the earth", unseen by most people, and the end of the world not being an event but a psychological transformation in which you see "not the world of solid things but a world of radiance".[72]

In a discussion with Mary Lutyens, Krishna spoke of himself as a freak. Buddha had gone through suffering and then threw it aside in enlightenment, he said. But Krishna said he was a freak who didn't go though "any" of that. Jesus may have been a freak, too, he said. Krishna believed that the "power" must have watched over his body from the moment it was born. Was it a question of the "power" wanting to manifest so that it created the boy or did the "power" see that Brahmin boy, an eighth child, and say that this was to be 'the' boy? The freak, Jiddu Krishnamurti, wanted to know if there were other people who had drunk the "waters" and would "carry on" the work.[73]

What most people would see as an out-of-control hubris in Krishna even had him, in a review his own *Notebook* published in May 1976, say that he had gone beyond the *Upanishads* and

Vedanta. Vedantists were maintaining the structure of knowledge whereas he began where tradition ended, asserting that freedom was "a first and last step", he wrote in a mock review. It's difficult to know whether in making such a statement, Krishna was aware of placing himself as part of a tradition, in going beyond it. He had always maintained that he did not have much knowledge of any system of philosophy, yet he was confident enough to assume authority about this ancient stream of thinking for the purposes of the review.[74]

Krishna continued on his self-illuminating lonesome trek to the threshold of his nineties without any obvious deterioration in his mind. But how long could his role as intellectual provocateur last? Krishna had said himself that he only lived to talk.

Krishna would not allow Mary Zimbalist to go with him to India in late-1985, when he was ninety, as she had been ill there the previous year. If he was about to die he'd phone her, he said, but he wouldn't die suddenly, he claimed, as it was all decided by "someone else". He couldn't tell her about it but knew that "the brain" would keep on as long as his body could, and his heart was still in good shape. Krishna's physician, Dr Parchure, travelled with him, assisting with his daily regime of exercises and giving him oil massages. Krishna still wanted to live to 120 but he knew that, regardless of whatever attempts he made to ameliorate the 'process' - through changes in diet, environment or exercise – it would have its way, and no less respect needed to be paid to the process of dying. Although Krishna was cut off from his closest companion, he dictated letters to Mary on a cassette recorder daily.[75]

Krishna's sense of timing, whether his own or that provided by a hidden "power", was certainly acute, as he channelled whatever knowledge he could through the forums arranged for him in the early 1980s. He gave a number of exceptional talks over those last few years of his life – in March 1982 he gave two talks to audiences of almost 3,000 people at Carnegie Hall in New York and in April 1983 he spoke to an even larger audience at the Felt Forum in Madison Square Garden. In the second Carnegie

Hall talk, in answer to the question, 'Does God exist?' Krishna said humans had invented 'God' out of misery and loneliness. "Personally" he had no belief in anything, he said, and if one was free from fear and sorrow there was no need for a 'god'. Presumably there was some difference between the 'personally-speaking' Krishna, who sounded a lot like an atheist or at the very least an agnostic, and the public figure who was 'protected' by someone or something – which some people could construe as 'god' - which he had told Mary Zimbalist about but couldn't explain. Krishna kept up his schedule of taxing public addresses as he approached the age of ninety. In 1982 and 1983 he took part in conferences with psychotherapists, arranged by Dr David Shainberg. In 1984 he was invited to take part in a symposium on 'Creativity in Science' at Los Alamos in New Mexico, and the following day spoke to a smaller audience of Fellows. He spoke to the Felt Forum in New York in April and gave a talk to the *Pacem in Terris Society* in the United Nations building. He returned there the next year but the audience was small and he said he wouldn't speak there again.[76]

More significantly, he was invited by Milton Friedman to give two talks at the Kennedy Centre in Washington and the hall was full. His performance was "radiant" and Lutyens chose to quote from a stand-out passage on sorrow from the talk:

> Can we look at sorrow as it actually is in us, and remain with it, hold it, and not move away from it? Sorrow is not different from the one who suffers. ... you will see for yourself, if you really look deeply, that there is an end to sorrow.[77]

But by far Krishna's finest sense of timing was his last talk of three held in Madras on 4 January 1986 – his last ever held in public, just six weeks before he died. His message ended on the theme of creation – the most "sacred" thing in life. If you'd made a mess of your life, change it today; if you were uncertain, be certain; think logically, otherwise you could not enter the world of creation, he said. He closed with the words, "It ends". Krishna held his hands in *namaskar* and after a pause, he said this was the last talk. "Do you want to sit together quietly," he asked? "All right, sirs, sit quietly for a while." After a few moments he asked,

"May we get up and go now?" and offered a final *namaskar* before leaving the platform. A mix of refined English and Brahmin cultural influences was evident in his demeanour.[78]

But it would be California that offered Krishna his last resting-place. Krishna did what he could to put affairs in order in the KFI, including appointing Dr P Krishna, who was Professor of Physics at the Benares Hindu University, as head of the Rajghat school. Professor Krishna, a nephew of Rukmini and cousin of Radha Burnier, was a little hesitant about taking on the responsibility but Krishna told him he felt in his heart that he was right for the job, and, as if he was running out of time, insisted Professor Krishna give him his acceptance without taking time to consider it.[79] At meetings in Madras before returning home, Krishna proscribed any of his centres becoming places of pilgrimage and forbade anyone from setting himself up as an authority on him or his teachings. A week after the last talk Krishna flew with Scott Forbes to Los Angeles via Singapore and Tokyo, suffering acute stomach pain during the 24-hour flight. On 13 January he saw Dr Gary Deutsch of Santa Paula and had a sonogram of his liver, gall-bladder and pancreas, which showed a "mass" on his liver. He was admitted to hospital a week later and X-rays showed obstruction of the bowel. He stayed in hospital for eight nights, with Mary Zimbalist, Dr Parchure, Scott Forbes, Erna and Theodor Lilliefelt taking it in shifts to stay with him. He was given "hyper-alimentation" intravenously to counteract his dramatic weight loss and morphine for the pain. He said the "other" could not reach him through the pain and he did not protest against the use of morphine, even though he had refused pain-killers all his life when he'd been going through the "process". Dr Parchure told him he "probably" had cancer, with the pancreas the primary source of malignancy. Krishna tape-recorded a request that his ashes be sent to three places – Ojai, Brockwood and India – but for the sites chosen not to become "holy" places of worship. He also asked for information about the traditional way of treating the corpse of a "holy" man in India. (When the answer came from Pundit Jagannath Upadhyaya in early February, Krishna said he did not want any ceremony.) On 30 January Krishna returned home from hospital to the *Pine Cottage* in Ojai. Perhaps a dozen close friends began to gather there from different parts of the world. On 7 February he asked for a tape recorder and recorded an exceptional statement about the "immense" intelligence that had been using his body for seventy years. The "Indians" had a lot of "damned" superstitions about it, he said: believing that through will the body could "go". But no one would find that "supreme" intelligence operating in a body again for many hundreds of years, was his conclusion. There would be none of "*that*" consciousness left behind when the body couldn't stand it any more, referring to the occupation of his own body. Krishnamurti was "very upset" when Scott Forbes tried to clarify what he'd said and he told him he had no right to interfere. Krishna now wanted to die. Pupul Jayakar visited him the day after he came home from hospital, carrying letters from Nandini, Sunanda and the Indian Prime Minister of India, Rajiv Gandhi, with whom he had dined the previous month. Pupul stayed until 16 February, leaving with a message for Nandini of Krishna's "real" - and then he corrected the word to "profound" - love. That night, after telling Mary Zimbalist to 'go to bed ... go to sleep', Krishna himself slept as she sat for hours, holding his left hand in hers. Scott Forbes and Dr Deutsch were also present as Krishna sank into a coma. His breath gradually slowed and his heart struck its last beat at ten minutes past midnight. Jiddu Krishnamurti had died three months short of his 91st birthday.

In the early hours of the morning, Mary, Dr Parchure and Scott washed Krishna's body and wrapped it in a length of *khadi* silk, with a warm cover he'd liked laid on top. Only a few people were allowed to see his corpse which was laid out on his bed in the sitting-room. One white camellia was placed at his feet. Mark Lee had made the arrangements for an early cremation that very same morning and Mary sat quietly beside her closest friend, now lost to her, holding his "child's feet, pliable as ever" as the time to leave drew near. She travelled with Krishna in the hearse as she'd promised to stay with him until the end. Only a few personal friends - Mary, the Lilliefelts, Asit Chandmal, Mark Lee,

Mahesh Saxena, Dr Parchure and Scott Forbes - were present at the cremation at 8 a.m. Krishna's ashes were kept to be finally scattered at seven sites – those places he had visited most often during his life.[80]

Krishna had spoken many times of the need to live with death. But perhaps his clearest statement came in a discussion with Pundit Jagannath Upadhyaya and Pupul. He told them that when a person is dying they do not need an intellectual understanding of what death is. A man is dying – unless the cause of his sorrow has been eliminated it cannot end - he has not eliminated sorrow – now he is dying. And he is not interested in philosophy. He needs someone who will hold his hand so that he knows the feeling of love. He needs a friend who has been living and dying all through life, never separating the two, and who understands the fear of death. Not a friend who *gives* love, as a separate being, but who is with the person facing the fear and says, 'when you die a part of me also dies'. A friend who says, 'Let us die - I understand your fear', so that death holds no fear.[81]

In telling this story Krishna was both the dying man and the friend. Both sufferer and comforter. Three days before his death, waiting for a shot of morphine to take effect, he said to Mary Zimbalist, "Too good to be true: sorrow I thought I had lost you". Mary was holding his hand when he passed into oblivion.[82]

Krishnamurti believed that people owe a guru nothing. One might point out how to dispel darkness but not expect devotion for the advice. Or another image: you're walking in the forest and another person suggests that if you walk a certain way you might arrive earlier. You walk, you arrive. It's as simple as that.[83]

Who was Krishnamurti? Guru, mystic or myth-maker, sinner or saint? It's impossible to say as he was so many different things to so many thousands of people: gnostic, charismatic, poet, friend, adversary, advisor, globetrotter. A poor but powerful child who became a child-like adult, a lover, a surrogate parent, a modernist, a traditionalist, a radical iconoclast, a conservative, a comforter, a questioner, a listener, a religious man, an atheist, an agnostic, an orator, a lecturer, a teacher, a world philosopher.

A chameleon from the jungle of human consciousness who'd escaped into thin air. At last he was free of others' image-making and judgements.

There is no resurrection, Krishna wrote in his last journal. That was superstition. But to live with death every day brought a sense of its "immensity" in place of fear.[84]

Controversy reigns over the value of Krishnamurti's teaching following his death and then the public exposure that he experienced a sexual life like so much of the rest of the human race.[85] The Foundations are considered by many to be too restrictive and protective of his image, no doubt their view based on Krishna's statements during his own lifetime that he wanted no one to be considered an authority on him, that there'd be no one like him again for hundreds of years, and that he wanted his teaching to continue in the schools. Millions of people under the age of forty have never heard of Krishnamurti, yet there's a persistence in his teaching, or at least in those aspects which emanate from the ancient wisdom of Advaitic Vedantist and Buddhist teaching, that breaks through in many forms of 'New Age' culture. Time will prove the ultimate test of the value of his life.[86]

Krishnamurti said he was nobody - that who he was, was not important. So what was important to find out in life? Krishna's answer, given to an unknown questioner from an audience, was to find out who and what you are.[87]

> He who consists of mind, whose body is the breath of life, whose form is light, whose idea is the real, whose self is space, through whom are all works, all desires, all scents, all tastes, who encompasses all this universe, who does not speak and has no care – he is my Self within the heart, smaller than a grain of rice or a barley-corn, or a mustard-seed, or a grain of millet, or the kernel of a grain of millet; this is my Self within my heart, greater than the earth, greater than the atmosphere, greater than the sky, greater than all these worlds. All works, all desires, all scents, all tastes belong to it: it encompasses all this universe, does not speak and has no care. This my Self within the heart is that Brahman. When I depart from hence I shall merge into it. He who believes this will never doubt.
>
> Chandogya Upanishad III, xiv, 3-5

Notes

Chapter 1 Boyhood Dreams

1 The author does not have a copy of Krishnamurti's birth certificate, unaware of whether it exists, considering the haphazard practice of birth registration in the late-19th century, but has taken the date from a horoscope published in *The Theosophist* April 1932 p 42. Earlier Theosophical Society accounts of Krishnamurti's birth give various dates, including 25 May 1896. Krishna's father, G Narianiah, gave the date as 4 May 1895 in a pamphlet published in 1913 to raise money to recover his sons in a custody court case. Although the dates differ, the tale of an astrologer declaring Krishna would be a great man is consistent. NSW State Records 5/7771.2 "Mrs Besant and the Alcyone Case" by Veritas 1913 Goodwin & Co Madras, a publication written in support of Krishna's father. The published horoscope was supplied by C. Jinarajadasa whose action in another significant matter concerning the verity of "astral" information has been questioned, so the author, while working with the birthdate information available, retains a measure of scepticism about the date. Information about the phase of the moon is supplied by Sydney Observatory. Astronomers calculated that on 11 May the moon rose at 20.21 hours and set on the morning of 12 May at 07.48. It would have had the appearance of a full moon but the exact full moon was the previous night, 10 May.

2 Krishnamurti – 'murti' in Sanskrit means model, embodiment or incarnation.

3 M Lutyens *The Boy Krishna* 1994 KF Trust Ltd Great Britain. All her biographical writing concerning Krishnamurti published during his lifetime was authorised by him.

4 M Lutyens (1994) makes the point that the English spelling of the name could be Geddu, Giddu, Jeddu or Jiddu. Krishnamurti's father namè is always spelt Geddu.

5 *The Theosophist* April 1932 p 42.

6 Statutory declaration given by Krishnamurti's nephew G Narayan January 1993 "J Krishnamurti Some Reminiscences by G Narayan". KFI Archives and M Lutyens (1994).

7 *Vargas* are astrological categories or divisions.

8 M Lutyens 1990 *The Life and Death of Krishnamurti* Rider London p 4. The Vedic horoscope was published in *The Theosophist* April 1932 pp 42-45. It has been interpreted by the Vedic astrologer Keven Barrett, with additional observations by Chris Turner from the Australian Association of Professional Astrologers.

9 M Lutyens (1994) p 14. Lutyens attributes this description of what is customary to Pupul Jayakar. P Jayakar. 1986 *Krishnamurti A Biography*, Harper & Row. San Francisco, p 17.

10 M Lutyens (1994) explains that at the age of eighteen. Krishnamurti, while on holiday at Varengeville in Normandy, wrote an autobiographical essay up to the year 1911, titled 'Fifty Years of My Life'. She quotes liberally from the sketch.

11 M Lutyens 1976 *Krishnamurti The Years of Awakening*. Avon. NY. reiterated in 1991 *The Life and Death of Krishnamurti* Rider London and also repeated by P Jayakar (1986). The mistake was corrected by Lutyens (1994). The *puja* room is where worship and sacred rituals are conducted.

12 During a visit to the house in December 1999, the author was shown the birth room and the *puja* room by the caretaker of the house. P Thyagamoorthy Sarma. Yantra patterns or *muggu*, are drawn in chalk on the floor of the birth room.

13 M Lutyens (1976) p 2. Thyagamoorthy explained to the author in 1999 that Krishnamurti's family was Velanadu Brahmin. Velanadu are popularly regarded as high-class Brahmins.

14 M Lutyens (1994) p 17.

15 M Lutyens (1994) p 16.

16 M Lutyens (1994) p 16.

17 Narasimha is said to have been Vishnu in his fourth incarnation, a lion among men.

18 M Lutyens (1994) p 18.

19 M Lutyen (1976) p 3.

20 M Lutyens (1976) p 4.

21 M Lutyens (1994) p 20. The author was told by the Theosophical Archivist at Adyar that all material relating to Krishnamurti was sent to the Krishnamurti Archives. The author was refused access to this material.

22 M Lutyens (1975) p 5. P Jayakar (1986) pp 19,20. Descriptions of auras have been a part of religious experience in both Eastern and Western creeds since the earliest dated records. Depictions have been found in temple caves and religious texts in India, Sri Lanka, Japan, Greece, Mexico and Peru. In the 16th century Paracelsus wrote of a vital force not enclosed in man but radiating around him like a luminous sphere. Although Krishna said that others in the family did not see his sister after her death, his father also claims to have seen his wife after her death.

23 President of the Hindu League and President of the TS from 1907.

24 M Lutyens (1994) p 16. Krishnamurti was aged eighteen when he wrote of this incident. *Karma* might be defined as the moral force and consequence of one's motives, thoughts and actions and is bound up with ideas of fate and reincarnation.

25 See HP Blavatsky 1972 *Isis Unveiled* Theosophical University Press Pasadena, 1962 *The Secret Doctrine* Theosophical Publishing House Madras & 1987 *Key to Theosophy* Theosophical Publishing House London. First published in 1888, *The Secret Doctrine* which began as a rewrite of *Isis Unveiled*, set forth Blavatsky's obscure cosmological explanation of a spiritual progress for the human race through successive evolutionary races and sub-races linked with different civilisations. She wrote of being "the reflection of an unknown light" and there was some speculation that this reflection of occult knowledge accounted for certain footnotes in her work being inverted – see Marion Meade 1980 *Madame Blavatsky The Woman Behind the Myth* Putnam's Sons New York p 180. However Meade shows that Blavatsky used trickery, including cutting a slit in a ceiling cloth to allow an envelope to fall through it from a second storey, to persuade others that her occult "Masters" were communicating with her and them, pp 217, 229. Blavatsky believed that following the decline of the Aryan 'root-race", a sixth would arise in the United States (and Australia), bringing physical and mental advancement for spiritual rejuvenation in humans. In 1922 the Society's Vice President C Jinarajadasa would speak of the "Australian face" and "definite characteristics appearing" and that "the very measurements of the cranium of Australians would soon be noticeably different from those of other races". Although Ceylonese, he was reported not to be an opponent of the racist White Australia immigration policy as he thought "young white races should be free to develop ... in their own way" but they could "no longer treat colored races as inferior", *Theosophy in Australia* May 1922 p 386. See also Leadbeater's booklet *Australia, the Home of a New Sub-Race*, mentioned in an article by Harold Morton, "The Powers Which Guide Australia", *The Australian Theosophist* 15 September 1928, p 41. The President, Mrs Besant, spoke in 1926 of a "New Age" and in 1927 of Blavatsky predicting in the second volume of *The Secret Doctrine* the coming of the sixth race in the United States which would develop from "peculiar children" and the "new human type, the sixth sub-race, now multiplying in California", *The Theosophist* February 1926 p 558, April 1927 p 6e, 6f and June 1927 p 269. She maintained these Californian children, according to "Bergson Intuition", recognised truth at sight rather than through reasoning. The French philosopher, Henri Bergson, was awarded the Nobel Prize for Literature in 1927 for his work which aimed to integrate research from biological science with a theory of consciousness and argued that intuition is deeper than the intellect. However the author has not found any evidence that Bergson agreed with Annie Besant that a new "sub-race" was developing in California. Mrs Besant also referred to "American anthropologists", including a Dr Hrdlika she described as the "greatest" of them, as saying that "perhaps" a sub-race was appearing most numerously in California, *Herald of the Star* March

1927 p 94. Dr Hrdlika was reported to be an anthropologist at the Smithsonian Institute whose psychological tests showed a "startling proportion of child prodigies". Gertrude Marvin Williams 1931 *The Passsionate Pilgrim A Life of Annie Besant* Coward-McCann NY p 329.

26 An excerpt from *The Secret Doctrine* Vol 3 pp 298-303 gives an impression of Blavatsky's anti-Darwinian stance as she argues a case for the existence of a 'third eye' in humans before their physical development and concomitant 'spiritual' regression into their current physical form. She proposes that the pineal gland is an atrophied 'third eye'. Natural selection was a pure myth, she said, as an explanation of the origin of variations, since survival of the fittest could only take place following "useful" variation. On the question of the source of Blavatsky's occult doctrine, Brendan French in his 2000 unpublished doctoral thesis *The Theosophical Masters: An Investigation into the Conceptual Domains of HP Blavatsky and CW Leadbeater* Vol I pp 80-81 says that "For Blavatsky, Egypt, as the crucible of Hermeticism, was the *fons et origo* of arcane lore ...[and] represented a primordial religious idyll". He maintains that Blavatsky's appropriation of Egyptian and Indian motifs might be viewed as a "synthetic universalist superstructure wedded to a preexisting, *thoroughly Western* infrastructure".

27 C Jinarajadasa in 1922 puts the number of Lodges at almost 1,350 worldwide and the due-paying membership at more than 45,000, *Theosophy in Australia* May 1922 p 404. Jill Roe 1986 *Beyond Belief Theosophy in Australia 1879-1939*, New South Wales University Press Sydney p 288 puts the 1925 membership of the Order of the Star in the East, set up for the World Teacher, at 40,000 people living in forty countries, two-thirds of whom were Theosophical Society members. Anne Taylor 1992 *Annie Besant A Biography* Oxford University Press p 328 says the Society's membership, estimated at 15,000 in 1907, peaked at 45,000 in 1928.

28 Handwritten letter signed by Blavatsky 1 April 1891 reproduced in *The Theosophist* June 1932 p 230. Annie Besant herself explained in her pamphlet in 1916 *A World Religion* Theosophical Publishing House Madras her understanding that the events on earth were projections or shadows thrown down on the earth by the spiritual truths of the universe and the need to awaken our faculties to know this.

29 G Tillett 1982 *The Elder Brother A biography of Charles Webster Leadbeater* Routledge & Kegan Paul London pp 42, 62. Tillett also exposes a discrepancy between Leadbeater's professed birth date and the actual date – 16 February 1854 and 17 February 1847.

30 The group, *Arya Samaj*, was founded by Dayananda Saraswati. According to NC Ramanujachary 1987 in "T Subba Row, 'The Secret Doctrine' and Madame HP Blavatsky", *Theosophical History* Vol 2 No 3 July, p 101, Blavatsky wrote an obituary for Swami Dayananda Saraswati in her journal when he died but their association had been very short-lived

and uneventful. Marion Meade (1980) pp 181-213, 254 says Saraswati's *Arya Samaj* agitated for aboliton of the caste system among other Hindu abuses. The purposes of the Theosophical Society and *Arya Samaj* seemed identical so an amalgamation was proposed, the Society incorporating *Arya Samaj* into its title about 1878. But by 1880 the Swami severed his connection with the Society, ordering his name be struck off the membership rolls, and afterwards printing handbills denouncing Blavatsky as an atheist and liar.

31 Lutyens(1976) p 11. A Trevor Barker (transcriber) 1975 *The Mahatma Letters to AP Sinnett* Theosophical University Press, Pasadena California Letter IX. To take an excerpt on p 44 as an example of the style: "Whether Imperator is a 'planetary' embodied or disembodied, whether he is an adept in flesh or out of it, I am not at liberty to say, any more than he would himself to tell S.M. who I am, or may be, or even who H.P.B. is. If he himself chooses to be silent on that subject S.M. has no right to ask *me*". See HE and WL Hare 1936 *Who Wrote the Mahatma Letters?* Williams & Norgate London. HE Hare pp 18-21 wrote that, after extensive research and sometime membership of the Theosophical Society by his brother, WL Hare, they had revealed in the book "the sandy foundations" provided by the "Mahatma Letters". He referred to "the ultimate authority of a hierarchy of 'Oriental sages' whose existence is fictitious, and whose teaching is discredited. F Edmund Garrett 1896 *Isis Is Very Much Unveiled* Westminster Gazette Office London p 9 says Blavatsky located the Mahatmas in the "recesses of the Himalayas" yet one of her most zealous disciples said they "now reside in an oasis of the Desert of Gobi". See B French (2000) p 200 for references to the Gobi desert and Tibet.

32 NC Ramanujachary (1987) p 96.

33 According to Ramanujachary (1987) p 100, T Subba Row followed a Raja Yoga school called 'Taraka'. G Feuerstein, *The Shambala Encyclopaedia of Yoga*, Shambala, Boston, 1997 p 305 describes this school as a Vedanta-based yoga widespread in medieval India, central to its approach being photistic phenomena occurring during meditation, considered to be a manifestation of the Absolute as 'deliverer'.

34 NC Ramanajachary (1987) pp 97-103.

35 NC Ramanujachary (1987) p 98.

36 Advaita Vedanta is defined by G Feuerstein (1997) as the metaphysics expounded in the Upanishads and scriptures based on the Upanishads. Shankara, believed to have lived 788- 822 CE, revived this ancient tradition, resulting in its renaissance in the face of the spread of Buddhism. He espoused non-duality, the knowledge found in mystical experience that there is only one being, without a second, and that being is Brahman/atman, or put more simply, God/individual self, as one whole. Scholars have noted that Adwaitism or Advaita philosophy plays a vital part in Krishnamurti's talks on 'the Unknown' and 'duality'. Discussed further in later chapters.

37 NC Ramanujachary (1987) p 99 reference taken from Introduction by Boris de Zirkoff to *The Secret Doctrine*, 1978, TPH, Adyar pp 2, 3, reportedly based on a letter held by Adyar Archives.

38 See J Roe (1986) p 18. Roe writes that Hodgson, a Bachelor of Arts from Melbourne and friend of Prime Minister Alfred Deakin, and the psychical researcher, Professor Henry Sedgewick, wrote the report on Blavatsky for the British Psychical Research Society.

39 See Vernon Harrison 1997, *HP Blavatsky and the SPR An Examination of the Hodgson Report of 1885*, Theosophical University Press Pasadena California p 3. Harrison says the Hodgson Report is not a model of what impartial and painstaking research should be but "the work of a man who has reached his conclusions early on in his investigation and thereafter, selecting and distorting evidence, did not hesitate to adopt flawed arguments to support his thesis". It might be argued that Harrison's case would receive greater acceptance if it found publication independently of the Theosophical Society.

40 J Roe (1986) p 11.

41 The size of the estate increased from 27 to 253 acres during the first five years of Annie Besant's Presidency. G Marvin Williams (1931) p 270.

42 In his biography of George Bernard Shaw, Hesketh Pearson describes Annie Besant, whom Shaw had persuaded to join the Fabians, as "easily the greatest public speaker in London, and possibly in Europe". He writes a wry anecdote of their attendance at the Bloody Sunday 1887 mass meeting of unemployed in Trafalgar Square when, faced by the forward section of the march being pursued and bludgeoned by police, Shaw dropped all attempts at heroics and told Besant, "You must keep out of this", whereupon she vanished, and he then cried, "Let every man get to the Square as best he can". Mrs Besant, described as indomitable, collected funds, enlisted newspaper support, "dashed into the police courts and stormed the witness stands", then "moved a resolution to return to the square [the next Sunday] and continue the fight to the bitter end in a speech of such magnificence that the applause shook the building". It turned out that there was no right of meeting in Trafalgar Square. Shaw and Besant used to play piano duets together and she serialised his novels in her magazine *Our Corner* and appointed him art critic. Their close relationship ended after a contract for them to live together as man and wife, supposedly drawn up by Besant, frightened Shaw off. Their correspondence was thrown into the fireplace and destroyed after this breach. H Pearson (1944) *Bernard Shaw His Life and Personality* Collins London pp 80-84, 113.

43 G Marvin Williams (1931) pp 189-97. It was the journalist and editor of the *Pall Mall Gazette*, and later *The Review of Reviews*, WT Stead, who gave *The Secret Doctrine* to Annie Besant for review. He later wrote of her that he never saw in her anything that was not consistent with the

character of a saint. See WT Stead 1946 *Annie Besant A Character Sketch 1891* Theosophical Publishing House Madras (with a Foreword by C Jinarajadasa) pp viii & 86. See also Annie Besant 1916 *A World Religion* Theosophical Publishing House Madras.

44 Annie Besant was an extraordinary figure in politics and public life in the late 19th and early 20th centuries. Her separation from an English Anglican minister in 1873 and the ensuing court case over custody of her children, which she lost, launched her into the national spotlight. The following year she became an office-holder in the National Secular Society and in turn became the close associate of the social reformer and free-thinker, Charles Bradlaugh, Dr EB Aveling and playwright George Bernard Shaw. She publicly supported birth control, political rights for women and socialism, joining the Fabian Society, and was famous as a prolific writer and forceful orator. Her meeting with Madame Blavatsky of the TS in 1889 was a major turning point in Besant's life, and she remained devoted to her until Blavatsky's death in 1891. Besant first visited India in 1893 and met the learned Dr Bhagavan Das in Benares and another friend, the mystic, Professor Gyanendra N. Chakravarti in Allahabad, who was said to have enchanted and influenced her over the next decade, until Leadbeater challenged him in this role. Mrs Besant remained on good terms with Chakravarti, however, having lunch with him during her golden jubilee year as a public speaker, 1924, according to Nethercot (1963) p 347. G Marvin Williams (1931) pp 210-11 says Chakravarti represented the Indian Theosophists at the 1893 World Parliament of Religions, that he was skilled in hypnotism and Besant had initially accepted him as her guru. Sylvia Cranston 1993 *HPB The Extraordinary Life and Influence of Helena Blavatsky* Putnam's Sons New York p 426 indicates that Chakravarti, who was a Theosophist, joined with Vivekananda in presenting Hinduism at the World Parliament. Besant set up the Central Hindu College for the education of boys in Benares in 1898. By 1913 she had become involved in Indian politics on a platform of self-government and was elected president of the Indian National Congress 1917-1923.

45 M Lutyens (1990) p 4.

46 Krishna's brother Nitya wrote to Leadbeater in 1923 that he had thought his mother died in 1907 but was mistaken as she died in 1905. 28 February 1923, KFI.

47 M Lutyens (1976) p 5-6.

48 M Lutyens (1990) p 5. The author has not sighted this document.

49 Veritas (1913) pp 19, 20. NSW State Records 5/7771.2. This account was published with Narianiah's support and is therefore probably the most accurate account of his point of view.

50 Krishnamurti's nephew, G Narayan, in a statutory declaration in 1993 said Shivaram was the eldest son and Krishna was the eighth of eleven chil-

dren, only six of whom survived. The cause of death of Krishnamurti's mother is also not given in Lutyens' biographies. Death of mother and child in or immediately after childbirth might account for the lack of an account of an eleventh child. In her refutation of Radha Rajagopal Sloss's biography of Krishnamurti, in 1996, *Krishnamurti and the Rajagopals*, KFA California, p 4, M Lutyens writes of Narianiah's "four surviving sons", once again leaving unclear the circumstances surrounding the deaths of other children. The situation is further confused perhaps by an account of Krishna and Nitya having one older brother, one younger brother, an adopted brother and two other boys, who were either distant relatives or friends of the family, living with them in Adyar before they moved onto the estate. Captain R. Balfour Clarke "The Childhood of Krishnaji" *Australian Theosophist* Aug 1928 pp 9-14. E Wood 1936 *Is This Theosophy?* Rider & Co London p 133 refers to four sons and three wards. In a letter to Narianiah in February 1912 Mrs Besant makes a reference to his 13 children. Lady Emily Lutyens (1957) pp 25, 27 knew Krishna well as an adolescent and makes two references to Narianiah having fourteen children.

51 G Tillett (1982) p 286. Tillett p 196 describes as "simply untrue" Leadbeater saying in 1922 that a 1908 committee which included eminent judges and barristers had cleared him of sex charges in 1906, since there were no lawyers on the in-house Society committee.

52 Transcript of interview with author 8 September 1999 held by author.

53 E Wood (1936) p 132.

54 Besant's biographer, Arthur H Nethercot 1963 *The Last Four Lives of Annie Besant* Rupert Hart-Davis 1963 pp 97, 107, 119-120 says Besant sent a telegram to the Blavatsky Lodge saying she would reinstate Leadbeater two years after he publicly repudiated his teaching in regard to masturbation but there is no record of his repudiation. Rather, Nethercot says Leadbeater wrote to Besant that one of his last reincarnations had been in ancient Greece - where pederast propensities had been regarded quite differently from at present.

55 M Lutyens (1976) p 22.

56 Balfour Clarke (August 1928) p 10.

57 Krishna's eyes were *sanpaku*, a Japanese term used to describe eyes where the whites are noticeable underneath the iris.

58 In Evelyne Blau 1995 *Krishnamurti 100 Years* Stewart Tabori & Chang NY p 50 Helen Knothe Nearing says that in 1921 Krishna called Mrs Besant 'Amma', which is 'Mother' in Tamil and Telugu. As Mary Lutyens explains in 1959 *To Be Young* Hart-Davis London p 121, many Theosophists referred to Mrs Besant as 'Amma'.

59 *The Theosophist* May 1932 pp125-128. Date of letter indecipherable. 'Maya' is a Sanskrit word from the Vedas generally understood as 'illusion', but more specifically, in most Shankara-based Advaitic (non-dual-

ity) schools of thought, it means 'relative existence', in contrast to the absolute 'Reality' which is non-dual.

60 HP Blavatsky 1962 *The Secret Doctrine* Theosophical Publishing House Madras p 300. For a comprehensive discussion of Blavatsky's ideas and their links with esoteric traditions including Hinduism, Buddhism, Hermeticism, Kabbalism and Neoplatonsim, as well as Blavatsky's challenge to Darwinism, see B French (2000) pp 81, 189-94, 197, 245.

61 G Marvin Williams (1931) p 312 points out that in *Isis Unveiled*, Blavatsky's purpose was to show that the apostolic succession was a fraud, which might be considered ironic considering she herself was accused of fraud. B French (2000) p 603 says Blavatsky tried to "remythify a universe she believed had been denuded of its numinosity" as "[N]either Church nor Academy offered sustenance to a world whose protective divinities were being undermined by materialist science and Positivist philosophy". B French (2000) p 236 gives the dates of Blavatsky's editorship (with some assistance from Mabel Collins Cook and Annie Besant) of *Lucifer* from 15 September 1888 until her death in 1891.

62 Maurice Maeterlinck (tr Bernard Miall) 1922 *The Great Secret* Methuen London p 204 believed that the "defects" of Blavatsky's method of exposition in *The Secret Doctrine* were "emphasised and aggravated" by her successors, Besant and Leadbeater, whose "gratuitous assertions, incapable of proof, seem to rain down thicker and thicker on every page". He also pointed to Scott-Elliot's work on Atlantis which he said began with references to historical texts but moved to "occult documents" and claims which Scott-Elliot discussed "as though they were on the same footing as historical and geographical evidence".

63 "Esoteric Teachings of HP Blavatsky" *The Theosophist* June 1932 p 229. Letter from Patricia Sinnett to Mr Christie 13 May 1891 published in *The Theosophist* May 1929 p 126. G Tillett (1982) p 53 says Blavatsky's mistake in an inscription to Leadbeater in a copy of her book, *The Voice of Silence*, calling him "WC Leadbeater" instead of "CW Leadbeater", has led to much speculation.

64 E Wood (1936) pp 294, 306. Tillett (1982) p 63 maintains that Mrs Besant had shown no inclination to psychic gifts prior to her meeting with Leadbeater but developed them overnight (as she said) under his influence and by 1895 they were publishing accounts of their joint astral investigations. Emily Lutyens 1957 *Candles in the Sun*, Rupert Hart-Davis London p 41 says that in 1912 Besant was clairvoyant but 'not long afterwards she deliberately laid aside her psychic powers in order to concentrate on her work for Home Rule for India, and thereafter she relied on CWL [Leadbeater] and one or two others for all occult revelations, putting her faith in them implicitly'.

65 Tillett interview with author (8 September 1999). G Feuerstein (1997) pp185-6.

66 Tillett (1982) p 7. Marvin Williams (1931) p 256-57 says that at the time of Leadbeater's forced resignation from the TS in 1906 he was zealous in writing to Besant about their close relationship, that it was supreme, and his membership of the TS, his position in the world and his other friendships were nothing by comparison, reminding her of their meetings 'out of the body and even in the presence of our Masters and of the Lord Himself'. Marvin Williams took the information from correspondence submitted as evidence in the case of G Narianiah vs Mrs Annie Besant in the Indian High Court Madras 15 April 1913.

67 G Marvin Williams (1931) p 254.

68 Tillett (1982) p 5.

69 E Wood (1936) p 305.

70 M Lutyens (1994) p 22-24.

71 G Marvin Williams (1931) pp 272-73 writes that on an American tour Besant had told newspaper reporters that Blavatsky's reincarnation had occurred in the body of a fourteen year old Hindu boy in 1892. But the idea was dropped and the boy sent on a trip to Tibet to study with the Mahatmas. According to A Nethercot (1963) p 192-93, Hubert van Hook, the son of an American theosophist, was also considered as a potential Saviour for a period before allegations of Leadbeater's sexual interference with the boy surfaced. Lutyens (1976) p 45 writes in a Footnote that Hubert swore that Leadbeater had misused him and although she admits that his testimony was "unshaken" she dismisses it as "not altogether reliable", claiming the young man was "extremely vindictive".

72 M Lutyens (1990) p 5. The Esoteric Section, set up by Blavatsky, was the inner core of the Society. Eligibility to join was only offered to those with a minimum two years membership of the Society.

73 *The Theosophist* June 1932 pp 238-245. Jinarajadasa chose and edited the extracts of correspondence.

74 M Lutyens (1976) p 23.

75 Lutyens (1994) p 26. Krishnamurti writes in 1982, *Krishnamurti's Journal* KFT, Hampshire, September 23 1973 p 26 that he didn't remember his childhood but was told years later by his teacher that he was caned practically every day because he couldn't study or remember anything he read or was told. The teacher was surprised that he had become the man who gave the lecture he'd just heard and was unnecessarily respectful.

76 Lutyens (1976) p 8 and *The Theosophist* June 1932 pp 238-245.

77 *The Theosophist* June 1932 pp 238-245.

78 *Theosophy in Australia* July 1922 p 458. Lutyens (1976) p 26-28. Lady Emily Lutyens (1957) pp 26-27.

79 *Theosophy in Australia* July 1922 p 458.

80 Derivative of the word 'halcyon' meaning peaceful, carefree, calm, from the Latin *alcyon* and Greek *alkuon*, kingfisher. In Greek myth the fabulous bird is associated with the winter solstice and calm weather. BP Wadia (*The Theosophist* Jan 1911 p 673) traced it as an ancient Persian name and this information was later expanded in exposing Leadbeater as a plagiarist. See Fn below. Annie Besant's biographer, Arthur Nethercot, notes that Leadbeater's amateur interest in astronomy gave rise to his choice of names of people who appeared in his descriptions of past lives. Nethercot says that Alcyone was pronounced 'Alkyone' by most Theosophists although a few argue for the 'Anglicised' 'Alsyone'. Arthur H Nethercot (1963) p 140.

81 *The Theosophist* June 1932 pp 238–245.

82 *The Theosophist* June 1932 pp 238–245.

83 E Blau (1995) p 15.

84 *The Theosophist* June 1932 pp 238 –245.

85 *Theosophy in Australia* July 1922 pp 454-458.

86 Lady Emily Lutyens 1957 *Candles in the Sun* Rupert Hart-Davis London p 23.

87 Lutyens (1976) p 25. Shiva Rao was a long-time tutor to Krishna, an editor of Mrs Besant's publication, *New India*, and later a representative in Madras of *The Hindu* newspaper.

88 *The Theosophist* June 1932 p 244. E Wood (1936) says candidly that he had spent ten thousand hours with Leadbeater in Adyar by 1913, working with him during that time to produce half of his total literary output, a not inconsiderable achievement. Nethercot (1963) p 141 makes the point that Wood was both a believer and a sceptic, wanting to believe in Leadbeater and Besant's revelations but too acute an observer to fail to notice discrepancies.

89 E Wood (1936) pp 135, 136, 139-142.

90 Tillett (1982) p 119.

91 Wadia's first recantation in *Occult Review* April 1923 p 246 came as a response to an article in the journal in January 1923 pp 30-38 by William Loftus Hare in which he exposed a passage from 'the Lives' as plagiarised from the *Shahnameh* by the ancient Persian poet, Firdausi, available in English translation since 1832. Hare said he believed "Leadbeater did not extract his Zarathustra date from the akashic records, but from a more cheap and handy volume" and challenged Wadia's testimony of Leadbeater's seership. See also *The Theosophist* Jan 1911 p 673, September 1911 pp 933-34 & May 1938 p 176 for Wadia statements. Also Tillett (1982) pp 118-122 & Hugh Gillespie *Canadian Theosophist* May 1934 pp 83-86. BP Wadia resigned from the Society in 1922 and a statement he addressed to colleagues was published as a supplement to the October 1922 edition. The author has not been able to locate this supplement. Wadia later became associated with the United Lodge of

Theosophists and anonymously edited a monthly magazine founded in 1930, *The Theosophical Movement*. In 1962, four years after his death, the Indian Institute of World Culture, which he also founded, published articles he wrote for *The Theosophical Movement* as a book, *Living the Life*. Wadia is credited with setting up the first trade union in India, the Madras Labour Union. Annie Besant wrote in October 1922 of the loss of Wadia who had been "drifting away from his old moorings" and wished him well. She said the "Non-Co-operation Press" was jubilant over him abandoning the Society but naturally those who wanted to separate India from Britain rejoiced over any weapon they could use against her as she stood for "Indian Freedom and respect for Law against mob-tyranny and anarchy". *The Theosophist* October 1922 pp 3, 8.

92 E Wood (1936) pp 141, 299-301, 317-318 writes that he believes "there is a *small* foundation of fact" in psychic experiences but there is "a vast superstructure which is completely false, being the product of that state of mind in which dreams originate". Following what he considered an unfair campaign against him for the Presidency of the Theosophical Society in 1933 by Arundale, Wood came to detest theosophical politics with its "perpetual circles of mutual admiration".

93 Lutyens (1991) pp 9-10 says Clarke and another woman vouched that the notes were written down by Krishna with great laboriousness and the only help he received was with spelling and punctuation. In her earlier work, M Lutyens (1976) p 47-8, writes that it's always been debatable whether Krishna wrote the work and as his original notes have not survived there is no way of telling to what extent Leadbeater revised them. In the same biography (1976) p 63, Mary Lutyens makes a point of defending Krishna's authorship of another work, *Education as Service*, written in 1912 which Lady Emily Lutyens (her mother) had declared obviously the work of his tutor, George Arundale. Mary Lutyens writes that in view of correspondence from Krishna saying he wrote it, Lady Emily overstated Arundale's part in its composition although Krishna's style would have been influenced by his tutor. Lady Emily Lutyens (1957) pp 27-28 wrote that someone closely associated with Krishna's early training told her that the teachings in the book [*At the Feet of the Master*] were dictated to Krishna by Leadbeater and that the style and matter left little room for doubt that its real inspiration was Leadbeater. She believed it would have been easy for him to impress on the dreamy boy's mind these sentences supposedly from 'the Master' and while Krishna was to some extent mediumistic he was never a conscious party to any fraud.

94 *Theosophy in Australia* July 1922 p 458.

95 E Wood (1936) pp 160-163. Leadbeater (1922) in *Talks On 'At the Feet of the Master'*. Theosophical Publishing House Adyar p 37 maintains that Krishna wrote the book, pontificating that he should bear testimony to it - to the "fact" that he "knew" and that he himself "saw", along with the

President, [even though she was not present] the scraps of paper, exercise books and so on, on which Krishna's sentences were written each morning. He said that having heard these teachings he had on several occasions used parts when speaking to members. The author has never been allowed access to such exercise books despite requests to the Theosophical Adyar Archives and to the Krishnamurti Archives so she cannot verify if they presently exist, or have ever existed. The contribution of another tutor, Dick Balfour Clarke, to the debate is his testimony in 1928 that he knew Krishna wrote the book at age thirteen because he saw him writing day by day with his own eyes what Krishna's Master had ostensibly said to him the night before during sleep. He then goes on to quote Leadbeater's account from 1925 in *The Masters and the Path*, Theosophical Publishing House, Adyar, that every night he, Leadbeater, had to take Krishna in his astral body to the house of the Master and then when Krishna had gone to Benares with Mrs Besant he wrote to Leadbeater and asked him to send to him all the notes Krishna had made of what the Master had said. Leadbeater said he arranged the notes as well as he could and typed them all out. As an indication of Leadbeater's awareness of a need for literary editing, he says he then checked the notes with the Master who altered a word or two and added some "connecting and explanatory notes, and a few other sentences", and then with the Lord Maitreya who read them and approved, saying "You should make a nice little book of this to introduce Alcyone to the world". Clarke also describes how after Mrs Besant's arrival in November the two boys moved into a bed-sitting room with a bathroom almost adjoining her own quarters. Leadbeater lived in a bungalow nearby but would have had free access to the main building. She left for Benares within a month and by early January had notified Leadbeater that her room was to be used for Krishna's major Initiation. See also R Balfour Clarke (Aug 1928) pp 9-14. See also M Lutyens (1976) p 47. The passage has been deleted from M Lutyens' abridged 1990 biography, *The Life and Death of Krishnamurti*, pp 9, 10, with a reference included that Balfour Clarke and "a lady living at Adyar" both vouched "for the fact that these notes were written down by Krishna himself with great laboriousness and that the only help he received was with spelling and punctuation". Krishna was awarded the Society's Subba Rao Medal in 1911 despite the fact that there was some controversy about whether the boy had written it, and the fact that Subba Rao fell out with Blavatsky and resigned from the Society in 1887, indicating the Theosophists' propensity for retrospective blindness to facts.

96 E Wood (1936) p 161.

97 Lady Emily Lutyens (1957) pp 27-28.

98 E Blau (1995) p 18.

99 CW Leadbeater 1979 *The Masters and the Path* Theosophical Publishing House Madras "The Way to the Master" p 52.

100 See also CW Leadbeater 1922 *Talks on At the Feet of the Master* Theosophical Publishing House Madras p 37 in which Leadbeater says the sentences were written down morning after morning "over a period of five months or so". In 1975 A Besant and CW Leadbeater *Talks on the Path of Occultism* Vol I p 3 "At the Feet of the Master" (first published 1926) Leadbeater says the book *At the Feet of the Master* was given by a "Master" to the young disciple J Krishnamurti, "called Alcyone...", when he was a boy of "thirteen" [sic] and his knowledge of English was "not perfect", so the instruction had to be "especially" clear. "The Master Kuthumi who had "marvellous" adaptability made it "wonderfully" simple, he said.

101 From author's research in Adyar Bookshop, Sydney, 20 July 1999.

102 Lutyens (1976) p 54 explains that Krishna's hair was cut shoulder length as Prince Siddartha had cut his hair to the shoulders with his sword when he left his home to seek enlightenment. Tillett (1982) p 151 writes that Krishnamurti was directed by the Master through Leadbeater to part his hair in the middle and underline his signature, both practices of deep esoteric significance. The hairstyle was an imitation of the Lord Buddha and a considerable number of Krishnamurti's disciples copied it.

103 Letter Besant to Krishna 19 December 1912 Huntington 9/22.

104 Lutyens (1991) pp 9, 45. Also E Blau (1995) p 13, which shows a page of Krishna's handwritten essay from 1913.

105 *Krishnamurti's Journal* 1982 KFI Madras p 23.

106 Lily Heber *The Man and his Message* 1931 Allen & Unwin London p 49-50.

107 Wood (1936) p 149.

108 Captain R. Balfour Clarke (Aug1928) pp 9-14. Clarke poetically claims he saw and touched "the cradle wherein that Holy Child was oft-times rocked to sleep by his well-beloved mother" in their Madanapalle home. He does not write whether it was made of cloth, as Pupul Jayakar maintains, or not. Considering the family had been moving about from town to town and Krishna's mother had had at least two more children after the birth of Krishna in the fifteen years before Balfour Clarke visited the home, the sanctity of the cradle might be questioned. Clarke gives the probable birthdate for Krishna as 25 May 1896, which has since been revised. He also writes that he was unusually thrilled and his interest in occult matters greatly stimulated when he was asked to attend in his sleep the astral occasion when Krishna was 'Accepted' by his Master, and he, Balfour Clarke, had a "personal fragmentary remembrance" of this when he woke the next morning. He showed great willingness to accept the descriptions of others' astral experiences which had occurred in the night as if they were "facts which were as real as the Central Railway Station in Sydney". There is no attempt by him to differentiate these astral experiences from dream.

109 Based on descriptions by R Balfour Clarke (1928) p 56. Lutyens (1976) pp 36-42. Lutyens (1991) p 11.

110 R Balfour Clarke (Sept 1928) pp 56-59. Lutyens (1976) p 36-7 says that Leadbeater wrote to Annie Besant on 12 January (the day after Krishna "woke") that Krishna had intended to write the description out by hand but it would have taken him two days and he was so tired that Mrs Russak, a Theosophist, offered to type it for him from Leadbeater's notes. Leadbeater goes on to say that the father behaved capitally, embraced Krishna affectionately, prostrated himself before Leadbeater and rejoiced exceedingly.

Chapter 2 A Sentimental Education

1 E Wood (1936) p 125-26.

2 Balfour Clarke (1928) pp 11, 12, 14.

3 Balfour Clarke (1928) p 11. Veritas (1913) p 27 sets the date of Narianiah's letter giving guardianship to Mrs Besant as 6 March 1909 but this is clearly incorrect as it is cited as subsequent to 14 December 1909. M Lutyens (1976) also refers to the guardianship document signed by Narianiah on 6 March 1910, p 68. In correspoendence with the author 23 January 2002 the Public Record Office in England makes the point that under English law there was no legal mechanism for adoption of children until 1927 so the arrangement must have been a private one.

4 E Wood (1936) pp148, 149, 150.

5 A Besant's talk to a Star Meeting at Ojai 11 January 1927 published in *The Theosophist* April 1927 p 15. It's interesting that in this version of the Initiation Besant is asked whether she will ***guard*** Krishna with her ***power*** whereas Leadbeater is asked whether he will ***guide*** him with his ***wisdom***, pointing up their respective roles.

6 E Wood (1936) p 162-63.

7 Correspondence Annie Besant to Krishna 24 Sentember, 3 October and 19 December 1912. Huntington 9/22.

8 Balfour Clarke (1928) p 157.

9 In the Madras High Court case Narianiah claimed he had considered Mrs Besant semi-divine.

10 F Morton writing in *The Triad* 10 June 1922 republished in *Theosophy in Australia* Aug 1922 p 486 says that he didn't know why he fell in love with Besant, dressed as she was in a shapeless dress and wearing no make-up, but he went on to describe her as good, sincere and strong.

11 Tillett (1982) p128. E Wood (1936) p 143.

12 G Marvin Williams pp 275-76.

13 G Marvin Williams (1931) pp 274-277, A Nethercot (1963) pp 159-160, E Lutyens (1976) pp 49-50. Lutyens' version glosses over the controversy, implying that the first Order was aimed at helping prepare the scene in

India while the second was enthusiastically taken up to turn it into an international organisation. It's interesting to note the emphasis laid on the belief that Krishna could "magnetise" by his touch, for example by touching ribbons, an idea which Franz Mesmer had made famous in the late 18th century and had grown out of Paracelsus' interest in the power of magnets in the 16th century. Joseph E Ross 1989 *Krotona of Old Hollywood 1866-1913* Vol I El Montecito Oaks Press Montecito California pp 148-49 says the Temple of the Rosy Cross (TRC) was established in July 1912 by Mrs Besant, Marie Russak and JI Wedgwood to study a range of Western esoteric or occult traditions. Ross cites a letter dated 7 July 1912 from C Jinarajadasa to AP Warrington in the United States which states that the London Temple's officers included GS Arundale as "Pontiff" and himself as "Preceptor". The officers were appointed by "Krishnaji", Jinarajadasa said. Yet Mrs Besant wrote to Krishna in 1912 that as he had said that he would like to enter the Temple of the Rosy Cross it was as well that he should. Letter dated 21 July 1912. Huntington 9/22. It's interesting that even in 1924 Krishna wrote an editorial filled with references to the rose of the soul – the scent of the rose, the happy rose, the powerful rose, the "beauteous" rose, the "Eternal" rose and the wise man who was a "disciple" of the "Rose". For Krishna the image of the rose also carried strong connotations of his feeling for Rosalind, undisclosed at this time. *Herald of the Star* January 1924 pp 2-4.

14 Onan, son of Judah, resisted intercourse with his deceased brother's widow, 'spilling his semen on the ground' since the progeny would not be his but his brother's child, and the Lord, displeased, slew him. Genesis 38:9-10.

15 A Nethercot (1963) p 156.

16 E Wood (1936) p 163.

17 A Nethercot (1963) pp 156-59. A pamphlet published in 1913 to raise funds for a legal appeal by Narianiah refers to the Hindu article being published on 13 March 1911, reprinted from an earlier article written and published by Dr Nair and a Dr U Rama Rao in the medical journal, *Antiseptic*.

18 A Nethercot (1963) p 163; M Lutyens (1976) p 51.

19 Clayre Percy and Jane Ridley (eds) 1988 *The Letters of Edwin Lutyens to his wife, Lady Emily*, Hamish Hamilton London p 220. Letter dated 8.8.1911.

20 Lady Emily Lutyens, (1957) pp 30-33. This memoir, published when Lady Emily was eighty three, reflected her disillusionment with Theosophy and Krishnamurti while maintaining her belief in him as "the purest and most beautiful human being I have ever come across, the perfect flower of humanity".

21 Veritas (1913) p 36. The letter is marked 'London 8th September 1911'.

22 Veritas (1913) p 37. Letters dated 9 & 22 June 1911. All Brahmin males wear a sacred thread across the chest from the time of their ritual initiation ceremony in adolescence.

23 M Lutyens (1976) p 55.

24 A Nethercot (1963) pp 169, 173; G Marvin Williams (1931) pp 276-7.

25 A Nethercot (1963) p 163 refers to Mrs Besant's unforgiving writing in Theosophical magazines and makes the point that while the Hindu University grew into perhaps the most impressive university in India, the first Director abandoned the Central Hindu College's textbooks on *dharma* as being incompatible with 'his brand of modern Hindu orthodoxy'.

26 A Nethercot (1963) pp 170-2; G Marvin Williams (1931) p 277; M Lutyens (1976) pp 58-60 for a full description of Leadbeater's version; M Lutyens (1990) p 15; Veritas (1913) p 42.

27 Veritas (1913) p 43.

28 M Lutyens (1976) p 60-61 says that according to Narianiah, Mrs Besant gave an undertaking about the boys being separated from Leadbeater, which leaves some uncertainty in the reader's mind about whether or not Mrs Besant was dishonest, whereas A Nethercot (1963) pp 172-3, 182 puts the onus on Mrs Besant as having assured the father of the separation. However Lutyens in this first version does make a point which is sympathetic to the father in writing that "poor" Narianiah must have been torn between his loathing and mistrust of Leadbeater and the advantages of an English education for his sons. In the later edited version (1991) p 15, Lutyens deletes all speculative and sympathetic comment. On the issue of the politics of the supporters of Narianiah, G Marvin Williams (1931) p 278 says that Mrs Besant attributed the lawsuit to "the Jesuits and the Tingley faction of the American Theosophists".

29 M Lutyens (1976) gives the detail of this subterfuge which was disclosed during the custody court case, explaining that Mrs Besant was anxious to get the boys out of India before Narianiah changed his mind again, whereas Nethercot (1963) p 173 says that before leaving the country, Mrs Besant received Narianiah's letter threatening a lawsuit unless she immediately returned his sons to him. The language of her letter, which is quoted by Lutyens, is brutal.

30 Mahatma Gandhi 1963 *The Collected Works of Mahatma Gandhi* Vol XI Government of India, Ahmedabad, letter to Pranjivan Mehta 8 May 1911, p 64.

31 Gandhi has acknowledged that he first became acquainted with the *Gita* in 1889 when two English Theosophist friends asked him to read Sir Edward Arnold's translation with them. He didn't really want to and felt ashamed and miserable, out of vanity, because he didn't know anything about the holy books from his own culture and couldn't read it in the original Sanskrit. He was immediately fascinated by the *Gita* and the last

nineteen stanzas from Chapter II remained "engraved" in his heart. MK Gandhi 1980 *The Bhagvadgita* Orient Ahmedabad p 9. MK Gandhi 1983 *An Autobiography* Penguin London p 76. Afterwards Gandhi read many other translations of the *Gita*. Nethercot (1963) p 45 says that in 1895 Mrs Besant had herself translated the *Gita* from Sanskrit into English with the assistance of a Hindu scholar Bhagavan Das. Gandhi also acknowledged that Madame Blavatsky's *Key to Theosophy* stimulated in him a desire to read books on Hinduism and "disabused" him of "the notion fostered by the missionaries that Hinduism was rife with superstition", (1963) Vol XXXIV "An Autobiography" Part I Chapter XX p 61. Gandhi also read Annie Besant's account of how she became a Theosophist. He said she was in the news for having turned to theism from atheism and this strengthened Gandhi's aversion to atheism. He met Blavatsky and Besant at the Blavatsky Lodge in London but declined his friends' invitation to join the Society which he considered a religious body. MK Gandhi (1983) pp 77-78. Gandhi fondly admired Annie Besant with whom he initially shared a goal of Indian Home Rule and about whom he once wrote to Lord Chelmsford, that she was "among the most powerful leaders of public opinion in India". In a tribute to Annie Besant in 1924 (1963) *Vol XXIV* Letter 281. 6 August 1924, Gandhi wrote that it was his misfortune to hold certain views as to policies and principles fundamentally different from her but it did not detract from his regard for as "a woman of high character, noble purpose, ceaseless energy and indomitable courage". She loved India with the devotion of a daughter, he said, and her courage "never shone so brilliant as when, at the risk of losing popularity, she opposed Non-co-operation". Despite their siginifcant political and religious differences of opinion, many respectful references to Mrs Besant are found in Gandhi's *Collected Works* for the period in which they were both prominent in Indian politics, and in a tribute the day she died, September 20, 1933, he wrote, "So long as India lives, the memory of the magnificent services rendered by Dr Besant will also live". Mahatma Gandhi (1963) Vol XI p 64 & Vol LVI p 11.

32 G Marvin Williams (1931) p 279; M Lutyens (1976) p 50. Lutyens puts the breakaway down to the decentralised structure of the Society in which sixteen thousand members were divided between six hundred lodges, allowing factions and rifts to occur, and does not mention the idolisation of Krishna as a factor. See also E Blau (1990) p 20.

33 Lady Emily Lutyens (1957) p 42 Letter from Annie Besant to Lady Emily dated 10 May 1912. Rudolf Steiner 1928 *The Story of My Life* Anthroposophical Publishing Co London pp 338-39.

34 *Theosophy in Australia*, June 1922 p 418. J Ross (1989) pp 199-200 shows a letter dated 13 November 1912 from Mrs Tingley to Dr Nanjunda Rao, who was supporting Krishna's father over custody, saying that she must show documents to her London lawyer before deciding to take

Errata

Page	*For*	*Read*
vii, line 3	Hapters	Chapters
xii, line 11	Bhagavad Gita	*Bhagavad Gita*
xvi, line 12	The Hindu	*The Hindu*
xvii, line 28	E	é
47, line 28	1912 January	January 1912
60, line 10	"love"	love"
60, line 24	favour". Aligning	favour" aligning
70, line 16	naivete	naiveté
145, line 17	Lady Emily; Kirby	Lady Emily, Kirby,
150, line 15	the drafting	drafting
163, line 14	liberation.69	liberation.[69]
165, line 5	Sphinx,	Sphinx
188, line 21	Then the meetings	The meetings
188, line 21	he gave six	gave six
191, line 7	cared for	looked after
193, line 12	outcaste	outcast
193, line 23	1933	1934
206, line 12	awareness people,	awareness, people
209, line 13	his"high	his "high
273, line 31	her.661	her.
287, line 24	was she	she was
334, line 14	Bircher-Brenner	Bircher-Benner
353, line 19	Luyens	Lutyens
372, line 15	me?83	me?[83]
406, line 7	1961and	1961, and
417, line 11	flush,	flush
469, line 22	discredited.	discredited,
553, Footnote 59	cultuvating	cultivating
553, *ibid.*	ans	and
554, Footnote 69 line13	to to	to
559, Footnote 48	whther	whether

action, and the Besant "party" used the name of Theosophy but did not work in a "practical" way.

35 A Nethercot (1963) pp 174-75. *The Times* 12 March 1912 p 6. On the same day the paper reported that 11 women suffragists had been committed for trial for window-breaking with 36 cases still to be heard. In her letter, Annie Besant cited 300 already in gaol and hundreds volunteering. By the end of the summer when Mrs Besant was on her way back to India, *The Times* published a letter from her saying it was better to break windows than heads. A walk by suffragists from Edinburgh to London which began mid-October kept the issue alive throughout the month causing one anonymous letter-writer to complain of the prejudice of the press in advertising the evil actions of militant suffragists. See *The Times* 14 October 1912 & October 24 p 10.

36 Mahatma Gandhi (1963) Vol XII No. 29 from *Indian Opinion* 19 April 1913. Gandhi disagreed with the English translation of *satyagraha* as 'passive resistance', saying it was instead a pure soul-force of love. Mahatma Gandhi (1963) Vol XIII Letter written about 2.9.1917.

37 Mahatma Gandhi (1963) Vol XIII pp 210- 218, 4 February 1916. Gandhi also suggested that Indian Princes strip themselves of their jewellery for their countrymen which would have been considered offensive to all Indian Maharajas and particularly those who shared the stage with him on that occasion.

38 Born in Ceylon in 1875, C Jinarajadasa was 'discovered' by Leadbeater who claimed the boy was his deceased brother reincarnated. Leadbeater kidnapped him from his parents and kept him on board a ship for three weeks but after a reconciliation with the parents, Jinarajadasa was allowed to go to England with Leadbeater and graduated from Cambridge in 1900.

39 'Beer and skittles' was a common expression of the time. Krishna used it in a letter in January 1922. M Lutyens (1976) p143.

40 A Nethercot (1963) p 180-81. Tillett (1982) p 146. Balfour Clarke (December 1928) p 158 observes that it seemed highly improbable that Krishna's father was planning a kidnapping but "to be on the safe side" they "tacitly formed a body-guard by day and by night round the two brothers". Nethercot describes Krishna and Nitya as running in and out of Warwick House while Lutyens (1996) p 11 denies Rajagopal Sloss's claim that they lived there.

41 Lady Emily Lutyens (1957) pp 50-51.

42 A Nethercot (1963) p184, 187.

43 Veritas (1913) pp 49-55. Narianiah was said to have been struck dumb by this letter, having paid homage to Mrs Besant which "most people pay only to the Supreme Being". Mrs Besant's reference to Narianiah having thirteen children is perhaps an indication of her hyperbole, although Lady Emily Lutyens makes reference to his fourteen children.

44 Veritas (1913) pp 56-59.

45 A Nethercot (1963) p 185.

46 Lady Emily Lutyens (1957) p 52-53 quotes from a letter from Leadbeater in October 1912 in which he refers to Narianiah as "Krishna's objectionable old man" and says he is a tool of that political party in India which is disaffected to the British Government and Mrs Besant has enemies, with attempts made on her life, because she warned the Government of the secret drilling of armed men during the Viceroyalty of Lord Curzon.

47 A Nethercot (1963) pp 186-87.

48 M Lutyens (1976) pp 67-69.

49 A Nethercot (1963) pp 189-194. On p 192 Fn 1 Nethercot says that in an interview in 1957, BP Wadia said that, although discredited at the trial, Lakshman's story about Leadbeater was true. He also said there were other authenticated examples of Leadbeater's sexual relations with boys, including that with Hubert van Hook. J Ross (1989) p 189 for letter from Mrs Besant to Warrington 31October 1912 complaining about the legal suit.

50 Reply in *The Times* 2 June 1913. Nethercot (1963) pp 193-198; M Lutyens (1976) p 75.

51 Letters dated 29 August, 10 October 1913. Huntington 9/9. In contrast to Leadbeater's summary of Narianiah's counsel, Ramaswami Aiyar, Annie Besant wrote of him as a brilliant young counsel and "a gentleman whose name for honour stands as high as his reputation for legal learning and ability". Four years later during internment, Mrs Besant wrote to him seeking his help and advice but he did not visit her as she had asked. A Nethercot (1963) pp 194-95, 263.

52 A Nethercot (1963) p 199-201.

53 In a letter to her husband on 10 August 1911, Lady Emily said that hero worship was the greatest joy of her life. "In my early youth I poured out all the devotion of my being on the thought of the Christ, and now the thought, the hope, the belief of His return absorbs me sometimes to the exclusion of everything else." C Percy and J Ridley (1988) p 221.

54 C Percy & J Ridley (1988) p 246. Letter dated 26.5.1912.

55 A Nethercot (1963) p 169 for Dr Rocke's appointment. The Nitya correspondence is dated 6 March, 11 April, 26 June, 31 July, 14, 22 August, 5, 11, 25 September, 7, 21 November 1913; 14, 23, 30 January 1914. Held by KFI.

56 Letter dated 28 March 1913 Huntington 9/8. Stories of Krishna's power to physically heal would recur throughout his life. In an interview with the author 24 December 1999, Professor P Krishna of the Rajghat Education Centre in Varanasi cited several cases he knew of Krishnamurti healing people.

57 Letter dated 20 August 1913, Huntington 9/2.

58 M Lutyens (1976) pp 80-82. Krishna first learnt to play golf while staying in a cottage near Crowborough in Sussex before dashing off to Genoa in October 1913. Telegram 31 October 1913. Huntington 20/8. See also correspondence Leadbeater to Krishna dated 10 October 1913 in which he says he notes what Krishna has to say about Devonshire but the Lord had a preference for islands, so Guernsey and the Channel Islands might be the best places for Krishna to settle. But if Krishna liked Torquay he could check it with the Lord. He reminded Krishna that the Master KH had advised him to avoid England until the court case was over. Leadbeater himself had had previous experience in lying low during a controversial period.

59 Krishna to Leadbeater 29 December 1913. KFI. Leena Sarabhai 1990 *Leaves from a Diary* Rite-Print-Pak Bombay p 2 says Krishna told her in 1933 that during the custody case he and Nitya "wandered" through Europe "in hiding" with Jinarrajadasa. Sarabhai says she wrote from recollection what Krishna told her in her diary so the language used may be questionable to some extent.

60 Krishna's correspondence to Leadbeater dated 30 April, undated, 3, 24, 31 July, 26 September, 29 December, 1913, held by KFI. Krishna's letter to Mrs Russak dated 20 August 1913, Huntington 9/2. G Tillett (1982) p 151 attaches occult significance to Krishna underlining his name.

61 Nitya's correspondence to Mrs Besant dated 11, 25 September, 10 October 1913, KFI.

62 Nitya's correspondence to Mrs Besant dated 11 & 25 September, 10 October 1913, 5 March, 5 November 1914 and one undated. Held by KFI.

63 C Percy & J Ridley (1988) pp 296, 301, 302. Letter dated 11.9.1914. Lady Emily (1957) pp 29, 43, 59-60 explains the significance and use of the blue ribbons which Leadbeater insisted should be the exact colour of the Lord Maitreya's aura. Regarding Edwin Lutyens' architectural work, there had been considerable press interest in Britain in the development of the new capital of India, removed from Calcutta to Delhi, over several years since the decision was finalised in 1912. See *The Times* 1 October 1912. Lutyens' commission for the city's design was worth a great deal to him in terms of money and status: in 1916 Edwin Lutyens warned his wife that if she came to India on a political mission for Indian Home Rule he would have to give up his New Delhi plans and it would spell ruin for them. Lady Emily Lutyens (1957) p 80.

64 C Percy & J Ridley (1988) pp 220, 304. Letters dated 8.8.1911, 19.9.1914. Lutyens' reference to 'Vedas' (Hindu sacred canon) is probably meant to be 'devas', meaning angel-like beings.

65 M Lutyens (1996) pp 9, 10 regarding Krishna and Lady Emily's love. In the Madras court custody case Mrs Besant had said that Krishna was not being prepared for the life of a Hindu *sannyasi*. She did not believe he would marry but there was no outward compulsion placed upon him.

Lutyens (1976) p 69. A few years later, in 1916, Jinarajadasa married an English woman, Dorothy Graham, and Krishna described the marriage as "most extraordinary", thinking Jinarajadasa the last person he would have thought of as getting married. Lutyens comments that the event sent a shock wave through the Society, as Initiates, especially, were not expected to marry and many marriages had been ruined by sexual abstinence. Lutyens (1996) p 17. Arundale's marriage in 1920 to Rukmini Devi, aged sixteen to his forty two years, and who was the daughter of a prominent Indian Sanskrit scholar and engineer, also caused controversy.

66 Lutyens (1976) pp 18. Letter dated February 1915. Lady Emily Lutyens (1957) p 76 on the break between Krishna and Arundale.

67 Lady Emily Lutyens (1957) pp 74-75. Arundale's letter dated 18.1.1915.

68 M Lutyens (1996) pp 12-16. Lutyens makes the point that Krishna was dogged all his life by people wanting his love exclusively.

69 Lady Emily Lutyens (1957) p 77. L Sarabhai (1990) pp 4,5.

70 M Lutyens (1976) p 89.

71 Other austerities advocated by Gandhi included brahmacharya, or abstinence from sex, and he in this same letter said it would be an excellent thing for a particular person to take in water through the nostrils and modify his diet, including some fasting. Mahatma Gandhi (1963) Vol XII p 146, letter to Jamnadas Gandhi dated 19.7.1913.

72 M Lutyens (1976) pp 98-100; Leadbeater, writing to Krishna from Sydney on 5 March 1916, said he could not understand why the hospital should object to Krishna's work on the grounds that he was Indian.

73 M Lutyens (1976) pp 103-108.

74 Lady Emily, who organised talks by Jinarajadasa in her home, joined the Indian Home Rule but when advised by Mrs Besant that she should keep out of it for fear of upsetting her husband, she resigned. A Nethercot (1963) p 249; Lady Emily Lutyens (1957) pp 79-80. Mrs Besant seems to have kept a tight rein on the political activities of Theosophists, in case their activities clashed with hers. After Ernest Wood shared a lecture platform with GK Gokhale, noted politician and social worker, in Poona in 1909 at a meeting which developed into a small riot after hecklers from the floor, including BG Tilak, caused trouble, Mrs Besant asked Wood not to engage in political activity in case the Society was suspected of being associated with it. Wood (1936) pp 128, 131. Leadbeater's politics must always have been a worry to Mrs Besant as Wood on p 137 describes him as a disbeliever in democracy and a good old Tory of the early Victorian style who seemed to be reactionary and uninformed in the extreme. Wood also observes of Mrs Besant, pp 125-26, that it was not until 1913 when she took up political work in India that she turned against the caste system, being generally in favour of strict Hindu custom, except child marriage for girls and the ban on widow remarriage. Wood's own political position, pp 221-25, was that the extreme left followed Gandhi in his pol-

icy of civil disobedience, and although Wood liked Gandhi, he believed his policy unpractical and he was not surprised when violence finally overtook Gandhi's philosophy of non-violence in Indian nationalism.

75 For letter of thanks for complimentary first issue dated 25 November 1915 see Huntington 20/8.

76 A Nethercot (1963) pp 232-261. M Lutyens (1976) p 106 says Mrs Besant never advocated separation between India and the British Raj and was fighting for Dominion Status for India. G Marvin Williams (1931) pp 295-300.

77 G Marvin Williams (1931) p 295. Mahatma Gandhi (1963) Vol XV p 26 wrote in 1918 that the policy of Tilak Maharaj and Mrs Besant was mistaken but their achievement heroic and their services impossible to measure, that it was from them that the young got a message of patriotism. Jawaharlal Nehru was powerfully influenced by Mrs Besant's Theosophists early in his life when he had a tutor who was a Theosophist, Ferdinand T Brooks. Brooks held weekly Theosophist meetings in his room. Jawaharlal attended and was inspired to join the Society at the age of thirteen, with Mrs Besant conducting the initiation ceremony. Jawaharlal's father before him had been a member and later resigned, putting up no protest against the boy's interest. Jawaharlal went on to attend school in England and soon lost interest in Theosophy, but later said that the initiation ceremony contained good advice. He continued to have "the warmest admiration" for Mrs Besant but not for Theosophists, whom he described as having a flat and insipid look denoting piety, and being "ordinary folk liking security better than risk". J Nehru 1962 *An Autobiography with Musings on Recent Events in India*, Allied Publishers Private Ltd, Bombay pp 14-16, 34. (First published 1932). See also Frank Moraes 1956 *Jawaharlal Nehru A Biography* Macmillan New York pp 26, 53 who says Motilal Nehru had been initiated into the Theosophical Society by Madame Blavatsky in India but ceased his association with it a short time after joining. He seemed to have no objection to Jawaharlal's theosophist tutor, Brooks' influence on his son. Moraes says Motilal always "cherished a high regard and respect for Mrs Besant".

78 Mahatma Gandhi (1963) Vol XIII p 464, letter dated 7.7 1917.

79 Mahatman Gandhi (1963) Vol XIII pp 510, pp 520-25. Meeting held 24.8.1917.

80 A Nethercot (1963) pp 262-66. Mrs Besant held the office of President of the Congress until 1923.

81 M Lutyens (1976) p 107. Lutyens makes the point that Krishna had little interest in either political movements or books. However his lack of interest in books is disputed by Susunaga Weeraperuma in an interview with the author (2000).

82 Undated letter Huntington 20/8. Annie Besant said all the people she worked with were in the Liberal League and she had no one to consult

with, scarcely seeing 'CP", and with deficits everywhere, she'd decided to sell *New India*.

83 Jawaharlal Nehru (1962) p 32. A Nethercot (1963) p 285 says that in an interview in 1956, LM Gulama Ahmad told him that Mrs Besant paid the cigar worker strikers' expenses for three months until they won.

84 G Marvin Williams (1931) pp 300-05, A Nethercot pp 283-301. Lady Emily Lutyens' take on the end of Annie Besant's political work in India is expressed in an article in *Theosophy in Australia* September 1925 pp 161-63. She describes the cruelty and sadism of the British Administration, including the Amritsar massacre, and gives a lenient slant on Mrs Besant's attitude to the Rowlett Act. She praises Gandhi as a "visionary" but says Mrs Besant was the only leader with the courage to oppose passive resistance and "from that moment her popularity vanished". The article is essentially critical of Gandhi's approach to politics. In correspondence from Nitya to Mrs Besant 17 July 1923 (KFI) he had praised Lady Emily's work with the Indian Union in England, but Mrs Besant discouraged Lady Emily from any political work.

85 Correspondence Krishna to Mrs Besant 22 January 1920 KFA, Nitya to Mrs Besant 10 September 1920 KFI.

86 A Nethercot (1963) p 294; Lady Emily Lutyens (1957) pp 86-88. M Lutyens (1976) p 127.

87 M Lutyens (1976) p 127-130.

88 Letter dated 29 January 1921 KFI.

89 Nitya to Mrs Besant 7 August, 1st September, 12 October 1921, undated, KFI; Krishna to Mrs Besant 8 August 1921, KFI. Krishna reports to Mrs Besant that Nitya is very well but still needing care 26 October 1921 KFA.

90 In E Blau (1995) pp 48-50, Helen Knothe Nearing thinks the Baron's car is an old Mercedes. In Helen Nearing 1992 *Loving and Leaving the Good Life* Chelsea Green Publishing Vermont p 39 she refers to an old Rolls Royce.

91 H Nearing (1992) p 40.

92 Inscription dated 6 November 1921. H Nearing (1992) p 41.

93 Letter dated 14 November 1921. H Nearing (1992) pp 42, 43.

94 M Lutyens (1976) p 138-40. Letters dated 9 September 1921 & 17 November 1921.

95 G Marvin Williams (1931) p 307-314; A Nethercot (1963) p 316-317. Wedgwood, a member of the extended family of the famous ceramics house, had been converted to Theosophy in 1911 after hearing Mrs Besant speak in York. He became General Secretary of the Society for England and Wales immediately before Arundale and introduced a ceremony called Rosy Cross which lasted a short time. In 1913 he was ordained a priest in the Old Catholic Church, or Jansenist Church, named after Bishop Cornelius Jansen, who broke away from the Church of Rome in the seventeenth century, claiming apostolic succession and rejecting papal

infallibility. Wedgwood went to Australia soon after his ordination. After consecrating Leadbeater in 1916, Wedgwood returned to England and charges of sexual perversion were laid against him by police. Mrs Besant wanted him to resign from the Theosophical Society but Leadbeater advised her otherwise in 1919 and the charges were not pressed. M Lutyens (1976) pp150-51. G Marvin Williams (1931) pp 313, 323 maintains that it was deemed advisable that Wedgwood resign after all and he stayed away from England due to the sensational press coverage. He established a European headquarters of the Church on a beautiful estate given him in Holland and returned to the Society after 27 months to become a powerful leader. According to Tillett(1982) pp 257 & 312 Fn2 Wedgwood contracted syphilis and towards the end of his life oscillated between sanity and unbalance. From 1937 he lived in a centre he established in Camberley and he died in 1951.

96 The "ocean of the Jiddu family" and the "womb-ocean" of Krishna's mother were referred to in Krishna's horoscope. Peter Washington 1993 *Madame Blavatsky's Baboon Theosophy and the Emergence of the Western Guru* Secker & Warburg London p 134 sees the cutting of Krishna from his roots as significant since he found himself "among the millions removed from one milieu but never at home in another". Washington says Krishna had lost his mother, his father, his family and his country so that he belonged to no one and nowhere, without ties and obligations, a condition which was a source of both spiritual authority and mischief and anguish.

Chapter 3 Antipodean Rudeness

1 *Herald of the Star* January 1922 p 2. Lady Emily Lutyens (1957) pp 88-89 says that by early 1921 Miss Dodge, who had been financing the *Herald of the Star* since 1915, could no longer do so and Wodehouse had given up its editorship, returning to India to teach, leaving Lady Emily as honorary editor so Krishnamurti wrote his own editorials, without guidance from anyone.

2 The wearing of headdress by Indians was common even with European dress. Bernard S Cohn 1996 *Colonialism and its Forms of Knowledge* Princeton University Press New Jersey pp 107-111, 143-149 makes the point that the British, in establishing themselves as rulers in India, constructed codes of conduct to distance themselves from their subjects. Covering of the head and feet were clear areas of distinction between Europeans and Indians. For example, if an Indian man wore European dress he would not wear a European hat. Many Indians traditionally wore turbans or caps but it was not the dress code in all regions, for example in south India (where Krishna was born) except for manual labourers, who wrapped a cloth about their heads for protection, or for many men during

special religious ceremonies. The turban, although worn by many groups in the north and west of India, became a salient, even political, feature of identification in male Sikh dress – with two types worn related to length of hair and social status. A tightly-wrapped turban of plain cloth accommodated the topknot, and another associated with rulership, was elaborately wrapped and had a plume and jewels attached. In developing his campaign against British rule, Gandhi's *khadi* cap became a symbol of independence, but Cohn says he was unable to find out when and how Gandhi created what became the uniform of the Indian National Congress, which included the cap. The most commonly-used photograph of Krishna's father shows him wearing a turban. The long-time official of the Theosophical Society and tutor to Krishna and Nitya, C Jinarajadasa, used to wear a small round purple velvet cap indoors as well as outdoors, ostensibly to protect his sensitive head from the "painful" rays of electric light, according to Nethercot (1963) p 181. Emma Tarlo 1996 *Clothing Matters Dress and Identity in India* Hurst & Co London pp 11, 12, 26, 64, 65 says it was the "Anglo-Ceylonese" Ananda Coomaraswamy who, earlier than Gandhi, pointed to the absurdity of imitating Englishmen. Tarlo emphasises the creative element of all clothing choices as people formulate their own self-image. It's hard to know the extent to which Krishna as a young man was determining his own self-image or following the expectations of his English benefactors in dressing up.

3 H Nearing (1992) p 43.

4 M Lutyens (1976) p 141, 145-46.

5 M Lutyens (1976) p 141-42. Part of the building had been a gift from Mrs Russak.

6 H Nearing (1992) p 44.

7 Nitya to Mrs Besant 12 October 1921 KFI. M Lutyens (1976) p 144. Krishnamurti's Journal (1982) pp 36-37. Krishna writes in the third person of two brothers. P Jayakar (1986) pp 44-45.

8 Nitya's letter to Jamnadas from Mt Lavinia Grand Hotel, Colombo, 21 March 1922 on the eve of his departure for Australia, Huntington 20/8. The political form of Krishna and Nitya's youthful political enthusiasm seems to have been the *Bharata Samaj* or *Children of India League* – which was established at the Theosophical headquarters at Adyar in May 1921. Mrs Besant is said to have consecrated the site of a Hindu temple under the direction of the League which worked towards the liberalisation and internationalism of Hinduism. An article on the *Bharata Samaj* in *The Theosophist* December 1922 pp 283-86, written by someone identified as "DHS", explained its aims of replacing complex rites with simple rules for worship and ritual, eradication of the caste system and admission of non-Hindus. Mrs Besant clearly yearned to be accepted as a Hindu but recognised, and had stated publicly, that she had no religion since she had not been born a Hindu, so this organisation might have been thought to

overcome that obstacle. The official organ of the *Bharata Samaj* was a monthly newsletter. *Bharata Dharma*, launched in November 1922 and edited by Pandit A Mahadeva Sastri. Lily Heber 1931 *Krishnamurti The Man and His Message* Allen & Unwin London pp 91, 92 says Krishnamurti supported the *Bharata Samaj* "without binding himself in any way by any form of membership". Krishna also wrote to an Indian friend (probably Jamnadas) 26 November 1923 from Ojai commiserating about an election loss and suggesting that the 'Masters' probably wanted him to do something else. Huntington 20/8.

9 G Marvin Williams (1931) pp 321-25.

10 Testimony of Thomas Leadbeater Martyn on 30 May 1922 pp 40. State Records 5/7771.2

11 NSW State Records 5/7771.2. Interview by Constable Murray with Hilda Martyn dated 31 May 1922. Statement by Thomas Martyn dated 1 June 1922.

12 Marvin Williams (1931) p 325.

13 *Theosophy in Australia* February 1922 p 320.

14 *NSW Industrial Gazette* 31 May 1922 p 1183.

15 A Nethercot (1963) pp 318, 321. *The Herald of the Star* July 1922 p 244.

16 *The Herald of the Star* July 1922 p 244 for Krishnamurti's description of the voyage. M Lutyens (1976) p 146. Although it was decided in November that Krishna would be going to Australia, he uses short notice as a reason for not writing his editorial notes for *The Herald of the Star* for May 1922, p 167. Lutyens says Krishna posted in Adelaide his July edition editorial notes, which contain a description of Perth and an essay on politics.

17 Nitya to Jamnadas 21 March 1922, Huntington 20/8.

18 *The Herald of the Star* July 1922 p 244. RMS is the abbreviation for Royal Mail Steamer; the ship was also known as *SS Omar*.

19 Krishna to Lady Emily 28 March 1922, KFA.

20 Letter dated 1 April 1922 on board the *Omar*, KFI.

21 *The West Australian* 3 April 1922 p 6. Lindsay was described as "a member of the well-known Lindsay family of artists" who had been in England and Europe for a year during which time he had married Miss Joan Weigall, a niece of the Governor of South Australia, who was "also an artist of merit". It is interesting to note that four stowaways who were on board another ship in the harbour that day claimed they'd escaped unemployment in Britain. The previous Friday eight stowaways were found on another ship – an indication of the lengths the poor of England would go to for work. See also *West Australian* 1 April 1922 pp 1 & 8 for details of ship and fares.

22 Letter dated 1 April 1922, KFA. M Lutyens (1976) p 146-47. Lutyens left off the final sentence about being Lord of Karma.

23 Letters to Lady Emily 30 March 1922 & 1 April 1922, KFA.

24 *West Australian* 3 April 1922 p 6 for ship's arrival. M Lutyens (1976) p 148 for ship's departure.

25 *Theosophy in Australia* May 1922 p 387. Senator Reid returned to Perth to meet Annie Besant on her arrival in May. An obituary to Senator Matthew Reid who died on 28 August 1947 at the age of ninety reported that he had made it easier for many "Indian brethren" to enter Australia, including Krishna but did not specify how. He was said to be a founder of the Labour Party in Queensland. C Jinarajadasa is quoted as saying that in WW I he stood "solidly" with Billie Hughes at odds with the rest of the Labor Party over conscription. *Theosophy in Australia* October-November 1947 p 10.

26 *Herald of the Star* July 1922 p 244. Also letter Krishna to Lady Emily 5 April 1922, KFA.

27 David Ellis *DH Lawrence, the dying* game *1922-1930*, 1998 Cambridge University Press, GB, pp 233-235. Letters dated 30 April 1922 & 4 April [sic] 1922. The date should read 4 May 1922.

28 M Lutyens (1976) P 147-48. Letter Krishna to Lady Emily 5 April 1922, KFA.

29 *Adelaide Advertiser* 8 April 1922 pp 10 & 14. A weather map on p 9 shows a high pressure system centred on the South Australian coast and stretching across the full extent of Australia which could have been expected to calm the waters of the Great Australian Bight and result in warm weather in Adelaide. *West Australian* 8 April p 8 shipping notices shows the *Omar* arrived Adelaide 7 April. An indication of disquiet over Italian immigrants in Australia comes in *The Age* 8 April 1922 p 16 which carries a report that the Queensland Premier had responded to criticism over the issue. He said that the Government was not encouraging Italians while discouraging Britons to emigrate and that the Italians were arriving of their own volition. Krishna had mentioned a Papal choir of 60 Italians on board in his letter to Lady Emily 28 March 1922, KFA. Australia had a racist White Australia policy at this time, favouring Britons and northern Europeans over Asians.

30 *Herald* (Melbourne) 8 April 1922 p 8. *West Australian* shipping notices p 6 - 10 April 1922 shows the *Omar* arrives Melbourne 8 April, 11 April shows the *Omar* departed Melbourne 10 April for Sydney, 13 April shows Omar arrived Sydney 12 April.

31 *The Herald* (Melbourne) 8 April 1922 p 8 &10 April 1922 p 11.

32 *The Age* 10 April 1922. The report was not an editorial but nevertheless clearly British Government propaganda.

33 *The Age* 13 April 1922 p 6. On the same page the *Omar* is listed as having arrived in Sydney the day before.

34 Krishna to Lady Emily 22 April 1922, KFA.

35 Departed Melbourne April 10, arrived Sydney April 12. *The Herald* (Melbourne) 10 April 1922 Mails and Shipping & *The Age* 11 April p 8 & 13 April p 6. Sydney Show report from *The Age* 13 April 1922 p 8.

36 M Lutyens (1976) pp 136-37.

37 M Lutyens (1976) p 149. Correspondence Krishna to Lady Emily 22 April 1922, KFA.

38 M Lutyens (1976) p 151. Correspondence Krishna to Lady Emily 22 April 1922, KFA.

39 The vote is recorded in *Theosophy in Australia* May 1922 p 382. M Lutyens (1976) pp152-53. The allegations by Mr and Mrs Martyn are further complicated by a statement that Wedgwood had also caused outrage in the household by making love to Mrs Martyn. This is not mentioned in either of the couple's testimonies to police but M Lutyens makes a reference to it, probably based on Nitya's account in a letter to Fabrizio Ruspoli dated 2 July 1922 of Wedgwood being flirtatious and Wedgwood and Mrs Martyn 'noticing' each other and then Wedgwood 'dropping' Mrs Martyn who turned bitterly against him. Leadbeater is also said to have insisted the Martyn couple occupy separate bedrooms. Nethercot (1963) Fn p 323.

40 M Lutyens 1959 *To Be Young* Hart-Davis London p 72; Lady Emily (1957) p 89; M Lutyens (1976) pp 135, 153. Nitya was treated by Dr Carton in Paris and Dr Rollier, a lung specialist, in Leysin before seeing an unnamed doctor in Sydney. Dr Rocke, a prominent member of the Society, was retired by 1922. Correspondence Krishna to Lady Emily 30 April 1922, KFA.

41 Correspondence Krishna to Lady Emily 30 April 1922, KFA.

42 Correspondence Krishna to Lady Emily 30 April, 1, 2 May 1922, KFA.

43 Mrs Besant received a Degree of Doctor of Letters from Benares Hindu University (the extension of her own Hindu College) on 14 December 1921. In Australia in 1922 the press mostly continued to address her as Mrs Besant, by which title she was widely known, and she said later that she did not mind what title was used. *Theosophy in Australia* April 1922 p 354 and June 1922 p 429.

44 Nethercot pp 33, 34, 118. See press articles: "Mrs Annie Besant" *Daily News* Perth 20 May 1908; "Annie Besant" *West Australian* Perth 23 May 1908; "The Life of Annie Besant" *Sunday Times* Perth 31 May 1908; "Theosophy" *Daily News* Perth 13 June 1908; "Madame Blavatsky Was She an Imposter?" *Daily News* Perth 20 June 1908; "Annie Besant Her Arrival in Brisbane" *Courier* Brisbane15 July 1908; Theosophy Mrs Besant's Lecture" *Daily Mail* Brisbane 16 July 1908; see also *Daily News* Perth 23 & 24 June; *Bulletin* Sydney 23 July; "Empty Heads in Politics" & "Reincarnation, An Old Superstition, Famous Imposters" *Evening News* Sydney23 & 25 July 1908; "The Unrest in India" *Star* Auckland 25 July 1908; "Annie Besant" *NZ Herald* Auckland 25 July 1908; "Man's Many Lives" *NZ Herald* 27 July 1908; "Man and his Destiny" *NZ Herald* Auckland 28 July 1908. File of press clippings held by Campbell Library, Blavatsky Lodge, Theosophical Society, Sydney.

45 Correspondence Krishna to Lady Emily 12, 19, 20 May, 2 June1922, KFA. Nitya's letter to a European Theosophist, Fabrizio Ruspoli, 2 July 1922, Huntington 9/4. M Lutyens (1976) pp 154-55. In the abridged biography (1990) pp 33-34 Lutyens leaves out all references to the 1922 Sydney press coverage of the Theosophical scandals and the resulting police inquiry in which Krishnamurti was involved, dealing only with Krishnamurti's dislike of Leadbeater's religious services and Nitya's ill-health.

46 M Lutyens (1976) p 155. Correspondence Krishna to Lady Emily 2 June 1922, KFA.

47 *Daily Telegraph* (Sydney) 10 May p 6.

48 *Daily Telegraph* 11 May 1922 p 5 and 15 May p 4.

49 *The Sun* (Sydney) 17 May 1922; *Dawn* was set up by Martyn and others to campaign against Leadbeater and to promote the 'Back to Blavatsky' movement. *Daily Telegraph* 17-20 May 1922 *Daily Mail* 17, 18 May 1922; *Sunday Times* 21 May 1922.

50 *Daily Telegraph* 22-26, 29-31 May 1922; *Daily Mail* 23 May 1922; *Sun 23*, 25, 26, 31 May 1922; after Mrs Besant's departure, *Ross's* newsletter 8 July 1922 pp 2-4 ran an article by H Bruno Thomas in which he said he could glimpse certain valid and practical arguments behind Leadbeater's advice and that the ease with which readers of the *Daily Telegraph* rose to the bait of scandal indicated how eager they were to be humbugged. He pointed out that members sympathetic to Leadbeater and Mrs Besant resigned from the Society's Sydney Lodge and set up the Blavatsky Lodge, ostensibly because the Sydney Lodge was too large, but this was a spurious argument. His opinion was that the words 'religion', 'morality' and 'loyalty' were a godsend to politicians, priests and pressmen who played upon the credulity of people for their own honour and advancement. For Mrs Besant's schedule see Nethercot (1963) p 322 - he does not acknowedge the source of the quoted 'thunderous acclamation' for her - and also *Theosophy in Australia* June 1922 p 421.

51 The letter from Joseph Fussell to the NSW Attorney-General, the Hon DR Hall, dated 1 June 1917, referred to a victim of Leadbeater suffering epilepsy as a result of the abuse he had received. (Apparently it was thought by some people that excessive masturbation caused epilepsy.) A report by Regent Street Police station on 26 August 1917 said that information had not been able to be obtained about whether Leadbeater still taught masturbation or self abuse. Articles had appeared in three editions of *Truth* beginning 18 June 1916. State Records 5/7771.2.

52 Regent Street police station was very close to where Leadbeater held services of the Liberal Catholic Church in Regent Street, near Central Station. The 1917 police report also made the point that Leadbeater seemed "to have a fairly large following here and to be in good monetary circumstances" and had been in ill health for two months suffering from

diabetes and heart trouble so could not be interviewed. He had moved from the Kollerstroms at Raymond Rd Neutral Bay to rooms at the Society's building, 'King's Hall', in Hunter St in the city, built since Leadbeater arrived in Australia. State Records 5/7771.2.

53 Testimony of Thomas Leadbeater Martyn on 30 May 1922 pp 35, 37, 40. State Records 5/7771.2

54 Testimony of Roy Bassingthwaight on 1st August 1922 pp 1, 3. State Records 5/7771.2.

55 Testimony of C Jinarajadasa 30 May 1922. Letter dated 14 April 1923 and reply dated 19 July 1923. State Records 5/7771.2

56 M Lutyens (1976) p 155-56 says that the date was 25 May – the day that was thought at that time to be Krishna's birthday – his twenty-seventh. Krishna writes that it was 25 May, his birthday, in a letter to Lady Emily dated 2 June 1922, KFA. But the interviews are dated as a whole in the police file as 30 May 1922. State Records 5/7771.2.

57 M Lutyens (1976) pp 155-56. Correspondence Krishna to Lady Emily 2 June 1922, KFA..

58 See *Daily Telegraph* 11 May 1922 article headed "Morven Garden". The Morven Garden School at Gore Hill was a Theosophical Society Australian Section school where principles of Theosophy were taught to 75 children every day. A great part of the annual convention on Good Friday 14 April had been devoted to discussion about its reform, led by a teacher, Dr van der Leeuw. Krishnamurti took part and was appointed as an honorary member of the 1922 Education Committee – see *Theosophy in Australia* May 1922 pp 387-398, 415. So he clearly knew a lot about the school. Yet in the police interview Krishnamurti at first said Morven schools had nothing to do with Theosophy and in his correction did not retract or clarify this statement. State Records 5/7771.2.

59 Testimony of Krishnamurti and Nityananda 30 May 1922 pp 14-16 plus corrections. State Records 5/7771.2

60 See A Nethercot (1963) p 326 & G Tillett (1982) pp 200, 208. Letter dated 2 June 1922, KFA.

61 Document from Assistant Law Officer CZ Wingall dated 11 August 1922. State Records 5/7771.2. See reports in *Daily Mail* 11 August 1922, *Daily Telegraph* 26 August 1922 & *Sun* 2 September 1922. J Roe (1986) p 269 makes this comment about Ley, which is borne out by the State Records file, and the reference to Perdiau.

62 Correspondence Nitya to Fabrizio Ruspoli 2 July 1922, Huntington 9/4.

63 *Daily Telegraph* clipping 23 April 1923 held by the Department of the Attorney General and Justice. See G Tillett (1982) pp 200, 208 for contents of the 'Precis' of the police report in which the Head of the Criminal Investigation Department said there were good grounds for believing Leadbeater was a sex pervert and the Inspector General of Police said Leadbeater's conduct should be kept under surveillance. See also *Dawn*

May 1923 & *Daily Guardian* 1 August 1923.

64 *Theosophy in Australia* April 1922 p 357.

65 *The Theosophist* October 1922 pp 5-6. Mrs Besant's monthly editorial was called "On the Watchtower".

66 *The Theosophist* November 1922 p 113

67 *The Theosophist* December 1922 p 226.

68 *Theosophy in Australia* December 1925 p 273.

69 G Marvin Williams (1931) p 326. G Tillett (1982) p 208.

70 Correspondence Krishna to Lady Emily 2 June 1922, KFA.

71 Extract from a letter DH Lawrence wrote from Thirroul to Mrs Jenkins 8 April 1922, Mitchell Library ML 673. It might be argued that Lawrence was in an alienated state on this trip – "In one part of myself I came to love it [Australia]". The more robust Frieda, on the other hand, really loved Australia. See reference in same letter, "Frieda loves it here", and her letter to Mrs Jenkins, "I love Australia – I feel I have 'packed all old Europe in the old Kit bag' and thrown it into the sea ...". Dickson Library Al 106/2. See also Jeffrey Meyers *DH Lawrence A Biography* 1993 Pan Macmillan London p 275.

72 A Nethercot (1963) p 320.

73 *Daily Telegraph* 19 May 1922 letter to the editor.

74 *Theosophy in Australia* May 1922 p 399.

75 *Theosophy in Australia* May 1922 p 395.

76 M Lutyens (1976) pp 156-57. Correspondence Krishna to Lady Emily 19 May 1922 & 2 June 1922, KFA.

77 M Lutyens (1976) p 156.

78 Term used by DH Lawrence in 20 May 1922 correspondence from D Ellis (1998) p 244. J Roe (1986) p 285 says crude Australians had laughed in Krishna's face so that he had gradually come to recognise the public derision he inspired "after years of private coddling by rich Europeans". She indicates her sympathy for "so dislocated a being, who by then saw no escape".

Chapter 4 Enlightenment

1 Krishna to Mrs Besant 26 June 1922, one day before the ship called in to Honolulu, KFI.

2 Nitya's letter at sea to Fabrizio Ruspoli dated 2 July 1922. Huntington 9/4.

3 Krishna to Mrs Besant 20 July 1922 & Nitya to Lady Emily 13 July 1922. KFI.

4 Krishna to Dr Rocke 29 August 1922 Huntington 9/13. He had offered her the position of Australian Representative of the Star on the International Committee before leaving Sydney (Huntington 14 June 1922 Huntington 9/8) and now said he was glad she had accepted it.

5 Nitya to Leadbeater 1 September 1922, KFI.

6 Krishna's statement dated 2 September 1922. Nitya's statement. KFI. See also M Lutyens (1976) pp 162-169 & pp 169-172.

7 A copy of the undated statement signed by Nitya is held by KFI. Excerpts were first published in 1975 in *Krishnamurti The Years of Awakening* Lutyens (1976) pp 162-177. Lutyens says Nitya's statement was written a fortnight after the occurrence.

8 Feuerstein (1997) p 251 defines *samadhi* as an ecstatic state, in which consciousness shines as the object of a meditation that precedes it, or there is a merging of subject and object. Lutyens (1976) P 168 explains that it is a Sanskrit word probably used by Nitya to mean a state of trance but she gives a definition that *samadhi* destroys death, leads to eternal happiness and confers the supreme 'Bliss of Brahman' or 'Reality'. Nitya to Leadbeater 1 September, 22 October, 10 December 1922, KFI; Nitya's account 11 February 1923, KFI.

9 R Rajagopal Sloss interview with the author Santa Barbara 18 October 2000. R Rajagopal Sloss 1991 *Lives in the Shadow with J Krishnamurti* Bloomsbury p60. M Lutyens (1996) p 30.

10 Statement signed by Warrington, KFI.

11 Letter dated 2 September 1922, KFI.

12 Letter dated 2 September 1922, KFI. It's notable that Krishna writes to Mrs Besant that he'll serve the Masters and her, and to Leadbeater that he'll serve the Masters and the Lord.

13 In an interview with the author in Santa Barbara 18 October 2000, Rosalind's daughter Radha Rajagopal Sloss said her father was agnostic and her mother's family had been freemasons who were excommunicated and became freethinkers and atheists. R Rajagopal Sloss (1991) p 77 also outlines her mother's religious attitude.

14 Krishna to Mrs Besant 28 February 1923, KFA; Lutyens (1976) p 159.

15 Nitya to Leadbeater 1 September 1922, KFI; Krishna to Leadbeater 2 September 1922, KFI; Nitya to Leadbeater 1 September & 18 November 1922, KFI; Nitya to Lady Emily Lutyens10 December 1922, KFI.

16 Interview with the author in Santa Barbara 18 November 2000. R Rajagopal Sloss (1991) p 60.

17 Nitya's letter to Leadbeater 22 October 1922, KFI; Nitya's letter to Mrs Besant 18 November 1922, KFI; entry for 6 October 1922 in Nitya's description of 'the process' written 11 February 1923 p 36, KFI. G Feuerstein (1997) pp 158, 162 explains kundalini-shakti or serpent power as a mysterious psychospiritual force encountered in Tantrism and *hatha yoga* in which a potent energy is released and rises up the spine to the top of the head. A Kashmiri public servant, Gopi Krishna (1903–1984), was a major exponent of kundalini-shakti in the West following publication of his book 1970 *Kundalini: Evolutionary Energy in Man* Stuart & Watwkins London, an account of his painful experience of kundalini in 1937 after seventeen years practising meditation. L Sarabhai (1990) p 9

says Krishna told her in 1933 that for about seven years he'd been experimenting to awaken *kundalini* and felt "unbearable" pain.

18 Correspondence dated 22 October 1922 & 18 November 1922, KFI. Lutyens (1976) p 176. It might be noted that Krishnamurti sanctioned Lutyens' biography of him. Correspondence Krishna to Mrs Besant 29 September 1922, KFA & 28 February 1923, KFA; Krishna to Lady Emily 8 December 1922, KFA; Lady Emily to Ruspoli 12 October 1922, Huntington 9/8; Nitya to Mrs Besant 18 November 1922, KFI; Krishna to Leadbeater 14 December 1922, KFI.

19 Krishna to Mrs Besaant 2 September 1922, KFI; Lady Emily to Ruspoli 12 October 1922, Huntington 9/8; Nitya to Mrs Besant 18 November 1922, KFI; Nitya to Lady Emily 10 December 1922 KFI; Krishna to Mrs Besant 28 February 1923, KFA.

20 Annie Besant's editorial October 1922 *The Theosophist* pp 3, 4, 6 and November 1922 *The Theosophist* p 114. The author has been unable to locate a copy of the supplement in either the Sydney or London libraries of the Theosophical Society nor any public libraries. Wadia also published a pamphlet 1922 *To All Fellow Theosophists and Members of the Theosophical Society* Los Angeles (see p 8) which the author has also been unable to locate. However an excerpt from Wadia's statement was published in *The High Country Theosophist* Boulder Colorado Vol 6 September 1991 pp 1-3. Wadia went on to become associated with the United Lodge of Theosophists in the United States and worked anonymously as the editor of *The Theosophical Movement*, a monthly magazine begun in 1930. A 'Note' by Wadia in *The Theosophist* January 1911 p 673-75 in praise of Leadbeater's 'Lives' stated that there was no middle course, Leadbeater was either a genuine and a scientifically-reliable seer or a fraud, and Wadia rejected the latter. However in *Occult Review* April 1923 p 246 BP Wadia made it clear that he "wholly" rejected his 1911 'Note', since he now had "confirming evidence". In the same issue on pp 30-38, W. Loftus Hare had exposed Leadbeater's article from *The Theosophist* October 1917 p 91 on the "Lives of Ulysses" as having been lifted from an ancient Persian text, the *Shahnameh*, written by the poet Firdausi published by John Murray in London in 1905. Hare claimed Leadbeater's "clairvoyance" was written "with less imagination and originality than any schoolboy's essay...", in effect providing evidence in accusing Leadbeater of plagiarism. Wadia's confirmed rejection of Leadbeater is also evidenced by his statement in May 1938 *The Theosophist* p 176 asking for space to refute the 1911 'Note', saying that in the 1920s he had written about it in the London *Occult Review* and referring to his letter of resignation 18 July 1922. He now considered his 1911 praise of Leadbeater not to be accurate, he said, in view of his later experience. Wadia died in 1958 after founding the Indian Institute of World Culture in Bangalore which published a centenary edition of his work in 1981.

21 Nitya to Mrs Besant 26 June 1922, KFI; Krishna to Mrs Besant 20 July & 2 September 1922, KFI & 20 October 1922, KFA; Krishna to Rosalind undated (probably September 1922), private source.

22 See Richard Van Fleck "The Electronic Reactions of Albert Abrams" 1998 *American Artifacts* No 39, Taneytown Maryland. Van Fleck maintains that Abrams' degree from the University of Heidelberg was confirmed by the AMA but not his degree from an institution called the University of Portland which was said not to exist. William Hudgings 1923 *Dr Abrahms' Electron Theory* New York republished on the internet by Delta Spectrum Research, Vibration Research Institute & Laboratories, Colorado. 'Abrams' is sometimes spelt 'Abrahms'.

23 M Lutyens (1976) pp 160-61; p 135 Lutyens writes that Krishna had suffered all his life from some unspecified trouble with his nose. Correspondence Nitya to Mrs Besant 18 November 1922 KFI; Krishna to Mrs Besant 1 January 1923, KFA.

24 Krishna to Mrs Besant 29 September & 20 October 1922, KFA; Nitya to Leadbeater 22 October 1922, KFI re depression; Nitya to Mrs Besant 18 November 1922, KFI; Krishna to Mrs Besant 8 December 1922, KFA; Nitya to Leadbeater 28 February 1923, KFI; Nitya to Mrs Besant 28 February & 1 March 1923, KFI. Nitya to Dr Rocke 1 March 1923, KFI.

25 Nitya to Leadbeater and Mrs Besant 28 February 1923, KFI; re 5,000 pounds donation, Nitya to Mrs Besant 1 March 1923, KFI.

26 Correspondence Nitya to Mrs Besant 28 February 1923, KFI, refers to fifty pounds raised at Hollywood; Krishna to Mrs Besant 28 February 1923, KFA, refers to $280 collected. See also Nitya to Mrs Besant 21June 1923, KFI; Krishna to Mrs Besant 21 March 1923, KFA and Nitya to Rosalind 10 May 1923, private source. Re $5,000 raised at TS convention see Nitya to Rosalind 1 June 1923 & Krishna to Rosalind 11 June 1923, private source.

27 Krishna wrote 'my own dearest' letters to several women, including Mrs Besant and Lady Emily, the possessive form of the expression perhaps inferred by each recipient as applying to that person alone. Although Krishna says this is his first letter to Rosalind, an undated letter written at the time he was writing a response to Wadia's pamphlet, possibly September 1922, is clearly a love letter to Rosalind in which Krishna says he misses her terribly, that she is like the sun to a flower, that he can't help it, he is sincere and he wants her to believe him. Private source.

28 10 May 1923, private source. Krishna again asks Rosalind to destroy a later letter, dated 27 May 1923, private source, but as Nitya was well aware of Krishna's feelings for Rosalind it's doubtful Nitya was the person Krishna feared would see the letter.

29 28 February 1923, KFA.

30 Nitya to Rosalind 24 May, 1, 4, 11 June 1923 & Krishna to Rosalind 27 May & 11 June 1923, private source. A telegram giving estimated date of

arrival was sent to Jamnadas Dwarkanath on 16 April 1923 signed 'Krishnitya'. Huntington 20/8. The closeness of the two brothers is attested by such combined signatures in telegrams or notes.

31 Letter dated 21 June 1923. Huntington 9/24.

32 Nitya to Mrs Besant 13 August 1923. KFI.

33 Nitya to Mrs Besant 13 August & 31 October 1923. KFI.

34 Nitya to Leadbeater 27 November 1923. KFI.
Nitya to Rosalind 23 August 1923 & Krishna to Rosalind 4 September 1923, private source. Nitya to Mrs Besant 23 August 1923. KFI.

35 E Blau (1995) pp 51-52.

36 Nearing (1992) pp 44-56. Nitya to Mrs Besant 28 December 1923. KFI. See J Krishnamurti 1995 *On Fear* HarperSanFrancisco for a compilation of Krishnamurti's thoughts on the subject of fear.

37 KFI and Huntington 9/12. The Huntington note has an annotation. "Received January 18 1924", perhaps indicating the date it came into someone else's possession, perhaps that of Rajagopal who deposited the material in the Huntington.

38 Mary Lutyens 1996 *Krishnamurti and the Rajagopals* KFA p 33. Lutyens says that Ruth Roberts was a beautiful, very tall English girl with whom Krishna had flirted in Sydney where she had been for a time a pupil of Leadbeater's. Nitya to Mrs Besant 23 August & 17 September, 1923. KFI.

39 Nitya to Mrs Besant 23 August 1923. KFI.

40 Lutyens (1975) p 127 says Rajagopal was seen as a possible rival to Krishnamurti in his role as 'World Teacher' in 1914 when Jinarajadasa brought him to England as Leadbeater's new "discovery". Rajagopal's daughter, Radha, says that he was born in Tamil Nadu on 7 September 1900, the fourth of seven children in a family belonging to the "Ayyangar Brahmin, Vaishnavite, one of the highest and strictest Hindu castes". His father was a judge and a Theosophist. Rajagopal Sloss (1991) p 40.

41 See *The Theosophist* December 1922 p 223 for reference to Dr van der Leeuw's psychology class. Oscar Kollerstrom, an acolyte of Leadbeater, also had an early interest in psychology. *Herald of the Star* June 1926 p 252, in an article on "Krishnaj", he says the mystic and the psychoanalyst both expose false "conceptions". Tillett (1999) told the author that some time after 1925 Kollerstrom abandoned the Theosophical Society and later had a psychoanalysis practice in London.

42 Nitya to Mrs Besant 31 October 1923. KFI. Lutyens (1996) p 33 says Rajagopal was asked to take a year off Cambridge to go to Ojai. Rajagopal Sloss (1991) p 74 says Rajagopal had completed his MA and LLB in 1925 and was offered a postgraduate place at Cambridge.

43 Nitya to Leadbeater 27 November 1923. KFI. M Lutyens (1996) pp 26, 34-5. According to Hindu legend, the Lord Krishna was said to have devotees or *gopis*, milkmaids who were charmed by his flute-playing into following him into the woods.

44 Nitya to Leadbeater 27 November 1923, KFI.

45 G Tillett interview with the author 8 September 1999. See also Tillett (1982) p 210 who says that Krishna's 'process' would not fit into Leadbeater's own scheme of spiritual development. Nitya to Dr Rocke 29 November 1923, Huntington 9/8; Nitya to Mrs Besant 28 December 1923, KFI.

46 Leadbeater to Nitya 1 January 1924, KFI. G Tillett (1982) p 210. Further details on the amphitheatre in Chapter 5.

47 Nitya to Leadbeater 25 January 1924, KFI.

48 G Tillett (1982) p 211.

49 See circular on US Adyar Committee letterhead which includes a fund for Brothers of Service, Huntington 9/12. Lutyens (1996) p 32 says Baillie-Weaver in England was in charge of all Krishna's and Nitya's financial affairs, and that in addition to the original purchase, Miss Dodge paid for another seven acres owned by the Trust which was called the Brothers' Association. Rajagopal Sloss (1991) p 65 makes the point that it was necessary for a trust to own the estate as 'Orientals', which incorrectly included Indians, could not own land in California at that time. She also says Krishna was astute enough to refuse to own property personally in tune with the idea that spiritual leaders should not be encumbered by materialism.

50 Krishna to Fabrizio Ruspoli 18 January 1924, Huntington 9/5; Krishna to Jamnadas 9 January 1924, Huntington 20/8. Krishna told Jamnadas he was lucky as most people don't get two opportunities. Jamnadas had won 1300 pounds on a horse race in 1919, and Nitya a lesser sum, so the allusion may have been to another win. Lutyens (1976) pp 114-115.

51 Nitya to Leadbeater 14 March, 21 April 1924, KFI; M Lutyens (1976) p 204; M Lutyens (1996) p 35.

52 Nitya to Leadbeater 25 April 1924, KFI. Lutyens (1996) p 36 makes the point that Rajagopal Sloss blames Krishna for the decision by Rosalind to go to the Theosophical Society in Sydney for an occult education from Leadbeater yet Nitya would have been just as much in favour of her going. The point might be made that there's evidence that Nitya was very keen, and whether it was originally his or Krishna's idea is irrelevant, as Nitya himself was keen to see Leadbeater, whom he believed to be a great occult teacher, in Australia or elsewhere. See Nitya correspondence to Leadbeater in 1923 and 1924, especially 26 March & 11 December 1924, KFI, in which he says he would not be in the way in Sydney and he would give a great deal to be with Leadbeater as he may not have another chance in this life.

53 Nitya to Rosalind 26 May & 7 June 1924, private source.

54 Krishna to Rosalind 4 August 1924 & 30 August 1924, private source

55 Nitya to Rosalind 30 August 1924, private source.

56 Krishna to Rosalind 4 August 1924, private source; M Lutyens (1996) pp 206-207. The hand-over of Castle Eerde was a protracted business as it was an historic site so the Dutch Government became involved. Krishna wrote to Mrs Besant on 17 September 1924, KFA, saying George was at Eerde getting affairs in order and on 19 October 1924, KFA, saying he expected it all settled before leaving for India in early November.

57 Nitya to Leadbeater 7 October & 11 December 1924 KFI.

58 H Nearing (1992) pp 52-53. Nearing says Lutyens claims Krishna had begun to lose interest in her in Pergine but elsewhere Lutyens (1996) p 36 writes that Helen was no less a favourite than she had been the year before. Lutyens (1976) p207 says that Rajagopal was also accommodated in the tower section of the castle. The author was not able to establish exactly when a turning point occurred in Krishna's attachment to Helen as the Knothe correspondence was withdrawn from her by the KFA on the grounds that the KFA had not yet decided on its access policy before she had completed its perusal. However Krishna's visit to Sydney in 1925 seems to have been a turning point.

59 Two-page document marked 'Received 18 January 1924' and dated '24 September 1924, Pergine', KFI. M Lutyens (1976) pp 210-211 says the message was received on 24 September and read out to the party by Nitya the following morning. Lutyens does not include the reference to Pergine becoming a centre. If the note that the message was received in January is correct, the place referred to would be Ojai. There is no indication who made the note or when.

60 Lutyens (1976) p 209. 'Gopis', the term Lutyens uses, is that applied to the shepherdesses who were love-sick for Lord Krishna and left their families to gather about him whenever they heard his flute.

61 Krishna's letter to Lady Emily 2 May 1922, KFA. H Nearing (1992) p 57. M Lutyens (1976) p 121 & (1996) p 33 on Krishna flirting.

62 M Lutyens (1959) pp 125-29; M Lutyens (1976) P 218; M Lutyens (1996) pp 25, 33-39; Nitya to Rosalind 30 August 1924 &19 October 1924 plus undated with same pen and paper, private source. Krishna writes to Mrs Besant 28 & 30 January 1925, KFI, that he is glad Mme de Manziarly will look after Nitya well as she is very capable and knows what he needs. See also 19/24 January 1925, KFI for Krishna's concern about Nitya going to Ooty for his health.

63 M Lutyens (1996) pp 28, 37.

64 *The Herald of the Star* January 1924 pp 2-4. *Herald of the Star* July 1926 p 264.

65 M Lutyens (1976) P 217.

66 Krishna to Mrs Besant 10 February1925, KFI; M Lutyens (1976) p 216. The author has visited the school which is run according to advice Krishnamurti gave about education during his lifetime. Details about the site are to be found in correspondence: Nitya to Rosalind re a woman giv-

ing $10,000 p.a., 19 October 1924, private source; Krishna to Nitya re role of Trilokar in assisting, 27 January 1925, KFI; Krishna to Nitya, re acreage and cost, 1 February 1925, KFI; Krishna comments to Nitya that there was no harm in buying the site as land was always useful, 10 February 1925, KFI; Krishna to Mrs Besant re the site 10 February 1925, KFI.

67 Reference to Mr Mackay and Leadbeater in correspondence Krishna to Mrs Besant 24 January 1925, KFI & Krishna to Nitya 1 February 1925, KFI.

Chapter 5 Pathless

1 *Herald* Melbourne 1 April 1925 p 8.

2 Letter dated March 1925, KFI.

3 Letter dated 23 March 1925, KFI.

4 Krishna's comment about Rosalind being a 'big bug' was an indication of her elevation in the occult hierarchy, 22 March 1925, private source, & Nitya wrote to Leadbeater 12 January 1925, KFI, to say how glad he was that Rosalind was 'accepted'. Krishna's correspondence to Rosalind dated 25 January & 6 February 1925, private source. Krishna had told Rosalind that he was serious in hoping that, being very wise, she would help Helen.

5 Letter dated 22 March 1925, private source.

6 References by Krishna to the pain in his head in letters to: Mrs Besant 24 January 1925; Rosalind 25 January 1925, private source; Nitya 27 January 1925, KFI; Mrs Besant 28 January 1925, KFI; Nitya 1 February 1925, KFI; Mrs Besant 3 February, 1925, KFI; Mrs Besant 8 April 1925, KFA.

7 *The Sun News-Pictorial* 1 April 1925 pp 3, 4. Whether or not Edwin Lutyens sculpted, he was by this time a renowned architect. See *The Age* 1 April 1925 pp 10, 11 & 2 April 1925 pp 8, 9; *The Herald* Melbourne 30 March 1925 p17, Shipping News, & 1 April 1925 p 8 & back page.

8 An indication of the mixed political stance of Theosophists in Australia is that, despite Mrs Besant's close association with the Labour Party in Britain, this did not transfer to its political counterpart in Australia. *Theosophy in Australia* January 1926 p 31 was moved to dissociate itself from the labour movement in Australia by pointing out that misunderstandings could occur over political "labels" and that the Australian Labor Party was different in outlook, aims and method from the British party. M Gandhi (1963) Vol XXV Letter to Annie Besant 18 September 1924 p 172, & pp 218-19 (message reported in *New India* 2 October 1924), & "Hand-spinning at Adyar" letter from Mme de Manziarly to Mrs Besant and her response that she would be willing "to spin half an hour a day, if it would help unity", p 384-85. Krishna to Mrs Besant 16 October 1924. Krishna to Jamnadas 20 March & 8 April 1925, Huntington 20/8. It's not,

however, absolutely clear what Krishna wanted the money raised for – but he was keen to raise money in Australia to establish an Indian university near Madanapalle, writing to Mrs Besant that he and Lady Emily would go to see some "big" people, and that he hoped the Maharaja of Mysore and the Duchess of Hawthorn would become patrons, 23 March 1925, KFI. Jamnadas would be gaoled over his political activities in the early 1930s; Ratansi would be Krishna's host in Bombay for many years to come. See Krishna to Rosalind 15 December 1932, private source.

9 See Krishna to Dr Rocke 14 June 1922, Huntington 9/8 & 29 August 1922, Huntington 9/13 in which he says Leadbeater had enthusiastically approved the appointment. M Lutyens (1976) p 218. Nitya to Dr Rocke 29 November 1923, Huntington 9/8. The foundation stone for the amphitheatre below Wyargine Street was laid on 28 July 1923 by Leadbeater. The theatre was designed by architects JE and ER Justelius and the builder J Jamieson of Marrickville. Its cost was reported in 1925 to have been 11,000 pounds. Founders' seats cost from 10 to 100 pounds, leased for 25 years, with their names engraved in bronze tablets. *Herald of the Star* March 1925 pp 95-96. However as was later made clear in the *Herald of the Star* September 1927, p 340 Krishna did not accept gifts of land or anything else personally as he was a *sannyasi*. Gavin Souter 1994 *Mosman A History* Melbourne University Press Melbourne pp 167-68 says the amphitheatre's construction cost was said to be about 16,000 pounds, paid for by the sale of members' seats and a loan of 4,000 pounds paid off within three years. *Theosophy in Australia* December 1925 p 273-74 ran an article presenting the amphitheatre at Balmoral, *The Manor* at Clifton Gardens and the Morven Garden School, despite its "collapse", as examples of justification for belief in Blavatsky's reported ideas about a spiritual "metropolis of the South".

10 G Tillett (1982) p 204; M Lutyens (1976) p 219. Krishna to Mrs Besant 8 April 1925, KFA.

11 *Sydney Morning Herald* 4 April 1925. M Lutyens (1976) pp 220-226. Krishna to Mrs Besant 6 May 1925, KFI.

12 *Theosophy in Australia* August 1925 pp 152-155 for a report of the convention. It's worth noting that one of the other speakers at the youth convention was the writer-to-be, Florence James, who offered her views about how to impress young people through mental training in this "new age".

13 Krishna to Nitya 6 & 10 February 1925, KFI; Krishna enclosed a copy of a letter from Helen and told Nitya to destroy it. Krishna also wrote to Mrs Besant that all his anxiety had gone since he'd received the Master's message that Nitya would be well, 10 February 1925, KFI.

14 The house, 'Nilgiri', was on the north side of Togo Parade, which was renamed Churchill Street during WW II to remove any association with Japan. The house was destroyed after a bushfire in 1957. Lutyens (1976)

p 221 says the Mackays bought the house in 1925 but council rate records show that the following year the owner was a Randwick builder named Hodgson. Information of Joan Smith. Blue Mountains Historical Society.

15 M Lutyens (1976) p 219-21. Krishna to Mrs Besant 8 & 22 April 1925. KFA.

16 Correspondence Krishna to Lady Emily 12 May 1925 & undated from Leura. KFA; Krishna to Dr Rocke 28 June 1925. Huntington 9/8. written after leaving Sydney, apologising for his interference. M Lutyens (1976) pp 224-225 says Krishna may not have been so much in tune with Helen now as she and Ruth were entrenched in *The Manor* way of life. Krishna was critical that Ruth never asked after Nitya's health.

17 R Rajagopal Sloss (1991) pp 72-3.

18 R Rajagopal Sloss (1991) p 72; M Lutyens (1959) pp 176-181.

19 The Sydney Observatory confirms that there was a full moon on 8 May 1925.

20 Krishna to Lady Emily 12 May 1925. KFA; Krishna to Mrs Besant 6 May 1925; Krishna to Ruspoli 27 April 1925. Huntington 9/5 & 12 May 1925. Huntington 9/8. M Lutyens (1976) p 224 says that altogether there were 70 advancements that Wesak in different parts of the Theosophical world.

21 M Lutyens (1976) p 221; G Tillett (1982) p 214. Lutyens p 224 says Krishna made the cheque book allusion in the *Herald of the Star* January 1925.

22 In respect to Nitya's illness it's interesting to read Krishna's chapter on "Care of the Physical Body" in 1926 *Self-Preparation* Star Publishing Trust Ommen pp 29-46 in which he tells all seekers it is their duty to have vigorous, strong, healthy bodies. Krishna to Mrs Besant from on board the *SS Sierra* 11 July 1925. KFI; Krishna to Lady Emily 12 July 1925, the day before reaching San Francisco KFA. M Lutyens (1976) p 225.

23 Krishna to Mrs Besant 24 July 1925. KFI. The brothers had named their home in Ojai 'Arya Vihara', which according to Lutyens (1976) p 195 means 'noble monastery'. In Sanskrit 'Viharin' has the meaning 'Krishna' or 'wanderer'. The name 'Ojai" was said by Mary Lutyens to be an American Indian word meaning 'nest', *Herald of the Star* January 1926 p 7.

24 R Rajagopal Sloss (1991) p 76.

25 Letters dated 11, 15, 16, 17, 18, 19, 20, 21, 25, 26, 27, 28, 29, 30 October & 8, 9, 10, 11 November 1925, KFI. Krishna travelled on the *SS Paris* to England and was joined by other Theosophists sailing on the *SS Ormuz* from Naples to India.

26 Eastern telegraph from Ojai 11 November 1925. Huntington 9/6.

27 M Lutyens (1976) p 237.

28 Shiva Rao's account and the quote from Krishna in M Lutyens (1976) pp 238-39. In an interview in January 1981 Krishna was only able to count to four in Telugu. N Lakshmi Prasad 1990 *Conversations with J Krishnamurti* Quest Wheaton p 14.

29 "Krishnitya" signature *Herald of the Star* May 1922 p 164. Poem in *Herald of the Star* September 1927 pp 324-25. *Herald of the Star* editorial January 1926 p 3.

30 M Lutyens (1976) pp 227-228, 236, G Tillett (1982) pp 218-219. Tillett quotes from Wood's article in the *Canadian Theosophist* Mar-April 1965 p 10 and his own interview with Balfour Clarke in 1979 to support the case that Leabeater didn't believe in the Huizen revelations. Wood had gone to live in Sydney in 1924 after consulting Krishnamurti. In an interview with the author in September 1999, Tillett says that it's quite clear that there was an unsuccessful expedition to find a Master in a castle, as a speech was published and it's recorded in Oscar Kollerstrom's diary, but as it is embarrassing, it has been reinterpreted in theosophical history as a holiday or as not having occurred. Gandhi (1963) Vol XXVI p 559 (interview with *New India* 29 April 1929) & Vol XXVII p 447, 464. G Marvin Williams (1931) p 330.

31 M Lutyens (1976) p 236.

32 G Tillett (1982) p 220. Tillett (1999) said he thought he was given the story by Mary Lutyens and he did not understand why the Krishnamurti Foundation of America had denied the claim. Mary Lutyens (1996) p 45 (published by KFA) denies the account.

33 Krishna to Nitya 9 November 1925, Huntington 9/6. Mary Lutyens (1996) p 47 seems to quote this letter incorrectly, citing Wedgwood instead of Arundale, whom Krishna had referred to as "Old George", as having a difference with Krishna.

34 *The Truth* Sydney 22 November 1925, front page.

35 G Tillett (1982) p 223 from M Lutyens (1976) p 246. Nitya described Wedgwood as a high panjandrum in correspodence to Ruspoli on 2 July 1922, Huntington 9/4.

36 M Lutyens (1976) p 241.

37 *New York Times* 26 December 1925 p 11 reported 5,000 people representing 37 nationalities attending the Madras Adyar convention. The *Times of India*, however, published a story on 25 December 1925 p 21 of a minister from Oxford preaching at St George's Church in New York that the hope that Christ would re-appear in physical manifestation was not now held by educated people.

38 M Lutyens (1976) pp 242-43. Madame Blavatsky had used this same banyan tree for public occasions. R Rajagopal Sloss (1991) p 81.

39 Lily Heber 1931 Krishnamurti *The Man and his Message*, George Allen & Unwin, London, pp 91-92.

40 M Lutyens (1976) p 245; R Rajagopal Sloss (1991) p 81.

41 M Lutyens (1976) p 246.

42 Obituaries *Herald of the Star* January 1926 pp 5-7. Krishna to Rosalind, 7, 17 & 20 April 1926, private source.

43 R Rajagopal Sloss (1991) p 80 quotes from an interview with Helen Knothe.

44 Nitya to Rosalind 19 October 1924, private source.

45 R Rajagopal Sloss (1991) p 77.

46 R Rajagopal Sloss (1991) p 83 and author's interview with Sloss October 2000.

47 Krishna to Rosalind 23 June 1926, private source. M Lutyens (1976) p 247.

48 Correspondence with Arthur Brisbane 17 May & 2 June 1926, Huntington 9/23; Krishna's letter dated 1 July 1926, Huntington 9/22.

49 Letter dated 8 July 1926, private source.

50 M Lutyens (1976) pp 248-50, 253. R Rajagopal Sloss (1991) pp 85-86 says Rosalind was naïve and "failed to find in his touch anything beyond the need to be mothered". Yet by now she was aged about 23 and is said by Sloss to have believed Krishna wanted the attention of a woman. Sloss also quotes from private papers Jinarajadasa's account of Mrs Besant's talk with Krishna. Leadbeater to Krishnamurti 28 July 1926, KFI. It's interesting that over several months leading up to this period there was a minor press controversy in a remote region of Australia with allegations that Krishnamurti was a "false prophet". The Reverend Kleindienst of the Townsville Methodist Church was reported in the Townsville *Daily Bulletin* 9 February 1926 as saying that to present Krishnamurti as the Messiah was a "monstrosity, in quarrel with both reason and faith". Kleindienst was supported by "the Reverend RE Bacon of Chartres [sic] Towers", an even less notable Queensland country town, on 24 May 1926. There followed a small publication printed in Charters Towers containing a startling quotation from a nonentity from Ceylon as saying of Theosophy that "Filthy as the work is, it should be recognised as a work of darkness and fraud" and including Kleindienst's conclusion that the "Messianic stunt" was "a travesty on the second coming – a daring and shameless blasphemy". The booklet found its way into the Mitchell Library collection of the State Library of NSW.

51 American Consulate Madras memorandum to the Secretary of State 26 April 1926 quoting *The Hindu* 1 May 1926, National Archives, Visa Division record Group No. 59.

52 M Lutyens (1976) p 255. The following year Edwin Lutyens stopped the publication of a story about Mary being engaged to Krishna and demanded she return home, but she stayed on in Holland. M Lutyens (1976) p 265.

53 Letter dated 11 September 1926, private source.

54 M Lutyens (1976) p 259.

55 M Lutyens (1976) p 258. M Lutyens (1996) p 56 speculates that Rosalind may have been jealous of Krishna's love for her, whereas she looked on Rosalind and Rajagopal as an engaged couple and saw no evidence that Krishna loved Rosalind.

56 C Percy & J Ridley (1988) p 408, letter dated 4 February 1927; M Lutyens (1976) p 258.

57 M Lutyens (1976) pp 258, 261.

58 M Lutyens (1976) p 257 explains that about sixty of Krishna's poems were published in-house in Theosophical or *Star* journals between 1923 and 1931 at which time he stopped writing poetry. *The Annual Obituary* 1986 St James Press Chicago p 116 cites Krishnamurti as "a mystic by nature and a poet by expression", despite the overwhelming proportion of prose in his published writing. Susunaga Weeraperuma (1974) & (1982) cite a total of 75 publications of poems, including both periodical and book republication. Weeraperuma says Krishna's first published poem was "Hymn of the initiate triumphant", in *Herald of the Star* January 1923, p 23. Poems and parables by Krishnamurti are collected in 1980 "From Darkness to Light" *The Collected Works of Krishnamurti Vol I* Harper & Row San Francisco. In John Tranter's correspondence with the author 28 July 2001, he playfully sums up Krishna's work: "As theology four out of ten. As poetry, in my opinion, two". J Krishnamurti 1927 *The Search* Star Publishing Trust & Allen & Unwin London. See also J Krishnamurti 1928 *The Pool of Wisdom* Star Publishing Ommen which contains three poems, "The Simple Union" (concerning the way to the heart of the "Beloved"), "The Garden Of My Heart" and "Come Away" (which repeats the refrains "Come away" and "I have found the way"). See also "My Beloved and I Are One" *Herald of the Star* August 1927 p 290. The theology expressed in this poem is a simplistic interpretation of Advaitism or non-duality. Lily Heber 1931 *The Man and His Message* Allen & Unwin London is so impressed by Krishna's poetry he included an excerpt on the same theme of purifying the "self" and finding the "Beloved". Recurring ideas used by Krishna as metaphor in poetry and prose include the light of love, a mountain to be scaled and the kingdom of happiness. Oscar Kollerstrom already in 1926 saw Krishna as artist giving way to Krishna as mystic (*Herald of the Star* June 1926 pp 251-52) yet in 1928 AE Wodehouse said Krishna had many unpublished poems in his desk and he saw him as "Orpheus" rather than "Shankaracharya" (*The Star* April 1928 pp 12-13).

59 *The Theosophist* December 1922 pp 312-14 article on the "Brotherhood of the New Age' written by John Cordes. The term "New Age" was used loosely in the early years of the twentieth century giving rise to a new journal established by GB Shaw in 1907. *The New Age*, edited by AR Orage up until 1922, provided what has been described by historian Wallace Martin as "an unparalleled arena of cultural and political debate". Wallace maintains that it provides a comprehensive record of the emergence of "modern" culture from the Victorian and Edwardian periods, as a left-wing forum for political and cultural debate for the 'intelligentsia', elaborating a Guild Socialist political theory after 1912. Towards the end

of his editorship. Orage developed an interest in the occult, especially in the Gurdjieff Institute. See Wallace Martin, 1967, *The New Age Under Orage*, Manchester University Press & Searchlight (pseud WD Frank) 1926 *Time Exposures*, Boni & Liveright New York, pp 151-156.

60 *Herald of the Star* May 1927 p168. M Lutyens (1976) pp 261-63.

61 M Lutyens (1976) p 272 & (1996) p 58. Lutyens explains only in the later work that the church was Liberal Catholic and not licensed to perform legal marriages and that Bishop Piggott who married them was "mixed up in the hysteria of the 'mad camp' in 1925". She also comments that it is a mystery why Rosalind married Rajagopal, whom she acknowledges was deeply in love with Rosalind. R Rajagopal Sloss (1991) p 93 says Rosalind felt keenly Krishna's disapproval of her and Rajagopal marrying. Nitya to Leadbeater 12 January 1925 KFI.

62 In author's interview Weeraperuma (2000), the disaffected former Krishnamurti acolyte, who knew Krishnamurti well for about thirty years, acknowledges that Krishna was "full of affection" even though he now believes he had a hypnotic effect on followers and was an imperfect spiritual teacher.

63 Correspondence: May 1927, KFA; 16 June 1927, KFA; 13 & 27 July, 1 August 1927, Huntington 9/22. M Lutyens (1976) pp 267-70.

64 Krishna to Mrs Besant May 1927 KFA. M Lutyens (1976) p 264-66. Jinarajadasa's letter marked in pencil Aug 1928, Huntington 11/14. The Upanishads, part of the sacred revelation called the Vedas, were composed about c200 BCE and added to the Vedas. They include the *Mahabharata* and the *Bhagavad Gita*. Mrs Besant's statement to Associated Press of America published *Herald of the Star* March 1927 p 93.

65 M Lutyens (1976) p 272. *The Theosophist* January 1928 p 391 and *The Star* February 1928 p 55. One of the donors was a Mrs Stead; the other was unnamed

66 Correspondence dated 26 February, 4, 10, 15 March, 7, 18 April, 3, 23, 27, 28 July, 1928, KFA.

67 Krishna to Mrs Besant 2, 22 August & 5 September 1928, KFA; Leadbeater to Krishna 15 August 1928, KFI.

68 Mrs Besant to Krishna 30 October 1928, Huntington 9/22.

69 Jinarajadasa to Krishna 11 February 1929, Huntington 11/15.

70 *Los Angeles Times*: 12 May 1928 p 3 Pt II, advertisement plus advertorial for address on15 May; 21 May 1928 p 6 Pt I report of sermon by Dr HC Culbertson at Plymouth Congregational Church; 22 May 1928 p1 article by *Times* Staff Representative Joseph Park.

71 Correspondence from Bourdelle December 1927 & undated proposal, Huntington 9/23. M Lutyens (1976) pp 271, 284. See reference to Bourdelle in Krishna's letter to Rosalind 3 August 1928, private source.

72 Krishna to Jamnadas Dwarkanath 21 May 1928. Huntington 20/8. Leadbeater to Krishna 18 July 1928. KFI; Krishna to Leadbeater 15 Aug 1928. KFI. M Lutyens (1976) Fn p 277 makes the point that the World Mother movement was short-lived. Rukmini went on to establish an Academy of Arts in Madras and was involved in the Theosophical Society for many years. unsuccessfully standing for office as the President in 1973 after the death of her brother Sri Ram who had held the post.

73 Krishna to Mrs Besant 22 August. 5 September. 19 & 23 November 1928. KFA; Krishna to Leadbeater 1 November 1928. KFI.

74 Krishna to Mrs Besant 29 January 1929 & 13 February 1929. KFA.

75 Letter undated from Hotel Bel Alp. Montroc Haute Savoie France refers to Mont Blanc as almost in Krishna's room. On the subject of cars. Krishna loved them. the classier the better. and he loved driving. At various times he had use of a Lincoln. a Packard. another Lincoln. a small. "cheap" Ford. and in his later years a Jaguar and a Mercedes. The cars were owned by the Rajagopals or his later companions or organisations. See Lutyens (1976) p 258. Lutyens (1983) p127. 134. Rajagopal Sloss (1991) p 222 and correspondence 18 April (KFA). 12 June (private source). 11 October (private source) 1928.

76 Letters to Rosalind include 12 June. 22 July. 11 October 1928. private source; Jinarajadasa to Krishna possibly June 1928 (may be 1926/7). Huntington 11/15. Jinarajadasa turned fifty in 1925.

77 Leadbeater to Krishna 16 January 1929. KFI.

78 M Lutyens (1976) p 291. Correspondence with Mrs Besant 22 March. 26 April. 13 May 1929. KFA.

79 M Lutyens (1976) pp 293-97. In October 1930 in Eerde Krishnamurti was still saying he had no followers or disciples as they would be a "limitation on truth" - Krishnamurti Australia pamphlet. *Life's Problems*.

80 Letters dated 12 August 1929. KFA; 13 August. London & August. Chicago. 1929. Huntington 9/22. The philosophy of unity is fundamental to Advaita philosophy.

81 Krishna to Mrs Besant 7 September 1929. KFA; Krishna to Rosalind 14 October 1929. 22 October 1929. private source.

Chapter 6 Ménage

1 Lady Emily Lutyens (1957) p 184. M Lutyens (1996) p 59 says when the Order of the Star was dissolved it had about 40,000 members. The deed of transfer returning the Castle to the Baron was signed on 26 March 1931. according to M Lutyens (1976) p 329. Krishna wrote to Rosalind in January 1931 that van Pallandt was now talking with Rajagopal in the negotiations and that greed was a terrible disease. without commenting who was greedy. 24 January 1931. private source. During WW II the estate was taken over as a Nazi concentration camp and is now the site of a school.

2 M Lutyens (1976) p 298 says the reopening made his resignation inevitable.
3 Lady Emily Lutyens (1957) p 176. Tillett (1982)p 230 and in an interview with the author says that by December 1927 Leadbeater was already declaring privately that "The Coming has gone wrong" despite Krishna's impression that Leadbeater was reverential to him.
4 M Lutyens (1976) p 299-300; Lady Emily Lutyens (1957) p 176.
5 Letters dated 4 February 1930 from Aden and 9 February 1930 from Port Said. KFA.
6 Lady Emily Lutyens (1957) pp 176-82. She dates Krishna's letter as 28 April 1930 from Ojai. Lady Emily was among many people who had been referring to Krishna as "Krishnaji", the "ji" used in India to convey respect and affection.
7 Lady Emily Lutyens (1957) pp 183-88.
8 M Lutyens (1976) p 302.
9 R Rajagopal Sloss (1991) p 107. M Lutyens (1996) pp 34, 36 , 44 in her refutation of aspects of the Sloss book is critical of Rosalind, calling her dishonest in going to the Theosophical Centre in Sydney and in promising Nitya she would stay with Krishna if she did not believe in occult Theosophy. Lutyens says she wonders how she herself could have believed what Leadbeater told them but at least she is not ashamed of admitting she once did.
10 M Lutyens (1976) p 329 & KFA Archives list of talks available on internet.
11 R Rajagopal Sloss (`991) pp 108-109.
12 Krishna to Rosalind 7 October 1930, private source.
13 M Lutyens (1976) p 329.
14 Krishna to Rosalind 11 November 1930, private source; KFA Archives list of talks available on internet.
15 R Rajagopal Sloss (1991) pp 108-109. See correspondence Leadbeater to Krishna 29 August 1913, Huntington 9/9.
16 R Rajagopal Sloss (1991) p 110.
17 Krishna to Rosalind 8 December 1930, private source.
18 Krishna to Rosalind 16 December, 1930, private source.
19 M Lutyens (1990) pp 82-83; R Rajagopal Sloss (1991) pp 111
20 Krishna to Rosalind 31 December 1930, private source.
21 Letter from Malati dated 2 January 1931 included in correspondence on Adyar Star letterhead dated 17 January 1931, private source.
22 Krishna to Rosalind 14 January 1931, private source. In the reference to a "bud" Krishna does not say when he offered it whether Rosalind took it and still has it or where it is, as it is still a bud. The reader cannot know whether it was an actual rosebud or whether he was using a metaphorical device, meaning a young Rosalind that had not yet blossomed.
23 Krishna to Rosalind 24 January 1931, private source.

24 Krishna to Rosalind 11, 12 February 1931, private source.

25 5 January & 5 February 1931, Huntington 11/15. The year of the letter dated 14 January is not marked and is most likely 1932 judging by its contents. Krishna wrote to Mrs Besant on 5 November 1931 that Rajagopal's and Rosalind's baby was very "nice" and on 11 December 1931 saying American papers were insisting they he and she had quarrelled, KFA. It's likely that the 1931 date for the 5 January letter is an oversight and should read 1932.

26 Krishna to Rosalind 30 March 1931, private source.

27 Krishna to Rosalind 13 April, 13 June 1931, private source.

28 13 July 1931, private source. The author presumes the existence of a telegram from Rajagopal, not having had access to his personal letters. It must be acknowledged that it was not common in the 1930s for fathers to be present at the birth of a child although few would have been out of the country.

29 R Rajagopal Sloss (1991) pp 110-111.

30 R Rajagopal Sloss(1991) pp 111-112.

31 Krishna to Rosalind 15 August 1931, private source.

32 M Lutyens (1976) p 303.

33 Krishna to Mrs Besant 5 November, 11, 18, 23, 29 December, 1931, 14 January, 1932, KFA; 20, 27 January 1932, KFI; 4 February, 8 April, 1932, KFA. The Sanskrit word *samadhi* carries meanings not necessarily associated with the Western concept of 'retreat'. *Samadhi* can be translated as 'ecstasy', being the final stage of a yogic path to self-realisation which is usually reached through complete sensory deprivation.

34 Krishna to Rosalind 17, 29 December 1931, private source.

35 Lady Emily Lutyens (1957) p 185. She attributes it to a statement made at Adyar in 1931 but Krishna did not go to Adyar in 1931.

36 M Lutyens (1976) pp 302-304. M Lutyens (1996) p 64 says Krishna had told Lady Emily when he first went to Paris that he longed for a happy home.

37 The date is a little uncertain as Krishna had given talks on Sundays from January to April 1932, covering the spring period, and the Ojai camp ran from 2-8 June, in the summer. R Rajagopal Sloss (1991) p 116-118.

38 M Lutyens (1996) p 62. Mary Zimbalist's interview with the author 15 November 2000.

39 R Rajagopal Sloss (1991) p 118.

40 M Lutyens (1996) p 64; R Rajagopal Sloss (1991) p 122.

41 Letters 21 July from Seattle, undated from Shawnigan Lake British Columbia and 15 August 1932, private source. Krishna sent on several letters from Lady Emily to Rosalind over the next year, asking her to destroy them after reading.

42 Lady Emily to Krishna 21 Aug 1932, KFI.

43 Jinarajadasa's letters to Krishna: 6 February, 12 May, 22 July, 1932, Huntington 11/15. Despite Jinarajadasa's warning about hair-tearing, the author retains a full head of hair. *Maya* is generally meant to indicate the illusory nature of what we see as the world.

44 A Rama Rao "The Teachings of Krishnamurti" *The Theosophist* June 1932 pp 246-49. Krishna's poem "The Search of the Beloved" was published in *The Star* October 1928 pp 3-7. Gandhi's correspondence with Sjt Rama Rao c/- Sjt Jamshed NR Mehta, Bonus Rd Karachi dated 11 February 1929, *Collected Works of Mahatma Gandhi* Vol XXXIX p 450. Gandhi's letter to J Krishnamurti 29 November 1928 *Collected Works* Vol XXXVIII p 119.

45 Krishna's letters to Rosalind dated 2, 13, 23 September, 8 October, 7, 11 November 1932, private source.

46 E Blau (1995) pp 67-70.

47 Krishna to Rosalind 15, 25, 27 November, 8 December 1932, private source.

48 Rajagopal to Rosalind 1932, Huntington 25/14.

49 Krishna to Rosalind 15, 29 December, 1932, private source.

50 M Lutyens (1983) p 24 for Benares talks and chicken pox; Krishna to Rosalind 13 February, 1 April 1933, private source.

51 Krishna to Rosalind 23 June 1933, private source.

52 C Percy & J Ridley (1988) p 430. Krishna is said to have stayed at the Lutyens home at 13 Mansfield St whenever he went to London.

53 R Rajagopal Sloss (1991) pp 120-21.

54 Krishna to Rosalind 17 September, 29 October, 30 November, 1933, private source. M Lutyens (1983) p 25.

55 Jinarjadasa to Krishna 11 September 1933 Huntington 11/15.

56 G Tillett (1982) p249; Nethercot (1963) pp 453-457. According to the London *Times* Mrs Besant left an estate valued at only 2,500 pounds, having made bequests to the Adyar Museum of Records and the Theosophical Society and having left her bookshop in Russell Street London to her son, Digby.

57 P Jayakar (1986) p 84.

58 *The Bombay Chronicle* 21 September 1933 from Gandhi (1963) Vol LVI pp 11,12. Jinarajadasa had published a brief biography of Mrs Besant the previous year in which he said the divergence between the two persisted because she believed mass action released forces which would degenerate into violence and be to the detriment of India's national life in the long term. C Jinarajadasa 1932 *A Short Biography of Anne Besant* Theosophical Publishing House Madras p 36.

59 Jinarajadasa to Krishna 11 September 1933 says this is how Mrs Besant describes him, Huntington 11/15. G Marvin Williams (1931) pp 347-350.

60 Jinarjadasa to Krishna 11 September 1933 Huntington 11/15.

61 M Lutyens (1983) p 25. Correspondence 16 January 1934 shows that the Indian Section of the Society of 26 December 1933 gave Krishna free use of Mrs Besant's house *Shanti Kunja* in Benares and two rooms at Adyar free of rent as provided in the deed of transfer by Mrs Besant and that Rajagopal replied with thanks from Krishna on 24 January 1934. Huntington 9/23. 'Vasanta Vihar' means spring of Krishna or wanderer.

62 M Lutyens (1983) p 26, letter dated 21 January 1934 written from Colombo on the way to Australia.

63 Letter dated 19 September 1933. Huntington 20/8.

64 Rajagopal to Rosalind 19 December 1933. Huntington 25/14. Krishna's reference in letter to Rosalind 23 September 1932.

65 M Lutyens (1983) p 26. Rajagopal to Rosalind 19 & 30 December 1933. Huntington 25/14.

66 *West Australian* Shipping Notices 5, 6, 12, 13, 14, 15 February 1934.

67 *West Australian* 3 February 1934 "The Teacher and his Creed" p 4. *Star* newsletter no. 2 April 1934.

68 KFA.

69 *West Australian* 7 February 1934 p 16 "Krishnamurti Indian Teacher in Perth. A Plea for Individualism".

70 *West Australian* 6 February 1934 p 3 "A West Australian Teacher Talks with Gandhi"

71 *Adelaide Advertiser* 10 February 1934 p 22. Extract from *The Advertiser* Adelaide published in *Star* newsletter no 2 April 1934. KFA.

72 *The Advertiser*, Adelaide, 14 February 1934 p 23.

73 KFA. "Vedanta" is the basis for a multiplicity of Indian philosophies. Krishnamurti's description of the mind working through opposites bears similarities to Advaita Vedanta. He would have developed an understanding of Vedanta philosophies from the Theosophical Society, both in written and spoken forms, as many books were available and people would have talked about many of the concepts written about by Blavatsky and Annie Besant who were both interested in Vedanta philosophies, without him having to have read very deeply the texts. Krishnamurti would not have needed to study Schopenhauer or Kant, who were both influenced by these ancient ideas, to espouse them.

74 RL Markel for the Star Publishing Trust to the Theosophical Publishing House, Adyar, 11 November 1930, Huntington 32/1.

75 *Herald* Melbourne 12 February 1934 p 8. Krishna had played golf well in Scotland in 1919 where he is reported to have won a "championship" at Muirfield, Gullane in East Lothian and in France in 1920, M Lutyens (1976) pp 112, 120.

76 *Herald* Melbourne 12 February 1934 p 11.

77 *Herald* Melbourne 29 January 1934 p 10.

78 KFA.

79 KFA.

80 KFA.

81 Discussion at Mackay home 23 February 1934. KFA. See Rohit Mehta 1973 *J Krishnamurti and the Nameless Experience* Samuel Weiser New York Preface and p 489 for reference to Krishnamurti's negative approach eg "emptying of the mind has to be total – even the products of order must be negated". See also Rohit Mehta & Shridevi Mehta 1990 *J Krishnamurti and Sant Kabir* Motilal Banarsidass New Delhi p 10 who writes that Krishnaji deals with problems with an "air" of negativity but his teachings are fundamentally positive.

82 On the question of aspects of Socrates' method of discourse being similar to that in the Vedantic tradition, Robert S Brumbaugh 1966 *The Philosophers of Greece* Allen & Unwin London pp 124, 125, 237 says that Socrates has been likened to a Hindu guru, citing Radhakrishnan (ed) 1955 *Philosophy East and West* II New York. He also points out Socrates' belief that people must do their own thinking and that after Socrates Greek thinkers could never forget the question, 'What am I ?', which is a question that underpins Indian philosophical thought. Theodore Zeldin 1998 *An Intimate History of Humanity* Vintage/Random House London pp 33, 34 describes Socrates as "the first known conversationalist", who introduced the idea that individuals needed someone else to stimulate them and who refused to teach, insisting that he was as ignorant as his pupil. Two contributors to Gregory Vlastos (ed) 1971 *The Philosophy of Socrates* Doubleday New York might be cited here: Gregory Vlastos in "The Paradox of Socrates" pp 9, 13 points to Socrates' searching for himself as well as wanting his partner in dialogue to find out about his soul for himself, and Richard Robinson in "Socratic Definition" pp 110-115 argues that the Socrates of Plato's dialogues is continually asking questions, first primary questions, usually ethical, followed by a series of secondary questions.

83 Savoy Theatre Sydney 22 February 1934, KFA.

84 L Heber (1931) p 93.

85 24 February 1934, KFA.

86 25 February 1934, KFA. Correspondence Rajagopal to Rosalind 1 March 1934, Huntington 25/14.

87 26 February 1934, KFA.

88 28 February, 1934, KFA.

89 21 March at Adyar Hall, Sydney, KFA. The article in the *Herald*, Melbourne 29 January 1934, p 10 said that Krishnamurti would sub-edit the shorthand writer's notes, deleting all that he thought superfluous or redundant.

90 Krishna to Rosalind 14 February 1934 on board *SS Otranto*, private source.

91 Rajagopal to Rosalind 19 February, 1, 2 March 1934, Huntington 25/14.

92 M Lutyens (1983) p 27. Leadbeater's ashes were sent to Adyar to remain with those of Mrs Besant in the garden of remembrance.

93 M Lutyens (1976) p viii. G Tillett (1982) pp 9-19. Interview with the author 8 September 1999.

94 21 March 1934. KFA.

95 *Krishnamurti Auckland, NZ – 1934*. Star Publishing Trust. Ommen. pp 3-11. 28 March 1934.

96 *Krishnamurti Auckland, NZ – 1934*. Star Publishing Trust. Ommen. pp 12-23. 30 March 1934.

97 *Krishnamurti Auckland, NZ – 1934*. Star Publishing Trust. Ommen. pp 24-33. 31 March 1934.

98 *Krishnamurti Auckland, NZ – 1934*. Star Publishing Trust. Ommen. pp 34-51. 31 March 1934.

99 *Krishnamurti Auckland, NZ – 1934*. Star Publishing Trust. Ommen. pp 52-64. 1 April 1934.

100 *Krishnamurti Auckland, NZ – 1934*. Star Publishing Trust. Ommen. pp 65-74. 2 April 1934. In an interview with the author 18 October 2000. Director of Krishnamurti Publications of America. Mark Lee. said such a misinterpretation was an aberration which might result in some people becoming highly agitated and even in some cases neurotic. He said Krishnamurti meditated for hours every day. and when he said not to use a technique he meant not to do it according to a particular pattern. J Krishnamurti 1983 *The Flame of Attention* Harper & Row San Francisco p 69.

101 *Krishnamurti Auckland, NZ – 1934*. Star Publishing Trust. Ommen. pp 75-85. 6 April 1934.

102 Extracts quoted in *Star* newsletter July 1934.

103 H Pearson 1944 *Bernard Shaw His Life and Personality* Collins London p 115. Nethercot (1963) p 449 dates the meeting as January 1933. when Krishnamurti visited Shaw on board the ship on which he was travelling. the *Empress of India*, berthed in Bombay. M Lutyens (1983) p 27-28 says Shaw had met Krishnamurti once or twice in London while lunching with Lady Emily yet for the quote credits Pearson. who only refers to Bombay.

104 M Lutyens (1983) p 29.

Chapter 7 In Love and War

1 *Star* newsletters April & December 1934. In December Rajagopal was printing talks from Auckland. Ojai. Italy and Norway and planning publication of *Thoughts on Life*.

2 M Lutyens (1996) p 23 writes that an April 1935 *New York Times* notice of the annual incomes for life for the Rajagopals. apparently jointly. was $4.000 and for Krishnamurti $5.000. The trusts were made in May 1931 and Miss Dodge died in December 1934. Krishnamurti and Rajagopal had earlier been given 500 and 400 pounds p.a. respectively.

3 Lady Emily to Krishna 14 August & 16 September 1934. KFI.
4 M Lutyens (1983) p 30.
5 Krishna to Rosalind 24 August 1934. private source.
6 Krishna to Rosalind 29 August 1934. private source.
7 M Lutyens (1983) p 31 says Rajagopal was to have a sinus operation at the end of August 1934 in the hope it cured his rheumatism but it was postponed.
8 In *The Song of Songs* or *Song of Solomon*. Old Testament, the quote is "sick of love, meaning 'sick with love'". Krishna's letter to Rosalind dated Monday 19 November 1934. then Tuesday and Wednesday nights. It's significant that in her 1975 biography of Krishna p159, M Lutyens includes a letter from him to her mother, Lady Emily, written in 1922 which is his first reference to Rosalind. in which he says that they are reading O. Henry and the Bible. Lutyens' aside is that *The Song of Solomon* is Krishna's favourite book in the Bible and what he did not mention was that Rosalind was a very pretty girl with fair, wavy hair and blue eyes like those of a Siamese cat. This indicates an early link between Rosalind and *The Song of Songs* in Krishna's mind. Further evidence that Krishna was cognisant of an erotic interpretation of *The Song of Songs* is to be found in a profile of Krishna taken from notes made in 1933/34 by L Sarabhai (1990) first published in Gujarati in 1955. On p 33 she says Krishna read aloud from *The Song of Songs* after saying that it was "so passionate" he should not read it aloud to young people. "It is really meant to illustrate the love of man and woman but was later on interpreted as the love of the Church for God," Sarabhai quotes Krishna as saying.
9 M Lutyens (1983) p 33.
10 M Lutyens (1983) p 31-32 says Robinson Jeffers' "Credo" was published in 1935. However it was first published in 1927 in *A Miscellany of American Poetry* and republished in 1930. so if it refers to Krishnamurti the poem must have been based on an impression of him before their meeting in Carmel in 1934. See 1968 SS Alberts *Bibliography of Robinson Jeffers* Franklin NY pp 3. 5.
11 Rom Landau 1935 *God is My Adventure* Nicholson & Watson London pp 355-385.
12 R Landau (1935) pp 367-78. 371.
13 From *Song of Songs* "set me as a seal upon thine heart". Krishna to Rosalind marked in pencil "January 1935". private source.
14 Krishna to Rosalind marked in pencil "1935" and "February 1935" and marked in the original by the day of the week only. For South American tour details see M Lutyens (1983) pp 36-39. Krishna had watched the operation on Rajagopal while he was anaesthetised. 13 January 1935. Huntington 23/6. R Rajagopal Sloss (1991) p 132 for reference to the abortion. Sloss does not say how an osteopath could abort a pregnancy. There's a bitter tone in the description even though Rosalind is said to

have acted for reasons of health rather than discretion. Sloss implies Krishna lacked compunction and did not take adequate contraceptive precautions and suggests her mother may have been naïve.

15 Unsigned letters to Rajagopal from Ommen 13 July 1934, Huntington 20/11, probably from A Folkersma, Manager at Ommen Star Camp. Mr & Mrs Vigeveno had sought refuge from Nazism and had been given accommodation at Ommen. They would remain attached to one or another of the organisations involved in disseminating Krishnamurti's teachings all their lives. See Rajagopal's letter to Mrs Vigeveno from Sydney 6 March 1934, Huntington 20/11. Rajagopal's letter to Mrs Vigeveno 15 May & 17 December 1935, Huntington 20/11.

16 Rajagopal to Rosalind 1 May, 1935 Huntington, 25/14. Rajagopal wrote to Rosalind on 14 June 1935 that Krishna had managed to correct and revise all the talks he'd given in Brazil, which was some achievement, he said, but not the Ommen talks. On creativity, Krishna once said that to be creative was not merely to produce poems, statues or children but to be in a state in which truth could come into being. J Krishnamurti 1999 *On Creativity* KFI Pune p 18 from (1956) *Education and the Significance of Life*.

17 Rajagopal to Rosalind 1, 10 May 1935 Huntington 25/14.

18 Rajagopal to Rosalind 17, 25, 31 May & 21 June 1935 1935, Huntington 25/14.

19 Rajagopal to Rosalind 1, 10, 17, 24 May & 7 June, 1935 Huntington 25/14.

20 Rajagopal to Rosalind 21 June 1935, Huntington 25/14. M Lutyens (1983) p 37. Krishna's comment in a letter to Madame Blech 22 July 1935, Huntington 9/23.

21 Rajagopal to Rosalind 5 July 1935, Huntington 25/14.

22 Krishna's letter dated 3 July 1935, Huntington 23/6. Rajagopal to Rosalind 5 July 1935, Huntington 25/14. See R Rajagopal Sloss (1991) p 135 for Rosalind's letter to Blanche Matthias 5 August 1935.

23 Krishna to Madame Blech 22 July 1935, Huntington 9/23. Krishna to Doris Gowlland 12 August 1935, KFA.

24 R Rajagopal Sloss (1991) p 135 alleges that Krishna and Rajagopal had serious misunderstandings over Krishna "lying" and "undercutting" him. She says Rajagopal believed Krishna should have been less critical and more patient with Theosophists who made up much of his audiences.

25 M Lutyens (1983) pp 36-7, quoting a letter from Krishna to Lady Emily.

26 M Lutyens (1983) p 39. R Landau (1935) p 363-366.

27 Doris Gowlland to Krishna 24 May 1935 & 11 Mar 1936 and his replies 12 August 1935 & 12 May 1936, KFA. Jinarajadasa's trip also mentioned in a letter Tidswell to Krishna 13 May 1935 Huntington 23/7 and in Rajagopal to Rosalind 17 May 1935, Huntington 25/14.

28 Rajagopal to Rosalind 24 May 1935, Huntington 25/14.

29 Jinarajadasa to Krishna 15 June, 30 July 1935, Huntington 11/15 & Jinarajadasa correspondence 27 November 1935, Huntington 11/14. Shankaracharya (788-820 CE) espoused Advaita or non-duality, that the sense of a distinction between God and one's self is an illusion. Similarly, the teaching of Gautama Buddha (ca 563-483 BCE) of the concept of impermanence is concerned with the insubstantiality, emptiness or void of what we see as reality.

30 Letter dated 30 January 1936, Huntington 11/14.

31 Letter dated 11 September 1938, Huntington 11/15. Few of Krishna's letters to Jinarajadasa were available to the author but the friendship continued through to Jinarajadasa's death in 1953.

32 Rajagopal to Rosalind 19 October 1935, Huntington 25/14. See similar reference to Krishna debating in Rajagopal correspondence 21 June 1935, Huntington 25/14. M Lutyens (1983) p 40 says Krishna went to Carmel with the Rajagopals, not specifying which Rajagopals, ie Rosalind and Radha. R Rajagopal Sloss (1991) pp 140-41.

33 Krishna to Lady Emily 21 April 1936, Huntington 9/30. R Rajagopal Sloss (1991) pp 140-42 quoting letter from Rosalind dated 28 June 1936. M Lutyens (1983) p 40.

34 Krishna's letter dated 11 June 1936, from H Nearing (1992) pp 53-57. She wrote part of her account in the third person. Helen's letters dated 1936, Huntington 20/8.

35 M Lutyens (1983) p 40. Yet in a letter to Dwarkanath Telang dated 21 July 1936 Krishna said he expected about 1500 people to attend the camp. R Rajagopal Sloss (1991) p 143 says she remembers waking one morning to see a large red rose above her crib and knowing it was there as a sign that her mother had gone to London with Krishna.

36 Nearing to Krishnamurti 25 October 1936, Huntington 20/8.

37 Krishna to van Pallandt 3 December 1936, Huntington 9/23. Pallandt had mentioned in a letter dated 8 November 1936 that Helen had sent him a copy of Nearing's letter to Krishnamurti, Huntington 9/23. Van Pallandt seemed to have been happy with Krishnamurti and the Ommen discussions, saying he had seen things differently since.

38 Krishnamurti to Nearing 7 December 1936, handwritten and typed, Huntington 20/8.

39 Letter dated 6 January 1936 mention "my wife" as a translator, which indicates that it was written by James Vigeveno, Huntington 20/11.

40 Deposition dated 27 December 1936, Huntington 25/14.

41 US National Archives and Department of Justice/FBI files released to the author under FOI provisions. KFA's Mark Lee, who also obtained some FBI files, told the author that "someone" from the "White House" had warned him that Krishnamurti was listed as an "undesirable alien" and if Lee pursued his enquiries with the agency it might set off an investigation into the KFA, so enquiries had been suspended for a number of years. In

a letter to the author dated 9 January 2002. Britain's MI5 refused to assist with a request for information held on Jiddu Krishnamurti on the grounds that it was the policy of successive Governments not to comment on the extistence of records on individuals or organisations.

42 M Lutyens (1983) p 40-41 says Mima Porter had owned a house in Ojai since 1930. From 1928 Carlo Suares published several articles and books about Krishnamurti in French, with a translation into English published in 1955. See Susunaga Weeraperuma (1974) & (1982).

43 R Rajagopal Sloss (1991) p 143. Krishna to Dwarkanath 27 November 1934 & 21 July 1936, Huntington 11/20. References to this activity found in: Krishna to Madame Blech 22 July 1935, Huntington 9/23; Jinarajadasa to Krishna 30 January 1936 & 12 December 1936, Huntington 11/15; Ernest Wood's letter 12 May 1935, Huntington 34/49.

44 M Lutyens (1983) p 42. RK Shringy 1977 *Philosophy of J Krishnamurti* Munshiram Manoharlal New Delhi pp 59, 156, 198-200, 218 points out that Krishna spoke of "constant awareness" which he later called "choiceless awareness". Shringy describes it as "self-discernment" or being aware of "what is", facing a problem without trying to solve it, or a means of awakening intelligence, only possible in the silence of the mind. Rohit Mehta wrote in the Foreword to Shringy's book that the words 'choiceless awareness' sum up Krishnamurti's philosophy. Similarly Robert Powell 1971 *Krishnamurti The Man And His Teaching* p 8 writes of the importance of having no "attitude" to Krishnamurti before coming to his teaching.

45 Letter from the Sulgrave marked June 1936, private source.

46 Letter written in pen is marked July 1936 in pencil, private source. Letter on Sarobia letterhead marked in pencil as 1936. The ship is from the Lloyd Triestino line. Radha told the author that her mother often didn't read Krishna's letters when she was very busy. R Rajagopal Sloss (1991) pp136-137 says Cheiro had told Rosalind that she, Krishnamurti and Rajagopal were inextricably bound together. Cheiro, or Count Louis Hamon (1866-1936), who had many famous clients, including politicians, actors and people in the arts, published copies of a number of hand prints in 1932 in *You and Your Hand* (revised in 1964 by Louise Owen, Arco New York). He had himself what was considered an extraordinary mark on his palm, a double line of head.

47 R Rajagopal Sloss (1991) p 138 – Radha's description of her mother.

48 Born in 1892, Richard Neutra had attended the Bauhaus school. Considered a master of modern design, using factory components to build elegant constructions of glass, concrete and steel, his best-known residences include the 1929 Lovell House and the 1947 Kauffman House. Radha says that her mother and Neutra became good friends but would have "vociferous" arguments about colour and Neutra said Rosalind had her way in the design of the apartment. R Rajagopal Sloss (1991) p 136.

Rosalind met Neutra through Kees Van der Leeuw, a friend of Krishna and the Rajagopals.

49 R Rajagopal Sloss (1991) pp 135-146.

50 M Lutyens (1983) p 43-44. See Krishna to Lady Emily 14 April 1937, Huntington 9/30. R Rajagopal Sloss (1991) p 147-153. Radha who was six at the time remembers that it was the first time she was acutely conscious that the three of them together without other friends about, was not as pleasant when they came in pairs, but they made a conscious effort to behave well towards each other. Krishna to Dwarkanath 21 July 1936, 23 July & 4 December 1937, Huntington 11/20 & 27 May 1938, Huntington 11/21. Arundale to Dwarkanath 18 June 1937, Huntington 36/1. Krishna describes the motels as both auto courts and auto camps. Krishna to Julia Cannon 10 December 1937, Huntington 9/23 says the trip went off well and was cheaper and more pleasant than staying in hotels. *Star Review* November 1929 pp 608-09, 614-626. Lawrence's article republished as "Men Must Work and Women As Well" in 1930 *Assorted Articles* Martin Secker London and 1968 *Phoenix II: Uncollected, Unpublished and Other Prose Works* Ed. Warren Roberts and Harry T Moore Heinemann London. R Rajagopal Sloss (1991) pp 150, 182.

51 Huxley's letter dated 16 September 1937, Huntington 20/8. Heard was a writer and former BBC commentator.

52 Krishna's letters dated 29 September 1937 & 26 January 1938, and Heard's 18 January, 8 April, 9 May, 16 June 1938, Huntington 20/8. R Rajagopal Sloss (1991) pp 153, 165-67. Huxley's biographer, Sybille Bedford (1987) Vol II p 295 makes it clear that Maria indulged Aldous in relationships with women he admired, even organising that he take them to dinner, often followed by love-making, much as Huxley described scenes in his novel, *Point Counter Point*. Bedford says Maria took what she describes as an "aristocratic" view of sex and it was a measure of the certainty between them. There's no evidence that Rosalind assumed such a view in relation to Krishnamurti. Krishna's letter to Lady Emily quoted in M Lutyens (1983) p 46.

53 A series of interviews conducted by Dr David K Dunaway in 1985 and 1986 with old friends of the Huxleys, including Maria's sister, Rose D'Haulleville (nee Nys), makes it clear that Maria's lesbianism was understood in the family but not publicly discussed. Huntington HM 56881. See also Sybille Bedford (1987).

54 Huxley and his wife Maria attended the Vedanta Society temple in Ivar Ave Hollywood for a time. Swami Prabhavananda told Huxley's biographer Sybille Bedford in 1969 that he had initiated Huxley whom he said had a brilliant mind and a noble soul. He expressed some discreet criticism of Huxley's experiments with LSD but mitigated this with the comment that he had to follow many roads. Sybille Bedford (1987) Vol II pp 75, 206. This last comment bears an echo of the conviction that all roads

lead to the same end - God-realisation - held by the 19th century spiritual sage Ramakrishna, in whose honour the American order was founded by Ramakrishna's devotee, Vivekananda. Isherwood also says of his relationship with Huxley in 1980 *My Guru and his Disciple*, Farrer, Strauss Giroux New York p 50 that when he was with Aldous and Maria Huxley they behaved as intimate friends but when he and Aldous were alone he felt uneasy because he was aware that Aldous found the homosexual "temperament" deeply distasteful, but as Aldous liked Chris Isherwood personally he fought against his prejudice.

55 This was also the view of Isherwood (1980) p 50 when he writes that Prabhavananda and Huxley were temperamentally far apart, the one being strongly devotional while the other was "much more akin to his friend Krishnamurti". Isherwood said Krishnamurti expounded a philosophy of discrimination between the real and the unreal, and, as a Hindu who had broken away from Hinduism, was "repelled by devotional religion and its rituals" and "greatly disapproved of the guru-disciple relationship". Huxley had told him Krishnamurti never meditated on 'objects' such as lotuses, lights, gods or goddesses and even believed that doing so might lead to insanity. See also Isherwood Diaries, 1996 Katherine Bucknell (ed) Methuen London, p 114, 31 July 1940 in which he says Huxley seemed to think Ramakrishna might have been a case of "borderline" sanity and was shocked to hear that Ramakrishna dressed up as a woman, thinking of his attitude to God as that of a loving wife. Isherwood was disturbed by what Huxley said, wondering whether their friend, Gerald Heard, was "barking up the wrong tree" with Vedantism but also aware that his doubts were being promoted by his "Ego" as a sabotage effort. Also see author's interview in November 2000 with James Sloss who as an adolescent used to walk with Huxley and Krishnamurti in the afternoons after school when the Huxleys stayed at Ojai. M Lutyens (1983) p 47-8 quotes a manuscript with a description of Huxley written in 1976 by Krishnamurti held at KFT.

56 R Rajagopal Sloss (1991) p 170.

57 S Bedford (1987) Vol II p 358. Huxley's second wife, Laura, and Rosalind were both present along with medical staff.

58 The shortened form of the title, *After Many a Summer*, is used in some publications. The title comes from aTennyson poem, *Tithonus*, about a search for immortality gone wrong, with aging immortality bestowed rather than youthful immortality. The symbolism of the swan, incidentally, is considered similar to that for the goose, being ecstasy, and a vehicle for the creator, Brahma, in Hindu myth.

59 A Huxley (1980) pp 45-50, 145, 157-58, 227.

60 Sybille Bedford (1987) p 379-80 takes the quote from an article by a friend of Huxley, Lawrence Clark Powell, Librarian of the University of California in *Westways*, December 1970.

61 Sybille Bedford (1987) p 379-80.

62 A Huxley (1980) p 179.

63 Krishna was well aware of the extraordinary political tensions in Europe in 1938, as he had read in Ojai in the spring, Stephen H Roberts 1937 *The House that Hitler Built* Methuen London. On pp 263, 363 Roberts describes Hitler's actions against Jews as "a campaign of annihilation – a progrom of the crudest form" and advises that war was inevitable as the ideology of Hitlerism was that of war. M Lutyens (1983) p 48.

64 Letter dated 8 July 1938, private source.

65 Letter dated 21 April 1938, private source.

66 Beatrice to Krishnaji 1 December 1938, Huntington 9/23. Rajagopal tells the Vigevenos Krishna has begun his Indian tour in a letter dated 14 November 1938, Huntington 20/11. R Rajagopal Sloss (1991) p 164. It's interesting to compare this description of Rosalind with that made by Sidney Field *Krishnamurti The Reluctant Messiah* Paragon New York p 41 who said she was a beautiful girl, blond, blue-eyed and had a guileless quality about her that was very attractive when his family first met Rosalind in 1928. Field had known Krishna since the 1920s through his parents whom he said were Theosophists who had moved to California from Costa Rica following a coup d'etat by an overzealous supporter of Krishnamurti.

67 Rajagopal to Vigevenos 14 November 1938, Huntington 20/11.

68 M Lutyens (1983) p 49-53. Lady Emily to Krishna 20 March 1939, KFI.

69 Krishna to Dwarkanath 1 & 29 August 1938, Huntington 11/21. Dwarkanath dealt with the question of groups and putting funding on a proper business footing in letters to Krishna following his trip 21 April, 9 June, 11 & 14 July 1939, & fundraising for tours is dealt with in the *Star Publishing Trust* newsletter from *Vasanta Vihar* 1 August 1939, Huntington 11/21. Krishna advised Dwarkanath to leave the idea of a separate fund in correspondence 8 August 1939, Huntington 11/21 and Dwarkanath's response on 13 October 1939 is that the idea had gone to sleep.

70 Jinarajadasa 11 September 1938, Huntington 11/15. Krishna to Dwarkanath 29 August 1938, Huntington 11/21. M Lutyens (1983) p 53.

71 Sexual questions raised at talks on 7 & 13 May 1939, KFA.

72 Auckland Town Hall 4 June 1939, KFA. Krishna wrote to Dwarkanath 13 October 1939 that he was a pacifist, Huntington 21/11.

73 1 June 1939 Auckland Town Hall, KFA.

74 15 June 1939, WEA Hall Auckland, KFA. Figure of attendance given by Krishna to Dwarkanath, 24 June 1939, Huntington 11/21. Such questions as the source of what is an illusion of a conscious free will are currently the subject of research by leading neurologists. Professor Susan Greenfield from Oxford University suggests that "the conscious feeling of who you are comes from the linguistic left side of the brain" and that the

feeling humans have of being consciously in control of their minds is just an illusion. BBC documentary. *Brain Story – The Final Mystery*. Pt IV. 2000.

75 Krishna to Lady Emily 16 June 1939. KFI. Krishna told Dwarkanath, 24 June & 8 August 1939. Huntington 11/21. that the reason for Rajagopal's return to Holland was that the military wanted the Ommen camp. *Star* newsletter article April 1939 article signed VCP. Huntington 36A/1. Dwarkanath to Krishna 11 & 14 July 1939 Huntington 11/21 re Krishna's health and powders from the Vaidya doctor being sent to Krishna .

76 Sybille Bedford (1987) p 381.

77 R Rajagopal Sloss (1991) p 166.

78 Letter dated 2 September 1939. Huntington 11/21. M Lutyens(1990) p 53 writes incorrectly that Patwardhan died suddenly of a brain haemorrhage in December 1939.

79 Krishna to Dwarkanath 13 October 1939. Huntington 11/21. M Lutyens (1983) p 50.

80 Krishna to Dwarkanath 2 September 1939. Huntington 11/21.

81 Isherwood to his mother 27 November 1939. Huntington CI 1915. Also Bucknell (1996) pp 49-51 for Isherwood's diary entry for 5 November 1939. Krishna was aged forty four. Peggy Kiskadden, a good friend of the Huxleys, remembers Maria bringing a young goat to the picnic although this recollection is questionable as she dated it as Easter, in an interview with Dr David Dunaway. Huntington Huxley Oral History transcripts HM 56885. Dr Dunaway's interview with Mary Anita Loos Huntington HM 56889.

82 Dr David Dunaway Huntington HM 56889. Anita Loos, probably best-known for 1925 *Gentlemen Prefer Blondes* Boni & Liverright New York.

Chapter 8 Relationships

1 Jinarajadasa to Krishna 4 March 1940. Huntington 11/15. In an interview with the author in October 2000, Radha said Rajagopal would try to help Krishna get a visa and ask him to put 'teacher' as his occupation on the immigration form but he would not and made it very difficult for Rajagopal.

2 Krishna to Dwarkanath 28 March 1940. Huntington 11/21.

3 M Lutyens (1996) p 68. Lutyens did not mention this in her earlier biography of Krishna written while Krishna was alive. It is noteworthy that some of Krishna's talks in Ojai and Sarobia in 1940 were published in 1943 *War abolished: one way to permanent peace* Currawong Publishing Sydney, in a series of "Unpopular pamphlets" as they were titled.

4 Sidney Field (1989) pp 94-97. Krishna's letter dated 13 November 1941. Field's letter dated 18 November 1941.

5 M Lutyens (1983) pp 55-56. Krishna to Dwarkanath 22 March 1940 mentions that Dwarkanath's last correspondence was delayed by about a month and was censored. Krishna's letter was sent by airmail as well as a copy by regular mail. All letters from India and some from Australia and New Zealand were censored, he said. FBI files obtained by the author under FOIA provisions reveal a report on Krishnamurti arriving in New York harbour on 26 August 1926, 25 February 1928, 30 December 1928, 13 December 1929, 19 October 1931, 12 September 1935 and 3 September 1937. It does not list his entries into the United States via San Francisco. It states that on 23 June 1944 he was granted the fifth extension to his visa, allowing him to remain in the United States until 1 May 1945. The FBI reports are dated 3 December 1943 and 30 March 1945. B Sanjia Rao (1989) p 22 claims Krishna had to spend nine years in California "virtually a prisoner on account of his pacifist views".

6 R Rajagopal Sloss (1991) pp 163-64.

7 R Rajagopal Sloss (1991) pp 167, 172, 173.

8 R Rajagopal Sloss (1991) pp 174-76, 185-6. Author's interview with Radha October 2000.

9 Sybille Bedford (1987) Vol II pp 6, 10. This picnic seems to be separate from the November 1939 picnic attended by Garbo, which would account for Peggy Kiskadden's confusion over Maria's goats at an earlier picnic where Garbo was present. R Rajagopal Sloss (1991) p 171 also refers to a picnic with the Huxleys, the Russells and some Hollywood personalities but does not specify the date.

10 Sybille Bedford (1987) Vol II pp 16, 21, 24. Maria said in October 1941 that she and Aldous stayed with "Rosalind and Krishnaji" in Ojai often. Rosalind's eyes must have been a remarkable feature, considering (1976) M Lutyen's reference p 159 to them as blue like those of a Siamese cat. Maria Huxley to Isherwood 16 July 1941, Huntington Isherwood Collection. Maria also mentions a letter from Leonard Wolff about the torture Virginia had felt before her suicide over her "insanity" coming upon her again and that she had been convinced she would not recover whereas he believed she would have.

11 Possibly 1940 *Authentic notes of discussions and talks given by Krishnamurti, Ojai and Sarobia 1940*, Star Publishing Trust Hollywood.

12 Huxley to Krishna 3 March 1941, Huntington 20/8.

13 D Rajagopal (ed) *Commentaries on Living*, Series I to III were published by Quest, the Theosophical Publishing House, by arrangement with KW Inc in 1956, 1958 and 1960, and according to Weeraperuma's bibliography, by Gollancz in 1956, 1959 and 1961. Author's interview with Donald Ingram Smith 16 February 1998. Later editors would also mine Krishna's dialogues of Q & A for publication, eg 1982 *Questions and Answers* KFT London.

14 R Rajagopal Sloss (1991) pp 170-71 and Sybille Bedford (1987) Vol II p 24: both Maria and Radha say the Huxleys visited often: pp 67-70 for quotes from *Science, Liberty and Peace. An Encyclopaedia of Pacifism* republished in Robert A Seeley 1986 *The Handbook of Non-Violence* Lawrence Hill Conn. Seeley says the book deserves to join the small shelf of pacifist classics, and that in studying it he came to appreciate the power of Huxley's mind and the magnitude of his achievement.

15 R Rajagopal Sloss (1991) pp 181-82, 188. In Patricia L Fry 1999 *The Ojai Valley* Matilija Press Ojai p 220 the actress Iris Tree is reported describing a "twilight procession of man and beast" down the road beside Arya Vihara, including Krishna often leading a cow and a calf on a evening stroll.

16 Author's interview with Radha October 2000. R Rajagopal Sloss (1991) p 180.

17 R Rajagopal Sloss (1991) pp 190-91 suggests that seeing her mother's dressmaker's form probably caused the woman's comment about a skeleton in the closet, seemingly unaware of the common meaning attached to the expression.

18 In an interview 18 October 2000 the author held with Mark Lee, Director of KFA Publications, he said that according to schedules held by the KFA, in the 1940s Krishna met up to 30 people a day for interviews throughout the year.

19 In an interview with the author (2000) Mark Lee said that this idea is an aberration and total misinterpretation of what Krishnamurti was saying by people who were neurotic.

20 M Lutyens (1983) p 61. Krishna uses this term "right" in a letter to Lady Emily 31 August 1943, Huntington 9/30, saying he engages in this activity every day for two hours at least and it's strenuous, creative, joyous, liberating and reveals the "Highest". S Field (1989) pp 75, 77, 81, 123. The word 'reality' is used without a capital 'R' although for Advaita Vedantists there is only one "Reality", found by turning away from the illusory world through mysticism. See Ninian Smart 1960 *World Religions: A Dialogue* Penguin Harmondsworth p 33. In Dunaway (1985) p 6 Field talks about Krishna's emphasis on facing physical and psychological "facts" rather than conceptualisation about awareness. The term "trip" was widely used in the 1960s - having originated from psychedelic drug-induced experiences, it came to be applied generally in conversation to describe exceptional sensations. In connection with this question of mental distress, it's interesting to note a letter to Krishna from one of his circle, Evelyn Wood, 4 November 1949, who says that Krishna and a timely treatment of electro-shock therapy had brought him nearer to "normality" than he had ever been in his life, Huntington 34/45.

21 S Field (1989) p 40. Field refers to Lawrence's view expressed in a *LA Times* article.

22 R Rajagopal Sloss (1991) p 184.
23 FBI reports on Krishnamurti dated 15 December 1943 and 30 March 1945 obtained by the author under FOIA provisions.
24 Krishna to Lady Emily 31 August 1931, Huntington 9/30. R Rajagopal Sloss (1991) p 182, 185.
25 R Rajagopal Sloss (1991) p 184.
26 In Bucknell (1996) p 345 Isherwood records on 14 May 1944 that he drove with the Huxleys to Ojai to hear Krishnamurti speak "in the famous oak grove". He described Krishnamurti as "really very nice ... a modest, slim, white-haired, boyish figure standing in the sunny shadows [who] obviously hates lecturing: he seemed terribly nervous and embarrassed, and winced visibly when people interrupted with questions". Isherwood also noted that there were present a few Theosophists - "bearded, smocked and sandalled" - who believed Krishnamurti would one day return to the movement.
27 M Lutyens (1983) pp 59-60.
28 M Lutyens (1983) p 60. Krishna to Lady Emily, 2 June 1945, Huntington 9/30.
29 Mary Zimbalist interview with the author, 15 November 2000. M Lutyens (1983) p 60.
30 R Rajagopal Sloss (1991) p 192.
31 Krishna to Dwarkanath 18 May 1940 & memo 18 May 1940 that the Star office was to be closed by 1 July 1940, Huntington 32/7. Rama Rao to Krishna 11 February 1941 & Krishna to Rama Rao 22 July 1941, Huntington 23/7. R Madhavachari to Krishnaji 29 October 1943, Huntington 11/16. Rama Rao to Krishna 19 June 1945, Huntington 23/17.
32 Helen to Krishna 2 February, 2 March, 17 & 24 April, 5 May, 1944, & Krishna's reply 28 April 1944, Huntington 20/8.
33 M Lutyens (1983) p 46 for reference to WH Bates. In the novel 1945*Time Must Have a Stop* Chatto & Windus London, Huxley develops an idea about paying attention to eternity to deliver ourselves from the tyrannies of tradition and progress. Huxley to Krishna 5 October 1944, Huntington 20/8. Heard to Krishna 6 October 1944, Huntington 20/8. P Jayakar (1986) p 92 says Krishna visited Trabuco for a week and did not like the "seething" and "violent" thoughts of others meditating there. Heard wrote to Krishna about another visit on 19 June 1947, Huntington 20/8. Sybille Bedford (1987) Vol II pp 30-32, 40-42, 81-82. Bedford explains Huxley and Heard's relationship as falling into a lull probably over Heard's autocratic "assumption of spiritual directorship". Heard abandoned Trabuco as a spiritual community in 1947 and it was eventually acquired by the Vedanta Society. Heard died in California in 1971.
34 Huxley to Krishna 4 March 1945, Huntington 20/8. Helen Boardman brought a $35,000 libel suit against the paper, *The Ojai*, in relation to a talk by Krishnamurti in the Oak Grove at Ojai which was dismissed in June 1946, Huntington 9/23.

35 Sybille Bedford (1987) Vol II p 61.

36 Sybille Bedford (1987) Vol II pp 59, 60, 64. Huxley to Krishna 19 July 1945 [misspelt 1845]. Huntington 20/8. Maria Huxley's letter undated. Huntington 20/8.

37 Sybille Bedford (1987) Vol II pp 55, 56, 64, 66.

38 A Huxley (1969)*The Perennial Philosophy* Chatto & Windus London p 7-8. See RC Zaehner (ed) 1938 *Hindu Scriptures* Dent London, Chandogya Upanishad (VI, x, 3) "This finest essence - the whole universe has it as its Self: That is the Real: That is the Self: That you are" and (VII, xxv, 1&2) which draws a parallel between the Infinite, the ego and the Self.

39 A Huxley (1969) pp 10-13.

40 Huxley to Isherwood 7 February 1942, Huntington Isherwood Collection. He also mentions works by Sri Aurobindo, Eckhart and Poulain. A Huxley (1969) p 27. S Field (1989) p 97. Dr David K Dunaway with Field, Huntington, Huxley Oral History transcripts HM 56879. R Rajagopal Sloss (1991) p 200.

41 Sybille Bedford (1987) Vol II p 133. Letter to Jeanne written in 1952.

42 Krishna to Rosalind 25 October, 22 & 29 November 1944, private source.

43 Krishna to Rosalind written in Sarobia and marked 'Thursday night" in pencil, private source.

44 R Rajagopal Sloss (1991) p 206-07.

45 R Rajagopal Sloss (1991) p 201-11. See A Huxley 1962 *Island* Harper New York p237 for a fictional treatment of educational ideas. M Lutyens (1983) p 64-65 quotes Krishna saying, in notes made by Mary Zimbalist, that he was ill a year and a half, whereas he was two months with fever and in recovery for six months, and that the doctor did not give him any medicine, whereas it was more likely that he refused medication.

46 M Lutyens (1983) p 65.

47 Jinarajadasa to editor 1 April 1943, Huntington 11/13; Jinarajadasa to Krishna 6 April 1943, Huntington 11/15.

48 Jinarajadasa to Krishna 22 February 1944, Huntington 11/15. In another letter to Krishna, Jinarajadasa sent a copy of a poem he wrote in 1910 about a direct vision of Krishna as the 'Face of the Lord' when he first saw a photo of him. The poem was printed in *The American Theosophist* in 1947. Jinarajadasa to Krishna and letter from Theosophical Society in America to Krishna, 1947, Huntington 11/13.

49 Jinarajadasa to Krishna 14 March 1944, Huntington 11/15.

50 Jinarajadasa to Krishna 9 October 1944, 21 November, 29 November (telegram) 1945, KFI; 9 &11 January, 17 February (telegram), 11 May, 4 July, 27 August , 7 October 1946, Huntington 11/15. Madhavachariar to Krishna undated [Nov1945] p 2 Huntington 11/16. Krishna to Rajagopal Iyengar 24 September 1946, Rajagopal to Rajagopal Iyengar 1 February 1947, Huntington 36/46. Sidney Dorne to Krishna 14 April 1946, Huntington 9/23. See advertisement in *The Indian Theosophist* Oct-Nov

1946 for *At the Feet of the Master*, costing 8 annas. Public Notices *The Hindu* 5 December 1946 notice of Star Publishing Trust changing its name to Krishnamurti Writings Incorporated, and correspondence 5 December 1946 re retrospective contracts as it was agreed the rights to *At the Feet of the Master* were held by the Star Publishing Trust but they were never legally copyrighted, Huntington 32/1.

51 Krishna to Madhavachariar 16 August 1947, Huntington 11/16. Krishna to Miss Bright 18 February 1947, Huntington 9/3. Swami to Chris 23 June 1947, Huntington, Isherwood Collection. Isherwood notes in his diary for 31 July 1940 that Krishnamurti, whose teaching, he says, is to Huxley's taste, never meditates on objects, even believing it might lead to insanity. By 14 June 1944 Isherwood quotes Prabhavananda as saying "Krishnamurti is transhient, I am eternal" and on 10 October 1944 he says Krishnamurti went to visit the Swami, even though the Swami was a little prejudiced following Mrs Besant's declaration years earlier, that Krishnamurti was an avatar. But Krishnamurti sat modestly at the back of a class, and then, when the Swami went over to him, they greeted each other with deep respect, "bowing again and again with folded palms". Then they had a long chat, becoming "very gay and Indian and laughing like schoolboys" and a bridge of communication was built between followers of the two. K Bucknell (1996) pp 114, 349, 373.

52 M Lutyens (1983) p 65. Lady Emily Lutyens (1957) pp 60, 188. R Rajagopal Sloss (1991) p 215 on Rajagopal's length of stay in Europe. Jinarajadasa had sent to Krishna a newspaper clipping about Sir Edwin Lutyens' estate of 42,000 pounds on his death dated 23 April 1944, Huntington 11/13.

53 Krishna to Rajagopal 19 August 1947, Huntington 9/7. Jinarajadasa had written to Krishna 11 June 1943 telling him a friend had heard on BBC radio a report that Ommen was one of two camps in Holland noteworthy for their brutality yet Krishna did not seem to feel at this stage that this was an obstacle in their return to KWINC, Huntington 11/15. Jinarajadasa makes a reference to Rajagopal's opportunity to become a US citizen in a letter to Krishna 4 July 1946, Huntington 11/15.

54 See Krishna from Wrightwood to Rosalind 27 July, 1946 in which he says he thinks of her constantly and she is very much in his heart, and 17 April 1947 Krishna to Rosalind in which he underlines "all" in sending all his love, private source. R Rajagopal Sloss (1991) p 215 says that from the time he left Ojai in 1947 his letters to Rosalind continually reaffirmed his love for her. M Lutyens (1983) P 66.

55 P Jayakar (1986) p 99-100. A *kurta* is long, loose shirt. Jayakar p 98-99 makes the point that with his change of clothes from Western to Indian attire upon arrival in India, Krishna's personality also changed, assuming more of a role as a teacher.

56 Description by Donald Ingram Smith, President of Krishnamurti Australia who says that she was not only beautiful facially but also had an extraordinary flowing grace in movement so that eyes were galvanised on her when she entered a room. M Lutyens (1983) p 66.

57 P Jayakar (1986) p 100.

58 Larry Collins & Dominique Lapierre 1976 *Freedom at Midnight* Vikas Publishing New Delhi pp 84-120, 317-344.

59 L Collins & D Lapierre (1976) pp 440-41 describe how the announcement on radio was held back for forty minutes after Gandhi's death until it was confirmed that his assassin was a Hindu, to avoid further bloodshed between Muslims and Hindus.

60 Krishna to Huxley 7 January, Huxley to Krishna 13 January 1948, Huntington 20/8.

61 P Jayakar (1986) pp 6-7, 105-09. For an account of Mahatma Gandhi's death see Stanley Wolpert 1996 *Nehru A Tryst with Destiny* Oxford University Press Oxford pp 428-30. Wolpert p 438 says that Nehru tried in vain to win back the support of former followers, ardent socialists, such as Achyut Patwardhan, to whom he offered ambassadorships. Nehru wrote to Patwardhan, 6 June 1948, that even though he had won the crown, many things oppressed his mind and he found himself in a harder prison than he had ever been before. Sahib Rao and Achyut Patwardhan were brothers who had been active in the independence movement in India. Sahib Rao had been closely associated with the work of Sarva Seva Singh, a Gandhian service organisation and had been gaoled. He was later overlooked in the first Constituent Assembly. Achyut was involved in the establishment of the Socialist Party of India. According to Jayakar, Achyut told Gandhi in late 1947 that he was going to spend time with Krishna, and Gandhi was very happy about this. In early 1949 Achyut returned to Delhi to edit a Socialist weekly, later breaking with the Party and politics. Pama, a younger brother, was a Poona businessman. His wife Sunanda took notes of Krishna's talks and transcribed them. She first met Krishnamurti at the age of twenty in 1947, described by Jayakar p 103 as "doe-eyed" and "lissom" at that time. In later years she was instrumental in establishing a school and study centre at Sahyadri near Poona, and wrote a memoir of Krishnamurti published by Penguin in 1999. Notice of radio talk 3 April 1948, Huntington 9/23. M Lutyens (1983) p 72 says Krishna gave a talk on All-India Radio on 6 November 1948.

62 P Jayakar (1986) pp 103-4, 111-120. Also P Jayakar 1995 *Fire in the Mind* Penguin New Delhi p viii.

63 Maria to Krishna postmarked 7 March 1948, typed 'le 3 mars 1948'; Krishna to Maria and Aldous 30 April 1948, Huntington 20/8.

64 Jinarajadasa to Krishna 11 October 1947, Huntington 11/15. P Jayakar (1986) pp 122-24. M Lutyens (1983) p 72.

65 Maurice Friedman spent many years in India studying mysticism, including a period in Sri Ramana Marharshi's ashram in Tiruvannamalai. P Jayakar (1986) pp 129-138. Friedman was not surprised by Krishna's activity and offered explanations to the sisters, who were at first embarrassed by it.

66 P Jayakar (1986) pp 139-40.

67 P Jayakar (1986) p 141. Dwarkanath to Miss Payne in England 29 May 1949 refers to Sunanda on whom Krishna "bestowed" a lot of attention, Huntington 23/7.

68 P Jayakar (1986) p 2-3.

69 P Jayakar (1986) pp 158-161; pp 255-277 publishes excerpts from Krishna's letters to Nandini June 1948-March 1960. Nandini's son's sight improved and he reportedly went on to study at the University of California, Berkeley, and teach at the University of Queensland in Australia.

70 P Jayakar (1986) pp 127-28 148-149. Pupul had known Nehru's daughter, Indira Gandhi, since their school days and the two became close in the last years of Indira's life. The description of carnations in bowls by Jayakar is evocative, since both men had a particular sensitivity to flowers, particularly roses, Nehru's signature image being a rose in his lapel. Nehru was going through extreme emotional difficulties in 1948 as he had lost both his great and close father figure, "Bapu" Mahatma Gandhi, in January as well as his closest love, Edwina Mountbatten, who returned to England in June, although he continued to see her intermittently. See MJ Akbar 1988 *Nehru The Making of India* Viking Penguin London pp 434, 458 and S Wolpert (1996) pp 430-32, 435-6, 439.

71 P Jayakar (1986) pp 152-53.

72 P Jayakar (1986) pp 156-57. She died in 1976 of a heart attack.

73 G Narayan, *Jiddu Krishnamurti Some Reminiscences* taken down by Quenby Dunlap during 1992 and compiled at Brockwood Park 1993, KFI. See published version G Narayan 1998 *As the River Joins the Ocean* Book Faith India Delhi.

74 R Rajagopal Sloss (1991) p 157.

75 Krishna to Lady Emily 1 May 1949, KFI.

76 H Nearing (1992) pp 56-59, 64.

77 M Lutyens (1983) p 66. P Jayakar (1986) p 98.

78 Krishna to Madhavachari 30 May, 15 & 20 June, 6 August 1949, Huntington 11/16. Krishna to Sanjeeva Rao 4 October 1949, Huntington 36/49.

79 R Rajagopal Sloss pp 215-16.

80 Letter Eve to Annie, Henderson, New Zealand 15 July 1948, Huntington 20/11.

81 Jinarajadasa's request to Madhavachari 15 June 1948, Huntington 36/35. TH Redfern of Cheshire to Rajagopal 26 October 1949, Krishna's reply

31 October 1949. Huntington 9/23. Letter from Subordinate Judge N Subramania Ayer BA BL 3 January 1948 and Krishna's reply 7 January 1948. Huntington 9/23.

Chapter 9 Self-Transformation

1 M Lutyens (1983) p 74. See J Krishnamurti 1951 *Krishnamurti's Talks 1949-1959* KWI Ojai

2 M Lutyens (1983) p 75 quotes an account of the talk by Professor G Venkatachalam 1966 *My Contemporaries* Bangalore. *Puja* means worship and *darshan* is a gift of vision given by a guru.

3 Smith interviews with the author 17 November 1997, 16 February 1998, and 22 October 1998. See also D Ingram Smith 1999 *The Transparent Mind A Journey with Krishnamurti*, Edwin House Publishing Ojai California. Smith's first book describing his meetings with Krishna published 1989 *Truth is a Pathless Land* Quest Wheaton.

4 Smith interview with the author 22 October 1998, broadcast 2SER 6 November 1998.

5 Krishna to Mr Solness 7 March 1953, Huntington 36/53.

6 Krishna to Lady Emily 21 January, 1 February 1950, KFI. Jinarajadasa to Madha 30 January 1950, Huntignton 36/35. Krishna to Jinarajadasa 3 February 1950 Huntington 9/28.

7 Jinarajadasa to Krishna 4 February, 5 October, late October, 1950 & to Rajagopal 11 February 1950, Huntington 9/31. Krishna to Jinarajadasa undated, 26 September, 13 October, 4 November 1950, Huntington 9/28. Rajagopal's view must have been that Mrs Besant, along with Leadbeater, received her instructions directly through the "Masters" and not in her capacity as President of the Theosophical Society. Jinarajadasa was still attending to copying correspondence for Krishna in 1953, Jinarajadasa to Krishna 8 June 1953, Huntington 9/31.

8 P Jayakar (1986) p 161.

9 *TIME* 16 January 1950. In a way Krishna was close to fifty, as he was fifty four when the article appeared and had been fifty two when he met Nandini in 1947.

10 P Jayakar pp 164, 183.

11 Krishna to Lady Emily 28 Mar 1950. KFI.

12 Vigeveno to Rajagopal 14 January 1950, Huntington 20/11.

13 Jinarajadasa to Madhavachari 24 April 1950, Huntington 11/13; Madhavachari to Jinarajadasa 26 April 1950, Huntington 34/12; draft of 'hand-out' of Feb-March 1950 discussions, dated 3 January 1950, Huntington 34/53; draft press release dated 21 March 1950, Huntington 34/50; Krishna to Evelyn Wood 29 April 1950, Huntington 36/54; Evelyn Wood to Krishna c/- Frederick Pinter 7 May 1950, Huntington 34/47; Evelyn Wood to Madhavachari 7 May 1950, Huntington 34/48; Evelyn

Wood to Rajagopal 7 May 1950. Huntington 34/54. Evelyn Wood to Pupul Jayakar 29 August 1950 Huntington 34/53.

14 R Rajagopal Sloss (1991) p 219.

15 R Rajagopal Sloss (1991) p 220.

16 R Rajagopal Sloss (1991) p 220. Author's interview with Radha October 2000.

17 R Rajagopal Sloss (1991) p 220. It's interesting to consider the definition of the word affair and whether it applies in this domestic situation which had been maintained over such a lengthy period.

18 The addressee for Krishna's letter dated 19 May 1950 is missing. Huntington 9/7.

19 M Lutyens (1983) p 77.

20 R Rajagopal Sloss (1991) p 221.

21 R Rajagopal Sloss (1991) p 221-22.

22 Author's interview with Smith 2 February 2001. In an interview with the author, James Sloss, Radha's husband, said that in looks Radha had Rajagopal's nose. M Lutyens (1983) p 78.

23 Krishna to Madhavachari 11 September 1950, Huntington 11/16; Krishna to Jinarajadasa 26 September 1950, Huntington 9/28. P Jayakar (1986) p 183.

24 R Rajagopal Sloss (1991) p 223.

25 Krishna to Madhavachari 2 December 1950, 12 January, 17 March 1951, Huntington 11/16.

26 At the end of his life Krishna made it clear that he wanted his teachings protected. On the question of what was his teaching, Krishna said in November 1974 that he didn't know himself; but the idea of the teaching and the taught was basically wrong, and that it was a matter of "sharing" rather than being taught. Pupal Jayakar & Sunanda Patwardhan (eds) 1982 *Within the Mind* KFI Madras p 8.

27 Sybille Bedford (1987) Vol II p 122.

28 R Rajagopal Sloss (1991) p 222.

29 Huxley to Krishna 23 July 1951 [mistyped as 1851] Huntington 20/8.

30 Rajagopal refers to a book on education made up of extracts from Krishna's talks he hopes to have published by Harpers so that it reaches "different" types of people through the book trade. Rajagopal to Dwarkanath 17 June 1953, Huntington 11/19. Author's interview with Smith (1997).

31 For compilations of Krishnamurti's writing on self-awareness see J Krishnamurti 1997 *Reflections on the Self* Rupa & Co esp p 163 "awareness is a process of discovery that becomes blocked through identification", & 1998 On Self-Knowledge KFI Chennai, a selection from talks from the 1940s.

32 J Krishnamurti 1956 *Education and the Significance of Life*, Gollancz London.

33 Krishna to Dwarkanath Telang 7 August 1951. Huntington 11/18. Verbatim material from Krishna's visit to Ceylon in 1949-50 was published as *Krishnamurti's Talks* by KWINC in Ojai in 1951. Other material such as summaries of discussions had been published in 1950 by Donald Ingram Smith in the Australian booklet *Voyage* in Sydney.

34 R Rajagopal Sloss (1991) p 226. P Jayakar (1986) p 185.

35 M Lutyens (1983) p 79. Professor R Srinivasan to Krishna and Krishna's reply 8 & 12 February 1952. Huntington 9/23. To Srinivasan's question about whether Krishna was the author of *At the Feet of the Master*, he replied that he'd given answers in public talks and did not like to answer any questions in correspondence. Jinarajadasa to Krishna 21, 22 January, 5 February 1952, Huntington 11/15. As explained in Chapter 1, the Indian calendar runs from sunrise, whereas by Western calculation the date is 12 May, 1895. Jinarajadasa also points out that the first part of the Upanishad is the Indian republic's motto.

36 Rajagopal to Krishna 21 April 1952. Huntington 20/11. R Rajagopal Sloss (1991) p 224.

37 M Lutyens (1983) p 79. P Jayakar (1986) pp185-86.

38 R Rajagopal Sloss (1991) pp 237-240.

39 R Rajagopal Sloss (1991) p 223, 240-41, 274; P Jayakar (1986) p 193. M Lutyens (1996) p 76.

40 P Jayakar (1986) pp 187-89. Among those attending were SM Joshi, active in the Gandhian movement, *Sarva Seva Sangh*, and Professor Dhopeshwarkar, who taught philosophy at Poona University and later wrote several books about Krishnamurti's teaching. Krishna had written to Madhavachari 7 May 1952 before this trip to India to say Miss Payne had been trying to see him in England but he had not seen her, and that she had sent 500 pounds anonymously [misspelt 'unanimously'] that they had returned to her. See also Doris Pratt to Madhavachari 6 May 1952 re cheque being returned.

41 For examples of Krishna's talks from this period see *Krishnamurti's Talks: To Boys and Girls ... Rajghat-Banaras 1952* (19 talks), *verbatim 1952* (10 talks), *verbatim 1953* (8 talks) *verbatim 1953* (10 talks) *verbatim 1954* (8 talks) KW Inc Ojai. P Jayakar (1986) pp 190-193.

42 G Narayan (1993) KFI and P Jayakar (1986) p 194-95.

43 S Weereperuma interview with the author by correspondence 26 July 2000. In contrast, Mark Lee (2000), who spent eight years at the Rishi Valley School and is now Director of Krishnamurti Publications of America, is happy about Krishna's role in his life. He says Krishna would talk about "cooking" certain people, and Lee assumes this included himself, which meant Krishna was "working" on them – talking with them at length, challenging them, forcing them to face certain things.

44 R Rajagopal Sloss (1991) pp 242-43. Rajagopal to Dwarkanath 17 June 1953, Huntington 11/19.

45 C Suares 1955 *Krishnamurti and the unity of man* Chetana Bombay first published in French was intended to replace the 1932 French publication, *Krishnamurti*. In relation to Krishna's interest in *The Song of Songs*, it might be noted here that Suares, a close friend of Krishna, published 1972 *The Song of Songs: the canonical Song of Solomon deciphered according to the original code of the Qabala* Shambala Berkeley California. Krishna to Madhavachari 13 July 1953, Huntington 11/16. Krishna correspondence dated 1 June 1953, Huntington 20/8.

46 Jinarajadasa to Krishna 8 June 1953, Huntington 9/31; Krishna to D Ingram Smith 27 July 1953, private source. R Rajagopal Sloss (1991) p 243.

47 M Lutyens (1983) p 82. Jinarajadasa to Krishna 8 June 1953, Huntington 9/31.

48 M Lutyens (1983) p 82.

49 M Lutyens (1983) pp 83-86.

50 J Krishnamurti 1958 *The First and Last Freedom* Gollancz London pp 9-18.

51 Correspondence cited earlier, 3 March 1941, Huntington 20/8.

52 M Lutyens (1983) pp 87-90. M Lutyens makes this observation in the 1983 biography of Krishna which he sanctioned so one might assume he agreed with this view of Rajagopal's role in the refusal. Rajagopal to Dwarkanath 10 October 1954, 17 March, 14 June 1955, Huntington 11/19.

53 R Rajagopal Sloss (1991) p 250.

54 R Rajagopal Sloss (1991) p 251. Sybille Bedford (1987) Vol II pp 140, 155, 160, 178, 186, 206-09. The year following Maria's death Aldous, with his friend, the Vedanta follower, Gerald Heard, took LSD for the first time and within two months had published *Heaven and Hell*, a sequel to *Doors of Perception*, about his experience with mescalin which he took first in 1953. He was also at this time concerned with the potential of education for humans to fulfill contradictory roles for both self and social group.

55 P Jayakar (1986) pp 198-201.

56 M Lutyens (1983) p 91. Annie Vigeveno to Rajagopal 4 June 1955. Rajagopal to the Vigevenos 14 June 1955, Huntington 20/11. Rajagopal to Dwarkanath 14 June 1955, Huntington 11/19.

57 M Lutyens (1983) p 93 dates Krishna's letters as 27 September, 22 October and from Sydney, November 1955. Lady Emily to Krishna 1 November 1956, KFI. Radha's interview with the author October 2000.

58 R Rajagopal Sloss (1991) p 251.

59 *Sun-Herald* 6 November 1955 p 33. By 1955 the amphitheatre had been demolished and replaced by a block of flats. EL Gardner 1963 *there is no religion higher than truth* Theosophical Publishing House London p 19 says that the stadium had been sold by 1930. Gavin Souter (1994) p 171

says that after the amphitheatre fell into disuse, part was used as a miniature golf course and then the impresario George Humphrey tried to make it a venue for vaudeville and theatre. In 1937 it was bought by the Roman Catholic Archdiocese of Sydney reportedly for 1900 pounds to build a convalescent home for nuns, but it was sold again for an undisclosed sum in 1950 and demolished to make way for a red brick block of flats, a development which the historian Jill Roe described as "suburbanisation" conquering all.

60 J Krishnamurti, 1956 *Talks by Krishnamurti in Australia, 1955, (Verbatim Report),* KWINC, Ojai.

61 Author's interview with Doneraile Burton 27 February 1999 Katoomba.

62 Circular from Spencer English, Killeaton St St. Ives dated 27 June 1955, private source. Krishna to Madhavachari 24 October, 23 & 26 November, 1955, Huntington 11/16.

63 R Rajagopal Sloss (1991) p 251.

64 Rosalind to Rajagopal 10, 25 December 1955, Huntington 25/14. Kitty Shiva Rao to Rajagopal 5 January 1956, Huntington 9/21.

65 R Rajagopal Sloss (1991) pp 252-54. *Samadhi* is that final ecstatic state of the yogic path which leads to liberation or *moksha*. It's questionable that Nandini ever reached such a state or that Krishna said that she had. M Lutyens' (1996) p 78 response to the question of first class travel was that Rajagopal, who controlled the purse-strings, always travelled first class by air if possible, and besides, Madhavachari's career had been on the railways and he hated flying.

66 P Jayakar (1986) pp 202-03.

67 R Rajagopal Sloss (1991) pp 254-255. M Lutyens (1983) p 94. Reference to Italian publisher in correspondence Contessa Topiaza Alliata di Salaparuta, Palermo, 9 June 1956, Huntington 9/21. Will dated 14 August 1956, Huntington 25/14.

68 Krishna to Madhavachari 7 September 1956, Huntington 11/16. See J Krishnamurti 1999 *The Revolution from Within* KFI Chennai pp 113, 120, 127 for talks in Brussels and Hamburg.

69 M Lutyens (1983) p 94. J Krishnamurti (1956) *Commentaries on Living*. Kitty Shiva Rao to Rajagopal 5, 7 October, 6, 28 November, 1956, Huntington 9/21. Rajagopal to Kitty Shiva Rao 25 January 1957, thanks her for *Hindustan Times* review by Sanjiva Rao, Huntington 9/21.

70 P Jayakar (1986) pp 203-07.

71 P Jayakar (1986) pp 192, 207-09. On pp 221-27 she describes Vinoba Bhave's first meeting with Krishna on 13 August 1959 when they spoke about many things including tradition and the role of the guru and "Vinobaji" left satisfied that Krishna was an incarnation of Lord Krishna. VimalaThakar 1989 *On An Eternal Voyage* Vimal Prakashan Trust, India. Letter from Vimala Thakar to the author 15 March 2001.

72 M Lutyens (1990) p 109 says the Sri Lankan talks were subversive so Krishna was surprised that the government allowed five to be broadcast. The talks were published verbatim by KWINC in Ojai 1960. The press also ran at least 11 provocative articles during January 1957 with headlines such as, "Revolt inwardly", "Religion – an idiotic label" and "Social morality has produced chaos in world" – see Susunaga Weeraperuma (1974) p 27. M Lutyens (1983) p 95. R Rajagopal Sloss (1991) P 259-61. Krishna to Lady Emily 11 April 1957, Huntington 11/16. Rajagopal to Kitty Shiva Rao17 April, 1957, Kitty Shiva Rao to Rajagopal 9 May 1957, Rajagopal to Kitty Shiva Rao, 14 May, 4 October 1957, Huntington 9/21. Rajagopal to Motwani 17 April 1957, KFI. Rajagopal to Bessie Simon 5 August 1957, Huntington 9/21. Rajagopal to Vanda Scaravelli 30 August 1957, Huntington 36A/8. Salvador Sendra to Rajagopal 23 October 1956 and reply 30 January 1957, Huntington 9/21. Byron Casselberry to Madhavachari 10 September 1958, Huntington 11/4.

73 Bircher-Benner advocated a diet of "living food" and respect for "the order of life". Ruth Kunz-Bircher 1980 *The Bircher-Benner Health Guide* Woodsbridge Press Santa Barbara pp 47, 71.

74 B Sanjiva Rao 1989 *Letter of Wisdom (1958-65)* Dipti Publications Pondicherry pp 20-23 says he had not a single rupee at his disposal when he was first asked to build a centre at Varanasi for Krishna during Mrs Besant's lifetime, and it was not until 1958 that Krishna intervened to take full responsibility for changes there. P Jayakar (1986) pp 211-214. See Asit Chandmal 1980 *One Thousand Suns Krishnamurti at Eighty-Five* Abrams New York.

75 R Rajagopal Sloss (1991) pp 263-266.

76 M Lutyens (1983) pp 98, 99. Casselberyy to Madhavachari 10 September 1958, Huntington 11/14.

77 P Jayakar (1986) pp 216-227.

78 The wife of a Los Angeles playwright who had known Krishna from the 1930s told the author that Krishna had been very impressed by the poodle's pedigree, using the observation as a comment about Krishna liking the upper class and good quality things, such as fine suits and cars, rather than "sticking up" for the common people. No doubt he genuinely cared for the dog in any case, as it was part of the family.

79 M Lutyens (1996) pp 80-81. Mary Cadogan says she read Krishnamurti on her honeymoon in 1950 and met him within a few years, becoming involved in the discussions during the 1950s, Mary Cadogan 1999 *KFA Newsletter* Vol 13 No 2 p 2. Among the generous friends who helped Krishna was the marchesa, Vanda Scaravelli. R Rajagopal Sloss (1991) pp 267-68.

80 R Rajagopal Sloss (1991) pp 268-69.

Chapter 10 Out with the Old, In with the New

1 Correspondence 18 & 30 January 1960. Huntington 11/14.

2 Correspondence 8 & 26 February 1960. Huntington 9/21. KFA Archives for published list of K's talks.

3 Rajagopal to Vanda Scaravelli 16 March 1960. Huntington 36A/8. M Lutyens (1996) p 81.

4 Doris Pratt to Rajagopal 18 May 1960. Huntington 23/5. M Lutyens (1996) p 82.

5 Biascoechea to Krishna 30 May 1960. Huntington 9/23; Biascoechea to Vanda Scaravelli 22 June 1960 and to Rajagopal 28 June 1960 & 10 July 1960, and Rajagopal's reply 2 July 1960, and telegrams from Biascoechea 17, 18, 19 August 1960. Huntington 36A/5; Rajagopal to Vanda Scaravelli 27 June 1960. Huntington 36A/8. M Lutyens (1996) pp 82-82.

6 M Lutyens (1990) p 112.

7 R Rajagopal Sloss (1991) p 268-70. Sloss uses the word "moratorium" and says Rosalind's notes indicate Krishna agreed not to give "any large public lectures" until the following year. It's not clear who initiated the request for Krishna to stop giving public talks to large audiences, or why, apart from Sloss's statement that Rosalind recommended it. However it is known that the FBI held a file on Krishnamurti. Perhaps Rajagopal and/or Rosalind simply wanted to prevent Krishna from creating new material which might cause further disputation over publication rights. KFA Archives for published list of K's talks. M Lutyens (1996) p 83.

8 Krishna to Doris Pratt 26 December 1960. Huntington 23/5. M Lutyens (1990) p 113.

9 M Lutyens (1990) p 113.

10 Doris to Rajagopal 15 June 1961. Huntington 23/5. Aryel Sanat 1999 *The Inner Life of Krishnamurti* Quest Wheaton pp 17, 27-8, 41, 50 makes the point that many people who have written about Krishnamurti's life equate a mystery surrounding Krishnamurti's process as "not appropriate to be examined further", yet Krishnamurti himself stated that certain aspects of his inner life were "amenable" to exploration, and that he wasn't making a mystery of the source of his work - it was "much too vast to be put into words". Sanat's bias toward Blavatsky and Leadbeater in his treatment of Krishnamurti is evident in his claims that K defended Leadbeater, and an unsubstantiated claim that Huxley was "following the lead of Blavatsky" in using the term "perennial philosophy" which Sanat claims Balavatsky meant in her use of completely different terms, such as 'occult philosophy', 'the Hermetic teachings', "*gupta vidya*", "occultism", "the ancient wisdom", "esoteric teachings", "the secret doctrine" and "theosophy".

11 M Lutyens (1996) p 86.

12 *Krishnamurti's Notebook*, 1976 Harper & Row, NY.

13 R Rajagopal Sloss (1991) pp 271-72. On the other hand, Mary Lutyens (1996) p 81 claims Rosalind fought the prospect of a divorce, yet offers no evidence to support the view.

14 Lutyens says Krishna did not receive a reply but later, in India, Rajagopal did send him a balance sheet which he could not understand. M Lutyens (1990) p 117 & (1996) p 89. Sybille Bedford (1987) Vol II p 285.

15 M Lutyens (1990) p 118.

16 Sybille Bedford (1987) Vol II p 296. Huxley's first wife, Maria, had died in 1955.

17 M Lutyens (1990) pp 119-20. Huxley to Krishna 10 October 1961 (misspelt 1960) & 29 October 1961, Huntington 36/29. The accommodation at *Vasanta Vihar* is rather spartan, the rooms sparsely furnished and the beds having thin mattresses. P Jayakar (1986) p 253 says she had promised to make the Huxley's stay a little more comfortable but was called away when her husband died. Laura Huxley to Mamaji, Huntington 36/28; Madhavachari to Rajagopal 1, 7 December 1961, Huntington 34/2; Madhavachari to Laura 7 December 1961, Huntington 34/12. Sybille Bedford (1987) Vol II p 297 gives Isaiah Berlin's account of the acknowledgement of Huxley's standing at the reception.

18 V Thakar 1989 *On an Eternal Voyage* Vimal Prakashan Trust Ahmedabad. Letter to the author 15 March 2001.

19 Madhavachari to Rajagopal 6, 9, April, 22 December 1962 & reply, Huntington 11/5; 25 April 1962, Huntington 34/2. Rajagopal to Biascoechea 17 December 1962 and reply 29 December 1962, Huntington 36A/5. Rajagopal thanks Biascoechea for medical details about Krishna and his whereabouts, and Biascoechea tells Rajagopal about Krishna treating intestinal worms by eating garlic. *Daily Mail* 5 February 1962; Madhavachari to the Managing Editor of the *Daily Mail*, 9 April 1962, Huntington 34/1. The question as to whether Indians are considered 'Oriental' is debatable.

20 M Lutyens (1983) p 120-21.

21 R Rajagopal Sloss (1991) p 267, 282.

22 M Lutyens (1983) pp 123-26. See letters from Barbara & Spencer English on Rajagopal's happiness 17 December 1962, Huntington 23/5 & Doris to Rajagopal on Mary Lutyens' reaction to his marriage 4 January 1964, Huntington 23/5.

23 M Lutyens (1983) pp 126-127, (1990) p 124. American art historian Bernard Berenson lived in a Florentine villa, *I Tatti*. Lutyens quotes from Berenson's diary for 7 May 1956 from Nicky Mariano (ed) *Sunset and Twilight*, Hamish Hamilton London 1964. Doris to Madhavachari 14 February 1963, Huntington 34/1.

24 M Lutyens (1990) p 125.

25 Krishna and Louis Zalk correspondence 6, 19, 31 August 1963, Huntington 10/8.

26 Correspondence between Madhavachari and Rajagopal 5, 12, 18, 26 September 1963. Rajagopal and Biascoechea 12 September 1963. Madhavachari to Sri Acharya Jugul Kishore 30 August 1963, Huntington 11/6. Biascoechea to Rajagopal 22 September 1963, Huntington 36A/5. Madhavachari to Rajagopal 18 (month misspelt) 1964, Huntington 11/7. Correspondence concerning purchase of house, 25, 26 September & 17 December 1962, Huntington 11/5. Rajagopal tells Madhavachari 31 May 1964 that Pupul Jayakar and Kitty Shiva Rao might be able to raise funds in America, Huntington 11/7.

27 Correspondence 26 September, 4, 13 October, 2,12, 16 November, 1963 Huntington 10/8; 10 December 1963, Huntington 10/8.

28 Doris to Rajagopal following publication of pamphlet in November 1963, Huntington 23/5.

29 EL Gardner 1963 *there is no religion higher than truth* Theosophical Publishing House London, pp 8, 9 10, 17. *Kriyashakti* is defined by G Feuerstein (1997) as 'action power' or that aspect of the Divine that is the source of all dynamism in nature.

30 S Hodson & M van Thiel (eds) *CW Leadbeater A Great Occultist*, undated and privately published in New Zealand, available Campbell Library, Theosophical Society, Sydney.

31 EL Gardner (1963) pp 19, 20.

32 Nethercot (1963) pp 449-451.

33 Doris to Rajagopal 20 November 1963, Huntington 23/5. These originally psychiatric medical terms had come into more general language by the 1960s and could be used in personality profiles without clear definition of their meaning in the context.

34 Sybille Bedford (1987) Vol II pp 346-349, 353-59. Aldous's article for *Show* magazine was completed, under great duress, the day before he died. Aldous was said to have told no one but Laura about his cancer until two months before he died because he wanted to keep on working right up to his death. A Huxley 1962 *Island* Harper & Row NY p 237 writes about "*moksha*-medicine" and adolescents who are helped to experience their "transcendental unity with all other sentient beings" . R Rajagopal Sloss (1991) p 280.

35 Krishna to Sir Julian February/March 1964, Huntington 36/53. Sybille Bedford (1987) Vol II p 336 quotes Krishna telling Chaman Nahal *Drugs and the Other Self*, Harper & Row, 1970, that Aldous used to discuss his experimental use of drugs with him and he wondered why he went so far, as everyone knew the human consciousness could be disturbed with stimulus – an alcoholic drink would do that much.

36 J Krishnamurti 1973 *The Awakening of Intelligence*, "The Art of Seeing", 3 January 1968. A Huxley 1967 (first published 1954) *The Doors of Perception* Penguin Middlesex, p 17 explains that his conversations were recorded on a "dictating machine" during his experiment in taking a

mescalin pill so that he could hear his description of flowers on a table, among other things. In the sequel, *Heaven and Hell* (1967) pp 72-73, Huxley said there were two methods of transporting oneself to one's "antipodes" – either to transport the soul by the aid of a chemical – mescalin or lysergic acid – or by the psychological vehicle of hypnosis. Yet he was aware of and valued the great insights of the Upanishads which were believed to have been the result of the exploration of states of consciousness by seers practising yoga 'naturally'.

37 M Lutyens (1983) p 128. Krishna actually met Lady Emily in 1911 when he was about to turn sixteen which was almost 53 years earlier. Doris Pratt discloses in a letter to Rajagopal 4 January 1964 that Mary Lutyens said she paid 1,500 pounds for her mother's correspondence with Krishnamurti used in her mother's book and wondered what happened to KWINC royalties. Krishna had offered to pay her to have the originals. Huntington 23/5.

38 P Jayakar (1986) p 28-86.

39 Doris Pratt's view of the 1963 Indian Talks was that they were badly edited. See Doris to Rajagopal 26 May 1964, Huntington 23/5. Her opinion expressed so decidedly would lead to conflict with Madhavachari. It is also interesting to note that she believed that Krishna's view that one could not find God at age sixty should have been edited out (she said Raja should never have allowed him to say this) raises a question about how much of what Krishnamurti said that might be controversial or offensive was deleted in publications. The Krishnamurti Foundation Trust in England went into production of LP records in 1971 eg *Mind in Meditation*, a talk given in Bangalore, India 31 January 1971, also published in print form.

40 R Rajagopal Sloss (1991) pp 281-84. Letter of resignation 9 October 1964, Rosalind's acceptance 3 December 1964, Krishna to Vigeveno 10 November 1964, Huntington 10/8. Krishna to Rosalind 13 July 1964 from Gstaad, Huntington 10/8. M Lutyens (1983) p 130 says Rajagopal agreed to put up the purchase price for the land on the understanding that after Krishna's death the land would revert to KWINC.

41 M Lutyens (1990) p 125.

42 Correspondence between Doris & Rajagopal 8, 11 March, 8 June 1964, Huntington 23/5. Correspondence between Naudé, Rajagopal, Balusundram, Madhavachari 13, 16, 20, 20 30 July 1965, Huntington 11/8. Rajagopal to the Biascoecheas 26 September 1965 alerts them to Madhavachari's SOS for the school at Rajghat, Huntington 11/6.

43 Doris to Rajagopal 6 February, 10, 28 August 1965 and Rajagopal's note about a Western Union cable 9 February 1965, Huntington 23/5. M Lutyens (1990) p 125.

44 M Lutyens (1996) p 93-94.

45 Madhavachari to Rajagopal 18 December 1964 Huntington 11/7 & 1 January, 8 November, 4, 18 December 1965, Huntington 11/8.

46 Doris to Rajagopal 6 February, 25 April, 23 May 1965, Casselberry to Doris 18 March 1965, Huntington 23/5; Madhavachari to Rajagopal 30 March, 30 July, 8 November 1965, Huntington 11/8; correspondence between Alain Naudé and Rajagopal 17 May, 18 August, 24 September, 13 October, 11, 14, 28 November, 1965 Huntington 36A/4.

47 Correspondence between Smith, Rajagopal & Madhavachari 15 February, 22, 30 March, 22 April 1965 & flyer for camp at Jolly Jumbuck, Terrigal, Huntington 9/21. Krishna to Smith, 31 March 1966, private source.

48 Doris to Rajagopal 20 October 1965, Huntington 23/5.

49 A Besant "The Great Work", *The Theosophist* June 1927, p 269. See also Joy Mills 1987 *100 Years of Theosophy* Theosophical Publishing House Wheaton p 93 who writes that Annie Besant was talking about a vision of establishing a "center of the new civilization in the Ojai valley" on "large acreage to be known as the Happy Valley land".

50 Doris to Naudé 19 February 1966, Huntington 23/5. Naudé to Rajagopal 27 March, 11 April, 23 May, 28 August 1966 from Rome, Paris & Gstaad & reply 29 April 1966, Huntington 36A/4. Correspondence between Krishna and Madhavachari 8, 13, 18 April, 21 May, 1966, minutes of meeting 26 April 1966, Madhavachari to Rajagopal 21 May, 13 June 1966 Huntington 11/9. P Jayakar (1986) p 287.

51 Author's interview with Mark Lee (2000). Lee says the boys' names have been withheld at their request.

52 R Rajagopal Sloss (1991) pp 285, 296-97. In October 1966 notification of an order from Edouard & Butler, New Bond St London for 9 poplin shirts for Krishna was sent to Doris Pratt, 20 October 1966, Huntington 36A/4. Lutyens (1983) pp 78 & 101 says Krishna's tailor *Myer & Mortimer* in Conduit St London had closed down in the 1950s so thereafter he patronised Huntsman in Savile Row for clothing and he went to Lobb's for his shoes. On p 196 she says that when in London, Krishna carried a "beautifully" rolled umbrella and hogskin gloves and his humanitarianism never extended to giving up the use of leather. Since meeting Leadbeater he had always been given fine clothes in whatever culture he was living, apart from his Ojai war years, so the quality of his clothing should have come as no surprise to Radha. Lutyens (1990) pp 143-44, says Krishna's barber wasTruefitt & Hill in Bond Street, and alterations to Krishna's clothes were often made at Huntsman to try to accord with his standard of "perfection". Lutyens also acknowledges that Krishna's interest in good clothes and cars, and escapist books, seemed "anomalous" to some people but it did not occur to him to change his "inclinations" in such "trivial" matters. See J Krishnamurti 1992 *On Right Livelihood* HarperSanFrancisco p 141 where he says that he earned his livelihood by talking to many people in many places, he'd been doing it for fifty years and he thought it was right for him, not imposed by anybody.

The Theosophist September 1927 pp 746-47. Mick Brown 1998 *The Spiritual Tourist* Bloomsbury London p 203 cites psychologist Anthony Storr's view that in clinical terms, "the voices, messages, the messianic beliefs of the mystic, the sense that they are somehow special or chosen ... are all classic symptoms of delusional behaviour", yet such characteristics are the "foundation stones for most of the world's great belief systems".

53 Madhavachari to Rajagopal 24 June, 2 July 1966 Huntington 11/9; Naudé explains to Rajagopal 29 June 1966 that Krishna is well taken care of and having treatment by a homeopath, Dr PierreSchmidt of Geneva, Huntington 36A/4. P Jayakar (1986) p 287. Allen Austill, Dean of New School to Kewal Motwani 30 September 1966, KFI. . Mary Cadogan to Naudé refers specifically to the talks in California following New York 10 November 1966, Huntington 36A/4. M Lutyens (1983) p 136. Mary Zimbalist accompanied Alain Naudé and Krishna to Lowell House at Harvard on 16 October 1966. A freelance journalist in New York, Marcia Kay Keegan, wrote a story for Associated Press about Krishna's lectures to "overflowing crowds" at the New School for Social Research but it was not used: "The world famous Indian philosopher and author of many books on self-realization stated that ... [spiritual] groups make men slaves to propaganda and conditioning", Huntington. 36A/4. Ginsberg had already had contact with Pupul Jayakar in 1962 when he took part in a peace march by Shankar Rao Deo, President of the Sarva Singh.

54 M Lutyens (1996) pp 96-101. A note was made by Rajagopal of a cheque for $400 given to Naudé for miscellaneous costs associated with Krishna's talks, all itemised, on 30 October 1966, Huntington 36A/4.

55 Madhavachari to Krishna 17 October 1966 says he believes Rajagopal will be nice and give favourable consideration to any suggestions he might make, Huntington 11/9. Madhavachari to Rajagopal 12 February 1967 says Krishna told him he would withdraw from KWINC but would not do anything unfriendly. Mary Cadogan to Naudé 19 October, 10 November 1966, Huntington 36A/4. Reg Bennett to Madhavachari 3, 22 April 1967, 21 February 1968, Huntington 36/7.

56 Doris to Naudé 15 October 1966 & National Educational Television to Naudé 31 October 1966, Huntington 36A/4. Casselberry to editor 2 August re article in June issue, 1966, Huntington 9/19. Rajagopal to Vanda 22 February 1967, 36A/8 for summary of success of the US trip.

57 Correspondence November and 12 December 1966, Huntington 11/9. Rajagopal to Madhavachari 4 March, 9 June 1967 & Casselberry to Madhavachari 30 October 1967 & reply 8 November 1967 & Madhavachari to Rajagopal 5, 9 August, 13 September, 6 October, 25 November 1967, Huntington 11/10. National Educational Television to Naudé 31 October 1966, Huntington 36A/4. Naudé to Casselberry 28 May 1967, Huntington 36A/4. Krishna spent the spring and summer of

1967 in Europe with Mary Zimbalist. Alain Naudé and Vanda Scaravelli. M Lutyens (1990) p 127-29. M Lutyens (1983) p 139 says Nandini also visited Krishna at Gstaad with her daughter.

58 Casselberry to Madhavachari 16 December 1967 and note dated 14 October 1967. Huntington 11/10.

59 Naudé to Rajagopal 15 January 1968. Huntington 36A/4. Naudé to Vigeveno 23 January 1968. Huntington 11/11.

60 R Rajagopal Sloss (1991) pp 290-94. M Lutyens (1996) p 102 makes the point that Rajagopal was refusing to show Krishna the records and Krishna did not want to see Rajagopal alone. believing he would be abused.

61 R Rajagopal Sloss (1991) pp 294-95.

62 M Lutyens (1983) pp 151-54. M Lutyens (1996) pp 104-05. George Digby. who had at one time worked with Ouspensky. was Keeper of the Department of Textiles at the Victoria and Albert Museum and a writer. Dorothy Simmons. who with her husband Montague. had managed a government school for twenty years advised Krishna on the establishment of Brockwood school in Hampshire. Notice of fundraising October 1968 by Cadogan. Huntington 36A/6.

63 M Lutyens (1983) p 145-53. Correspondence between Mary Cadogan. Byron. Rajagopal & Krishna 17. 27 April. 7. 24. 28 May 1968. Huntington 23/5.

64 Rajagopal's stand seems to have been in stark contrast to his view in a speech reported in *The Herald of the Star* October 1926 p 416 in which he said that his ideal of an organisation was for it to be flexible so that the "World Teacher" could use it as he liked. He wanted it to be "perfect" he said, yet able to be changed should the "Teacher" want to change it.

65 Madhavachari to Rajagopal and telegram to and from Krishnamurti. 25 March, 14 April. 4. 13. 14. 19 May. 22. 27 August 1968. Huntington 11/11. Dwarkanath personal and confidential to Casselberry. Huntington 11/17. P Jayakar (1986) p 288-94.

66 Various correspondence including 21 May 1968. Huntington 9/21.

67 Alan Hooker to Rajagopal 23 August 1968. Huntington 9/21. See also Rajagopal's and Helen and Alan Hooker's correspondence. 9. 16. 20 July. 21 August 1968 & letter to the KWINC Board 23 August. 1968. Huntington 9/21 & 9/12.

68 Frank Noyes document 29 August 1968. Huntington 36A/7. Rajagopal to Krishna 16 September 1968 & reply 28 September. 1968 Huntington 36A/6.

69 Correspondence between Casselberry & Bennett 14 December 1968. 27 March, 27 April. 11 May. 16 May 1969. Huntington 10/3. Casselberry's continued use of the honorific "ji" seems curious in this context but the author is not suggesting he himself had a dual personality. Casselberry to Sudhakar Dikshit 27 September 1968, Huntington 36/35.

70 R Rajagopal Sloss (1991) pp 297-98. From the context, it's likely that Rosalind meant "principals". M Lutyens (1996) p 108 makes the point that Rosalind had previously "banished" Krishna from Ojai. According to M Lutyens (1983) p 158, among Krishna and Mary's visitors in Malibu at this time was Christopher Isherwood and Deborah Kerr and her husband Peter Viertel.

71 Copies of Vigeveno's 7-page open letter dated July 1969 are found in many folders of the Huntington Rajagopal collection, including over 40 copies in 20/10, as well as in 34/43 and 20/3. Vigeveno to Krishna 4 August 1969, Huntington 20/3. Vigeveno was said to have written notes for the letter soon after surgery. However he remained loyal to Rajagopal, resigning from the Board of the K&R Foundation in November 1973 due to age and ill health, while emphasising that his feelings and interest in the work of the Foundation had not diminished. Huntington 20/3. Vigeveno's daughter Gabriele Blackburn 1996 *The Light of Krishnamurti* Idylwild Books Ojai pp 122-23 says that her parents felt tied to Rajagopal for his effort in carrying out Krishnaji's warning to them to leave Holland during WWII but the split weighed heavily on them. She says her father made notes for a letter to Krishnaji under heavy medication following surgery and Rajagopal "edited" the notes into a statement her father signed. After her father had a heart attack, to avoid conflict in his life he was not told of the lawsuits.

72 S Weereperuma 1982 *Supplement to a Bibliography of the Life and Teachings of Jiddu Krishnamurti*, Chetana, Bombay p 112, citing *Rajneesh Foundation Newsletter* vol 5 no 8 16 April 1979 pp 4-6 & Rashneesh 1976 *Only one sky: on the tantric way of Tilopa's Song of Mahamudra*, EP Dutton New York pp 165-67 & 196-97.

73 F Noyes to Vigevenos 9 August 1969, Huntington 36A/7. During the author's brief and largely unproductive phone conversation with Naudé 8 December 2000 he said he and Krishnamurti had been very close and he probably knew him better than anyone else but he would not agree to be interviewed by me if I was also going to interview Radha Rajagopal Sloss or use any material from her. M Lutyens (1990) p 131-32.

74 Erna Lilliefelt 1995 *Formation of the Krishnamurti Foundation of America and the Lawsuits which Took Place ...* KFA Ojai pp 5-7.

75 M Lutyens (1996) pp 109-112. Shiva Rao had tried in 1969 to regain use of *Vasanta Vihar* for Krishna, writing to Rajagopal for permission, 19 November 1969, Huntington 9/21.

76 Author's copies of different editions. M Lutyens (1990) pp 128-29. AD Dhopeshwarkar 1967, *J Krishnamurti and Awareness in Action*, Popular Prakashan Bombay, printed by MH Patwardhan at Sangam Press.

77 P Jayakar (1986) pp 295-97. Krishna to Balasundaram 13 March 1969, Huntington 36/45.

78 Widow marriage is a reference to "suttee", the practice of widows being burned on their husband's funeral pyre. This was a custom in India but is said not to be sanctioned in the Hindu texts.

79 *The Star* August 1928 p 3-7; *Australian Theosophist* February 1929 pp 207, 209 interview by Miss Kisch of South Africa; *Star Review* December 1929 p 669; *The Star* January 1928 pp 11-13. Author's interview with Ahalya Chari (1998). Jayakar (1988) pp 317-18.

80 Madhavachari to Rajagopal 31 October 1966, Huntington 11/9; P Jayakar (1986) pp 210-11 puts the healing of Shankar Rao as the winter of 1963. She says news of the "miracle" spread through the Sarva Sangh movement across the country and crowds came to see Krishna in Bombay, trying to touch his hand as he walked from a meeting to his car.

81 Information based on author's interviews plus P Jayakar (1986) pp 111, 494. Leena Sarabhai 1990 *Leaves from a Diary* Rite-Print-Pak, Bombay p 13 also wrote in 1933 that Krishnamurti could certainly heal, citing examples of a man with a broken "spine", and a blind woman being healed.

82 S Patwardhan 1991 *A Vision of the Sacred My Personal Journey with Krishnamurti* Penguin New Delhi p 99. Susunaga Weeraperuma (2000) and (1988) pp 74-85. In correspondence with the author Weeraperuma maintains that Krishna's ability to heal the sick does not necessarily qualify him as an enlightened being. Back on 14 February 1932 Krishna said he had done "healing" but was not doing it then as he wanted to "heal" the mind and the heart. The power which healed wounds was the same which healed minds and hearts so they were serene and free from all fear. See J Krishnamurti 1933 *Talks and Writings* Star Publishing Trust Los Angeles. A section of this book, "Thoughts on Life", comprising aphorisms taken from his notebook, is similar to the 1999 publication, RE Mark Lee (ed) 1999 *The Little Book of Living* Penguin New Delhi.

83 V Thakar (1989) p 32, 37, 44. The account was first published in 1966 and Madahavchari sent a copy of the book to Rajagopal, 31 October 1966, Huntington 11/9.

84 M Lutyens (1983) p 119.

Chapter 11 Science and Revolution

1 P Jayakar (1986) pp 297-99.

2 Krishna to Enrique Biascoechea dated 3 March 1970, to Anneke Korndorffer 16 March 1970, to Leon de Vidas 31 March 1970, KFI. M Lutyens (1983) pp 165 & p 169 for attendance figure. De Vidas had been instrumental in organising the Saanen gatherings. He resigned in 1969 and died two years later. His place was taken by Edgar Graf.

3 M Lutyens (1983) p 156 says that in San Juan, Krishna and Naudé visited Pablo Casals, now aged 95, whom they'd previously met in Europe.

4 KFA Archives list. Scott Forbes 1995 "Education as a Religious Activity" *The Theosophist* May pp 338 – 47. Forbes, a director of Brockwood school in the 1980s, says Krishna believed schools should be beautiful and sacred places. Javier Gomez Rodriguez 1995 *Souvenir 1995* KFI Madras, writing as a former pupil and teacher at Brockwood, says that there is ample evidence of its emphasis on psychological exploration and wholeness touching "a core of deep persoanl significance" for most staff and students. M Lutyens (1983) pp 136, 139, 156-158, 160-61, 168. Lutyens says she went "with others" to see Brockwood Park on 23 October 1968 and five days later a decision was made by the Foundation trustees to buy the estate, despite an objection by M. Blitz who resigned, believing financially it was too soon to start up a school. George Wingfield Digby and his wife, Nelly, who had previously worked with Ouspensky were editing Krishna's talks for publication at this time but the author is not aware whether they were trustees. Lutyens (1983) p 152 makes a note that Krishna once visited Ouspensky who had reportedly remarked of Krishna that he was like no ordinary mortal in attaining "that state".

5 Krishna to trustees 30 March 1970, KFI, to Anneke Korndorffer 16 March 1970, to Mary Cadogan 16 March 1970, KFI.

6 J Krishnamurti 1970 *The Only Revolution* Victor Gollancz London.

7 Mary Zimbalist to Donald 22 July 1970, private source.

8 Bennett to Madhavachari 21 February 1968, Huntington 36/7. Casselberry to Bennett 14 December 1968, 27 April 1969; Bennett to Casselberry 11 May 1969 & Casselberry to Spencer English 27 March, 16 May 1969, Huntington 10/3. Bennett also kept up a corrrespondence with Casselberry after Krishna's visit, writing on 14 September 1972 to him that he had screened films to four enthusiastic groups in Cairns, Huntington 10/3.

9 Circular *Krishnamurti Visit* dated May 1970.

10 *Krishnamurti's Fifth Visit*, 1970 by Smith, private source. This was actually Krishna's sixth visit to Australia. Smith had met Krishna twenty one years earlier, although no doubt he had "watched" him from afar for thirty years.

11 Author's interview with Mary Zimbalist (2000) and a number of Sydney residents who attended the talks, including Betty Carmody, 18 July 2001, who said she remembers the occasion as startling as it had been a burning, personal question she had wanted to ask. See 1970 *Talks and Dialogues Sydney Australia* Krishnamurti Books Sydney.

12 Author's interview with Mary Zimbalist (2000).

13 Author's interview with a former adherent 3 June 2000. The testimonies of most associates of Krishna were that away from the public platform he was a shy, retiring personality.

14 Author's interview with Smith 13 June 2000 and Rino Donvito 27 February 1999. An organisation called 'Krishnamurti Australia' now operates out of Bundall in Queensland to disseminate Krishnamurti's teaching.

15 *Sun Herald* 22 November 1970, p 21. An indication of the increased interest in "religion" at the time was a story, p 17, headed "...cult" about the establishment of a Maharishi Mahesh Yogi or TM centre in Sydney which claimed 3,000 practitioners in Australia. Not acquainted with the nuances of Krishnamurti's view about 'the religious mind', the mainstream press would have considered Krishna simply 'anti-religion' at this time.

16 V Thakar (1989) p 37.

17 P Jayakar (1986) p 300. J Krishnamurti (1972) *Tradition and Revolution*. Orient Longman New Delhi. *Sadhana* means one's spiritual practice. M Lutyens (1983) p 182 & (1990) p 135. Lutyens dropped the reference to Krishna as a Brahmin in the later version. This is in tune with a current downplaying of the fact that most of the people who are at present involved with the KFI are from the Brahmin class.

18 AD Dhopeshwarkar 1970 *J Krishnamurti and Mind in Revolution*, Chetana Bombay. In his earlier work, 1967 *J Krishnamurti and Awareness in Action* Popular Prakashan, Bombay (printed by MH Patwardhan) pp 4, 15. Dopeshwarkar says that to Krishnamurti "knowledge means self-knowledge ... a clear perception of our own mind in action", and that "awareness" is the central theme of his teaching – at its earliest stage, "observation 'without condemnation, without justification and without identification'". See also AD Dhopeshwarkar 1972 *Meditation and Life* Chetana Bombay for a discussion of "choiceless awareness".

19 Krishna to Anneke 16 March 1970, KFI; Vigeveno to Krishna marked "Draft" 13 April & 17 July 1970, Huntington 20/3. Casselberry to Mrs Clarke 14 May 1971, Huntington 10/3. Vigeveno to Krishna 3 January 1972, July 1972 and reply 28 July 1972, Huntington 20/3. Kitty Shiva Rao had also written 24 January 1969 that although Rajagopal was exhausted from so many adversities his mind was calm and his conscience clear, Huntington 36A/9. R Rajagopal Sloss (1991) pp 302-03.

20 M Lutyens (1990) p 132, 135.

21 M Lutyens (1990) p 132. M Lutyens (1983) pp 157, 162-64, 169-70. The *Bulletin* had been set up by Gerard Blitz at Club Mediterranée's head office. P Jayakar (1992) pp 295-97, 316-17. On the question of sex, Weeraperuma (2000) says that in Colombo in January 1957 Krishna stated that he had no sex life. It was most likely true as his acknowledged sexual partner, Rosalind, was not with him then. However Weeraperuma maintains that "you cannot have something pure in an impure vessel" and that as Nirvana is that state in which all cravings have ceased, "sex is the very negation of Nirvana". He says Krishna was "an ordinary man as

regards sex ... yet he claimed to be Liberated". In Weeraperuma 1983 *That Pathless Land* Chetana Bombay p 59, 60. Weraperuma had written that "a serious person cannot possibly afford the sexual dissipation of his precious energies" and that it was possible to "*watch* the sexual drive objectively and passively", clearly believing that was Krishnamurti's view.

22 M Lutyens (1983) p 171. J Krishnamurti 1977 *The Urgency of Change* Harper & Row, New York, pp 73-76. Mary Lutyens is credited as the editor. The back covers states that it provides a synthesis between the potential beauty of life and the brutal myth mankind too often makes of living. 'The word is not the thing' was a fundamental recurring idea in Krishna's talk: in (1963) *Life Ahead* p 121 he had said that the word, the symbol, the image, the idea were not the truth. Krishna's view was in accord with his emphasis on negation at this time - that negation of the false was the "truth". 1971 *Krishnamurti Foundation Bulletin* No. 10 Summer p 11.

23 M Lutyens (1983) p 162. J Krishnamurti 1970 *The Only Revolution* pp 20, 132, 156.

24 Arjun Appadurai 1997 *Modernity at Large Cultural Dimensions of Globalization* University of Minnesota Press Minneapolis pp 37, 168, 173. Juan Carlos Kreimer 1998 *Krishnamurti for Beginners* Writers and Readers Publishing New York p 66 and Walter Anderson 1983 *The Upstart Spring: Esalen and the American Awakening* Addison-Wesley Boston confirm that William Anderson, who had been influenced by Krishnamurti in his youth, participated in the establishment of the Esalen Institute at Big Sur, linked with the Movement for Human Potential and Gestalt therapy. It might be useful to note here the attribution to William Blake of the use of the term "the doors of perception" as in "If the doors of perception were cleansed, everything would appear to man as it is, infinite" - see Huston Smith (2000) p 74. Krishnamurti used the terms "Door of Liberation" (*The Star* March 1928 pp 57-61) and "Door of the Eternal" (*Star Review* May 1929 p 247-49). Krishnamurti was the only door through which one could see liberation, he said, and one must cast aside one's particular mode of thought to establish oneself in the universal thought beyond the door. The door or portal of liberation was in one's heart, he said. There were some who had passed through and they did not cast a shadow as they had become one with eternal light.

25 Peter Washington 1993 *Madame Blavatsky's Baboon* Secker & Warburg London pp 357, 360-61. P Jayakar (1986) p 223. Author's interview with Jane Hammond at Brockwood December 1998 about Krishna's impact on an audience.

26 Program *In Doubts and Certainties* produced by Shirley du Boulay, BBC 7 December 1970.

27 Blume from Bern to Mrs Vigeveno 2 July 1975, Huntington 20/7.

28 Krishna to Jamnadas 24 May 1970, 19 April, 1973, to Shiva Rao 30 September 1970, to Kitty 9 November 1970, to Kewal Motwani 28 July 1970, 18 March, 25 November 1974, 14 August 1975, KFI. M Zimbalist to Motwani 16 May 1971, KFI. Shiva Rao to Rajagopal 4 September & 17 December 1970, Huntington 9/21. Donald Ingram Smith interview with the author, 2 February 2001.

29 P Jayakar (1986) p 217. Author's interview with someone who took a strong interest in Krishna's health over the last decade of his life and did not want to be named; M Lutyens (1990) also points out in a footnote p 137 that Krishna practised yoga as a form of physical exercise "only". Author's interview with TKV Desikachar 12 December 1998, Chennai. Desikachar dedicated his 1995 book, *The Heart of Yoga*, Inner Traditions, Vermont, to "J Krishnamurthi, who taught me how to be a good yoga student". He also thanks Vanda Scaravelli in the acknowledgements. The word 'yoga' from the Sanskrit root, *yuj* 'to yoke', carries the meaning of union with God through control of the mind and senses. There are considered to be four main paths of yoga – jnana or gnosis/knowledge; raja or royal/perception; karma through work/action; bhakti through love/devotion.

30 Desikachar to Naudé 12 October, 8 November 1966, Huntington 36A/4. TKV Desikachar (text compiled by Mala Srivatsan) 1997 *Sri Krishnamacharya The Purnacarya*, Krishnamacharya Yoga Mandiram, Chennai pp 80-81. M Lutyens (1990) p 137.

31 Krishna to Desikachar 6, 24 May, 22 June, 1970, KFI.

32 Author's interview with Desikachar (1998).

33 Krishna to 'Frydman' in Bombay 16 March 1970, KFI. Friedman, a Polish engineer and former Theosophist, had become a spiritual pilgrim in India many years earlier, staying for some years in Gandhi's ashram near Wardhar, in Maharashtra, and at Tiruvannamalai with Sri Ramana Maharshi.

34 Madhavachari to Krishna 17 October, Madhavachari to Rajagopal 31 October 1966, Huntington 11/9. Krishna to Adikaram 6 May 1979, KFI..

35 V Thakar (1989) pp 51-52, 57-65

36 Vimala Thakar's correspondence with the author, 15 March 2001. Vimala Thakar now alternates her time between two centres, 'Shivkul', Dalhousie, Himachal Pradesh and 'Shivkuti', Mount Abu, Rajasthan.

37 This query recalls Olcott's questioning in 1880 of Swami Dayananda Sarasvati of the *Arya Samaj* on behalf of Madame Blavatsky about whether one could possess occult powers and perform supernatural acts without years of discipline and study of yoga. Marion Meade (1980) p 218.

38 Discussion with 93-year old swami (unnamed) 1 February 1971, Bangalore. KFA. *Samskara*, or "activator", means a person's past or psychological imprints which are not passive but dynamic forces in a per-

son's psychic life which propel consciousness into action. *Shastras* are spiritual texts.

39 In an interview with the author 25 November 1999, Professor Krishna Nath said Krishnaji liked to tell the joke. There are variations on it, including that the yogis sat meditating for several hundred yerars.

40 J Krishnamurti *Notebook* (1976). KFA cites a conversation in Bombay 6 February 1971 in which Pupul Jayakar and Krishnamurti both use the third person. M Lutyens (1983) p 216. Lutyens (1988) pp 92, 93 describes Krishna recording on tape a meeting with a "Pandit" from Benares he would not identify who had told him in Madras about Tibetan manuscripts from 600 or 900 AD which predicted the coming of the Lord Maitreya, giving the name "Krishnamurti" as the vehicle for the manifestation. Achyut and Sunanda Patwardhan were present and she took notes of the Pandit's words. Jayakar (1988) pp 30-31 says Sunanda Patwardhan's transcription is held by the KFI but it has not been sighted by the author. Jayakar says that Pandit Jagannath Upadhyaya of Varanasi (Benares) told Krishna in January 1985 that he had found a copy of the *Kala Chakra Tantra*, based on a secret doctrine, lost in India but preserved in Tibet, which included information on the subject of a "Krishnamurti" given to Mrs Besant by the Tantric Swami Vishudhanand (and his disciple Gopinath Kaviraj) of Varanasi, in 1909.

41 M Lutyens (1990) p 129. K Satchidananda Murty (1991) p 35 refers to Sankara's *Vivekacudamani* as pointing to an immediate perception, *saksatkara*, of the one non-dual Reality of the nature of consciousness and bliss, devoid of all attributes.

42 T McCarthy interview conducted 1 June 1970 for Canadian broadcasting. In the author's interview with McCarthy 20 August 1999 she said that she went to Krishnamurti's talks in England, India and California and his "universality" was apparent to her.

43 Available on video beginning from "Transformation" Pt 5 *The Conscious and Unconscious Mind* . D 31, KFI and published as 1978 *The Wholeness of Life* Dialogues 5-7, Gollancz, London, pp 79-138. The question of Krishna's vacancy of mind, what and how much he remembered and whether this was the result of a "transformation" of his mind, remains a debatable point. See M Lutyens (1983) p 34 concerning Krishna's memory of his childhood and M Lutyens (1990) pp 159-68 concerning his "vacancy" and what may have "manifested" through him.

44 Available on video as *Where Knowledge and Silence Go Together*, recorded 18-28 February, D17, KFI.and published as 1991 *A Wholly Different Way of Living*, Dialogues XVII & XVIII Gollancz London pp 238-69.

45 P Jayakar (1986) p 301.

46 M Lutyens (1990) pp 129-30, 134-137. Author's interview with Zimbalist (2000). Author's interview with Mark Lee, 18 October 2000. Lee had taught at the Rishi Valley school and become its principal, over a period of 8 years, after first meeting Krishna in Switzerland in 1965.

47 At Krishnamurti gatherings even today time is set aside for a walk at sunset by the very people who do not regard themselves as Krishnamurti "followers".

48 M Lutyens (1990) pp 99, 155. G Narayan had been a teacher for twenty five years, first at Rishi Valley, at Krishna's request, and then at a Steiner school in England. He had married a teacher from Brockwood and they had a daughter, Natasha.

49 Krishna and Ivan Illich dialogue Varanasi 27 November 1972.

50 J Krishnamurti 1972 *The Flight of the Eagle*. Harper & Row New York.

51 M Lutyens (1983) p 153.

52 M Lutyens (1990) pp 139-140. Reviewer was John Stewart Collis. The idea of the same water in different receptacles is used as an example in the teachings of many Indian gurus.

53 John E Coleman (1971) *The Quiet Mind* Rider London p 90 says that Krishnamurti never allowed photographs if he could help it as he was afraid some people might misuse them, possibly to "deify" him. But Krishna did permit Coleman to take a photograph for publication. Coleman recounts an incident when Krishna was agitated as a Japanese man tried to photograph him at a talk and called out to him to stop. Lutyens (1990) p 140 says Krishna had refused to have photographs taken of himself for over thirty years until 1968 when he allowed Mark Edwards to take some. Yet photographs of Krishna with family and friends in Ojai and other places during the 1940s are archived in the Huntington Library and some have been published in R Rajagopal Sloss's book (1991).

54 It might be recalled that Huxley had studied Vedantism for a period in the 1930s so Krishna would have discussed many Vedantist concepts with him. Bohm had first gone to a talk by Krishnamurti at Wimbledon in 1961 after reading *The First and Last Freedom*. He was the author of several books on quantum theory and would go on to publish in 1980 *Wholeness and the Implicate Order*. See also J Krishnamurti 1977 *Truth & Actuality* Gollancz London for dialogues with Bohm.; David Bohm & F David Peat 2000 *Science, Order, and Creativity* Routledge New York p 257 for reference to Krishnamurti on how "through awareness and attention to the overall movement of thought, the mind comes to a state of silence".

55 The journal runs from 14 September to 25 October 1973, falters, with an entry on 29 October, and does not resume until 1 April 1975 in Malibu. Entry for 2 October 1973 taken as an example.

56 M Lutyens (1983) pp180-81.

57 Letter to Hilde 13 October 1972, Huntington 20/1 and memo regarding *Vasanta Vihar* 15 June 1974, Huntington 20/2. Shiva Rao to Rajagopal 19 July 1974, Huntington 9/21. Madhavachari to Rajagopal 4 January 1975, Huntington 34/2. M Lutyens (1983) p 185.

58 Shiva Rao to Rajagopal 4 February, 19 July 1974, Huntington 9/21. M Lutyens (1983) p 160. R Rajagopal Sloss (1991) p 303. Attorney's letter

25 February 1975. Huntington 20/4. Rajagopal to Spencer 26 March 1975. Huntington 10/3. Shri S Rajam. Indian representative of K & R Foundation. letter of appointment 5 December 1975. Rajam to Terry Christensen 12. 18 December 1975. Huntington 11/1.

59 Correspondence 24 April. 4 May 1973. Huntington 9/21. M Lutyens (1983) p 181. R Rajagopal Slòss (1991) p 304. In the event the KFA established the Oak Grove school where Krishna had given his talks in Ojai in 1975 with an intent to help children learn a way to live that was "whole. sane and intelligent" rather than merely cultuvating intellect. memory ans skills. See Oak Grove School brochure folder 1999.

60 R Rajagopal Sloss (1991) pp 303-04. Interview with the author. November 2000.

61 J Krishnamurti 1974 *Krishnamurti on Education* Orient Longman New Delhi & 1975 *Beginnings of Learning* Victor Gollancz London.

62 Lutyens (1990) p 141. J Krishnamurti *Krishnamurti on Education* (1974) Harper & Row New York. Authentic Report of Talks in Saanen Switzerland 1974. KFT. Beckenham.

63 J Krishnamurti 1972 *The Impossible Question* Gollancz London. See first quote and dust jacket.

64 Fritjof Capra 1988 *Uncommon Wisdom* Century Hutchinson London pp 24-30. Capra. a physicist with a strong interest in eastern mysticism and the philosophical implications of science. was the author of *The Tao of Physics*. with sales of more than half a million copies.

65 The account by M Lutyens (1990) p 149 of the meeting with the Maharishi Mahesh is much more dismissive. She says the yogi came along "beamingly" to talk to Krishna. carrying a flower. and that K's abhorrence of gurus soon put a stop to their conversation. She adds that Krishna told her later that he would have liked to see the Maharishi's balance sheet. and there's no sense in her writing that Krishna himself had been the beneficiary of gifts by wealthy patrons. P Jayakar (1986) p 312-13. She describes the scene on 19 November 1974 when Krishna was asked the question in his sitting room overlooking the Ganges in Varanasi. A talk in Madras 10 January 1968 from J Krishnamurti *The Awakening of Intelligence* (1973) p 206.

66 J Krishnamurti 1996 *Questioning Krishnamurti* HarperCollins London pp 236-42. Observation on the dialogue in San Diego on15 February 1972 by someone present was given to the author in confidence. M Brown (1988) p 199 says Chogyam Trungpa Rinpoche was notorious for "giving teachings reeking of alcohol".

67 M Lutyens (1983) p 207.

68 0 R Rajagopal Sloss (1991) pp 200. 217.

69 John Wren-Lewis 1996 *Journal of Humanistic Psychology* Vol 36 Issue 1 "Flesh-and-blood Buddha or stained glass saint?" proposes that not even as much as "delusions of avatarhood" but "the more limited idealization

involved in the world teacher role forced ... [Krishnamurti] to an evasion of his own human 'what is' and this was his undoing". This view raises the question of the origin of the idea or idealisation of the role of 'world teacher' that Wren-Lewis believes "forced" Krishnamurti to evasion and how it could have been possible for the idealisation and evasion to have been anything other than part of who Krishnamurti was, and, ipso facto, the basis for what he could achieve as the person he was. The view has a resonance with the Leadbeaterian view that something had "gone wrong", as if there is a standard from which Krishna fell away. The word "undoing" in itself carries a negative connotation implying failure. But it may be argued as vital that Krishnamurti is recognised as neither an avatar nor a human with moral weakness – as the two extremes which are often proposed – in order to to understand the relevance of his life to all humankind, made up of individuals with capacities for mystical understanding of the meaning, value and purpose of their lives.

Chapter 12 Yoga and the Nameless

1 J Coleman (1971) pp 75-76. Peter Michel 1995 *Krishnamurti Love and Freedom* Bluestar Communications Woodside p 97 points out that Krishnamurti did not feel as close to Krishna or Christ as to the Buddha, telling a meeting of Trustees in Ojai in 1977 that he had doubts about the historical authenticity of Christ.

2 Paul Carus 1904 *The Gospel of Buddha According to Old Records* Open Court Publishing Chicago. Weeraperuma's correspondence with the author (2000). After having been devoted to Krishna for about forty years, Weeraperuma has turned against him in late life, saying 'he turned out to be a playboy with feet of clay" and that "whenever K talked he was under the sway of satanic powers". He says he gave Krishna books on Zen Buddhism and Krishna was also conversant with Sri Ramana Maharshi's books and "always pretended this [knowledge] was part of his 'Otherness' and came mysteriously into his consciousness".

3 *Questioning Krishnamurti* (1996) pp 18-21, 33-38. Walpola Rahula was author of the *Encyclopaedia Brittanica* entry on the Buddha

4 Weeraperuma's correspondence with the author (2000). Krishnamurti claimed he had found "Liberation" *The Star* March 1928 p 61, May 1928 p 4, June 1928 p 4. He said "Liberation" was not withdrawal from the world but detachment from all things of the world.

5 There are many variations on this story. The Sufi poet, Jalaludin Rumi's version of the elephant in the dark, written 700 years ago, 1979 *Masnavi I Ma'navi: Teachings of Rumi* (trns) E H Whinfield Octagon Press London p 122 begins, "Some Hindoos were exhibiting an elephant in a dark room ...". Idries Shah 1974 *The Elephant in the Dark Geneva University Lectures 1972/73* Octagon Press London Preface seems to

overlook the reference to Hindus as the source of the story in saying that the Islamic interpretation of the resemblance of so many Sufi ideas to those of several religious and esoteric systems is that religion is of one origin, differences being due to local or historical causes".

6 Krishna's June 1926 talk published *Herald of the Star* August 1926. Weeraperuma's correspondence with the author (2000).

7 Weeraperuma's correspondence with the author (2000). Weeraperuma's books on Krishnamurti include: 1974 *A Bibliography of the Life and Teachings of Jiddu Krishnamurti* EJ Brill Leiden: 1982 *Supplement to a Bibliography of the Life and Teachings of Jiddu Krishnamurti*, Chetana, Bombay: 1983 *That Pathless Land* Chetana Bombay: 1988 *J Krishnamurti as I Knew Him* Motilal Banarsidass Delhi. M Lutyens (1983) p 183. Gregory Tillett's interview with the author (1999). Krishnamurti's comments about dress 11 January 1926 published in *Herald of the Star* March 1926 p 98: "... pay attention to these little things. How you behave at meetings, what kind of clothes you put on, how you dress, how you look, how tidy you are and all these little things which make for beauty, for real life". See also Mima de Manziarly Porter's article "The Man Krishnaji" *Herald of the Star* April 1926 p 163 about Krishna's "body beautiful" and ordered life. Krishna had identified himself as a pacifist, for example, saying he was a pacifist by nature *Herald of the Star* September 1926 p 383 and that he was on the side of pacifists *Herald of the Star* December 1927 p 458. He pointed out to Theosophists that many were satisfied in thinking they had all the knowledge they needed from reading their few "special" books. *Herald of the Star* May 1927 p 167.

8 Author's interview with Professor Krishna Nath of the Keshi Vidyapitha in Varanasi, now retired, 25 November 1999.

9 M Lutyens (1990) p 114 for terms Krishna used. Eric Warmington & Philip Grouse (eds) 1956 *Great Dialogues of Plato*, Mentor, New York, p 429. See also Leo Strauss 1972 *Xenophon's Socrates* Cornell University Press New York pp 4-7 for a discussion of Socrates having 'the *daimonion*' give him divinatory signs.

10 Author's interview with Professor Krishna Nath (1999). In a memorial to Krishnamurti, Achyut Patwardhan 1986 "A Message for All Times" *The Theosophist* March p 234 wrote that the most basic postulate of Krishnamurti was that "the Ego is not an entity but a transient bio-psychic process emerging through the operations of our brain cells" and that our brains represented the evolutionary progress of the race stretching over hundreds of thousands of years.

11 P Jayakar (1986) pp 314, 398-404.

12 P Jayakar (1986) pp 338-343. On p 148 Krishna speaks of Nehru's fine, sensitive mind wasted in politics. M Lutyens (1983) p 194-95. Katherine Frank 2001 Indira *The Life of Indira Nehru Gandhi* HarperCollins London p 373.

13 P Jayakar (1986) pp 343-347. K Frank (2000) p 410. Inder Malhotra 1989 *Indira Gandhi A Personal and Political Biography* Hodder & Stoughton London p 193 also reports that Indira Gandhi asked Jayakar to persuade Krishnaji to resume his annual visits. Jayakar makes a link between Indira Gandhi's tears with Krishna and those she shed when she met the Shankaracharya of Kanchi Kamakoti Peetham in Tamil Nadu, in the direct line of teachers descended from Adi Shankara in the C8th. In *The Illustrated Weekly of India* 26 January 1975 p 13, Indira Gandhi is quoted as saying that she was not a devotee of anybody and when she had met the Shankacharya he did not talk so there was no discussion and "the versions given out were not quite correct". She had told him she did not want anything for herself or her family but blessings for the people of India. LK Jha had been principal private secretary to Prime Minister Lal Bahadur Shastri and then to Indira Gandhi before she appointed PN Haksar in 1967 to replace him. K Frank (2001) p 410.

14 P Jayakar (1986) p 347-48.

15 K Frank (2001) pp 443-44.says it was rumoured that Brahmachari was such an integral part of Mrs Gandhi's life that he may have been her lover. KFA. P Jayakar (1986) pp 348-353.

16 K Frank (2001) p 447-48 makes the point that Dhirendra Brahmachari prospered after Sanjay's death as their business dealings had been intertwined for years. He dealt in arms and had his own TV show. His influence over Indira Gandhi was greater than ever and she believed that she might have prevented Sanjay's death if she had completed certain visits to shrines she had neglected to visit. Brahmachari's influence over Mrs Gandhi was gradually lessened by her son, Rajiv, through the early 1980s until in 1984 the swami was told that 'Madame' no longer had the time to see him. *The Illustrated Weekly of India*, 8 June 1986 p 6 claimed the "Rasputin" figure had used his "proximity" with the first family to build up an enormous fortune and incredible political clout and went into hiding after the death of Indira Gandhi.

17 Speech given 20 December 1980. KFA. P Jayakar (1986) pp 353-356.

18 P Jayakar (1986) p 357-60.

19 Krishna to "My dear Mrs Gandhi" 12 January 1982, KFI. P Jayakar (1986) p 361-62.

20 Indira to "Krishnaji" 5 January 1983. KFI.

21 Krishna to Indira 15 Janaury 1983.

22 P Jayakar (1986) pp 362-363.

23 Krishna to "My dear Indiraji" 6 January 1984. KFI.

24 P Jayakar (1986) pp 365-68. M Lutyens 1988 *Krishnamurti The Open Door* John Urray London p 90. K Frank (2001) pp 484-85, 487, 492-93. Indira Gandi wrote in a note in the autumn of 1984 that she had found calm and peace of mind and if she was to die a violent death, the violence would be in the thought and action of the assassin, not in her dying.

25 P Jayakar (1986) pp 323-326.

26 P Jayakar (1986) pp 335, 404-05. This holistic image shares a resonance with the *Ch'i wu lun* (*The Inner Chapters or 'the sorting which evens things out'*) by Chuang Tzu which is an exposition of a synthesising vision in contrast to the intellectual analysis of Confucians, among others. AC Graham 1981 *Chuang Tzu The Inner Chapters*, Allen & Unwin London. P 48.

27 R Rajagopal Sloss (1991) p 307-08 says that twenty years later Vanda Scaravelli showed her her account of Krishna experiencing the 'process' and it seemed to Radha that it was a "probable performance" by Krishna so Vanda would become devoted to him.

28 P Jayakar (1986) pp 245-50. Jayakar says Krishna's word 'wheels' refers to the *chakras*. *Chakra* carries several connotations, including the 'wheel of becoming' or cosmos, a circle of initiates, and most commonly, psychoenergy points in the body depicted as lotuses. Letters to Nandini dated 25 March, unknown date from Rome, 12, 18 May, 1, 16 June, 4, 19 July, 1961. M Lutyens (1983) p 168 says K became President of KFI in 1978.

29 P Jayakar (1986) pp 342, 410-11. In 1981 when Radha visited Krishna at Pupul Jayakar's home in Delhi, it was Nandini who ushered her out to the taxi when she thought the meeting had become too taxing for Krishna. R Rajagopal Sloss (1991) p 310.

30 M Lutyens (1983) p 65, 139, 168, 215. Author's interview with Mary Zimbalist (2000). Lutyens ((1990) p 105 says Rosalind was "humanly jealous" of Nandini in 1949. R Rajagopal Sloss (1991) p 289. Roland Vernon (2000) p 247 says Krishnamurti enjoyed the company of women and became "intimate" friends with several without naming them or providing evidence of who they were.

31 M Lutyens (1990) p 153-54.

32 P Washington (1993) pp 306-07 suggests that Raja clung to Krishna in the mid-70s through litigation, indicating his possessiveness and that the triangle was not simply one in which Krishna was at fault in betraying his friend and abusing his mistress, but that the dynamics of the relationship between the three were subtle and that they had complex mutual needs. See also pp 352, 357.

33 R Rajagopal Sloss (1991) pp 310-14. M Lutyens (1996) pp 114-16. Rajagopal dates the letter as 8 June 1983 but Mary Zimbalist dates its receipt by Krishna as 7 July 1982.

34 M Lutyens (1996) pp 118-120. R Rajagopal Sloss (1991) pp 314, 321.

35 Clipping from an Ojai Valley paper, probably the *Ojai Valley News*, held by the author.

36 See KFA Archives List.

37 M Lutyens (1996) p 123. Author's interview with Radha Burnier, 10 December 1999. P Jayakar (1986) pp 405-06 describes the scene in Mrs Besant's room where Radha Burnier took Krishna before lunch one day

in 1980 but does not say she was present and heard him say the word. "Pax". Author's interview with Tillett (1999). 1980 was also the year of publication of Krishnamurti's *Collected Works*. In a review, Professor Ralph Buultjens (1995) *Souvenir 1995* p 70 reflects on the question of whether Krishna was an agnostic or an atheist, and concludes that he was neither, quoting him as saying that God was a living eternal reality but it couldn't be described and had to be realized for oneself.

38 Author's interview with Anthony Wood of the NSW School of Hypnotic Sciences, formerly the stage performer 'Jason', 10 July 2001. V Thakar (1989) p 39 says Krishna once asked her if she wanted to know how she had been healed because she herself wanted healing powers and when she answered no, he asked whether she was afraid it might be hypnotism, and she said no, that she would not associate mesmerism or hypnotism with him.

39 Sakurazawa Nyoiti (George Ohsawa) 1965 *You Are All Sanpaku* (trans) William Dufty University Books NY pp 9, 10, 15-17. The book refers to two articles by Tom Wolfe in the New York *Herald Tribune*, 18 August 1963 and 12 January 1964. See photo of Indira Gandhi as a girl, with *sanpaku* eyes.

40 M Lutyens (1983) p 194. Hypnotist, Paul McKenna, and subjects on BBC Radio 18 November 2000. Author's interview with Mary Zimbalist (2000). Friedrich (Grohe 1991) p 48 writes that often people seemed hypnotised after a talk by Krishnamurti and he would tell them not to be mesmerized.

41 Margaret Goldsmith 1934 *Franz Anton Mesmer The History of an Idea* Arthur Baker London pp 9, 62-63.

42 Ravi Ravindra 1995 *Krishnamurti :Two Birds on One Tree* Quest Wheaton pp 25 – 28 points to two distinct parts to Krishnamurti: a "deep spiritual essence" and a "relatively superficial personality, formed by his personal history … [which] was discordant". Ravindra suggests a "radical split" in Krishnamurti might have been a form of "sacred schizophrenia". Mick Brown 1998 *A Personal Odyssey Through the Outer Reaches of Belief* Bloomsbury London p 203.

43 Martin Gardner *Skeptical Inquirer* July 2000 v24 i4 p 20. David Peat 1997 *Infinite Potential The Life and Times of David Bohm* Addison Wesley, Reading Mass pp 200, 225, 273-75, 285, 299, 305-06. See also THE LINK newsletter (Krishnamurti Link International) No 15 1998 pp 7-9. F Capra (1988) p 66. Susunaga Weeraperuma (2000) also says that Krishna scolded students who misbehaved sexually and strongly recommended sexual abstinence to him.

44 D Bohm in Lucinda Vardey 1995 *God in All Worlds* Millennium Sydney pp 724-25. D Bohm "A Brief Introduction to the Work of Krishnamurti" brochure, KFA Ojai. The statement recalls Krishna's comment that the meditation of the universe is the ground of creation, P Jayakar (1986) p

436. See also J Krishnamurti 1996 *Total Freedom* HarperSanFrancisco p 352 (talk dated 20 April 1985) "So one has to inquire into what thinking is. ... The speaker has been asking this question for sixty years".

45 J Krishnamurti & Dr David Bohm 1985 *The Ending of Time* Harper & Row New York. See also J Krishnamurti & David Bohm 1986 *The Future of Humanity* KFT London of dialogues in June 1983. M Lutyens (1990) pp 169-70. Mary Cadogan edited the talks anonymously. See also "Key Brain Growth Goes on Into Teens" *Washington Post* 9 March 2000 p A01; "Growth patterns in the developing brain..." *Nature* 8 March 2000 pp 190-93.

46 M Lutyens (1990) pp187-88. A dialogue between Iris Murdoch and Krishna is published in 1996 *Questioning Krishnaumurti* Thorsons San Francisco p 99. An indication of Bohm and Krishna's friendship is shown in Krishna comforting Bohm in a visit to Birkbeck College a couple of days before Bohm had triple heart by-pass surgery in 1981, M Lutyens (1988) p 43.

47 P Jayakar (1986) p 407; M Lutyens (1983) p 171. Sri Lanka later passed legislation concerning an archive for Krishnamurti material. See J Krishnamurti 1988 *Sri Lanka Talks 1980* KFT London.

48 M Lutyens (1990) pp 180, 183. Critchlow has also designed the guru, Sai Baba's hospital at Putta Parthi in Andra Pradesh, India. Friedrich Grohe (1991) p 49 says he placed his rented apartment at Rougemont at Krishna's disposal for the 1985 talks, where he was visited by the actor, Richard Gere, who, after intense conversation with Krishnamurti, asked whther he might hug him as he was leaving.

49 Asit Chandmal 1995 *One thousand suns, Krishnamurti at 85*, Aperture, NY p 7 says he drew on almost fifteen hundred photographs for the work.

50 M Lutyens (1990) p 204.

51 R Rajagopal Sloss (1991) pp 320-21, 323. On p 319 Radha says Krishna succumbed to cancer at the age of 92. Lutyens (1996) p 122 says that it had been fifty-one years since Krishna had met Rukmini and he found it awkward as he didn't know what to say to her.

52 *Ojai Valley News* 31 January 1996.

53 *Ojai Valley News* 30 April 1993.

54 M Lutyens (1983) p 184, on Krishna saying in 1972 that he might live until he was 90 and M Zimbalist must outlive him; (1990) p 188 re Mary Zimbalist writing a book and p 190 re telling Mary Lutyens at lunch in 1985 that he knew when he would die and she gathered it would be in 2-3 years. The reference to him being around for the completion of the Brockwood Centre is not precise as Krishna died the following year whereas the Centre was not completed until September 1987 but there's no indication what the planned date of completion was at the time of the conversation. P Jayakar (1986) p 499 says Krishna told her in 1985 that in Rougemont, Switzerland in July of that year he found out when he

would die – the day and place. He said the "manifestation" had begun to fade. The date 17 February was believed to be Leadbeater's birthdate but this was later shown to be incorrect. Leadbeater had told people his birthdate was 17 February 1847 whereas G Tillet (1982) p 264 found a birth certificate which authenticates 16 February 1854 as the date. Krishna would certainly have believed the date to be 17 February at the time of his own death. Author's interview with M Zimbalist (2000). In an interview with the author E Blau (2000) also likened Krishnamurti to the "world teachers", Jesus Christ, Buddha and Mohammed.

55 M Lutyens (1996) p 121.

56 M Lutyens (1990) pp 184, 210.

57 P Jayakar (1986) pp 409-10, 439-41. In an interview with the author (1999), Leadbeater's biographer, Gregory Tillet, says it's a mystery to him why Krishnamurti taught "almost an antithesis" of the Theosophist teaching once he broke free, and a mystery about the source of what he taught, if he didn't make it up, as it seemed "a bit more sophisticated" than if he had done so. Tillett criticises Krishnamurti on the grounds of hyposcrisy over materialism. Author's interview with M Zimbalist (2000).

58 M Lutyens (1983) p 183 says he was a mystery to her in writing the biography and she had to go deeply into questions about who he was and what the 'process' was to write it. Her final statement on the 'process' in her last biographical work - a rebuttal of Radha's book - (1996) p 126 quotes Krishna saying that it was beyond love and the brain could never understand it but he was blessed to have been given the experience. P Washington (1993) p 365.

59 M Lutyens (1990) p 83-84, 211. Author's interview with Professor Krishna Nath (1999). Professor PK Krishna gave the author a copy of a booklet of chants that Krishna used to sing and which was used in the Rajghat school. The "sage" who met Krishnamurti in the 1950s and who shuns publicity, UG Krishnamurti, is quoted in an article in *The Illustrated Weekly of India*, 25 May 1986 pp 58-59 as saying that Jiddu Krishnamurti accepted the role of messiah despite his dissolution of the organisation built around him. " For all I know, a sort of delusional separation from the messiahhood mission may have occurred in him. But did he actually free himself from the mission set for him? His delusional concepts projected as a truth and the illusion of experiencing something that is not there falsified his teaching," he said.

60 M Lutyens (1990) p 168. P Jayakar (1986) p 491.

61 P Jayakar (1986) pp 435-36.

62 P Washington (1993) pp 365-66.

63 M Lutyens (1990) p 172.

64 Author's interview with TKV Desikachar (1998). Dr Parchure 1997 "Look At How He Lived" *The Presence That Stays* Jiddu Krishnamurti Centre Hyderabad, admits he may have had esoteric experiences with

Krishna but he cannot say because he is sworn to secrecy. Friedrich Grohe 1991 *The Beauty of the Mountain* (self-published) p 36 says Krishnamurti practised yoga throughout his life, emphasising that yoga was good for the body but "had nothing to do with spiritual enlightenment". M Lutyens (1990) p 180, 190. Author's interview with Ahalya Chari (1999).

65 Author's interview with staff member who wished to remain anonymous.

66 Author's interviews with Kathy Forbes, Colin Foster. M Krohnen (1997) pp 15, 16, 99, 151, 201, 294-95. Krishna's irritability must have increased in his last years, as Lutyens' biography p 189 includes a description of Mary pointing out to him in 1985 that he had become a little "rough" with her in his manner, and he said that it was because he wanted her to hasten to have a new "brain" and later, on reflection, said he'd become hypersensitive and had probably fallen into the habit of picking on her which was unforgiveable.

67 C Jung 1973 *On the Nature of the Psyche* Routledge & Kegan Paul London pp 108-09, 125. Krishna's description of the 1922 occurrences included "... over my head I saw the Star, bright and clear" and "I have seen the Light ... Never can I be in utter darkness; I have seen the glorious and healing Light". Lutyens (1976) p 171; and in 1972 he had tried to describe an energy that woke him in the night as "a sense of extraordinary fire, a light burning in the mind", Lutyens (1988) p 40.

68 M Lutyens (1990) p 166.

69 C Jung (1973) pp 111-125.

70 Krishna came more and more to discuss the question of the evolution of the psyche, particularly in the context of computerisation, Jayakar (1988) pp 412, 418, 452, 466, 468-74. See *Questioning Krishnamurti* (1996) p 192 where Krishna tells Bernard Levin that the word is not the thing - it is only a communication by people who have seen something and want to communicate it to others but you could not have light from another. See also (1988) *Sri Lanka Talks 1980* p 26. See P Jayakar (1986) Chapter 39 for a discussion of consciousness as the common ground.

71 Joseph Campbell 1960 *The Masks of God: Primitive Mythology* Secker & Warburg London pp 253-54. Campbell refers to William James' and Paul Radin's views that spontaneous intuitions occur in sensitive people no less in "primitive than in higher societies". Stephen Larson 1988 *The Shaman's Doorway - Opening Imagination to Power and Myth* Station Hill Press New York p 80. See also Paul Gillen 1982 *Hope Beheld: the Ideology of Spiritualism* unpublished PhD dissertation, Macquarie University Sydney p 147, "the goal of progress is a dangerous one: the 'psychic sense' which the medium aims to 'develop' is not easily distinguishable from, and can become, madness". The contribution by R Vernon 2000 *Star in the East* Constable London p 127 to the question of Krishnamurti's experiences in relation to shamanism, or even trance or hypnosis recognised by modern psychoanalysis "as a way of disgorging

repressed emotion", is to say that it is not inconceivable that Krishna's "suffering and awakening at Ojai were symptoms of a nervous stress disorder". But he rejects Radha's "theory" that Krishna's aim, consciously or otherwise, was to gain sexual intimacy with Rosalind and other women, and points to the "staggering consistency" of Krishna's symptoms over the years.

72 Joseph Campbell 1988 *The Power of Myth* Doubleday New York p 230. It might be useful to compare these views with those of Agehananda Bharati 1976 *The Light at the Center* Ross-Erikson, Santa Barbara pp 61, 200 who believes that all mystics know euphoria but give different descriptions of it and that mysticism, per se, constitutes what is "*illicit*".

73 M Lutyens (1990) pp 164-65.

74 M Lutyens (1983) p 212.

75 M Lutyens (1990) pp 195-96. M Lutyens (1988) p 150 says Krishna even persisted with his Bates' eye exercises(which Huxley had advocated) right up until his death.

76 M Lutyens (1990) pp 173-74, 179, 181-2, 185. Mary Cadogan (1999) also wrote of some protection surrounding Krishnamurti. KFA List of Archives.

77 M Lutyens (1990) p 185-86.

78 KFI Video T75, also published 1989 as *The Future is Now: Last Talks in India* Harper & Row New York. M Lutyens (1990) p 199.

79 M Lutyens (1988) p 119. In an interview with the author 24 December 1999 Professor Krishna said he came very close to Krishna when Krishna asked him and his wife to take the job. He also recounted a closeness the last day he ever saw Krishna and asked him for something and Krishna touched his cheek and held his hand and he felt Krishna's body throbbing.

80 M Lutyens (1990) pp 199, 201-8. M Lutyens (1988) pp 152-54. P Jayakar (1986) p 498-502. Jayakar describes Mahesh Saxena as a "pilgrim" who gave up his job as head of the central police in Delhi to become a "seeker", living in the Himalayas until he arrived in Rajghat, met Krishna and later became Secretary of the Indian Krishnamurti Foundation. M Lutyens (1996) pp 123, 153-54. The ashes were scattered in Ojai, at Brockwood and in India on the Ganges, at Rajghat, Varanasi, at Gangotri, the source of the river, and off Adyar Beach in Chennai. Mark Lee told the author (2000) that there were seven sites but would not specify their location. Krishna had asked that his body be cared for after death as he had always cared for it. He did not want anyone to see his corpse and as few people as possible to attend his cremation. It is interesting to note that the cremation occurred very soon after death before severe deterioration might have occurred. In some Indian religious traditions much emphasis is placed on identifying from which orifice the *prana* or life force leaves the body and there is a belief that a master yogi can consciously die. For instance, in Paramahansa Yogananda 1977 *Autobiography of a Yogi* Self-

Realization Fellowship Los Angeles the Director of the Forest Lawn Memorial-Park Mortuary in Los Angeles, Mr Harry T Rowe, is reported to have written a notarised letter saying that no visible disintegration was visible in the body of Paramahansa Yogananda twenty days after his death on 7 March 1952, and this state of perfect preservation of a body was unparalleled in the mortuary annals. It might be noted that although Krishna had not favoured Aldous Huxley's use of LSD, saying everyone knew that human consciousness could be disturbed with stimulus, even by an alcoholic drink, both he and Aldous made use of psycho-tropic drugs to pass into death. See Sybille Bedford (1987) Vol II p 336 citing Krishnamurti talking with Chaman Nahal 1970 *Drugs and the Other Self*, Harper & Row New York. Rosalind Rajagopal attended Huxley's death but there's no evidence how she was informed of Krishna's.

81 P Jayakar (1986) p 485-87. See J Krishnamurti 1992 *To Live with Death* (recorded February 1965) KFI Chennai p 12. Death demands a mind that is not afraid, he says.

82 M Lutyens (1990) p 207.

83 M Lutyens (1990) p 141 cites a conversation with Swami Venkatesananda in 1973. V Thakar (1989) p 44.

84 *Krishnamurti to Himself His Last Journal* 1988 KFI Madras p 133.

85 The exposé was made by Rajagopal Sloss. In an interview with the author (2000), Rajagopal Sloss described the flood of response she received to her revelations. In its response, 1995 *Statement by the Krishnamurti Foundation of America about the Radha Sloss book*, the KFA cited extracts from Krishna's talks in which he encouraged people not to deny their sexuality, eg p 14, saying that if one denied it, as most religions denied it, one must cut off one's tongue and put out one's eyes and never look at anything. R Vernon (2000) p 247 points to Krishna's close relationship with Mary Zimbalist over the last twenty years of his life as a demonstration that Krishna "was not an asexual being, but greatly enjoyed the company of women and became intimate friends with several of them". Krishna also shared a close relationship with Vanda Scaravelli.

86 After repeated requests for access to the KFA and other archives over a period of several years, the author was told by the Executive Director of the KFA on 18 November 2000 that it was "not ready to open the archives for access" as it still had no policy on the matter. R Vernon (2000) p 255 points to the "tight-knit band of inner helpers ... whose behaviour at times resembled that traditionally associated with sectarian communities". He says Krishna's close circle "showed symptoms of a consistent discipular condition", a "circus" that Krishnamurti continued to allow to be reconstituted "at least in order to look after his administrative needs". S Weeraperuma 1988 *J Krishnamurti as I Knew Him* Motilal Banarsidass Delhi pp 45-47 says he wrote in 1968 to Krishna about the establishment

of the "Foundation" being at odds with his own "cautioning ... against spiritual organizations", particularly on the issue of permission to quote from his work, and Krishna did not reply but later told him it was quite a sensible letter. M Cadogan 2001 "The Challenges Then and Now" *The Link* No 21 questions whether Krishnamurti would see fear, strife, fragmentation, petty bureaucracy and clinging to the past in "staleness and futility" in the current work of the Krishnamurti Foundations. M Lutyens (1983) p 222 says that from 1978 to 1980 Krishna wrote thirty seven letters to the schools about his views, including his concern with "the cultivation" of the "whole" person, 1981 & 1985 *Letters to the Schools Vols I & II* available from the Krishnamurti Foundations. The Indian Government acknowledged Krishnamurti's standing in issuing a commemorative stamp in 1987. See first day cover 11 May 1987 illustration Rajagopal Sloss (1991) opp. p 243.

87 The final chapter of *Questioning Krishnamurti* (1996) p 252 echoes Sri Ramana Maharshi's perennial advice to spiritual seekers to ask themselves, "Who Am I?"

References

J Krishnamurti:

1926 *Self-Preparation* Star Publishing Trust Ommen
1927 *The Search* Star Publishing Trust & Allen & Unwin London
1933 *Talks and Writings* Star Publishing Trust Los Angeles
1934 *Krishnamurti Auckland, NZ – 1934*, Star Publishing Trust, Ommen
1928 *The Pool of Wisdom* Star Publishing Ommen
1940 *Authentic notes of discussions and talks given by Krishnamurti, Ojai and Sarobia 1940*, Star Publishing Trust Hollywood
1943 "War abolished: one way to permanent peace" *Unpopular pamphlets* Currawong Publishing Sydney
1944 *Authentic Report of Ten Talks May-July* Star Publishing Trust Ojai.
1951 - 1954 *Krishnamurti's Talks 1949-1954* KWINC Ojai
1956, 1958, 1960 D Rajagopal (ed) *Commentaries on Living*, Series I to III Quest, the Theosophical Publishing House Wheaton (Gollancz 1956, 1959 and 1961)
1956 *Education and the Significance of Life*, Gollancz London
1956 *Talks by Krishnamurti in Australia, 1955, (Verbatim Report)*, KWINC, Ojai
1958 *The First and Last Freedom* Gollancz London
1963 *Life Ahead* Gollancz London
1964 *Think on These Things* Harper & Row New York (published in England as *This Matter of Culture*)
1969 *Freedom From the Known* Gollancz London
1970 *The Only Revolution* Gollancz London
1970 *The Penguin Krishnamurti Reader* Penguin Harmondsworth
1970 *Krishnamurti Talks and Dialogues Sydney Australia* Krishnamurti Books Sydney
1971 *Talks and Dialogues* Avon New York
1971 *Mind in Meditation* KFI Madras
1972 *Tradition and Revolution*, Orient Longman New Delhi
1972 *The Flight of the Eagle* Harper & Row New York
1972 *The Impossible Question* Gollancz London
1972 *Tradition and Revolution* Orient Longman New Delhi
1972 *The Second Penguin Krishnamurti Reader* Penguin Harmondsworth
1973 *The Awakening of Intelligence* Gollancz London
1974 *Krishnamurti on Education* Orient Longman New Delhi
1974 *Krishnamurti on Education* Harper & Row New York
1974 *Authentic Report of Talks in Saanen Switzerland* KFT, Beckenham
1975 *Beginnings of Learning* Victor Gollancz London
1976 *Krishnamurti's Notebook* Harper & Row New York
1977 *The Urgency of Change* Harper & Row New York

1977 *Truth & Actuality* Gollancz London
1978 *The Wholeness of Life* Gollancz. London
1980 *Meditations* Harper & Row New York
1980 "From Darkness to Light" *The Collected Works of Krishnamurti Vol I* Harper & Row San Francisco
1981 & 1985 *Letters to the Schools* Vols I & II KFT London
1982 *Krishnamurti's Journal* KFT London
1982 *Questions and Answers* KFT London
1982 Pupal Jayakar & Sunanda Patwardhan (eds) *Within the Mind* KFI Madras
1983 *The Flame of Attention* Harper & Row New York
1985 (with David Bohm) *The Ending of Time* Harper & Row New York
1986 (with David Bohm) *The Future of Humanity* KFT London
1988 *Krishnamurti to Himself His Last Journal* KFI Madras
1989 *The Future is Now: Last Talks in India* Harper & Row New York
1991 *A Wholly Different Way of Living* Gollancz. London.
1991 *Beyond Violence* Gollancz London
1992 *On Right Livelihood* HarperSanFrancisco
1992 *To Live with Death* KFI Chennai
1995 *On Fear* HarperSanFrancisco
1996 *Total Freedom* HarperSanFrancisco
1996 *Questioning Krishnamurti* HarperCollins London
1997 *Reflections on the Self* (ed Raymond Martin) Rupa & Co Calcutta
1998 *On Self-Knowledge* KFI Chennai
1999 *The Revolution from Within* KFI Chennai
1999 *On Creativity* KFI Pune
1999 *The Little Book of Living* (ed RE Mark Lee) Penguin New Delhi

Books

Rig Veda, Upanishads
The Song of Songs or *Song of Solomon*, *Ecclesiastes* and *Psalms Old Testament King James Bible*

MJ Akbar 1988 *Nehru The Making of India* Viking Penguin London
SS Alberts 1968 *Bibliography of Robinson Jeffers* Franklin NY
Alcyone (pseud) 1928 *At the Feet of the Master* Theosophical Society Adyar
Walter Anderson 1983 *The Upstart Spring: Esalen and the American Awakening* Addison-Wesley Boston
Arjun Appadurai 1997 *Modernity at Large Cultural Dimensions of Globalization* University of Minnesota Press Minneapolis
Ramesh S Balsekar 1989 *A Duet of One* Advaita Press Redondo Beach
Ramesh S Balsekar 1992 *Consciousness Speaks* Advaita Press Redondo Beach

Ramesh S Balsekar 1996 *A Net of Jewels* Advaita Press Redondo Beach

A Trevor Barker (compiler) 1975 *The Mahatma Letters to AP Sinnett* Theosophical University Press. Pasadena

Sybille Bedford 1987 *Aldous Huxley A Biography* Collins/Paladin London.

Annie Besant 1916 *A World Religion* Theosophical Publishing House Madras

Agehananda Bharati 1976 *The Light at the Center* Ross-Erikson Santa Barbara

Gabriele Blackburn 1996 *The Light of Krishnamurti* Idylwild Books Ojai

Evelyne Blau 1995 *Krishnamurti 100 Years* Stewart Tabori & Chang New York

HP Blavatsky 1962 *The Secret Doctrine* Theosophical Publishing House Madras

HP Blavatsky 1987 *Key to Theosophy* Theosophical Publishing House London

HP Blavatsky 1972 *Isis Unveiled* Theosophical University Press Pasadena

David Bohm 1983 Wholeness and the Implicate Order Routledge & Kegan Paul London

David Bohm & F David Peat 2000 *Science, Order, and Creativity* Routledge New York

Mick Brown 1998 *The Spiritual Tourist* Bloomsbury London

P Brunton 1934 *A Search in Secret India* Rider London

Katherine Bucknell (ed) 1996 *Diaries / Christopher Isherwood* Methuen London

Mary Cadogan 1999 "Working with Krishnamurti" *KFA Newsletter* Vol 13 No 2

Joseph Campbell 1960 *The Masks of God: Primitive Mythology* Secker & Warburg London

Fritjof Capra 1988 *Uncommon Wisdom* Century Hutchinson London

Paul Carus 1904 *The Gospel of Buddha According to Old Records* Open Court Publishing Chicago

Asit Chandmal 1995 *One thousand suns, Krishnamurti at Eighty-Five* Aperture. New York

Cheiro (Count Louis Hamon) 1964 (revised by Louise Owen*) You and Your Hand*. Arco New York Sarasvati Chennakesavan 1960 *The Concept of Mind in Indian Philosophy* Asia Publishing House Bombay Bernard S Cohn 1996 *Colonialism and its Forms of Knowledge* Princeton University Press New Jersey

John E Coleman 1971 *The Quiet Mind* Rider London

Larry Collins & Dominique Lapierre 1976 *Freedom at Midnight* Vikas Publishing New Delhi

Sylvia Cranston 1993 *HPB The Extraordinary Life and Influence of Helena Blavatsky* Putnam's Sons New York

Surendranath Dasgupta 1949 *A History of Indian Philosophy*. I. Cambridge University Press

TKV Desikachar 1995*The Heart of Yoga*. Inner Traditions. Vermont

TKV Desikachar (text by Mala Srivatsan) 1997 *Sri Krishnamacharya The Purnacarya*. Krishnamacharya Yoga Mandiram. Chennai

AD Dhopeshwarkar 1967. *J Krishnamurti and Awareness in Action* Popular Prakashan Bombay

AD Dhopeshwarkar 1970 *J Krishnamurti and Mind in Revolution* Chetana Bombay

AD Dhopeshwarkar 1972 *Meditation and Life* Chetana Bombay

David Ellis 1998 *DH Lawrence, the dying* game *1922-1930* Cambridge University Press

G Feuerstein 1997 *The Shambala Encyclopaedia of Yoga*. Shambala. Boston.

Sidney Field 1989 *Krishnamurti The Reluctant Messiah* Paragon New York

René Fouéré 1964 *The Man and his Teaching* Chetana Bombay

Katherine Frank 2001 *Indira The Life of Indira Nehru Gandhi* HarperCollins London

Brendan French in his 2000 unpublished doctoral thesis *The Theosophical Masters: An Investigation into the Conceptual Domains of HP Blavatsky and CW Leadbeater* Vols I & II

EL Gardner 1963 *there is no religion higher than truth* Theosophical Publishing House London

MK Gandhi 1963 *The Collected Works of Mahatma Gandhi* Vol XI Government of India, Ahmedabad

MK Gandhi 1980 *The Bhagvadgita* Orient Ahmedabad

MK Gandhi 1983 *An Autobiography* Penguin London

F Edmund Garrett 1896 *Isis Very Much Unveiled* Westminster Gazette Office London

Paul Gillen 1982 *Hope Beheld: the Ideology of Spiritualism* unpublished PhD dissertation, Macquarie University Sydney.

Margaret Goldsmith 1934 *Franz Anton Mesmer The History of an Idea* Arthur Baker London

AC Graham 1981 *Chuang Tzu The Inner Chapters*. Allen & Unwin London

Friedrich Grohe 1991 *The Beauty of the Mountain* (self-published)

Paula Hamilton "Inventing the Self: Oral History as Autobiography", in *Shaping Lives Reflections on Biography* 1992 Ian Donaldson, Peter Read and James Walter (eds) Humanities Research Centre Australian National University Canberra p113

HE and WL Hare 1936 *Who Wrote the Mahatma Letters?* Williams & Norgate London.

Lily Heber 1931 *The Man and his Message* Allen & Unwin London

A Huxley 1980 *After Many A Summer* The Folio Society London

A Huxley 1945 *Time Must Have a Stop* Chatto & Windus London

A Huxley 1962 *Island* Harper & Row NY

A Huxley 1969 *The Perennial Philosophy* Chatto & Windus London

A Huxley 1967 *The Doors of Perception and Heaven and Hell* Penguin Middlesex

Christopher Isherwood 1980 *My Guru and his Disciple*. Farrer, Strauss Giroux New York

Pupul Jayakar 1986 *Krishnamurti A Biography*, Harper & Row, San Francisco

Pupul Jayakar 1992 *Indira Gandhi An Intimate Biography* Pantheon New York

Pupul Jayakar 1995 *Fire in the Mind* Penguin New Delhi

Robinson Jeffers 1927 "Credo" *A Miscellany of American Poetry* Harcourt Brace New York

C Jinarajadasa 1932 *A Short Biography of Annie Besant* Theosophical Publishing House Madras

C Jung 1973 *On the Nature of the Psyche* Routledge & Kegan Paul London

Kolak, Daniel & Martin, Raymond (eds) 2002 *Wisdom Without Answers* Wadsworth/Thompson Learning Belmont CA

Juan Carlos Kreimer 1998 *Krishnamurti for Beginners* Writers and Readers Publishing New York

Gopi Krishna 1970 *Kundalini: Evolutionary Energy in Man* Stuart & Watkins London

Michael Krohnen 1997 *1001 Lunches with J Krishnamurti* Penguin Delhi

Harish Kumar (ed) 1997 *The Presence That Stays* Jiddu Krishnamurti Centre Hyderabad

Ruth Kunz-Bircher 1980 *The Bircher-Benner Health Guide* Woodsbridge Press Santa Barbara

Rom Landau 1935 *God is My Adventure* Nicholson & Watson London

Stephen Larson 1988 *The Shaman's Doorway - Opening Imagination to Power and Myth* Station Hill Press New York

DH Lawrence 1930 "Men Must Work and Women As Well" *Assorted Articles* Martin Secker London

CW Leadbeater 1922 *Talks On 'At the Feet of the Master* Theosophical Publishing House Madras

CW Leadbeater & Annie Besant 1975 Talks on the Path of Occultism Theosophical Publishing House Madras

CW Leadbeater 1979*The Masters and the Path*. Theosophical Publishing House, Madras

Erna Lilliefelt 1995 *Formation of the Krishnamurti Foundation and the Lawsuits Which Took Place ...* KFA Ojai

Emily Lutyens 1957 *Candles in the Sun*, Rupert Hart-Davis London

Mary Lutyens 1959 *To Be Young* Hart-Davis London

Mary Lutyens 1976 *Krishnamurti The Years of Awakening*. Avon, NY.

Mary Lutyens 1983 *Krishnamurti The Years of Fulfilment* Farrer Straus Giroux New York

Mary Lutyens 1988 *Krishnamurti The Open Door* John Murray London

Mary Lutyens 1990*The Life and Death of Krishnamurti* Rider London

Mary Lutyens 1990 *Krishnamurti: His Life and Death* St Martin's Press New York

Mary Lutyens 1994 *The Boy Krishna* KFT England

Mary Lutyens 1996 *Krishnamurti and the Rajagopals*. KFA California

Maurice Maeterlinck (tr Bernard Miall) 1922 *The Great Secret* Methuen London

Janet Malcom 1991 *The Journalist and the Murderer* Bloomsbury London

Inder Malhotra 1989 *Indira Gandhi A Personal and Political Biography* Hodder & Stoughton London Nicky Mariano (ed) 1964 *Sunset and Twilight*. Hamish Hamilton London

Wallace Martin. 1967. *The New Age Under Orage*. Manchester University Press

Gertrude Marvin Williams 1931 *The Passsionate Pilgrim A Life of Annie Besant* Coward-McCann New York

Marion Meade 1980 *Madame Blavatsky The Woman Behind the Myth* Putnam's Sons New York

Rohit Mehta 1973 *J Krishnamurti and the Nameless Experience* Samuel Weiser New York

Rohit Mehta & Shridevi Mehta 1990 *J Krishnamurti and Sant Kabir* Motilal Banarsidass New Delhi

Y Keshava Menon 1976 *The Mind of Adi Shankaracharya* Jaico Publishing House Mumbai

Jeffrey Meyers 1993 *DH Lawrence A Biography* Pan Macmillan London

Peter Michel 1995 *Krishnamurti Love and Freedom* Bluestar Communications Woodside

Joy Mills 1987 *100 Years of Theosophy* Theosophical Publishing House Wheaton

Frank Moraes 1956 *Jawaharlal Nehru A Biography* Macmillan New York

Meaghan Morris 1992 "I Don't Really Like Biography" *Writing Lives: Feminist Biography and Autobiography*. Australian Feminist Studies Adelaide

Chaman Nahal 1970 *Drugs and the Other Self*. Harper & Row. NY

Hajime Nakamura 1964 *Ways of Thinking of Eastern Peoples* East-West Center Press Honolulu

G Narayan 1998 *As the River Joins the Ocean* Book Faith India Delhi

Helen Nearing 1992 *Loving and Leaving the Good Life* Chelsea Green Publishing Vermont

Jawaharlal Nehru 1962 *An Autobiography with Musings on Recent Events in India*. Allied Publishers Private Ltd. Bombay

Arthur H Nethercot 1963 *The Last Four Lives of Annie Besant* Rupert Hart-Davis

Martha C Nussbaum 2001 *Upheavals of Thought: The Intelligence of Emotions* Cambridge University Press

Sakurazawa Nyoiti (George Ohsawa) 1965 *You Are All Sanpaku* (trans) William Dufty University Books New York

Vikram Parchure 1995 *Souvenir 1995* KFI Madras

Sunanda Patwardhan 1991 *A Vision of the Sacred My Personal Journey with Krishnamurti* Penguin New Delhi

Hesketh Pearson 1944 *Bernard Shaw His Life and Personality* Collins London

David Peat 1997 *Infinite Potential The Life and Times of David Bohm* Addison Wesley, Reading Mass

Clayre Percy and Jane Ridley (eds) 1985 *The Letters of Edwin Lutyens to his wife, Lady Emily*, Hamish Hamilton London

Robert Powell 1971 *Krishnamurti The Man And His Teaching* marca impressions USA

R Rajagopal Sloss 1991 *Lives in the Shadow with J Krishnamurti* Bloomsbury London

Rajneesh 1976 *Only one sky: on the tantric way of Tilopa's Song of Mahamudra*, EP Dutton New York Ravi Ravindra 1995 *Krishnamurti: Two Birds on One Tree* Quest Wheaton

Jill Roe 1986 *Beyond Belief Theosophy in Australia 1879-1939*, New South Wales University Press Sydney

Joseph E Ross 1989 *Krotona of Old Hollywood 1866-1913* Vol I El Montecito Oaks Press Montecito California

Rumi (trns) E H Whinfield 1979 *Masnavi I Ma'navi: Teachings of Rumi* Octagon Press London

Aryel Sanat 1999 *The Inner Life of Krishnamurti* Quest Wheaton

Leena Sarabhai 1990 *Leaves from a Diary* Rite-Print-Pak Bombay

K. Satchidananda Murty 1991 *Philosophy in India* Indian Council of Philosophical Research New Delhi Searchlight (pseud - WD Frank) 1926 *Time Exposures*, Boni & Liveright New York

Robert A Seeley 1986 *The Handbook of Non-Violence* Lawrence Hill Conn.

Idries Shah 1974 *The Elephant in the Dark Geneva University Lectures 1972/73* Octagon Press London

RK Shringy 1977 *Philosophy of Krishnamurti* Munshiram Manoharlal New Delhi

Robert Skidelsky 1988 "Only Connect: Biography and Truth" in Eric Homberger & John Charmley (eds) *The Troubled Face of Biography* Macmillan London

Ninian Smart 1960 *World Religions: A Dialogue* Penguin Harmondsworth

D Ingram Smith 1999 *The Transpqrent Mind A Journey with Krishnamurti*, Edwin House Publishing Ojai California

Huston Smith 2000 *Cleansing the Doors of Perception The Religious Significance of Entheogenic Plants and Chemicals* Tarcher/Putnam

Gavin Souter 1994 *Mosman A History* Melbourne University Press Melbourne

Henry P Stapp 1993 *Mind Matter and Quantum Mechanics* Springer-Verlag New York

WT Stead 1946 *Annie Besant A Character Sketch 1891* Theosophical Publishing House Madras

Rudolf Steiner 1928 *The Story of My Life* Anthroposophical Publishing Co London

C Suares 1955 *Krishnamurti and the unity of man* Chetana Bombay

C Suares 1972 Song *of Songs: the canonical Song of Solomon deciphered according to the original code of the Qabala* Shambala Berkeley

Emma Tarlo 1996 *Clothing Matters Dress and Identity in India* Hurst & Co London

Anne Taylor 1992 *Annie Besant A Biography* Oxford University Press

Vimala Thakar 1989 *On An Eternal Voyage* Vimal Prakashan Trust, Ahmedabad

G Tillett 1982 *The Elder Brother A biography of Charles Webster Leadbeater* Routledge & Kegan Paul London

Lucinda Vardey 1995 *God in All Worlds* Millennium Sydney

Veritas 1913 "Mrs Besant and the Alcyone Case" Goodwin & Co Madras

Roland Vernon 2000 *Star in the East* Constable London

Eric Warmington & Philip Grouse (eds) (trns WHD Rouse) 1956 *Great Dialogues of Plato* Mentor New York

Peter Washington 1993 *Madame Blavatsky's Baboon Theosophy and the Emergence of the Western Guru* Secker & Warburg London

Susunaga Weeraperuma 1974 *A Bibliography of the Life and Teachings of Jiddu Krishnamurti* EJ Brill Leiden

Susunaga Weereperuma 1982 *Supplement to a Bibliography of the Life and Teachings of Jiddu Krishnamurti*, Chetana, Bombay

Susunaga Weeraperuma 1983 *That Pathless Land* Chetana Bombay

Susunaga Weereperuma 1988 *J Krishnamurti as I Knew Him* Motilal Banarsidass Delhi

Stanley Wolpert 1996 *Nehru A Tryst with Destiny* Oxford University Press Oxford

Ernest Wood 1936 *Is This Theosophy?* Rider & Co London

Ernest Wood 1977 *Zen Dictionary* Pelican Harmondsworth

Paramahansa Yogananda 1977 *Autobiography of a Yogi* Self-Realization Fellowship Los Angeles

Robert M Young "Darwin and the Genre of Biography, p 1, from 1987 *One Culture: Essays in Science and Literature*, University of Wisconsin Press, Madison.

RC Zaehner (ed) 1966 *Hindu Scriptures* Dent London

Boris de Zirkoff 1978 Foreword to HP Blavatsky *The Secret Doctrine*, TPH, Adyar

Journals/Magazines/ Newspapers

Adelaide Advertiser
The Annual Obituary 1986
The Australian Financial Review
The Bombay Chronicle
Canadian Theosophist 1965
Courier Mail Brisbane
Daily Bulletin Townsville 1926
Daily Guardian 1923
Daily Mail Brisbane
Daily Mail London
Daily News Perth
Daily Telegraph Sydney
Dawn
Evening News Sydney
Herald Melbourne
Herald of the Star
The Hindu
The Illustrated Weekly of India
The Indian Theosophist
Journal of Humanistic Psychology
KFI Bulletin
Krishnamurti Foundation Bulletin
The Link
Los Angeles Times
Lucifer
The Mountain Path
Nature
New York Times
New York Herald Tribune
NSW Industrial Gazette 1922 May
NZ Herald
Ojai Valley News
Rajneesh Foundation Newsletter
Ross's newsletter 1922
Skeptical Inquirer
Star Auckland
The Star
The Star Review
Sunday Times Perth
Sun-Herald Sydney
The Age
The American Theosophist

The Australian Theosophist
The High Country Theosophist Boulder Colorado
The Sun Sydney
Sydney Morning Herald
Theosophist
The Star
The Times
The Times of India
The Theosophist
Theosophy in Australia
The West Australian
TIME
Truth 1916
Voyage Sydney
Washington Post

Balfour Clarke 1928 "The Childhood of Krishnaji" *The Australian Theosophist* August/Sep
Annie Besant 1916 *A World Religion* Theosophical Publishing House Madras
David Bohm "A Brief Introduction to the Work of Krishnamurti" brochure KFA
Hugh Gillespie 1934 *Canadian Theosophist* May
Javier Gomez Rodriguez 1995 "The Prison and the Rose" *Souvenir 1995* KFI Madras
Vernon Harrison 1997 *HP Blavatsky and the SPR An Examination of the Hodgson Report of 1885* Theosophical University Press Pasadena
S Hodson & M van Thiel (eds) *CW Leadbeater A Great Occultist*, undated and privately published in New Zealand
C Jinarajadasa 1946 Foreword *Annie Besant A Character Sketch 1891* Theosophical Publishing House Madras
F Morton 1922 "Annie Besant" *The Triad* June
G Narayan January 1993 "J Krishnamurti Some Reminiscences by G Narayan". KFI Archives.
NC Ramanujachary 1987 in "T Subba Row, 'The Secret Doctrine' and Madame HP Blavatsky", *Theosophical History*
D Ingram Smith *Krishnamurti's Fifth Visit* 1970
Richard Van Fleck 1998 "The Electronic Reactions of Albert Abrams" *American Artifacts* No 39 Taneytown Maryland
BP Wadia 1911 "Notes on Life XXVIII" (Jan) & "Reviews" (Sep) *The Theosophist*
BP Wadia 1922 *To All Fellow Theosophists and Members of the Theosophical Society* Los Angeles first published 1922 *The Theosophist* (supplement) October.
BP Wadia 1923 *Occult Review* April

BP Wadia 1938 "The Lives of Alcyone" *The Theosophist May*
BP Wadia 1962 *Living the Life* Indian Institute of World Culture Bangalore

Electronic

J Krishnamurti 1971 *Mind in Meditation* KF Records LP3
Shirley du Boulay (prod) 1970 *In Doubts and Certainties* BBC TV.
Susan Greenfield from Oxford University. BBC documentary. *Brain Story – The Final Mystery Pt IV* 2000
William Hudgings 1923 *Dr Abrahms' Electron Theory* New York republished on the internet by Delta Spectrum Research. Vibration Research Institute & Laboratories. Colorado
T McCarthy 1970 interview with J Krishnamurti 1 June for broadcast in Canada.
Paul McKenna 2000 interview BBC Radio 18 November
www.csp.org
www.human-nature.com.

Interviews

Ravi Aluganti. Evelyne Blau. Doneraile Burton. Radha Burnier. Ahalya Chari. Lee Chittick. Betty Carmody. Rino Donvito. TKV Desikachar. Colin Foster. Kathy Forbes. Scott Forbes. Darcy Gray. Jane Hammond. Alan Kishbaugh. Professor P Krishna. K Krishnamurti. Mark Lee. Marcia Murray. Tara McCarthy. Professor Krishna Nath. Radha Rajagopal Sloss. Grayson Rogers. OR Rao. John Scott. James Sloss. Donald Ingram Smith. Stephen Smith. Gregory Tillett. Vimala Thakar. Susunaga Weeraperuma. Mary Zimbalist.

Other sources

Documentation obtained under FOI provisions in Australia. Britain and the United States.
Documentation from the Public Record Office. Richmond , Surrey.
Original documents of the D Rajagopal Collection of the Huntington Library. San Marino.
Original documents of the Christopher Isherwood Collection of the Huntington Library, San Marino.
Transcriptions of interviews by Dr David Dunaway 1985 held by the Huntington Library, San Marino.

INDEX

D

F

G

H

I

J

N

O

P

R

S

T

V

W

Y

Z